COLINVAUX'S

LAW

OF

INSURANCE

AUSTRALIA
The Law Book Company Ltd.
Sydney : Melbourne : Brisbane : Perth

CANADA
The Carswell Company Ltd.
Toronto : Calgary : Vancouver : Ottawa

INDIA
N. M. Tripathi Private Ltd.
Bombay
and
Eastern Law House Private Ltd.
Calcutta

M.P.P. House
Bangalore

ISRAEL
Steimatzky's Agency Ltd.
Jerusalem : Tel Aviv : Haifa

PAKISTAN
Pakistan Law House
Karachi

COLINVAUX'S
LAW
OF
INSURANCE

SIXTH EDITION

EDITED BY

ROBERT MERKIN

Professor of Law, University of Sussex

LONDON
Sweet & Maxwell
1990

First Edition	1950
Second Edition	1961
Third Edition	1970
Fourth Edition	1979
Fifth Edition	1984
Sixth Edition	1990

Published in 1990 by
Sweet and Maxwell Limited of
South Quay Plaza, 183 Marsh Wall, London E14 9FT
Computerset by Promenade Graphics Ltd., Cheltenham
and printed in Great Britain by
Richard Clay Limited,
Bungay, Suffolk

British Library Cataloguing in Publication Data
Colinvaux, Raoul 1916–1984
The law of insurance.—6th ed.
1. England. Insurance. Law
I. Title   II. Merkin, Robert
344.20686

ISBN 0–421–38570–7

©
Sweet & Maxwell Limited
1990

PREFACE

Raoul Colinvaux died in 1984, shortly before the publication of the fifth edition of this work. Since the publication of the first edition in 1950, *Colinvaux's Law of Insurance* (as this work has now, appropriately, been renamed) has been invaluable to practitioners, to judges and to students of Law, becoming famous for its concise statements of principle and for the author's idiosyncratic yet illuminating style. Raoul Colinvaux was beyond all argument unduly modest in his genuine belief that he was primarily an author whose subject just happened to be Law.

I had somewhat mixed feelings when offered the opportunity by Sweet & Maxwell to edit the sixth edition of *Colinvaux*. My initial reaction was delight at taking over a work which I had myself used both as a student and subsequently as a teacher and author. This was, however, tempered by a deep concern: how could I possibly maintain the original author's style and erudition and, more generally, avoid compromising the distinctiveness of *Colinvaux* while at the same time seeking to inject a good deal of new material into the work? I concluded that I could not copy Raoul Colinvaux and that I should not try to do so. Thus, while much of the original structure, and some of the text, of this book remain the same, readers of previous editions will notice various changes, for the most part influenced by judicial and legislative activity since the publication of the previous edition.

In addition to discussing or noting recent authorities, I have recast a number of chapters whose structure had been overtaken by events. The most significant changes here are to the chapters on Reinsurance, Agents and Marine Insurance. I have added much new material on the international aspects of insurance (Chapter 1) and the Third Parties (Rights against Insurers) Act 1930 (Chapter 19). I have also tried to compensate for the growth of the number of authorities by a limited amount of excisions, notably by removing much of the material on American regulatory law and marine insurance and by replacing a good deal of the complex legislative material contained in Chapter 13 with rather briefer summaries of regulation under English law and European Communities Law. In the event the present edition of *Colinvaux* is some fifty pages shorter than its predecessor. I cannot of course pretend that Raoul Colinvaux would have gone about the preparation of the new edition in remotely the same way, but I can at least hope that the end result is worthy of previous editions.

I have received much assistance and guidance from the Publishers, to whom I extend my grateful thanks. Barbara, my wife, remained supportive and understanding throughout the lengthy period of editing *Colinvaux*; this was finally completed despite my daughters Eleanor, Lucy and (newly-arrived) Sophie Rose.

This book takes into account all material available to me as of the end of April 1990, although the very occasional footnote was added at proof stage.

Eastbourne   R.M.
June 1990

TABLE OF CONTENTS

PART ONE

Policies of Insurance

PART TWO

Parties to Insurance Contracts

PART THREE

Special Types of Insurance

APPENDIX

TABLE OF CASES

xiii

TABLE OF STATUTES

[References throughout this table are to paragraphs. **Bold** *type indicates where statutory matter is printed verbatim.]*

TABLE OF STATUTORY INSTRUMENTS

TABLE OF RULES OF THE SUPREME COURT

TABLE OF E.C. INSTRUMENTS

TABLE OF INTERNATIONAL CONVENTIONS

Part One

POLICIES OF INSURANCE

CHAPTER 1

THE CONTRACT OF INSURANCE

1. NATURE OF THE CONTRACT

Aleatory contracts   1–01

Contracts of insurance, like wagering contracts, are *aleatory* contracts "depending on an uncertain event or contingency as to both profit and loss"[1]; for financial or other consideration the insurer agrees to pay or otherwise benefit the assured on the happening of a specified event or contingency which is outside the control of the insurer. "Insurance is a contract upon speculation."[2]

However, unlike insurance contracts, wagering contracts are not enforceable in English law, so that the distinction between them is crucial. The major distinguishing factor is risk of loss: in insurance the assured is moved to effect a policy by the risk of loss, and does not create the risk of loss by the contract itself, as is the case in a pure wager.

> "I apprehend that the distinction between a policy and a wager is this: a policy is, properly speaking, a contract to indemnify the insured in respect of some interest which he has against the perils which he contemplates he will be liable to."[3]

Much will thus turn on the unilateral intention of the "assured" as well as upon the proper construction of the words used[4]: In what sense can we consider the plaintiffs as gamblers?" was the question posed by Lord Ellenborough C.J. in *Robertson* v. *Hamilton*.[5] The genuine expectation of an interest in the future will, therefore, be sufficient to make a contract one of insurance.[6]

Need for a general definition   1–02

It rarely occurs, in cases determinable on common law principles, that any question as to the exact meaning of insurance is really material, for, other than the doctrine of *uberrima fides*, the law of insurance has few significant principles of its own. Nevertheless a definition may be important for a number of statutory purposes. The most wide-ranging relevant statute is the Insurance Companies Act 1982, which regulates all forms of insurance business including "effecting and carrying out contracts of insurance," a term which is not exhaustively defined in the

---

[1] Webster's *New International Dictionary* (2nd ed.). See Dr. Smith's *Latin-English Dictionary*, under the heading "alea" *et seq.* for the origin of the word "aleatory" which gives the key to the nature of insurance contracts. See also *Oxford English Dictionary*; 2nd ed. of Shorter O.E.D.: "ALEATORY Dependent on the throw of a die; hence, dependent on uncertain contingencies, as an *aleatory contract.*"
[2] *Per* Lord Mansfield in *Carter* v. *Boehm* (1766) 3 Burr. 1905.
[3] *Wilson* v. *Jones* (1867) L.R. 2 Ex. 139, 150, *per* Blackburn J.
[4] *Tomlinson* v. *Hepburn* [1966] A.C. 451.
[5] (1811) 14 East 522, 533.
[6] See the M.I.A. 1906, s.4(2)(*a*), *infra*, 3–30.

I.C.A. 1982[7] and which the courts have been called upon to construe on a number of occasions both under this Act and its predecessors.[8] Other statutes under which the point might arise are the Unfair Contract Terms Act 1977, which imposes general controls over contractual exclusion clauses but excludes from its ambit contracts of insurance, and the Third Parties (Rights against Insurers) Act 1930, which transfers the benefits and burdens of a contract of insurance against liability to the plaintiff victim of an insolvent assured.

1–03 The meaning of "insurance"

In *Prudential Insurance* v. *I.R.C.*,[9] Channell J. said that insurance was a contract which bore a number of characteristics:

> "It must be a contract whereby for some consideration, usually but not necessarily in periodical payments called premiums, you secure to yourself some benefit, usually but not necessarily the payment of a sum of money, upon the happening of some event. Then the next thing that is necessary is that the event should be one which involves some amount of uncertainty. There must be either uncertainty whether the event will ever happen or not, or if the event is one which must happen at some time there must be uncertainty as to the time at which it will happen."[10]

1–04 *Premium*. Most forms of insurance entail money payments by the assured to the insurer, and this is assumed to be the case by the I.C.A. 1982.[11] Where money payments are made, they will not always be referred to as premiums: in the case of mutual insurance, for example, consideration takes the form of "calls" by the mutual insurer on its members.[12] Difficulty has in the past been encountered where insurance forms a part of some wider arrangement, so that sums payable by the assured have been in consideration of a non-insurance benefit with insurance being provided incidentally and free: in such circumstances the absence of an apportionable premium has been held to preclude a finding of insurance.[13] The modern view would doubtless be that in the world of commerce there is no such thing as a free gift, and that some part of the assured's payment would be subjected to a notional apportionment as consideration for insurance benefits.[14]

---

[7] A partial definition is provided by s.95. It should be noted that the I.C.A. 1982 regulates the effecting of transactions which are not insurance contracts as such, for example, bonding arrangements: s.95(*a*). It is thus possible for a contract of guarantee to be regulated by the 1982 Act while not attracting the duty of utmost good faith applicable to insurance contracts proper at common law: see *infra*, 1–07.

[8] Notably the Life Assurance Companies Act 1870, the Insurance Companies Act 1974 and the Insurance Companies Act 1981.

[9] [1904] 2 K.B. 658.

[10] *Ibid.* at p. 663. Channell J. went on to say that the event must be adverse to the assured. This however, overlooks the possibility of contingency insurance, generally in the form of endowment life assurance, where the policy moneys are payable at a given time or on death, whichever is sooner: see the comments of Buckley L.J. in *Gould* v. *Curtis* [1913] 3 K.B. 84, 94–96.

[11] s.95(a) refers to the granting of insurance "in return for one or more premiums."

[12] The M.I.A. 1906, s.85(2) recognises that mutual insurance does not fit the accepted pattern in this regard.

[13] *Hampton* v. *Toxteth Co-operative Society* [1915] 1 Ch. 721, but contrast *Nelson* v. *Board of Trade* (1901) 84 L.T. 565.

[14] *cf. Attorney-General* v. *Imperial Tobacco* [1980] 1 All E.R. 866. There are nevertheless doubts as to whether a "mixed grill," consisting of insurance and non-insurance benefits is a contract *of* insurance within the I.C.A. 1982, or a contract *for* insurance and outside the statute: see *Medical Defence Union* v. *Department of Trade* [1979] 2 All E.R. 421, 432, *per* Megarry V.-C.

Money or corresponding benefit. The usual form of consideration to **1–05**
be provided by an insurer is money, although property policies may well
confer upon the insurer an option to reinstate or replace damaged or
lost property: the latter is probably what Channell J. had in mind when
referring to "some benefit, usually but not necessarily the payment of a
sum of money." The extent to which the provision of services by the
insurer may constitute insurance was considered by Templeman J. in
D.T.I. v. *St. Christopher Association*,[15] the policies in which provided
chauffeur services to persons prevented from driving by reason of dis-
qualification or otherwise. The learned judge concluded that the provision of "money's worth" did not preclude a finding of insurance.
Similarly, in *Medical Defence Union* v. *Department of Trade*[16] Megarry
V.-C. was of the view that the provision of legal services could legitima-
tely be regarded as an insurance benefit. However, while it is apparent
from both decisions that insurance may be based upon the provision of
services to be paid for by the insurer, it is also apparent that the provision of "benefit" in general may not suffice.

The insurer's obligation. A contract of insurance necessarily places **1–06**
some obligation upon the insurer. In the *Medical Defence Union* case
the service provided by the insurer was the right to have a claim fairly
considered and not the right to an indemnity. Although the evidence
showed that the MDU had never refused to meet a valid claim by the
arbitrary exercise of discretion, Megarry V.-C. felt compelled to con-
clude that discretionary benefits were inconsistent with insurance: "One
is in a different world from the world of insurance when the only contractual right is a right to have a claim fairly considered."[17]

Guarantees and bonds 1–07

The I.C.A. 1982 regulates the carrying on of the business of performance and other bonds, and similar contracts of guarantee.[18] For other
purposes, however, a contract for the provision of a bond or guarantee
is not a contract of insurance and will not attract the duty of utmost good
faith or the other incidences of insurance.[19]

Indemnity 1–08

"Indemnity" it has been said, "is the controlling principle in insurance law."[20] This is an over-simplification. By reference to that "principle" many difficulties arising on insurance contracts can be settled.[21]
Except in insurance on life and against accident[22] the insurer usually
contracts to indemnify the assured for what he may actually lose by the
happening of the event upon which the insurer's liability is to arise. In

---

[15] [1974] 1 All E.R. 395.
[16] [1979] 2 All E.R. 421.
[17] [1979] 2 All E.R. 421, 429.
[18] s.95(a), and Sched. 2, class 15.
[19] *The Zuhal K and the Selin* [1987] 1 Lloyd's Rep. 151; *Travel & General Insurance Co.* v. *Barron*
1988, *The Times*, November 25. Chap. 21, *infra.*
[20] Brett L.J. in *Castellain* v. *Preston* (1883) 11 Q.B.D. 380, 386.
[21] See Chap. 8, *infra*, for an enumeration of the consequences of this principle.
[22] See §§ 16–02 *et seq., infra.*

no circumstances, it has been said, is the assured entitled to make a profit from his loss.[23] This is not strictly accurate.

There is no *general* rule requiring interest or indemnity. The true principle of English law is that all contracts entered into are enforceable by the parties to them irrespective of their subject-matter, provided this is neither illegal, immoral nor contrary to public policy.[24] It is in fact "a principle of public policy that persons who enter into contractual engagements should be required to fulfil them."[25] Apart from policies without interest or by way of wagering which have been prohibited by Acts of Parliament,[26] contracts of insurance are no exception to this general rule. The principle that the assured should recover no more than his loss may therefore, be modified by the express terms of the policy.[27]

1–09 *Contract of indemnity defined.* Notwithstanding the caveats above, it is possible to define the insurance species of contract of indemnity, of which marine insurance is an established subspecies, quite simply.

By section 1 ("Marine insurance defined") of the Marine Insurance Act 1906:

> "A contract of marine insurance is a contract whereby the insurer under-takes to indemnify the assured, in manner and to the extent thereby agreed, against marine losses, that is to say, the losses incident to marine adventure."

Applying that definition generally: A contract of indemnity (of the insurance species) is a contract whereby the insurer undertakes to indemnify the assured, in manner and to the extent thereby agreed, against losses. There is no requirement as to how the assured is to be indemnified; there is, in particular, no requirement of indemnity by money payment.[28]

1–10 *Other contracts of indemnity.* Although contracts of insurance are often members of one species of the *genus* contract of indemnity, there are also other species well recognised by the law. Thus, as was seen above, contracts of guarantee have never been regarded as contracts of insurance, although contracts of guarantee insurance have,[29] yet the object of each may be to indemnify a creditor against failure of the debtor to pay his debt. It is not always necessary to determine whether the contract is one of insurance or guarantee as they share many charac-teristics.[30]

---

[23] *Castellain* v. *Preston, supra*; Younger L.J., in *Matthey* v. *Curling* [1922] A.C. 180, 219.

[24] See *Fender* v. *Mildmay* [1938] A.C. 1, *per* Lord Wright at p. 36.

[25] *Beresford* v. *Royal* [1938] A.C. 586, 604, *per* Lord Macmillan. See also *Janson* v. *Driefontein Mines* [1902] A.C. 484.

[26] See Chap. 3, *infra*.

[27] *Maurice* v. *Goldsbrough Mort* [1939] A.C. 452 (P.C.).

[28] See *supra*, § 1–05 and § 1–06. See also Chap. 11, *infra*, on Reinstatement.

[29] For the distinction, see § 21–02, *infra*, which arises from the adjectival as opposed to nounal use of term "guarantee."

[30] See *Lucas* v. *Export Credits Dept.* [1974] 1 W.L.R. 909 (H.L.), where a government department contracted to indemnify an exporter against the risk of failure by foreign buyers to pay. They delayed, and the department paid the indemnity. The exporter eventually recovered in excess of the guarantee, and repaid the department, who wanted their share of the excess also, but they lost in the Lords, who considered it irrelevant whether the contract was one of insurance or guarantee.

Contingency insurance. So-called "contingency insurance"—the **1–11** undertaking by the insurer to pay on the happening of an event irrespective of the loss—is not an indemnity insurance at all. Life and, usually, accident insurance is of this nature, but there are other cases, as where in a liability policy the insurer agrees to pay any claim (though it may be a bad one) unless leading counsel advises that it can be successfully contested.[31]

Valued policies. There is nothing to prevent the parties agreeing in the **1–12** policy on the value of the thing insured. If they do so the assured will be entitled, in the absence of fraud,[32] to recover the agreed value in the event of a total loss, or, if the loss be partial, a proportion (the depreciation in its actual value) of the agreed value.[33] It will not be open to the insurers to say that that was not the true value,[34] and that the assured can only recover the extent of his loss if it be less. There is nothing illegal about such a contract, provided the over-valuation is not so gross as to amount to a wager.[35] Despite dicta in *Castellain* v. *Preston*[36] and elsewhere it is clear then that a contract of insurance that gives the assured more than an indemnity may be enforceable, provided it is not invalid on other grounds.[37] A contract is only prima facie one of pure indemnity, but it may be framed otherwise,[38] and whether or not a policy is intended to be a valued policy is mainly a matter of construing the policy itself.[39] Convenience alone is a sufficient reason why valued policies should be allowed by law,[40] and they have been held not to be wagering policies for this reason.[41] The contract contained in them has been described as "not an ideal contract of indemnity, but of indemnity according to the conventional terms of the bargain."[42]

The valuation is conclusive only as to the value of the thing lost; it does not affect the insurers' right of subrogation,[43] for the rules of indemnity apply to valued policies in all other respects.[44] After payment of a loss at the policy valuation the insurers will be entitled to any moneys recoverable by the assured from a third party in respect of the loss up to the insured value.

But where the over-valuation by the assured is so gross that, had the insurers known the facts, it would have affected their willingness to take

---

[31] Devlin J. in *West Wake Price* v. *Ching* [1957] 1 W.L.R. 45, 51.

[32] Kerr J. in *Berger* v. *Pollock* [1973] 2 Lloyd's Rep. 442.

[33] *Elcock* v. *Thomson* [1949] 2 K.B. 755, applied by New York Supreme Court to a marine policy in *Compania Maritima Astra* v. *Archdale* [1954] 2 Lloyd's Rep. 95; [1954] A.M.C. 1674.

[34] *Bruce* v. *Jones* (1863) 1 H. & C. 769.

[35] *Lewis* v. *Rucker* (1761) 2 Burr. 1167. See Lord Campbell in *Irving* v. *Manning* (1847) 1 H.L.C. 287, 308; *City Tailors* v. *Evans* (1922) 38 T.L.R. 230. In *Glafki Shipping* v. *Pinios Shipping, The Maria No. 2* [1984] 1 Lloyd's Rep. 660 Hobhouse J. held that the proper construction of M.I.A. 1906 s.4 was that a marine policy made on interest could not become a wager merely because of over-valuation of the subject-matter.

[36] (1883) 11 Q.B.D. 380.

[37] *Irving* v. *Manning, supra, per* Patteson J. at p. 307.

[38] *City Tailors* v. *Evans* (1922) 38 T.L.R. 230, 234.

[39] *Blascheck* v. *Bussell* (1916) 33 T.L.R. 74; *Brunton* v. *Marshall* (1922) 10 Ll.L.R. 689.

[40] *Barker* v. *Janson* (1868) L.R. 3 C.P. 303.

[41] Lord Eldon in *Lucena* v. *Craufurd* (1806) 2 Bos. & P.N.R. 269, 322.

[42] *Per* MacKinnon J. in *Goole Steam Towing Co.* v. *Ocean Marine* [1928] 1 K.B. 589, 594; 17 Asp.Mar. Law Cas. 409, 411.

[43] Selborne L.C. in *Burnand* v. *Rodocanachi* (1882) 7 App.Cas. 333, 335. As to subrogation rights, see Chap. 8, *infra.*

[44] See n. 37.

the risk, they may be entitled to avoid the contract[45] on the ground of misrepresentation or non-disclosure of a material fact.[46] This applies also to unvalued policies where the assured has overstated the value of the insured subject-matter.[47] In the absence of fraud, an excessive over-valuation is not itself a ground for repudiating the contract; the insurer can avoid on the ground of misrepresentation only where it would have affected his judgment as a prudent insurer in fixing the premium or determining whether or not to take the risk.[48]

Valued policies, though common in the case of insurance on ships and profits, are rare in the case of goods and buildings on land.[49]

These principles are partially codified by the Marine Insurance Act 1906, s.27:

> (1) A policy may be either valued or unvalued.
> (2) A valued policy is a policy which specifies the agreed value of the subject-matter insured.
> (3) Subject to the provisions of this Act, and in the absence of fraud, the value fixed by the policy is, as between the insurer and assured, conclusive of the insurable value of the subject intended to be insured, whether the loss be total or partial.
> (4) Unless the policy otherwise provides, the value fixed by the policy is not conclusive for the purpose of determining whether there has been a constructive total loss.[50]

1–13　　*Sum insured.* The agreement by the insurers to indemnify the assured is rarely an unqualified one; nearly always their liability is limited to a named amount known as the "sum insured." Where the value of the thing lost exceeds this sum, this sum is all that they are bound to pay; where the value of the thing lost is less, they are bound, except in the case of a valued policy, to pay no more than its actual value. There the principle of indemnity comes into operation to limit their liability to the loss actually suffered by the assured, for their undertaking is to pay that loss only.

Rates of premium are generally computed in proportion to the sum insured. Insurers therefore generally accept the assured's valuation for the purpose of fixing the sum insured. By over-insurance they will earn a higher premium, and yet remain liable for the actual loss only. They are more likely, in fact, to object to under-insurance, on the ground that in the event of a partial loss, and subject to any average conditions,[51] they may be liable to the full extent of the loss notwithstanding the lowness of the premium in proportion to the value of the thing insured.

---

[45] *Thames & Mersey Marine Insurance* v. *Gunford* [1911] A.C. 529; *Hoff* v. *De Rougemont* (1929) 34 Com.Cas. 291.

[46] See *Inversiones Manria* v. *Sphere Drake Insurance, The Dora* [1989] 1 Lloyd's Rep. 69, and Chap. 5, *infra.*

[47] *Berger* v. *Pollock* [1973] 2 Lloyd's Rep. 442.

[48] *Ibid.* Kerr J. at p. 465. In that case a valuation of £20,000 was not considered a material misrepresentation entitling the underwriters to avoid liability where the court subsequently, with knowledge of all the facts and the assistance of expert opinion, arrived at a figure of £5,000.

[49] But see *Elcock* v. *Thomson, supra.*

[50] s.27(3) is subject to ss.18–20 (utmost good faith): *The Dora, op. cit.* It is also subject to s.27(4) so that, in determining whether a vessel is a constructive total loss because the cost of repairs would exceed the repaired value (s.60(1)), the repaired value is to be assessed by actual market value and not by agreed value. In practice, however, s.27(4) is normally ousted by agreement.

[51] See Chap. 18, *infra.*

Insurable value. The object of a contract of insurance is to indemnify **1–14** the assured in respect of the commercial value of the thing lost. Insurance is not to compensate him for his feelings, at the burning of an heirloom, for instance,[52] but only for his loss so far as it is estimable in money on ordinary business principles.

It appears then that although prima facie the insurer indemnifies the assured, his liability may be limited in several respects, and a contract of insurance is not necessarily one of perfect indemnity.[53]

2. PRINCIPLES APPLICABLE

How insurance contracts are special **1–15**

The law relating to contracts of insurance is part of the general law of contract.[54] Contracts of insurance are, however, a species of that special class of contract, contracts of utmost good faith. Special rules therefore apply in insurance law relating to non-disclosure and misrepresentation[55] which differ from the rules applicable to contracts generally. Moreover, a "warranty" in insurance law is a very different concept to that of the ordinary contractual warranty. Otherwise there is no principle in insurance law which is at variance with the ordinary principles of the law of contract.

Case law **1–16**

Insurance law may be divided into marine and non-marine insurance law. The common law of insurance has been developed mainly by marine decisions. Since non-marine insurance policies on property have for centuries almost invariably included a clause providing for the settlement of disputes by arbitration, it had been comparatively rare for such disputes to come before the courts. The advent of compulsory motor vehicle and employers' liability insurance, and the abandonment of arbitration in "consumer" cases, have gone far to redress the balance between these two branches of insurance law in this respect, but it remains essential to look to marine decisions for much of the basic law applicable to insurance generally.

A lack of reported case law has hampered the development of insurance law throughout its history, and it is only since Lord Mansfield became Chief Justice in 1756 that even marine decisions have provided a satisfactory body of insurance law. Before that date no more than 60 insurance decisions in all had been reported,[56] and since at that time the whole case was left to a jury of merchants without any minute statement from the Bench of the principles of law on which insurances were established, those cases were of little value. Lord Mansfield, however, instituted the radical innovation of instructing the jury in full upon the rules of insurance law in each case and it is his judgments, principally in mar-

---

[52] But see *Re Egmont's Trusts* [1908] 1 Ch. 821, 826.
[53] *Aitchison* v. *Lohre* (1879) 4 App.Cas. 755.
[54] See *per* Roskill L.J. in *Cehave* v. *Bremer* [1976] Q.B. 44, 71, *infra*, § 2–01, n. 1. Thus the first edition of this work questioned at p. 2 whether the doctrine of frustration could apply to contracts of insurance.
[55] See Chap. 5, *infra*.
[56] See Park, *Marine Insurance*, Introduction.

ine cases, which now form the backbone of English, American and Commonwealth insurance law. Marine principles were codified by the Marine Insurance Act 1906.

1–17   *Marine insurance.* This is defined by section 1 of the Marine Insurance Act 1906 as insurance "against . . . losses incident to marine adventure." As regards mixed sea and land risks, section 2 provides:

> (1) A contract of marine insurance may, by its express terms, or by usage of trade, be extended so as to protect the assured against losses on inland waters or on any land risk which may be incidental to any sea voyage.
> (2) Where a ship in course of building, or the launch of a ship, or any adventure analogous to a marine adventure, is covered by a policy in the form of a marine policy, the provisions of this Act, in so far as applicable, shall apply thereto; but, except as by this section provided, nothing in this Act shall alter or affect any rule of law applicable to any contract of insurance other than a contract of marine insurance as by this Act defined.

As a matter of practice, cargo policies are written on a "warehouse to warehouse" basis, so that both land and sea risks are included.

Marine adventure and *maritime perils* are defined by section 3:

> (1) Subject to the provisions of this Act, every lawful marine adventure may be the subject of a contract of marine insurance.
> (2) In particular there is a *marine adventure* where—
>> (*a*) Any ship goods or other moveables are exposed to maritime perils. Such property is in this Act referred to as "insurable property";
>> (*b*) The earning or acquisition of any freight, passage money, commission, profit, or other pecuniary benefit, or the security for any advances, loan, or disbursements, is endangered by the exposure of insurable property to maritime perils;
>> (*c*) Any liability to a third party may be incurred by the owner of, or other person interested in or responsible for, insurable property, by reason of maritime perils.
> "*Maritime perils* means the perils consequent on, or incidental to, the navigation of the sea, that is to say, perils of the seas, fire, war, perils, pirates, rovers, thieves, captures, seisures, restraints, and detainments of princes and peoples, jettisons, barratry, and any other perils, either of the like kind or which may be designated by the policy."

The list of maritime perils set out in the M.I.A. has been held not to be exhaustive, although the concluding words "or which may be designated by the policy" do not permit the insurance of non-marine risks as marine risks simply by designating them to be marine risks.[57]

Marine insurance law has, owing to its long and peculiar history, been more influenced by continental jurisprudence than other branches of the common law. Lord Mansfield, for instance, did not hesitate to cite foreign sources, such as the great Ordonnance de la Marine of 1681, as authorities for propositions of marine law. It is not therefore always safe to rely on marine decisions as sources of non-marine insurance law unless it is clear, from judicial dicta or otherwise, that the same principles are applicable. Thus it has been laid down that the principle of

---

[57] *Continental Illinois National Bank* v. *Bathurst. The Captain Panagos D.P.* [1985] 1 Lloyd's Rep. 625.

utmost good faith and the rights of subrogation and contribution apply to both types of insurance. In the case of insurable interest, on the other hand, while marine decisions are of great assistance in determining non-marine questions, the statutes relating to interest differ widely in the case of marine and non-marine insurance.[58] And even where the principles are identical, their application may vary. Thus, while in the case of both types of insurance the assured is bound to disclose material facts,[59] previous refusals to insure by other insurers will generally be held to be material in non-marine but not in marine cases.[60]

Marine and terrestrial law compared. Generally speaking it may be **1–18** assumed that the rules of law are identical,[61] subject to the differences set out in the following table. This table takes no account of rules obviously applicable only to one or other branch of the law, such as rules relating to the implied warranty of seaworthiness[62] or constructive total loss in marine insurance law or the rules of reinstatement which belong peculiarly to the law of fire insurance. Doctrines peculiar to maritime law, such as the liability of participants in a maritime adventure to general average contribution in the event of an extraordinary sacrifice to avert a common peril, and the concept of the warranty of legality[63] likewise have no application in the field of non-marine insurance law.

Marine Insurance Law	Non-Marine Insurance Law
(a) A contract of marine insurance cannot be enforced unless it is embodied in a formal policy, Marine Insurance Act 1906, s. 22.[64]	(a) A contract of non-marine insurance is required to be in no special form, and is enforceable even if it is only oral.[65]
(b) Owing to the special form of a Lloyd's policy, which is made in the assured's own name and in the name of every other person to whom the same may appertain, the assured may assign the benefit of a marine policy on parting with the subject-matter.[66]	(b) With the exception of life insurance policies, non-marine policies cannot be effectively assigned without the consent of the insurers.[68]
(c) Policies of marine insurance are "subject to average" in the fire insurance sense by virtue of s. 81 of the Act.[67]	(c) Other insurances are only "subject to average," in that sense, if expressly made so.[69]
(d) The amount recoverable under a marine policy is measured by the value at	(d) In non-marine insurance it is the value at the time of the loss that supplies the

---

[58] See Chap. 3, *infra.*

[59] See Chap. 5, *infra.*

[60] See *London Assurance* v. *Mansel* (1879) 11 Ch.D. 363, 368, and § 5–22, *infra.* But the question of materiality is a pure fact provable by evidence and thus this is not a case where a rule of law is applicable only to non-marine insurance within s.2(2) of M.I.A. 1906.

[61] See Lord Blackburn in *Thomson* v. *Weems* (1884) 9 App.Cas. 671, 684; Morris J. in *Elcock* v. *Thomson* [1949] 2 K.B. 755. But M.I.A. 1906 enacts (s.2(2), § 1–17, *supra*) generally that nothing in it "shall alter or affect any rules of law applicable to any contract of insurance other than a contract of marine insurance." This rule has not always prevailed when non-marine insurance questions have been considered in the courts.

[62] But roadworthiness is relevant to motor vehicle and transport insurance law and "seaworthiness" may be pertinent accordingly to non-marine problems by way of analogy or to secure consistency in insurance law.

[63] *Euro-Diam Ltd.* v. *Bathurst* [1987] 1 Lloyd's Rep 178, affirmed [1988] 2 All E.R 23.

[64] § 1–23, *infra.*

[65] See § 1–22, *infra.*

[66] See M.I.A. 1906, ss.50, 51.

[67] § 10–07, *infra.*

[68] See §§ 23–82 *et seq., infra.*

[69] See §§ 18–28 *et seq., infra.*

the commencement of the risk and not by the value at the time of the loss, s. 16.[70]

measure of indemnity. *Re Wilson and Scottish Insurance.*[72]

Adjustments "new for old" are regulated by custom, s. 69(1)[71] of the Act.

Adjustments "new for old" are not so regulated.[73]

(e) A contract of marine insurance may be ratified after loss.[74]

(e) A contract of non-marine insurance may not be ratified after loss.[75]

(f) In marine insurance cases the court is empowered to order the production of the ship's papers for inspection by the underwriters.[76]

(f) The insurers have no similar privilege in non-marine cases, *Tannenbaum* v. *Heath*,[77] *Daily Express* v. *Mountain*.[78] In such cases the ordinary rules of discovery apply.[79]

(g) Any statement of fact bearing upon the risk introduced into the policy is to be construed as a warranty.[81]

(g) The ordinary rules of construction apply in determining whether such statements are warranties.[80]

(h) Express warranties must be set out or incorporated by reference in the policy, s. 35(2) of the Act.[82]

(h) Warranties need not be incorporated in the policy itself.[83]

(i) The premium is generally repayable if the risk is not run.[84]

(i) Special rules govern this question.[85]

1–19   *Foreign case law.* It should be borne in mind that in recent years English courts, and in particular the House of Lords, have adopted a far less parochial approach to decisions of foreign courts—particularly those of Australia and the United States of America. Apart from English law there is in existence a great body of case law in America, Canada, Scotland and Ireland and elsewhere which is of assistance in ascertaining the principles of general insurance law. The law of most of those countries, with the exception of Scotland, is based on the principles of Anglo-Saxon law, and even in Scotland the principles of commercial law are practically identical with those of England. But although all this law is of assistance to English courts none of it is binding upon them.[86] Although most statutes affecting insurance are common to both England and Scotland,[87] the common law has developed in each in its own way; and where questions of public policy are in issue the law of one country is no guide to the law of another.[88]

With regard to the force of American decisions, it has been laid down in insurance cases that while cases in the United States Supreme Court

---

[70] § 8–07, *infra.*

[71] [1920] 2 Ch. 28; and see § 8–05, *infra.*

[72] See § 8–08, *infra.*

[73] See § 8–08, *infra.*

[74] S.86 of M.I.A. 1906.

[75] See § 15–04, *infra.*

[76] R.S.C., Ord. 31, r. 12A(*b*).

[77] [1908] 1 K.B. 1032.

[78] (1916) 32 T.L.R. 592.

[79] R.S.C., Ord. 31, r. 12.

[80] See *infra*, § 6–09, and particularly terms of s.33 (*nature of warranty*) of Act of 1906.

[81] *Per* Lord Blackburn in *Thomson* v. *Weems* (1884) 9 App.Cas. 671, 684.

[82] *Ibid.* § 6–09.

[83] See § 6–17, *infra.*

[84] See § 7–09, *infra*, for special marine rules.

[85] See § 7–10, *infra.*

[86] Wright J. in *Halifax Building Society* v. *Keighley* [1931] 2 K.B. 248, 252.

[87] As to the weight to be accorded in England to Scots decisions on a common statute see *Cording* v. *Halse* [1955] 1 Q.B. 63; *Watson* v. *Nikolaisen* [1955] 2 Q.B. 286; *Kahn* v. *Newberry* [1959] 2 Q.B. 1; *Abbott* v. *Philbin* [1960] Ch. 27.

[88] See *Beresford* v. *Royal* [1937] 2 K.B. 197, 216, *per* Lord Wright M.R.; [1938] A.C. 586, 600, *per* Lord Atkin.

are entitled to respect in English courts,[89] cases in state courts are of comparatively little value.[90] But even where decisions of the Supreme Court are cited, the differences mentioned above have to be taken into consideration. Subject to such differences it has often been said in our courts that it is desirable to have uniformity in the law of contracts as far as possible in both England and America[91] or the Commonwealth,[92] and in the absence of any English authorities on a point,[93] and taking into account such differences, English courts would no doubt tend to apply American or Commonwealth decisions. But they are a most unsafe guide to English law where English authorities are available, and in matters of construction English and American decisions have sometimes shown a remarkable divergence.[94]

Reference to such decisions is therefore generally omitted in the present work except where there is no English authority, marine or otherwise, upon the point in question. Scottish and Irish decisions, on the other hand, where applicable, are freely cited in this work, since the common right of appeal to the House of Lords has preserved a common legal development in the three countries. English decisions have no more authority in Scotland,[95] or elsewhere, than have Scottish decisions in England.

3. FORMATION OF THE CONTRACT

Offer and acceptance   1–20

The first requisite of any valid contract is that there should be mutual agreement—*consensus ad idem*—between the parties. So to form any binding contract there must be a definite promise by one party and an acceptance by the other. Negotiations may carry on for a considerable time between them, but no valid contract can come into being until one accepts without qualification the final proposal of the other.[96]

Time. It is important to know the exact time when an agreement to insure comes into being as until then:

(a) should the casualty insured against occur, the insurer will not be bound,[97] and

---

[89] Lord Herschell in *The Bernina* (1883) 13 App.Cas. 1, 10. As to similar attitude of U.S. Sup.Ct. to H.L. decisions see *Standard Oil* v. *United States* [1951] 2 Lloyd's Rep. 36; [1951] A.M.C. 1.

[90] James L.J. in *North British* v. *London, Liverpool & Globe*, 46 J.L.Ch. 538; Hamilton J. in *American Surety Co.* v. *Wrightson* (1910) 27 T.L.R. 91, 93.

[91] See n. 89.

[92] Lord Stormonth-Darling in *Salvation Army Assurance* v. *British Legal Life*, 1908 S.C. 1138, 1143, as regards England and Scotland.

[93] Lord Esher M.R. in *Stewart* v. *Merchants' Marine* (1885) 16 Q.B.D. 619, 622; Roche J. in *Simmonds* v. *Cockell* [1920] 1 K.B. 843, 844.

[94] See *Re Hooley Hill Rubber and Royal* [1920] 1 K.B. 257, *per* Scrutton L.J. at p. 272 and *per* Duke L.J. at p. 274.

[95] *Hutchison* v. *National Loan Fund Life* (1845) 7 D. (Ct. of Sess.) 147; *Life Association of Scotland* v. *Forster* (1873) 11 M. (Ct. of Sess.) 351.

[96] But why cannot there be a contract to negotiate? Lord Wright said *obiter* that there could be in *Hillas* v. *Arcos* [1932] All E.R. 494 (H.L.); "if there is good consideration . . . " "though in the event of repudiation by one party the damages may be nominal . . . " Lord Denning M.R. in *Courtney* v. *Tolaini* [1975] 1 All E.R. 716 (C.A.) rejected that dictum as bad law, because no court could estimate the damages. See (1976) 126 N.L.J. 95.

[97] Unless the insurance is "lost or not lost," see § 1–33, *infra*.

(b) the duty to disclose all material facts still binds both the assured and the insurer.[98]

There is, however, a crucial distinction between the making of the contract and the commencement of the risk, as the former commonly precedes the latter. The insurer is not bound to meet a casualty occurring after formation and before attachment of risk, but the duty of disclosure comes to an end on formation whether or not the risk then attaches.

1–21   *Acceptance of offer.* For the contract to be complete the acceptance by one party of the offer of the other must be unconditional.[99] It is necessary to distinguish between an acceptance and a counter-offer[1]; in the case of the latter the contract is only completed on the acceptance of the counter-offer. Thus, where the insurers accept the assured's proposal subject to payment of a certain premium the contract becomes binding only on the tender to the insurer of that premium.[2] Tender of the premium then amounts to an acceptance of the insurers' counter-offer by the assured. The offer or the acceptance may be implied from the conduct of the parties; thus, where the insurers tender a policy in conformity with the assured's proposal, that also amounts to acceptance,[3] though delivery of a different kind of policy does not.[4] Even the failure of the insurers to decline an application for insurance may amount to acceptance,[5] at least where the insurer has indicated expressly or impliedly that a contract is to come into being unless it communicates a rejection of the proposer's offer. Such cases should be distinguished from those in which the insurers provisionally accept the risk subject to the premium being paid within a fixed time. In such a case a binding contract is concluded on acceptance of the risk,[6] although its performance by the insurers may be contingent on their receipt of the premium. A contract of insurance is normally contingent on the risk being run, and if it never attaches the premium is repayable.[7]

While the offer must be unconditional it does not matter if it does not contain the actual terms of the policy: indeed, an offer by the proposer will be taken to be one on the insurer's usual terms or, where there have been previous dealings, on terms previously agreed to by the parties.[8]

If A proposes for a policy the terms of which he is familiar with, actually or constructively, and such proposal is acceptable to the insurers, and a policy is signed and posted to the proposer, the contract of insurance is complete.[9] There must, however, be agreement as to all

---

[98] See § 5–04, *infra.*

[99] See, *e.g. Taylor* v. *Allon* [1966] 1 Q.B. 304; § 1–33 (v), *infra.*

[1] *Canning* v. *Farquhar* (1886) 16 Q.B.D. 727, 733; *Re Yager & Guardian* (1912) 108 L.T. 38, 43, *per* Lord Alverstone C.J.

[2] *Canning* v. *Farquhar, supra.* It is not clear from this case whether tender or acceptance of the premium makes the contract binding. The view expressed in the text is, it is submitted, correct in principle.

[3] *General Accident Insurance* v. *Cronk* (1901) 17 T.L.R. 233; *Rust* v. *Abbey Life Assurance Co.* [1979] 2 Lloyd's Rep. 334.

[4] *South East Lancashire Insurance* v. *Croisdale* (1931) 40 Ll.L.R. 22.

[5] *Smith* v. *Merchants' Fire of New York* [1925] 3 W.W.R. 91.

[6] *Harrington* v. *Pearl Life* (1914) 30 T.L.R. 613.

[7] *Tyrie* v. *Fletcher* (1777) 2 Cowp. 666, 668.

[8] *Adie & Sons* v. *Insurances Corpn.* (1898) 14 T.L.R. 544.

[9] *Sanderson* v. *Cunningham* [1919] 2 Ir.R. 234.

the principal terms, such as the subject-matter, the risk and the sum insured. An agreement to agree cannot constitute a binding contract, but an agreement on the usual terms,[10] or at the usual rate of premium offered by a company, may do so. So provisional cover offered and accepted "at a premium to be arranged" has been held to be binding.[11]

While acceptance of an offer within a reasonable time normally constitutes a binding contract, an offer by the insurers to insure is subject to an implied condition that the risk does not materially change prior to acceptance. Such an offer cannot be fairly regarded as an offer continuing after the risk has changed.[12]

Under certain circumstances, however, an offer may be held to continue for an unlimited period; thus a policy may contain a continuing offer to accept surrender of it on terms, in which case a binding contract is concluded by acceptance of this offer at any time.[13]

When a contract is made by post, acceptance is complete as soon as the letter of acceptance is put into the post-box, but where a contract is made by direct communication, such as Telex, the contract is complete only when the acceptance is received by the offeror, since generally an acceptance must be notified to the offeror to make a binding contract.[14]

Whether writing needed. At common law any oral contract for valu- **1–22** able consideration is valid, and contracts of insurance are no exception to this rule.[15] There is at present no statutory requirement of writing to render contracts of non-marine insurance either valid or enforceable.[16] In Scotland, however, contracts of insurance are *obligationes litteris* and must be constituted in writing.

Marine insurance in this respect is now governed by sections 22 *et seq.* **1–23** of the Marine Insurance Act 1906. Section 22 renders a contract of marine insurance inadmissible in evidence unless it is embodied in a marine policy in accordance with the Act, and section 23 states that such policy must specify the name of the assured or of some person who effects the insurance on his behalf. *Specification* of the insured subject-matter is governed by section 26:

(1) The subject-matter insured must be designated in a marine policy with reasonable certainty.
(2) The nature and extent of the interest of the assured in the subject-matter insured need not be specified in the policy.
(3) Where the policy designates the subject-matter insured in general terms, it shall be construed to apply to the interest intended by the assured to be covered.

---

[10] In *Nicolene* v. *Simmonds* [1953] 1 Q.B. 543 a contract of sale subject to "usual conditions" was held complete although there were no usual conditions; that clause was ignored as meaningless. But see *Fitzgerald* v. *Masters* (1956) 40 Austr.L.J. 412, 414, *per* Dixon C.J. and Fullager J. In *British Electrical* v. *Patley* [1953] 1 W.L.R. 280, a similar case: *held*, no contract. Contrast contracts by slip negotiated at Lloyd's where the parties will understand the customary hieroglyphics used.
[11] *Gliksten* v. *State Assurance* (1922) 10 Ll.L.R. 604.
[12] *Canning* v. *Farquhar, supra,* at p. 733.
[13] *Ingram-Johnson* v. *Century Insurance,* 1909 S.C. 1032.
[14] *Entores* v. *Miles* [1955] 2 Q.B. 327; *Brinkibon* v. *Stahag Stahl* [1982] 1 All E.R. 293.
[15] *Murfitt* v. *Royal* (1922) 38 T.L.R. 334; *Kaines* v. *Knightly* (1681) Skinner 54; *Bhugwandass* v. *Netherlands India Sea & Fire* (1888) 14 App.Cas. 83.
[16] As to contracts of guarantee see § 21–05, *infra.*

(4) In the application of this section regard shall be had to any usage regulating the designation of the subject-matter insured.

and *subscription* by section 24:

(1) A marine policy must be signed by or on behalf of the insurer, provided that in the case of a corporation the corporate seal may be sufficient, but nothing in this section shall be construed as requiring the subscription of a corporation to be under seal.

(2) Where a policy is subscribed by or on behalf of two or more insurers, each subscription, unless the contrary be expressed, constitutes a distinct contract with the assured.

1–24 The policy

A contract of insurance is, however, generally embodied in a formal document called a "policy," a term borrowed from the Italian merchants who introduced the practice of insurance into this country.[17] While the word is generally used to describe such a formal document, it may be used to describe any contract of insurance however informal.[18] The Life Assurance Act 1774, s.2, contemplates that insurance will be made by a formal policy, but does not enact that it shall so be made and provides only that the policy shall contain the name of the person interested in it.[19]

1–25 *Lloyd's policies.* Lloyd's policies generally (including non-marine) emanate from Lloyd's Policy Signing Office (L.P.S.O.) where the terms of the slip[20] are translated into those of a policy based on Lloyd's current form of policy for the purpose of the insurance effected. "When L.P.S.O. put their stamp on a policy . . . and issue it, they bind the underwriters as completely and effectively as if each underwriter had signed for himself."[21] "When underwriters set up this policy signing office they entrusted to it the task of signing policies which will bind them, leaving it to the members of that office to carry out any necessary check and test before they issue the policy."[22] L.P.S.O. have actual authority to bind underwriters.[23]

1–26 *Stamp.* There are cogent commercial reasons for the issue of such a document and by the Stamp Act 1891,[24] it was enacted that the insurers were bound under penalty to issue a stamped policy within a month after receiving the premium. But this provision now applies only to policies of life insurance.[25] The insurers' failure so to issue a stamped policy

---

[17] The Italian "polizza" is derived from, polyptych, a tablet of several folds (as distinguished from diptych, triptych, etc.), used in late Latin for an account or memorandum book.

[18] *Re Norwich Equitable Fire* (1887) 57 L.T. 241; *Forsikringsaktieselskabet National* v. *Att.-Gen.* [1925] A.C. 639, 642.

[19] *Hodson* v. *Observer Life* (1857) 8 E. & B. 40; *Evans* v. *Bignold* (1869) L.R. 4 Q.B. 622.

[20] § 1–29, *infra.*

[21] *Per* Lord Denning M.R. in *Eagle Star* v. *Spratt* [1971] 2 Lloyd's Rep. 116 (C.A.) reversing Brandon J., at p. 128.

[22] *Ibid. per* Phillimore L.J.

[23] *Ibid. per* Megaw L.J. at p. 129. See also § 1–30.

[24] s.100.

[25] Annuities are excluded. The Finance Act 1959, s.30(1) had simplified the position under the Act of 1891 by inserting a duty of 6d. on any "Policy of Insurance other than Life Insurance" not differentiating between classes of policy outside life insurance. That duty was abolished by the Finance Act 1970, Sched. 7, Pt. I, 1(2)(*b*), ("so that a policy of insurance other than life insurance shall be kept from all stamp duties.") The same Act abolished the duties of 2d. on cheques and receipts: Sched. 7, Pt. I, 2(2).

only, however, subjected them to a penalty and did not affect the validity or the enforceability by the assured of the contract.[26]

Proposal. The first step in the making of a contract of insurance is the **1–27** *proposal* or *application* by means of which the assured gives to the insurers particulars of the risk which he wishes them to undertake. Before that he will probably have found out from the insurers, either directly or through an agent, the terms on which they are usually willing to grant insurances of the kind he wants, but, where the contract is subsequently reduced into writing, its terms will not be affected by anything which is said or done at this stage.[27]

Cover notes. The applicant may want immediate protection pending **1–28** the acceptance of his proposal and prior to the issue of a formal policy, and the insurers may be willing to give it provided they are free to withdraw from the temporary bargain after they have made inquiries. Such cover may be given informally,[28] but normally the insurers give the applicant a formal document known as a "cover note."[29] Such a note is in fact a temporary or provisional contract of insurance, quite distinct from the contract embodied in the policy, and the fact that the assured changes his mind and decides to negotiate with another company does not affect the cover already given him by such a note.[30] The conditions of the policy are not therefore binding upon the assured unless they are incorporated expressly or by reference in the cover note,[31] as they generally are. If the assured pays all, or part, of the premium, the insurers may combine the receipt with the cover note,[32] in which case it is known as a *deposit receipt.*

The cover note usually states that it is to be in force for a limited period of time, or until a policy is delivered, unless meanwhile the insurers give notice to the assured that they have decided not to accept his proposal.[33]

But a temporary cover note renewing a policy and sent to the assured does not of itself constitute a contract of insurance unless the assured takes some step to accept it; it may be treated simply as an offer to insure for the future.[34]

Slip. The formation of insurance contracts at Lloyd's is initiated by **1–29** means of a slip. This is a brief document prepared by the broker acting

---

[26] Contrast assignment of policies not duly stamped: see § 16–37, *infra.*

[27] *Dunn* v. *Campbell* (1920) 4 Ll.L.R. 36. In *Pearl Life* v. *Johnson* [1909] 2 K.B. 288 the recitals to a life policy by deed stated that it was made on the basis of *a* proposal; the proposal had not in fact been signed by the policy holder or her authority, and premiums had been paid. *Held*, that the insurers were estopped from contending that there was no contract.

[28] *Murfitt* v. *Royal* (1922) 38 T.L.R. 334.

[29] *Thompson* v. *Adams* (1889) 23 Q.B.D. 361, 366, *per* Mathew J.; *Re Yager and Guardian* (1912) 108 L.T. 38, 40.

[30] *Mackie* v. *European Assurance* (1869) 21 L.T. 102. But see *Taylor* v. *Allon, infra.*

[31] *Re Coleman's Depositories* [1907] 2 K.B. 798; *Symington* v. *Union Insurance of Canton* (*No.* 2) (1928) 141 L.T. 48; *Queen Insurance* v. *Parsons* (1881) 7 App.Cas. 96.

[32] *Mackie* v. *European Assurance* (1869) 21 L.T. 102, 104; *Re Yager and Guardian* (1912) 108 L.T. 38, 40.

[33] See *Mackie* v. *European Assurance, supra*; and *Levy* v. *Scottish Employers' Insurance* (1901) 17 T.L.R. 229.

[34] *Taylor* v. *Allon* [1966] 1 Q.B. 304.

on behalf of the assured[35] containing short particulars of the risk and indicating in the customary shorthand the cover that the assured requires. The slip will be presented to a selected series of underwriters, beginning with the leading underwriter, *i.e.* one who has a reputation in the market as an expert in the kind of cover required and whose lead is likely to be followed by other underwriters in the market. The broker and leading underwriter go through the slip together, agree on any amendments to the broker's draft and fix the premium. The leading underwriter then initials (*i.e.* signs) the slip for his proportion of the cover and the broker then takes the initialled slip round the market to other insurers, who initial it for such proportion of the cover as each is willing to accept. Once the slip is fully subscribed it will be presented to L.P.S.O. for a policy to be issued on behalf of each subscribing under-writer.[36] Once the leading underwriter has initialled a slip it is common for subsequent underwriters to rely upon his market experience and to initial the slip simply by following his lead. In these circumstances it is not open to those underwriters to assert that false statements made to the leading underwriter by the broker are also deemed to have been made to them: irrespective of the rights of the leading underwriter, sub-sequent underwriters to whom nothing has expressly been said cannot avoid the policy[37] or sue the broker.[38]

1–30   The essential characteristic of the Lloyd's procedure is that the final contract of insurance will have been subscribed to by a number of underwriters, and it becomes essential to know whether an underwriter is bound by the terms of the slip when he initials it, or whether he becomes bound at some later stage, for example where the slip becomes fully subscribed or the L.P.S.O. has issued a formal policy. The issue may arise in the following ways: can an underwriter withdraw from the slip if the broker cannot obtain full subscription?; can the assured with-draw from the slip if the broker cannot obtain full subscription?; is the assured's duty of disclosure maintained until full subscription even in favour of those underwriters who have initialled the slip?; can under-writers who have initialled the slip insist upon being party to changes made to it by subsequent underwriters?

The view taken by early cases was that a slip was a completed contract of insurance in its own right, and not merely an offer of insurance by the initialling underwriter or a temporary contract pending full inquiries by the underwriter.[39] Consequently, underwriters were bound to issue a policy in accordance with the terms of the slip. This approach was con-sistent with the Marine Insurance Act 1906, s.21, which provides that the contract "is deemed to be concluded when the proposal of the

---

[35] It is established that a Lloyd's broker is the agent of the assured and not the agent of the under-writer: *American Airlines* v. *Hope* [1974] 2 Lloyd's Rep. 301, 304, *per* Lord Diplock. See also *General Accident* v. *Tanter, The Zephyr* [1984] 1 Lloyd's Rep 75, reversed in part on other grounds [1985] 2 Lloyd's Rep. 529.

[36] See para. 1–25.

[37] *Bank Leumi Le Israel BM* v. *British National Insurance Co.* [1988] 1 Lloyd's Rep. 71.

[38] *General Accident* v. *Tanter, The Zephyr* [1985] 2 Lloyd's Rep. 529.

[39] *Thompson* v. *Adams* (1889) 23 Q.B.D. 361; *Haase* v. *Evans* (1934) 48 Ll.L.R. 131; *Grover* v. *Matthews* [1910] 2 K.B. 401.

assured is *accepted by the insurer*, whether the policy be then issued or not; and, for the purpose of showing when the proposal was accepted, *reference may be made to the slip . . . .*" (emphasis added). Further, section 89 provides that where there is a duly stamped policy, reference may be made to the slip in any legal proceeding. However, in *Jaglom* v. *Excess Insurance*[40] Donaldson J. described as erroneous the proposition that a slip is an offer which is accepted by each underwriter who takes a line: in his opinion, each underwriter who takes a line is merely making and not accepting an offer. This reasoning was *obiter*, and was a convenient method of disposing of a hypothetical problem which had been raised in that case, namely, that of a subsequent underwriter who insists upon changes to the slip: Donaldson J.'s approach would have allowed all earlier underwriters to take advantage of those changes.

Despite Donaldson J.'s opinion, the traditional view that the initialling of a slip is the acceptance of an offer was adopted by the Court of Appeal in *Eagle Star Insurance* v. *Spratt*[41] and the House of Lords in *American Airlines* v. *Hope*.[42] The matter was put beyond all doubt by the Court of Appeal in *General Reinsurance Corporation* v. *Forsakringsaktiebolaget Fenna Patria*.[43] Paper was here shipped from British Columbia to Europe for sale, and was stored in a warehouse at Antwerp. The paper was insured under policies issued by the defendants, who reinsured under two separate contracts, one for the whole risk (whole account cover) and one for loss by fire or flood (specific cover). The specific cover was for 15 million finmarks with an excess of 15 million finmarks, and had been entered into by 28 reinsurance companies of which the plaintiff was one. A fire destroyed all the paper on February 11, 1977. On February 14, 1977, not knowing the extent of the fire, the defendants instructed their brokers to prepare a slip amending the specific cover retrospectively from January 1, 1977 to 15 million finmarks in excess of 25 million finmarks; the plaintiffs and one other of the 28 specific cover reinsurers initialled the amendment slip. After hearing of the extent of the fire, the defendants sought to withdraw the amendment slip. This was vigorously resisted by the plaintiffs, whose liability under the amendment was limited to their share of 2 million finmarks with the whole account reinsurers being liable for 20 million finmarks, whereas without the amendment the plaintiffs' liability would have been their share of 15 million finmarks and the whole account reinsurers would have been liable only for 10 million finmarks. The plaintiffs thus sought a declaration that the amendment was binding upon the defendants.

At first instance Staughton J. held that the defendants were entitled to cancel the amendment slip before it had become fully subscribed, on the ground that the custom and practice of the London market entitled an insured or reinsured person to cancel before it had been initialled by all of the original underwriters. The Court of Appeal, reversing this decision, held that the existence of such a custom had not been proved.

[40] [1972] 2 Q.B. 250.
[41] [1971] 2 Lloyd's Rep. 116.
[42] [1972] 2 Lloyd's Rep. 301.
[43] [1982] Q.B. 1022.

The judgments reaffirm the well-established principle that the initialling of a slip creates a binding contract as between assured and underwriter, and that this applies to original and to amendment slips alike. Only one exception to the binding nature of this contract was admitted by the Court of Appeal: if a slip is oversubscribed, the broker is entitled to "write down" proportionately the liability of each of the subscribing underwriters in order to reduce subscription to 100 per cent. Oversubscription and writing down are common, particularly in the reinsurance market, but do give rise to difficulties where an underwriter initials a slip for a substantial line on the assumption that there will be a subsequent signing down, but in fact the signing down does not materialise.[44]

1–31   In order to permit variations, the slip will often contain a "leading underwriter" clause, providing that amendments may be agreed by the leading and will bind all other signatories to the slip: this is referred to as a "tba L/U" (to be agreed by leading underwriter) provision. Such a clause does not entitle the assured to demand amendments to the slip: it merely has the effect of authorising the leading underwriter to make amendments which bind all other underwriters,[45] although it will not be effective to authorise the leading underwriter to enter into different forms of insurance on behalf of following underwriters.[46]

1–32   In the case of marine insurance, the slip is thought to be nothing more than an "honour" contract, because no action can be brought on a contract of marine insurance by virtue of the Marine Insurance Act 1906, s.22 unless and until a stamped policy has been issued.[47] However, if a loss does occur, it is usual to deliver a stamped policy in accordance with the slip, even if the insurers deny liability, so that the assured is at least able to bring an action against them.

1–33   *Loss before issue of policy.* Cases where the loss occurs before the issue of a policy require special care.

   (a) *Where no binding contract has been formed.* An offer to insure cannot be accepted after the loss so as to bind the insurers.[48]
   (b) *Where there is provisional cover, e.g.* a cover note, the assured will of course be able to recover.
   (c) Where the insurer is not on risk, but *there is a binding contract to issue a policy*, the doctrine of frustration applies[49]; thus if the assured becomes mortally ill before the policy is issued and the

---

[44] See *General Accident* v. *Tanter, The Zephyr* [1985] 2 Lloyd's Rep. 529, in which the Court of Appeal awarded damages to a leading reinsurer against a broker whose statement that the slip would be oversubscribed (a "signing indication") proved not to be justified. Subsequent underwriters, who were not given a signing indication but who relied upon the oversubscription of the leading underwriter to act in a similar fashion, were held not to have a cause of action against the broker.

[45] *Barlee Marine Corporation* v. *Mountain* [1987] 1 Lloyd's Rep. 471.

[46] *Inversiones Manria* v. *Sphere Drake Insurance* [1989] 1 Lloyd's Rep. 23.

[47] *Lishman* v. *Northern Marine* (1875) L.R. 10 C.P. 179; *Re Yager and Guardian* (1912) 108 L.T. 38. There is some conflict in the older cases on the question of whether a slip constitutes a policy in its own right.

[48] *Canning* v. *Farquhar* (1886) 16 Q.B.D. 727.

[49] This doctrine is fully considered in Carver, *Carriage by Sea* (13th ed., British Shipping Laws), Vol. 2, §§ 817 *et seq.*

risk begins to run[50] the contract is automatically dissolved. "An agreement to undertake to relieve against risks necessarily assumes that when it comes to be fulfilled by issuing the policy the events are still risks, and does not apply if before fulfilment, and there being no delay for which the insurer is alone responsible, the events have been converted into certainties."[51] This does not mean that a mere change in the risk dissolves the contract, however commercially disastrous to the insurer[52]; the peril insured against must virtually have become a certainty.

(d) Where the loss occurs, *unknown to the insurers but known to the assured*, and they afterwards issue a policy which they were not bound to issue, they will be entitled to avoid it on the ground of the failure of the assured to disclose the loss.[53]

(e) Where the loss occurs, *unknown to both parties*, prior to the contract of insurance. In that case, unless the policy is made "lost or not lost" as marine policies normally are, the policy will be void on account of mutual mistake as to a matter going to the root of the contract. Thus where a life insurance policy was renewed by agreement, and unknown to both parties the "life" was already dead, it was held that the whole transaction was founded on a mistake and that the assured could not therefore recover.[54] The principle is the same as in the case in which the sale of a life policy after the assured had died was held void.[55]

Thus, in no case can the assured recover where the loss occurs before the beginning of the term covered by the policy,[56] nor, it will be seen from the above propositions, will a policy normally have retrospective effect unless it is made "lost or not lost." Voyage policies and policies of reinsurance may, however, have retrospective effect without those words.[57] But even a life policy may be retrospective provided the intention of the parties is made clear.[58]

Policies under seal. The requirement that a deed should be **1–34** "delivered" is now a mere formality and where a policy purports to be signed, sealed and delivered, but has never left the office of the company, it is not open to them to deny due delivery.[59] Delivery may be inferred from execution,[60] and actual delivery to the assured or his agent is quite unnecessary. Delivery of any deed, including an insurance policy, may be the subject of a condition, in which case the deed is known as an escrow. Deeds must now be not only sealed but also, by section 73 of the Law of Property Act 1925, signed.

---

[50] *Harrington v. Pearl Life* (1914) 30 T.L.R. 613; see § 4–19, *infra.*
[51] *Sickness & Accident Assurance Association* v. *General Accident Assurance Corporation* (1892) 29 S.L.R. 836, 840, *per* the Lord President.
[52] *Cf.* Lord Sumner, *Larrinaga* v. *Société Franco Americaine* (1923) 29 Com.Cas. 1, 18, 19.
[53] *Canning* v. *Farquhar, supra,* and see authorities cited, § 5–04, n. 19, *infra.*
[54] *Pritchard* v. *Merchants' Life* (1858) 3 C.B. (N.S.) 622.
[55] *Scott* v. *Coulson* [1903] 2 Ch. 249.
[56] *Oceanic Steamship Co.* v. *Faber* (1907) 23 T.L.R. 673; and see § 4–28, *infra.*
[57] *Marine Insurance* v. *Grimmer* [1944] 2 All E.R. 197.
[58] Byles J. in *Pritchard* v. *Merchants' Life, supra,* at pp. 644, 645.
[59] *Xenos* v. *Wickham* (1867) L.R. 2 (H.L.) 296.
[60] *Roberts* v. *Security* [1897] 1 Q.B. 111. As to this case see also *Equitable Fire* v. *Ching Wo Hong* [1907] A.C. 96.

1–35 *Receipt and acceptance of policy.* Whereas the insurers will be bound by policies under seal irrespective of the assent of the assured, the binding nature of a policy under seal depends entirely on whether or not the proposed policy is to be on the insurer's usual terms. The general rule is that the assured's offer to the insurer is deemed to be on the terms of the insurer's standard policy of that type,[61] so that both parties will be bound by those terms.[62] Conversely, if the policy is to be on different terms, neither the assured nor the insurer will be able to take advantage of a policy that the assured has not seen or received.

If the insurers are under a prior contractual duty to issue a policy, and tender a policy not in accordance with the earlier agreement (*e.g.* an agreement contained in a slip) the assured may refuse to accept it,[63] but if he has accepted such a policy his only remedy is an action for its rectification.[64] He will not be bound any the less by any conditions in it because he has not read them.[65]

1–36 *Whether whole contract embodied in policy.* The general rule of contract that, where the terms of a contract are reduced into writing, oral evidence is not admissible to vary or contradict them and the writing alone can be looked at as containing the terms of the contract, is applicable to policies of insurance.[66] However, this does not mean that the whole of the contract between the parties will necessarily be embodied in the policy: warranties frequently appear in the proposal alone.[67] Moreover, statements of a promissory nature in a prospectus delivered by the insurers to the assured may form part of a collateral agreement between them and bind the insurers, although no mention is made of them in the policy,[68] but such statements cannot be called in aid to construe the terms of the policy itself.[69] But a statement in a prospectus that loans would be made at the rate of 4 per cent. on an assurance company's policies was held not to amount to a collateral agreement to charge no higher rate[70]; and the publication in a prospectus of a company's practice in the distribution of profits was held not to affect its right to vary that practice by altering its by-laws, where the policy was issued subject to the deed of settlement of the company (by which they could be altered) and its by-laws.[71] In *Sun Life of Canada* v. *Jervis*,[72] it was held that an illustration setting out the benefits the assured would

---

[61] *General Accident* v. *Cronk* (1901) 17 T.L.R. 233; *Rust* v. *Abbey Life* [1979] 2 Lloyd's Rep 334. Suggestions to the contrary in *Alliss-Chalmers* v. *Fidelty Deposit* (1916) 32 T.L.R. 263 can no longer stand.

[62] See, however, *Re Coleman's Depositories* [1907] 2 K.B. 798, in which a majority of the Court of Appeal held that the assured under a cover note was not bound by the notice of loss provisions contained in the insurer's usual policy, as they had not been brought to its attention.

[63] *South East Lancashire* v. *Croisdale* (1931) 40 Ll.L.R. 22.

[64] See § 1–37, *infra.*

[65] *Watkins* v. *Rymill* (1883) 10 Q.B.D. 178.

[66] *Quin* v. *National Assurance* (1839) Jones & Carey 316 (Ire.); *Beacon Life* v. *Gibb* (1862) 1 Moo.P.C.C.(N.S.) 73, 97; Greer L.J. in *Newsholme Brothers* v. *Road Transport Insurance* [1919] 2 K.B. 356.

[67] See §§ 6–18, 6–19, *infra.*

[68] *Thiselton* v. *Commercial Union Ass. Co.* [1926] 1 Ch. 888. See also *Sun Life of Canada* v. *Jervis* (1943) 113 L.J.K.B. 174; [1944] A.C. 111; *Excess Life* v. *Firemen's Ins. of Newark, New Jersey* [1982] 2 Lloyd's Rep. 599, Webster J.

[69] *British Equitable Ass. Co.* v. *Baily* [1906] A.C. 35, 41, *per* Lord Lindley.

[70] See n. 68.

[71] See n. 69.

[72] (1943) 113 L.J.K.B. 174.

receive formed part of the contract between him and the company, since the proposal form was incomprehensible unless read in conjunction with it.

Rectification of the policy. Should the policy contain terms contradic- **1–37** tory to or inconsistent with a prior contract between the parties the assured may bring an action for its rectification, or the insurers may claim rectification in an action by the assured upon the policy.[73]

Thus where the proposal was made by reference to an illustration setting out the scale of the policy holder's benefits, and a policy was subsequently executed on less advantageous terms after acceptance of the proposal by the company, it was held that the assured was entitled to rectification of the policy in order to give effect to the contract contained in the illustration and the proposal.[74]

The right to rectification, clearly, arises if there has been a prior contract binding on the insurers,[75] such as that evidenced by a slip,[76] and the burden of proving such a contract is on the assured. If it appears that the assured intended one thing and the insurers intended something else, the assured has no right to insist on a policy of the kind he wants,[77] though he may be able to recover any premiums he may have already paid as money paid to the insurers under a mistake of fact.[78] It is also clear from recent decisions[79] that the court may rectify a contract provided there was a common continuing intention of the parties as to any provision in it which that provision, properly construed, does not represent, even where it is impossible to prove a concluded and binding contract between the parties antecedent to the agreement which it is sought to rectify, provided that intention has found expression. Mere clerical errors may be rectified on this principle.[80]

There is a strong presumption that the policy embodies the real contract between the parties, and a strong case is required to rebut that presumption and to support a claim for rectification, especially after the loss.[81] But a party to a policy is entitled to rectification even after taking arbitration proceedings,[82] provided the policy moneys have not been paid,[83] if he can make out a sufficiently strong case.

Renewal. "Self-renewing policies." Policies of insurance are not **1–38** renewable beyond their original term unless they are expressed to be so, and where there is no provision for renewal they can only therefore be renewed by a new agreement between the parties.

---

[73] *Motteux* v. *London Assurance* (1739) 1 Atk. 545; *Mutual Reserve* v. *Foster* (1904) 20 T.L.R. 715; *Letts* v. *Excess Insurance* (1916) 32 T.L.R. 361.
[74] *Sun Life of Canada* v. *Jervis* (1943) 113 L.J.K.B. 174.
[75] *Hvalfangerskapet* v. *Unilever* (1932) 42 Ll.L.R. 215, 220; *Mackenzie* v. *Coulson* (1869) L.R. 8 Eq. 368, 375.
[76] *Letts* v. *Excess Insurance, supra*; *Holgate* v. *London and Cheshire Insurance* (1922) 13 Ll.L.R. 486; *Scottish Metropolitan* v. *Stewart* (1923) 15 Ll.L.R. 55; *Eagle Star* v. *Rainer* (1927) 27 Ll.L.R. 173.
[77] *Fowler* v. *Scottish Equitable* (1858) 28 L.J.Ch. 225; *South-East Lancashire* v. *Croisdale* (1931) 40 Ll.L.R. 22; *Hvalfangerskapet* v. *Unilever, supra*.
[78] *Fowler* v. *Scottish Equitable, supra*.
[79] *Joscelyn* v. *Nissen* [1970] 2 Q.B. 86; *Mint Security* v. *Blair* [1982] 1 Lloyd's Rep. 188; *Pindos Shipping* v. *Raven* [1983] 2 Lloyd's Rep. 449.
[80] *Nittan (UK)* v. *Solent Steel Fabrication* [1981] 1 Lloyd's Rep. 633.
[81] *Henkle* v. *Royal Exchange* (1749) 1 Ves.Sen. 317.
[82] *Crane* v. *Hegeman-Harris* [1939] 1 All E.R. 662; [1939] 4 All E.R. 68.
[83] See *Caird* v. *Moss* (1886) 33 Ch.D. 22, discussed in *Crane's* case, *supra*.

Where there is a provision for renewal it may, as is usual in life policies, give the assured an unconditional right to renew, or as is generally the case in connection with other policies, renewal may be conditional on the assent of both parties.[84] The latter class includes policies which may be renewed by tender of a further premium by the assured and by the acceptance of that premium by the insurers,[85] and also those policies, known as "self-renewing," which provide that they shall be automatically renewed unless either of the parties shall give notice of an intention not to renew.[86]

It is a matter of construction whether or not a policy is self-extending. In *Jones Construction Co.* v. *Alliance Assurance Co.*[87] a contractor's all risks policy covered the building of a dam in Iraq, and provided for any period subsequent to that stated where the assured paid the premium and the insurer accepted it. It was held that the insurers were only accepting the risk, subject to their volition, for the stated period.

In *Webb and Hughes* v. *Bracey*,[88] a solicitor's indemnity policy provided that "in the event of non-renewal by underwriters" certain benefits would accrue to the assured. The assured failed to take steps to obtain a renewal of the policy from the underwriters. *Held*, that this was not non-renewal by them.

In *Kirby* v. *Cosindit*,[89] the insurance (a policy covering for builder's risks) provided: "Extension held covered at a premium to be arranged." Ten days' notice to the assured by the representative Lloyd's underwriter to pay a premium for the extension was held by Megaw J. (*obiter*) to be unreasonable: there was no sum which could be defined except by agreement; meanwhile Lloyd's were presumably bound by their contract.

1–39   Life policies may be expressed to be either:

(a) an annual contract, which the assured has the right to renew,[90] by payment of a further premium, or

(b) an entire contract for life, subject to forfeiture on the failure of the assured to pay any of the annual premiums.[91]

The distinction is important where the death occurs during the days of grace.[92] English policies generally fall into the first category, but they may fall into the second one, as where a debtor insures his life in favour

---

[84] As to apparent hybrid see *Re Commercial Travellers and Duck* [1951] 1 D.L.R. 576.

[85] *Sun Fire* v. *Hart* (1889) 14 App.Cas. 98.

[86] *Solvency Mutual* v. *Froane* (1861) 7 H. & N. 5. Thus in Belgium motor insurance policies are "*self-renewing*," and go on from year to year unless one side or the other gives notice cancelling them; *per* Devlin L.J. in *Poland* v. *Julien Praet* [1961] 1 Lloyd's Rep. 187, 190. As to notice of cancellation of builder's risk policy see *Kirby* v. *Cosindit* [1969] 1 Lloyd's Rep. 75.

[87] [1961] 1 Lloyd's Rep. 121.

[88] [1964] 1 Lloyd's Rep. 465.

[89] [1969] 1 Lloyd's Rep. 75.

[90] *Pritchard* v. *The Merchants' Life* (1858) 3 C.B.(N.S.) 622, 643, *per* Willes J.; *Phoenix Life* v. *Sheridan* (1860) 8 H.L.C. 745, 750; *Stuart* v. *Freeman* [1903] 1 K.B. 47.

[91] *New York* v. *Statham* (1876) 93 U.S. 24, 30; *McMaster* v. *New York*, 183 U.S. 25, 35 (1901); see also Jessel M.R. in *Fryer* v. *Morland* (1876) 3 Ch.D. 675, 685; *Re Anchor Assurance* (1870) L.R. 5 Ch. 632, 638; *Re Harrison and Ingram, ex p. Whinney* [1900] 2 Q.B. 710, 718.

[92] See § 7–05, *infra*.

of his creditor and covenants to pay the premiums, for there the assured has not only an option but a duty to renew.[93]

If the assured fails to renew by the appointed day a policy renewable by payment of a further premium, his right to do so can only be revived by the assent of the insurers, and if they give this assent subject to conditions a new contract will be formed thereby.[94]

4. CONFLICT OF LAWS

Significance of topic 1–40

A great deal of insurance and reinsurance business is international in nature, and the London market is one of world's leading centres for the placing of risks. In the event of a dispute it becomes important to determine two issues: (a) whether an action may be brought in England; and (b) whether or not the action is brought in England, the system of law which is to be applied to the contract.

Jurisdiction 1–41

Presence. The jurisdiction of the English courts over an insurance dispute rests not upon the nationalities of the parties or on any connection between the contract and England, but rather on the procedural question of whether the English High Court is entitled to sanction the issue of a writ against the proposed defendant. If the defendant is to be found in England a writ may be served on him. In the case of an individual, mere temporary physical presence is sufficient for these purposes.[95] In the case of a company registered in England service may be effected at its registered office.[96] In the case of a company registered in Scotland service may be effected at its principal place of business in England as long as a copy of the writ is sent to its Scottish registered office.[97] In the case of a company incorporated outside Great Britain (an "oversea" company) service may be effected on a person authorised to receive service[98] or, in the absence of any such authorisation, at any place of its business in Great Britain.[99]

Submission. A defendant who does not have a physical presence in 1–42 England may nevertheless have submitted to the jurisdiction of the English courts. In international insurance and reinsurance agreements it is common for the parties, or one of them, to agree to submit to the exclusive or non-exclusive jurisdiction of the English courts, and in such a case the court may give leave to serve a writ upon a defendant who is outside the jurisdiction.[1] The court has a general discretion to refuse to issue a writ, although this is only likely to be exercised in the case of a

---

[93] See *Seligman* v. *Eagle Insurance* [1917] 1 Ch. 519, 524, *per* Neville J. See also McNair, *Legal Effects of War* (2nd ed.), pp. 259–261.
[94] *Handler* v. *Mutual Reserve* (1904) 90 L.T. 192.
[95] *Maharanee of Baroda* v. *Wildenstein* [1972] 2 Q.B. 283. For the procedures involved, see *Barclays Bank of Swaziland* v. *Hahn* (1989) *The Times*, May 19.
[96] Companies Act 1985, s.725(1).
[97] Companies Act 1985, s.725(2), (3).
[98] Companies Act 1985, ss.691, 695.
[99] Companies Act 1985, s.691. As to what constitutes a place of business, see: *Re Oriel* [1986] 1 W.L.R. 180; *Cleveland Museum of Art* v. *Capricorn International* (1989) *The Times*, October 4.
[1] R.S.C. Ord. 11, r. 1(1)(*d*)(iv).

non-exclusive jurisdiction agreement.[2] In the absence of express agreement to submit to the jurisdiction of the English courts, implied submission may be found in the conduct of the defendant following the plaintiff's attempts to commence proceedings in England, for example in conferring unconditional jurisdiction upon solicitors to accept service on his behalf[3] or in contesting the case on its merits and not merely on procedural grounds. A plaintiff who commences an action in the English courts has clearly submitted to the jurisdiction in respect of counter-claims in the action, but not in respect of an entirely different dispute between the parties.[4]

1–43 *Assumed jurisdiction: non-European Communities cases.* Where a defendant is outside the jurisdiction and has not submitted to the jurisdiction of the English courts, the High Court may nevertheless give leave for service of a writ against him. In order to obtain leave for service outside the jurisdiction the plaintiff must bring himself within one or more of the grounds listed in R.S.C. Ord. 11, r. 1 and must also satisfy the court that the case is a proper one for the exercise of its discretion. In insurance and reinsurance cases the relevant grounds for leave are as follows:

(1) The defendant is domiciled or ordinarily resident within the jurisdiction.[5] Domicile refers to the permanency of the defendant's home,[6] while ordinary residence is a lesser concept requiring at least some form of habitual residence.[7] This ground would appear not to be material to companies, as domicile and ordinary residence have been held to refer to the place of incorporation.[8]

(2) An injunction is sought ordering the defendant to do or to refrain from doing anything within the jurisdiction (whether or not damages are also claimed).[9]

(3) The claim is brought against a person duly served within or out of the jurisdiction and a person out of the jurisdiction is a necessary or proper party thereto.[10]

(4) The claim is brought in respect of a breach of contract which was made within the jurisdiction.[11] As far as English law is concerned, an agreement is

---

[2] See § 1–46, *infra.* Jurisdiction agreements which are ambiguous as to their exclusivity will commonly be construed as conferring exclusive jurisdiction on the named courts: *Sohio* v. *Gatoil* [1989] 1 Lloyd's Rep. 588. However, an ambiguous clause in an insurance contract will, by contrast, be construed as conferring non-exclusive jurisdiction, as otherwise the assured might be constrained to sue only in the named place: *Beresford* v. *New Hampshire Insurance* [1990] 2 All E.R. 321.

[3] *Sphere Drake Insurance plc* v. *Sigorta Anonim Sirketi* [1988] 1 Lloyd's Rep. 139, where no submission was found as the defendant had reserved his rights in this regard. *Cf. Esal* v. *Pujara* [1989] 2 Lloyd's Rep. 479. In *Finnish Marine* v. *Protective National Insurance* [1989] 2 All E.R. 929 it was held that seeking a stay of English proceedings does not amount to submission to the jurisdiction of the English courts.

[4] *Factories Insurance Co.* v. *Anglo-Scottish General Commercial Insurance* (1913) 29 T.L.R. 312.

[5] R.S.C. Ord. 11, r. 1(1)(*a*).

[6] *Re Fuld (No. 3)* [1968] P. 675.

[7] *Levene* v. *I.R.C.* [1928] A.C. 217.

[8] *Jones* v. *Scottish Accident* (1886) 17 Q.B.D. 421; *Watkins* v. *Scottish Imperial* (1889) 23 Q.B.D. 285.

[9] R.S.C. Ord. 11, r. 1(1)(*b*).

[10] R.S.C. Ord. 11, r. 1(1)(*c*). In *Goldean Ocean Assurance* v. *Martin* [1989] 2 Lloyd's Rep. 390 it was held that every co-insurer under a single policy is a necessary or proper party to English proceedings against any one of them.

[11] R.S.C. Ord. 11, r. 1(1)(*d*)(i). This ground does not apply where the applicant is not a party to the contract in question even though its operation affects him. Moreover, the ground cannot be relied upon to obtain a declaration that a contract is void. On both issues, see *Finnish Marine* v. *Protective National Insurance* [1989] 2 All E.R. 929. However, if the action is brought in respect of a breach, the *defence* that no contract exists does not deprive the English court of jurisdiction: *Britannia Steamship* v. *Ausonia* [1984] 2 Lloyd's Rep. 98; *Marc Rich* v. *Societa Italiana* [1989] 1 Lloyd's Rep. 548.

made when the offer is accepted, so that jurisdiction will exist if the acceptance took place in England. Thus the posting of a letter of acceptance in England,[12] the receipt of a telex or fax message in England[13] or the initialling of a Lloyd's slip in England[14] will all confer jurisdiction on the court to give leave for service abroad.

(5) The claim is brought in respect of a breach of contract which was made by or through an agent trading or within the jurisdiction.[15] Acceptance by a broker in England, while acting for an insurer or assured outside the jurisdiction, will bring this ground into operation; further, it would seem that the conducting of negotiations in England by a broker will have the same effect even though final authorisation and acceptance take place elsewhere.[16] An agent acting beyond his authority may confer jurisdiction upon the English courts.[17]

(6) The claim is brought in respect of a breach of contract where the proper law of the contract is, by its terms or by implication, English law.[18]

(7) The claim is brought in respect of a breach of contract committed within the jurisdiction.[19] Actual breach of an insurance contract will generally take the form of refusal to pay, so that the place of breach may be taken to be the place at which payment was due.[20] It is suggested that anticipatory breach, *i.e.* a communication by one of the parties that he does not intend to fulfil his future obligations, takes effect at the place of its receipt and not at the place of its sending.[21]

(8) The claim is founded on a tort and the damage was sustained, or resulted from an act committed, within the jurisdiction.[22] In the insurance context an action in tort is most likely to be brought against a broker by the assured, and the court will have jurisdiction to hear the claim if the broker's negligent act or omission took place in England or if it resulted in failure by the insurer to pay sums which, but for the broker's negligence, would have been payable in England.

If the plaintiff establishes any ground within R.S.C. Ord. 11, r. 1, he **1–44** must nevertheless go on to persuade the High Court that the case is a proper one for leave for service outside the jurisdiction to be given. The question in every case is whether the matter is more appropriately dealt with in some other jurisdiction, whether or not proceedings have been commenced in that jurisdiction, or whether England is a more appropriate forum. If the proper law of the agreement is the law of some other place, whether by agreement or by implication, it will generally be the case that the dispute is more appropriately dealt with in that place and leave will be refused.[23] However, the discretion may be exercised in the

---

[12] *Household Fire* v. *Grant* (1879) 4 Ex.D. 216.
[13] *Brinkibon* v. *Stahag Stahl* [1982] 1 All E.R. 293.
[14] *Citadel Insurance* v. *Atlantic Union* [1982] 2 Lloyd's Rep. 543.
[15] R.S.C. Ord. 11, r. 1(1)(*d*)(ii).
[16] *Afia Worldwide* v. *Deutsche Ruck* (1983) 133 New L.J. 242.
[17] *National Mortgage Agency* v. *Gosselin* (1922) 38 T.L.R. 832 but the ground is not satisfied where the applicant's action is for a declaration that his agent was unauthorised: *Finnish Marine* v. *Protective National Insurance* [1989] 2 All E.R. 929.
[18] R.S.C. Ord. 11, r. 1(1)(*d*)(ii). The concept of proper law is discusse *infra*, §§ 1–51–1–56.
[19] R.S.C. Ord. 11, r. 1(1)(*e*).
[20] *Citadel Insurance* v. *Atlantic Union* [1982] 2 Lloyd's Rep. 543.
[21] *Cooper* v. *Knight* (1901) 17 T.L.R. 299, but see *Holland* v. *Bennett* [1902] 1 K.B. 867. In *Mutzenbecher* v. *La Asequradora Espanola* [1906] 1 K.B. 254 both postng and receipt took place in England, so that the position was clear. In *Atlantic Union Underwriting* v. *Compania di Assicurazione di Milano* [1979] 2 Lloyd's Rep. 240 Lloyd J. suggested, wrongly it is submitted, that the place at which the anticipatory breach was treated as repudiatory by the innocent party constituted the place of breach: the R.S.C. refer to breach and not to termination.
[22] R.S.C. Ord. 11, r. 1(1)(f).
[23] *Mackender* v. *Feldia* [1967] 2 Q.B. 590; *Atlantic Underwriting Agencies* v. *Compania di Assicurazione di Milano* [1979] 2 Lloyd's Rep. 240. Even if English law is the proper law, other factors may point towards a hearing in some other jurisdiction: *Amin Rasheed* v. *Kuwait Insurance* [1984] A.C. 50. See *infra* § 1–45.

plaintiff's favour if there is no obvious other forum for the dispute to be heard, if there are substantiated grounds for believing that a fair trial cannot be obtained in the natural forum, or if all relevant witnesses are in England and proceedings in England would be the most convenient course of action.[24]

1-45   Where the proper law of the insurance contract is English law, it does not necessarily follow that England is the most convenient forum for the hearing of the dispute. In *Amin Rasheed Shipping* v. *Kuwait Insurance*[25] a Liberian shipping company based in Dubai insured its vessel with the defendant insurer, based in Kuwait, under a Lloyd's standard marine policy. The policy was issued in Kuwait and claims were also payable there. The dispute concerned the circumstances of the loss, the insurer alleging that the vessel had been engaged in smuggling when the loss occurred, and the relevant witnesses were in Saudi Arabia, Bangladesh and India. The House of Lords, having ruled that the contract was governed by English law, further held that this fact did not compel the English courts to assert jurisdiction: the dispute had no connection with England, the witnesses were not in England and there was no reason to suspect the competence of the Kuwaiti courts in applying English law. Nevertheless, if the contract has some connection with England, then the court is likely to give leave for service outside the jurisdiction whether[26] or not[27] there is a choice of law clause nominating English law.

1-46   *Stay of domestic proceedings.* Even where the court has jurisdiction to hear a dispute, whether based on presence, submission or exorbitant jurisdiction under the R.S.C. Ord. 11, it has an inherent jurisdiction to stay those proceedings in favour of actual or potential proceedings in another jurisdiction. The power to stay has been exercised in four types of case. First, if the insurance agreement contains arbitration provisions, court proceedings will normally be stayed in favour of arbitration; moreover, if the arbitration agreement has an international flavour, the grant of a stay will be mandatory under the Arbitration Act 1975.[28] Secondly, if the parties have agreed that their dispute is to be heard by the courts or tribunals of some other country, the English courts will not interfere with their agreement and will stay domestic proceedings unless there is compelling evidence that England would be a more convenient forum or that the defendant in the foreign proceedings would not receive a fair trial.[29] Thirdly, if proceedings are pending in

---

[24] *Et Soules et Compagnie* v. *Handgate* [1987] 1 Lloyd's Rep. 142; *Amanuel* v. *Alexandros Shipping* [1986] Q.B. 464. Factors pointing towards England have been held to include: the ability of the victor in an English action to recover his costs (*Roneleigh* v. *MII Exports* (1989) *The Times*, February 23); the availability of an action against the defendant's liability insurers under the Third Parties (Rights against Insurers) Act 1930 (*Irish Shipping* v. *Commercial Union* [1989] 2 Lloyd's Rep. 144); and the danger that foreign public policy rules may preclude an action in that jurisdiction (*Seashell Shipping* v. *Mutualidad de Sequeros* (1988) *The Times*, August 11; *Kloeckner* v. *Gatoil* [1990] 1 Lloyd's Rep. 177).
[25] [1983] 2 All E.R. 884. See also *Insurance Co. of Ireland* v. *Strombus International Insurance* [1985] 2 Lloyd's Rep. 138.
[26] *Britannia Steamship Insurance* v. *Ausonia Assicurazione* [1984] 2 Lloyd's Rep. 98.
[27] *Islamic Arab Insurance* v. *Saudi Egyptian American Reinsurance* [1987] 1 Lloyd's Rep. 315; *Seashell Shipping* v. *Mutualidad de Sequros* (1988) *The Times*, August 11.
[28] See 9–24 *et seq.*
[29] *The Eleftheria* [1970] P. 94.

another jurisdiction, and that jurisdiction is the natural and most convenient forum for the resolution of the dispute, English proceedings will be stayed on the *lis alibis pendens* principle. This rule was laid down by the House of Lords in *The Abidin Daver*,[30] and is to be disregarded only where:

> "the would-be plaintiff can establish objectively by cogent evidence that there is some personal or judicial advantage that would be available to him only in the English action that is of such importance that it would cause injustice to him to deprive him of it."[31]

Fourthly, the doctrine of *forum non conveniens*, introduced into English law by the House of Lords in *The Abidin Daver*, authorises the English courts to stay domestic proceedings whether or not proceedings in another jurisdiction have been commenced, if an alternative forum exists and is more appropriate for the resolution of the dispute.[32] The proper law of the contract will be an important, but not conclusive, factor in the court's decision on whether or not to stay English proceedings.[33]

Stay of foreign proceedings. Where proceedings have been commenced in another jurisdiction, the defendant in those proceedings may seek an injunction in the English courts preventing the plaintiff from pursuing his action; such a course is permissible only where the plaintiff in the foreign proceedings is subject to the jurisdiction of the English courts, by presence, submission or exorbitant jurisdiction under the R.S.C. This power may be exercised by the English court on *lis alibis pendens* grounds, *i.e.* where proceedings concerning the same dispute have been commenced in England and are more appropriately brought in England,[34] or on *forum non conveniens* grounds but only where the foreign proceedings may be regarded as vexatious.[35] **1–47**

Jurisdiction in the European Communities. By virtue of the Civil Jurisdiction and Judgments Act 1982, the U.K., with effect from January 1, 1987, became a party to the European Communities' Convention on Jurisdiction and the Enforcement of Judgments in Civil and Commercial Matters, signed in Brussels in 1968. Ultimately, all of the member states of the EC will be parties to this Convention. The effect of the Convention is to replace domestic jurisdiction rules with a set of common principles operating throughout the EC. The Convention is material to insurance disputes over jurisdiction in two respects: it lays down a series **1–48**

---

[30] [1984] A.C. 398.

[31] [1984] A.C. 398, 412, *per* Lord Diplock. On this principle the English courts will not permit a "forum-shopping" action brought in England for a declaration of the plaintiff's non-liability, when the plaintiff is or is about to be sued in some other jurisdiction: *The Volvox Mollandia* [1988] 2 Lloyd's Rep. 361; *Sohio* v. *Gatoil* [1989] 1 Lloyd's Rep. 588; *First National Bank of Boston* v. *Union Bank of Switzerland* [1990] 1 Lloyd's Rep. 32.

[32] The relevant principles and burdens of proof are set out in the judgment of Lord Goff in *Spiliada Maritime* v. *Cansulex* [1986] 3 All E.R. 843.

[33] *El du Pont* v. *Agnew* [1987] 2 F.T.L.R. 487: English court best placed to consider matters of English public policy—stay refused. In co-insurance cases, the overriding factor is finding a jurisdiction in which all of the parties can be sued: *Golden Ocean Assurance* v. *Martin* [1989] 2 Lloyd's Rep. 390. This will generally be England, as few other countries operate a system of jurisdiction as broad as that under Ord. 11 of the R.S.C.

[34] *Charm Maritime* v. *Kyriakou* [1987] 1 F.T.L.R. 265.

[35] *Societe Nationale Industrielle* v. *Jak* [1987] 3 All E.R. 510; *El du Pont* v. *Agnew* [1988] 2 F.T.L.R. 41.

of generally applicable rules for determining jurisdiction; and it lays down an additional series of rules for determining jurisdiction in insurance cases, which are in some cases without prejudice to the generally applicable rules. Where the courts of two or more contracting states potentially have jurisdiction over the same action, the court before which proceedings are first brought is to have exclusive jurisdiction.[36] The Convention is to be applied by national courts, but any dispute as to its proper interpretation may, and ultimately must, be referred to the European Court of Justice for preliminary ruling. The reports on the Convention prepared by Professors Jenard and Schlosser are also of authority.

1–49   The guiding principle under the Brussels Convention is that a defendant is to be sued in the place of his domicile.[37] Domicile is defined for these purposes as meaning, in the case of an individual, residence coupled with a substantial connection or, in the case of a company, the place of its incorporation or the place in which its central management is located.[38] The general rule of domicile is ousted in a number of cases listed in Art. 5: in the case of breach of contract, the plaintiff may sue in the place of performance of the obligation in question[39]; in the case of tort the plaintiff may sue where the harmful act occurred[40]; and where the action arises out of the activities of a branch or agency, the plaintiff may sue in the place in which the branch or agency is located.[41] Moreover, the parties are free to agree that the courts of any one contracting state are to have exclusive jurisdiction in the event of a dispute.[42] The jurisdiction rules are subject to the overriding principle that a defendant who appears before a national court first seised of the action, other than

---

[36] Art. 21. This applies whether or not the plaintiff is domiciled in a contracting state: *Overseas Union* v. *New Hampshire Insurance* (1988) *The Times*, September 27. This point has now been referred to the European Court of Justice by the Court of Appeal. If two "related" but not identical actions are brought in different Contracting States, the court seised of the later action *may* stay that action to avoid the risk of irreconcilable judgments: Art. 22, and see *Virgin Aviation* v. *CAD Aviation* (1990) *The Times*, February 2.

It is important to determine, for the purpose of both Arts. 21 and 22, which court is "first seised" of an action. Under English law an English court is seised of an action *in rem* for the arrest of a vessel when the writ is served or the vessel arrested (*The Freccia del Nord* [1988] 1 Lloyd's Rep. 388) and is first seised of other actions on the date of the issue of the writ (*Kloeckner* v. *Gatoil* [1990] 1 Lloyd's Rep. 177).

[37] Art. 2.

[38] Arts. 52 and 53; C.J.J.A. 1982, ss. 41 and 42. Special rules relate to the domicile of an insurer: see *infra*, n. 45.

[39] This is not necessarily the term which has been broken, but rather is the term which characterises the contract: *Tessili* v. *Dunlop* case 12/76 [1976] E.C.R. 1473. As far as the English courts are concerned, the "obligation in question" is that upon which the claim is founded, so that a party may be sued in the Contracting State in which he broke the contract: *Medway Packaging* v. *Meurer* (1989) *The Financial Times*, October 20.

[40] This is either where the wrongful act was committed or where the damage was ultimately inflicted: *Bier* v. *Mines de Potasse* case 21/76 [1976] E.C.R. 1735. *Cf. Minster Investments* v. *Hyundai* (1988) *The Times*, January 26.

[41] See *Blankaert and Willens* v. *Trost* case 139/80 [1981] E.C.R. 819. An insurance broker, as an independent person, is not a branch or agency for these purposes: *New Hampshire Insurance* v. *Strabag Bav* (1990) *The Financial Times*, February 21.

[42] Art. 17. The effect of this provision is to convert a non-exclusive jurisdiction clause into one conferring exclusive jurisdiction on the named court: *Beresford* v. *New Hampshire Insurance* [1990] 2 All E.R. 321. It was held in *Kloeckner* v. *Gatoil* [1990] 1 Lloyd's Rep. 177 that if an action is brought in another Contracting State in defiance of a jurisdiction clause, nominating England, an English court may itself determine the validity of the clause even though it is not the court first seised of the action.

to contest its jurisdiction confers exclusive jurisdiction on that court[43]: submission will equally override any exclusive jurisdiction agreement reached between the parties.[44]

The general rules of jurisdiction are supplanted by specific rules relat- **1–50** ing to insurance matters (excluding reinsurance but including both consumer and commercial policies[44a]), contained in Articles. 7 to 12A of the Brussels Convention. An insurer may be sued in the contracting state of his domicile,[45] in the contracting state of the assured's domicile or, in the case of co-insurance, in the contracting state in which the leading insurer has been sued.[46] Where the insurance is on real property, the assured has the further option of bringing proceedings in the courts of the place in which the harmful act occurred.[47] Where the insurance is against liability, the assured may, instead of following any of the general jurisdiction rules or special insurance rules, commence his action in the courts of the place in which the harmful act occurred, and may join the insurer as co-defendant in the courts in which an action is brought against the assured in respect of which the insurer may be liable.[48] An action against the assured by the insurer may be brought only in the courts of the assured's domicile.[49]

The purpose of the additional jurisdiction provisions is consumer protection. For this reason, the Convention seeks to restrict the insurer's right to enter into jurisdiction agreements with the assured. An agreement conferring jurisdiction upon the courts of a contracting state is valid only in any one of the following circumstances[50]: it is entered into after the dispute between insurer and assured has arisen; or it does not confer exclusive jurisdiction upon the courts of any one contracting state; or the parties were at the date of the policy domiciled in the same contracting state and the agreement confers jurisdiction upon the courts of that state; or the assured was not at the date of the contract domiciled in a contracting state unless the insurance was compulsory or related to real property. The restrictions on jurisdiction agreements are lifted in respect of various commercial risks, including marine, aviation and transport, and financial loss.

Proper law   **1–51**

Significance. Where an English court has jurisdiction over an insurance dispute, it must apply the proper law of the agreement to the sub-

---

[43] Art. 18. Merely acknowledging receipt of a writ is not, however, submission to jurisdiction: *The Sydney Express* [1988] 2 Lloyd's Rep. 257.
[44] *The Sydney Express, op. cit.*
[44a] *Arkwright Mutual* v. *Bryanstone Insurance* [1990] 2 All E.R. 335; *New Hampshire Insurance* v. *Strabag Bav* (1990) *The Financial Times*, February 21.
[45] Art. 8. If the insurer is domiciled outside the E.C. but has a branch or agency in any contracting state, the insurer is deemed to be domiciled in accordance with the location of the branch or agency. This right is available to a plaintiff himself domiciled outside the European Communities: *Beresford* v. *New Hampshire Insurance, supra.*
[46] Art. 7.
[47] Art. 9: see n. 40, [1990] 2 All E.R. 321.
[48] Arts. 9 and 10.
[49] Art. 11.
[50] Arts. 12 and 12A.

stantive issues which arise; this may or may not be English law.[51] If the proper law is a foreign law, it is assumed to be consistent with English law unless the contrary is proved as a matter of fact by the evidence of appropriate experts.[52] The determination of the proper law depends upon the intentions of the parties "to be ascertained in each case on a consideration of the terms of the contract, the situation of the parties, and generally on all the surrounding facts."[53]

1–52   *Express choice of law.* If the parties have expressly nominated a governing law for their agreement, the English courts will honour their decision even if the chosen law has no independent connection with the agreement.[54] This principle is not applicable, however, if the choice of law is intended to achieve some purpose contrary to public policy,[55] if the agreement is insufficiently certain to enable a proper law to be identified,[56] or, possibly, if the agreement would be unlawful under the nominated law.[57] Not all references to a system of law are to be construed as a choice of that law as the proper law, as it may be that the parties have the more limited intention of incorporating specific rules of a system of law into a contract governed by another system of law.[58]

1–53   *Implied choice of law.* Where there is no express choice of law clause it may nevertheless be possible to ascertain an intention from the remaining terms of the policy. The presence of an arbitration clause which specifies that arbitration is to be held in a specific place is an important, while not conclusive,[59] indication that the law of that place is intended to be the proper law. Similarly, mandatory jurisdiction clauses, such as "In the case of any dispute under the policy, the . . . Company agrees to be bound in all things by the jurisdiction and decision of the English Courts," provide a strong indication that the proper law is that of the nominated jurisdiction,[60] although an optional "suable" clause—stating that any suit *may* be brought within a particular jurisdiction—will not have any impact on the ascertainment of the proper law.[61]

---

[51] English procedural law will of course be applicable to the proceedings: *South Carolina Insurance* v. *Assurantie Maatschappij "de Zeven Provincien"* [1986] 3 All E.R. 487, which demonstrates that the procedures of another jurisdiction may be used to obtain evidence from that jurisdiction for use in English proceedings.

[52] *Callwood* v. *Callwood* [1960] A.C. 659; Civil Evidence Act 1968, s.4.

[53] Lord Wright in *Mount Albert B.C.* v. *Australasian Temperance Association* [1938] A.C. 240.

[54] *Vita Food Products* v. *Unus Shipping* [1939] A.C. 277; *Anderson* v. *Equitable Assurance Society* [1926] All E.R. Rep 93.

[55] Lord Wright in *Vita Food Products* v. *Unus Shipping* [1939] A.C. 277, 291.

[56] *Compagnie D'Armement Maritime* v. *Compagnie Tunisienne de Navigation* [1971] A.C. 572.

[57] This was argued in *Perry* v. *Equitable Life* (1929) 45 T.L.R. 468, although a final decision on the point was not required.

[58] *Ex parte Dever* (1887) 18 Q.B.D. 660. Contrast *Spurrier* v. *La Cloche* [1902] A.C. 446, where, in the absence of an express choice of law provision, the House of Lords regarded a limited incorporation clause in relation to arbitration as evidencing a broader intention for the entire agreement to be governed by the system referred to by the parties.

[59] *Royal Exchange* v. *Sjoforsakrings Aktiebolaget Vega* [1902] 2 K.B. 384; *Maritime Union* v. *Assecuranz Union von 1865* (1935) 52 Ll.L.R. 16; *Norske Atlas Insurance* v. *London General Insurance* (1927) 43 T.L.R. 541; *Afia Worldwide* v. *Deutsche Ruck* (1983) 133 New L.J. 242. See also *Bankers and Shippers Insurance* v. *Liverpool Marine* (1926) 24 Ll.L.R. 85; *First Russian Insurance* v. *London and Lancashire Insurance* [1928] 1 Ch. 922. *Compagnie d'Armement Maritime* v. *Compagnie Tunisienne* [1971] A.C. 572.

[60] *Royal Exchange* v. *Vega, op. cit.*.

[61] *Armadora Occidental* v. *Mann Insurance* [1977] 2 Lloyd's Rep. 406 ("New York suable" clause); *Cantieri Navali Riunita* v. *Omne Justitia* [1985] 2 Lloyd's Rep. 428.

The effect of a "Follow London" clause was considered by the Court of Appeal in *Armorada Occidental* v. *Mann Insurance*.[62] Here two policies were broked and issued in San Francisco to twenty-nine "one-ship" companies run in London but registered in Panama and Liberia: the insurers were from five countries, 39 per cent. of the risk being underwritten by American insurers, 20 per cent. by English insurance companies and 10 per cent. by Lloyd's. The policy contained a "Follow London" clause, which provided that:

> "Assurers herein shall follow Lloyd's underwriters and/or British insurance companies in regard to accounts, terms, conditions, alterations, additions . . . and settlement of claims hereunder."

The Court of Appeal, affirming the judgment of Kerr J., held that the clause was of paramount importance. As was said by Lord Denning, "[the clause] shows that the contract is to be construed and interpreted and applied according to English law."

Other cases: the intention of the parties. In the absence of an express **1–54** choice of law clause and of any contractual provision which gives a persuasive indication of the proper law, the court must ascertain the proper law by seeking to determine in an objective fashion the intention of the parties. In practice an English court will, by weighing competing factors, seek to establish the system of law with which the contract has its greatest connection. This process may on occasion produce a "dead-heat" between competing factors such as the domicile of the parties, the place of performance and the currency of the agreement, but the court is obliged ultimately to come to some conclusion,[63] commonly because the power for it to give leave for service outside the jurisdiction will depend upon whether the proper law of a contract is English law.

At one time it was believed that the location of the insurer's head office was a significant factor in determining proper law, largely because final acceptance will normally be made at head office and also because a policy issued from head office will be in the language and form appropriate to the location of the head office.[64] Whether or not this presumption was ever justified, it is now clear that the proper test in insurance matters is the "centre of gravity" test laid down by Kerr L.J. in *Citadel Insurance* v. *Atlantic Union*,[65] namely that most weight will be given to the place of the making of the contract and of its subsequent administration. This case concerned a contract between a Canadian reinsurer and a Greek reinsured, which was broked and operated in London: the Court of Appeal, rejecting the view of Bingham J. that the London connection was simply one of mechanics, held that the use of the London market and the presence of all of the relevant documents in London were con-

---

[62] [1977] 2 Lloyd's Rep. 406.
[63] *The Assunzione* [1954] p. 150; *Coast Lines* v. *Hudig and Veder Chartering* [1972] 2 Q.B. 34; *Atlantic Underwriting Agencies* v. *Compagnie di Assicurazione di Milano* [1979] 2 Lloyd's Rep. 240.
[64] Life authorities are *Pick* v. *Manufacturers' Life* [1958] 2 Lloyd's Rep. 93 and *Rossano* v. *Manufacturers's Life* [1963] 2 Q.B. 352, although contrast *Buerger* v. *New York Life* [1927] All E.R. Rep. 342, where it was assumed without argument that life policies issued in Russia by a New York insurer were governed by Russian law. Marine authorities are *Greer* v. *Poole* (1880) 5 Q.B.D. 272, *Armadora Occidental* v. *Mann Insurance* [1977] 2 Lloyd's Rep. 406 and *Atlantic Underwriting Agencies* v. *Compania di Assicurazione di Milano* [1979] 2 Lloyd's Rep. 240.
[65] [1982] 2 Lloyd's Rep. 543, 549–550.

clusive factors in favour of English law. This approach had been anticipated by earlier decisions,[66] and would now appear to be firmly established.[67] While the place of formation and of subsequent administration
will today generally provide the proper law, exceptional circumstances
may point to a different conclusion. In *Amin Rasheed Shipping* v. *Kuwait Insurance*[68] the policy was in standard Lloyd's form and was issued by
a Kuwaiti insurer to a Liberian assured: the "centre of gravity" was
undoubtedly Kuwait. A majority of the House of Lords, following the
majority of the Court of Appeal, was of the view that English law was
the proper law, for the reason that Kuwait did not possess an insurance
code so that a policy in English form could be understood only by reference to English rules. Goff L.J. in the Court of Appeal, whose opinion
on the matter was accepted by Lord Wilberforce on appeal, argued
strongly that everything pointed towards Kuwaiti law as the governing
law.

1–55   *Matters governed by the proper law.* Where the English courts are
seised of an action on an insurance policy, the domestic rules of the
proper law[69] will be applied. This has a number of consequences: words
and phrases will be construed in accordance with their proper law meaning as opposed to the law of the forum or of the place of performance[70];
any dispute as to the formation of the contract will be determined by the
rules of the putative proper law[71]; a contract will be enforced if the parties have complied with formalities laid down by the proper law,[72] but
only where the procedural rules of the forum applicable to that class of
contract do not prevent enforcement[73]; the limitation periods operating
under the proper law are to be applied in place of English limitation
periods[74]; and a contract lawful by its proper law[75] will be enforced in
England unless it offends English public policy[76] or it is to be performed

---

[66] *Royal Exchange* v. *Vega* [1902] 2 K.B. 384.

[67] *Afia Worldwide* v. *Deutsche Ruck* (1983) 133 New L.J. 242; *Britannia Steamship Insurance* v.
Ausonia Assicurazione [1984] 2 Lloyd's Rep. 98; *Islamic Arab Insurance* v. *Saudi Egyptian American
Reinsurance* [1987] 1 Lloyd's Rep. 315.

[68] [1983] 2 All E.R. 884.

[69] As opposed to the conflict of laws rules of the proper law, as these might have the effect of requiring some other law to be regarded as the proper law: *Amin Rasheed* v. *Kuwait Insurance* [1983] 2 All
E.R. 884, 888 *per* Lord Diplock.

[70] *Rowatt Leaky & Co.* v. *Scottish Provident* [1927] 1 Ch. 55, where this rule deprived the words of a
technical meaning established in the place of performance but not elsewhere. But see *Forsakringsaktieselskapet Vesta* v. *Butcher* [1989] 1 All E.R. 402, where the House of Lords held that the English proper
law of a reinsurance agreement did not prevent its meaning being determined in accordance with Norwegian law as the proper law of the underlying insurance: this ensured that the reinsurer's liability
matched that of the reinsured.

[71] *Albeko Shumaschinen* v. *Kamborian Shoe Machine Co.* (1961) 111 Sol. Jo. 519; *The Parouth*
[1982] 2 Lloyd's Rep. 351, *Britannia Steamship Insurance* v. *Ausonia Assicurazione* [1984] 2 Lloyd's
Rep. 98; *Marc Rich* v. *Societa Italiana* [1989] 1 Lloyd's Rep. 548. Express choice of law clauses are
apparently to be disregarded, possibly because these are normally to be construed as governing disputes under the valid contract and not the question whether the contract is valid *ab initio*: *Mackender* v.
Feldia [1967] 2 Q.B. 590.

[72] *Van Grutten* v. *Digby* (1862) 31 Beav. 561. Alternatively, it is sufficient if the formalities laid down
by the place in which the contract was made have been complied with: *Guepratte* v. *Young* (1851) 4 De
G. & Sm. 217.

[73] For example, the requirement of the M.I.A. 1906 that a contract of marine insurance is to be
embedded in a policy: *cf. Leroux* v. *Brown* (1852) 12 C.B. 801.

[74] Foreign Limitation Periods Act 1984. The English courts have a discretion to disapply the Act in
cases of "undue hardship". See: *The Komninos S* (1990) *The Financial Times*, January 16; *Jones* v.
Trollope & Colls (1990) *The Times*, January 26.

[75] See *Kahler* v. *Midland Bank* [1950] A.C. 24, where the contract was unlawful under its proper law.

[76] *Boissevain* v. *Weil* [1950] A.C. 327; *Addison* v. *Brown* [1954] 2 All E.R. 213.

contrary to English law in England.[77] In the case of assignment of a policy, the proper law of the policy governs the substantive validity of its assignment[78] as well as priorities between competing assignees,[79] while the law of the place of assignment governs formal validity.

Payment of the proceeds. Policy moneys, like debts or other things in **1-56** action, are recoverable—subject to any contrary provision in the policy—where the debtor (normally, in the present context, the insurer) resides[80] or, in the case of a company, carries on business.[81] Where a company carries on business in two or more countries, the moneys are recoverable where they are primarily payable by express or implied term of the contract.[82] The ultimate title to policy moneys upon the death of the assured depends upon the law of the domicile of the assured at the date of his death, as that law governs questions of succession.[83]

Sometimes policies sued upon in England express the policy moneys to be payable in a foreign currency. Prior to 1975 it was settled law that an English court could not award sums in a foreign currency: the rule was that the judgment would be in sterling, the rate of exchange being fixed at the date at which the cause of action arose.[84] In the case of an insurance policy, given that a claim is treated as an action for breach of contract giving rise to unliquidated damages, the rate of exchange would be fixed at the date of the claim. The underlying principle was nevertheless widely regarded as unsatisfactory, for the plaintiff would receive a windfall if sterling had appreciated against the currency of account between the date of his action and the date of judgment, but would be left worse of in the event of the depreciation of sterling in that period. Consequently, in 1975 in *Miliangos* v. *Frank (Textiles)*[85] the House of Lords invoked its 1966 Practice Statement[86] and overruled its own earlier decision in *Re United Railways of Havana.*[87]

Consequently, an English court may now order payment by the defendant either in foreign currency or in sterling equivalent at a rate of exchange fixed at the date at which the court authorises the enforcement of its judgment. The *Miliangos* case concerned a claim for liquidated damages under a contract governed by the law of the currency of account. However, subsequent cases have made it clear that the principle is applicable to claims for unliquidated sums (such as claims under insurance policies),[88] and to claims under contracts the proper law of which is English law as long as the plaintiff's loss was suffered in a foreign currency.[89]

---

[77] *Clugas* v. *Penaluna* (1791) 4 T.R. 466.
[78] *Pender* v. *Provincial Bank of Scotland* 1940 S.L.T. 306, but contrast *Lee* v. *Abdy* (1886) 17 Q.B.D. 309, which seems no longer to represent English law.
[79] *Le Fevre* v. *Sullivan* (1855) 10 Moo.P.C. 1.
[80] *Jabbour* v. *Custodian of Israeli Absentee Property* [1954] 1 W.L.R. 139.
[81] *Jabbour, ibid.* at p. 146.
[82] *New York Life* v. *Public Trustee* [1924] 2 Ch. 101.
[83] *Re Maldonado* [1954] p. 233; *Haas* v. *Atlas Insurance* [1913] 2 K.B. 209.
[84] *Re United Railways of Havana* [1961] A.C. 1007; *Anderson* v. *Equitable Assurance* [1926] 134 L.T. 557.
[85] [1976] A.C. 443.
[86] *Practice Statement (Judicial Precedent)* [1966] 1 W.L.R. 1234.
[87] [1961] A.C. 1007.
[88] *Société Francaise* v. *Belcan* [1985] 3 All E.R. 378.
[89] *The Despina R* and *The Folias* [1979] A.C. 685.

1–57 Appendix: Choice of law in the European Communities

These above rules as to determination of the proper law, while remaining of general application, are shortly to be superseded in fundamental respects. First, the United Kingdom is about to implement into English law the Rome Convention of 1980; the implementing Bill, the Contracts (Applicable Law) Bill 1989, is expected to receive the Royal Assent in 1990. Secondly, as regards non-life insurance, the Second Directive on Non-life Insurance establishes choice of law rules to be applied to policies covering risks within member states; these are to be implemented by statutory instrument before June 1990. Thirdly, as regards life insurance, the draft Second Life Insurance Directive establishes choice of law rules applicable to assureds resident within member states. It may be that, when all of these measures are implemented, little will remain of existing principles.

1–58 *The Rome Convention.* This Convention, when operative and applicable, recognises party autonomy by permitting them to choose the governing law, subject only to public policy considerations; present English law is to the same effect. However, in the absence of express choice, the Convention parts company with English law. The "applicable law" is to be "the law of the country with which [the contract] is most closely connected." There is a rebuttable presumption this law is that of "the country where the party who is to effect the performance which is characteristic of the contract has, at the time of the conclusion of the contract, his habitual residence, or, in the case of a body corporate or unincorporate, its central administration." This presumption may be rebutted where "it appears from the circumstances as a whole that the contract is more closely connected with another country."

1–59 The Rome Convention does *not* apply to "contracts of insurance which cover risks situated in the territories of the Member States of the European Economic Community." This provision means that there is no overlap between rules in the Second Non-Life and draft Second Life Directives and the Rome Convention. The location of a risk is to be determined by national law, although this matter is to be resolved by implementing legislation in accordance with the rules established in those Directives. The Rome Convention does, however, apply to reinsurance. Consequently, the London market must brace itself against the uncertainties of an entirely fresh set of rules the operation of which is presently far from clear. Will, for example, the English courts, in the absence of express choice of law clauses, continue to give primacy to the seat of the arbitration, or will they apply the as yet uncertain Rome Convention presumption?

1–60 *The Second Non-Life Directive.* The rules for selecting the governing law of a non-life policy in respect of a risk located within a member state are as follows. It will be appreciated that party autonomy is severely restricted by these rules:

(a) If the assured is habitually resident or has its central administration in the member state in which the risk is located, the governing law is the law of that member state, although the parties are free to contract out of the law if that law so allows.

(b) If the assured's residence or administration and the risk are located in different member states, the parties may choose the law of either of those states.

(c) Where the policy covers business risks located in different member states, the choice of law may be that of any of those states.

(d) As regards (b) and (c), the parties may in addition choose any law permitted by the law of any of the relevant member states.

(e) In (a), (b) and (c), when the events insured against are located in a member state other than that in which the risk is located, the parties may also choose the law of that member state.

(f) In the case of a large or mass risk, the parties have an unfettered choice of law.

(g) Where the contract is connected only with one member state but the law of a different state is chosen, the choice of law may be overriden by public policy requirements.

(h) An express choice of law must be made with reasonable certainty. In the absence of a clear choice of law, the governing law is that of the state with which the contract is most closely connected; this is rebuttably presumed to be the country in which the risk is located.

The draft Second Life Directive. The proposed choice of law rules in **1–61** this document are as follows:

(a) The applicable law is the law of the place in which the policy-holder has his habitual residence or, in the case of a company, has its head office. However, where that law permits it, some other law may be chosen.

(b) Where the policy-holder has taken the initiative in seeking a policy, and he is a national of a member state other than that in which he has his residence, the parties may choose the law of the member state of his nationality.

CHAPTER 2

CONSTRUCTION OF THE POLICY

1. CONSTRUCTION OF WORDS

General principle of construction   2–01

A policy of insurance is to be construed like any other contract[1]; it is to be construed in the first place from the terms used in it, which terms are themselves to be understood in their primary,[2] natural, ordinary[3] and popular[4] sense. The meaning of a word in a policy is that which an ordinary man of normal intelligence would place upon it,[5] it is to be construed as it is used in the English language by ordinary persons.[6] Thus it has been held that "gas" in an insurance policy is to be given its ordinary or popular sense and not a philosophical or scientific meaning, and "fire" does not include explosion,[7] although explosion, scientifically speaking, might involve ignition. So popular phrases must be given their popular and not their literary meaning[8]: thus death "by the hands" of the assured has been held to include death by drowning.[9]

Words in context   2–02

The above generality is not applicable when it is clear from the context that the words are not used in a colloquial popular sense. Thus the word "flood" in the phrase "storm, tempest or flood" does not cover a case where a householder's bathroom is affected by upward seepage of water to a depth of three inches, as the context of the word requires an event violent, sudden or abnormal.[10] Similarly, heavy rain is not in itself likely to constitute a storm.[11]

---

[1] Considering whether a provision in a contract should be construed as a condition or a warranty, Roskill L.J. said in *Cehave* v. *Bremer* [1976] Q.B. 44, 71 (approved by Lord Wilberforce in *Reardon Smith* v. *Hansen-Tangen* [1976] 1 W.L.R. 989, 998): "It is desirable that the same legal principles should apply to the law of contract as a whole and that different legal principles should not apply to different branches of that law." See 1–15, *supra*, n. 54.

[2] Farwell L.J. in *Yangtze Assurance* v. *Indemnity Marine* [1908] 2 K.B. 504, 509.

[3] Parke B. in *Glen* v. *Lewis* (1853) 8 Ex. 607, 618; Brett L.J. in *West India Telegraph Co.* v. *Home & Colonial Marine* (1880) 6 Q.B.D. 51, 58; *Thomson* v. *Weems* (1884) 9 App.Cas. 671, 687, *per* Lord Watson *Thames & Mersey Marine* v. *Hamilton, Fraser* (1887) 12 App.Cas. 484, 493, *per* Lord Bramwell; Lord Esher M.R. in *Leo Steamship Co.* v. *Corderoy* (1896) 1 Com.Cas. 379, 385; Smith L.J. in *Re George and Goldsmiths Insurance* [1899] 1 Q.B. 595, 608; Lord Macnaghten in *Thompson* v. *Equity Fire* [1910] A.C. 592, 597 (P.C.).

[4] Wilmot C.J. in *Drinkwater* v. *London Assurance* (1767) 2 Wils. 363; Lord Dunedin in *Curtis's & Harvey* v. *North British* [1921] A.C. 303, 311 (P.C.); *Stanley* v. *Western Insurance* (1868) L.R. 3 Ex. 71.

[5] McCardie J. in *Yorke* v. *Yorkshire Insurance* [1918] 1 K.B. 662, 666.

[6] Fry L.J. in *Hart* v. *Standard Marine* (1889) 22 Q.B.D. 499, 503; *Stanley* v. *Western Insurance* (1868) L.R. 3 Ex. 71, 73, *per* Kelly C.B.

[7] *Re Hooley Hill Rubber & Chemical Co. Ltd* [1970] 1 K.B. 257.

[8] Maugham L.J. in *Algemeene Bank* v. *Langton* (1935) 40 Com.Cas. 247, 259.

[9] *Borradaile* v. *Hunter* (1843) 5 M. & G. 639.

[10] *Young* v. *Sun Alliance* [1976] 2 Lloyd's Rep. 189.

[11] *Anderson* v. *Norwich Union* [1977] 1 Lloyd's Rep. 253. By way of contrast, the Scottish courts have held that a heavy fall of snow is, in the absence of high winds, capable of constituting a storm: *Glasgow Training Group* v. *Lombard Continental* (1988) *The Times*, November 21.

37

2–03 Technical words

The general rule is also subject to well-defined limitations summed up by Parke B. in *Clift* v. *Schwabe*.[12] "Terms of art or technical words must be understood in their proper sense, unless the context controls or alters their meaning; ancient words may be explained by contemporaneous usage; and words which have acquired a particular sense by usage in particular districts, occupations or trades,[13] must be read (the usage being established as a matter of evidence) in their acquired sense."

Terms of legal art are to be given their technical meaning. Thus "riot" is to be interpreted when it occurs in an insurance policy with the special meaning attached to it by the criminal law,[14] and "theft" is to be construed in accordance with the Theft Act 1968.[15] This rule does not apply to such words as "hold-up," which do not occur in Acts of Parliament relating to the criminal law, or are not otherwise known to English law as technical phrases.[16] Thus, in *Clift* v. *Schwabe*,[17] "commit suicide" was given its popular sense, including suicide while insane, and not the limited meaning of the technical phrase *felo de se* which refers only to sane suicide. Suicide ceased to be a crime by virtue of the Suicide Act 1961.

Besides, many words, though not otherwise technical legal words of art, have come to have a fixed meaning or a fixed construction in insurance policies.[18] The meaning of such phrases as "civil commotion" and "perils of the sea"[19] have been determined by judicial decisions which are now part of the law of the land. Once a phrase has been given a definite meaning by the courts for a long period, not even a court of higher jurisdiction will overrule earlier decisions on the matter.[20]

Such cases aside, it should not be forgotten that ordinary words may have a secondary technical meaning which the context of the policy indicates to be the intended meaning. In *Commonwealth Smelting* v. *Guardian Royal Exchange*[21] the Court of Appeal ruled that there was no "explosion" where a piece of metal caused the outer casing of a motor to shatter; some physical or chemical reaction was required before there could be said to have been an explosion.

2–04 The ejusdem generis rule

The general rule of construction that where general words are linked with particular words they must be construed as limited to the same

---

[12] (1846) 3 C.B. 437, 469.

[13] And sports. Thus where a life policy excluded from full benefit death as a result of "motor racing, motor speed hill climbs, motor trials or rallies" the Commercial Court held that the phrase "motor racing" and the following words were used in a technical sense, and that evidence was admissible as to their meaning in the sport. *Scragg* v. *U.K. Temperance* [1976] 2 Lloyd's Rep. 227, Mocatta J.

[14] *London & Lancashire Fire* v. *Bolands* [1924] A.C. 836, a principle codified to some extent by the Public Order Act 1986; see § 18–13 *infra*.

[15] *Grundy (Teddington)* v. *Fulton* [1983] 1 Lloyd's Rep 16; *Dobson* v. *General Accident* [1989] 3 All E.R. 927.

[16] Maugham L.J. in *Algemeene Bankvereeniging* v. *Langton* (1935) 40 Com.Cas. 247, 259.

[17] (1846) 3 C.B. 437.

[18] Vaughan Williams L.J. in *London & Manchester Plate Glass* v. *Heath* [1913] 3 K.B. 411, 416.

[19] Brett L.J. in *West India Telegraph Co.* v. *Home & Colonial Marine* (1880) 6 Q.B.D. 51, 59.

[20] Lord Dunedin in *Becker, Gray* v. *London Assurance* [1918] A.C. 101, 108; *Thames & Mersey Marine* v. *Hamilton, Fraser* (1887) 12 App.Cas. 484, *per* Lord Halsbury L.C. at p. 491; *per* Lord Herschell at p. 494; Lord Halsbury in *Andersen* v. *Marten* [1908] A.C. 334, 340.

[21] [1984] 2 Lloyd's Rep 608.

genus as the particular words applies to policies of insurance.[22] Thus an insurance of a vessel against the perils of the seas, men-of-war, fire, etc., and "all other perils," has been held not to cover the explosion of a donkey boiler.[23] So the meaning to be attached to a word can often be ascertained by considering the words with which it is linked: *noscitur a sociis*. Thus "household furniture, linen, wearing apparel and plate" has been held to include household linen but not linen drapery goods bought on speculation.[24] The parties to a policy may however make it clear that the rule is not to apply.[25]

2. CONSTRUCTION OF POLICY AS A WHOLE

Just as individual words and phrases will be construed in their ordinary **2–05** meaning, so also will the policy as a whole. It has often been said that the intention of the parties is paramount, but it is only the intention of the parties as declared by the words of the policy which may be taken into account.[26] The task of the court is to reach the meaning of the parties through the words they have used,[27] assuming that they mean what they say, and looking only at the policy.

It follows accordingly that the terms and conditions of a policy must be literally[28] construed according to their natural and ordinary meaning,[29] even though the result is harsh and technical.[30] In construing them the ordinary rules of grammar must be observed.[31] It is only where the result of applying such rules will make a clause meaningless that they may be ignored, as where the word "not" is added in error.[32]

But effect must, if possible, be given to every word in the policy,[33] and a reasonable construction must therefore be given to each clause in order to give effect to the plain and obvious intention of the parties as collected from the whole instrument.[34] It is no objection to a clause,

---

[22] Lord Coleridge C.J. in *Mair* v. *Railway Passengers Assurance* (1877) 37 L.T. 356, 358; but see Denman J. at p. 359.

[23] *Thames & Mersey Marine* v. *Hamilton Fraser* (1887) 12 App.Cas. 484. The standard marine clauses do now, however, cover such perils.

[24] *Watchorn* v. *Langford* (1813) 3 Camp. 422.

[25] *Sun Fire* v. *Hart* (1889) 14 App.Cas. 98 (P.C.).

[26] Lord Kenyon C.J. in *Tarleton* v. *Staniforth* (1794) 5 T.R. 695, 699; Lawrence J. in *Marsden* v. *Reid* (1803) 3 East 572, 579; Tindal C.J. in *Stavers* v. *Curling* (1836) 3 Bing.N.C. 355, 370; Crompton J. in *Braunstein* v. *Accidental Death* (1861) 1 B. & S. 782, 797; Collins L.J. in *Re George and Goldsmiths Insurance* [1899] 1 Q.B. 595, 610; Bankes L.J. in *Koskas* v. *Standard Marine* (1927) 137 L.T. 165, 167.

[27] Lord Halsbury L.C. in *Thames & Mersey Marine* v. *Hamilton, Fraser* (1887) 12 App.Cas. 484, 490.

[28] Lord Fitzgerald in *Cory* v. *Burr* (1883) 8 App.Cas. 393, 405; Lord Watson in *Sun Fire* v. *Hart* (1889) 14 App.Cas. 98, 104; Warrington L.J. in *Re United London and Scottish, Brown's Claim* [1915] 2 Ch. 167, 172.

[29] Lord O'Hagan in *Pearson* v. *Commercial Union* (1876) 1 App.Cas. 498, 510.

[30] Viscount Haldane in *Dawsons* v. *Boninn* [1922] 2 A.C. 413, 424.

[31] Willes J. in *Ionides* v. *Universal Marine* (1863) 14 C.B.(N.S.) 259, 289; Lord Esher M.R. in *Price* v. *Al Ships' Small Damage Insurance* (1889) 22 Q.B.D. 580, 584; Lord Sumner in *London & Lancashire Fire* v. *Bolands* [1924] A.C. 836, 848; Roche J. in *Holmes* v. *Payne* [1930] 2 K.B. 301; Lord Russell in *Anglo-International Bank* v. *General Accident* (1934) 48 Ll.L.R. 151, 155.

[32] *Glen's Trustees* v. *Lancashire & Yorkshire Accident* (1906) 8 F. (Ct. of Sess.) 915, 917, 918, *per* Lord Dunedin.

[33] Lord Sumner in *Yorkshire Insurance* v. *Campbell* [1917] A.C. 218, 224 (P.C.); Atkin L.J. in *City Tailors* v. *Evans* (1927) 38 T.L.R. 230, 234; Scrutton L.J. in *Roberts* v. *Anglo-Saxon Insurance* (1927) 96 L.J.K.B. 590, 594.

[34] Erskine J. in *Borradaile* v. *Hunter* (1843) 5 M. & G. 639, 657.

however, that it is redundant,[35] or inserted out of an excess of caution.[36] Effect must be given to a clause nonetheless though it is contained on a separate slip of paper pasted to the policy, if in fact it forms part of it.[37] Sometimes it is plain that a particular provision cannot apply to the facts of a particular contract.[38] An effort must however be made to construe a policy adapted for some unusual subject-matter so as to give each provision in it some meaning. Thus, in *Beacon Life* v. *Gibb*[39] a policy framed for buildings was used for the insurance of a ship. It was held that provision against keeping gunpower on "the premises" was applicable, and that evidence of usage relating to the carriage of gun-powder on ships was therefore inadmissible.

2–06 Deletions

It is permissible in construing a document to pay attention to words struck out.[40] Where the parties deliberately delete words from a printed form this is often a most useful guide to their intended meaning.

2–07 Ut res magis valeat quam pereat

The policy must if possible be construed to make it an effective legal document: thus where it is ambiguous it will be presumed to be made with the person who had an interest in the subject-matter,[41] and a policy must not, where there are two constructions open, be given a meaning that will render it a wagering contract and therefore unenforceable.[42] Similarly, it is prima facie to be assumed that a motor-vehicle policy affords the cover required by statute.[43]

Thus a word must not be given its technical signification if the effect is to make the provision in which it occurs inoperative. So "legally" in the phrase "legally assigned" was not given its technical meaning, as opposed to "equitably," at a time when legal assignments in this sense were not possible.[44]

2–08 Conflicting clauses

Where after every effort to reconcile them, two clauses of a contract of insurance appear plainly in conflict, it is necessary to consider the comparative weight to be given to each of them.[45] In such a case three rules are applicable to determine which clause shall prevail:

---

[35] See Roche J. in *Curtis* v. *Mathews* [1918] 2 K.B. 825, 830; affirmed [1919] 1 K.B. 425.

[36] One leans towards treating words as adding something rather than as mere surplusage, Somervell L.J. in *S.A. Maritime* v. *Anglo-Iranian* [1954] 1 W.L.R. 492, 495, but less so in construing a commercial document than a statute, Devlin J. *ibid.* [1953] 1 W.L.R. 1379, 1384.

[37] Lord Halsbury L.C. in *Bensaude* v. *Thames & Mersey Marine* [1897] A.C. 609, 612.

[38] Atkin L.J. in *City Tailors* v. *Evans, supra*; Lord Penzance in *Dudgeon* v. *Pembroke* (1877) 2 App.-Cas. 284, 293. See also Rigby L.J. in *Hydarnes S.S. Co.* v. *Indemnity Mutual Marine* [1895] 1 Q.B. 500, 509; *Home Insurance of New York* v. *Victoria-Montreal Fire* [1907] A.C. 59 (P.C.); *Forsikringsaktie-selskapet Vesta* v. *Butcher* [1989] 1 All E.R. 402.

[39] (1862) 1 Moo.P.C.C.(N.S.) 73.

[40] Harman J. in *City and Westminster Properties* v. *Mudd* [1959] 1 Ch. 129, 140, 141, and cases there cited; *The London Explorer* [1972] A.C. 1, 15, 16, *per* Lord Reid. Judicial dicta to the contrary (*per* Lord Sumner in *Sassoon* v. *International Banking Corp.* [1927] A.C. 711, 721; Lord Finlay in *Ambatie-los* v. *Anton Jurgens* [1923] A.C. 175, 185) are in practice ignored.

[41] *Sutherland Marine* v. *Kearney and Noonan* (1851) 16 Q.B. 925.

[42] *Coker* v. *Bolton* [1912] 3 K.B. 315.

[43] Lord Wright in *Digby* v. *General Accident* [1943] A.C. 121, 141.

[44] *Dufaur* v. *Professional Life* (1858) 25 Beav. 599.

[45] Lord Birkenhead in *Mountain* v. *Whittle* [1921] 1 A.C. 615 at p. 621.

(a) the rule that the policy should be construed more strongly against the insurers[46];

(b) where printed and written or typewritten words are in any kind of conflict greatest weight should be given to the written words, and greater weight should be given to typewritten than to printed words[47];

(c) if a contract is contained in more than one document greater weight should be given to the later in date[48]; where the later instrument conflicts with the earlier it is presumed to be the intention of the parties so to vary it.[49]

But there is no rule that large print is to be preferred to small print, and a clause must not be ignored simply because it is difficult to read[50] except in an extreme case.[51]

It is only exceptionally that these rules come into operation: the primary rule is that effect should be given if possible to every part of the contract, whether the parts are in writing or printed,[52] or whether they occur earlier or later in the policy[53] or in date.[54] Thus if a part of the contract is contained in the proposal, and a part in the policy, effect must be given if possible to both those documents.[55] The proposal conditions and the express conditions of the policy must be read together and so far as may be, reconciled, so that every part of the contract may receive effect. It is only if there is a final and direct inconsistency that the terms of the policy, on account of the third rule, must prevail.[56]

Even in that event the court will not allow the insurer to take advantage of a clause in the policy varying the rights of the assured in the proposal where the assured would be entitled to come to the court and claim rectification of the policy.[57]

Recitals   2–09

Where the policy contains recitals recourse may be had to them in construing an ambiguous clause in the policy,[58] but where the operative words are unambiguous the recitals cannot be resorted to to vary their grammatical meaning.[59]

Incorporated documents   2–10

The terms of an insurance agreement may be contained in more than one document, where there is incorporation by reference into the

---

[46] See § 2–11, *infra.*

[47] *Glynn* v. *Margetson* [1893] A.C. 351. But typed words in wide terms may be limited by a narrower clause in print which would otherwise be repugnant to them: *Berk* v. *Style* [1956] 1 Q.B. 180.

[48] *Williams* v. *Agius* [1914] A.C. 510.

[49] Roche J. in *Kaufmann* v. *British Surety Insurance* (1929) 45 T.L.T. 399; 33 Ll.L.R. 315, 318.

[50] *Koskas* v. *Standard Marine* (1927) 137 L.T. 165, *per* Scrutton L.J. at pp. 168, 169, and *per* Bankes L.J. at p. 167.

[51] For such a case see *Harvey* v. *Ventilatorenfabrik Velde* (1988) *The Financial Times* 11 November.

[52] Blackburn J. in *Joyce* v. *Realm Marine* (1872) L.R. 7 Q.B. 580, 583.

[53] Erle J. in *Harrison* v. *Ellis* (1857) 7 E. & B. 465, 481.

[54] Bankes L.J. in *Koskas* v. *Standard Marine* (1927) 137 L.T. 165, 167.

[55] Lord Treyner in *Reid* v. *Employers' Accident* (1899) 1 F. (Ct. of Sess.) 1031, 1036.

[56] Lord Wright in *Izzard* v. *Universal Insurance* [1937] A.C. 773, 780.

[57] *Collett* v. *Morrison* (1851) 9 Hare 162; *Wood* v. *Dwarris* (1856) 11 Ex. 493; *Re Bradley and Essex Accident* [1912] 1 K.B. 415.

[58] Swinfen Eady L.J. in *Blascheck* v. *Bussell* (1916) 33 T.L.R. 74, 75.

[59] Lord Russell of Killowen in *Anglo-International Bank* v. *General Accident* (1934) 48 Ll.L.R. 151, 155.

policy. It is common to provide that the terms of the proposal form are deemed to be a part of the policy itself, by means of a "basis of the contract" clause in the proposal, although insurers generally do not rely upon such incorporation as against indivduals.[60] Incoporated terms are to be given the same weight as terms in the policy itself, although the courts have refused to give effect to incorporation provisions insofar as they seek to incorporate terms which are plainly inconsistent with the policy[61] or which are onerous and have not properly been brought to the attention of the assured.[62]

2–11 Contra proferentem rule

Quite apart from contradictory clauses in policies, ambiguities are common in them and it is often very uncertain what the parties to them mean.[63] In such cases the rule is that the policy, being drafted in language chosen by the insurers, must be taken most strongly against them.[64] It is construed *contra proferentes*, against those who offer it. In a doubtful case the turn of the scale ought to be given against the speaker, because he has not clearly and fully expressed himself.[65] Nothing is easier than for the insurers to express themselves in plain terms.[66] The assured cannot put his own meaning upon a policy,[67] but, where it is ambiguous, it is to be construed in the sense in which he might reasonably have understood it.[68] If the insurers wish to escape liability under given circumstances, they must use words admitting of no possible doubt.[69]

But a clause is only to be construed *contra proferentes* in cases of real ambiguity.[70] One must not use the rule to create an ambiguity, one must find the ambiguity first.[71] Even where a clause by itself is ambiguous if, by looking at the whole policy, its meaning becomes clear, there is no room for the application of the doctrine.[72] So also where if one meaning is given to a clause, the rest of the policy becomes clear, the policy should be construed accordingly.[73]

---

[60] By virtue of the Statements of Insurance Practice. For "basis" clauses generally, and the effect of the Statements upon them, see Chap. 6 *infra*.

[61] *Home Insurance of New York* v. *Victoria-Montreal Fire* [1907] A.C. 59 (P.C.); *Pine Top Insurance* v. *Unione Italiana Anglo-Saxon Reinsurance* [1987] 1 Lloyd's Rep. 476; *Forsikringsaktieselskapet Vesta* v. *Butcher* [1989] 1 All E.R. 402, 407, *per* Lord Griffiths.

[62] See generally *Interfoto Picture Library* v. *Stiletto Visual Programmes* [1988] 2 W.L.R. 615; *Circle Freight* v. *Medeast Gulf Exports* [1988] 2 Lloyds's Rep. 427.

[63] Wilmot C.J. in *Drinkwater* v. *London Assurance* (1767) 2 Wils. 363, 364.

[64] Lord Kenyon in *Tarleton* v. *Staniforth* (1794) 5 T.R. 695, 699; Blackburn J. in *Fowkes* v. *Manchester & London Life* (1863) 3 B. & S. 917, 929, 930; Willis J. in *Fitton* v. *Accidental Death* (1864) 17 C.B.(N.S.) 122, 135; Kelly C.B. in *Smith* v. *Accident* (1870) L.R. 5 Ex. 302; *Re Etherington and Lancashire & Yorkshire Accident* [1909] 1 K.B. 591, 596; Blackburn J. in *Thomson* v. *Weems* (1884) 9 App.Cas. 671, 682; Viscount Sumner in *Lake* v. *Simmons* [1927] A.C. 487, 508–511. See *Taylor* v. *National Insurance Corporation* [1989] 6 C.L. 248.

[65] Wilmot C.J. in *Drinkwater* v. *London Assurance* (1767) 2 Wils. 363, 364; *Houghton* v. *Trafalgar* [1954] 1 Q.B. 247.

[66] Cockburn C.J. in *Notman* v. *Anchor* (1858) 4 C.B.(N.S.) 476, 481.

[67] *Life Association of Scotland* v. *Forster* (1873) 11 M. (Ct. of Sess.) 351, 371.

[68] Blackburn J. in *Fowkes'* case, *supra*, cited by Lord Deas in *Forster's* case, *supra*, at p. 369.

[69] Lord Russell of Killowen in *Provincial* v. *Morgan* [1933] A.C. 240, 250.

[70] Lord Denman C.J. in *Hare* v. *Barstow* (1844) 8 Jur. 928, 929.

[71] Lindley L.J. in *Cornish* v. *Accident Insurance* (1889) 23 Q.B.D. 453, 456; and in *Cole* v. *Accident Insurance* (1889) 5 T.L.R. 736, 737; *Alder* v. *Moore* [1960] 2 Lloyd's Rep. 325.

[72] du Parcq J. in *Passmore* v. *Vulcan Boiler & General Insurance* (1936) 154 L.T. 258, 259. *Young* v. *Sun Alliance* [1976] 2 Lloyd's Rep. 189.

[73] Lord Sumner in *Yorkshire Insurance* v. *Campbell* [1917] A.C. 218, 223 (P.C.).

Sometimes the assured or a broker is responsible for the wording of a part of the policy, and in such cases the rule may not be applicable,[74] and evidence will be admissible to show who in fact was responsible.[75] Where a proposal is accepted without qualification by the insurers, plainly ambiguous statements by the assured in it are to be construed against them,[76] but tricky or misleading statements will be construed against the assured.[77] In any case the rule applies with full force to warranties and other such engagements by the assured, which are drafted by the insurers, and in drafting them the insurers are bound to use unequivocal language such as persons of ordinary intelligence may, without difficulty, understand.[78]

Surrounding circumstances   2–12

In construing a policy, regard may be had to the surrounding circumstances[79] such as the nature of the transaction and the known course of business and the forms in which such matters are carried out, but regard may not be given to, and in this respect evidence is not admissible of, particular facts that occurred at the inception of the transaction or during the negotiations.[80] The old rule, that parol evidence is not admissible to explain the construction of a written instrument,[81] applies to policies of insurance as to any other instrument.[82]

Custom   2–13

While evidence may not be given in order to show that a policy was meant to be understood in a particular way, evidence may be given of a custom of the trade subject to which the policy was executed.[83] Such a custom must be a general custom of the trade.[84] However, no custom can ever be admitted to contradict the plain terms of the policy,[85] usage may be admissible to explain what is doubtful, it is never admissible to contradict what is plain.[86] Custom cannot be relied on to modify the natural meaning of a policy, it was said in a fire insurance case.[87] In fact it is rare for a plea of custom to be raised, and still rarer for it to succeed, in non-marine insurance cases.

---

[74] Lord Watson in *Birrell* v. *Dryer* (1884) 9 App.Cas. 345, 354.
[75] *Quin* v. *National Assurance* (1839) Jones & Carey 316 (Ire).
[76] Bankes L.J. in *Dunn* v. *Campbell* (1920) 4 Ll.L.R. 36, 39. See also *de Maurier (Jewels)* v. *Bastion Ins. Co.* [1967] 2 Lloyd's Rep. 550, 559, 560. (Cases of the construction of brokers' slips.)
[77] *Condogianis* v. *Guardian* [1921] 2 A.C. 125.
[78] *Life Association of Scotland* v. *Forster* (1873) 11 M. (Ct. of Sess.) 351, 364, 371.
[79] What, in fact Lord Wilberforce refers to in *Reardon-Smith* v. *Hansen-Tangen*, [1976] as the "factual matrix" in which the parties were, which forms an objective setting in which the contract is to be construed.
[80] Lord Sumner in *Yorkshire Insurance* v. *Campbell* [1917] A.C. 218, 225; Lord Esher M.R. in *Hydarnes Steamship Co.* v. *Indemnity Mutual Marine* [1895] 1 Q.B. 500, 504.
[81] Lord Mansfield in *Loraine* v. *Thomlinson* (1781) 2 Dougl. 585, 587.
[82] *Weston* v. *Emes* (1808) 1 Taunt. 115, 117; Blackburn J. in *Burges* v. *Wickham* (1863) 3 B. & S. 669, 696, *Newsholme Brothers* v. *Road Transport and General Insurance* [1929] 2 K.B. 356. The parol evidence rule is, however, falling into general disfavour: *Howard Marine* v. *Ogden* [1978] 2 All E.R. 1134.
[83] *Crofts* v. *Marshall* (1836) 7 C. & P. 597.
[84] Lord Lyndhurst C.B. in *Blackett* v. *Royal Exchange* (1832) 2 G. & J. 244, 249; Lord Denman C.J. in *Crofts* v. *Marshall, supra,* at p. 605.
[85] Lord Campbell C.J. in *Hall* v. *Janson* (1855) 4 E. & B. 500, 509, 510.
[86] See n. 84.
[87] Lush J. in *Australian Agricultural Co.* v. *Saunders* (1875) L.R. 10 C.P. 668, 677.

2–14 Latent ambiguity

So, also, while evidence may not be given to explain an ambiguity which appears on the face of the policy, a *patent* ambiguity, it is admissible to explain a *latent* ambiguity.[88] Thus where premises are insured against fire, evidence is admissible to prove the identity and extent of the premises insured,[89] and evidence may similarly be admissible to prove that the property insured was on risk at the time of the loss.[90] Such questions are questions of fact, and are properly decided on the evidence adduced.

2–15 Construction question of law

The construction of a policy is a question of law for the court, and not a question of fact.

2–16 Other jurisdictions

British policies of insurance are frequently construed in foreign countries who have very different standards of construction. Thus, in *Gerdhart* v. *Continental Insurance Co.*[91] an exclusionary clause in a householder's comprehensive insurance was ignored by the Supreme Court of New Jersey on the ground that it was "neither conspicuous nor plain and clear."

---

[88] Lord Denman C.J. in *Hare* v. *Barstow* (1844) 8 Jur. 928, 929.
[89] *Hordern* v. *Commercial Union* (1887) 56 L.J.P.C. 78.
[90] *Hunting* v. *Boulton* (1895) 1 Com.Cas. 120; see also *Kaufmann* v. *British Surety Insurance* (1929) 45 T.L.R. 399.
[91] [1967] 1 Lloyd's Rep. 380, 384.

CHAPTER 3

INSURABLE INTEREST

1. GENERAL PRINCIPLES

The insurable interest requirement   **3–01**

There is no single overriding general rule of English law which requires the assured to possess any interest in the subject matter insured under the policy. The insurable interest requirement is in fact based upon a series of independent principles, which apply differently to the various classes of insurance contract.

    (i) *Interest required by statute.* The Life Assurance Act 1774 imposes an insurable interest requirement in respect of life policies, and the Marine Insurance Act 1906 operates similarly in respect of marine policies. These statutes override any provision to the contrary in the policy.

    (ii) *Interest required by the policy.* The policy will generally require the assured to have insurable interest, either directly, or indirectly by providing that the assured must prove that he has suffered a loss. Policies of this nature are *indemnity* policies.

    (iii) *Anti-wagering legislation.* By the Gaming Act 1845, s.18, all contracts by way of gaming or wagering—including purported contracts contracts of insurance[1]—are null and void.

Statutory interest   **3–02**

Marine Insurance Act 1746. Before the Revolution of 1688 the English common law refused, on grounds of public policy, to enforce a claim made under a contract of insurance which had been used as a cloak for a gambling transaction, but after that period the rule was relaxed and by a series of decisions the validity of wager policies was gradually established.[2] This let in a "mischievous form of gaming" and caused the legislature to intervene. The Marine Insurance Act 1746 forbade the making of policies on British ships or on "any goods, merchandises or effects laden or to be laden" on the "interest or no interest or without further proof of interest than the policy, or by way of gaming or wagering or without benefit of salvage to the insurer."

Life Assurance Act 1774. After the passing of the 1746 Act it was still **3–03** possible to gamble on lives and other events not within the prohibition until 1774, when another statute, known by the misleading title of the Life Assurance Act, forbade the making of any policy:

    "on the life of any person or other event wherein the person whose benefit

---

[1] Mathew J. in *Howard* v .*Refuge* (1866) 54 L.T. 644.
[2] See Lord Kenyon in *Craufurd* v. *Hunter* (1798) 8 T.R. 13. 23; Roche J. in *Williams* v. *Baltic* [1924] 2 K.B. 282, 289. But see Lord Eldon in *Lucena* v. *Craufurd* (1806) 2 Bos. & Pul. 269, 321.

or on whose account such policy shall be made shall have no interest, or by way of gaming or wagering."[3]

It further provided that there must be inserted in every policy the name of the person "for whose benefit or on whose account it was made."[4] There seems to have been some fear that restrictions on insurances "bona fide made by any person" on "ships, goods and merchandises" would hamper the trade of the country, and so those insurances were expressly excluded from the scope of the 1774 Act.[5] In addition, the Court of Appeal has in more recent times held that the 1774 Act does not apply to policies on real property,[6] so that the Act is in effect limited to life policies.

3–04   *Marine Insurance Act 1788.* In the year 1785 a further Act was passed "for regulating insurances, on ships and on goods, merchandises or effects" with the object of putting an end to the practice of issuing policies in blank, without inserting in them the name of the assured. This Act led however to "great mischiefs and inconveniences" and was repealed by the Marine Insurance Act 1788 which required only the name of one person interested or concerned to be inserted. The 1788 Act was repealed and replaced by the Marine Insurance Act 1906 but only "so far as it relates to marine insurance," so that it remains in force as regards goods.

3–05   *Gaming Act 1845.* The Act of 1774 applied only to policies of insurance: gaming contracts which were held not to be such policies were outside its scope.[7] By contrast, the Gaming Act 1845, s.18, applies to all wagering contracts, including purported contracts of insurance. Certain contracts may, however, resemble wagers on lives but fall outside the scope of both Acts, as where A sold his expectation under B's will to C for £2,000, also assigning a life policy to C on his own life, and it was held that neither Act applied.[8] The 1845 Act will only strike down an insurance agreement if the policyholder has no insurable interest at the inception of the policy and no reasonable expectation of acquiring any interest: if he has a reasonable expectation of obtaining interest, he cannot be said to be gambling.

3–06   *Marine Insurance Act 1906.* The Marine Insurance Act 1746, and the Marine Insurance Act 1788 insofar as it related to marine insurance, were repealed by the Marine Insurance Act 1906, which imposes a specific regime of insurable interest for marine insurance. This is considered separately below.[9]

3–07   *Statutory interest classified.* It follows that three separate classes have now to be distinguished in considering the interest required by statute:

(i) *Marine insurance,* governed by the Marine Insurance Act 1906.

---

[3] s.1.
[4] s.2. This was amended by the Insurance Companies Amendment Act 1973, s.50, for the benefit of group life insurances.
[5] s.4. Ships were in any event regulated by the 1746 Act.
[6] *Mark Rowlands Ltd.* v. *Berni Inns* [1985] 3 All E.R. 473.
[7] See *Roebuck* v. *Hammerton* (1778) 2 Cowp. 737; *Paterson* v. *Powell* (1832) 9 Bing. 320.
[8] *Cook* v. *Field* (1850) 15 Q.B. 460.
[9] *Infra* 3–29 *et seq.*

(ii) *Insurances on real and personal property,* governed by the Act of 1788 and the Gaming Act 1845.

(iii) *Life insurances,* governed by the Life Assurance 1774 and the Gaming Act 1845, although the latter probably adds nothing to the former.

Contractual interest 3–08

Insurable interest is not only used in insurance law as a term of art to describe a statutory requirement; the term is also used to describe the assured's interest in the subject matter of the loss under a policy of indemnity. A contract of insurance on goods or land, for example, is construed as a contract of indemnity if there is nothing in the policy to indicate a contrary intention: the insurer is not obliged to pay under such a policy if the assured has no interest at the time of the loss. And even if the terms of the contract are not clear on the point, there is a tendency of the courts to construe those terms in such a way as to necessitate interest in the assured as a condition precedent to his claim. For otherwise the contract might be void as a wager, and it must be construed *ut res magis valeat quam pereat.*[10]

But there are many cases where the policy does indicate an intention by the insurer to pay even though the assured has no interest at the time of the loss, and such a policy is not necessarily a wager, as, for example, where the assured as agent or trustee insures the interests of a third party.[11]

Thus, in *Thomas* v. *National Farmers' Union Mutual Insurance Society*[12] the tenant of a farm insured hay and straw against fire. The policy stipulated that it should cease "to be in force as to any property . . . which shall pass from the insured to any other person otherwise than by operation of law . . . " The tenant moved from the farm, and the property in the hay and straw passed to the landlord by virtue of the Agricultural Holdings Act 1948. The hay and straw were subsequently destroyed by fire. Diplock J. held the assured entitled to recover under the policy: it had not ceased to be in force although the assured had ceased to have an interest.

2. NATURE OF INSURABLE INTEREST

"The definition of insurable interest has been continuously expanding, **3–09** and dicta in some of the older cases, which would tend to narrow it, must be accepted with caution."[13]

The governing principle is that the interest must be an enforceable one. The mere hope, however strong, of acquiring an interest is not enough.[14] It has been said that a party has an interest in an event if he

---

[10] See *Coker* v. *Bolton* [1912] 3 K.B. 315.
[11] See *infra* 3–34 *et seq.*
[12] [1961] 1 W.L.R. 386.
[13] Walton J. in *Moran Galloway* v. *Uzielli* [1905] 2 K.B. 555, 563. See conflicting dicta in *Lucena* v. *Craufurd* (1806) 2 Bos. & P.N.R. 269 and *Ebsworth* v. *Alliance Marine* (1873) L.R. 8 C.P. 596.
[14] *Lucena* v. *Craufurd, supra.*

will gain an advantage if it happens and suffer a loss if it does not.[15] But
the advantage or loss must depend on his legal rights. Thus a shareholder has no insurable interest in the assets of a company. The sole
substantial shareholder in a one-man company will suffer a certain loss
in the event of the loss of the company's property, but he has no interest
in it.[16] Mere probability of detriment is not enough, and one cannot
insure a thing merely because there is a chance that some collateral ben-
fit may arise should it not be lost.[17] A shareholder has no interest in a
company's liability for wrongful acts.[18] But there is nothing to prevent
him from insuring his own shares, in which he has an insurable interest,
against loss suffered owing to the failure of an adventure in which the
company is engaged, however difficult the calculation of his loss, and in
Wilson v. *Jones*[19] the adventure of laying down a submarine cable was
insured by a shareholder in that way.

The true principle appears to be that enunciated by Finch J. in
National Filtering Oil Co. v. *Citizen's Insurance Co. of Missouri*[20] that
"if there be a right in or against the property which some court will
enforce . . . , a right so closely connected with and so much dependent
for value upon the continued existence of it alone, as that a loss of the
property will cause pecuniary damage to the holder of the right against
it, he has an insurable interest." It is now clear from the authorities that
some contractual or proprietary right, whether legal or equitable so long
as it is enforceable in the courts, is essential to found insurable interest.
But a husband who is living with his wife has an insurable interest in her
property, for he is by law entitled to share her enjoyment of it,[21] and
she, no doubt has a similar insurable interest in his property, as their
rights and duties are largely reciprocal.[22] But a father has no insurable
interest in the possible personal liability of his child in tort "since natural
love and affection does not give such an interest in law."[23] Nor does the
general concern of a trade union in the welfare of its members give it an
insurable interest in their losses or liabilities.[24]

3–10 Expectancy

While a mere expectancy will not give an insurable interest, a legal
right depending on an expectancy will. So in a case of an agreement to
sell an expectancy under a will for £2,000, and to repay the purchase
money if the expectation was not realised, the purchaser was held to
have an insurable interest in the life of the vendor of the expectancy.[25]

Similarly, an expectancy founded on legal rights may afford an insurable interest. One has no legal right to expect profits from a sale of one's
goods, but provided the assured has an insurable interest in goods, he

---

[15] Blackburn J. in *Wilson* v. *Jones* (1867) L.R. 2 Ex. 139, citing Lawrence J. in *Barclay* v. *Cousins* (1802) 2 East 544, 546–551 and in *Lucena* v. *Craufurd, supra.*
[16] *Macaura* v. *Northern Assurance* [1925] A.C. 619.
[17] Lord Ellenborough in *Routh* v. *Thompson* (1809) 11 East 428.
[18] *Levinger* v. *Licenses & General* (1836) 54 Ll.L.R. 68.
[19] (1867) L.R. 2 Ex. 139.
[20] (1887) 13 N.E. 337.
[21] *Goulstone* v. *Royal* (1858) 1 F. & F. 276.
[22] See Vaughan Williams L.J. in *Griffiths* v. *Fleming* [1909] 1 K.B. 805, 815.
[23] Lord Wright in *Vandepitte* v. *Preferred Accident* [1933] A.C. 70, 80.
[24] *Prudential Staff Union* v. *Hall* [1947] K.B. 685.
[25] *Cook* v. *Field* (1850) 15 Q.B. 460.

also has an insurable interest in the profits he may expect to make from them.[26] Mere expectation of profit, without any interest in the goods, will not however be sufficient to give an insurable interest.[27] So also where one has an insurable interest in premises, one can insure against loss of profits due to their destruction[28] provided one does so in express terms.[29]

Equitable interest   3–11

A strict legal interest in property is not necessary to create an insurable interest, an equitable interest is sufficient.[30] Lord Eldon could say in 1808 that it had always been held that a *cestui que trust* had an insurable interest in respect of his equitable interest.[31]

Interest under contract   3–12

Anyone who by contract is liable to pay any money in case of the loss of anything has an insurable interest in that thing.[32] It is on this principle that insurers can always reinsure property insured by them with other companies. On this ground, a shipper may insure his freight,[33] or a consignee his commission.[34] A purchaser of goods will have an insurable interest in them if they are at his risk under the contract of sale, whether or not the property in them has passed to him,[35] and the insurers will have no right to call on the assured to exercise a possible option to be released from such a contract.[36]

Bare legal estate   3–13

A bare legal title, such as that of a trustee, unaccompanied by the equitable interest, will always support an insurance.[37] Thus the personal representatives of a deceased have an insurable interest in all his property.[38]

Pecuniary interest   3–14

It has been said that insurable interest must be a pecuniary interest.[39] "It must be in a reasonable sense capable of valuation in money."[40] But the difficulty of such valuation is no bar. Thus profits which might be

---

[26] *Barclay* v. *Cousins* (1802) 2 East 544; *Eyre* v. *Glover* (1812) 16 East 218; *Royal Exchange* v. *M'Swiney* (1850) 14 Q.B. 646; *Stockdale* v. *Dunlop* (1840) 6 M. & W. 224.

[27] Lord Eldon in *Lucena* v. *Craufurd* (1806) 2 Bos. & P.N.R. 269, 325.

[28] *City Tailors* v. *Evans* (1921) 91 L.J.K.B. 379.

[29] *Re Sun Fire and Wright* (1834) 3 N. & M. 819; *Re Wright and Pole* (1834) 1 A. & E. 621.

[30] Ashhurst J. in *Smith* v. *Lascelles* (1788) 2 T.R. 187, 188; *Hill* v. *Secretan* (1798) 1 Bos. & P. 315; Lord Eldon in *Lucena* v. *Craufurd* (1802) 3 Bos. & P. 75, 103; *Samuel* v. *Dumas* [1924] A.C. 431, 443, 444, 450, 460.

[31] *Ex p. Yallop* (1808) 15 Ves. 60, 67, 68.

[32] Parke J. in *Miller* v. *Warre* (1824) 1 C. & P. 237, 239; (1825) 4 B. & C. 538; *Stock* v. *Inglis* (1884) 12 Q.B.D. 564; *Anderson* v. *Morice* (1876) 1 App.Cas. 713.

[33] *Thompson* v. *Taylor* (1795) 6 T.R. 478; *Flint* v. *Flemyng* (1830) 1 B. & Ad. 45; *Devaux* v. *J'Anson* (1839) 7 Scott 507.

[34] *King* v. *Glover* (1806) 2 Bos. & P.N.R. 206; *Knox* v. *Wood* (1808) 1 Camp. 543.

[35] *Anderson* v. *Morice* (1876) 1 App.Cas. 713, 724, *per* Hatherley L.C.

[36] *Inglis* v. *Stock* (1885) 10 App.Cas. 263.

[37] Ashhurst J. in *Smith* v. *Lascelles* (1788) 2 T.R. 187; *Camden* v. *Anderson* (1794) 5 T.R. 709; Lord Eldon in *Ex p. Yallop* (1808) 15 Ves. 60, 67, 68; *Ex p. Houghton* (1810) 17 Ves. 251.

[38] *Tidswell* v. *Ankerstein* (1792) Peake 204; *Stirling* v. *Vaughan* (1809) 11 East 619; *Bailey* v. *Gould* (1840) 4 Y. & C. 221; *Re Betty, Betty* v. *Att.-Gen.* [1899] 1 Ch. 821.

[39] Lord Tenterden in *Halford* v. *Kymer* (1830) 10 B. & C. 724, 728; *Macaura* v. *Northern, supra.*

[40] *Simcock* v. *Scottish Imperial* (1902) 10 S.L.T. 286.

exceedingly difficult to calculate are commonly insured by valued policies. And legal obligations, such as the obligation of a wife towards her
husband, may give an insurable interest in the life of another—although
they cannot be strictly described as "pecuniary." Nor can the unlimited
interest of a man in his own life be so described.[41] Again, it has been
said that it is not necessary that a pecuniary loss must follow from the
event insured against: it is sufficient that such loss might follow.[42] In
short, pecuniary loss affords a most unsatisfactory test as to the existence of an insurable interest.

3–15 Engagement binding in honour only

An engagement binding in honour only is not enough to support an
insurable interest.[43] Thus a purchaser of goods under a contract which
was enforceable under section 4 of the Sale of Goods Act 1893 had no
insurable interest in them.[44] Where a bank manager promised, without
consideration, not to call in a loan within his lifetime, it was held that
the borrower had no insurable interest in his life.[45] The expectation of
an *ex gratia* payment by the Crown will not support an insurance.[46] A
discharge in bankruptcy extinguishes the debt for all purposes[47] and the
insurable interest of the creditor ceases thereby even if the debtor subsequently promises to pay and is therefore under a moral obligation to
do so.

3–16 Defeasible interest

The fact that the interest of the assured is liable to be defeated by a
third person or is voidable does not invalidate a policy under the Life
Assurance Act 1774.[48]

3–17 Possession

Possession, even where improper, usually supports an insurance.
Thus the captors of a ship had an insurable interest in it whether the capture were legal or not, for if not they were liable to be called to account
in a Court of Admiralty in the event of its loss.[49] A bailee has an insurable interest in so far as he is liable to the owner in the event of the loss
of the goods entrusted to him, or in so far as his reward under a contract
of bailment depends upon the safety of the goods and is secured by a
lien on them.[50] A person in possession as the apparent or presumptive
owner has a full insurable interest: thus a bankrupt remaining in possession of his estate has an insurable interest in it.[51] Again, a person
whose property is liable to be seized by the Customs and Excise

---

[41] Kennedy L.J. in *Griffiths* v. *Fleming* [1909] 1 K.B. 805, 820–823; see § 16–00, *infra*.
[42] Lord O'Hagan in *Anderson* v. *Morice* (1876) 1 App.Cas. 713, 742.
[43] *Stockdale* v. *Dunlop* (1840) 6 M. & W. 224; *Stainbank* v. *Fenning* (1851) 11 C.B. 51; *Stainbank* v.
Shepard (1853) 13 C.B. 418.
[44] *Stockdale* v. *Dunlop, supra*.
[45] *Hebdon* v. *West* (1863) 3 B. & S. 579.
[46] *Routh* v. *Thompson* (1809) 11 East 428, 432, 433, *per* Lord Ellenborough.
[47] *Heather* v. *Webb* (1876) 2 C.P.D. 1; see *Ellis* v. *M'Henry* (1871) L.R. 6 C.P. 228, for effect of discharge in England and other countries.
[48] *Hill* v. *Secretan* (1798) 1 Bos. & P. 315; *Dwyer* v. *Edie* (1788) 2 Park (8th ed., 1842) 914.
[49] Lord Kenyon in *Boehm* v. *Bell* (1799) 8 T.R. 154, 161.
[50] See §§ 3–39 *et seq., infra*.
[51] *Marks* v. *Hamilton* (1852) 7 Ex. 323; *Goulstone* v. *Royal* (1858) 1 F. & F. 276.

authorities has an insurable interest in it, even though public policy precludes an action on the policy.[52] But mere possession, without responsibility gives no insurable interest,[53] as where the assured allowed timber belonging to a company to lie on his land, but owed no duty to the company in respect of its safe custody.[54]

Interest need not be stated 3–18

It is not necessary to state in a policy of insurance the precise nature of the interest, or whether the property be absolute or special. A person who has different kinds of interest in property may cover them all by one insurance without stating in the policy the number or nature of the interests.[55] Only the subject-matter of the insurance need be correctly described. A consignor, a consignee, a prize agent (as such), may all insure; they are not bound, however, to specify what their interest is.[56]

Creditors and debtors 3–19

It follows from these principles that a creditor has an insurable interest, to the extent of the amount owing when the insurance is made,[57] in the life of his debtor,[58] and in the life of anyone else whose death will or may take away from the creditor some security which, but for the death, would have been available to satisfy the debt.[59] So also a surety has an insurable interest in the life of his co-surety to the extent of the co-surety's proportion of the debt,[60] and also in the life of the principal debtor,[61] and a joint debtor has an insurable interest in the life of the other joint debtor.[62]

A creditor has an insurable interest in any property of his debtor over which he has a lien[63] or similar interest[64] or which has been mortgaged to him to secure payment of the debt,[65] and it makes no difference whether or not the debtor has insured such property.[66]

But a bare debt does not, by itself, give a creditor an insurable interest in things belonging to his debtor[67] although the debtor may, by reason of the loss or injury of these things, be less able to pay what he owes. The creditor must have some right against the thing itself, such as a right *in rem* against a vessel,[68] in order to support an insurance of it.

---

[52] *Geismar* v. *Sun Alliance* [1978] Q.B. 383.
[53] Keating J. in *North British* v. *Moffatt* (1871) L.R. 7 C.P. 25, 30, 31. It may, however, support an insurance covering another's interest; see § 3–39, *infra*. As regards tenants, see § 3–44, *infra*.
[54] Lord Buckmaster in *Macaura* v. *Northern* [1925] A.C. 619, 628.
[55] *Carruthers* v. *Sheddon* (1815) 6 Taunt. 14.
[56] *Crowley* v. *Cohen* (1832) 3 B. & Ad. 478.
[57] *Dalby* v. *India & London Life* (1854) 15 C.P. 365, overruling *Godsall* v. *Boldero* (1807) 9 East 72; *Law* v. *London Indisputable Life* (1855) 1 K. & J. 223; *Hebdon* v. *West* (1863) 3 B. & S. 579.
[58] *Anderson* v. *Edie* (1795) 2 Park (8th ed., 1842) 914; *Lindenau* v. *Desborough* (1828) 8 B. & C. 586.
[59] *Henson* v. *Blackwell* (1845) 4 Hare 434.
[60] *Branford* v. *Saunders* (1877) 25 W.R. 650.
[61] *Lea* v. *Hinton* (1854) 4 De G.M. & G. 823.
[62] *Davitt* v. *Titcumb* [1989] 3 All E.R. 417.
[63] Buller J. in *Wolff* v. *Horncastle* (1798) 1 Bos. & P. 316, 323; Walton J. in *Moran Galloway* v. *Uzielli* [1905] 2 K.B. 555, 562, 563.
[64] *Briggs* v. *Merchant Traders' Insurance* (1849) 13 Q.B. 167.
[65] See §§ 14–25 *et seq.*, *infra*.
[66] Lord Halsbury L.C. in *Westminster Fire* v. *Glasgow Provident* (1888) 13 App.Cas. 699, 709.
[67] Buller J. in *Wolff* v. *Horncastle, supra*; *Stainbank* v. *Fenning* (1851) 11 C.B. 51; *Macaura* v. *Northern* [1925] A.C. 619.
[68] Walton J. in *Moran Galloway* v. *Uzielli, supra*.

There is nothing, however, to prevent the creditor insuring against the insolvency of the debtor caused by the loss of the debtor's assets,[69] or against default in payment.[70]

3. TIME WHEN INTEREST MUST ATTACH

3–20   *Contractual interest.* The nature of the interest required is similar in the cases of both statutory and contractual interest, but a distinction must be drawn as to when the assured's interest must attach to the subject-matter insured. In the case of contractual interest, subject to the express terms of the contract, it is the time of the loss that is all-important; unless the assured can prove interest at that time he cannot recover, for he has suffered no loss for which an indemnity is payable.[71] The only exception to this principle exists in the marine context, where the assured insures "lost or not lost" and acquires an interest after the loss.[72] Consequently, in the case of insurance on real or personal property or, for that matter, against liability, it is sufficient for the assured to prove his loss and there is no need for him to demonstrate that he had an insurable interest at the inception of the policy.

The Gaming Act 1845, s.18, does, however, affect this principle in that the policy will fall foul of this provision if the assured neither possessed, nor had any reasonable expectation of acquiring, an insurable interest at the inception of the policy. If the policy is a wagering policy on this ground, it is void and cannot be revived by the fact that the assured does subsequently acquire an insurable interest.

3–21   *Statutory interest.* The Life Assurance Act 1774, s.1, provides that no insurance shall be made on any event wherein the assured "shall have no interest." This was construed in *Dalby* v. *India and London Life*[73] to mean *no interest at the time of the contract.* Consequently, given that life policies are not contracts of indemnity and thus do not contain any contractual requirement for interest, it is sufficient if the assured possesses insurable interest at the inception of the contract rather than at the date of death. For this reason, life policies are freely assignable by sale or auction. The Gaming Act 1845 has no impact upon policies within the 1774 Act, as its requirements are less strict than those of the 1774 Act itself.

Section 3 of the 1774 Act goes on to say that "no greater amount shall be recovered than the amount or value of the interest"; this limits the amount recoverable to the amount of interest at the time of the contract without any reference to amount of interest at the time of the loss.[74] But where the interest consists of a debt owing to the assured that debt need

---

[69] *Waterkeyn* v. *Eagle Star* (1920) 5 Ll.L.R. 42, 43, *per* Greer J.
[70] See § 21–15, *infra.*
[71] *Anderson* v. *Morice* (1876) 1 App. Cas. 713.
[72] *Sutherland* v. *Pratt* (1843) 11 M. & W. 296, a rule now codified in the M.I.A. 1906, proviso to s.6(1).
[73] (1854) 15 C.B. 365.
[74] *Dalby's* case, *supra* n. 73.

not be made up in full at the time the insurance is taken out, so that where A was obliged to maintain B and entitled to be repaid the maintenance money, it was held that his insurable interest extended to each sum of money as it was successively expended[75] and not merely to sums already expended at the time the policy was taken out.

It was at one time thought, consistently with the wording of section 3 **3–22** of the 1774 Act, that the Act applied to all insurances other than those on "ships, goods and merchandises"; so that insurance on buildings was within the Act. This belief produced a number of serious inconveniences: a building could not be insured other than by a person with an actual insurable interest in it, so that no insurable interest could exist by the purchaser of a building in the course of completion; the wording of section 3 restricting the amount recoverable to the assured's interest at the inception of the policy caused difficulties where the assured insured as agent or trustee on behalf of himself and another; and the requirement in section 2 concerning the insertion of the names of all interested parties into policy could not be complied with by, for example, landlords insuring on behalf of themselves and present and future tenants, or mortgagees insuring on behalf of themselves and present and future mortgagors. Fortunately, in 1975 the Court of Appeal decided, in *Mark Rowlands Ltd.* v. *Berni Inns*,[76] that the 1774 Act applied only to life policies and did not extend to indemnity insurances: the Court described the Act as an "ancient statute" and held that the words "other event or events" contained in the Act did not extend to indemnity insurances but caught only "insurances which provide for the payment of a specified sum upon the happening of an insured event." Consequently, the previous difficulties affecting policies on buildings have been removed.

4. CONSEQUENCES OF LACK OF INTEREST

Insurance companies and underwriters do sometimes seek to evade **3–23** their just obligations on the ground of want of interest, and it is the duty of the court always to lean in favour of an insurable interest, if possible, for after the underwriters or company have received the premium the objection that there was no insurable interest is often a technical objection and one which has no real merit as between the assured and the insurer.[77] "Time was," said Buller J. in 1798,[78]

"when no underwriter would have dreamed of making such an objection; if his solicitor had suggested a loophole by which he might escape he would have spurned at the idea."

There is nothing illegal about the insurers paying on a policy other

---

[75] *Barnes* v. *London Edinburgh & Glasgow Life* [1892] 1 Q.B. 864, 867, *per* A.L. Smith J.
[76] [1985] 3 All E.R. 473. The point arose in this case in the context of s.2.
[77] Brett M.R. in *Stock* v. *Inglis* (1884) 12 Q.B.D. 564, affirmed (1885) 10 App. Cas. 263.
[78] In *Wolff* v. *Horncastle* (1798) 1 Bos. & p. 316, 320–321.

than a life policy without interest,[79] and, except in the case of marine policies,[80] a policy will not be invalid simply because it contains a provision that the insurers will pay, interest or no interest.[81]

3–24 Statutory interest

A policy falling within the Life Assurance Act 1774—*i.e.* a life policy—which is made without interest at the date of its inception is illegal and not merely void. This was held to be the effect of the words "no insurance shall be made" without interest, in the section 1 of the Life Assurance Act 1774, by the Court of Appeal in *Harse* v. *Pearl Assurance*.[82] Consequently, the assured can neither recover under the policy nor reclaim his premiums.[83] As the policy is illegal, it is the duty of the court to refuse jurisdiction in the event that a claim under the policy should come before it, even though the insurer does not seek to plead illegality.

3–25 Contractual interest

A policy outside the Life Assurance Act 1774 which is made without interest is prima facie lawful, unless it falls foul of the Gaming Act 1845, s.18. If the policy is not a wager, but the assured has no interest at the date of the loss–either because he has never obtained any interest or because he has obtained interest but has subsequently lost it[84]—he cannot suffer any loss and thus the indemnity principle prevents any recovery by him. The case of *Macaura* v. *Northern Insurance*[85] illustrates the position. In that case Mr. Macaura insured, against fire, cut timber upon his estate. The timber was subsequently sold to a one-man company of which he was the sole effective shareholder. The greater part of the timber was destroyed by fire. The insurers refused to pay on the ground that Mr. Macaura, being a mere shareholder, had no insurable interest in the assets of his company, and on a submission to arbitration under the terms of the policy their contention was upheld. The court also upheld their contention, but it was further argued on behalf of Mr. Macaura that since he had no interest the policy was a wager and void, and that the arbitrators had therefore no authority to entertain the submission. This failed. "No gaming contract was ever made," said Lord Sumner,[86] this was:

> "a contract of indemnity under which the assured must have and prove interest at the time of the loss. This part of the law of insurance, quite independently of the Gaming Act, though the consequence of failure to provide

---

[79] *Worthington* v. *Curtis* (1875) 1 Ch.D. 419; *Attorney-General* v. *Murrany* [1904] 1 K.B. 165; Shearman J. in *Hatley* v. *Liverpool Victoria Friendly Society* (1918) 88 L.J.K.B. 237; *Carmichael's Case* 1920 S.C. (H.L.) 195. This is so because a policy within the Life Assurance Act 1774 which is made without interest is unlawful. See below.

[80] M.I.A. 1906, s.4(2)(b).

[81] *Anctil* v. *Manufacturers' Life* [1899] A.C. 604.

[82] [1904] 1 K.B. 558.

[83] Unless he can establish an exception to the rule *in pari delicto potior est conditio defendentis*: see the general discussion of return of premiums in Chap. 7, *infra*.

[84] If he has never obtained interest, he is entitled to a return of the premium, on the principle that the premium is returnable for total failure of consideration if the risk has never run. By contrast, if he has lost interest, the risk has run and the premium is not returnable at all: see Chap. 7, *infra*.

[85] [1925] A.C. 619.

[86] At p. 632.

interest is the same—namely, that the policy is unenforceable by an uninterested assured."

5. INSERTION OF NAMES OF PERSONS INTERESTED

Insurance on goods 3–26
Where the insurance is on goods, the name of one person interested only, is to be inserted in the policy, by reason of the Marine Insurance Act 1788. This limited provision is in all cases complied with automatically, as the name of at least one person interested is always inserted in the policy as the named assured. If the insurance is effected by an agent, it would seem to suffice if the agent's name is inserted in the policy.

Insurance on lives 3–27
Where the insurance is on a life or lives, within the Life Assurance Act 1774, section 2 of the Act requires the insertion of all persons interested in the policy. However, various forms of life policies insure a class of persons, as opposed to an individual, and members of that class may change during the currency of the policy: a group life policy taken out by an employer for the benefit of its employees is the commonest example here. It will be appreciated that section 2 cannot be complied with in this type of case, and for that reason section 2 was amended by the Insurance Companies Amendment Act 1973, section 50(1). This provides that section 2 does not invalidate a policy for the benefit of unnamed persons within a specified class or description:

> "stated with sufficient particularity to make it possible to establish the identity of all persons who at any given time are entitled to benefit under the policy."[87]

Where the requirements of section 2 are not complied with, the policy is illegal even if founded on a valid interest.[88]

Other cases 3–28
Leaving aside the special case of marine insurance, considered below, other forms of insurance are unaffected by any requirement that the names of one or more persons interested are to be inserted in the policy. Thus, in the case of insurance on buildings, the policy is not invalidated by section 2 of the 1774 Act where it contains only the name of the landlord even if it has been taken out for the joint benefit of the landlord and his tenants.[89] A similar rule doubtless applies in the case of insurance by a mortgagee on behalf of himself and the mortgagor. On the same principle, a liability policy is valid even if it does not contain the names of all the persons who are able to seek indemnity under it.[90]

---

[87] s.50(2) makes this provision retroactive.
[88] *Evans* v. *Bignold* (1869) L.R. 4 Q.B. 622.
[89] *Mark Rowlands Ltd.* v. *Berni Inns* [1985] 3 All E.R. 473.
[90] *Williams* v. *Baltic* [1924] 2 K.B. 282 had reached this conclusion prior to the adoption of the general principle in *Mark Rowlands* that the 1774 Act was confined in its operation to policies of life insurance.

6. INSURABLE INTEREST IN MARINE POLICIES

3–29 The Marine Insurance Act 1906

The Marine Insurance Act 1746, and also the Act of 1788 "so far as it relates to marine insurance" were repealed by the Marine Insurance Act 1906. The Act codifies the many marine decisions on what constitutes an insurable interest, and provides that defeasible or contingent interests[91] and partial interests are insurable,[92] and that the insurer under a contract of marine insurance has an interest in his risk and may reinsure in respect of it.[93] A detailed discussion of exactly when an insurable interest will exist is found in paras. 3–09–3–19.

3–30 Contracts by way of gaming or wagering

The M.I.A. 1906, s.4, provides as follows:

(1) Every contract of marine insurance by way of gaming or wagering[94] is void.

(2) A contract of marine insurance is deemed to be a gaming or wagering contract—

(a) where the assured does not have an insurable interest as defined by this Act, and the contract is entered into with no expectation of acquiring such an interest; or

(b) Where the policy is made "interest or no interest," or "without further proof of interest that the policy itself," or "without benefit of salvage to the insurer," or subject to any like term:[95]

Provided that, where there is no possibility of salvage, a policy may be effected without benefit of salvage to the insurer.

Where the policy is made by way of gaming or wagering the assured cannot claim on the policy, nor can he reclaim his premium for total failure of consideration,[96] although if the policy is made on interest but is void simply because it is one of the forms prohibited by section 4(2)(b) the premium will be recoverable.[97]

3–31 The "insurable interest" referred to in section 5(2)(a), is defined by section 6.

6.—(1) Subject to the provisions of this Act, every person has an insurable interest who is interested in a marine adventure.

(2) In particular a person is interested in a marine adventure where he stands in any legal or equitable relation to the adventure or to any insurable property at risk therein, in consequence of which he may benefit by the safety or due arrival of insurable property, or may be prejudiced by its loss, or by damage thereto, or by the detention thereof, or may incur liability in respect thereof.

---

[91] s.7(1). S.7(2) gives a specific example of this: where a buyer of goods has insured them, he has an insurable interest even though he has the right to reject the goods for breach of condition (under the Sale of Goods Act 1979, s.11) or to treat them at the seller's risk by reason of delay in delivery (under the Sale of Goods Act 1979, s.20(2)).

[92] s.8.

[93] s.9(1). S.9(2) goes on to provide, in the line with the privity rule, that the original assured has no rights against the reinsurer.

[94] Mere overvaluation of an actual interest does not render a contract void for gaming or wagering: *Glafki Shipping* v. *Pinios Shipping* [1984] 1 Lloyd's Rep. 660.

[95] This provision renders void any marine policy containing a "p.p.i." or equivalent clause, even if the policy is made on interest: *Cheshire* v. *Vaughan* [1920] 3 K.B. 240.

[96] M.I.A. 1906, s.84(3)(c).

[97] *Re London County Commercial Reinsurance Office* [1922] 1 Ch. 67.

This definition is in effect a codification of the principles laid down by Lord Eldon in *Lucena* v. *Craufurd.*[98]

Time when interest must attach 3–32

Section 6(1) laid down the principle that the assured must be interested in the subject matter at the date of the loss, although he need not be interested when the insurance is effected. The former rule is simply a recognition that a contract of marine insurance is a contract of indemnity, so that if the assured has no interest he cannot be have suffered any loss. The latter rule is apparent from section 5, as it is there stated that a policy made without interest is made by way of gaming or wagering only where the assured has no reasonable expectation of acquiring an interest.

There are nevertheless two situations in which an assured without interest at the date of the loss is entitled to recover. First, if the policy has been made "lost or not lost," and a loss has occurred before the assured has acquired his interest, the assured may recover as long as he was not aware of the loss when the contract was entered into.[99] Secondly, the assured who has exercised some right or option over the insured subject matter after it has been lost, thereby obtaining insurable interest in it, can recover if he was not aware of the loss at the date of acquiring the interest.[1]

Criminal sanctions 3–33

Whereas gaming or wagering contracts had been unenforceable for many years, nothing had been done to render them criminal until the passing of the Marine Insurance (Gambling Policies) Act 1909, which provides:

1.—(1) If—
   (a) any person effects a contract of marine insurance without having a bona fide interest, direct or indirect, either in the safe arrival of the ship in relation to which the contract is made or in the safety or preservation of the subject-matter insured, or a bona fide expectation of acquiring such an interest; or
   (b) any person in the employment of the owner of a ship, not being part owner of the ship, effects a contract of marine insurance in relation to the ship, and the contract is made "interest or no interest," or "without further proof of interest than the policy itself," or "without benefit of salvage to the insurer," or subject to any other like term,

the contract shall be deemed to be a contract by way of gambling in loss of maritime perils, and the person effecting it shall be guilty of an offence.

7. INSURANCES COVERING OTHER INTERESTS

Before considering this question, it is necessary clearly to understand 3–34 the general principles of contract, agency and trusteeship applicable. We start with two general rules:

---

[98] (1806) 2 Bos. & Pul. 269.
[99] s.6(1), proviso.
[1] s.6(2).

(a) the assured must have the requisite interest in the subject-matter insured at the appropriate time, and

(b) only a person who is a party to a contract can sue under it.[2]

3–35 Insurance by agent

The rules of agency provide the first modification of these principles: an agent without interest may effect a valid and enforceable contract of insurance on behalf of a principal who has interest,[3] and either the agent[4] or the principal himself can sue upon such a contract.[5] The limitation on this modification is that such insurances must be duly authorised or ratified by the principal.[6]

3–36 Insurance by trustee

The second modification is provided by the rules of trusteeship. A party to a contract can constitute himself a trustee for a third party of rights under a contract and thus confer rights on the third party.[7] Where more than one person has an interest in the same subject-matter and one of them insures to the extent of the whole value, constituting himself a trustee to the extent of the others' interest of any benefit he may receive under the policy,[8] he cannot actually benefit to more than the extent of his own interest, and the principle of indemnity will not be offended. Thus, Bowen L.J. said in *Castellain* v. *Preston*[9]: "A person with a limited interest may insure either for himself and to cover his own interest only, or he may insure so as to cover . . . the interest of all others who are interested in the property." Thus a person without any interest at all can insure, provided he holds himself trustee for interested parties and provided interest in such insurance is not required by statute. So a trade union may insure against its members' losses of *goods*, provided it regards itself as their trustee in respect of any moneys it may receive under the policy.[10] Such an insurance is not a wager and illustrates the principle that lack of interest is not fatal to the assured at common law.

3–37 *Question of construction.* These principles were applied by the House of Lords in *Tomlinson* v. *Hepburn*.[11] Carriers insured cigarettes, the property of a third party, which were stolen. They insured not as agents but on their own behalf. It was held that, on its true construction, the policy was not a personal liability policy but a goods policy, and that

---

[2] *Dunlop* v. *Selfridge* [1915] A.C. 847, 853, *per* Viscount Haldane; *Midland Silicones* v. *Scruttons* [1962] A.C. 446.

[3] *Provincial Insurance* v. *Leduc* (1874) L.R. 6 P.C. 224, 244. *Transcontinental Underwriting* v. *Grand Union Insurance* [1987] 2 Lloyd's Rep. 409; *Pan Atlantic* v. *Pine Top Insurance* [1989] 1 Lloyd's Rep. 568.

[4] The agent necessarily holds the proceeds on trust for the principal.

[5] *Browning* v. *Provincial Insurance* (1873) L.R. 5 P.C. 263, 272, 273.

[6] See §§ 15–04 *et seq.*, *infra*.

[7] *Vandepitte* v. *Preferred Accident* [1933] A.C. 70, 79, *per* Lord Wright. See also *Lloyd's* v. *Harper* (1880) 16 Ch.D. 290. Contrast *Re Engelbach's Estate* [1924] 2 Ch. 348. Doubted in *Beswick* v. *Beswick* [1968] A.C. 58. As to how such rights should be enforced, see *Harmer* v. *Armstrong* [1934] 1 Ch. 65.

[8] *Sidaways* v. *Todd* (1818) 2 Stark. 400; Campbell L.C.J. in *Waters* v. *Monarch Fire & Life* (1856) 5 E. & B. 870, 881; *London & North-Western Ry.* v. *Glyn* (1859) 1 E. & E. 652.

[9] (1883) 11 Q.B.D. 380, 398.

[10] *Prudential Staff Union* v. *Hall* [1947] K.B. 685.

[11] [1966] A.C. 451. And see *Petrofina (U.K.) Ltd.* v. *Magnaload Ltd.* [1983] 2 Lloyd's Rep. 91, applying the principles to contractors' all risks insurance.

accordingly the carriers were entitled to recover in full from the insurer irrespective of whether they were personally liable to the third party. But the law required the carriers to account to the owner of the goods who had suffered the loss.

Lord Reid restated these principles in a speech agreed with by Lord Guest and Lord Wilberforce. He made clear, however, that the intention of the assured, uncommunicated to the insurer, was irrelevant to the issue raised, contrary to views previously expressed by the judiciary and in textbooks, including this one.

"A bailee can if he chooses merely insure to cover his own loss or personal liability to the owner of the goods either at common law or under contract and if he does that of course he can recover no more under the policy than sufficient to make good his own personal loss or liability. But equally he can if he chooses insure up to his full insurable interest—up to the full value of the goods entrusted to him. And if he does that he can recover the value of the goods though he has suffered no personal loss at all."[12] The question whether the bailee is insuring goods or liability is purely one of construction of the policy.

Apart from life policies, which are governed by section 2 of the Life Assurance Act 1774, a policy of insurance taken out in the name of a person who has an insurable interest,[13] of his own in every part of the subject-matter,[14] whoever may have the beneficial interest in it,[15] will extend to include, besides his own interest, all other interests which the assured intended to protect, according to the true construction of the policy.[16] Thus a joint tenant or a tenant in common has such an interest in the entirety as will enable him to insure the whole, including the interests of other joint tenants or tenants in common.[17]

Moreover, provided the intention is clear, a non-marine policy on goods may be taken out by one who has no insurable interest at all covering the interests of others, whether or not he is acting as their agent or whether or not they ratify the transaction.[18]

Thus, it was held in *Waters* v. *Monarch Fire & Life*, that a bailee liable only for negligence may insure the goods bailed to their full value against any loss,[19] and it has also been held that the owner of a motor-vehicle may insure against third party liability incurred in its use by himself or others.[20] And where the assured has possession, even although he has no interest at all, he can make an insurance also covering the interest of the owner of the subject-matter insured.[21]

---

[12] [1966] A.C. 451 at p. 467 *per* Lord Reid.

[13] A dictum of Brett J. in *Ebsworth* v. *Alliance Marine* (1873) L.R. 8 C.P. 596, 637, 638, implying that the assured must have a legal as opposed to equitable interest appears to be wrong. See Bovill C.J. in the *Ebsworth* case, at pp. 608, 609, and the many cases cited in that case, especially *Robertson* v. *Hamilton* (1811) 14 East 522 and *Irving* v. *Richardson* (1831) 2 B. & Ad. 193; Bowen L.J. in *Castellain* v. *Preston* (1883) 11 Q.B.D. 380, 398 *et seq*.

[14] Lord Eldon in *Page* v. *Fry* (1800) 2 Bos. & P. 240, 242; Lord Ellenborough in *Robertson* v. *Hamilton* (1811) 14 East 522, 532; Crompton J. in *Waters* v. *Monarch Fire & Life* (1856) 5 E. & B. 870, 882.

[15] Lord Eldon in *Page* v. *Fry, supra*.

[16] See *North British* v. *Moffatt* (1871) L.R. 7 C.P. 25.

[17] *Page* v. *Fry, supra*.

[18] *Prudential Staff Union* v. *Hall* [1947] K.B. 685.

[19] (1856) 5 E. & B. 870, approved in *Tomlinson* v. *Hepburn* [1966] A.C. 451; see also *London & North-Western Ry.* v. *Glyn* (1859) 1 E. & E. 652.

[20] *Williams* v. *Baltic* [1924] 2 K.B. 282. See § 20–15, *infra*.

[21] Keating J. in *North British* v. *Moffatt* (1871) L.R. 7 C.P. 25, 30, 31.

3–38   *Intention.* The question whether the assured intended to protect the
interests of others is one of construction, and the answer to it depends
on the circumstances of each particular case.[22] The wording of the policy
itself may provide valuable evidence in this respect.[23] If the assured was
under no duty to insure on behalf of anyone else and if there is nothing
to show that he intended to do so, the presumption will be that he
intended to protect his own interest and nothing more.[24] In one case
where the rules of a building society, entitled the mortgagees to insure
property mortgaged at the mortgagor's expense, the insurance moneys
being applicable "to the payment of the amount secured," it was held
that an insurance by them covered the mortgagor's interest.[25]

If insurance companies wish in granting policies to a person such as a
carrier with a limited interest to limit their responsibility to his interest,
they should be careful to employ precise words to that effect in the body
of the policy.[26]

3–39   *Bailees for reward.* It is especially important in the case of insurances
of goods by bailees, factors, wharfingers and the like, to determine
whether or not the interest of the owners is also covered, for their own
interest is normally limited in extent to the amount of their liability for
loss of the goods to the owners.[27] This liability, any special contract or
custom apart,[28] usually extends at common law only to loss by their negligence,[29] so that if the goods are lost by fire and without negligence on
their part, they will be unable to recover anything under a fire policy
covering their own interest only,[30] unless they have a lien on goods for
their charges, in which case these alone are recoverable.[31]

3–40   *Goods "in trust."* It is usual for bailees such as wharfingers to insure
their own goods and goods *"in trust or on commission,"* and it is well
established that such an insurance covers both their own interest, a lien
for warehouse rent for instance, and the interest of the owners of such
goods. They are entitled therefore, as against the insurers, to recover
the entire value of the goods, whether the owners have assented to the
assurance or not.[32] *"In trust"* in this context means goods with which the
assured has been entrusted, not goods held in trust in the technical sense
of *as trustees.*[33] The bailee is not technically a trustee of such goods for
the owners, but he will be a trustee of any insurance moneys which he
receives under such policy in excess of his interest.[34]

A similar phrase, *goods entrusted to others,* was held in *Lake* v. *Sim-*

---

[22] See *Rayner* v. *Preston* (1881) 18 Ch.D. 1, 10; *Yangtze Insurance* v. *Lukmanjee* [1918] A.C. 585
(P.C.).
[23] *Waters* v. *Monarch Fire & Life* (1856) 5 E. & B. 870; *London & North-Western* v. *Glyn* (1859) 1 E.
& E. 652; *North British* v. *Moffatt* (1871) L.R. 7 C.P. 25.
[24] *Armitage* v. *Winterbotton* (1840) 1 Man. & G. 130.
[25] *Nichols* v. *Scottish Union* (1885) 2 T.L.R. 190.
[26] Erle J. in *Waters* v. *Monarch, etc., supra.*
[27] *London & North-Western Ry.* v. *Glyn, supra.*
[28] *North British* v. *London, Liverpool & Globe* (1877) 5 Ch.D. 569.
[29] *Coggs* v. *Bernard* (1703) 1 Sm.L.C. (13th ed.) 175.
[30] *Sidaways* v. *Todd* (1818) 2 Stark. 400.
[31] *Crowley* v. *Cohen* (1832) 3 B. & Ad. 478.
[32] *Donaldson* v. *Manchester Insurance* (1836) 14 Sh. (Ct. of Sess.) 601; *Waters* v. *Monarch Fire &*
Life (1856) 5 E. & B. 870; *Cochran* v. *Leckie's Trustee* (1906) 8 F. (Ct. of Sess.) 975.
[33] Campbell L.C.J. in *Waters* v. *Monarch Fire & Life, supra.,* at p. 880.
[34] *Ibid.* at p. 881.

mons[35] not to extend to goods whose possession has been obtained by another by fraud amounting to larceny by a trick.

The policy in *London and North-Western Ry.* v. *Glyn*,[36] an insurance of goods by carriers, contained a clause: "goods in trust are to be insured as such, otherwise the policy will not extend to cover such property."[37] The subject-matter was described as "goods their own and in trust as carrier." It was held that that policy covered the owner's interest as well as their own, and that carriers were not limited in their claim against the insurers to an amount representing their liability to the owners, the words of the policy not being sufficient to limit the insurers' liability in that way.

Seller in possession. A seller who remains in possession of the goods **3–41** after both risk and property have passed to the buyer is in a similar position to any other bailee, and though he may have no interest left in the goods, he will still be able to make an insurance covering the buyer's interest. In *North British* v. *Moffatt*,[38] such sellers insured goods "the assured's own, *in trust or on commission, for which they are responsible*," but it was held that since they were no longer responsible, the risk having passed, the words were insufficient to cover the goods in question. And in a later case, *Engel* v. *Lancashire and General Assurance*,[39] it was held that even where the bailee is responsible for losses due to his negligence, but the loss occurs otherwise, such words preclude him from recovery.

Such words in effect, therefore, preclude the assured from covering interests other than his own. They do, however, have the effect of giving the owner of the goods an equitable interest, as *cestui que trust*, in any insurance moneys received, so that if the bailee becomes bankrupt the owner will have a preferential claim on the insurance moneys as against the bailee's other creditors.[40]

Distribution of benefit. The fact that the assured may be entitled to **3–42** insure interests other than his own does not of course mean that executors,[41] trustees[42] and others who have an insurable interest which is derived from their legal title can use this right for the purpose of private gain. If they insure and provide the premiums out of their own pockets they will be allowed to reimburse themselves out of any insurance money which comes into their hands, but they must account for the rest of it to those who have the beneficial interest.[43] So also the owner of

---

[35] [1927] A.C. 487. But in *Rigby* v. *Reliance Marine* [1956] 2 Q.B. 468, road transport contractors gave X, under a mistake as to his identity, a collection order addressed to shipping agents, who held the goods and gave them to X who absconded with them: *held*, that the goods were entrusted to the contractors and held "in trust" by them.

[36] (1859) 1 E. & E. 652.

[37] Such a provision does not mean that the assured cannot recover at all where he holds goods on trust, but simply that he cannot recover more than his own interest in them. The effect of the clause is to cut down the common law right of a bailee with possession to insure the owner's interest if he intends to do so, by requiring that such intention must be expressed in the policy. *Ibid.* and see also *South Australian Central Ins.* v. *Randell* (1869) L.R. 3 P.C. 101, 111, 112.

[38] Keating J. in (1871) L.R. 7 C.P. 25.

[39] (1925) 41 T.L.R. 408.

[40] *Cochran* v. *Leckie's Trustee* (1906) 8 F. (Ct. of Sess.) 975.

[41] *Lea* v. *Hinton* (1854) 5 De G.M. & Co. 823.

[42] *Re Emmett, ex p. Andrews* (1816) 1 Madd. 573; *Holland* v. *Smith* (1806) 6 Esp. 11.

[43] *Re Emmett, ex p. Andrews* (1816) 1 Madd. 573.

goods voluntarily insured by a bailee may recover any benefit received by him under the policy in an action for money had and received,[44] provided that the bailee, when insuring, intended to cover the owner's interest.[45] Even if the bailee is bankrupt the owner, as beneficially entitled thereunder, will be entitled to preferential ranking on any sum recovered under this policy as against the bailee's other creditors.[46]

But an assured who has, of his own free will and at his own expense included the interests of others in a policy of his own is entitled to keep, out of the money which he gets under it, enough to meet his own loss. Others, whose interests he covered, can only lay claim to what, if any, is left over. Thus where the sellers of goods who retained possession of them, the risk having passed to the buyers, included "goods on the premises, sold and paid for but not removed" under floating policies covering also their own goods, it was held that they were entitled to appropriate to their own losses the whole of a sum received from their insurers under these policies, the insurance money being insufficient to cover their losses alone. It would have been held otherwise, however, had they been under any obligation to the buyers to make the insurance.[47]

3–43   While a bailee who insures his own interest and that of his principal is entitled to deduct any charges accrued due to him, it was held by the Privy Council in *Maurice* v. *Goldsbrough Mort*[48] that such a bailee was not entitled to deduct prospective profits and charges which he might have earned, although the effect would be that his principal would receive more than an indemnity. The ground for this decision was that an insurance of goods does not cover profits unless they are expressly included.[49]

If a policy in the name and on the life of another be effected for his own benefit by a person who has no insurable interest in such life, and the insurance company, on the death of the person whose life is insured, pays the insurance money to the person effecting the insurance, he is entitled to retain money as against the legal personal representative of the deceased. Illegality under the Life Assurance Act 1774 does not affect the rights *inter se* of rival claimants to the insurance money if the insurers in fact choose to pay it.[50]

Thus a person who has an insurable interest entitling him to cover by a policy of his own the interests of others can, if he wishes, effect an insurance which will protect all the interests in the subject-matter. Under it he will be able to recover, as trustee, in an action brought in his own name, the entire loss suffered by all concerned, and thus enforce performance in favour of the beneficiaries by the insurers. If the policy

---

[44] *Sidaways* v. *Todd* (1818) 2 Stark. 400.
[45] *Armitage* v. *Winterbotton* (1840) 1 Man. & G. 130.
[46] *Cochran* v. *Leckie's Trustees* (1906) 8 F. (Ct. of Sess.) 975.
[47] *Dalgleish* v. *Buchanan* (1854) 16 Ct. of Sess. (2nd ser.) 322; *Martineau* v. *Kitching* (1862) L.R. 7 Q.B. 436; *Ferguson* v. *Aberdeen* 1916 S.C. 715.
[48] [1939] A.C. 452.
[49] See § 4–14, *infra*.
[50] *Worthington* v. *Curtis* (1875) 1 Ch.D. 419; see also *Hadden* v. *Bryden* (1899) 1 F. (Ct. of Sess.) 710; *Att.-Gen.* v. *Murray* [1904] 1 K.B. 165. See also § 16–13, *infra*.

holder refuses to sue the insurers, the beneficiaries can sue joining him as a defendant.[51]

Life insurance. Life insurance policies are peculiar in that an assured **3–44** with interest may, provided the arrangement is not a fraudulent one, insure, in effect for the benefit of someone without interest, by either making himself a trustee of the policy for the beneficiary or by subsequently assigning it to him.[52]

But if a life is insured by A as trustee for B, B's name must, by section 2 of the Act, be inserted in the policy. Thus where a husband obtained a loan from his wife's trustees on his obtaining surety for its repayment, and the surety stipulated that the husband should insure his wife's life, the husband having induced the wife to insure her own life in her own name without references to its being for her husband, it was held that, as the husband was primarily interested in the policy, it was illegal and void.[53]

Insurances on buildings. Insurances on buildings are in a peculiar pos- **3–45** ition, and, as a result of the Fire Prevention (Metropolis) Act 1774, giving persons interested a right to insist on reinstatement in case of fire,[54] anyone with a limited interest, *e.g.* a tenant from year to year, may insure, to the extent of the whole value[55] if he intends to cover the owner's interest. The owner may then insist on reinstatement in case of fire, but it is doubtful whether the assured may be paid more than the value of his own interest.[56] The difficulty does not arise where a tenant has covenanted to repair.[57] In *Gold* v. *Patman*[58] a building contractor covenanted with the owner to insure adjoining properties against collapse. It was held that this required insurance only of his liability for negligence and not the absolute liability of the owner.

Insurances founded on assured's interest alone. Insurance including **3–46** other interests should be contrasted with cases in which an assured with a limited interest is responsible, by contract or otherwise, for the whole loss. In such a case the insurance is founded upon his own insurable interest alone,[59] and strangers to the contract have no lien upon or control over any benefit he may receive,[60] although they do get an indirect advantage inasmuch as the assured, by making insurance, has provided a fund by which he is able to meet claims made upon him.

Similarly where someone without interest insures for his own benefit alone, and the insurers, though under no liability to do so, pay him

---

[51] Lord Wright in *Vandepitte* v. *Preferred Accident* [1933] A.C. 70, 79.
[52] See *Royal Exchange* v. *Hope* [1928] Ch. 179; *Ashley* v. *Ashley* (1829) 3 Sim. 149.
[53] *Evans* v. *Bignold* (1869) L.R. 4 Q.B. 622.
[54] See §§ 11–07 *et seq.*, *infra*.
[55] *Simpson* v. *Scottish Union* (1863) 1 H. & M. 618, 628.
[56] *Castellain* v. *Preston* (1883) 11 Q.B.D. 380.. See also *Leppard* v. *Excess Ins.* [1979] 1 W.L.R. 512 (C.A.) (insured entitled only to market value of house burnt down less site value). For policies which effectively required insurers to reinstate see *Pleasurama* v. *Sun Alliance* [1979] 1 Lloyd's Rep. 389.
[57] *Ibid.* at p. 400.
[58] [1958] 1 W.L.R. 697.
[59] In this respect contrast *Waters* v. *Monarch Fire & Life* and *London & North-Western Ry.* v. *Glyn*, *supra*, with *North British* v. *Moffatt, supra*.
[60] *Re Law Guarantee Trust* [1915] 1 Ch. 340; *Re Harrington Motor Co.* [1928] Ch. 105. For a statutory exception to this principle, see § 19–14, *infra*; Third Parties (Rights against Insurers) Act 1930.

under the policy, a stranger to the policy who has an interest in the loss will have no claim to the money paid.[61]

3–47 Co-insurance

The preceding paragraphs have considered the case in which a policy have been taken out by one on behalf of another, or on behalf of himself and another. This situation must be distinguished from that in which there are two parties to a policy, each with an insurable interest. If the parties have an undivided interest in the insured subject matter (such as joint ownership), the policy is properly referred to as a joint, whereas if the parties have different interests (such as landlord and tenant) the policy is properly referred to as composite. The legal differences between joint insurance and composite insurance are the following:

(a) If one assured under a joint policy has been guilty of misrepresentation or some other breach of duty, neither can recover. Conversely, misrepresentation or breach of duty by a mortgagor does not affect the rights of the mortgagee under the policy.[62]

(b) Deliberate destruction of the insured subject matter by a joint assured will prevent any recovery under the policy, whereas such misconduct by one party to a composite policy will not defeat the rights of the other party[63] unless loss of that type is excluded by the policy.[64]

(c) The insurer may discharge its liability under a joint policy by payment to any of the joint assureds, whereas under a composite policy each assured must be paid in respect of his own interest.[65]

8. ILLEGAL CONTRACTS OF INSURANCE

3–48 Tendency to sin irrelevant

It has been the general policy of the courts to declare contracts with a *tendency* to lead to crime, immorality, or other effects prejudicial to the public, void on the ground of public policy.[66] Thus, the rule that seamen cannot validly insure their wages has sprung up in many countries on the ground that such insurances would have a tendency to induce seamen to relax their efforts to bring a ship to port, being more interested one must suppose in their wages than their safety.[67] But, owing partly perhaps to the control by legislation of insurances without interest and by way of wagering, the law of insurance has departed from the general law of contract in this respect, and no policy is void in England simply on the ground that it *might* lead to crime.[68] Thus a poisoner may persuade his

---

[61] *Grant* v. *Hill* (1812) 4 Taunt. 380; *Armitage* v. *Winterbottom* (1840) 1 Man. & G. 130; *Worthington* v. *Curtis* (1875) 1 Ch.D. 419.

[62] *Woolcott* v. *Sun Alliance* [1978] 1 Lloyd's Rep. 629.

[63] *Lomard* v. *N.R.M.A. Insurance* [1969] 1 Lloyd's Rep. 575; *The Alexion Hope* [1988] 1 Lloyd's Rep. 311. *Cf. Davitt* v. *Titcumb* [1989] 3 All E.R. 417, a policy on the joint lives of A and B, where A murdered B: *held* that A could derive no benefit from the policy but B's estate was entitled to receive the proceeds.

[64] *Samuel* v. *Dumas* [1924] A.C. 431.

[65] *General Accident* v. *Midland Bank* [1940] 2 K.B. 388

[66] *Egerton* v. *Brownlow*, (1853) 4 H.L.C. 1.

[67] *Fender* v. *St. John Mildmay* [1938] A.C. 1, 13, *per* Lord Atkin.

[68] *Wainewright* v. *Bland* (1835) 1 Moo. & R. 481; *Beresford* v. *Royal Exchange* [1938] A.C. 586.

victim to insure his life in his favour for a sum however excessive, or the insurers may engage to pay on the sane suicide of the assured, and, in either case, unless the crime which it encourages is proved to have been committed,[69] the policy is valid and enforceable. Thus, also, insurance has been held valid notwithstanding that it might operate as a restraint on marriage.[70]

Contract with an enemy   3–49

But contracts of insurance with enemies or of enemy property are in rather a special position. The general rule of contract is that, although individual cases of trading with the enemy may operate to his detriment,[71] all contracts made with an enemy are void because such contracts in general might enhance his resources[72]; it is on account of their tendency to assist the enemy that such contracts are void.[73] The courts were slow to adapt these principles to contracts of insurance, but it was first decided in 1802–03 that policies taken out on enemy ships against capture by British ships were illegal and therefore void if made during the war,[74] and, if made before it, they were abrogated by it.[75] *Potts* v. *Bell*,[76] in 1800, had decided that no valid contract of insurance can be made during the war between a person in this country and an enemy in a territorial sense, and in 1803 the principles was enunciated that all insurances of enemy property are contrary to the public interest and that a loss occurring during the war cannot be recovered. It is now clear that all contracts with an enemy insuring property are illegal if made after the outbreak of war, or, if made before it, are abrogated by it.[77] But a loss before the outbreak of war is recoverable after the restoration of peace.[78]

Illegal interest no interest   3–50

A policy founded on an illegal interest, which is not itself recoverable in the courts, will always be void if it falls within the Life Assurance Act 1774, for such an interest is no interest at all. Thus the holder of a note given for money won at play cannot validly insure the life of the maker.[79]

Policies on illegal adventures   3–51

There are a number of marine decisions which show that a policy of insurance on an illegal adventure is itself illegal, but caution must be

---

[69] *Wainewright* v. *Bland, supra,* p. 486, *per* Lord Abinger.
[70] *Re Michelhams Will Trusts* [1964] 1 Ch. 550.
[71] *Rodriguez* v. *Speyer Bros.* [1919] A.C. 59, 66.
[72] Lord Dunedin in *Ertel Bieber* v. *Rio Tinto Co.* [1918] A.C. 260, 273, speaking of *The Hoop* (1799) 1 C.Rob. 196.
[73] *Theodor Schneider* v. *Burgett and Newsam* [1916] 1 K.B. 495.
[74] *Kellner* v. *Le Mesurier* (1803) 4 East 396.
[75] *Furtado* v. *Rogers* (1802) 3 Bos. & P. 191.
[76] (1800) 8 T.R. 548.
[77] See Lord Ellenborough's judgments in *Kellner* v. *Le Mesurier, supra*; *Gamba* v. *Le Mesurier* (1803), 4 East 407, and *Brandon* v. *Curling* (1803) 4 East 410. As regards life insurance, see § 16–07, *infra*.
[78] *Janson* v. *Driefontein Mines* [1902] A.C. 484.
[79] *Dwyer* v. *Edie* (1788) 2 Park (8th ed.) 914.

exercised in considering these cases, for not only may marine policies be void on the ground of public policy, but they also contain an implied warranty that the adventure insured is a lawful one,[80] and these two principles may not operate in the same way. Moreover, where the illegality causes loss, as where the master of a ship was engaged in smuggling with the connivance of the owner, and the ship was therefore arrested,[81] the principle considered below that an assured cannot recover an indemnity for his crime operates. Where the illegality exists, or is contemplated by the assured, at the time the policy is taken out, as where deck-cargo had been loaded on a ship contrary to statute,[82] it is clear that the marine policy is wholly void for illegality.[83]

3–52 Illegal use of subject-matter

It would not seem that the mere illegal use of the thing insured would by itself make a policy on it void although illegality may provide the insurer with a defence (see below). Thus in *Leggate* v. *Brown*[84] a policy on a motor-tractor was expressed to be operative while the vehicle was being used "with not more than two trailers attached at any time." The assured used it with two *laden* trailers attached, an offence by the Road Traffic Act 1930, s.18(1)(b). It was held that the insurers could have been liable under the policy had a third party been injured while the vehicle was so used. So, where a factory was temporarily used for the drawing of an illegal lottery, this was held in an American case not to render a fire policy on the factory void.[85] The test that has sometimes been applied in America is whether there was an illegal design at the time of taking out the insurance.[86] It is clear that the policy will never be void on the ground of such illegality unless the assured himself was privy to it[87]: he is not in this respect answerable for the illegal acts of his agents or servants.

Moreover an insurance on an adventure remains valid although, by the outbreak of war, for instance, it becomes illegal for the assured to continue with the adventure, if he thereupon abandons it.[88] Nor does the mere fact that property is in enemy territory make an insurance of it illegal.[89]

Where a policy is void for illegality, the fact that the defendants do not wish to raise this point will not necessarily assist the plaintiff, for the court is always empowered to take the point itself if it comes to its notice, and refuse to give judgment on the policy.[90]

---

[80] M.I.A. 1906, s.41. The warranty of legality is confined to marine policies: *Euro-Diam* v. *Bathurst* [1988] 2 All E.R. 23.

[81] *Pipon* v. *Cope* (1808) 1 Camp. 434, as explained. *Trinder* v. *Thames & Mersey Marine* [1898] 2 Q.B. 114 at p. 129.

[82] *Cunard* v. *Hyde* (1859) 2 E. & E. 1.

[83] *Ibid*. Lord Campbell at pp. 7 and 8.

[84] (1950) 66 T.L.R. (Pt. 2) 281.

[85] *Boardman* v. *Merrimack Mutual* 62 Mass. (8 Cush.) 583 (1851). Contrast *Kelly* v. *Home Insurance*, 97 Mass. (1 Browne) 288 (1867); *Johnson* v. *Union Marine*, 127 Mass. (13 Lathrop) 555 (1879).

[86] *Carrign* v. *Lycoming Fire Ins.*, 38 Am.Rep. 687 (Vermont) (1881); *Hinckley* v. *Germania Fire*, 140 Mass. 38 (1885).

[87] *Wilson* v. *Rankin* (1865) L.R. 1 Q.B. 162.

[88] *British Marine* v. *Sanday* [1916] 1 A.C. 650.

[89] *Nigel Gold Mining Co.* v. *Hoade* [1901] 2 K.B. 849.

[90] *Gedge* v. *Royal Exchange* [1900] 2 Q.B. 214, 220, *per* Kennedy J.

Insurances made by unauthorised insurers 3–53

Under section 2 of the Insurance Companies Act 1982, "no person shall carry on any insurance business in the United Kingdom unless authorised to do so."[91] Similar words had appeared in earlier insurance companies legislation. In *Phoenix* v. *A.D.A.S.*[92] the Court of Appeal held, resolving some disagreement at first instance,[93] that the intention of the legislation was to render illegal any policy issued by an authorised insurer. This ruling affects policies issued before January 12, 1987, as on that date section 132 of the Financial Services Act 1986 came into force. This provides that a policy issued by an unauthorised insurer is merely unenforceable at the instance of the insurer, although the court does have a discretion to enforce the agreement if the insurer's conduct had not been culpable and if it is otherwise just and equitable for enforcement to be allowed.

9. LOSS FOLLOWING A CRIMINAL ACT

Governing principles 3–54

It is an old so-called "principle" of insurance law that the assured cannot (in most circumstances) recover under an insurance policy in respect of a loss which has followed his own crime. But this may be on either or both of two grounds. First, the assured will not be able to recover where his own "wilful misconduct" has brought about the loss.[94] Wilful misconduct can, however, arise without the commission of a crime, and its key feature is that the assured has brought about his own loss. The wilful misconduct rule is an application of the general principle that insurance covers events fortuitous as regards the assured, and not acts which the assured deliberately commits in order to bring about a loss. Secondly, he may be unable to recover on the ground of public policy, an uncertain and continually fluctuating branch of the common law.

These principles overlap—as where the beneficiary under a life policy murders the assured[95]—but are not identical. Thus, an assured who sets fire to his own property does not commit an unlawful act (unless he intends to make a fraudulent claim on his insurers), but will be unable to claim on his policy due to his own wilful misconduct in bringing about the loss. Conversely, public policy may operate in the absence of wilful misconduct. Thus in *Amicable Insurance* v. *Bolland*[96] it was decided by the House of Lords that the assignees in bankruptcy of a forger who had been executed for his own crime could not recover under a life policy taken out by him on his own life. "Is it possible that such a contract could be sustained?" said Lord Lyndhurst,[97]

---

[91] For discussion of authorisation, see Chap. 13.

[92] [1987] 2 All E.R. 152, followed in *Re Cavalier Insurance* [1989] 2 Lloyd's Rep. 430, in which it was further held that the assured could recover his premiums despite the illegality.

[93] *Bedford Insurance* v. *Institutio de Ressaguros do Brasil* [1984] 3 All E.R. 766 (illegality); *Stewart* v. *Oriental Fire* [1984] 3 All E.R. 777 (legal, but unenforceable by insurer); *Phoenix* v. *Halvanon* [1986] 1 All E.R. 908 (legal, but unenforceable by insurer).

[94] See *infra* 4–03 *et seq.*

[95] *Cleaver* v. *Mutual Reserve* [1892] 1 Q.B. 147. The principle that the beneficiary cannot recover in these circumstances is enshrined in the Forfeiture Act 1982. *Cf. Davitt* v. *Titcumb, supra* n. 63.

[96] (1830) 4 Bligh (N.S.) 194.

[97] At pp. 211, 212.

"Is it not void[98] upon the plainest principles of public policy? Would not such a contract (if available) take away one of those restraints operating on the minds of men against the commission of crimes?"

It is clear that the assured could not be said deliberately to have brought about his own loss, but public policy nevertheless defeated the claim. A further distinction between wilful misconduct and public policy concerns the terms of the policy. Where a person is unable to recover on account of public policy, no term in the contract, however express it may be, will assist him, but where it is an implied term of the contract alone which prevents a person from recovering an express term may well assist him.[99]

3–55   The rule *ex turpi causa non oritur actio* does not, like the general rule relating to contracts against public policy, render the contract itself void. It only prevents the criminal himself, or anyone deriving title from him after the crime, from recovering. Thus in *Cleaver* v. *Mutual Reserve*[1] James Maybrick insured his life in this wife's favour. On his death his executors would normally have held the moneys as trustees for her. She poisoned him, and was therefore not able to benefit under the trust, but it was held nevertheless that the executors were entitled to recover for the benefit of *his* estate. Again, in *Hardy* v. *Motor Insurers Bureau*[2] the Court of Appeal ruled that the fact an insurer was not obliged to make payment under the policy following a deliberate unlawful act by the assured, did not prevent an action on the policy by a third party upon whom a direct right of action has been conferred by statute.

3–56   Leaving aside the possibility of wilful misconduct, which operates irrespective of criminality and only where the act in question brings about the loss, not every act of criminality by the assured will deprive him of the right to recover under the policy. The relevant principles are to be found in the judgment of the Court of Appeal in *Euro-Diam* v. *Bathurst*.[3] The assured insured a quantity of diamonds under a Lloyd's policy and sold them on a sale or return basis to a customer in Germany. The true price to be paid was understated on the invoice, in order to allow the purchaser to avoid turnover tax in Germany. The diamonds were lost in Germany, and the assured claimed under the policy. The underwriters contested liablility on the basis that the assured had assisted in the commission of an unlawful act—tax evasion—and was precluded from recovering by the *ex turpi causa* rule. The Court of Appeal, allowing the assured's action on the policy, set out the guiding principles on the application of *ex turpi causa* in the insurance context.

   (i) The guiding rule was that the court would not assist a plaintiff who had been guilty of illegal or immoral conduct of which the court should take notice. The court should be prepared to dis-

---

[98] The policy was not *void*; the forger's assignees could simply not claim on it on the principle *ex turpi causa*.
[99] See the suicide cases, discussed below.
[1] [1892] 1 Q.B. 147. See also *Davitt* v. *Titcumb, supra*.
[2] [1964] 2 Q.B. 745, approved by the House of Lords in *Gardner* v. *Moore* [1984] 1 All E.R. 1100.
[3] [1988] 2 All E.R. 23.

allow recovery where a successful action would be affront to the public conscience in that the court would be seen to be assisting in an illegal or immoral design.

(ii) The *ex turpi causa* defence will prima facie succeed in a number of cases, including: (a) where the plaintiff is forced to found his claim upon his own illegal act; (b) where the grant of relief to the plaintiff would enable him to benefit from his own criminal conduct; (c) in residual circumstances falling outside the above.

(iii) The *ex turpi causa* principle is to be approached pragmatically and with caution, so that not every act of illegality prevents recovery.

Applying these principles, the Court of Appeal held that the assured had a right to recover: the illegality was not causative of the loss, the assured did not benefit from the underinvoicing, and the insurers were unaffected (given that the insured value was not the invoiced value but the market value).

As a result of *Euro-Diam*, it now follows that the assured will be **3–57** denied recovery only where two requirements are fulfilled. First, his unlawful or immoral act must have been causative of the loss, or in the absence of this, the assured's action under the policy must be an attempt to benefit indirectly from his unlawful act. Secondly, public policy must militate against recovery. The Court of Appeal in *Euro-Diam* approved the earlier decision of Talbot J. in *Geismar* v. *Sun Alliance*[4] by an application of these guidelines. In that case the assured householder had, unknown to his insurers, smuggled jewellery into England. His failure to declare the jewellery to the customs authorities rendered it liable to immediate forfeiture. Talbot J. held that, although the policy was not illegal, the courts should not assist the assured in seeking to derive a profit from the act of smuggling, even though such benefit was sought indirectly through an indemnity under an insurance policy. The Court of Appeal in *Euro-Diam* held this reasoning to be correct.

Suicide 3–58

Beresford v. *Royal Insurance*[5] was the leading authority on this matter. The deceased insured his life in 1925. In 1934 he shot himself in order that his personal representatives should benefit under the policy. He was found to be sane at the time and his suicide therefore amounted to a crime. However, it was an express term of the policy that sane suicide within one year of the taking out of the policy should avoid it, so that it was a necessary implication that after that time had elapsed the policy moneys were payable on sane suicide.[6] The House of Lords nevertheless denied coverage on public policy grounds.

> "The absolute rule is that the courts will not recognise a benefit accruing to a criminal from his crime . . . His executor or administrator claims as his representative, and, as his representative, falls under the same ban.[7]

---

[4] [1977] 2 Lloyd's Rep. 62.
[5] [1938] A.C. 586.
[6] *Ibid.* p. 596.
[7] *Ibid.* p. 599.

However, by the Suicide Act 1961, s.1: "The rule of law whereby it is a crime for a person to commit suicide is hereby abrogated." The *Beresford* case would clearly have been decided differently had this statute then been in force: there would have been no public policy ground for denying recovery, and the insurers had implicitly undertaken liability for sane suicide occurring after one year from the inception of the policy. It might also be noted that the common law misdemeanour of attempted suicide had ceased to exist, although a suicide faked by one who has taken out a life policy may amount to the crime of attempting to obtain the policy moneys by deception.[8]

3–59 Criminal acts of negligence

In *Haseldine* v. *Hosken*,[9] it was held that an indemnity policy taken out by a solicitor could not cover his liability in respect of an intentional criminal act. He had entered into a champertous agreement, but though he clearly understood its terms he did not apparently realise that it was criminal. This case, is however, the furthest that the law has gone: the principle has never been applied to an indemnity policy in the case of mere acts of negligence even though they were criminal. Thus, it was held in *Tinline* v. *White Cross*[10] and *James* v. *British General*,[11] that motor manslaughter does not preclude the assured recovering under a motor policy that includes third party risks. Doubt was thrown on those cases by the Court of Appeal in *Haseldine* v. *Hosken*[12] but they have not been overruled, and many thousand motor insurance claims must in fact have been paid despite the fact that the assured was guilty of some driving offence.

Lord Denning M.R. said in *Gray* v. *Barr*[13] that it was settled beyond doubt by these cases, that in the category of "motor manslaughter" the insured was entitled to recover (even if, it seems, his conduct is wilful and culpable); and Salmon L.J. said[14] that "it seems now to be settled law that a motorist can rely on his policy of insurance to indemnify him in respect of his liability for any injuries which he has caused otherwise than on purpose." But where the lethal weapon is not a motor vehicle, and particularly where it is a gun, the courts have in recent years taken a different view in cases of manslaughter in which the assured does a dangerous act with the intention of frightening or harming someone, or with the realisation that it is likely to do so (as in the case of reckless driving), and hold that it is contrary to public policy to allow the accused to profit by his crime (always provided that the weapon was not a motor car).[15]

It has been said of the distinction: "The court has to weigh the gravity of the anti-social act and the extent to which it will be encouraged by enforcing the right sought to be asserted against the social harm which

---

[8] *D.P.P.* v. *Stonehouse* [1977] 3 W.L.R. 143.
[9] [1933] 1 K.B. 822.
[10] [1921] 3 K.B. 327.
[11] [1927] 2 K.B. 311.
[12] *Per* Scrutton L.J. at pp. 833–835; Greer L.J. at p. 838.
[13] [1971] 2 Q.B. 554.
[14] At p. 581.
[15] See *Gray* v. *Barr* [1971] 2 Q.B. 554, *per* Lord Denning M.R. at p. 568; pp. 581–582 *per* Salmon L.J. and Phillimore L.J. at pp. 587–588.

will be caused if the right is not enforced."[16] It may thus be seen that even though a criminal act is causative of loss, the court is nevertheless able to allow the assured to recover if public policy is on balance in favour of recovery.

---

[16] *Per* Diplock L.J. in *Hardy* v. *Motor Insurers' Bureau* [1964] 2 Q.B. 745, 768.

CHAPTER 4

THE RISK

1. EXTENT OF RISK

THE most important part of insurance is determination of the risk. The **4–01**
insurer can only adjust his premium profitably if he knows accurately
the nature of the risk which he is asked to take upon himself, and it is
even more essential to the assured to know precisely the extent of his
cover, so that he may take out additional insurance if it is required, and
so that he may avoid uneconomical double insurance.

Negligence   4–02
Casualties insured against, include those caused by negligence. The
principle is an old one.[1] It does not matter whether the negligence is that
of the assured,[2] his servants or a stranger.[3] An insurance of goods on
land will usually cover the negligence of a carrier, his servant and
agents.[4] Thus, where the assured placed her jewellery in a grate to hide
it from thieves, and later negligently lit a fire there, it was held that she
was entitled to recover under a fire policy for damage resulting to it.[5]
Similarly, an accident policy covers accidents caused by the negligence of third parties or of the assured himself,[6] as where the assured
negligently crosses a railway line and is knocked down,[7] or carelessly
drinks a dose of poison instead of medicine.[8]
It is perfectly possible, however, to exclude liability where the assured
or his servants or agents bring about an insured peril by negligence.
Thus personal accident policies may exclude liability where the assured
exposes himself to obvious risk of injury[9] or danger,[10] liability and property policies may exclude liability where the assured has failed to take
reasonable care[11] and marine policies normally require the assured to
exercise "due diligence" for certain classes of risk and to exercise

---

[1] *Austin* v. *Drewe* (1815) 4 Camp. 360, 362.
[2] *Shaw* v. *Robberds* (1837) 6 Ad. & El. 75, 84, *per* Denman L.C.J.
[3] *Dobson* v. *Sotheby* (1827) Moo. & M. 90.
[4] *Boehm* v. *Combe* (1813) 2 M. & S. 172 *Busk* v. *Royal Exchange* (1818) 2 B. & Ald. 73.
[5] *Harris* v. *Poland* [1941] 1 K.B. 462.
[6] Lord M'Laren in *Clidero* v. *Scottish Accident* (1892) 19 R. (Ct. of Sess.) 355, 363.
[7] *Cornish* v. *Accident Insurance* (1889) 23 Q.B.D. 453.
[8] *Cole* v. *Accident Insurance* (1889) 5 T.L.R. 736.
[9] *Cornish* v. *Accident Insurance*, *supra*.
[10] *Marcel Beller* v. *Hayden* [1978] Q.B. 694 (wording not appropriate to exclude negligent exposure
to danger).
[11] Such clauses are construed narrowly, on the basis that liability and property policies are intended
to insure against negligence. Consequently, nothing less than recklessness will defeat the assured's
claim: *Fraser* v. *Furman* [1967] 3 All E.R. 57; *Woolfall & Rimmer* v. *Moyle* [1942] 1 K.B. 66; *Lindon
Alimak* v. *British Engine Insurance* [1984] 1 Lloyd's Rep. 416; *Aluminium Wire and Cable Co.* v. *Allstate Insurance* [1985] 2 Lloyd's Rep. 280; *Port-Rose* v. *Phoenix* 1986, unreported; *Sinnott* v. *Municipal
Insurance* [1989] 9 C.L. 297; *M/S Aswan* v. *Iron Trades Mutual* [1989] 1 Lloyd's Rep. 289; *Sofi* v. *Prudential* 1990, unreported; *Devco Holder* v. *Legal and General* 1988, unreported.

"reasonable endeavours"[12] to mitigate loss following the occurrence of an insured peril.

4–03 Wilful misconduct

But while it matters not that a loss is due to the assured's negligence he will never, in the absence of express words,[13] be entitled to recover where the loss is due to his wilful misconduct,[14] as where he intentionally sets fire to his house,[15] or scuttles his ship,[16] or where such acts are done by another with his privity or consent.[17] For insurance is against fortuitous events only, and in such a case the assured has not merely exposed the goods to the chance of injury, he has injured them himself.[18]

4–04　　But *Beresford* v. *Royal*[19] makes it clear that the parties may, by their contract, even extend the risk to cover cases where the assured wilfully causes the loss with his own hand, though it might be contrary to public policy to allow him to recover on such an insurance.

This rule is directed against *misconduct* only, and does not cover cases where the assured properly, and without any fraud or *dolus* on his part, causes the loss in question,[20] as where he causes the loss in the performance of a duty to the State under whose law the policy was made. Thus, where the captain of a British vessel set fire to it to prevent it falling into the hands of French privateers, it was held that the loss fell within the fire cover provided by the policy.[21]

4–05　　The prohibition extends only to the misconduct of the assured himself. Thus, the fact that a man's wife wilfully destroys his property will not preclude him from recovering from his insurers in respect of the loss, unless it can be shown that he was a party to her action.[22] So, also, a loss caused by the wilful misconduct of his servants is within the risk covered by a policy,[23] unless it is expressly excluded. Similarly, an injury due to the wilful or even criminal act of a stranger falls within an accident policy,[24] unless the assured is a party to the act.

4–06　　Some risks, however, from their nature, exclude any wilful human agency. Thus, "collapse" of a building has been held not to include demolition in obedience to an order of the London County Council, or intentional destruction of a building by house-breakers.[25]

---

[12] See *Stephen* v. *Scottish Boatowners Mutual* [1989] 1 Lloyd's Rep. 135.

[13] As in *Beresford* v. *Royal* [1938] A.C. 586.

[14] *Thurtell* v. *Beaumont* (1824) 1 Bing. 339; Lord Atkin in *Beresford* v. *Royal* [1938] A.C. 586, 595; Lord Wright in *Yorkshire Dale S.S. Co.* v. *Minister of War Transport* [1942] A.C. 691, 704.

[15] Scrutton L.J. in *Upjohn* v. *Hitchens* [1918] 2 K.B. 48, 58, and *City Tailors* v. *Evans* (1921) 38 T.L.R. 230, 233, 234.

[16] *Samuel* v. *Dumas* [1924] A.C. 431; M.I.A. 1906, s.55(2)(*a*).

[17] *Midland Insurance* v. *Smith* (1881) 6 Q.B.D. 561; *Samuel* v. *Dumas, supra.*

[18] *Per* Lord Sumner in *British Marine* v. *Gaunt* [1921] 2 A.C. 41, 57.

[19] [1938] A.C. 586.

[20] *Thompson* v. *Hopper* (1858) E.B. & E. 1038; *Trinder* v. *Thames & Mersey Marine* [1898] 2 Q.B. 114.

[21] *Gordon* v. *Rimmington* (1807) 1 Camp. 123. See also *Rickards* v. *Forestal* [1942] A.C. 50.

[22] *Midland Insurance* v. *Smith* (1881) 6 Q.B.D. 561.

[23] *Shaw* v. *Robberds* (1837) 6 Ad. & El. 75, 84, *per* Denman L.C.J.; *Lind* v. *Mitchell* (1928) 45 T.L.R. 54, 56, *per* Scrutton L.J.

[24] *Letts* v. *Excess Insurance* (1916) 32 T.L.R. 361.

[25] *Allen Billposting* v. *Drysdale* [1939] 4 All E.R. 113.

Misconduct of part-owner   **4–07**

Where two persons both have an interest in a thing, and one of them destroys it, the other will be able to recover under a policy covering his interest, provided he is quite innocent and so long as his interest is not so inseparably connected with that of the wrongdoer, that his loss or gain necessarily affects them both.[26] This principle applies in favour of an innocent mortgagee, where the mortgagor scuttles his ship[26] or sets fire to his building.[27] Moreover, in the latter case, an assignment before the loss to the mortgagee of the mortgagor's policy, assented to by the insurers, will probably enable him to recover in respect of his interest,[27] for in fire insurance such assignment amounts to a new contract between the mortgagee and the insurers. The mortgagor may take out the insurance for the mortgagee's benefit, but by paying the mortgagee the insurers will have no subrogation rights against the guilty mortgagor.[28]

Other implied limitations   **4–08**

There are other implied limitations on the liability of the insurer besides losses caused by the wilful misconduct of the assured. They include:

(i) *Wear and tear*.[29] The casualty must be a fortuitous one, and no damage such as could be expected to occur in normal circumstances. There must be some abnormal circumstance, accident or casualty even when the insurance is expressed to be against "all risks."[30] The purpose of a policy is to secure an indemnity against accidents which may happen, not against events which must happen.[31] Thus, damage to a ship by rats is not covered by a marine policy,[32] and damage by smoke and heat, as distinct from flames, is not included in the risk covered by a fire policy.[33]

(ii) *Inherent vice*.[34] Risks insured against do not, without clear **4–09** words,[35] include the inherent vice of the subject-matter insured, *i.e.* its natural behaviour, being what it is, in the circumstances under which it is. The risk must be something which happens to it from without.[36] Putrescence of meat through delay is an example of such inherent vice.[37] Thus, an insurance of cargo against fire does not cover fire caused by spontaneous combustion,[38] although insurance against the risks of heat, sweat and spontaneous combustion will cover heat damage arising from

---

[26] *Samuel* v. *Dumas* [1924] A.C. 431. See *supra.* para. 3–47.

[27] See *Central Bank of India* v. *Guardian Assurance* (1936) 54 Ll.L.R. 247 (P.C.).

[28] *Mark Rowlands* v. *Berni Inns* [1985] 3 All E.R. 473.

[29] See M.I.A. 1906, s.55(2)(*c*).

[30] Lord Birkenhead in *British Marine* v. *Gaunt* [1921] 2 A.C. 41, 46–47.

[31] Lord Herschell in *The Xantho* (1887) 12 App.Cas. 503, 509.

[32] *Hunter* v. *Potts* (1815) 4 Camp. 203; M.I.A. 1906, s.55(2)(*c*); but see *Hamilton* v. *Pandorf* (1887) 12 App.Cas. 518, as explained in *Leyland* v. *Norwich Union* [1918] A.C. 350.

[33] *Austin* v. *Drewe* (1815) 4 Camp. 360, as explained in *Harris* v. *Poland* [1941] 1 K.B. 462.

[34] See also n. 29.

[35] *Soya* v. *White* [1983], Lloyd's Rep. 122. See illustrations considered by Sellers J. in *Berk* v. *Style* [1956] 1 Q.B. 180; and *Overseas Commodities* v. *Style* [1958] 1 Lloyd's Rep. 546.

[36] Lord Sumner in *British Marine* v. *Gaunt* [1921] 2 A.C. 41, 57. It was thus held in *Noten* v. *Harding* [1989] 2 Lloyd's Rep. 527 that mould caused by condensation dripping onto leather gloves was not inherent vice as an external force had been involved. The fact that the water causing the loss had been emitted by the leather itself was held by Phillips J. to be immaterial.

[37] *Taylor* v. *Dunbar* (1869) L.R. 4 C.P. 206.

[38] See *Boyd* v. *Dubois* (1811) 3 Camp. 133; *Sassoon* v. *Yorkshire Insurance* (1923) 14 Ll.L.R. 167; affirmed 16 Ll.L.R. 129.

inherent vice.[39] So insurances of animals, or, formerly, insurances of slaves, do not include death by natural causes. So also, an accident policy does not cover death from natural disease, even if it is not expressly excepted,[40] though the risk covered by an ordinary life policy includes death by disease or senile decay.[41]

4–10   (iii) *Risks that it is not lawful to cover.* Certain risks, such as the capture of an enemy ship by a British vessel, cannot be lawfully insured, and such risks are therefore impliedly excepted from any policy.[42]

4–11 *"All risks" policies*

The best illustration of these limitations is to be found in cases where "all risks" or "all losses" are insured against.[43] Such policies are common today, especially in the case of insurances of jewellery. In *British Marine* v. *Gaunt*,[44] where wool was insured against "all risks" from the sheep's back in Patagonia to warehouses in Europe, the House of Lords held that "all risks" did not include wear and tear, inherent vice, own act of assured, British capture, or risks that it was not lawful to cover.[45]

In that case the wool was badly damaged from an unknown cause, and the loss was held to fall within the policy. "If the casualty was fortuitous it needed not to be a calamity."[46]

Under an "all risks" transit policy,[47] it is prima facie sufficient, to establish a claim, to prove that the goods were undamaged before transit and arrived damaged.[48]

It has been held that seizure of goods by an administrator in bankruptcy, or a wrongful conversion of them amounting to theft, are losses falling within such a policy.[49]

There is no magic, however, in using the term "all risks"—the words may be used to refer to the quantum of loss, in which case they do not cover all casualties but merely mean that the loss will be payable in full whatever its actual amount.[50] The meaning of the phrase is a matter of construction in each case.[51]

4–12 "Loss" of subject-matter insured

Another limitation on the protection given by all insurance policies is the principle that the insurers are only liable for loss of, or damage to, the subject-matter of the insurance.

---

[39] *Soya* v. *White, supra.*

[40] *Winspear* v. *Accident Insurance* (1880) 6 Q.B.D. 42; *Isitt* v. *Railway Passengers Assurance* (1889) 22 Q.B.D. 504.

[41] The fortuity there is not the occurrence of death, which is certain, but the hour at which it occurs.

[42] *Brandon* v. *Curling* (1803) 4 East 410. *Cf. Janson* v. *Driefontein Mines* [1902] A.C. 484.

[43] See *Schloss Bros.* v. *Stevens* [1906] 2 K.B. 665.

[44] [1921] 2 A.C. 41.

[45] *Per* Lord Sumner at pp. 57–58.

[46] *Per* Lord Sumner at p.58. Under an "all risks" policy the insurer bears the burden of proof of showing loss by an excepted cause: *Fuerst Day Lawson* v. *Orion Insurance* [1980] 1 Lloyd's Rep. 656.

[47] Lloyd's ordinary "Lloyd's Goods in Transit Policy" (L.P.O. 55A (1.4.68)) covers *inter alia* (subject to specific exclusions) goods in transit against "all risks of loss of or destruction of or damage to" them, Clause C.

[48] *Electro Motion* v. *Maritime Ins.* [1956] 1 Lloyd's Rep. 420; but contrast *Theodorou* v. *Chester* [1951] 1 Lloyd's Rep. 204, and see *Gee & Garnham* v. *Whittall* [1955] 2 Lloyd's Rep. 562 where inherent vice was alleged.

[49] *London Leather Processes* v. *Hudson* [1939] 2 K.B. 724.

[50] *Per* Hamilton J. in *Vincentelli* v. *John Rowlett & Co.* (1911) 105 L.T. 411, 414.

[51] For a case where a contractor's "all risks" policy excluded "faulty design," see *Queensland Government Railways* v. *Manufacturers' Mutual Ins.* [1969] 1 Lloyd's Rep. 214 (High Ct. of Australia).

Thus the protection given by insurances on goods only extends to loss of, or damage to, the goods insured. Where goods were insured under a marine policy and they were held up in Paris while it was besieged, it was held that the assured was entitled to recover.[52] "It is well established that there may be a loss of the goods by a loss of the voyage during which the goods are being transported, if it amounts, to use the words of Lord Ellenborough, 'to a destruction of the contemplated adventure.' "[53] But under a marine policy the adventure is insured,[54] the insurance is not only an insurance of the goods but also an insurance of their safe arrival.[55] Such cases[56] have no application to non-marine policies on goods. Thus, where the owner of timber, insured against war-risks, was unable to bring it to allied territory because it lay, in the hands of his agent, in enemy territory, it was held that there was no loss under the policy.[57]

It follows that to establish a loss of goods insured against "all losses" it is not enough to show that they are in enemy territory and the owner cannot regain possession of them.[58] Some evidence of seizure is necessary.[59] But if a pearl necklace appears prima facie to be lost, with no real hope of recovery, then there is a loss within the terms of such a policy,[59] and the fact that it is subsequently recovered does not change the position, it simply means that the insurer will be entitled to it, if he has already paid, by way of salvage.[60] Mere unlikelihood of recovery does not constitute a loss under a non-marine policy, though it would constitute a constructive total loss under the Marine Insurance Act 1906,[61] for that doctrine has no application, at any rate in this respect,[62] outside marine insurance law.[63]

In *Webster* v. *General Accident*,[64] the assured parted with possession **4–13** of a motor-car to a rogue on the fraudulent representation that he had a buyer for it. The rogue sold it by auction in his own name and misapplied the proceeds. The assured knew where the car was, but was told by the police and his solicitor that an attempt to recover it would be hopeless. Parker J. held that there was a "loss" of the car within the meaning of a policy. "The test as it seems to me," he said, "is whether, after all reasonable steps to recover a chattel have been taken by the assured, recovery is uncertain."[65] But it was held otherwise in *Eisinger* v. *General Accident*,[66] where the assured sold his car to a rogue who

---

[52] *Rodocanachi* v. *Elliot* (1874) L.R. 9 C.P. 518.
[53] *Ibid. per* Bramwell B. at p. 522.
[54] See s.3 of M.I.A. 1906.
[55] *Rickards* v. *Forestal* [1942] A.C. 50.
[56] See also *British Marine* v. *Sanday* [1916] 1 A.C. 605; *Fooks* v. *Smith* [1924] 2 K.B. 508.
[57] *Mitsui* v. *Mumford* [1915] 2 K.B. 27, followed in *Campbell* v. *Denman* (1915) 21 Com.Cas. 357, and by the House of Lords in *Moore* v. *Evans* [1918] A.C. 185.
[58] *Moore* v. *Evans*, *supra*.
[59] *Holmes* v. *Payne* [1930] 2 K.B. 301.
[60] See § 8–02, *infra*.
[61] M.I.A. 1906, ss.60, 61. See *Polurrian* v. *Young* [1915] 1 K.B. 922; *The Bamburi* [1982] 1 Lloyd's Rep. 312.
[62] See § 8–01, *infra*.
[63] *Moore* v. *Evans*, *supra*, pp. 193–197, *per* Lord Atkinson.
[64] [1953] 1 Q.B. 520.
[65] At p. 532, but *quaere*. There seems to have been no hope of recovery in that case.
[66] [1955] 1 W.L.R. 869. *Cf. Metal Scrap* v. *Federated Conveyors* [1953] 1 Lloyd's Rep. 221.

gave him a worthless cheque for it. "It is a clear case of obtaining a car by false pretences. But that passed the property in the car. You cannot say that the claimant has lost the car; what he has lost is the proceeds of sale."[67]

In regard to a question in a proposal form whether the assured had sustained a "loss" it was held that a loss was no less a loss although the previous insurers had indemnified the proposer.[68]

4–14 *Loss of profits*

It also follows that where the assured desires to cover himself against loss consequential on the loss of property, he must be careful to ensure that the subject-matter of the desired insurance is properly described in the policy.[69] Thus, where the policy simply covers loss of goods, their value alone can be recovered and nothing can be recovered in respect of loss of profits.[70] Though profits may be insured, they must be described as such.[71] It was held accordingly that where consignees insured wool on trust they had to pay over the whole of the insurance moneys to the owners, and that they could retain nothing on account of their loss of commission.[72] So, also, an insurance on goods does not cover the loss in value of uninjured goods due to damage to other goods which are part of the same consignment.[73] But realised profits due to a rising market may be covered on an unvalued policy of goods alone, as their market price at the time of the loss will be the measure of the insurer's liability,[74] and future profits must be distinguished from realised profits in this respect. Where the policy is a valued one, however, no such distinction can be drawn.[75] If the same policy covers goods at a valuation and also profits unvalued, the valuation will be taken as the agreed value when the risk begins.[76]

4–15 *Consequential loss*

So, also, only damage to the fabric of the building will be covered under an ordinary fire insurance policy, it was held in *Re Wright and Pole*.[77] There an inn was burnt down and it was held that such consequential losses as rent, the hire of other premises and the loss of custom while the inn was being rebuilt were unrecovered. Nor, where business premises are burnt down, can wages or loss of profits be recovered under an ordinary fire policy.[78]

---

[67] Lord Goddard C.J. at p. 871. Contrast *Dobson* v. *General Accident* [1989] 3 All E.R. 927, where this form of misappropriation was held to constitute "loss by theft".

[68] *Roberts* v. *Avon Ins.* [1956] 2 Lloyd's Rep. 240.

[69] *Glover* v. *Black* (1763) 3 Burr. 1394.

[70] Lord Wright in *Maurice* v. *Goldborough Mort* [1939] A.C. 452, 461. See also *Emanuel* v. *Hepburn* [1960] 1 Lloyd's Rep. 304 (transit insurance against "physical loss or damage or deterioration" held not to cover loss of market).

[71] *Ibid.* citing *Lucena* v. *Craufurd* (1806) 2 Bos. & P.(N.R.) 269; *Mackenzie* v. *Whitworth* (1875) 1 Ex.D. 36, 43. See also Parke B. in *Stockdale* v. *Dunlop* (1840) 6 M. & W. 224, 232–233.

[72] See n. 70.

[73] *Cator* v. *Great Western Insurance of New York* (1873) L.R. 8 C.P. 552.

[74] See § 8–05, *infra*.

[75] See Pollock C.B. in *Smith* v. *Reynolds* (1856) 1 H. & N. 221, 224.

[76] See Scrutton L.J. in *Williams* v. *Atlantic Assurance* [1933] 1 K.B. 81, 90.

[77] (1834) 1 Ad. & El. 621.

[78] *Menzies* v. *North British* (1847) 9 D. (Ct. of Sess.) 694; see also *Westminster Fire* v. *Glasgow Provident* (1888) 13 App.Cas. 699, and Pollock C.B. in *Theobald* v. *Railway Passengers Assurance* (1854) 10 Ex. 45, 58. But see *City Tailors* v. *Evans* (1921) 38 T.L.R. 230.

Insurers may undertake to pay in respect of consequential loss "*x* per cent. of the ultimate net loss as may be paid" on the main policy. In calculating that percentage amounts received by the insurers under the main policy on account of their subrogation rights should, subject to express wording, be disregarded.[79]

Similar principles apply to accident insurance. The assured is ordinarily entitled to the costs of medical attendance and expenses to which he is put by the accident, but not to the loss of business or professional profits.[80]

Goods named by reference to named place   **4-16**

Where goods, the subject-matter of an insurance, are named in the policy by reference to a named place, it is a question of construction which of the following classes of goods is covered.

(i) *All goods in that place when a loss happens.* Such insurances have been made on goods in canal boats[81] and in lighters.[82] Such a policy would obviously cease to apply to goods removed. It will not, on the other hand, become exhausted when goods to the amount named in it have been carried, but only when losses to that amount have been paid.[83] In order to prevent the assured from making his policy cover in effect a larger amount of goods than are fairly insurable at the premium paid, such "floating" policies usually provide that the liability of the insurers shall only be rateable. Thus, if it be on a fluctuating amount of goods in a warehouse, and the value of the goods there at the date of a fire exceed the sum insured, the owner will be his own insurer for the balance.[84]

(ii) *Named goods in that place when the policy is taken out, but only so* **4-17** *long as they are not removed.* A policy of fire insurance on two ricks of hay in a haggard was held to fall into this category in an Irish case; it did not therefore include hay that had been removed and replaced since the insurance was effected.[85] But had it not contained a condition against removal of the hay without notice, it might have fallen into the next category. The condition against removal may make express provision for removal with the assent of the insurer.[86]

Where furniture was insured "whilst in store at the Pall Mall Depositories," and owing to lack of covered space, it was left in two lift vans

---

[79] *Bailliere, Tindall & Cox* v. *Drysdale* (1949) 82 Ll.L.R. 736. "Ultimate net loss" clauses commonly expressly require subrogation recoveries to be taken into account.

[80] *Theobald* v. *Railway Passengers Assurance, supra.*

[81] *Crowley* v. *Cohen* (1832) 3 B. & Ad. 478.

[82] *Joyce* v. *Kennard* (1871) L.R. 7 Q.B. 78. See also *Crozier* v. *Phoenix* (1870) 13 New.Br. (2 Han.) 200; *London and Lancaster* v. *Graves* (1883) 43 Am.Rep. 35; *British American* v. *Joseph* (1857) 9 Lr.Can.Rep. 448; *Butler* v. *Standard Fire* (1879) 4 Ont.App. 391; *Lyons* v. *Providence* (1881) 43 Am.Rep. 32, 33.

[83] See n. 81.

[84] See § 18–28, *infra.*

[85] *Gorman* v. *Hand-in-Hand* (1877) Ir.R. 11 C.L. 224. See also *Harrison* v. *Ellis* (1857) 7 E. & B. 465 (marine policy on goods).

[86] *McClure* v. *Lancashire Insurance* (1860) 13 Ir.Jur. 63. Or for a limited right of removal: *Pearson* v. *Commercial Union* (1876) 1 App.Cas. 498, 505.

place in an enclosed yard and covered with tarpaulins, it was held that the furniture was "in store" within the meaning of the policy.[87]

4-18   (iii) *Goods merely identified by the place in which they are when the policy is effected.* In this case the removal of the goods will not affect the assured's right to recover.[88]

In the first two cases the risk is limited by the place, in the third case the place merely identifies the subject-matter of the insurance. A policy covering the third class would not generally be appropriate where goods are insured against fire, because fire risk is essentially local.[89]

Where there was an exclusion in an all risks policy on furs of those in the "shop portion of L. Ltd." it was held that this meant only those premises at the time of the contract, and not premises subsequently acquired by L. Ltd. It was a reference to premises not persons.[90]

2. PERIOD COVERED

Policies for fixed period

4-19 Computation of time

The general rule is that a period measured "after"[91] or "from"[92] a named day, does not include the day named.[93] Thus, it has been held, terms of years last during the whole anniversary of the day from which they are granted,[94] but each case must depend on its own circumstances and subject-matter.[95] This general rule has been applied to time policies of insurance. Thus in *Isaacs* v. *Royal*,[96] a policy of six months "from February 14 until August 14" was held to exclude February 14 and therefore to include August 14. The same reasoning was applied in *South Staffordshire Tramways* v. *Sickness and Accident*,[97] the policy being "for twelve calendar months from November 24, 1887." It was held that that policy did not cover November 24, 1887, and that a loss on November 24, 1888, was therefore covered. Where this rule applies, the insurance extends throughout the last day, irrespective of the hour at which it was made. The total period sometimes gives assistance in construing a particular policy. "From one day until another" can, where the intention is clear, include both days[98]; so an insurance from January 1 to

---

[87] *Wulfson* v. *Switzerland General* (1940) 56 T.L.R. 701. But "warehouse" has been held not to include a loaded lorry in a locked open compound: *Leo Rapp* v. *McClure* [1955] 1 Lloyd's Rep. 292. In *Boag* v. *Economic Ins.* [1954] 2 Lloyd's Rep. 581 goods in a lorry at factory B of the assured in transit from his factory A to docks were held not to be "stock-in-trade" of factory B for the purpose of a floating policy.

[88] Many such cases appear in American reports. See *McClure* v. *Girard Fire* (1876) 22 Am.Rep. 249; *London & Lancaster* v. *Graves, supra; Noyes* v. *North-Western* (1885) 54 Am.Rep. 641.

[89] *Pearson* v. *Commercial Union* (1876) 1 App.Cas. 498, 505.

[90] *Simon Brooks* v. *Hepburn* [1961] 2 Lloyd's Rep. 43.

[91] *Lester* v. *Garland* (1808) 15 Ves. 248.

[92] *Isaacs* v. *Royal* (1870) L.R. 5 Ex. 296.

[93] See also *Watson* v. *Pears* (1809) 2 Camp. 294; *Webb* v. *Fairmaner* (1838) 3 M. & W. 473; *Bellhouse* v. *Mellow* (1859) 4 H. & N. 116.

[94] *Pugh* v. *Leeds* (1777) 2 Cowp. 714; *Ackland* v. *Lutley* (1839) 9 Ad. & El. 879.

[95] A. L. Smith L.J. in *Re North* [1895] 2 Q.B. 264, 272.

[96] See n. 92.

[97] [1891] 1 Q.B. 402.

[98] Rowlatt J. in *Scottish Metropolitan Assurance* v. *Stewart* (1923) 39 T.L.R. 407, 409.

December 31 would no doubt be construed as intended to give cover for a year and therefore to include both days.[99] Where the policy is renewable, the period of the new term will be presumed to begin when the old term ran out, and this may assist in construing the original term, but no such assistance can be afforded where the assured enters into a new contract with a new company.[1]

The parties are free to fix the term in which way they choose, *e.g.* for 30 days from a named event—then if the event occurs at 11.30 a.m. on one day it will expire at 11.30 a.m. 30 days later.[2] Unless a contrary intention appears "month" means calendar month.[3]

All losses within policy period covered 4–20

A policy for a period covers all losses within that period up to the amount insured. If half a dozen small fires occur, the insurer must pay in respect of each. The only mode of extinguishing his liability for losses occurring during the period is by his actually paying the full amount insured. Even if the assured has already suffered damage to the full sum insured, but has been indemnified from other sources, his insurer will continue to be liable for further losses.[4] On the other hand, as soon as the sum insured has been paid by the insurer, his liability is exhausted, although the period has not expired.

Transit risks

Transit policies 4–21

Contracts of insurance are not always made for a fixed space of time. In the business of marine insurance it is common practice to grant policies for a named voyage[5]; and, although this was not often done in connection with risks on land, "transit" policies are now often issued against accidents to persons whilst they are travelling from one place to another, or on goods whilst they are being sent from one place to another by land, sea or air.[6] In these cases the risk begins when the journey or the transit begins[7] and it ends when the destination is reached, unless the policy otherwise provides.

---

[99] See *Hough* v. *Head* (1885) 55 L.J.Q.B. 43, where the word "inclusive" made such a construction the only possible one.

[1] *Sickness & Accident* v. *General Accident* (1892) 19 R. (Ct. of Sess.) 977.

[2] *Cornfoot* v. *Royal Exchange* [1904] 1 K.B. 40, 43. This case was distinguished in *Cartwright* v. *MacCormack* [1963] 1 W.L.R. 18, where a cover note for motor-vehicle insurance ran from 11.45 a.m. on one day for 15 days "*from* the commencement date of risk." It lasted for 15 full days after the day of commencement.

[3] Law of Property Act 1925, s.61(*a*).

[4] *Smith* v. *Colonial Mutual Fire* (1880) 6 Vict.L.R. 200.

[5] See Marine Insurance Act 1906, s.25 (*voyage and time policies*): "(1) Where the contract is to insure the subject-matter 'at and from,' or from one place to another or others, the policy is called a 'voyage policy,' and where the contract is to insure the subject-matter for a definite period of time the policy is called a 'time policy.' A contract for both voyage and time may be included in the same policy."

A policy is a "time policy" in this Act even though the specified period of its duration may be extended or determined by the parties, *Compania Maritima San Basilio S.A.* v. *Oceanus Mutual* [1973] 3 W.L.R. 265 (C.A.). For the legal consequences of the distinction between time and voyage policies, see Chap., 23.

[6] *Boehm* v. *Combe* (1813) 2 M. & S. 172.

[7] *Halhead* v. *Young* (1856) 6 E. & B. 312, *per* Lord Campbell C.J. at p. 324.

Transit risks may also be covered by floating[8] or declaration[9] time policies on goods,[10] but the same principles apply to any particular transit of any particular goods, so far as the extent of transit risks is in issue.

As to the period covered, four questions frequently arise involving: (i) commencement of transit; (ii) interruption of transit; (iii) deviation in transit; and (iv) termination of transit.

4–22   (i) *Commencement of transit*

In *Crow's Transport* v. *Phoenix Assurance Co.*[11] goods were insured against all risks in transit by a firm of hauliers. The policy covered goods "temporarily housed during the course of transit." Cartons of gramophone records were delivered to the hauliers by day when their drivers were resting, and were stolen. It was held, by the Court of Appeal, that the goods were "in transit" within the meaning of the policy when stolen. "When you take a parcel to the post office or to a railway station and you hand it over and get a receipt, the goods are in transit from the moment the post office or the railway takes them."[12] The commencement of transit, it seems, is the moment of acceptance by the carrier unless the policy otherwise provides, for so far as both the consignor and the carrier are concerned the transit has then begun.

Thus where the contract is governed by the Carriage of Goods by Road Act 1965 (applying the Geneva Convention of 1956)[13] the carrier, by Article 17(1) shall be liable for loss of or damage to the goods "between the time when he takes over the goods" and delivery. The time of taking over is clearly when he has received them against a consignment note for checking.[14] By Lloyd's standard forms of policy for international carriers (Lloyd's Goods in Transit (C.M.R.) Policy) the underwriters agree " . . . to indemnify the Insured against the Insured's legal liability as a Carrier under the provisions of the Convention for loss of or damage to goods whilst in transit per Insured's vehicle . . . including any loading . . . ." The transit begins, it is submitted, when the mantle of liability is donned under the Convention by the carrier— namely, on taking over the goods. The "transit," applying common sense (even though common law be inapplicable) then begins; in other words, the policy then attaches. The words are not "in transit *in* the Insured's vehicles" but *per* them, a pertinent distinction. They cannot be *in* them when being loaded, or prior to loading.

The question when the risk commences under a marine policy depends upon the subject matter insured. In the case of a policy on a

---

[8] See, *e.g. Tomlinson* v. *Hepburn* [1964] 1 Lloyd's Rep. 416; [1966] 1 Q.B. 21 (C.A.); [1966] A.C. 451 (H.L.); *Sadler Bros. Co.* v. *Meredith* [1963] 2 Lloyd's Rep. 293.

[9] See, *e.g. Bartlett & Partners* v. *Meller* [1961] 1 Lloyd's Rep. 487.

[10] See § 14.40, *infra.*

[11] [1965] 1 W.L.R. 383.

[12] At p. 388, *per* Lord Denning M.R., Salmon L.J. *dubitante. Quaere* words *obiter* of Roskill J. in *Sadler Bros. & Co.* v. *Meredith* [1963] 2 Lloyd's Rep. 293, 307: "Transit has in its nature the element of carriage . . . and the carriage starts . . . when the goods are placed on the vehicle." Ackner J. noted the conflict of views, in *S.C.A. (Freight)* v. *Gibson* [1974] 2 Lloyd's Rep. 533, but did not need to decide between them as the goods in question had already been loaded.

[13] Convention on the Contract for the International Carriage of Goods by Road. This Convention applies where the place for the taking over of the goods and the place designated for delivery are in two different countries of which at least one is a Contracting State: art. 1(1).

[14] Act of 1965. Sched. (Geneva Convention), Arts. 4 to 9.

vessel or freight the risk may commence "at and from" a port or "from" a port: in the former case the risk commences when the contract is concluded (or, if the vessel is not in the port at that time, when it arrives in port in good safety), while in the latter the risk commences when the vessel commences her voyage.[15] In the case of a cargo policy, the modern practice is to insure on a "warehouse to warehouse" basis, so that the risk commences from the time when the goods leave the warehouse or place of storage at a named place.

(ii) *Interruption of transit*   4–23
The general rule is that the insurance covers the duration of the transit. In *Sadler* v. *Meredith*[16] Roskill J. held that, in the policy concerned, "transit" meant the passage or carriage of goods from one place to another; goods were still "in transit" when a van (which was stolen) was temporarily parked. The only relevant words in the policy were "in transit": this, therefore, is a key decision.

Vehicle "left unattended"   4–24
It is usual in the case of transit by a motor vehicle for the policy to exclude the insurer's liability where the loss occurs at a time when the vehicle is "left unattended" or, more specifically, not locked in a garage overnight. The phrase "left unattended" has been considered in a number of cases; these demonstrate a fine line between what and what is not permissible conduct on behalf of the assured.

In *Starfire Diamond Rings* v. *Angel*[17] the Court of Appeal determined, under a jewellers' block policy, that a car from which jewellery was stolen was left unattended when the driver left the car, locked and with its windows shut, in a lay-by. He walked 37 yards to stand behind some bushes to urinate, and was able to see the car throughout. All three judges of the Court of Appeal, reversing Barry J., were in agreement that the expression "left unattended" was not "susceptible of any prolonged exegesis."[18] This ruling was applied by Phillimore J. in *Ilford* v. *General Accident Fire & Life Assurance Corporation*,[19] where it was held that a van was left unattended when the driver went into a shop for 15 minutes and not in a position to keep the van under observation.

These cases may be contrasted with a number of others. In *Plaistow Transport* v. *Graham*[20] the relevant clause in a transit policy read: "Warranted Vehicles garaged in locked garage at night except when employed in night journeys but then never unattended." The driver was asleep in his lorry in a lay-by on a night journey when, during the journey, goods were stolen from the vehicle. Nield J. held that the lorry was not unattended. In *Langford* v. *Legal and General*[21] a car was held not to have been left unattended when it was parked on the assured's drive

---

[15] M.I.A. 1906, sched. 1 paras. 2 and 3.
[16] [1963] 2 Lloyd's Rep. 293.
[17] 1962] 2 Lloyd's Rep. 217.
[18] *Ibid.*, at p. 220, per Diplock L.J.
[19] [1967] 2 Lloyd's Rep. 179. See also *Lowenstein* v. *Poplar Motor Transport* [1968] 2 Lloyd's Rep. 233; *Cohen* v. *Plaistow Transport* [1968] 2 Lloyd's Rep. 587.
[20] [1966] 1 Lloyd's Rep. 639.
[21] [1986] 2 Lloyd's Rep. 103.

for a few moments in a position not visible from the house. In *O'Donog-hue* v. *Harding*[22] a similar decision was reached in relation to a car which had been filled with petrol and then locked while the driver paid for the petrol by credit card: the only time at which he could not see the car was for the few seconds during which he was signing the credit card slip, in which period a theft occurred by means of the use of a duplicate key to the car.

(iii) *Deviation in transit*

S.C.A. (*Freight*) v. *Gibson*[23] was a case under a Lloyd's Goods in Transit (C.M.R.) Policy covering the road transit of books from Ciampino, near Rome, to Manchester. The insured carrier sent two of his lorries to the consignor's premises at Ciampino. One was fully loaded, one half loaded, at nightfall. The drivers took the loaded lorry to Rome that night on a joy ride before taking both en route to Manchester next day. The lorry taken overturned and the load of books was damaged. Ackner J. held the underwriters not liable. This form of policy covers cases "where in the normal course of transit the goods . . . are temporarily housed on or off the vehicles . . . ." The judge held that if the books were "temporarily housed" they were not in the "normal course of transit."[24]

However, earlier on in his judgment Ackner J. said[25]: "A deviation which is wholly unrelated to the usual and ordinary method of pursuing the adventure would prevent the goods being 'in transit' within the meaning of the policy." The use of the word "deviation" suggesting as it does the application of section 46 of the Marine Insurance Act 1906,[26] is dangerous in this context, since any deviation *inter alia* wholly discharges the insurers from liability "as from the time of deviation."[27] There is no warrant, it is submitted, by reason of an implied warranty or otherwise, for importing this doctrine, understood in maritime insurance, *in toto* into the law of transit insurance generally. A departure from the route on a frolic is not part of the transit, but that does not *per se* mean that the assured cannot resume the transit and remain insured, in the absence of an express provision in the policy to that effect.

4–25 (iv) *Termination of transit*

When the transit ends is, theoretically, a difficult problem. Suppose the insurance were to cover "goods in transit" and nothing more: there is no authority to determine, for instance, whether transit would end on the arrival of a land vehicle at the *terminus ad quem* or on the completion of unloading of the goods.

This problem has arisen for centuries in the context of marine voyage policies. In the case of vessels, it has been traditional for the voyage to terminate when the vessel has been moored at anchor for twenty-four

---

[22] [1988] 2 Lloyd's Rep. 281.
[23] [1974] 2 Lloyd's Rep. 533.
[24] At p. 536.
[25] p. 535.
[26] *Infra*, Chap. 23.
[27] *Ibid.* s.46(1).

hours in good safety,[28] although this is commonly supplemented by a further period of (often) thirty days.[29] In the case of goods, policies were at one time written on the basis that the risk would terminate when the goods were "safely landed,"[30] but it is now the practice under the standard "warehouse to warehouse" clause for the policy to determine on delivery of the goods to the final warehouse at the port of destination.

Terrestrial policies usually give a similar guide. Thus, in *Tomlinson* v. *Hepburn*[31] a policy of transit on goods covered risks "including loading and unloading. Including risk during halts and/or whilst garaged and/or elsewhere overnight." In this case, cigarettes, having arrived on a lorry at the *terminus ad quem*, were stolen overnight before unloading. The words in the policy, held Roskill J., widened the meaning which might otherwise attach to the word "transit."[32] Cover continued until unloading was completed. This judgment was upheld in the Court of Appeal and the House of Lords.

"Lloyd's Goods in Transit Policy"[33] and "Lloyd's Goods in Transit (C.M.R.) Policy"[34] both by different drafting methods afford transit cover "to any address" (within a territorial limit) and "in transit" is provided to include "unloading . . . and unpacking."

A policy covering risks during conveyance by land does not cover risks arising after goods have been put in barges for conveyance by inland waterways.[35]

Deviation generally   4–26

By section 46(1) of the Marine Insurance Act 1906:

> "Where a ship, without lawful excuse, deviates from the voyage contemplated by the policy, the insurer is discharged from liability, as from the time of deviation. . . . "

Deviation, which is necessarily only relevant to voyage policies—as opposed to time policies, as these do not specify any route—will occur where the vessel deviates from the voyage specified in the policy or, in the absence of a specified voyage, from the customary route.[36] Minor deviation will suffice to give the insurer the right to terminate[37] and the fact that the vessel has regained its route is no defence to the assured.[38] Section 49 provides a list of situations in which deviation by the insured vessel is excused.[39]

---

[28] On the meaning of "good safety," see *Lidgett* v. *Secretan* (1870) L.R. 5 C.P. 190.
[29] *Cornfoot* v. *Royal Exchange* [1904] 1 K.B. 40; the extension period runs from, and terminates at, the exact time of day at which the voyage would otherwise have terminated.
[30] The M.I.A. 1906, sched. 1 rule 5 defines this phrase. See Chap. 23.
[31] [1964] 1 Lloyd's Rep. 416, Roskill J.; [1966] 1 Q.B. 21, C.A.; [1966] A.C. 451 (H.L.).
[32] [1964] 1 Lloyd's Rep. 416, 421, 422.
[33] L.P.O. 55A (1.4.68).
[34] L.P.O. 78 (1.11.67).
[35] *Ewing* v. *Sicklemore* (1918) 35 T.L.R. 55.
[36] ss.46(2), 47.
[37] Despite the inference from s.46(1) that termination is automatic on deviation, it would seem that the insurer merely has the option to terminate. Deviation must actually occur; it is not enough that a deviation is intended without having been put into effect: s.46(3).
[38] s.46(1).
[39] For further discussion of this and deviation generally, see Chap. 23, *infra*.

Policies without stipulated termination

4-27 Although there must be some point of time at which the risk begins it is
not essential that there should be any stipulation in the contract with
regard to the time when it is to come to an end. Insurers sometimes
grant policies by which they agree, in consideration of a single premium
paid at the outset, to indemnify the assured or to pay a sum of money on
the happening, after the risk has been undertaken, of some named event
whenever, if at all, this takes place. In one kind of fidelity guarantee,
administration bonds, the insurers bind themselves to make good, up to
the amount for which the bond is given, any loss caused by the default of
the administrator without regard to the time when he was guilty of the
act or omission leading to the default, for these bonds fix no limit of
time. It should be remembered that, notwithstanding the death of a
party, agreements are generally enforceable against or by his personal
representatives.[40]

Time of loss

4-28 The loss must occur during the term of insurance, and the time of the
loss will, subject to contrary wording, be taken to be the time of the
original accident insured against. But this was not always held to be so in
marine cases. In *Hough* v. *Head*,[41] an insurance of freight, the ship met
with an accident during the period of the insurance which was not discovered until after its termination, and it was held that the loss was not
covered by the policy. But that was because freight had been paid
throughout the policy term, and there had, therefore, been no *loss* of
freight during that time. Lord Mansfield laid it down in *Meretony* v.
Dunlope[42] that where a peril insured against occurred, but a ship was
kept afloat until after the termination of the policy, the shipowner could
not recover. But that decision is no longer sound law,[43] and on simple
insurances of buildings, ships or goods on land it may be generally said
that the time of the loss *is* the time of the accident. Where the owner of a
vessel insures against loss from latent defect, he is not covered where an
old defect is merely discovered during the term of the policy.[44] And
where a vessel is seized during the currency of a policy the underwriters
are not relieved from liability because it has not been condemned by a
Prize Court during that period,[45] although the loss cannot be assessed
until it is so condemned.

The principle was worked out in marine cases, but it applies generally. Cases such as *Moore* v. *Evans*,[46] in which jewels were in enemy territory but not yet seized during the currency of the policy, illustrate its
application. Even if such goods are taken into enemy territory under
pressure of the enemy's government, there will be no loss during the

---

[40] *Lloyd's* v. *Harper* (1880) 16 Ch.D. 290. See also *Beswick* v. *Beswick* [1968] A.C. 58.
[41] (1885) 55 L.J.Q.B. 43.
[42] Cited by Willes J. in *Lockyer* v. *Offley* (1786) 1 T.R. 252, 260.
[43] *Knight* v. *Faith* (1850) 15 Q.B. 649.
[44] *Oceanic* v. *Faber* (1907) 23 T.L.R. 673.
[45] Lord Loreburn in *Andersen* v. *Marten* [1908] A.C. 334, 339.
[46] [1918] A.C. 185.

currency of the policy unless the goods are actually requisitioned during that period.[47]

In the same way, where an accident predates the inception of the policy, and damage becomes manifest only during the currency of the policy, the assured will generally not be able to recover. In *Kelly* v. *Norwich Union*[48] the Court of Appeal held that the "events" insured against in a property policy were the accidents giving rise to damage and not the manifestation of the damage itself: consequently, the assured could not recover for cracking damage becoming apparent during the currency of the policy which was the result of a pipe bursting before the insurer had come on risk.

The same position as that in *Hough* v. *Head* might occur in an insur-   **4–29** ance by a landlord of his rent. So also in liability insurance cases it is the date when the liability arises, not the date of the casualty, which is vital. Thus in the case of insurance against liability under the Workmen's Compensation Acts where it was the time of the certified disablement that fixed the employer's liability,[49] it was that date that must fall within the period covered if the insurers were to be liable.[50]

In fidelity insurance it is the date of the misappropriation, not its discovery that must fall within the term of the policy.[51] Such an insurance is comparable, in this respect, with an insurance of a ship against barratry or scuttling.

3. PROXIMITY RULE

The rule of proximity in insurance law, depending as it does on the pre-   **4–30** sumed intention of the parties to a commercial document,[52] is a very simple one. Only the *proximate* cause of a loss is to be looked to. By "proximate" cause is not meant the latest, but the direct,[53] dominant,[54] operative and efficient[55] one. If this cause is within the risks covered, the insurers are liable in respect of the loss; if it is within the perils excepted[56] the insurers are not liable. A loss may be the combined effect of a whole number of causes, but, for the purposes of insurance law, one direct or dominant cause must wherever possible be singled out. The time-honoured maxim *causa proxima non remota spectatur* must be

---

[47] *Fooks* v. *Smith* [1924] 2 K.B. 508.
[48] [1989] 2 All E.R. 888.
[49] s.43 of the Workmen's Compensation Act 1925.
[50] *Ellerbeck Collieries* v. *Cornhill Insurance* [1932] 1 K.B. 401.
[51] *Allis Chalmers* v. *Fidelity Deposit* (1916) 32 T.L.R. 263 (H.L.); *Ward* v. *Law Property* (1856) 4 W.R. 605; *Pennsylvania Insurance* v. *Mumford* [1920] 2 K.B. 537.
[52] Lindley L.J. in *Reischer* v. *Borwick* [1894] 2 Q.B. 548 at p. 550; Lord Sumner in *Becker, Gray* v. *London Assurance* [1918] A.C. 101, 112; *Leyland* v. *Norwich Union* [1918] A.C. 350, 362, *per* Viscount Haldane; 370, *per* Lord Shaw.
[53] Lord Sumner in *Becker, Gray* case, *supra*, at p. 114.
[54] *Leyland* case, *supra*, *per* Lord Dunedin at p. 363.
[55] *Ibid. per* Lord Shaw, at pp. 369, 370. Viscount Cave in *Samuel* v. *Dumas* [1924] A.C. at p. 447.
[56] *Ionides* v. *Universal Marine, infra; Marsden* v. *City & County Insurance, infra; Cory* v. *Burr* (1883) 8 App.Cas. 393; *Lawrence* v. *Accidental Insurance* (1881) 7 Q.B.D. 216. *Wayne Tank Co.* v. *Employers Liability Assurance Corp.* [1974] Q.B. 57 ([1973] 2 Lloyd's Rep. 237), (C.A.), reversing Mocatta J. [1972] 2 Lloyd's Rep. 141.

understood to have this meaning.[57] Even where the policy expressly
excludes "*all* consequences of hostilities," it has been held, this warranty does not extend beyond losses caused *proximately* by hostilities.[58]

There is no difference, as will appear, in the application of the law of
proximity, between marine and non-marine insurance law.[59]

4–31 Words sufficient to displace rule

But the rule can be displaced by express words, as where a policy
against death by accident excepted death "directly or *indirectly* caused
by war," for an indirect proximate cause is an absurdity. Scrutton J.
held therefore that an officer who was killed by a train when visiting his
sentries could not take advantage of the policy, though the train was the
proximate cause of his death.[60] So, in *Smith* v. *Accident Insurance*[61] it
was held that erysipelas resulting from an accident fell within the exception of disease "following such accidental injury, whether causing death
directly *or jointly* with such accidental injury," though the accident
proximately caused the death. Loss "originating from" fire has, on the
other hand, been construed to mean loss proximately caused thereby[62]
and "independently and exclusively of all other cases" has been held to
add nothing to resulting "directly" from an accident.[63] Where a policy
covered "loss on the property of the assured directly damaged" by an
accident to a steam-jacketed bleacher tank, and "indirect results" were
excepted, the Privy Council applied the ordinary rule of proximity.[64]

4–32 Whether there can be more than one proximate cause

Lindley L.J.'s judgment in *Reischer* v. *Borwick*[65] supports a view that
there may be more than one proximate cause of a loss.[66] That was a case
of collision damage being increased by the action of the sea. But the
other two members of the Court of Appeal clearly regarded the collision
alone as the proximate cause of the loss, and the House of Lords' approval of the case in *Leyland* v. *Norwich Union*[67] proceeds on this ground.

---

[57] See Scrutton L.J. in *Samuel* v. *Dumas* [1923] 1 K.B. 592, 619; [1924] A.C. 431. In *Turner* v. *North-ern Life* [1953] 1 D.L.R. 427 the assured, a poacher, fired at the car of another poacher, who, firing to scare the assured off, accidentally killed him. *Held*, the death was "indirectly" caused by the assured's illegal act; it was the foreseeable result of it.

[58] Willes J. in *Ionides* v. *Universal Marine* (1863) 14 C.B.(N.S.) 259; *Liverpool & London War Risks* v. *Ocean S.S. Co.* [1948] A.C. 243.

[59] See, *e.g.* M.I.A. 1906, s.55(1).

[60] *Coxe* v. *Employers' Liability Insurance* [1916] 2 K.B. 629; *American Tobacco* v. *Guardian* (1925) 69 S.J. 621 (C.A.) gives another example of such a clause. See also *Spinney's* (*1948*) *Ltd.* v. *Royal Insurance Co. Ltd.* [1980] 1 Lloyd's Rep. 406 and *Oei* v. *Foster* [1982] 2 Lloyd's Rep. 170.

[61] (1870) L.R. 5 Ex. 302.

[62] *Marsden* v. *City & County Insurance* (1865) L.R. 1 C.P. 232.

[63] *Fidelity & Casualty Co. of New York* v. *Mitchell* [1917] A.C. 592. See also *Re Etherington* [1909] 1 K.B. 591.

[64] *Boiler Inspection Co.* v. *Sherwin-Williams* [1951] A.C. 319, 333.

[65] [1894] 2 Q.B. 548, 550–551. *Pink* v. *Fleming* (1890) 25 Q.B.D. 396, 397, *per* Lord Esher is a clear authority against Lindley L.J.'s suggestion that once a risk covered operates, all subsequent damage on the ordinary contractual measure of damages principle is covered.

[66] Lord Buckmaster in *Board of Trade* v. *Hain SS. Co.* [1929] A.C. at p. 539, supports this view, but this was an *obiter dictum* in a case on a charterparty. See also in support of it Scott L.J. in *Ocean S.S. Co.* v. *Liverpool & London War Risks* [1946] K.B. 561, 575; [1948] A.C. 243. It is criticised by Devlin J. in *Heskell* v. *Continental Express* [1950] 1 All E.R. 1033, 1048 and *West Wake Price* v. *Ching* [1957] 1 W.L.R. 45, 49.

[67] [1918] A.C. 350.

Lord Dunedin's judgment in that case[68] makes it clear that, if there are two causes, one or other of them must be chosen as the proximate one.[69] In Bacon's words, "It were infinite for the law to judge the causes of causes, and their impulsions one of another; therefore it contenteth itself with the immediate cause, and judgeth of acts by that, without looking to any further degree."[70] It was, however, strenuously argued in *Liverpool & London War Risks* v. *Ocean S.S. Company*[71] that there could be more than one proximate cause of a loss, but the House of Lords gave no support to that submission.

The modern view is, however, that it is perfectly possible to have concurrent proximate causes of a loss, and in such a case the ability of the assured to recover will depend upon whether one of the concurrent proximate causes is an excluded peril. In *Wayne Tank Co.* v. *Employers Liability Ltd.*[72] the assured's policy provided cover for losses caused by accidents, but specifically excluded liability for damage caused by the nature or condition of goods supplied by the assured. Premises were destroyed as a result of the installation of defective equipment by the assured. The Court of Appeal ruled that the installation of defective equipment was the proximate cause of the loss so that recovery was not possible, but that the case could equally have been decided on the ground that the installation of the equipment (excluded peril) and the failure to monitor it (insured peril) were concurrent causes of the loss and that the specific exclusion relating to equipment precluded recovery.

The position is different where there are concurrent causes of loss, neither of which is a specifically excluded peril. In *Lloyd Instruments* v. *Northern Star Insurance*[73] an unseaworthy vessel sank in adverse weather conditions which a seaworthy vessel would have been able to withstand. The loss thus had concurrent causes: unseaworthiness, which was not an excluded peril but which nevertheless did not fall within the policy,[74] and perils of the sea, a peril covered by the policy. The Court of Appeal held that in the absence of the operation of an express exclusion, the assured is entitled to recover where there have been concurrent causes of loss at least one of which is an insured peril. Thus where a gang of thieves steal goods covered by theft and burglary policy, and the assured's servant connives at the theft, it is unnecessary to determine whether the enterprise of the thieves or the disloyalty of the servant caused the loss; in either event it will be covered. But if theft by the assured's servant is excepted, then the disjunction may become vital.[75]

---

[68] At p. 363. See also his remarks in *Fidelity & Casualty Co. of New York* v. *Mitchell* [1917] A.C. 592, 596.

[69] See also Lord Sumner in *Samuel* v. *Dumas* [1924] A.C. 431, 467.

[70] Quoted by Byles J. in *Everett* v. *London Assurance* (1865) 19 C.B.(N.S.) 126, 133.

[71] [1948] A.C. 243.

[72] [1973] 2 Lloyd's Rep. 237, following observations in the dissenting speech of Lord Summer in *Samuel* v. *Dumas* [1924] A.C. 431, 467.

[73] [1987] 1 Lloyd's Rep. 32.

[74] As the policy was a time policy, there was no seaworthiness warranty. Consequently, unseaworthiness operated as a defence to the insurer only if the vessel had been sent to sea in an unseaworthy state with the privity of the assured: Marine Insurance Act 1906, s.39(5). This was not, however, the case, so that unseaworthiness did not bar a claim but was merely a peril which was not covered by the policy.

[75] See *Saqut & Lawrence* v. *Stearns* [1911] 1 K.B. 426.

4–33 Rules for determining proximate cause

The proximity rule has been worked out in marine cases, but it applies generally.[76] While it is simple to enunciate, it is difficult to apply, but a number of sub-rules may be deduced from the authorities.

Such rules must be applied with caution, for common sense is the final arbiter in determining what is the proximate cause of a loss. The "choice of the real or efficient cause from out of the whole complex of the facts must be made by applying common-sense standards. Causation is to be understood as the man in the street, and not as either scientist or the metaphysician would understand it."[77] However, although common sense may be taken to have originally actuated the courts in decisions on proximity, they have now settled many cases of difficulty "to the great convenience of the business world," and they will not in such cases seek afresh to reason the matter out.[78] Since proximity is a question of law, and since the matter was governed by many decisions of the House of Lords which could not be reversed even by that tribunal, the courts could not alter such decisions even though some were neither convenient nor even logical.[79]

4–34   (i) *The risk insured against must in fact operate.*[80] Thus the abandonment of a voyage through fear of capture is not loss by capture.[81] The danger of losing goods by seizure is not loss by seizure.[82] Nor would the unloading of coal to avoid spontaneous combustion be loss by fire, tough it would fall within the words of a policy covering loss by fire *and other losses.*[83] In the case of fire policies this principle may be recognised in the rule that there must always be actual ignition.

4–35   (ii) *Once the risk operates, damage to the subject-matter due to efforts to check the progress of the casualty, is covered,*[84] for the proximate cause of such damage is the risk insured against.[85] Thus, in *Symington* v. *Union Insurance of Canton,*[86] cork was insured against fire. A fire broke out some distance away and to prevent it spreading local authorities threw some of the cork into the sea. It was held that the loss of this cork was covered, on the ground that damage by water to save the consequence of fire and the destruction of property to prevent it spreading were both proximately caused by the fire.[87] The test is, "Is it a fear of something that will happen in the future or has the peril already happened and is it so imminent that it is immediately necessary to avert the

---

[76] See now s.55(1) of Marine Insurance Act 1906; Lord Sumner in *Samuel* v. *Dumas, supra,* at p. 467, and in *Becker, Gray* v. *London Assurance* [1918] A.C. 101.

[77] Lord Wright in *Yorkshire Dale S.S. Co* v. *Minister of War Transport* [1942] A.C. 691, 706. See also *Boiler Inspection Co.* v. *Sherwin-Williams* [1951] A.C. 319, 333, 334, *per* Lord Porter.

[78] *Yorkshire Dale Case* [1942] A.C. 691 at p. 700, *per* Lord Atkin.

[79] See *Liverpool & London War Risks* v. *Ocean S.S. Co.* [1948] A.C. 243.

[80] *Kacianoff* v. *China Traders* [1914] 3 K.B. 1121, *per* Lord Reading C.J.

[81] *Becker, Gray* v. *London Assurance* [1918] A.C. 101.

[82] *Moore* v. *Evans* [1918] A.C. 185.

[83] *Knight of St. Michael* [1898] P. 30.

[84] See § 18–07, *infra,* for the detailed application of this principle in fire insurance. See also M.I.A. 1906, s.78(4).

[85] Kelly C.B. in *Stanley* v. *Western Insurance* (1868) L.R. 3 Ex. 71, 75.

[86] (1928) 97 L.J.K.B. 646.

[87] *Per* Greer L.J. at p. 652; see also *Johnstone* v. *West of Scotland* (1828) 7 Sh. (Ct. of Sess.) 52.

danger by action?"[88] It is only in the latter case that the insurers are liable.[89]

(iii) *An accident facilitating the loss must be distinguished from an acci-* **4–36** *dent causing the loss.* Thus, where the goods are put under a restraint of princes that facilitates their ultimate seizure, it is the seizure and not the restraint that is the proximate cause of the loss.[90] Where an air-raid facilitates the stealing of goods from a building, stealing and not the air-raid is the proximate cause of their loss,[91] and where a fire encourages a mob to plunder, and a plate glass is broken thereby, it is the lawlessness of the mob and not the fire which is the proximate cause.[92]

Nor will events merely occurring during warlike operations be proximately caused by such operations. Thus, if an omnibus is proceeding with dimmed lights in a blackout ordered by the Government as a protection against attack by hostile aircraft, and by reason of the lack of light it collides with a wayfarer or another omnibus, the resulting injury is not proximately caused by a warlike operation. Nor is a fall during a blackout proximately caused by a warlike operation.[93]

(iv) *Novus actus interveniens.*[94] It will be seen from the cases cited **4–37** above that where human intervention, occurring after the peril insured against, causes the loss, that intervention (unless its object was to mitigate the loss), and not the insured peril, is the proximate cause. The cases of a man run down in a fit,[95] of stealing during an air-raid,[96] and of breaking glass during a fire,[97] illustrate this point. So an increase of damage due to the negligence or misconduct of the assured has been held in marine cases not to be proximately caused by the original casualty,[98] and the same principle applies in fire insurance law.[99]

The fresh intervention must be something accidental, and not such acts as acts of obedience to one's government,[1] as we have seen, efforts to arrest the progress of a casualty which are a natural consequence of it.

---

[88] *Per* Scrutton L.J. at p. 650.

[89] See also *Glen Falls Ins.* v. *Spencer* (1956) 3 D.L.R. (2d) 745 (Can.), insurance of car against fire but not collision. Accident caused by driver attempting to put out fire in dashboard: *held*, accident caused by fire.

[90] *Fooks* v. *Smith* [1924] 2 K.B. 508.

[91] *Winicofsky* v. *Army & Navy Insurance* (1919) 35 T.L.R. 283.

[92] *Marsden* v. *City & County Insurance* (1865) L.R. 1 C.P. 232.

[93] Atkin L.J. in *Britain S.S. Co.* v. *The King* [1919] 2 K.B. 670, 696, 697; approved [1921] 1 A.C. 99. But see his dictum in *Yorkshire Dale S.S. Co.* v. *Minister of War Transport* [1942] A.C. 691, 700, 701. See also *Liverpool & London War Risks* v. *Ocean S.S. Co.* [1948] A.C. 243. The view adopted in the text appears to be supported by the U.S. Sup.Ct. (by a majority) in *Standard Oil* v. *United States* [1951] 2 Lloyd's Rep. 36; [1951] A.M.C. 1, in which our H.L. decisions on marine policies are criticised as being not altogether reconcilable. Americans seem to approach these problems in a somewhat different, though wholly rational way.

[94] As to the applicability of this test see Atkinson J. in *Smith* v. *Cornhill Insurance* (1938) 54 T.L.R. 869, 872.

[95] *Lawrence* v. *Accidental Insurance* (1881) 7 Q.B.D. 216.

[96] *Winicofsky* v. *Army & Navy, supra.*

[97] *Marsden* v. *City & County, supra.*

[98] *Tanner* v. *Bennett* (1825) Ryan & Mood. 182; *Currie* v. *Bombay Insurance* (1869) L.R. 3 P.C. 72; *Lind* v. *Mitchell* (1928) 45 T.L.R. 54.

[99] See § 18–07, *infra.*

[1] See *Czarnikow* v. *Java Sea Insurance* [1941] 3 All E.R. 256; *British Marine* v. *Sanday* [1916] 1 A.C. 650. See also *Rickards* v. *Forestal* [1942] A.C. 50.

4–38   It would follow from a strict application of the *novus actus* principle that where, after the occurrence of a fire, the assured loses goods by theft, the loss by theft would not be caused proximately by the fire. However, it is clearly desirable that theft and other losses during removal of goods from the scene of a fire should be covered, as otherwise the assured might be tempted to leave them to burn, and insurance companies have not, therefore, in fact contested such losses in this country.[2] In Canadian cases such losses have been held to be covered under a simple insurance against fire.[3] Similarly it has been held here, in an old marine case,[4] that where a ship is run ashore owing to a fire, and goods are landed, pilferage of the goods by landsmen is a peril of the sea.

On the other hand loss due to the assured failing in his implied duty under the policy to minimise it, is clearly referable to his own act or omission rather than to the peril insured against, and the insurers would not therefore be responsible for such a loss.[5]

The *novus actus* rule is possibly an instance of a wider rule that where a loss is brought about by a natural cause and a human agency, the latter cause dominates and is therefore proximate, since man by his will dominates the world.[6]

4–39   (v) *The death-blow cases.* The converse of the *novus actus interveniens* principle is that where a casualty due to human agency is followed by natural causes that contribute to the loss, the chain of causation is not broken. Thus, where, in *Leyland* v. *Norwich Union*,[7] a torpedo gave a ship her death-blow, though her final loss was due to a storm, it was held that it was the torpedo which proximately caused her loss. Accident cases, where an accident and a natural disease both contribute to the death of the assured, are on an analogous footing.

4–40 *Accident cases*

The courts have tended to give the proximity rule an interpretation generous to the assured in such cases. In fact in *Smith* v. *Cornhill Insurance*,[8] Atkinson J. suggested[9] that once there is an accident all its results are covered, on the principle of workmen's compensation decisions, until a *novus actus interveniens* breaks the chain of causation. In that case the assured, injured in a motor accident, fell into water in a dazed condition, and thereupon died of shock, and it was held that her death was proximately caused by the motor accident. In *Fidelity and Casualty of New York* v. *Mitchell*[10] the Privy Council held that disablement due

---

[2] See *Levy* v. *Baillie* (1831) 7 Bing. 349. But see *Marsden* v. *City & County Insurance, supra* n. 17.
[3] *Thompson* v. *Montreal Insurance* (1850) 6 U.C.Q.B. 319; *McLaren* v. *Commercial Union* (1885) 12 Ont.App. 279. See also: *Witherell* v. *Marine Insurance* (1861) 49 Me. (5 Hub.) 200; *Balestracci* v. *Fireman's Insurance* (1882) 34 Louis.Ann. (41 Louis.) 844; *McPherson* v. *Guardian Insurance* (1893) 7 Newfoundland L.R. (1884–96) 768.
[4] *Bondrett* v. *Hentigg* (1816) Holt N.P. 149, *per* Gibbs C.J.; see also *The Knight of St. Michael* [1898] P. 30.
[5] See Scrutton L.J. in *City Tailors* v. *Evans* (1921) 38 T.L.R. 230, 233, 234.
[6] See Lord Normand in *Liverpool & London War Risks* v. *Ocean S.S. Co.* [1948] A.C. 243, 271–273.
[7] [1918] A.C. 350.
[8] (1938) 54 T.L.R. 869.
[9] At p. 872.
[10] [1917] A.C. 592.

to the assured's latent tuberculosis, which was brought on by an accident, was proximately caused by the accident, and in *Isitt* v. *Railway Passengers Assurance*[11] and *Re Etherington*[12] deaths due to pneumonia, of which an accident and cold were the dual causes, were likewise held proximately to have been caused by the accidents. Where an accident caused a hernia which was followed immediately by a surgical operation intended to relieve the patient but which caused death,[13] and where a dog-bite gave the assured hydrophobia,[14] it was more obvious that the accident proximately caused the death. It matters not how trivial the original accident may have been. Thus, gangrene from a cut has been held covered by an accident policy,[15] though death by dislodgment of a gallstone consequent upon a fall has been held not to be within such a policy.[16]

Scottish and American cases have not always gone to the same lengths as English cases in this regard.[17]

Where a natural event has given rise to an accident, the courts have invariably held that, for the purposes of an accident policy, the accident is a *novus actus interveniens* and the assured is able to recover. Thus, where a man in the course of a fit fell into a stream and was drowned the accident and not the fit was held to be the proximate cause of the loss,[18] and where a man in the course of a fit fell onto a railway line and was run over the proximate cause of death was held to be the accident, despite the presence in the policy of a provision that it applied only where "such accidental injury is the direct and sole cause of death."[19]

Fire cases   **4–41**

Fire insurance cases have been treated by the courts on similar lines. Thus where a fire attacks the fabric of a building and causes the roof or walls to fall in, damage due to such fall is proximately caused by the fire.[20] So also damage within the building itself due to an explosion caused by the fire will be proximately caused by the fire; but damage so caused to other buildings, it was decided in *Everett* v. *London Assurance*,[21] will be too remote.

A distinction is expressly drawn in fire insurance cases between the spread of a fire due to natural causes, such as a shift in direction of the wind, and the intervention of a new and unexpected cause which makes the fire a fresh fire, and therefore breaks the chain of causation.[22] The

---

[11] (1889) 22 Q.B.D. 504.

[12] [1909] 1 K.B. 591.

[13] *Fitton* v. *Accidental Death* (1864) 17 C.B.(N.S.) 122.

[14] Wright J. in *Mardorf* v. *Accident Insurance* [1903] 1 K.B. 584, 588.

[15] *Waller* v. *Northern Assurance* (1884) 64 Iowa 101; *The Times*, January 26, 1887: see also *Western Commercial* v. *Smith*, 85 Fed. Rep. 401 (1898).

[16] *Cawley* v. *National Employers' Accident* (1885) 1 T.L.R. 255.

[17] *Anderson* v. *Scottish Accident* (1889) 27 Sc.L.R. 20; *National Masonic Accident* v. *Shyrock*, 73 Fed. Rep. 774 (1896).

[18] *Winspear* v. *Accident Insurance* (1880) 6 Q.B.D. 42.

[19] *Lawrence* v. *Accidental Insurance* (1881) 7 Q.B.D. 216.

[20] Scrutton L.J. in *Re Hooley Hill Rubber Co.* [1920] 1 K.B. 257, 271; *Johnston* v. *West of Scotland Insurance* (1828) 7 S. (Ct. of Sess.) 52.

[21] (1865) 19 C.B.(N.S.) 126; see §§ 18–08, 18–09, *infra*.

[22] Bingham J. in *Tootal* v. *London & Lancashire Fire* (1908) Welford, *Fire* (3rd ed.), 498, 499, 500; *The Times*, May 21, 1908; *Walker* v. *London & Provincial* (1888) 22 L.R.Ir. 572.

case of *Everett* v. *London Assurance*[23] may be considered in a similar light, the explosion being, as regards damage to other houses, a new and unexpected cause.

4–42 *Consequential loss (breakdown) insurance*

In *Burts and Harvey* v. *Vulcan & General Ins. Co.*[24] there was "sudden and accidental damage" (covered by the policy) owing to defective metal in an industrial appliance. The insurers were held liable notwithstanding an exclusion clause against *"corrosion, erosion."* The exclusion was intended to relate to corrosion and erosion in the ordinary use of the appliance, and not to such damage arising out of failure of a component.[25]

4. BURDEN OF PROOF

4–43 The burden of proof is upon the assured to show that the loss was proximately caused by a peril insured against.[26] To prove a prima facie case the assured need not prove how the casualty occurred, or what particular peril caused it: he need merely prove that the cause fell within the perils insured against. Thus where the assured under a marine policy covering the usual perils of the sea but warranted "free of capture" proves that the vessel is at the bottom of the sea, he discharges his burden of proof.[27] So, where the assured is found drowned, this fact is prima facie proof of loss under an accident policy,[28] for the presumption in such a case is against suicide.[29] So, where the insurance is against "all risks," the assured discharges his burden of proof by showing that the loss was occasioned accidentally, without proving in what the exact nature of the casualty consisted.[30]

Once the assured has produced a prima facie case the burden shifts to the insurers if they wish to show that it was in fact a cause excepted by the policy which proximately caused the loss.[31] The difficulty in applying this principle occurs where the expected peril is expressed as a limitation on the cover afforded, and not as an exception to it, and it seems that in that case it is for the assured to prove that the loss falls within the cover afforded. Thus where the insurance was against loss from any cause except dishonesty of servants, Lush J. held that the burden was on the assured to prove that the loss was not due to his servant's dishonesty.[32]

---

[23] See n. 21.
[24] [1966] 1 Lloyd's Rep. 161.
[25] See *per* Lawton J. at p. 170.
[26] *Austin* v. *Drewe* (1816) 6 Taunt. 436; *Everett* v. *London Assurance* (1865) 19 C.B.(N.S.) 126; *Marsden* v. *City & County Insurance* (1865) L.R. 1 C.P. 232; *London Plate Glass* v. *Heath* [1913] 3 K.B. 411; *Century Bank* v. *Young* (1914) 84 L.J.K.B. 385; Lord Sumner in *British Marine* v. *Gaunt* [1921] 2 A.C. 41, 58. *Rhesa Shipping* v. *Edmunds, The Popi M.* [1985] 2 All E.R. 712.
[27] Bailhache J. in *Macbeth* v. *King* (1916) 115 L.T. 221.
[28] *Macdonald* v. *Refuge* (1890) 17 R. (Ct. of Sess.) 955.
[29] *Harvey* v. *Ocean* [1905] 2 Ir.R. 1.
[30] *British Marine* v. *Gaunt* [1921] 2 A.C. 41.
[31] *Greaves* v. *Drysdale* (1935) 53 Ll.L.R. 16; L.J. Clerk in *Macdonald* v. *Refuge* (1890) 17 R. (Ct. of Sess.) 955, 957; *Motor Union* v. *Boggon* (1923) 130 L.T. 588, *per* Lord Birkenhead at p. 591.
[32] *Hurst* v. *Evans* [1917] 1 K.B. 352. Questioned by Bailhache J. in *Munro Brice* v. *War Risks* [1918] 2 K.B. 78, 87, reversed on facts [1920] 3 K.B. 94.

Where the expected peril is, however, expressed as such[33] or where it is expressed as a condition[34] or a warranty,[35] there can be no doubt that it is for the insured, if he can, to prove that the loss falls within its scope.

In any case the burden of proof may be displaced by the express terms of the policy itself. The burden of proof of any particular fact, or of its non-existence, may be placed on either party by an agreement made between them.[36] However, if the assured is required to prove that the loss was covered by the policy, prima facie evidence of an excepted peril must be adduced by the insurer.[37]

Proof of arson or fraud 4-44

If the insurers wish to set up as a defence that the assured himself fired premises, it was at one time thought that such evidence must be adduced as would be required to convict the assured upon an indictment for arson, such as to persuade a jury beyond reasonable doubt of his guilt.[38] This rule has been followed in Canada,[39] but courts in the United States have inclined to hold that evidence not strong enough to support a conviction for arson would be strong enough to defeat the claim of the assured.[40] Now it is clear that English law itself knows no such rule: no general standard can be laid down. On the one hand the degree of probability proved must be commensurate with the gravity of any charge in any case (whether civil, criminal or divorce)[41]; on the other, the court should be equally reluctant to make underwriters pay a fraudulent claim as to find the assured guilty of making one.[42] Further, if the assured alleges a burglary, which the insurers deny, the onus remains on him throughout of proving that a burglary in fact occurred.[43]

In *Slattery* v. *Mance*[44] Salmon J. decided, on a claim under a marine policy covering perils of the sea, for loss of a vessel by fire, that once the assured had shown that the loss was caused by fire, the onus of proving, on a balance of probabilities, that the fire was caused or connived at by the assured rested on the underwriter who so asserted. There was no principle that when the facts were peculiarly within the knowledge of a person against whom an assertion of arson was made, then that person

---

[33] *American Tobacco* v. *Guardian* (1925) 69 S.J. 621; *Re National Benefit* (1933) 45 Ll.L.R. 147.

[34] *Gorman* v. *Hand-in-Hand* (1877) Ir.R. 11 C.L. 224; but see Palles C.B. in *Walker* v. *London & Provincial* (1888) 22 L.R.Ir. 572, 574–575.

[35] *Macbeth* v. *King, supra; Bond Air Services* v. *Hill* [1955] 2 Q.B. 417; *Soya* v. *White* [1980] 1 Lloyd's Rep. 491.

[36] *Levy* v. *Assicurazioni Generali* [1940] A.C. 791, approving Scrutton L.J. in *Re Hooley Hill Rubber Co.* [1920] 1 K.B. 257, 273.

[37] *Spinney's (1948) Ltd.* v. *Royal Insurance* [1980] 1 Lloyd's Rep. 406.

[38] *Thurtell* v. *Beaumont* (1824) 1 Bing. 339; Willes J. in *Britton* v. *Royal* (1866) 4 F. & F. 905, 908; *Herbert* v. *Poland* (1932) 44 Ll.L.R. 139; *London Assurance* v. *Clare* (1937) 57 Ll.L.R. 254.

[39] *Hercules* v. *Hunter* (1836) 15 S. (Ct. of Sess.) 1318; *Lambkin* v. *Ontario Marine & Fire* (1855) 12 U.C.Q.B. 578.

[40] See *May on Insurance* (2nd ed.), p. 889; Sansum, *Ins.Dig.*, pp. 148–150; *The Vainqueur José* [1974] 2 Lloyd's Rep. 398, U.S. District Ct., and cases there referred to.

[41] *Hornal* v. *Neuberger Products* [1957] 1 Q.B. 247; *Grunther* v. *Fed. Employers* [1976] 2 Lloyd's Rep. 259 (C.A.). This principle has been consistently reaffirmed in a number of cases dealing with loss by fire. See: *Watkins & Davies Ltd.* v. *Legal and General* [1981] 1 Lloyd's Rep. 674; *S. & M. Carpets* v. *Cornhill Insurance* [1982] 1 Lloyd's Rep. 423; *Broughton Park Textiles* v. *Commercial Union* [1987] 1 Lloyd's Rep. 94; *Polvitte* v. *Commercial Union* [1987] 1 Lloyd's Rep. 379.

[42] Viscount Sumner in *Lek* v. *Matthews* (1927) 29 Ll.L.R. 141, 164.

[43] *Regina Fur* v. *Bossom* [1958] 2 Lloyd's Rep. 425.

[44] [1962] 1 Q.B. 676.

must assume the burden of proving that the loss was not caused or connived at by him. The onus of proving that the loss was not accidental was
on the underwriter. This approach was approved by the Court of
Appeal in *The Alexion Hope*.[45]

---

[45] [1988] 1 Lloyd's Rep. 311. This case also decides that where the assured's claim is for perils of the
sea, the assured must show that the loss was fortuitous, as fortuity is an element of this form of loss, but
that where the claim is for barratry the insurer must demonstrate that the assured was privy to the misconduct of the crew if the claim is to be defeated.

CHAPTER 5

NON-DISCLOSURE AND MISREPRESENTATION

1. DUTY OF DISCLOSURE

Uberrima fides   **5–01**
While a misstatement by one party by which the other is induced to
enter into a contract will generally entitle the latter to rescind the contract, mere non-disclosure does not usually do so. In the case of certain
contracts, however, the law demands a higher standard of good faith
between the parties, and "there is no class of documents as to which the
strictest good faith is more rigidly required in courts of law than policies
of assurance."[1] "As the underwriter knows nothing and the man who
comes to him to ask him to insure knows everything, it is the duty of the
assured, the man who desires to have a policy, to make a full disclosure
to the underwriters without being asked of all the material circumstances, because the underwriters know nothing and the assured knows
everything. This is expressed by saying that it is a contract of the utmost
good faith–*uberrima fides.*"[2] Moreover, this utmost good faith is
required not only from the assured but also from the insurer,[3] and the
insurer is therefore under a similar duty of disclosure. The doctrine
applies substantially to all kinds of insurance, including life insurance.[4]

The principles governing utmost good faith were codified in sections **5–02**
17 and 18 of the Marine Insurance Act 1906. These rules have proved to
be of general application.
Section 17 (*insurance is uberrima fidei*) provides:

"A contract of marine insurance is a contract based on the utmost good
faith, and, if the utmost good faith be not observed by either party the contract may be avoided by the other party."

Section 18 (*disclosure by assured*) provides:

(1) Subject to the provisions of this section, the assured must disclose to the
insurer, before the contract is concluded, every material circumstance which
is known to the assured, and the assured is deemed to know every circumstance which, in the ordinary course of business, ought to be known by him. If
the assured fails to make such disclosure, the insurer may avoid the contract.
(2) Every circumstance is material which would influence the judgment of a
prudent insurer in fixing the premium, or determining whether he will take
the risk.

---

[1] *Mackenzie* v. *Coulson* (1869) L.R. 8 Eq. 368, 375, *per* James V.-C. *Uberrima fides* has been applied
as a doctrine of equity or the common law to differing extents and with differing rules of application to
partnership agreements, company promotion, family settlements, title to land and so forth. See *Chitty
on Contracts* (2nd ed.) §§ 411 to 423; and *March Cabaret* case, *infra*, n. 9.
[2] *Rozanes* v. *Brown* (1928) 32 Ll.L.R. 98, 102, *per* Scrutton L.J.
[3] *Re Bradley and Essex Accident* [1912] 1 K.B. 415, 430, *per* Farwell L.J.; *Provincial* v. *Morgan*
[1933] A.C. 240, 250. *La Banque Financière* v. *Westgate* [1988] 2 Lloyds Rep. 513. See *infra* para. 5–10
et seq.
[4] Vaughan Williams L.J. in *Joel* v. *Law Union* [1908] 2 K.B. 863, 878.

(3) In the absence of inquiry the following circumstances need not be disclosed, namely:—

(*a*) Any circumstance which diminishes the risk;

(*b*) Any circumstance which is known or presumed to be known to the insurer. The insurer is presumed to know matters of common notoriety or knowledge, and matters which an insurer in the ordinary course of his business, as such, ought to know;

(*c*) Any circumstance as 'to which information is waived by the insurer;

(*d*) Any circumstance which it is superfluous to disclose by reason of any express or implied warranty.

(4) Whether any particular circumstance, which is not disclosed, be material or not is, in each case, a question of fact.

(5) The term 'circumstance' includes any communication made to, or information received by, the assured.

5–03 Effect of non-disclosure

Where the assured conceals something he knows to be material such *concealment* is fraud.[5] But in any case the effect of mere non-disclosure on an insurance contract is to some extent the same as the effect of misrepresentation: the party aggrieved, when the matter comes to his knowledge, may choose either to carry on with the contract or not.[6] It is *voidable* at the *election* of the aggrieved party, as opposed to that class of contract which is *void* by operation of law.[7]

The duty to disclose is not an implied term of the contract itself.[8] Unlike fraud, negligence or a breach of condition,[9] non-disclosure never by itself gives rise to a claim for damages. Avoidance of the whole contract is the only remedy.[10] Once the aggrieved party (i) knows all the facts,[11] and (ii) has had a reasonable time in which to make up his mind,[12] he must make his election once and for all. He need not exercise it, however, until he does know all the facts; being put on inquiry is not sufficient.[12] Thus where, although the assured has suppressed or misrepresented a fact, he discloses it to the insurance office before they pay a claim, they cannot after payment recover back the money.[13] Similarly where the insurers receive notice that the risks insured against have been misrepresented, concealed or incompletely disclosed and accept further premiums on the same policy, they lose their right to avoid it.[14]

Either party may apply to the court for a declaration as to whether the

---

[5] Rolfe B. in *Dalglish* v. *Jarvie* (1850) 2 Mac. & G. 231, 243.

[6] *Morrison* v. *Universal Marine* (1873) L.R. 8 Exch. 197.

[7] See *Armstrong* v. *Turquand* (1858) 9 I.C.L.R. 32; *Mackender* v. *Feldia* [1967] 2 Q.B. 590.

[8] See *Joel* v. *Law Union, supra*, at p. 886. Dicta referring to non-disclosure as an implied term of the contract, *e.g. per* Parke B. in *Moens* v. *Heyworth* (1842) 10 M. & W. 147, 157, do not, it is thought, represent the law; see *Merchants' & Manufacturers' Insurance* v. *Hunt* [1941] 1 K.B. 295, 313, *per* Scott L.J. "The duty to disclose is not based upon an implied term of the contract at all; it arises outside the contract; it applies to all contracts *uberrimae fidei* and is not limited to insurance contracts; it also applies, for instance to contracts of partnership, contracts of surety, certain family settlement contracts and other similar types of contractual relationships": *per* May J. in *March Cabaret* v. *London Ass.* [1975] 1 Lloyd's Rep. 169, 175. The matter has been put beyond doubt by the Court of Appeal in *La Banque Financière, supra* n. 3, and *Bank of Nova Scotia* v. *Hellenic Mutual, The Good Luck* [1989] 2 Lloyd's Rep. 238.

[9] See Chap. 6, *infra*.

[10] *Glasgow Assurance* v. *Symondson* (1911) 104 L.T. 254, 258, *per* Scrutton J; *La Banque Financière, supra* n. 3.

[11] See Lord Russell of Killowen in *Evans* v. *Bartlam* [1937] A.C. 473, 483.

[12] *McCormick* v. *National Motor* (1934) 40 Com.Cas. 76, 81, 82, *per* Scrutton L.J.; *Simon, Haynes* v. *Beer* (1946) 78 Ll.L.R. 337.

[13] *Bilbie* v. *Lumley* (1802) 2 East 269; *Wing* v. *Harvey* (1854) 5 De G.M. & G. 265.

[14] *Scottish Equitable* v. *Buist* (1877) 4 R. (Ct. of Sess.) 1076.

policy is binding, but the remedy is a discretionary one.[15] While it will be granted where the insurers have made a definite assertion denying the validity of the policy,[16] it will be refused where the office might obtain possession, on the death of the life insured, of material information which they could not for the moment obtain.[17]

Time of non-disclosure 5–04

The duty of disclosure primarily applies to negotiations preceding the formation of the contract,[18] but full disclosure must be made up to the moment when a binding contract is concluded[19] of any fresh facts affecting the risk. A contract of insurance is concluded when the assured's proposal is accepted by the insurer whether or not the policy has then been issued[20]; in the case of a Lloyd's slip the assured owes a duty of disclosure to each individual successive underwriter, as every initialling constitutes a separate contract.[21] Moreover, as the renewal of most non-life policies constitutes the creation of a fresh contract, the duty of disclosure arises on each successive renewal[22]; this is not the case with life assurances, as such policies are entire and the insurer's consent for renewal is not required.[23] Where the insurer gives an open cover to the assured, permitting the assured to allocate fresh risks to the cover, the duty of disclosure arises prior to the formation of the open cover itself[24] but does not apply in respect of each individual risk allocated to the cover unless it is clear that the open cover is non-obligatory so far as the insurer is concerned or unless the open cover has been issued to a broker and not directly to the assured.[25]

There may, however, be exceptional cases in which the duty of utmost 5–05 good faith extends beyond the time of the formation of the policy, although the scope of these exceptions is unclear. Thus where the assured deliberately failed to disclose to the insurer, when submitting a claim, that the insured vessel had entered into a war zone without the requisite notice to the insurer, it was held that the insurer could avoid the policy for breach of the duty of utmost good faith.[26] Again, where the assured had deliberately grounded the insured vessel, and there had been a subsequent total loss by fire, it was held that the grounding constituted a breach of the assured's duty of utmost good faith and that a claim for the subsequent loss by fire could be sustained only if the

---

[15] The remedy extends to questions of construction also, even where the policy is held to be governed by foreign law: *Pick* v. *Manufacturers Life* [1958] 2 Lloyd's Rep. 93. See generally R.S.C. Ord. 15, r. 16, as construed by the House of Lords in *Gouriet* v. *U.P.O.W.* [1978] A.C. 35.

[16] *Sparenborg* v. *Edinburgh Life* [1912] 1 K.B. 195.

[17] *Honour* v. *Equitable Life U.S.A.* [1900] 1 Ch. 852.

[18] *Whitwell* v. *Autocar Fire* (1927) 27 Ll.L.R. 418.

[19] *British Equitable* v. *G.W.R.* (1869) 20 L.T. 422; *Canning* v. *Farquhar* (1886) 16 Q.B.D. 727; *Allis Chalmers* v. *Fidelity Deposit* (1916) 32 T.L.R. 263; *Looker* v. *Law Union* [1928] 1 K.B. 554.

[20] M.I.A. 1906, s.21, stating a general principle.

[21] See *supra.* para. 1–30.

[22] *Pim* v. *Reid* (1843) 6 Man. & G.I., 25, *per* Cresswell J.; *Re Wilson and Scottish Insurance* [1920] 2 Ch. 28; *Lambert* v. *C.I.S.* [1976] 2 Lloyd's Rep. 189.

[23] See *supra.* para. 1–39.

[24] *Glasgow Assurance* v. *Symondson* (1911) 104 L.T. 254.

[25] *Berger* v. *Pollock* [1973] 2 Lloyd's Rep. 442. *Cf. The La Pointe* [1986] 2 Lloyd's Rep. 513.

[26] *Black King Shipping* v. *Massie, The Litsion Pride* [1985] 1 Lloyd's Rep. 437. The claim was independently deniable for fraud.

insurer chose to waive that breach of duty.[27] The continuing duty of utmost good faith is similarly owed by the insurer to the assured, but not to the assignee of the proceeds of the policy as such assignee owes no duties of this nature to the insurer.[28] However, the assured cannot recover damages in respect of a breach by the insurer, but may only rescind the contract.[29]

5–06 Agency and utmost good faith

Where insurance is effected by an agent on behalf of the assured, the agent is obliged to make full disclosure to the insurer. Section 19 of the Marine Insurance Act 1906 thus provides:

> Where an insurance is effected for the assured by an agent, the agent must disclose to the insurer—
> (a) Every material circumstance which is known to himself, and an agent to insure is deemed to know every circumstance which in the ordinary course of business ought to be known by, or to have been communicated to, him; and
> (b) Every material circumstance which the assured is bound to disclose, unless it come to his knowledge too late to communicate it to the agent.

Where, however, the policy is effected by the assured, he is bound to disclose facts known to the agent which ought to have been communicated to him by the agent in the course of the agency,[30] although the position is otherwise as regards facts which the agent was not obliged to disclose to the assured in respect of the transaction in question.[31]

5–07 Facts which need not be disclosed

The assured is not, however, bound to disclose the following facts unless the insurer expressly questions him about them.

(i) *Facts which he does not know.* A man "can only disclose what he knows"[32] and is therefore bound to disclose nothing else.[33] But the rule of marine insurance law[34] that the assured "is deemed to know every circumstance, which, in the ordinary course of business, ought to be known by him"[35] would, no doubt, have general application. And it will afford the assured no excuse that he did not know that a fact was material.[36] Knowledge of the existence of the duty of disclosure is irrelevant.

(ii) *Facts which diminish the risk.*[37] Thus, the assured need not dis-

---

[27] *Continental Illinois National Bank* v. *Alliance Assurance, The Captain Panagos* [1986] 2 Lloyd's Rep. 470, where the fire was in any event found to have been set fraudulently by the assured.
[28] *Bank of Nova Scotia* v. *Hellenic Mutual, The Good Luck* [1989] 2 Lloyd's Rep. 238.
[29] *La Banque Financière* v. *Westgate Insurance* [1988] 1 Lloyd's Rep. 513.
[30] *Fitzherbert* v. *Mather* (1785) I.T.R. 12; *Blackburn* v. *Vigors* (1887) 12 App.Cas. 531.
[31] *Blackburn* v. *Haslam* (1888) 21 Q.B.D. 144; *Australia Bank* v. *Colonial and Eagle Wharves* [1960] 2 Lloyd's Rep. 241.
[32] Goddard in *Hearts of Oak Building Society* v. *Law Union Insurance* [1936] 2 All E.R. 619, 625; Lord Campbell C.J. in *Wheelton* v. *Hardisty* (1857) 8 E. & B. 232, 269.
[33] *Joel* v. *Law Union* [1908] 2 K.B. 863; *Whitwell* v. *Autocar Insurance* (1927) 27 Ll.L.R. 418.
[34] See M.I.A. s.18(1).
[35] M.I.A. 1906, s.18(1); *Proudfoot* v. *Montefiore* (1867) L.R. 2 Q.B. 511, 519; *Blackburn* v. *Vigors* (1887) 12 App.Cas. 531, 537, 541.
[36] See § 5–17, *infra.*
[37] M.I.A. 1906, s.18(3)(a); *Carter* v. *Boehm* (1766) 3 Burr. 1905, 1910, *per* Lord Mansfield.

close that the insured yacht will spend much of the period of the insurance in the builders' yard, for it is at less risk there than on the open sea.[38]

(iii) *Facts within the knowledge of the insurers.*[39] In the words of section 18(3)(*b*) of the Marine Insurance Act the assured need not disclose "any circumstance which is known or presumed to be known to the insurer. The insurer is presumed to know matters of common notoriety or knowledge, and matters which an insurer in the ordinary course of business, as such, ought to know." Actual knowledge is not essential, if the insurer had the means of knowing the fact,[40] or if he ought to have known it.[41] He will be presumed to know what is known generally and what other insurers in the same business know.[42] Trade usages[43] and matters ascertainable by perusing Lloyd's lists[44] have been thus held to be matters within the knowledge of the insurers. That principle is not confined to marine insurance. Thus in *Woodcott* v. *Excess Insurance*[45] the assured was able to recover under his fire policy, as his criminal record had been disclosed to the insurer's agent, even though neither the agent nor the assured had communicated the information to the insurer.

(iv) *Facts of which information is waived by the insurer.*[46] If the insurers forbear to ask questions after they have learnt something which ought to have put them on their inquiry, they will be held to have waived their right to fuller and more precise information.[47] So if the assured supplies the insurers with particulars which ought to put them on their guard, and they fail to ask further questions, they cannot subsequently complain.[48] Another example of such waiver is where the assured leaves blanks in the proposal form and the insurers ask no further questions on the matter.[49] If the assured communicates verbally facts material to be known, *e.g.* that he was in the R.N.R., while in his written answers to the questions on his proposal form he describes himself as a "fisherman," the verbal communication, followed by acceptance of the premiums by the insurer, will constitute a waiver by the insurer of the non-disclosure.[50]

---

[38] *Inversiones Manria* v. *Sphere Drake Insurance, The Dora* [1989] 1 Lloyd's Rep. 69.

[39] *Bates* v. *Hewitt* (1867) L.R. 2 Q.B. 595; Vaughan Williams L.J. in *Joel* v. *Law Union* [1908] 2 K.B. 863, 878, 879; *Hales* v. *Reliance* [1960] 2 Lloyd's Rep. 391.

[40] Erle C.J. in *Foley* v. *Tabor* (1861) 2 F. & F. 663, 672.

[41] Lord Mansfield in *Carter* v. *Boehm*, *supra*.

[42] *Harrower* v. *Hutchinson* (1870) L.R. 5 Q.B. 584, *per* Kelly C.B. See *North British Fishing* v. *Starr* (1922) 13 Ll.L.R. 206; insurer deemed to know pattern of loss in fishing boat trade.

[43] *Vallance* v. *Dewar* (1808) 1 Camp. 503, 508; *British Marine* v. *Gaunt* [1921] 2 A.C. 41, 59–62, *per* Lord Sumner.

[44] *Friere* v. *Woodhouse* (1817) Holt N.P. 572; *Foley* v. *Tabor* (1861) 2 F. & F. 663; contrast *London General* v. *General Marine* [1921] 1 K.B. 104.

[45] [1979] 1 Lloyd's Rep. 231, for the retrial, see [1979] 2 Lloyd's Rep. 210.

[46] M.I.A. 1906, s.18(3)(*c*).

[47] Lord Mansfield in *Carter* v. *Boehm*, *supra*; Scrutton L.J. in *Greenhill* v. *Federal Insurance* [1927] 1 K.B. 65, 85. See *Roberts* v. *Plaisted* [1989] 2 Lloyd's Rep. 341.

[48] Scrutton L.J. in *Becker* v. *Marshall* (1922) 12 Ll.L.R. 413, 414.

[49] See § 5–08, *infra*.

[50] *Ayrey* v. *British Legal & United Provident Assurance Co.* [1918] 1 K.B. 136; 87 L.J.K.B. 513; 118 L.T. 255.

(v) *Facts which it is superfluous to disclose by reason of any express or implied warranty.*[51] So where the assured warrants that the insured vessel will be used only for pleasure purposes, his failure to disclose his intention to use the vessel as a demonstration model does not permit the insurer to use utmost good faith as a defence.[52]

2. NON-DISCLOSURE AND PROPOSAL FORMS

5–08 Where, as is usual in non-marine insurance, the applicant for insurance is asked to fill in a proposal form containing a list of questions, there is a presumption against him that such questions refer to material facts.[53] In such a case the parties are considered to have agreed the difficult question as to which facts are material.[54] Thus where the assured's answers are literally true, the insurer is nevertheless not prevented from relying on non-disclosure in respect of an answer which is misleading, incomplete or evasive. However, if a question is unclear or ambiguous, the courts are generally slow to apply the doctrine of non-disclosure to answers which are true on a reasonable construction of the question. Thus, where the assured answered a question as to the cost of her car honestly, the fact that some of the cost was made up by the part-exchange of another car was held not to be material,[55] and where a firm applies for insurance and is asked whether the proposer has been a claimant on a fire policy before, the question will normally be construed to refer to claims by the firm itself and not by its individual partners.[56] Moreover, where it is clearly the case that the assured has not given a complete answer, or has failed to answer a question, and the insurer is nevertheless content to issue a policy, the insurer runs the risk of being held to have waived further disclosure. So where an insurer was told that the insured vessel was carrying cargo, but made no inquiry as to the nature of the cargo, the insurer was held to have waived disclosure of the fact that the cargo was inflammable.[57] All will, however, depend upon the nature of the question, for in other cases it has been held that a blank left on a proposal form in response to an express question is capable of amounting to an answer in the negative.[58]

Where the assured has put the insurer in a position to obtain the required information no question of non-disclosure can arise.[59]

---

[51] M.I.A. 1906, s.18(3)(*d*), generally applicable: *De Maurier (Jewels)* v. *Bastion Ins. Co.* [1967] 2 Lloyd's Rep. 550, 557.

[52] *Inversiones Manria* v. *Sphere Drake Insurance, op cit.*

[53] Lord Dundas in *Dawsons Ltd.* v. *Bonnin* (1921) S.C. 511, 518; *Glicksman* v. *Lancashire and General* [1925] 2 K.B. 593, 608, *per* Scrutton L.J.; [1927] A.C. 139, 144, *per* Lord Dunedin.

[54] Lord Cranworth in *Anderson* v. *Fitzgerald* (1853) 4 H.L.C. 484, 503; Jessel M.R. in *London Assurance* v. *Mansel* (1879) 11 Ch.D. 363.

[55] *Brewtnall* v. *Cornhill Insurance* (1931) 40 Ll.L.R. 166.

[56] *Davies* v. *National Fire of New Zealand* [1891] A.C. 485; *Ewer* v. *National Employers Mutual* [1937] 2 All E.R. 193. Contrast *Glicksman* v. *Lancashire & General* [1927] A.C. 139, where there was a close relationship between the proposing partner and the firm.

[57] *Mann* v. *Capital and Counties Insurance* [1921] 2 K.B. 300. See also: *Perrins* v. *Marine & General* (1859) 2 E. & E. 317; *Cohen* v. *Standard Marine* (1925) 21 Ll.L.R. 30; *Markovitch* v. *Liverpool Victoria Friendly Society* (1912) 28 T.L.R. 188; *Roberts* v. *Plaisted* [1989] 2 Lloyd's Rep. 341.

[58] *Roberts* v. *Avon Insurance* [1956] 2 Lloyd's Rep. 240; *Forbes* v. *Edinburgh Life* (1832) 10 S. (Ct. of Sess.) 451.

[59] *Wheelton* v. *Hardisty* (1857) 8 E. & B. 232, 269, 270, *per* Lord Campbell C.J.

The assured is bound not only to make true answers to the questions **5–09** put to him but also spontaneously to disclose any fact exclusively within his knowledge which it is material for the insurer to know,[60] nor does the existence of written questions and answers excuse him from answering oral questions truthfully.[61] While the presumption is that matters dealt with in the proposal form are immaterial there is no corresponding presumption that matters not so dealt with are not.[62] Thus, in life insurance cases the fact that the assured warrants his answers in the proposal form *only* to be true does not mean that he is excused the duty to make full disclosure of all facts material to the risk when he is afterwards questioned by the insurer's doctor.[63] Again, where a question was asked in a proposal form as to previous refusals to insure by other companies, it was held that the assured was bound to disclose that his last insurer had failed to invite him to *renew* a policy.[64]

Where the insurer has not asked a specific question, it follows from the above principles that the assured cannot normally argue that such omission amounts to an implied waiver of disclosure,[65] although by not asking questions about a matter insurers do run a greater risk of a finding of immateriality.[66] Further, where the insurer asks a limited question, there is authority for the proposition that information beyond that question has been waived[67]: this has been applied in motor insurance, where questions limited to motoring convictions were held to have waived the disclosure of non-motoring convictions.[68] Matters were taken a step further in *Hair* v. *Prudential*,[69] in which Woolf J. held that a statement on the proposal form by which the assured warranted that his answers were true operated as an implied waiver of information about which specific questions had not been asked.

The insurer's duty of disclosure   5–10

The reciprocal nature of the duty of disclosure, while long established in principle,[70] was little explored until the *Gemstones* litigation, *Banque Keyser Ullman* v. *Skandia Insurance*,[71] on appeal *La Banque Financière* v. *Westgate Insurance*.[72] This Case involved massive frauds by a number of persons, but in essence the plaintiff banks had obtained credit policies which, due to the fraud of an employee of the brokers, were insufficient to cover the primary debtor's fraudulent default. The fraud of the

---

[60] Dampier J. in *Huguenin* v. *Rayley* (1815) 6 Taunt. 186; Lord Campbell C.J. in *Wheelton* v. *Hardisty* (1857) 8 E. & B. 232, 270; *Glicksman* v. *Lancashire & General* [1927] A.C. 139; *Bond* v. *Commercial Assurance* (1930) 35 Com.Cas. 171.

[61] See Gurney B. in *Wainewright* v. *Bland* (1836) 1 M. & W. 32, 35.

[62] *Schoolman* v. *Hall* [1951] 1 Lloyd's Rep. 139.

[63] Vaughan Williams L.J. in *Joel* v. *Law Union* [1908] 2 K.B. 863, 876–878.

[64] *Holt's Motors* v. *South-East Lanes Insurance* (1930) 35 Com.Cas. 281.

[65] *Arterial Caravans* v. *Yorkshire Insurance* [1973] 1 Lloyd's Rep. 169. But see *Roberts* v. *Plaisted* [1989] 2 Lloyd's Rep. 341, where the Court of Appeal signalled a possible change to this harsh principle.

[66] Scrutton L.J. in *Newsholme Bros.* v. *Road Transport & General* [1929] 2 K.B. 356, 362, 263; *McCormick* v. *National Motor & Accident* (1934) 40 Com.Cas. 76, 78.

[67] Vaughan Williams L.J. in *Joel* v. *Law Union* [1908] 2 K.B. 863, 878.

[68] *Revell* v. *London General Assurance* (1934) 50 Ll.L.R. 114; *Taylor* v. *Eagle Star* (1940) 67 Ll.L.R. 136.

[69] [1983] 2 Lloyd's Rep. 667.

[70] M.I.A. 1906, s.17; *Carter* v. *Boehm* (1766) 3 Burr. 1905. See also the authorities in n. 3, *supra*.

[71] [1986] 2 F.T.L.R. 601.

[72] [1988] 2 Lloyd's Rep. 513.

broker was known to a senior employee of the leading insurers, and the banks argued that the failure of the insurers to disclose the brokers' employee's fraud constituted a breach of the insurers' duty of utmost good faith resulting in loss to the banks. Both Steyn J. and the Court of Appeal held that there had been a breach of this duty, but the Court of Appeal overturned Steyn J.'s view that damages were available for breach of this duty: the only remedy was rescission, which on the facts was of little use in any event. The scope of the insurer's duty of disclosure:

> "must at least extend to disclosing all facts known to him which are material either to the nature of the risk sought to be covered or the recoverability of a claim under the policy which a prudent assured would take into account in deciding whether or not to place the risk for which he seeks cover."[73]

While this principle is wide, the non-availability of damages in effect limits its utility to those cases in which the facts withheld by the insurer relate to the assured's very decision whether or not to insure, for example where the assured took out insurance on a vessel which was known to the insurer to have arrived safely at its destination.[74] In a later case, *The Good Luck*,[75] the Court of Appeal went on to hold that in appropriate circumstances the insurer's duty of utmost good faith may subsist beyond the creation of the contract,[76] although this is rarely likely to be of use to the assured given the absence of a remedy in damages.

It was further argued in *La Banque Financière* that the fact that a contract of insurance is one of utmost good faith creates the necessary proximity and special relationship between insurer and assured sufficient to give rise to a duty of care in tort: it was suggested that any such duty would impose on the insurer a "duty to speak," failure to do so giving rise to damages. The Court of Appeal, reversing Steyn J., rejected this reasoning, on the basis that awarding tort damages would simply sidestep the principle that damages do not lie for breach of the duty of utmost good faith. It was subsequently argued in *The Good Luck* that the assignee of insurance proceeds could mount a tort action of this nature even though no duty of utmost good faith was owed by the insurer to the assignee. Once again the Court of Appeal rejected the argument, here on the basis that imposing tortious duties would interfere with the contractual arrangements between insurer and assignee contained in the letter of undertaking issued by the insurer to the assignee.

3. MISREPRESENTATION

5–11 The principles governing misrepresentation have been codified in section 20 of the Marine Insurance Act, which is of general application. Section 20 provides:

---

[73] *Ibid. per* Slade L.J. at p. 545.
[74] This example is given by Lord Mansfield in *Carter* v. *Boehm, op cit.*
[75] *Bank of Nova Scotia* v. *Hellenic Mutual* [1989] 2 Lloyd's Rep. 238.
[76] In accordance with *The Litsion Pride* [1985] 1 Lloyd's Rep. 437; see *supra.* para. 5–05.

(1) Every material representation made by the assured or his agent to the insurer during the negotiations for the contract, and before the contract is concluded, must be true. If it be untrue the insurer may avoid the contract.

(2) A representation is material which would influence the judgment of a prudent insurer in fixing the premium, or determining whether he will take the risk.

(3) A representation may be either a representation as to a matter of fact, or as to a matter of expectation or belief.

(4) A representation as to a matter of fact is true, if it be substantially correct, that is to say, if the difference between what is represented and what is actually correct would not be considered material by a prudent insurer.

(5) A representation as to a matter of expectation or belief is true if it be made in good faith.

(6) A representation may be withdrawn or corrected before the contract is concluded.

(7) Whether a particular representation be material or not is, in each case, a question of fact.

It is plain from section 20(1) that the right to avoid is not confined to cases in which the assured has been guilty of fraud. The principle, said Roche J. in *Graham* v. *Western Australian Insurance*, a case relating mainly to non-marine risks, had been settled for years,

> "that if there is information given, be it quite innocent, which is not a matter of contract, and never becomes a matter of contract, yet, nevertheless, if it is inaccurate, it can be used to avoid the policy or policies in question."[77]

Thus if the fact misstated by the assured is material, the policy is voidable and it will not avail him that he acted with perfect good faith and honesty of intention.[78] There are a number of dicta[79] and one decision[80] to the effect that life insurance is an exception to the general rule that an innocent misrepresentation may afford grounds for avoiding a policy of life insurance, but there is no modern authority for this view. The position in misrepresentation differs from that in non-disclosure, in that a policy will not be voidable because the assured fails to disclose material facts of which he was not aware: innocence is thus a defence to non-disclosure.

What constitutes misrepresentation   5–12

A representation can be material only if it is of fact. Statements of intention or of opinion are thus to be treated as false only if the assured did not genuinely have the stated intention or hold the stated opinion.[81] Thus where the assured stated his expectation as to the date of departure of certain vessels, it was held to be an insufficient answer to his claim that the vessels had in fact already departed[82] In such a case, provided the assured speaks truly as to his own state of mind, the fact that his belief or expectation is not in accordance with the actual facts will

---

[77] (1931) 40 Ll.L.R. 64, 66.

[78] *Anderson* v. *Pacific Insurance* (1872) L.R. 7 C.P. 65, 68; *Golding* v. *Royal London Auxiliary Insurance* (1914) 30 T.L.R. 350, 351.

[79] See Vaughan Williams L.J. in *Joel* v. *Law Union* [1908] 2 K.B. 863, citing Lord Cranworth in *Anderson* v. *Fitzgerald* (1853) 4 H.L.C. 484, 504.

[80] *Scottish Provident* v. *Boddam* (1893) 9 T.L.R. 385.

[81] *Wheelton* v. *Hardisty* (1857) 8 E. & B. 232, in which the assured stated his "belief" as to the particulars of a life assured: see *infra*, para. 16–27 *et seq.*

[82] *Barber* v. *Fletcher* (1779) 1 Doug K.B. 305.

not vitiate the policy. A statement by the assured that he is in good health in reference to a posposed life policy will generally be construed to mean in good health to his own knowledge,[83] but it is otherwise where he states without any limitation that he is of temperate habits.[84] A plain "no" to a question in a motor-vehicle insurance proposal has not been construed to relate to the proposer's knowledge; the policy is voidable if such answer is untrue in fact.[85]

5–13 Effect of misrepresentation

The effect of misrepresentation on the contract is precisely the same as that of non-disclosure: it affords the aggrieved party a ground for avoiding the contract. This right does not depend upon any implied term of the contract but arose originally, it has been said, by reason of the jurisdiction originally exercised by the courts of equity to prevent imposition.[86] Previous editions of this work had taken the view that the right of avoidance in insurance law is a common law concept distinct from the equitable remedy of rescission operating in other areas of contract law.[87] The point would appear to be important mainly in determining whether the Misrepresentation Act 1967 is applicable to insurance contracts. However, in the one case in which the point has arisen it was assumed that the 1967 Act was applicable in principle to insurance contracts,[88] and in more recent cases discussing the basis of utmost good faith no distinction has been drawn between misrepresentation in insurance and operating generally.[89]

5–14   *The Misrepresentation Act 1967.* Under section 2(2) of this Act the Court is empowered to award damages, in lieu of rescission, to the innocent party; this recognises that rescission may operate unfairly. This provision is apparently applicable to insurance, although the view has been expressed that it ought not to be given effect to where the insurer seeks to avoid a policy issued to a commercial assured.[90] The 1967 Act is, therefore, to be used only to relieve a consumer or private assured who has acted innocently in falsely stating a fact.

5–15 Time of misrepresentation

Like non-disclosure, only a misrepresentation prior to the formation of the contract will give the insurers a ground for avoidance.[91] The insurers have no right, on the other hand, to avoid the contract if the assured informs them of the truth after making the misrepresentation

---

[83] *Life Association of Scotland* v. *Forster* (1873) 11 M. (Ct. of Sess.) 351. See also *Delahaye* v. *British Empire Mutual Life* (1897) 13 T.L.R 245. See § 16–25, *infra*.

[84] *Thomson* v. *Weems* (1884) 9 App.Cas. 671.

[85] *Merchants & Manufacturers Insurance* v. *Hunt* [1941] 1 K.B. 295; *Zurich* v. *Leven*, 1940 S.C. 406.

[86] Luxmoore L.J. in *Merchants & Manufacturers Insurance* v. *Hunt* [1941] 1 K.B. 295, 318. The jurisdiction at common law, in marine cases at least, long antedated the fusion of law and equity, but the *dictum* does usefully point to the nature of the concept. *Cf.* also n. 8, *supra*.

[87] See the 5th Ed., § 5–09.

[88] *Highland Insurance* v. *Continental Insurance* [1987] 1 Lloyd's Rep. 109.

[89] *La Banque Financière* v. *Westgate Insurance* [1988] 2 Lloyd's Rep. 513. But note that in insurance law a misrepresentation is operative whether or not the insurer was actually misled, although in the general law a misrepresentation must subjectively affect the party seeking rescission: *Museprime Properties Ltd.* v. *Adhill Properties Ltd.* (1990) *The Times*, March 13.

[90] *Highland Insurance* v. *Continental Insurance*, *supra*. n. 88 (a reinsurance case).

[91] See M.I.A. 1906, s.20(1); see § 5–04, *supra*.

but before the formation of the contract.[92] Where a statement, true
when made, turns out to be untrue before completion, the assured must
correct it.[93] The rule applies to statements of intention, and if the
assured changes his mind before the contract is complete, he must
inform his insurers, though he is not bound to do so if he changes his
mind subsequently.[94]

Burden of proof 5–16

The burden of proving non-disclosure or misrepresentation is on the
insurers: *Joel* v. *Law Union*.[95]

4. WHAT FACTS ARE MATERIAL

The test 5–17

Everything is material which might influence a prudent insurer in
determining whether he will take the risk and, if so, at what premium
and on what conditions.[96]

In determining the question whether a particular fact is one which
ought to be disclosed, the test to be applied is not what the assured
thinks,[97] nor even what the insurers think,[98] but whether a prudent and
experienced insurer might be influenced in his judgment if he knew of
it.[99] It is not necessary to show that a prudent insurer's decision *would*
have been influenced by the fact; it suffice that his decision *might* have
been so influenced.[1] There are dicta to suggest that the test is, "What
would a reasonable assured consider material?"[2] but section 18(2) of the
Marine Insurance Act 1906 adopts the test of the judgment of a prudent
insurer and, since marine and non-marine insurance law are identical in
this respect,[3] this test may be regarded as the proper one.[4] What is
regarded as material by the "more experienced and intelligent insurers"

---

[92] *Golding* v. *Royal London Auxiliary Insurance* (1914) 30 T.L.R. 350.

[93] *Canning* v. *Farquhar* (1886) 16 Q.B.D. 727.

[94] *Benham* v. *United Guarantee* (1852) 7 Ex. 744.

[95] [1908] 2 K.B. 863.

[96] See M.I.A. 1906, ss.18(2), *supra* § 5–02, and 20(2), *supra*, § 5–11, as construed by the Court of
Appeal in *C.T.I.* v. *Oceanus Mutual* [1984] 1 Lloyd's Rep. 476.

[97] *Lindenau* v. *Desborough* (1828) 8 B & C. 586, *per* Bayley J. at p. 592 and *per* Littledale J. at p.
593; *Dalglish* v. *Jarvie* (1850) 2 Mac. & G. 231; *Bates* v. *Hewitt* (1867) L.R. 2 Q.B. 595, 607, 608, *per*
Cockburn C.J.; Jessel M.R. in *London Assurance* v. *Mansel* (1879) 11 Ch.D. 363, 368; Channell J. in
Re Yager and Guardian (1912) 108 L.T. 38, 44, 45; Finlay J. in *Beauchamp* v. *National Mutual* [1937] 3
All E.R. 19, 22; Lord Blackburn in *Brownlie* v. *Campbell* (1880) 5 App.Cas. 295, 954.

[98] See Cockburn C.J. in *Bates* v. *Hewitt* (1867) L.R. 2 Q.B. 595; Scrutton J. in *Glasgow Assurance* v.
Symondson (1911) 104 L.T. 254, 257.

[99] See Blackburn J. in *Ionides* v. *Pender* (1874) L.R. 9 Q.B. 531; Bowen L.J. in *Tate* v. *Hyslop* (1885)
15 Q.B.D. 368, 379; *Rivaz* v. *Gerussi* (1880) 6 Q.B.D. 222, *per* Baggallay L.J. at p. 227; *per* Brett L.J.
at pp. 227–229, and *per* Cotton L.J. at pp. 230, 231.

[1] *C.T.I.* v. *Oceanus Mutual, supra*. This is harsh on the assured and indeed curious, for the M.I.A.
1906, ss.18(2) and 20(2) both use the word "would" and not the word "might."

[2] Gibbs C.J. in *Durrell* v. *Bederley* (1816) Holt N.P. 283, 286; *Swete* v. *Fairlie* (1833) 6 C. & P. 1;
Fowkes v. *Manchester & London* (1862) 3 F. & F. 440; Fletcher Moulton L.J. in *Joel* v. *Law Union*
[1908] 2 K.B. 853, 884; Lord President Inglis in *Life Association of Scotland* v. *Forster* (1873) 11 M.
(Ct. of Sess.) 351; see also, equivocally, Lord Sterndale M.R. in *Becker* v. *Marshall* (1922) 12 Ll.L.R.
413, 414.

[3] Bayley J. in *Lindenau* v. *Desborough* (1828) 8 B. & C. 586, 592; Jessel M.R. in *London Assurance*
v. *Mansel* (1879) 11 Ch.D. 363, 367; Vaughan Williams L.J. in *Joel* v. *Law Union* [1908] 2 K.B. 863,
878. *Lambert* v. *C.I.S.* [1975] 2 Lloyd's Rep. 485 (C.A.); *C.T.I.* v. *Oceanus Mutual, supra*.

[4] See also Scrutton J. in *Glasgow Assurance* v. *Symondson, supra*. The Privy Council adopted the
test of a reasonable insurer in *Mutual Life of New York* v. *Ontario Metal Products* [1925] A.C. 344,
350–353; also applied by the C.A. in *Zurich* v. *Morrison* [1942] 2 K.B. 53.

carrying on the business in question at the time is what matters,[5] and the general practice of insurers is relevant in this respect.[6]

Courts, acting as juries, have in practice for many years tended to test the view of insurers by reference to the test of what a reasonable man, in the shoes of the assured, would have considered material,[7] although this practice cannot survive *C.T.I.* v. *Oceanus*, despite widespread opposition to this case, particularly from commercial arbitrators.

5–18   Not every fact which increases the risk is a material one: there must be a possibility that the insurers might attach some importance to it in assessing the premiums.[8] Thus it was held to be immaterial that a lorry was garaged in a wooden shed which had been used to store hay, the insurance being a comprehensive motor-vehicle one, and the percentage of the premium allocated to the fire risk being very small.[9] But it might have been held otherwise had the insurance been against fire only.[10]

Finally, it is the circumstances existing at the time when a fact ought to be disclosed, *i.e.* before the formation of the contract, and not their results, which are to be considered in determining whether any given fact is material.[11] A state of affairs is not material simply because it causes the loss in question.[12]

5–19 Materiality question of fact

The question of materiality is a pure question of fact in each case,[13] and the decided cases therefore give no more than an indication of what conclusion an arbitrator would reach in any particular case.

5–20 Types of material fact

Facts may be material because they render the subject-matter insured exceptionally liable to destruction by the peril insured against, or because they indicate that the proposer is not a person whose proposal may be accepted as a matter of course without careful consideration. An example of the former is afforded by the case of *Bufe* v. *Turner*,[14] in which the assured, having one of several warehouses next but one to a boat-builder's shop which took fire, on the same evening after that fire was apparently extinguished insured his warehouse without informing the insurers of the neighbouring fire. In addition a fact may be material if it might influence the premium, whether or not that fact affects the physical or moral hazard. Thus where the insurer issued a policy on a yacht at a discounted premium, on the understanding that the assured

---

[5] Atkin J. in *Associated Oil Carriers Ltd.* v. *Union Insurance of Canton* [1917] 2 K.B. 184, 192.

[6] *Girdlestone* v. *North British* (1870) L.R. 11 Eq. 197. Hence the importance of employing expert brokers to effect insurance: see *Ogden* v. *Reliance* [1975] 1 Lloyd's Rep. 52, Sup.Ct.Aust., Macfarlan J.

[7] The authorities are carefully considered by McNair J. in his judgment in *Roselodge* v. *Castle* [1966] 2 Lloyd's Rep. 105, 129–131.

[8] *Dawsons* v. *Bonnin* [1922] 2 A.C. 413, *per* Viscount Haldane at pp. 420, 421.

[9] *Ibid.*

[10] *Ibid. per* Viscount Finlay at p. 429.

[11] *Seaton* v. *Burnand* [1900] A.C. 135.

[12] *Dawsons* v. *Bonnin* [1922] 2 A.C. 413.

[13] *Anderson* v. *Fitzgerald* (1853) 4 H.L.C. 484; *Hoare* v. *Bremridge* (1872) L.R. 8 Ch. 22; Viscount Dunedin in *Glicksman* v. *Lancashire & General* [1927] A.C. 139, 144.

[14] (1815) 6 Taunt. 338; see §§ 18–19, 18–27, *infra*, for fire insurance examples, and §§ 16–25 to 16–33, *infra*, for life insurance examples.

intended to insure four yachts per year, the assured's false statement in this regard was held to be material.[15]

Moral hazard 5–21

The character of the assured has long been held to be material to the risk.[16] Such fact affects the "moral hazard," as it is termed. It may be said generally that, although the assured is not necessarily bound to disclose that his character is a bad one, it would be unsafe on his part not to disclose the following information:

(a) previous losses and claims under other policies,[17]
(b) in the case of motor vehicle insurance, previous convictions for motoring offences,[18] and in other cases convictions material to the risk,[19]
(c) any changes of name on his part,[20] and
(d) his nationality and racial origin.[21]

Previous refusals 5–22

As regards previous refusals of other insurers to undertake similar risks, these are not regarded as material in marine insurance,[22] but are generally held to be material in non-marine insurance,[23] in which insurers have shown by constantly asking questions in their proposal forms as to previous refusals that they regard that matter as material. Thus, in *Locker & Woolf* v. *Western Australian Insurance*[24] it was decided that, where the insurers asked a question as to previous refusals in a proposal form for fire insurance, a previous refusal in respect of an application for motor vehicle insurance was material and ought to have

---

[15] *Inversiones Manria* v. *Sphere Drake, The Dora* [1989] 1 Lloyd's Rep. 65.

[16] *Lynch* v. *Dalzell* (1729) 4 Bro.P.C. 431.

[17] See Lord Shaw in *Condogianis* v. *Guardian* [1921] 2 A.C. 125, 131; *Morser* v. *Eagle Star* (1931) 40 Ll.L.R. 254; *Becker* v. *Marshall* (1922) 12 Ll.L.R. 413; *Rozanes* v. *Bowen* (1928) 32 Ll.L.R. 98; *Farra* v. *Hetherington* (1931) 47 T.L.R. 465; *Simon, Haynes* v. *Beer* (1946) 78 Ll.L.R. 337; *Arterial Caravans* v. *Yorkshire Insurance* [1973] 1 Lloyd's Rep. 169.

[18] *Dunn* v. *Ocean* (1933) 47 Ll.L.R. 129; *McCormick* v. *National Motor* (1934) 40 Com.Cas. 76; *Zurich* v. *Leven*, 1940 S.C. 406.

[19] In *Schoolman* v. *Hall* [1951] 1 Lloyd's Rep. 139 (burglary insurance), a jury held material convictions of the assured for larceny over a period of seven years ending 14 years before the date of the policy. In *March Cabaret* v. *London Ass., supra*, the assured failed to disclose a conviction for handling stolen property on renewing a fire policy. May J. held the insurers not liable on it. In *Lambert* v. *Cooperative Insurance* [1975] 2 Lloyd's Rep. 485 (C.A.) a wife took out an all-risks policy covering her jewellery and that of her husband. She failed to disclose that he had been convicted, on one occasion, of receiving. The insurers failed to pay in respect of a loss on that ground, and the C.A. gave judgment in their favour. In *Woolcott* v. *Sun Alliance* [1978] 1 All E.R. 1253 a conviction for armed robbery was held to be material in relation to a fire policy. In *Reynolds* v. *Phoenix* [1978] 2 Lloyd's Rep. 440 it was held that a conviction for receiving stolen goods was not material to a fire policy, and similarly in *Roselodge* v. *Castle* [1966] 2 Lloyd's Rep. 113 a conviction for bribing a policeman was held to be immaterial to a policy on goods. The conviction cases should now, however, be read subject to the Rehabilitation of Offenders Act 1974. Where the assured has been charged with an offence and is awaiting trial when the contract of insurance is entered into, the charge must be disclosed even though the assured intends to plead innocence: *The Dora, supra*, n. 13. *Reynolds* v. *Phoenix, op. cit* even indicates that the assured must disclose criminality which has not been the subject of charge or conviction!

[20] *Gallé Gowns* v. *Licenses & General* (1933) 47 Ll.L.R. 186; but see *Britton* v. *Royal* (1866) 4 F. & F. 905; *Horne* v. *Poland* [1922] 2 K.B. 364, 365, *per* Lush J.

[21] *Horne* v. *Poland, supra*; *Becker* v. *Marshall, supra*. These cases probably do not survive the Race Relations Act 1976.

[22] Scrutton J. in *Glasgow Assurance* v. *Symondson* (1911) 104 L.T. 254.

[23] *Glicksman* v. *Lancashire & General* [1925] 2 K.B. 593, 608, 611; [1927] A.C. 139; *Holt's Motors* v. *South East Lancashire Insurance* (1930) 35 Com.Cas. 281, 282, 283, *per* Scrutton L.J.; *Re Yager and Guardian* (1912) 108 L.T. 38; *Taylor* v. *Yorkshire Insurance* [1913] 2 Ir.R. 1. But see *contra* Malins V.-C. in *Re General Provincial Life* (1870) 18 W.R. 396, 397.

[24] [1936] 1 K.B. 408.

been disclosed. The fact that the subject-matter differed did not reduce the increased moral hazard indicated by that refusal.[25] But MacKinnon J. held in *Ewer* v. *National Employers Mutual*[26] that the fact that the assured, the proprietor of a garage, had made a number of claims under policies indemnifying him from liability as a carrier was not material on his taking out a fire policy. He did not appear to be impressed by the arbitrator's finding in the case above that the previous refusal was material.[27] Those cases illustrate the difficulty of laying down any general principles as to the test of materiality, since it is a pure question of fact depending upon the circumstances of each case.

5–23 Existence of other insurances

The existence of other insurances against the same risks is generally material in the case of life[28] or accident[29] policies where, the principles of indemnity not applying, such insurances are of special importance. Besides, life insurance companies are always interested to know what other offices have done with respect to the same lives. Other insurances against other risks, such as fire policies or other policies of indemnity,[30] will not be material since their existence will tend to lessen the liability of the insurer on account of the principle of contribution.[31]

5–24 Failure to disclose as moral hazard

The fact that the insurer would have accepted the risk had disclosure been made does not necessarily mean that the fact was not material,[32] for the test is whether a *prudent insurer might* have been influenced and not whether the *insurer in question was* influenced.[33] But facts have been held not to be material where their disclosure would merely have caused delay pending inquiries[34]; moreover previous breaches of duty by the assured are immaterial facts.[35]

5–25 Over-insurance

Deliberate and intentional over-insurance has been held to be a material fact which should be disclosed, especially where the policy is a valued one.[36] The value of a thing may depend upon the use to which it is to be put and it may be worth more to the owner than its market value,[37] but where the value put upon it by the assured is based upon what he believes to be a reasonable prospect of appreciation, he should

---

[25] Slesser L.J. at p. 414.
[26] [1937] 2 All E.R. 193.
[27] At p. 201.
[28] Jessel M.R. in *London Assurance* v. *Mansel* (1879) 11 Ch.D. 363, 370; see also Lord Abinger in *Wainewright* v. *Bland* (1835) 1 M. & Rob. 481, 487.
[29] *Re Marshall and Scottish Employers' Liability* (1901) 85 L.T. 757, 758, *per* Wright J.
[30] See *Simpson S.S. Co.* v. *Premier Underwriting Association* (1905) 92 L.T. 730; *McDonnell* v. *Beacon Fire* (1857) 7 U.C.C.P. 308.
[31] See §§ 8–26 *et seq.*, *infra*; *Donaldson* v. *Manchester Insurance* (1836) 14 S. (Ct. of Sess.) 601.
[32] Wright J. in *Re Marshall and Scottish Employers' Liability* (1901) 85 L.T. 757, 758.
[33] *C.T.I.* v. *Oceanus Mutual*, *op. cit.*
[34] *Mutual Life of New York* v. *Ontario Metal Products* [1925] A.C. 344 (P.C.).
[35] *C.T.I.* v. *Oceanus* [1984] 1 Lloyd's Rep. 476 (Lloyd J.).
[36] *Ionides* v. *Pender* (1874) L.R. 9 Q.B. 531; *Hoff* v. *De Rougemont* (1929) 34 Com.Cas. 291; *Haase* v. *Evans* (1934) 48 Ll.L.R. 131; Willes J. in *Britton* v. *Royal* (1866) 4 F. & F. 905. The law is more generous when the policy is unvalued *Berger* v. *Pollock* [1973] 2 Lloyd's Rep. 442.
[37] Lord Shaw in *Thames & Mersey Marine* v. *Gunford* [1911] A.C. 529, 542.

make it plain to the insurer that the value stated is not immediate but speculative.[38] Such over-valuation will entitle the insurer to avoid the policy even if it cannot be shown to be fraudulent. The gross over-insurance by an agent of his own interest in an adventure will be material in the insurance by him of his principal's interest in it, notwithstanding that the agent's own insurance was effected by means of an "honour" policy.[39] If the assured insures his property for its purchase price, the fact that its market value is less is not a material fact.[40]

Facts affecting subrogation rights 5–26
Sometimes facts affecting the subrogation rights of the insurers are material. Thus where the owner of goods makes a special contract with a carrier relieving him of all liability, such fact may affect the premium or the willingness of the insurers to take the risk, in which case it must be disclosed.[41]

Tricky conduct 5–27
The assured may be too clever by half. Thus when one described army surplus leather jerkins (unused for 20 years) as "new men's clothes in bales for export" Megaw J.[42] held that, since the underwriters, were not told (i) that the goods were Government surplus or (ii) that they were at least 20 years old, any claim by the assured could be answered by a plea of non-disclosure.

Evidence of materiality 5–28
The opinion of experts is admissible evidence to prove whether a fact is material as to prove technical questions generally, and the evidence of doctors has therefore always been held to be admissible in determining whether facts relating to the assured's state of health, as, for instance, previous mental trouble, are material ones.[43] Thus it was held that doctors might be asked in evidence whether a veronal habit or insomnia troubles from which the proposer suffered were material.[44]

The courts were slow, on the other hand, to admit the opinion of underwriters, insurance brokers, and other such persons engaged in insurance business as to whether any particular facts were material. The question of materiality in old marine insurance cases being left for the jury alone to decide, it was not thought proper that they should be influenced by the opinion of underwriters or brokers on the matter.[45] It might indeed be felt that such persons would show a bias against the assured, but for many years now their opinion as to the materiality of any given fact has been as freely admitted in evidence as that of other

---

[38] *Hoff* v. *De Rougemont, supra.*
[39] *Thames & Mersey Marine* v. *Gunford, supra.*
[40] *The Dora, supra.*
[41] *Tate* v. *Hyslop* (1885) 15 Q.B.D. 368, 377.
[42] *Anglo-African Merchants* v. *Bayley* [1969] 1 Lloyd's Rep. 268.
[43] *Lindenau* v. *Desborough* (1828) 8 B. & C. 586; see also Denman C.J. in *Campbell* v. *Rickards* (1833) 5 B. & Ad. 840, 847.
[44] *Yorke* v. *Yorkshire Insurance* [1918] 1 K.B. 662, 669–671, *per* McCardie J.
[45] *Carter* v. *Boehm* (1766) 3 Burr. 1905, 1918, *per* Lord Mansfield; *Durrell* v. *Bederley* (1816) Holt N.P. 283; *Rickards* v. *Murdoch* (1830) 10 B. & C. 527; *Campbell* v. *Rickards* (1833) 5 B. & Ad. 840.

experts,[46] and the old decisions excluding such evidence are no longer good law.[47] The natural effect of admitting such evidence has been a gradual increase in the field of material facts.

5. STATEMENTS OF INSURANCE PRACTICE

5–29 History and status of the Statements

The Unfair Contract Terms Act 1977, which came into force on February 1, 1978 and which submits exclusion clauses in standard form contracts to a "reasonableness" test, excludes from its scope, by Schedule 1 paragraph 1(a), "any contract of insurance (including a contract to pay an annuity on human life)." The insurance industry agreed, as the price of this exemption, to draw up voluntary codes of practice. This was achieved by the publication of two Statements of Insurance Practice in 1977: these as revised in 1981, are observed by members of the Association of British Insurers and of Lloyd's. There is no formal sanction against an insurer who fails to comply with the Statements. However, the Insurance Ombudsman Bureau, which has been in existence since 1981 and the membership of which includes almost every major British insurer (and from the beginning of 1989, Lloyd's), is empowered to hear cases and to make recommendations and awards "in accordance with good insurance practice," phrase which in the Bureau's terms of reference includes compliance with the two Statements of Insurance Practice. The Statements modify to a considerable degree the right of insurers to plead non-disclosure, misrepresentation, breach of warranty[48] and breach of claims conditions,[49] but apply only to the assured in their private capacities.

5–30 Statement of (Non-life) Insurance Practice

The provisions of the Statement which affect non-disclosure and misrepresentation are as follows:

(a) There will be a statement prominently displayed on the proposal form drawing the attention of the proposer to the consequences of failure to disclose facts which an insurer would regard as likely to influence the acceptance and assessment of the proposal, and warning that if the proposer is in doubt as to the materiality of any fact he should disclose it.

(b) Matters which insurers have generally found to be material will be the subject of clear questions in proposal forms.

(c) Except where fraud, deception or negligence is involved, an insurer will not unreasonably repudiate liability on the grounds of non-disclosure or misrepresentation of a material fact where

---

[46] *Quin* v. *National Assurance* (1839) Jones & Carey 316 (Ex.Ch.Ire.); *Ionides* v. *Pender* (1874) L.R. 9 Q.B. 531; 535, Scrutton J. in *Glasgow Assurance* v. *Symondson* (1911) 104 L.T. 254, 257. See also *Reynolds* v. *Phoenix Assurance Co.* [1978] 2 Lloyd's Rep. 440 at pp. 457–459.

[47] McCardie J. in *Yorke* v. *Yorkshire Assurance, supra,* at pp. 669, 670; Scrutton L.J. in *Hoff* v. *De Rougemont* (1929) 34 Com.Cas. 291, 299–303; McNair J. in *Roselodge* v. *Castle* [1966] 2 Lloyd's Rep. 105, 129.

[48] See Chap. 6.

[49] See Chap. 9.

knowledge of that fact would not materially have influenced the insurer's judgment in the acceptance or assessment of the insurance. This does not apply to marine or aviation policies.

(d) Renewal notices should contain a warning about the duty of disclosure including the necessity to advise changes affecting the policy which have occurred since the policy inception or last renewal date, whichever was the later.

Statement of Long-Term Insurance Practice   **5–31**

The provisions of the Statement which affect non-disclosure and misrepresentation are as follows:

(a) An insurer will not unreasonably reject a claim. In particular, an insurer will not reject a claim on grounds of non-disclosure or misrepresentation of a matter that was outside the proposer's knowledge. However, fraud or deception will, and negligence may, result in adjustment or rejection.

(b) If the proposal calls for the disclosure of a material fact there will be a statement prominently displayed drawing attention to the consequences of failure to disclose facts which an insurer would regard as likely to influence the acceptance and assessment of the proposal, and warning that if the signatory is in doubt as to the materiality of any fact he should disclose it.

(c) Matters which insurers have generally found to be material will be the subject of clear questions in proposal forms.

CHAPTER 6

CONDITIONS AND WARRANTIES

1. LEGAL EFFECT OF CONDITIONS

MOST policies contain a certain number of clauses declaratory of the terms **6–01**
on which they are granted. Some of these terms consist only of a statement
of the legal effect which the policy would have had, had they not been
inserted, whilst others enlarge or restrict the rights of the assured or impose
upon him obligations or duties in excess of those implied by law. It may be a
difficult question of construction whether or not a term in the policy is
simply declaratory of, or intended to alter, the general legal position.[1]

Terms in insurance contracts are generally referred to as either conditions or warranties. The use of the term "condition" in insurance contract law is sometimes confusing and often differs from its use in other
branches of the law of contract where it generally denotes a fundamental term on breach of which the innocent party may elect to treat the
contract as repudiated. What is described as a condition in an insurance
contract may have this effect, but equally may be merely a collateral
stipulation. Some conditions in insurance contracts do not strictly speaking confer obligations on the insured but are merely declaratory of or
extend rights conferred on the insurer by the general law.[2] Furthermore, a warranty in an insurance policy is always a fundamental term,
breach of which entitles the insurer to repudiate the policy.

A term other than a warranty imposing an obligation on the insured
must be declared to be a condition precedent in order that a breach does
not merely give a right to damages to the insurer. However, such a condition may either be precedent to the validity of the contract or merely
precedent to the insurer's liability for a particular loss, depending on the
true construction of the contract.

Conditions precedent to validity   6–02
Conditions precedent to the validity of the contract generally impose
continuing obligations on the insured, such as an obligation in a motor
policy to maintain the vehicle in an efficient condition.[3]

It appears that it is open to an insurer to make compliance with any
obligation imposed on the insured fundamental, even if the obligation is
not a continuing one and normally would be the subject of a condition
precedent to liability.[4]

---

[1] See, for instance, *McCormick* v. *National Motor Insurance* (1934) 40 Com.Cas. 76, where Scrutton
L.J. treats a condition as declaratory of the law (p. 81) while Greer L.J. treats it otherwise (p. 87).
[2] For example, in respect of subrogation.
[3] For example, *Jones* v. *Provincial Ins. Co. Ltd.* (1929) 35 L1.L.R. 135, § 6–10, *infra*; *Brown* v. *Zurich General Accident Co.* [1954] 2 Lloyd's Rep. 243.
[4] See *Cox* v. *Orion Insurance Co. Ltd.* [1982] R.T.R. 1, where the insurers were held entitled to
repudiate the policy for breach by the insured of a condition requiring him to deliver particulars of any
accident, loss or damage, and all the conditions in the policy were declared to be "conditions precedent
to any liability of the company to make any payment under this policy."

6–03   Upon discovering a breach of a condition precedent to the validity of the contract, the insurer may elect to treat the contract as repudiated, or to affirm it.[5] If an insurer affirms the policy notwithstanding a breach of condition by the assured he will be liable under it in the event of a loss.[6] If he elects to treat it as repudiated, he will have a good answer to any action upon it in respect of losses occurring after the date of the assured's breach. Such election does not have the same effect as avoidance, *e.g.* for non-disclosure. For in one case, the party aggrieved, by relying on a condition of contract, accepts its existence as a binding contract: in the other he disputes the existence of any binding contract at all.[7] The aggrieved party must exercise his election in a reasonable time; mere lapse of time may not matter in the circumstances of a particular case.[8]

This distinction has the further technical effect that, while an action may be brought in a court of law to rescind a policy of insurance which the assured has obtained by his failure to disclose a material fact, no such action lies in the case of a breach of a condition of the policy.[9] The better view, however, is that the court has jurisdiction to grant a declaration in either case once a dispute has arisen.[10] A more important consequence is that anyone seeking to avoid a contract, as distinct from mere repudiation of liability under it, probably cannot set up a clause of the contract, an arbitration clause for instance,[11] in his defence.

The words "void" or "voidable" were at one time used, both in the conditions themselves and judicially[12] to denote the effect on a policy of a breach of a fundamental condition. Such words are only used however as inapt descriptions of the right to repudiate for breach of condition.[13] The use of the word "void" does not therefore exclude the affirmation of the contract by the party aggrieved.[14]

6–04 Waiver and estoppel

Where the party aggrieved by a breach of condition elects to carry on with the contract, he is often said to have "waived" the breach of condition,[15] The use of the word "waiver" in this sense has, however, been criticised, and it should be distinguished from the more usual use of that term in the law of contract, to express an agreement between the parties for good consideration not to enforce rights which have already

---

[5] See Lord Atkin and Lord Wright in *Hain S.S. Co.* v. *Tate & Lyle* (1936) 52 T.L.R. 617, 619, 622 for the general law on this matter. See also Sale of Goods Act 1979, s.11(1). It is usual to describe the former election as "acceptance" of the party in default's "repudiation": *Heyman* v. *Darwins* [1942] A.C. 356, 361, 373, 379, 398. See generally *Johnson* v. *Agnew* [1980] A.C. 367.

[6] *West* v. *National Motor* [1955] 1 W.L.R. 343.

[7] Bankes L.J. in *Woodall* v. *Pearl Assurance* [1919] 1 K.B. 593, 604.

[8] *Allen* v. *Robles* [1969] 2 Lloyd's Rep. 61.

[9] *Brooking* v. *Maudslay* (1888) 38 Ch.D. 636.

[10] See *Sparenborg* v. *Edinburgh Life* [1912] 1 K.B. 195.

[11] See § 9–30, *infra.*

[12] See, for instance, Lord Esher in *Hambrough* v. *Mutual Life* (1895) 11 T.L.R. 190, 192–193; Viscount Finlay in *Dawsons* v. *Bonnin* [1922] 2 A.C. 413, 428, 429.

[13] See such cases as *Woodall* v. *Pearl Assurance* [1919] 1 K.B. 593; *Metal Products* v. *Phoenix Assurance* (1925) 23 Ll.L.R. 87.

[14] *Armstrong* v. *Turquand* (1858) 9 I.C.L.R. 32; *Wing* v. *Harvey* (1854) 5 De G.M. & G. 265. The principle is implicit in such decisions as *Ayrey* v. *British Legal* [1918] 1 K.B. 136. See Scrutton L.J. in *McCormick* v. *National Motor Insurance* (1934) 40 Com.Cas. 76, 81. *Quaere* Greer L.J. at p. 87.

[15] *e.g.* by Greer L.J. in *Evans* v. *Employers Mutual* [1936] 1 K.B. 505, 514; by Lawrence J. in *Ayrey* v. *British Legal* [1918] 1 K.B. 136, 140.

accrued.[16] The election to affirm, on the other hand, is a unilateral act irrespective of agreement.

A formal election to affirm on the part of the insurers is not essential to prevent them setting up the defence of breach of a condition to a claim by the assured. So acceptance by the insurers of premiums after discovery of the breach of a condition by the assured evinces an election on their part to affirm the policy.[17] Here also the doctrine of estoppel comes to the assured's assistance.

Where the defendants, with full knowledge of the facts,[18] by their acts or conduct lead the plaintiff reasonably to suppose that they did not intend to treat the contract as at an end for the future, on account of his breach of a condition, they are "estopped" from setting up the breach as a defence.[19] Thus where, in a marine insurance case, the insurers accepted abandonment to them of the vessel lost, they were estopped from setting up the breach of warranty, of which they were already aware, in answer to a claim.[20] The insurers, so to be estopped, must have full knowledge of the breach,[21] but in this connection the knowledge of their agent may be imputed to the insurers themselves.[22] Thus where agents had accepted life insurance premiums and paid them to the company with knowledge that the assured had broken a condition,[23] and where in a motor insurance case a clerk of the insurers had notice of such a breach and the insurers had subsequently paid a claim under the policy,[24] the insurers have been held to be estopped from setting up the breach of condition as a defence. Atkin J.'s judgment in *Ayrey* v. *British Legal*[25] is valuable as showing the reasoning behind these decisions: as the agent in that case had no authority to contract on behalf of the insurers he had no authority to "waive" the breach in the strict sense, but the insurers were nevertheless liable on the policy on the ground of estoppel.

Conditions precedent to recovery 6–05

Conditions precedent to the insurer's liability for a particular loss, which may conveniently be described as conditions precedent to recovery, generally cover obligations not of a continuing nature such as giving notice and particulars of loss. A breach by the insured will not entitle the insurer to treat the contract as repudiated and the insured may recover for a second loss if he duly complies with the condition.[26]

An insurer may elect not to rely upon a breach of such a condition or be estopped from doing so, as described in paragraph 6–04. In addition it

---

[16] See Lord Russell of Killowen's remarks in *Nippon Kaisha* v. *Dawsons Bank* (1935) 51 Ll.L.R. 147, 150 (P.C.); Lord Sumner in *Atlantic Shipping Co.* v. *Louis Dreyfus* [1922] 2 A.C. 250, 261, 262; Bramwell B. in *Croft* v. *Lumley* (1858) 6 H.L.C. 672, 705.

[17] *Armstrong* v. *Turquand* (1858) 9 I.C.L.R. 32, 55; *Hemmings* v. *Sceptre Life* [1905] 1 Ch. 365.

[18] *Ayrey* v. *British Legal* [1918] 1 K.B. 136, 142; and see Lord Russell in *Evans* v. *Bartlam* [1937] A.C. 473, 483; *Scottish Equitable* v. *Buist* (1877) 4 R. (Ct. of Sess.) 1076, 1081.

[19] *Bentsen* v. *Taylor* [1893] 2 Q.B. 274, 283, *per* Bowen L.J.

[20] *Provincial Insurance* v. *Leduc* (1874) L.R. 6 P.C. 224.

[21] See Scrutton L.J. in *McCormick* v. *National Motor Insurance* (1934) 40 Com.Cas. 76, 81, 82.

[22] See §§ 15–10 *et seq.*, *infra*.

[23] *Wing* v. *Harvey* (1854) 5 De G.M. & G. 265; *Ayrey* v. *British Legal* [1918] 1 K.B. 136.

[24] *Evans* v. *Employers Mutual* [1936] 1 K.B. 505. *Cf. McKay* v. *Eagle Star* (1879) 18 M.C.R.(N.Z.) 83; *Canada Landed Credit* v. *Canada Agricultural Insurance* (1870) 17 Grant (U.C.) 418.

[25] See n. 23.

[26] *Hood's Trustees* v. *Southern Union General Ins. Co. of Australasia* [1928] Ch. 793, 806.

seems that an insured may be excused from breach where performance would be futile or unnecessary because of extraneous circumstances. In *Barrett Bros.* v. *Davies*,[27] the insured had failed to give the insurers particulars of loss as required by a condition precedent in the policy. However, the insurers had learnt all the relevant facts from the police and it was held by a majority of the Court of Appeal[28] that the insured's breach was thereby excused.

But conduct on the part of the insurers by which the assured is not prejudiced and which is not inconsistent with an intention, by the insurers, to repudiate the contract cannot be relied on by the assured as an election to affirm it. Thus the issue of a policy where an insurance is only covered by a slip is not necessarily an election to affirm.[29]

6–06 Conditions as collateral stipulations

A stipulation in the policy is not necessarily a condition precedent to validity or liability. In fact, unless the insurers use apt words to show that its performance is a condition precedent in either of the senses described above, or that it forms the basis upon which they contract, a stipulation in a policy will be construed merely as collateral to the main contract, breach of which gives right to an action or counterclaim for damages, but in no way relieves the insurers from their liability. Such collateral stipulations rarely occur in insurance policies, but this is only because insurers are careful to give stipulations in their policies the force of full conditions. Where they have not clearly done so it is a matter of construction whether a condition precedent or collateral agreement was intended, the guiding principle being that if the insurers wish a clause to be a condition precedent they must say so quite clearly.[30] Thus, in *Re Bradley and Suffolk Accident*[31] a term in an employer's liability policy that the assured should keep a proper wages book was held to be merely a collateral agreement relating to the adjustment of premium, the breach of which would not discharge the insurers from liability. So in *Stoneham* v. *Ocean, Railway and General*[32] it was held that a stipulation that "in case of fatal accident notice must be given to the company within seven days" was not a condition precedent to recovery. In the absence of such notice the company could only recover damages for the increased expenses of investigation.

2. WARRANTIES AND REPRESENTATIONS

6–07 Meaning of "warranty" in insurance law

From an early date insurers have not only relied on their right to avoid for misrepresentation, but have adopted the practice of inserting clauses in their policies to which they have given the name of "warranties," by which the right of the assured to recover is made to depend

---

[27] [1966] 1 W.L.R. 1334.
[28] Lord Denning M.R. and Danckwerts L.J.; Salmon L.J. *dubitante.*
[29] *Morrison* v. *Universal Marine* (1873) L.R. 8 Ex. 197.
[30] Rowlatt J. in *Jones and James* v. *Provincial* (1929) 46 T.L.R. 71, 73.
[31] [1912] 1 K.B. 415.
[32] (1887) 19 Q.B.D. 237.

upon the existence of a given fact or state of things defined in the clause. By this device the insurers are able to grant policies without troubling to make inquiries about matters covered by warranties.

The use of the word "warranty" in this sense should be clearly dis- **6–08** tinguished from its use in other branches of the law of contract. The usual use of the term is to denote a promise, collateral to the main contract,[33] breach of which entitles the party aggrieved only to damages, leaving him still liable to perform his part of the main contract. A warranty in a policy of insurance, on the other hand, corresponds with a condition in any other contract,[34] and breach of it entitles the party aggrieved to repudiate his liability under the rest of the contract as from the date of breach. In relation to contracts of insurance the two words, condition and warranty, are often used interchangeably.[35]

Terms of Marine Insurance Act   6–09

Since the common law of insurance has been developed mainly by marine decisions it is apposite to set out the result concisely stated in section 33 to 35 of the Marine Insurance Act 1906:

Section 33 (*nature of warranty*):

(1) A warranty, in the following sections relating to warranties, means *a promissory warranty*, that is to say, a warranty by which the *assured undertakes* that some particular thing shall or shall not be done, *or* that some condition shall be fulfilled, or whereby he *affirms* or negatives the existence of a particular state of facts.

(2) A warranty may be *express or implied*.[36]

(3) A warranty, as above defined, is a condition which must be *exactly complied with*, whether it be material to the risk or not. If it be not so complied with, then, subject to any express provision in the policy, the insurer is discharged from liability as from the date of the breach of warranty, but without prejudice in any liability incurred by him before that date.

Section 34 (*when breach of warranty excused*):

(1) Non-compliance with a warranty is excused when, by reason of a *change of circumstances*, the warranty ceases to be applicable to the circumstances of the contract, or when compliance with the warranty is rendered *unlawful* by any subsequent law.

(2) Where a warranty is broken, the assured cannot avail himself of the defence that the breach has been *remedied*, and the warranty complied with, before loss.

(3) A breach of warranty may be *waived* by the insurer.

Section 35 (*express warranties*):

(1) An express warranty may be in any form of words from which the intention to warrant is to be inferred.

(2) An express warranty must be included in, or written upon the policy, or must be contained in some document incorporated by reference into the policy.

---

[33] Viscount Haldane in *Dawsons* v. *Bonnin* [1922] 2 A.C. 413, 423.
[34] Lord Wright in *Provincial Insurance* v. *Morgan* [1933] A.C. 240, 253, 254.
[35] See *Barnard* v. *Faber* [1893] 1 Q.B. 340, *per* A. L. Smith L.J. at p. 345 and *per* Bowen L.J. at pp. 343, 344; *Ellinger* v. *Mutual Life* [1905] 1 K.B. 31, *per* Collins M.R. at p. 35 and *per* Stirling J. at pp. 37, 38; Cave L.C. in *Palatine* v. *Gregory* [1926] A.C. 90, 93.
[36] Implied warranties are relevant only to marine insurance: see *infra*. § 6–21.

(3) An express warranty does not exclude an implied warranty, unless it be inconsistent therewith.[37]

There follows, in sections 36 to 41, consideration of implied warranties, such as neutrality, seaworthiness and legality, pertinent only to marine insurance.

6–10 Exact compliance

A warranty must always be exactly[38] complied with. It makes no difference that a breach of it occurred without the fault,[39] or even the knowledge,[40] of the assured, or owing to someone else's fault,[41] or that the risk is not increased by its breach.[42] It does not matter if the loss is totally unconnected with it, and would have happened in any event.[43] Thus where it was warranted under a motor policy that the assured would "take all reasonable steps to maintain the vehicle in an efficient condition," and he removed the foot-brake, leaving only a hand-brake, and an accident occurred, it was held that he was not entitled to recover, although the exact cause of the accident could not be ascertained.[44] Moreover, even a temporary breach of warranty which is remedied by the date of the loss will afford a defence to the insurer.[45]

6–11   It follows from the rule that a warranty must be exactly complied with, that exact compliance with it is enough. Thus, where a policy on cotton mills contained a warranty that they should be worked by day only, the mere turning of one steam engine in them during the night was held not to be a breach.[46] The working of the part of a mill is not the working of the mill within the meaning of such a warranty.[47] But though only exact compliance is necessary, the ordinary rules of construction apply in determining what is exact compliance. Thus in *Condogianis* v. *Guardian*[48] the assured was asked if he had made claims before and if so when and on what company. He replied, "Yes. 1917. Ocean," and warranted his answer to be true. He had also made other claims. It was held by the Privy Council that although his answer was literally true in an academic sense, it was nevertheless untrue in the eyes of the law, because on a fair and reasonable construction of the answer it was not true.

6–12   Similarly, where a proposal in writing for the insurance of a motor charabanc against accident was made and signed with a warranty that the statements and particulars contained in it were true, and reference

---

[37] This is necessarily relevant only to marine insurance.

[38] Lord Mansfield in *De Hahn* v. *Hartley* (1786) 1 T.R. 343, 345, 346; see also M.I.A. 1906, s.33(3).

[39] *Philips* v. *Baillie* (1784) 3 Doug. K.B. 374.

[40] *Trickett* v. *Queensland Insurance* [1936] A.C. 159, 165, *per* Lord Alness; Lord Mackenzie in *Hutchison* v. *National Loan Fund Life* (1845) 7 D. (Ct. of Sess.) 467, 476.

[41] *Worsley* v. *Wood* (1976) 6 T.R. 710.

[42] *Newcastle Fire* v. *Macmorran* (1815) 3 Dow. 225.

[43] *Maynard* v. *Rhode* (1824) 1 C. & P. 360; *Glen* v. *Lewis* (1853) 8 Ex. 607; *Foley* v. *Tabor* (1861) 2 F. & F. 663; *Beacon Life* v. *Gibb* (1862) 1 Moo.P.C.C.(N.S.) 73.

[44] *Jones and James* v. *Provincial* (1929) 46 T.L.R. 71.

[45] M.I.A. 1906, s.34(2).

[46] *Whitehead* v. *Price* (1835) 2 Cr.M. & R. 447.

[47] *Mayall* v. *Mitford* (1837) 6 Ad. & El. 670.

[48] [1921] 2 A.C. 125; see also *Cazenove* v. *British Equitable* (1859) 6 C.B.(N.S.) 437; *Holt's Motors* v. *South-East Lancashire Insurance* (1930) 35 Com.Cass. 281.

was made in it to a previous accident in 1920, and a statement that damage to cattle belonging to third parties was measured at £80, but it was not stated that there had been any damage to the car, and it was proved at the trial that a sum of £45 had been paid for damage to the car, as well as a sum of £70 for damage to cattle, it was held that that was a wilful misstatement invalidating the policy.[49]

But where a man was asked whether he had been insured before, it was held that this question referred only to the premises which he was then proposing to insure, and that the answer "No" was therefore true although he had taken out other insurances on other premises.[50]

It was held that, where a man was questioned as to his calling, and described himself as an "esquire" whereas he was in fact engaged in trade as an ironmonger and said nothing about it, this did not amount to a statement false in fact.[51] At most he had not stated all that he might have stated; but that only made his statement imperfect, not untrue,[52] and the court would not deem such an omission to amount to a misrepresentation. Again, where the assured warranted that is security procedures would not be "varied" it was held that isolated charges did not amount to variation,[53] and an occupancy warranty does not mean that premises may never be left unattended.[54]

In fact, the question whether or not a warranty has been broken, once the facts have been ascertained, is always simply one of construction of the words constituting the warranty.[55] The question is therefore one of law for the court.[56]

Opinions 6–13

It may often be difficult to determine whether the assured has warranted a state of affairs or, in the alternative, the state of his mind. The tendency of the courts has been to treat questions apparently eliciting the assured's opinopn as demanding statments of fact. Thus where the assured was asked whether he was temperate it was held that he had warranted a matter of fact rather than of opinion,[57] and an assured who warranted "no known adverse facts" was held to have warranted that there were no adverse facts of which he ought reasonably to have known.[58]

Burden of proof 6–14

The burden of proving that a warranty has been broken lies upon the insurers.[59] It follows that, if they dispute the assured's right to recover

---

[49] *Furey* v. *Eagle Star* [1922] W.C. & Ins.Rep. 149, 225.
[50] *Golding* v. *Royal London Auxiliary Insurance* (1914) 30 T.L.R. 350.
[51] *Perrins* v. *Marine & General Travellers' Insurance* (1859) 2 E. & E. 317.
[52] *Ibid.* at p. 323.
[53] *Mint Security* v. *Blair* [1982] 1 Lloyd's Rep. 188.
[54] *Hair* v. *Prudential* [1980] 1 Lloyd's Rep. 52.
[55] Lord Watson in *Thomson* v. *Weems* (1884) 9 App.Cas. 671, 683, 687; cited in *Condogianis* v. *Guardian* [1921] 2 A.C. 125, 131; see, *e.g. Simmonds* v. *Cockell* [1920] 1 K.B. 843; *Provincial Insurance* v. *Morgan* [1933] A.C. 240, 247, 255, 256.
[56] Avory J. in *Dunn* v. *Ocean Accident* (1933) 45 Ll.L.R. 276, 280, affirmed, 47 Ll.L.R. 129.
[57] *Thompson* v. *Weems* (1884) 9 App.Cas. 671.
[58] *Kelsall* v. *Allstate Insurance* (1987) *The Times*, March 20.
[59] *Stebbing* v. *Liverpool & London & Globe* [1917] 2 K.B. 433, 438; *Bond Air Services* v. *Hill* [1955] 2 Q.B. 417.

on the policy on the ground that he stated in the proposals that he had
not had certain diseases, whereas he in fact had one of them at the time,
they will be obliged to give particulars of the symptoms of the disease
alleged.[60]

6-15 Materiality irrelevant

The great advantage of warranties to insurers is that their breach
entitles them to repudiate quite irrespective of their materiality. A misrepresentation, in order to entitle the insurer to avoid, must not only be
untrue but also material. A breach of warranty entitles him to repudiate
whether it is material or not.[61] This is one of the cardinal principles of
the law of contract which specially applies to insurance law. For once a
representation is given the force of a warranty it becomes a condition of
the contract, and it is not then of any importance whether or not it is
material; the parties would not have made it a part of the contract if they
had not thought it material, and they have a right to determine for themselves what they shall deem to be material.[62] Thus in *Dawsons* v. *Bonnin*,[63] a motor-vehicle case, a misrepresentation by the assured as to the
place where a vehicle was garaged was held to be immaterial, but the
assured was precluded by it from recovering under the policy since he
had warranted it to be true. Again, in *Forsakringsaktieselskapet Vesta* v.
Butcher[64] the House of Lords accepted that as a matter of English law
the insurer of a fish farm could treat its obligations as discharged by
the assured's failure to maintain a twenty-four hour watch, even
though the presence of a watch could not possibly have averted or
minimised the loss by storm damage. Lord Griffiths described the principle of law involved as "One of the less attractive features of English
insurance law."[65]

6-16 Other advantages to insurers

Other advantages of making representations warranties are: (i) The
insurer need not, if they are untrue, avoid the whole contract, but can
simply deny liability on it, and can rely on an arbitration clause, if one is
in the policy. (ii) He will have no difficulty in proving that the assured
made a misrepresentation, if the contract containing the warranty is
resolved into writing, for extrinsic evidence will be admissible to vary it.
But where the insurer relies on answers to questions by the assured strict
proof is necessary as to what the assured said at the time, even though
the answers were reduced into writing and signed.[66]

Having regard to these advantages it is not surprising to find the

---

[60] *Marshall* v. *Emperor Life* (1865) L.R. 1 Q.B. 35; *Girdlestone* v. *North British* (1870) L.R. 11 Eq.
197.
[61] M.I.A. 1906, s.33(3). See Lord Mansfield in *Pawson* v. *Watson* (1778) 2 Cowp. 785, 788; Eldon
L.C. in *Newcastle Fire* v. *Macmorran* (1815) 3 Dow. H.L. 225, 263; Cranworth L.C. in *Anderson* v.
Fitzgerald (1853) 4 H.L.C. 484, 503, 504; Viscount Dunedin in *Glicksman* v. *Lancashire & General*
[1927] A.C. 139, 143.
[62] Lord Blackburn in *Thomson* v. *Weems* (1884) 9 App.Cas. 671, 683, 684, cited by Viscount Haldane in *Dawsons* v. *Bonnin* [1922] 2 A.C. 413, 423.
[63] *Supra.*
[64] [1989] 1 All E.R. 402.
[65] *Ibid.* at p. 406.
[66] *Joel* v. *Law Union* [1908] 2 K.B. 863.

assured's answers in the proposal form being given the force of warranties in the case of most forms of insurance.[67] This practice might operate unfairly to the assured, and has been condemned by the judiciary from time to time,[68] but their condemnation has not prevented its development in this country. Legislation has however proved unnecessary[69] as no reputable English insurer would normally rely on a purely technical defence to meet an honest claim, and insurers of consumer risks have in any event agreed not to reject a claim for breach of warranty unless the breach was causative of the loss.[70] In Canada, legislation has been enacted to limit the unbounded right of the parties at common law to make whatever warranties they choose,[71] and the conversion of immaterial representations into warranties has been prohibited.[72]

3. HOW WARRANTIES ARE MADE

The methods by which representations have been made warranties have **6–17** exhibited many variations, some major and some minor, in detail.[73] Warranties may be included in the terms of the policy itself. They may be written on its face, in the margin for instance,[74] or incorporated in it by reference to another document, generally the proposal form. In policies of marine insurance any statement of fact bearing upon the risk introduced into the written policy is, by whatever words and in whatever place, to be construed as a warranty,[75] but this rule is not, in this extreme form, applicable to other policies.[76] No particular form of words is, however, necessary so long as the intention is clear,[77] and, therefore, it is of little importance whether the words "warranty" or "warranted" are used or not.[78]

Clauses providing that something shall be a condition precedent to the insurers' liability,[79] or that if certain things are not done the policy will be void,[80] or of no force, or of no effect, or that all benefits under it will be forfeited[81] have been held to have the effect of warranties.

---

[67] Greer L.J. in *Holt's Motors* v. *South-East Lancashire Insurance* (1930) 35 Com.Cas. 281, 287.

[68] Lord St. Leonards in *Anderson* v. *Fitzgerald* (1853) 4 H.L.C. 484, 507, 508; Fletcher Moulton L.J. in *Joel* v. *Law Union* [1908] 2 K.B. 863, 885.

[69] But, as regards industrial assurance, see Industrial Assurance and Friendly Societies Act 1948, s.9, requiring a proposer only truly to state his knowledge and belief as regards his state of health.

[70] *Infra.* para. 6–24 *et seq.*

[71] See, *e.g.* Ontario Insurance Act 1914, s.156, discussed in *Mutual Life of New York* v. *Ontario Metal Products* [1925] A.C. 344; New Brunswick Fire Insurance Policies Act 1913, discussed in *Palatine Insurance* v. *Gregory* [1926] A.C. 90; Quebec Insurance Act 1909.

[72] See *Mutual Life* v. *Ontario Products, supra.*

[73] Lord Wright in *Provincial Insurance* v. *Morgan* [1933] A.C. 240, 251.

[74] Lord Mansfield in *Bean* v. *Stupart* (1778) 1 Doug. K.B. 11, 14; *Birrell* v. *Dryer* (1884) 9 App.Cas. 345.

[75] See M.I.A. 1906, s.35, *supra*, § 6–09.

[76] Lord Blackburn in *Thomson* v. *Weems* (1884) 9 App.Cas. 671, 684.

[77] Channel B. in *Wheelton* v. *Hardisty* (1858) 8 E. & B. 232, 302.

[78] *Bean* v. *Stupart* (1778) 1 Doug. 11; *Sceales* v. *Scanlan* (1843) 6 L.R.Ir. 367, 371, 372, *per* Lefroy B.; A. L. Smith L.J. in *Barnard* v. *Faber* [1893] 1 Q.B. 340, 345; Lord Parmoor in *Union Insurance of Canton* v. *Wills* [1916] A.C. 281, 287 (P.C.); Viscount Finlay in *Dawsons* v. *Bonnin* [1922] 2 A.C. 413, 428, 429.

[79] *Jones and James* v. *Provincial* (1929) 46 T.L.R. 71; *Allen* v. *Universal Automobile Insurance* (1933) 45 Ll.L.R. 55, 57, 58, *per* Lord Wright.

[80] *Sceales* v. *Scanlan* (1843) 6 L.R.Ir. 367, 375; *Glen* v. *Lewis* (1858) 8 Ex. 607.

[81] *Glen* v. *Lewis, supra.*

6–18 Answers in proposals

In *Thomson* v. *Weems*[82] the policy itself provided that if anything averred in the declaration "shall be untrue, this policy shall be void," and it was held that these words had the effect of giving the assured's statements in the declaration the force of warranties. In *Dawsons* v. *Bonnin*[83] the same effect was held to result from a recital in the policy that the proposal should be the "basis of the contract." In *Anderson* v. *Fitzgerald*[84] only 14 out of 27 answers in the proposal were made the subject of a warranty in the policy. Even where the whole proposal is made the basis of the contract, this will not convert representations not contained in the proposal, such as the answers of the assured to questions put by the medical officer of the company, into warranties.[85]

The general scheme now in use is that there is a proposal form, signed by the assured, containing various particulars and answers to various questions, and a declaration that the answers are to be the basis of the contract and an agreement to accept the company's policy. The policy itself contains a recital incorporating the proposal and declaration.[86] The use of "basis" clauses has to some extent been limited under the 1977 Statements of Insurance Practice.[87]

6–19 Warranties need not be incorporated in policy

But, other than in marine insurance[88] there is no need for a warranty to be incorporated into the policy itself, by reference or at all. There is no reason why a policy should not be signed subject even to an oral condition or warranty that is not even referred to in the policy.[89] An answer in the proposal form will have the effect of a warranty if it is clear, either from the terms of the form or otherwise, that it was the basis on which the parties contracted.[90] The practice of warranting the truth of the assured's answer in this way, without any reference to the matter in the policy, is especially common in the case of insurances other than life,[91] to which the practice of converting representations into warranties has in the course of time extended. The practice is, however, a most unwelcome one, as should the assured not have kept a copy of the proposal form he may be under a grave disadvantage, especially where representations in the proposal of a promissory nature are made into warranties and relate to the assured's future conduct.[92]

6–20   Even the practice of incorporating the proposal form into the policy by reference has been frequently criticised by the judges as puzzling to the assured, who may find it difficult to fit the disjointed parts together in such a way as to get a true and complete conspectus of what his rights

---

[82] (1884) 9 App.Cas. 671.

[83] [1922] 2 A.C. 413.

[84] (1853) 4 H.L.C. 484.

[85] *Joel* v. *Law Union* [1908] 2 K.B. 863.

[86] Lord Wright in *Provincial* v. *Morgan* [1933] A.C. 240, 251.

[87] See *infra* paras. 6–29 *et seq.*

[88] M.I.A. 1906, s.35(2), *supra.* para. 6–09.

[89] Walton J. in *Anglo-Californian Bank* v. *London & Provincial Marine* (1904) 10 Com.Cas. 1.

[90] *Duckett* v. *Williams* (1834) 2 Cr. & M. 348; *Condogianis* v. *Guardian* [1921] 2 A.C. 125; *Rozanes* v. *Bowen* (1928) 32 Ll.L.R. 98.

[91] See, *e.g. Locker and Woolf* v. *Western Australian Insurance* [1936] 1 K.B. 408.

[92] See *Beauchamp* v. *National Mutual* [1937] 3 All E.R. 19.

and duties are and that acts on his part may involve a forfeiture of the insurance.[93] The practice of not even referring in the policy to a proposal which the assured has warranted to contain true answers is even more objectionable. The marine rule that an express warranty must be included in the policy or incorporated by reference into it[94] might well have been applied generally.

If there is any doubt, the answer to a question in the proposal form will be construed as a representation and not as a warranty,[95] especially where it is not material.[96] But, once the assured has clearly warranted his answers to be true, the fact that there is a clause in the policy to the effect that *material* misrepresentations make the policy void, will not assist him. The insurers will still be entitled to repudiate the policy if his answers are untrue, whether they are material or not.[97] This is even so where the warranty only appears in the proposal form and no reference is made to it in a policy containing such a clause.[98] But where a provision in a policy that the proposal should be the "basis" of the contract went on to stipulate that false and fraudulent answers should make the contract void it was held that a false but not fraudulent answer did not do so, for the insurers had thus given a meaning of their own to "basis" of the contract.[99]

4. KINDS OF WARRANTY

No implied warranties   6–21

Implied warranties, such as the warranty of seaworthiness, which occur in marine insurance,[1] have no counterpart in other branches of insurance. There is no implied warranty in a fire policy, for instance, that the assured will do nothing to increase the risk.[2] The fact that the life insured under a life policy is already dead may make the policy void,[3] but this is on the ground of a mutual mistake of fact: there is no implied warranty in such a policy that the life insured is in good health or even alive. An implied term that the risk will not materially change may, however, be imported into an agreement to issue a policy.[4] In the same way the marine warranty of legality[5] has no non-marine counterpart.[6]

Warranties relating to present and future   6–22

Warranties may be divided into (i) warranties relating to a fact or state of affairs stated to exist at the time of the contract; and (ii) warranties as to future facts or states of affairs.

---

[93] Lord Wright in *Provincial* v. *Morgan* [1933] A.C. 240, 252.
[94] M.I.A. 1906, s.35(2) *supra*, § 6–09; *Bean* v. *Stupart* (1778) 1 Doug.K.B. 11, 12n.
[95] Channell B. in *Wheelton* v. *Hardisty* (1858) 8 E. & B. 232, 302.
[96] Viscount Finlay in *Dawsons* v. *Bonnin* [1922] 2 A.C. 413, 429.
[97] *Dawsons* v. *Bonnin*, *supra*.
[98] *Condogianis* v. *Guardian* [1921] 2 A.C. 125.
[99] *Scottish Provident* v. *Boddam* (1893) 9 T.L.R. 385.
[1] See *infra*. Chap. 23.
[2] *Shaw* v. *Robberds* (1837) 6 A. & E. 75.
[3] *Pritchard* v. *Merchant's Life* (1858) 3 C.B.(N.S.) 622; see § 1–33, *supra*.
[4] *Harrington* v. *Pearl Life* (1914) 30 T.L.R. 613.
[5] M.I.A 1906, s.41.
[6] *Euro-Diam* v. *Bathurst* [1988] 2 All E.R. 23.

(i) *Warranties as to existing facts*, *e.g.* that the assured is in good health. Such a warranty will be given prior to the making of the contract, so that if the insurer exercises his right to terminate the contract as from the date of breach the effect will be to prevent the insurer from ever having come on risk. Consequently a breach of such a warranty is similar in its legal effect to an ordinary pre-contractual material misrepresentation,[7] and the premium will not be recoverable.[8]

(ii) *Warranties as to the future*, *e.g.* that the assured will not venture abroad, or that he will fit a mortise lock within a given time to his front door. The breach of such a warranty does not prevent the risk from running and leaves untouches any right which has already vested in the assured at the time of the breach.[9] Thus he may still claim for a partial loss that occurred before the breach, and there is no possibility of return of premium unless the contract stipulates otherwise. Representations can never have continuing effect, even if they relate to the future,[10] unless they can be construed as warranties.[11]

6–23   Where the answers given by the assured are warranted to be true the question whether or not there has been a breach will often turn upon whether or not the question and answer are construed as relating solely to the present, or also to the future, state of affairs. The cases necessarily turn on their own facts.

In a number of cases the warranty has been held to relate to the present only. Thus, in a fidelity policy the question "How often is [the assured] required to send statements of cash received?"[12] and in an employer's liability policy the question "Is your machinery properly fenced?"[13] were held not to be seeking promises as to the future but merely asking about existing states of affairs. A similar interpretation was put upon the question "Are any of your drivers under 21?"[14] In *Grant* v. *Aetna Insurance*[15] a vessel was insured and was described by the assured as "now lying in the T dock and intended to navigate the St. Lawrence as a freight boat, and to be laid up for the winter in a place approved by this company." The vessel was destroyed 11 months later by fire, and had remained in dock the whole time, and the Privy Council held that the words were not a warranty as to the ship's future movements but merely expressed an intention that the vessel should navigate as mentioned. More recently, in *Hair* v. *Prudential*[16] a warranty that premises were occupied was held not to amount to a promise that this state of affairs would continue.

By contrast, the courts have held that questions relating to the usual

---

[7] *Anderson* v. *Fitzgerald* (1853) 4 H.L.C. 484.

[8] See *infra.* 7–15 *et seq.*

[9] M.I.A. 1906, s.33(3); Lord Parmoor in *Union Insurance of Canton* v. *Wills* [1916] 1 A.C. 281, 286, 287.

[10] *Shaw* v. *Robberds* (1837) 6 A. & E. 75; *Benham* v. *United Guarantee* (1852) 7 Ex. 744.

[11] *Beauchamp* v. *National Mutual* [1937] 3 All E.R. 19.

[12] *Hearts of Oak* v. *Law Union* [1936] 2 All E.R. 619.

[13] *Woodfall* v. *Rimmer & Moyle* [1941] 3 All E.R. 304.

[14] *Sweeney* v. *Kennedy* (1949) 82 Ll.L.R. 295.

[15] (1862) 15 Moo. P.C. 516.

[16] [1983] 2 Lloyd's Rep. 667.

address at which vehicles will be garaged,[17] to the use of explosives in a business[18] and to the storage of inflammable material[19] all sought to obtain promises as to the future and were not merely statements of existing intention.

It should be noted that the mere fact that a warranty is described as **6–24** "promissory" does not mean that it relates to the future as opposed to a present state of affairs. Section 33(1) of the Marine Insurance Act 1906 indeed describes all warranties as promissory, and it is clear that the word is here used in a collective sense, seeking to distinguish warranties from excepted perils.[20] So, also in non-marine insurance law, any representation which is warranted to be true is sometimes spoken of as being, for that reason, of a promissory nature.[21] Goddard J. in *Hearts of Oak* v. *Law Union*[22] speaks of those clauses which "have been called in the House of Lords promissory," as if members of that House had used the term to describe warranties as to the future. A perusal of their decisions,[23] however, shows that the adjective "promissory" has been used by their Lordships only to describe those representations which amount to warranties.

Clauses descriptive of the risk   **6–25**
Such "promissory warranties" or conditions precedent to the insurer's liability must be clearly distinguished from clauses in a contract describing or limiting the risk. It is customary for a policy, having defined the risk, to cut down its scope by means of exceptions or excepted perils. Such excepted perils are frequently printed among the conditions of the policy. They are not however conditions in the usual sense, but rather operate as limitations on the risk covered by the policy, exempting the insurers from liability for certain kinds of loss which would otherwise be covered by it.[24] So the occurrence of an excepted peril will not preclude the assured from recovery unless it is also the proximate cause of the loss.[25] In the case of the breach of a promissory warranty the cause of the loss is immaterial, and any breach of the warranty entitles the insurers to repudiate even if it has had nothing whatever to do with the loss.

Thus, in *Provincial Insurance* v. *Morgan*,[26] the assured stated that a **6–26** lorry he insured was to be used to carry coal, and the cover was limited to transportation in connection with his business. He also warranted his answers to be true. He occasionally used the lorry to carry timber, but was involved in an accident when carrying coal only. It was held that the

---

[17] *Dawsons* v. *Bonnin* [1922] A.C. 413.
[18] *Beauchamp* v. *National Mutual* [1937] 3 All E.R. 19.
[19] Hales v. *Reliance Fire* [1960] 2 Lloyd's Rep. 391.
[20] See Scrutton L.J. in *Morgan* v. *Provincial* [1932] 2 K.B. 70, 80.
[21] See, *e.g.* Lord Wright in *Provincial* v. *Morgan* [1933] A.C. 340, 254.
[22] [1936] 2 All E.R. 619, 623.
[23] *Dawsons* v. *Bonnin*, *Provincial* v. *Morgan*, *supra.*
[24] Duke L.J. in *Re Hooley Hill Rubber and Royal* [1920] 1 K.B. 254, 274; Lord Sumner in *Lake* v. *Simmons* [1927] A.C. 487, 507.
[25] See §§ 4–30 *et seq.*, *supra.*
[26] [1933] A.C. 240.

effect of his statement was only to limit the risk to the use of the lorry while carrying coal, and that he could recover. His statement did not amount to a warranty that the lorry would only be used to carry coal.[27] Similarly, in another motor-vehicle case, a statement by the assured that a cab was only to be driven in one shift per 24 hours was held to be only a description of the risk, and was not construed as a warranty.[28]

And in *De Maurier (Jewels)* v. *Bastion Insurance Co.*[29] Donaldson J. held that a "warranty" regarding locks and alarms fitted to vehicles was "not of a promissory character"; it delimited and was part of the description of the risk.

The principle is not limited to motor cases. In *C.T.N. Cash & Carry* v. *General Accident*[30] an obligation on the assured—described in the policy as a "warranty"—to ensure that its cash kiosk was attended at all times during business hours, was held to be a term descriptive of the risk. This finding permitted the insurers to deny liability for a loss occurring while the kiosk was unattended, for had the term been a warranty it was clear that the insurers had waived its breach.

On the other hand in *Palatine Insurance* v. *Gregory*,[31] fire insurances on timber were made "subject to the fifty feet clear space clause attached." The clear space clause read: "Warranted by the assured that a clear space of fifty feet shall hereafter be maintained between the property hereby insured and any sawmill." It was held that this clause amounted to a promissory warranty, and was not merely a limitation on the cover afforded.

5. BREACH OF WARRANTY

6–27 The insurer's rights

Section 33(3) of the Marine Insurance Act 1906 provides that the insurer "is discharged from liability as from the date of the breach of warranty." It is nevertheless clear that in both marine and non-marine insurance breach of warranty does not operate as an event which automatically discharges the insurer, but rather merely gives the insurer the option to terminate the contract as from the date of breach. This was made clear by the Court of Appeal in *The Good Luck*,[32] in which it was held that the insurer's contractual obligation to inform the assured's mortgagee if the insurance should "cease" did not apply to a case in which the assured's breach of warranty remained under consideration by the insurer.

Where, however, the insurer wishes to deny liability following the assured's breach of warranty, he must determine the policy: it is not open to the insurer to affirm the policy and to reject the assured's

---

[27] Lord Wright in *Provincial* v. *Morgan* [1933] A.C. 240, 254.
[28] *Farr* v. *Motor Traders Mutual* [1920] 3 K.B. 669; see also *Roberts* v. *Anglo-Saxon Insurance* (1927) 43 T.L.R. 359.
[29] [1967] 2 Lloyd's Rep. 550, 558, and see *Facer* v. *Vehicle and General Ins. Co.* [1965] 1 Lloyd's Rep. 113.
[30] [1989] 1 Lloyd's Rep. 299.
[31] [1926] A.C. 90, 92.
[32] *Bank of Nova Scotia* v. *Hellenic Mutual* [1989] 2 Lloyd's Rep. 238.

claim.[33] This rule is inconvenient for insurers and unjust for assureds, and is commonly overcome by policy wording which renders compliance with all warranties as a condition precedent to the assured's right to recover. Under such wording the insurer may terminate the policy for breach of warranty, or simply refuse to pay under the condition precedent while maintaining the policy.[34]

The insurer's right to terminate for breach of warranty is not removed where the breach has been remedied by the time of the loss.[35] This follows from the principle that a breach of warranty is operative even though not causative of the loss.

The assured's rights   6–28

Where the assured is in breach of warranty he may be able to make out one of three defences. First, the insurer may have waived compliance with the warranty, for example, by itself issuing a further policy to the assured in breach of a warranty in the original policy to the effect that the assured would not procure further insurance.[36] Secondly, the insurer may, following breach, waive such breach or be estopped from denying liability.[37] Thirdly, non-compliance with a warranty is excused where the warranty ceases in the circumstances to be applicable or where compliance with it would not be lawful.[38]

The assured will not be entitled to a return of his premium where the insurer terminates the policy for breach of a continuing warranty, as in such a case the risk has been run. Morever, if the insurer terminates the policy for breach of a warranty as to present facts, the risk will not attach and the assured can reclaim his premium provided that he had not been guilty of fraudulent misstatement.[39]

6. STATEMENTS OF INSURANCE PRACTICE

The background and scope of the Association of British Insurers *State-* 6–29
ments of Insurance Practice of 1977 were discussed in Chapter 5. It will be recalled that there are two Statements, one for life assurance and one for general business, in each case applicable only to "consumer policies." The Statements have some impact on the practical application of the law of warranties.

Statment of (Non-life) Insurance Practice   6–30

This statement has the following effects on the law of warranties:

(a) The declaration at the foot of the proposal form is to be limited to completion according to the proposer's knowledge and belief.

(b) So far as is practicable insurers are to avoid asking questions

---

[33] *West* v. *National Motor* [1955] 1 All E.R. 800; *C.T.N. Cash & Carry* v. *General Accident* [1989] 1 Lloyd's Rep. 299.

[34] *Mint Security* v. *Blair* [1982] 1 Lloyd's Rep. 188.

[35] M.I.A. 1906, s.34(2), codifying marine cases in which the vessel had ceased to be unseaworthy by the date of the loss: *Quebec Marine* v. *Commercial Bank of Canada* (1870) L.R. 3 P.C. 234.

[36] *Samuel* v. *Dumas* [1924] A.C. 431.

[37] For waiver and estoppel, see *supra*, § 6–04.

[38] M.I.A. 1906, s.34(1).

[39] See M.I.A. 1906, s.84: § 7–15 *et seq.*, *infra*.

which would required expert knowledge beyond that which the proposer could reasonably be expected to possess or obtain, or which would require a value judgment on the part of the proposer.

(c) Except where fraud, deception or negligence is involved, an insurer will not unreasonably repudiate liability to indemnify a policyholder on the grounds of a breach of warranty or condition where the circumstances of the loss are unconnected with the breach. This provision is not however, applicable to marine and aviation policies.

6–31 Statement of long-term Insurance Practice

This statement has the following effects on the law of warranties:

(a) An insurer is not unreasonably to reject a claim, although fraudulent misrepresentation will, and negligent misrepresentation may, result in rejection or adjustment of a claim.

(b) An insurer is not to reject a claim for misrepresentation of a matter outside the knowledge of the proposer.

(c) Insurers are to avoid asking questions which would require knowledge beyond that which the proposer could reasonably be expected to possess.

CHAPTER 7

THE PREMIUM

1. PAYMENT

THE premium is the price for which the insurer undertakes his liabilities. **7–01**
It may be a consideration other than a money payment; *e.g.* in a mutual
insurance it may consist of a liability to contribute to the losses of other
members of the mutual society.[1]

The Marine Insurance Act 1906, s.85(2) thus provides:

> "(2) The provisions of this Act relating to the premium do not apply to
> mutual insurance, but a guarantee, or such other arrangement as may be
> agreed upon, may be substituted for the premium."

A premium is in no respect a prerequisite of a contract of insurance:
all that is necessary is the undertaking by the insurer for good consideration. The policy may be by deed, in which case no premium or other
consideration flowing from the assured is necessary to render the insurer
bound.

The premium more usually, however, takes the form of a money payment. It has been defined as "a price paid adequate to the risk,"[2] but the
adequacy of the premium is purely the insurer's concern. The amount of
the premium may be of assistance, however, in showing the scope of the
policy,[3] for it is measured by the insurer's estimate of the risk formed
upon an average of his previous experience of similar risks,[4] together
with an allowance for office expenses and other charges and profit.[5]

It is generally the case that the precise amount of the premium is fixed
in advance of the commencement of the risk, although this is not always
so, particularly in respect of marine insurance. Section 31(1) of the Marine Insurance Act 1906 thus provides that if the parties have agreed to
determine a premium at some later date, but fail to do so, a reasonable
premium is payable. Further, many marine hulls and freight policies
contain provisions whereby the assured is "held covered" at a premium
to be arranged in specified circumstances in which the risk has
increased: here, section 31(2) of the Marine Insurance Act 1906 similarly stipulates that a reasonable premium is payable in the absence of
agreement between the parties. In determinining what is reasonable,
the courts will take account of market rates and the degree of extra risk
accepted by the insurer,[6] and may refuse to give effect to a "held

---

[1] *Lion Ins. Assocn.* v. *Tucker* (1883) 12 Q.B.D. 176, 187, *per* Brett M.R.; *Great Britain 100 A1 S.S. Insurance* v. *Wyllie* (1889) 22 Q.B.D. 710, 722, *per* Fry L.J.
[2] Lawrence J. in *Lucena* v. *Craufurd* (1806) 2 Bros. & P.N.R. 269, 301.
[3] Collins L.J. in *Re George and Goldsmiths' Insurance* [1899] 1 Q.B. 595, 611.
[4] Cockburn C.J. in *Chapman* v. *Pole* (1870) 22 L.T. 306, 307; Lord Blackburn in *Thomson* v. *Weems* (1884) 9 App.Cas. 671, 681.
[5] Lord Cairns in *Re Albert Life* (1871) L.R. 14 Eq. 72n.
[6] *Greenock S.S. Co.* v. *Maritime Insurance* [1903] 1 K.B. 367; *Mentz, Decker & Co.* v. *Maritime Insurance* [1910] 1 K.B. 132; *Hewitt* v. *London General* (1925) 23 Ll.L.R. 243.

covered" clause if the insurer can demonstrate that the risk had increased in a manner which was uninsurable on the market.[7]

7–02 Prepayment of premium

Actual payment of the premium is not necessary to the creation of a complete and binding contract of insurance, and a stipulation that the insurance shall not attach until the premium is paid will not be implied.[8] It is not uncommon, however, for insurers so to stipulate either in the policy,[9] or by some other means,[10] and the courts will enforce such a stipulation,[11] unless it has been waived by the insurers.[12] The mere fact that the policy both stipulates prepayment of the premium and, contrary to the truth, acknowledges receipt of it will not necessarily amount to such a waiver.[13] Where, however, such an acknowledgment is contained in the recital of a policy by deed, the company will be estopped from denying that the premium has in fact been paid.[14]

The Marine Insurance Act 1906, s.52, which is not applicable to other forms of policy, states:

> "Unless otherwise agreed, the duty of the assured or his agent to pay the premium, and the duty of the insurer to issue the policy to the assured or his agent, are concurrent conditions, and the insurer is not bound to issue the policy until payment or tender of the premium."

This provision does not prevent a contract from coming into being, but merely prevents its enforcement, as section 22 of the 1906 Act provides that evidence of a marine insurance contract is inadmissible unless embodied in a policy.

7–03 Mode of payment

The premium must be paid in money,[15] unless some other mode of payment is substituted by agreement.[16] Thus the manager of a company has no authority to accept a promissory note by way of premium.[17]

When the insurers accept money from the assured in circumstances from which it can reasonably be inferred that he intended the money, or some of it, to be applied in the payment of particular premiums, but the insurers fail to appropriate the money in their books to the premiums in question, they cannot afterwards complain that the premiums have not been paid.[18]

---

[7] *Liberian Insurance Agency* v. *Mosse* [1977] 2 Lloyd's Rep. 560.

[8] Mathew J. in *Kelly* v. *London & Staffordshire Fire* (1883) 1 Cab. & El. 47, 48.

[9] *Roberts* v. *Security Co.* [1897] 1 Q.B. 111; *Equitable Fire* v. *Ching Wo Hong* [1907] A.C. 96 (P.C.); *Re Yager & Guardian* (1912) 108 L.T. 38.

[10] *Looker* v. *Law Union* [1928] 1 K.B. 554 (in acceptance of assured's proposal).

[11] *Phoenix Life* v. *Sheridan* (1860) 8 H.L.C. 745.

[12] *Goit* v. *National Protection* (1844) 25 Barb.(N.Y.) 189; *Supple* v. *Cann* (1858) 9 Ir.C.L. 1; *Bodine* v. *Exchange Fire* (1872) 51 N.Y.App. 117; *Cooper* v. *Pacific Mutual* (1871) 8 Am.Rep. 705; *Hodge* v. *Security Insurance* (1884) 33 Hun.N.Y. 583; *Farnum* v. *Phoenix* (1890) 17 Am.St.Rep. 233.

[13] *Equitable Fire* v. *Ching Wo Hong, supra*; *Newis* v. *General Accident* (1910) 11 C.L.R. 620.

[14] *Roberts* v. *Security Co., supra*.

[15] *Montreal Assurance* v. *McGillivray* (1859) 13 Moo.P.C.C. 87; *London & Lancashire Life* v. *Fleming* [1897] A.C. 499. In fact insurers usually regularly accept payment by cheque, and in such circumstances they could hardly rely on default of a payment on the ground that it was not in cash. *Cf. Tankexpress* v. *Compagnie Financière* [1949] A.C. 76, 93, 98, 103.

[16] *Prince of Wales Life* v. *Harding* (1858) E.B. & E. 183.

[17] See n. 16.

[18] *Kirkpatrick* v. *South Australian Insurance* (1886) 11 App.Cas. 177 (P.C.).

If the insurers indicate a particular mode of paying the premium, the assured who complies with such request will not be responsible if the money is lost, providing he observes any instructions qualifying such request.[19] But the general rule is that a debtor must seek out and pay his creditor[20] and, therefore, if the assured chooses, for his own convenience, to send money, in any form, through the post, he does so at his own risk.[21] A request to use the post will, however, readily be implied,[22] but mere passive acceptance of money paid in this way will not amount to a request even if such course of dealing has been followed for a number of years.[23]

Payment of broker   7–04

Outside the sphere of marine insurance and also policies issued by Lloyd's, any dealings with the premium by the broker will be on behalf of the assured and not on behalf of the insurer. Consequently, if the assured makes payment to the broker, but the broker does not pass on such premium to the insurer, the insurer is not deemed to have received the premium. Similarly if the premium is not paid and the insurer brings an action for it, the assured is the proper defendant whether or not the broker has received the premium.[24] The position is, however, different in relation to marine policies and Lloyd's policies. The rule here is that the broker is personally liable to the insurer for the premium,[25] in accordance with the fiction that a premium received by the broker is deemed to have been paid by him to the insurer and loaned back to him by the insurer.[26] Losses nevertheless remain directly payable by the insurer to the assured and not to the broker.[27]

Many insurers and brokers operate an accounting system whereby all premiums are retained, and all losses paid, by the broker, and settlements are made between broker and insurer at the end of fixed accounting periods. It is the practice for policies to state that the premium has been received by the insurer even though this is not the case, and such a statement is binding as between insurer and assured but not as between insurer and broker.[28]

Days of grace   7–05

In cases in which the premium is payable periodically, or the policy is renewable by payment of a further premium, it is the custom of insurance companies to send the assured a reminder shortly before a premium falls due. They are, however, under no legal obligation to observe

---

[19] *Robb* v. *Gow Bros.* (1905) 8 F. (Ct. of Sess.) 90, 107.
[20] Lord Esher in *Norman* v. *Ricketts* (1886) 3 T.L.R. 182.
[21] *Pennington* v. *Crossley & Son* (1897) 77 L.T. 43.
[22] *Mitchell-Henry* v. *Norwich Union* [1918] 2 K.B. 67.
[23] See n. 21.
[24] *Wilson* v. *Avec Audio-Visual Equipment* [1974] 1 Lloyd's Rep. 81.
[25] M.I.A. 1906, s.53(1). The similar position in relation to Lloyd's was accepted without dispute in *Julian Praet* v. *Poland* [1960] 1 Lloyd's Rep. 416.
[26] *Edgar* v. *Fowler* (1803) 3 East 222; *Edgar* v. *Bumstead* (1809) 1 Camp. 411; *Universo Insurance of Milan* v. *Merchants Marine* [1897] 2 Q.B. 93. Differing juridical bases for the rule were put forward in *Power* v. *Butcher* (1829) 10 B. & C. 329.
[27] M.I.A. 1906, s.53(1).
[28] M.I.A. 1906, s.54.

this custom[29] unless they or their agents have, expressly or impliedly, undertaken to do so. But most of such policies allow a certain number of days—called "days of grace"[30]—beyond the due dates for the payment of premiums. Policies which give the assured the right to renew by paying a renewal premium nearly always contain such a provision enlarging the time in which the premium may be paid.

A provision of this kind does not extend the term of the insurance[31] or the time allowed to the assured for the doing of other acts or exercising other privileges, so that a clause in a life policy that where it had acquired a surrender value it should remain in force for "twelve calendar months from the date upon which the last premium became due" was held to mean 12 months from the commencement, not from the expiration, of the 30 days of grace allowed by the policy.[32]

7–06 Loss during days of grace

Whether or not the insurers will be liable where the premium is paid within the days of grace but after the occurrence of the loss depends on the facts of each case and requires careful consideration.

If the insurers have a right to refuse the renewal premium, and elect not to carry on with an insurance which they are not bound to renew, then it is clear that their liability will cease on the last day of the period for which the insurance was expressed to run, and the tender of the renewal premium by the assured during the days of grace will not alter the position.[33]

But where the assured has a right to continue with the policy a distinction must be drawn between cases in which the policy subsists until he forfeits his rights under it by non-payment of an instalment of the premium, and those cases in which the policy is renewable on payment by him of an additional premium. In the former case the insurers' liabilities continue throughout the days of grace. Thus, in *Stuart* v. *Freeman*[34] a life insurance policy was renewable annually, by payment of the appropriate premium, but instalments of the premium were payable quarterly, and the policy was liable to forfeiture on non-payment of such quarterly instalments within the days of grace allowed. The assured died within the days of grace and a quarterly instalment was duly paid later by an assignee of the policy. It was held he was entitled to recover. But judicial dicta in that case and in *Pritchard* v. *Merchant's Life*[35] conflict as to the position where the assured dies during the days of grace and before the payment of a *renewal* premium. In *Pritchard's* case the policy was revived both after the days of grace had expired and after the death of the assured, pursuant to an arrangement in the policy, and it was held that the insurers were not liable. It seems that the question must depend on the construction of each particular policy, and it is usual therefore to

---

[29] *Windus* v. *Tredegar* (1866) 15 L.T. 108.
[30] For a case where the last day of grace fell on Easter Day, see *Firth* v. *Western Life Ass.* (1957) 8 D.L.R. (2d) 129 (Can.Sup.Ct.).
[31] *Salvin* v. *James* (1805) 6 East 571.
[32] *McKenna* v. *City Life* [1919] 2 K.B. 491.
[33] *Tarleton* v. *Staniforth* (1794) 5 T.R. 695; *Simpson* v. *Accidental Death* (1857) 2 C.B.(N.S.) 257.
[34] [1903] 1 K.B. 47.
[35] (1858) 3 C.B.(N.S.) 622.

insert a provision that the insurers will be liable in the event of death during the days of grace but before payment of the premium, to put the matter beyond doubt.

Insurers' remedies for non-payment of premium   7–07

(i) *Action.* Where a premium becomes due to the insurers under a contract of insurance they are entitled to bring an action for its payment. The assured cannot escape liability for it on the ground that, as by the terms of the contract the insurers are not liable for any loss which may happen before it is paid, there is no consideration for his promise to pay it[36]; for the original contract of insurance supplies such consideration. Thus, where a policy was expressed to be treated as a renewal contract unless notice was given by either party not to renew, and no such notice was given, the assured was held liable to pay the renewal premium in a claim for it by the insurer.[37]

In an Irish case[38] it was decided that the insurer's only remedy in such a case is an action for damages, and not an action for the premium since he has not been on risk, but in English law the insurer is entitled to sue the assured for the premium itself.[39]

(ii) *Forfeiture.* Where the risk, or the renewal of the risk, does not 7–08 begin to run until the premium, or the renewal premium, is paid no provision for forfeiture is necessary. Where, however, the premium is payable by instalments while the risk is being run it is usual for the insurers to insert a provision in the policy providing for its forfeiture in the event of premiums not being duly paid, subject to any days of grace which may be allowed. Such a forfeiture will be enforced by the courts unless the insurers are estopped by their conduct from relying on it.[40]

2. REPAYMENT

Principles generally applicable   7–09

The general rule applicable to claims by the assured for the return of premium is that if the insurers have never been on risk they have not earned the premium and ought to return it. "Equity," says Lord Mansfield,[41] "implies a condition that the insurer shall not receive the price of running a risk if he runs none." The principle has been pushed to great lengths in marine cases. In such cases "if the risk is not run, though it is by the neglect or even the fault of the party insuring, yet the insurer shall not retain the premium,"[42] although there appears to be no English decision applying the principle in this wide form to non-marine policies of insurance.

---

[36] *Municipal Mutual* v. *Pontefract* (1917) 116 L.T. 671.
[37] *Solvency Mutual* v. *York* (1858) 3 H. & N. 588.
[38] *Phoenix Insurance* v. *Four Courts Hotel* [1935] Ir.R. 628.
[39] *General Accident* v. *Cronk* (1901) 17 T.L.R. 233.
[40] See *Scottish Equitable Life* v. *Buist* (1877) 4 R. (Ct. of Sess.) 1076; (1878) 5 R. (Ct. of Sess.) 64 (H.L.); *Wing* v. *Harvey* (1854) 5 De G.M. & G. 265.
[41] *Stevenson* v. *Shaw* (1761) 3 Burr. 1237, 1240. See now ss.84(1) and 84(3)(b) of the M.I.A. 1906.
[42] *Ibid.* at p. 1240.

Once, however, the insurer has been at risk under a valid and enforceable policy the premium is in no case recoverable at common law. Thus where the lease of a house expires while an insurance by the lessee is still current,[43] or where the assured sells his interest in a building he has insured,[44] he will not be entitled to a return of premium in whole or in part if the risk has in fact been run for however short a time.

The risk taken is entire. If it has once attached no apportionment of premium can take place[45] even if the policy subsequently becomes forfeited.[46] Insurance premiums are expressly excluded from the Apportionment Act 1870.[47] Thus, where the assured under a life policy commits suicide the policy may by its terms not be enforceable but the insurers will not be liable to return the premiums for the risk has attached.[48]

7–10   *Provision in policy for partial return.* Marine policies generally contain provisions which allow for partial return of premiums on a proportionate basis,[49] and some non-marine policies may contain equivalent terms where, for example, the policy is cancelled[50] or the risk is reduced.[51] Where the insurer is given a discretion as to such partial return of premium, the courts will not interfere with the insurer's exercise of discretion provided that it was reasonable.[52]

7–11   *Liability for return of premium.* Where the premium, or a proportionate part of the premium, is returnable, it is recoverable by the assured from the insurer if it has been paid, but if it has not been paid it may be retained by the assured or his agent.[53] If a premium be paid to the agent of an insurer in respect of a contract known, or which ought to be known, to be outside the scope of his agency, it is not recoverable from the insurer[54] unless he subsequently ratifies the contract by accepting the premium or otherwise. If the contract is beyond the powers of an insurance company they cannot strictly speaking ratify it, but they will nevertheless be liable to return the premium.[55] Premiums paid to a collecting society or industrial assurance company under a policy issued by them are generally recoverable if the policy was *ultra vires*.[56]

7–12 Return of premium in specific cases

The marine rules have been codified in section 84(3) of the Marine Insurance Act 1906. These are of general application, with two excep-

---

[43] *Sadlers Company* v. *Badcock* (1743) 2 Atk. 554.
[44] *Lynch* v. *Dalzell* (1729) 4 Bro. P.C. 431.
[45] Unless the premium is by the terms of the policy apportioned to particular aspects of the risk, some of which do not attach. This rule is contained in s.84(2) of the M.I.A. 1906, but there is no post-1906 marine case or indeed any non-marine case in which it has been applied.
[46] *Tyrie* v. *Fletcher* (1777) 2 Cowp. 666.
[47] Apportionment Act 1870, s.5.
[48] Lord Mansfield C.J. in *Tyrie* v. *Fletcher* (1777) 3 Cowp. 666, 668; *Bermon* v. *Woodbridge* (1781) 2 Doug. K.B. 781.
[49] See s.83 of the M.I.A., which recognises this fact. The relevant return provisions are contained in the Institute of London Underwriters hull and freight clauses, revised 1983.
[50] *Sun Fire* v. *Hart* (1889) 14 App.Cas. 90, 100.
[51] *Parr's Bank* v. *Albert Mines* (1900) 5 Com.Cas. 116.
[52] *Madby* v. *Gresham Life* (1861) 29 Beav. 439.
[53] M.I.A. 1906, s.82.
[54] *Re Arthur Average, De Winton's Case* (1876) 34 L.T. 942.
[55] *Re Phoenix Life, Burges and Stock's Case* (1862) 2 J. & H. 441.
[56] Industrial Assurance Act 1923, s.5.

tions: insurable interest rules differ as between classes of insurance; and the marine doctrine that where the assured has over-insured a proportionate part of the premium is returnable has no place outside marine insurance.[57] The return of premium rules are considered in the following paragraphs.

(i) *Where the company issues a policy which the assured is not bound to* **7–13** *accept, and which he rejects, any premium paid by him is recoverable*

Thus, where the policy did not accord with the terms of a contract of life insurance the court ordered it to be cancelled and the premiums to be refunded as paid under a mistake.[58] But the premium will not be recoverable in such a case where the assured is entitled to rectification of the policy.[59]

Under this principle premiums paid under a policy which the company had not the power to issue will be recoverable.[60]

(ii) *Premiums paid under a policy which is void, as being made under a* **7–14** *mistake of fact, are recoverable*

So also are premiums paid under a non-existent policy which the assured erroneously believed to be in existence.[61] This rule is an application of the general principle that money paid under a mistake of fact is always recoverable, though a contrary rule applies where it is paid under a mistake of law.[62]

Thus, a house may be insured in the mistaken belief that it is standing, when in fact it has already been burnt down, and a life may be insured in the belief that the *cestui qui vie* is still living when he is in fact dead[63]—in each of which cases the premium must be returned.

(iii) *Where the insurer repudiates liability for breach of warranty* **7–15**

(a) *Where the breach occurs before completion of the contract,* as where an intemperate assured warrants himself to be temperate in his habits. In such a case the risk never attaches, the premiums therefore never become due, and may, if paid, be recovered back as money paid without consideration.[64]

(b) *Where the breach is of a warranty relating to the future and is made after the risk has attached.* In this case it appears clear from the principles of the marine cases,[65] and *a fortiori* in the case of non-marine insurance, that premiums paid before the breach cannot be recovered. But premiums paid after the breach to cover future periods will be recoverable nevertheless.[66] Thus, where the assured under a life policy warrants that he will not go

---

[57] Lush J. in *Wolenberg* v. *Royal Co-operative Society* (1915) 84 L.J.K.B. 1316.
[58] *Fowler* v. *Scottish Equitable Life* (1858) 28 L.J.Ch. 225.
[59] *General Accident Insurance* v. *Cronk* (1901) 17 T.L.R. 233.
[60] *Re Phoenix Life* (1862) 2 J. & H. 441; *Flood* v. *Irish Provident Assurance* (1912) 46 Ir.L.T. 214.
[61] *Lower Rhine Insurance* v. *Sedgwick* [1899] 1 Q.B. 179.
[62] *Kelly* v. *Solari* (1841) 9 M. & W. 54.
[63] See Byles J. in *Pritchard* v. *Merchant's Life* (1858) 3 C.B.(N.S.) 622, 645.
[64] Lord Blackburn in *Thomson* v. *Weems* (1884) 9 App.Cas 671, 682.
[65] See, *e.g. Annen* v. *Woodman* (1810) 3 Taunt. 299 and *Langhorn* v. *Cologan* (1812) 4 Taunt. 330.
[66] See *Bunyon on Life Insurance* (5th ed.), p. 113.

abroad, and does so, renewal premiums paid after he does so would, at common law, be recoverable.[67]

As a result of these rules it has been usual, for many years, to insert a term in life insurance policies that in the event of breach of warranty by the assured, the premiums shall be forfeited, and in such a case the fact that the breach precedes the attachment of the risk does not entitle the assured to recover premiums paid,[68] and, similarly, where the breach occurs after the risk has attached such a term precludes the assured from recovering premiums paid after such breach.[69]

7–16 (iv) *Where the insurer avoids the policy for misrepresentation or non-disclosure on the part of the assured*

(a) *Where the misrepresentation is an innocent one, or where the non-disclosure does not amount to a fraudulent concealment.* Here the marine rule is clear—the premium is recoverable on the ground that the risk has never attached,[70] and this rule applies generally to non-marine cases.[71]

(b) *Where the assured has acted fraudulently.* Here again the marine rule is clear; the assured cannot recover any premiums he had paid, for, although the risk has never attached, the court will not allow him to set up his own fraud as a basis of a claim.[72] Should the assured come to the court to reclaim a premium paid under a non-marine policy under such circumstances, he would no doubt be refused relief on the same ground; but where, on the other hand, it is the insurer who comes to the court to claim rescission of the policy on the ground of the assured's fraud, a different principle applies. Since such rescission is a purely equitable remedy, the court will apply the maxim that "he who seeks equity must do equity" and may, therefore, in its discretion, refuse the insurer relief unless he is willing to repay premiums already paid.[73] The premium is sometimes ordered in such a case to be applied towards payment of the costs,[74] however gross the fraud of the assured.[75]

7–17 (v) *Where the assured avoids the policy on the ground of misrepresentation by the insurer*

It would appear obvious on principle that any premiums paid should be recoverable in every such case, as the insurers are never on risk and no question of fraud on the part of the assured arises. And the law, it is

---

[67] See Bray J. in *Sparenborg* v. *Edinburgh Life* [1912] 1 K.B. 195, 204.

[68] *Duckett* v. *Williams* (1834) 2 C. & M. 348; *Howarth* v. *Pioneer Life* (1912) 107 L.T. 155.

[69] *Sparenborg* v. *Edinburgh Life, supra.*

[70] Gibbs J. in *Feise* v. *Parkinson* (1812) 4 Taunt. 640, 641; Parke B. in *Anderson* v. *Thornton* (1853) 8 Ex. 425. See the M.I.A. 1906, s.84(3)(*a*).

[71] See *Anderson* v. *Fitzgerald* (1853) 4 H.L.C. 484, 507; *Mulvey* v. *Gore District Mutual Fire* (1866) 25 U.C.Q.B. 424; Wright J. in *Biggar* v. *Rock Life* [1902] 1 K.B. 516, 526.

[72] *Chapman* v. *Fraser* (1793) 1 Park (8th ed.) 456.

[73] *De Costa* v. *Scandret* (1723) 2 P.Wms. 170; *Barker* v. *Walters* (1844) 8 Beav. 92, 96; *London Assurance* v. *Mansel* (1879) 11 Ch.D. 363, 372.

[74] *Whittingham* v. *Thornburgh* (1690) 2 Vern. 206; *De Costa* v. *Scandret, supra.*

[75] *Prince of Wales Assurance* v. *Palmer* (1858) 25 Beav. 605.

respectfully submitted, must be taken therefore to be that such premiums are always recoverable,[76] despite the dicta of Buckley L.J. in *Kettlewell* v. *Refuge*[77] suggesting that this is only so where the insurers are guilty of fraud.

(vi) *Illegal insurance*   7–18
The general rule is that premiums paid under an unlawful policy, as where the assured has not the interest required by statute,[78] are not recoverable.[79] If an illegal insurance be effected, the parties being *in pari delicto*, the assured can neither recover the insurance money nor the premiums he has paid, in the event of a loss.[80] Nor can he recover back his premiums where no loss has occurred, once the risk has been run.[81] The principle applied is that if the parties enter into an unlawful contract the law will not normally lend its hand to get them out of their difficulties[82]; *in pari delicto potior est conditio possidentis*. There are however several exceptions to this general rule, and a premium paid under an unlawful policy is recoverable:

(a) *Where the assured gives notice to the insurers abandoning the contract before the risk has begun to run.*[83] Though the rule that the premium is recoverable in such a case has been criticised,[84] it is the well-established policy of the law to give the assured a *locus penitentiae*, a chance of repentance, while the unlawful contract is still executory.

(b) *Where the parties enter into an unlawful contract under a mutual mistake of fact, believing it to be a lawful one.*[85]

(c) *Where the assured, who was himself blameless, was induced to make the contract by the fraud of the insurer.*[86] Thus, where the insurer fraudulently represented that interest was unnecessary under a life policy, an innocent assured was held entitled to recover the premium he had paid[87]; but it has been held otherwise where the insurer's misrepresentation as to interest was an innocent one.[88] The principle behind this exception is that where the insurer's conduct is fraudulent the parties cannot be said to be *in pari delicto*, equally to blame.

---

[76] *Carter* v. *Boehm* (1766) 3 Burr. 1905; *Duffell* v. *Wilson* (1808) 1 Camp. 401; *Foster* v. *Mutual Life* (1904) 20 T.L.R. 15 (H.L.); *Merino* v. *Mutual Life* (1904) 21 T.L.R. 167; *Molloy* v. *Mutual Life* (1905) 22 T.L.R. 59; *Kettlewell* v. *Refuge* [1909] A.C. 243.

[77] [1907] 2 K.B. 242.

[78] *M'Culloch* v. *Royal Exchange* (1813) 3 Camp. 406.

[79] Lord Mansfield in *Lowry* v. *Bourdieu* (1780) 2 Dougl. 468, 470; Lord Ellenborough in *Palyart* v. *Leckie* (1817) 6 M. & S. 290; *Howard* v. *Refuge* (1886) 54 L.T. 644.

[80] *Kelly* v. *Solari* (1841) 9 M. & W. 54.

[81] *Lowry* v. *Bourdieu*, *supra*; *Paterson* v. *Powell* (1832) 9 Bing. 320.

[82] Lord Mansfield in *Busk* v. *Walsh* (1812) 4 Taunt. 290, 292.

[83] *Lowry* v. *Bourdieu*, *supra*; *Busk* v. *Walsh*, *supra*; *Kearley* v. *Thomson* (1890) 24 Q.B.D. 742.

[84] Lord Mansfield in *Busk* v. *Walsh*; Lord Ellenborough in *Palyart* v. *Leckie*, *supra*.

[85] *Oom* v. *Bruce* (1810) 12 East 225, 226; *Hentig* v. *Staniforth* (1816) 5 M. & S. 122, 123–125.

[86] *Drummond* v. *Deey* (1794) 1 Esp. 151; *Howarth* v. *Pioneer Life* (1912) 107 L.T. 155.

[87] *British Workman's Assurance* v. *Cunliffe* (1902) 18 T.L.R. 502; *Hughes* v. *Liverpool Victoria Friendly Society* [1916] 2 K.B. 482.

[88] *Harse* v. *Pearl Life Assurance* [1904] 1 K.B. 558; *Phillips* v. *Royal London Mutual* (1911) 105 L.T. 136.

(d) *Where the statute creating the illegality was passed to protect assureds as a class.*[89]

7–19 (vii) *Where the assured has a defeasible interest which is defeated during the currency of the risk, the premium is not returnable.*[90]

In such a case the risk has commenced, so that return is not possible.

7–20 (viii) *Where the assured has no insurable interest during the currency of the policy, the possibility of return of premium varies with the class of insurance.*

In marine insurance, the premium will be recoverable, as long as the assured was not gambling, in that he had expected to obtain an insurable interest.[91] Ordinary non-marine indemnity insurance apparently operates in the same way. Life polices made without insurable interest are unlawful under the Life Assurance Act 1774 so that prima facie the premiums are not recoverable.[92]

7–21 (ix) *Overinsurance*

In non-marine insurance, the assured may not recover surplus premiums where he has overinsured under one or more policies. The marine rules differ. Where the assured has overinsured under an unvalued policy[93] a proportionate part of his premium is returnable to him.[94] Where the assured has overinsured by double insurance, a proportionate part of the several premiums are returnable to him, although this rule does not apply where the overinsurance was deliberate and it does not apply in respect of a policy which has at any time born the entire risk.[95]

---

[89] *Re Cavalier Insurance* [1989] 2 Lloyd's Rep. 430.
[90] M.I.A. 1906, s.84(3)(*d*).
[91] M.I.A. 1906, s.84(3)(*c*).
[92] See § 7–18.
[93] Overinsurance under a valued policy is not possible, as the valuation agreed between the parties is conclusive: M.I.A. 1906, s.27(3).
[94] M.I.A. 1906, s.84(3)(*e*).
[95] M.I.A. 1906, s.84(3)(*f*).

CHAPTER 8

INDEMNITY

1. FORMS OF LOSS

Total, partial and constructive total loss   8–01

Non-marine insurance recognises two forms of loss: total loss, which may be defined as destruction or damage which causes the insured subject matter to lose its identity, or the assured's irretrievable deprivation of the insured subject matter[1]; and partial loss, which is any lesser form of loss. Marine insurance recognises an intermediate form of loss, known as "constructive total loss." This arises where[2]:

(a) the subject matter is reasonably abandoned on account of its actual total loss appearing to be inevitable;

(b) the subject matter could not be preserved from actual total loss without expenditure which would exceed its market value when the expenditure had been incurred;

(c) the assured has been deprived of possession and it is unlikely that he can recover possession within a reasonable time;

(d) the assured has been deprived of possession and the cost of recovery would exceed market value when recovered;

(e) repairing the damage would exceed the repaired value (in the case of a ship) or the value on arrival (in the case of goods).

Cases (a), (b), (d) and (e) are technically partial losses in non-marine insurance, but in practice the insurer will pay for a total loss. By contrast, case (c) is no loss at all in non-marine insurance. In *Moore* v. *Evans*[3] jewellery was insured against all risks by a non-marine policy. Some of the jewels insured had been consigned to Brussels and on the German occupation of Belgium the assured claimed against the insurers for their full value. It was argued on his behalf that the marine doctrine of constructive total loss was applicable, but the Court of Appeal rejected this argument, holding further that there was no actual loss in this case. But there is a loss under such a policy where the goods insured are lost "in all probability."[4]

An assured under a marine policy who wishes to treat a constructive total loss as a total loss must serve a notice of abandonment on the insurer; his failure to do so will allow the insurer to treat the loss as a partial loss only.[5] Notices of abandonment have no role outside marine insurance.

---

[1] Based on the definition in the M.I.A. 1906, s.57.
[2] M.I.A. 1906, s.60.
[3] [1971] 1 K.B. 458.
[4] *Ibid.* Bankes L.J. at pp. 468, 469.
[5] M.I.A. 1906, ss. 61 and 62 deal with the need for, and the form of, a notice of abandonment.

8–02 Abandonment and salvage

Where the insurer has paid for a total loss, he is entitled to claim whatever may remain of the insured subject matter by way of abandonment. The doctrine of abandonment is not confined to marine insurance. As Brett L.J. said in *Kaltenbach* v. *Mackenzie*[6]:

> "I concur in what has been said by Lord Blackburn,[7] that abandonment is not peculiar to policies of marine insurance; abandonment is part of every contract of indemnity. Whenever, therefore, there is a contract of indemnity and a claim under it for an absolute indemnity, there must be an abandonment on the part of the person claiming indemnity of all his right in respect of that for which he receives indemnity."

Abandonment should, therefore, be distinguished from notice of abandonment, the former conferring upon the insurer a right of salvage while the latter merely being the formal device whereby the assured can convert a marine constructive total loss into an actual total loss.

Abandonment and salvage are relevant only to total losses. If the thing insured is not totally destroyed but remains wholly or in part in a deteriorated or damaged condition, the assured can claim only the value of the injury actually done. The insurer's right of salvage is likely to be of limited use in the case of a total loss, although in the case of a marine constructive total loss there will frequently be something of value remaining in existence. Nevertheless, it is settled law that a fire insurer is entitled to claim any old materials left by the fire by way of salvage,[8] and similarly the insurer was held to be entitled to claim jewellery which the assured had believed to have been destroyed by fire but which was found intact after the insurer had paid the claim.[9] It is also clear that the insurer in *Moore* v. *Evans*[10] would, had it paid for a total loss, have been entitled to claim the jewellery on its return to the assured.

Where the assured has suffered a total loss and abandons what remains of the insured subject matter to the insurer, the assured ceases to be the owner of the property in question.[11] It is unclear whether the insurer automatically becomes the owner on abandonment or whether he is entitled to refuse to accept the responsibilities of ownership so that the property becomes a *res nullius*.[12]

2. MEASURE OF INDEMNITY

8–03 A claim under a policy of indemnity is a claim for unliquidated damages.[13] The precise amount which the assured is entitled to recover depends upon whether the policy is valued or unvalued, whether the loss is total or partial and whether the policy is marine or terrestrial.

---

[6] (1878) 3 C.P.D. 467, 470.

[7] *Rankin* v. *Potter* (1873) L.R. 6 H.L. 83, 118. See also *Mason* v. *Sainsbury* (1782) 3 Dougl. 61.

[8] *Oldfield* v. *Price* (1860) 2 F. & F. 80, and see Brett L.J. in *Kaltenbach* v. *Mackenzie* (1873) 3 C.P.D. 467, 470.

[9] *Holmes* v. *Payne* [1930] 2 K.B. 301.

[10] [1917] 1 K.B. 45.

[11] *Boston Corporation* v. *France Fenwick* (1923) 15 Ll.L.R. 85.

[12] See Greer L.J. in *Oceanic Steam Navigation Co.* v. *Evans* (1934) 50 Ll.L.R. 1, at p. 3.

[13] *Jabbour* v. *Custodian of Israeli Absentee Property* [1954] 1 W.L.R. 139; *Edmunds* v. *Lloyd Italico* [1986] 1 All E.R. 249.

Valued policies   **8–04**

Where the policy is a valued one, *i.e.* where the agreed value of the subject matter is specified in the policy,[14] the amount of indemnity is the agreed value; this rule, which rests upon the principle that the valuation agreed between the parties is conclusive,[15] applies in both marine and non-marine insurance. In the case of a total loss, the assured is thus entitled to the full sum insured.[16] In the event of a partial loss, the assured may recover the relevant proportion of the agreed value. In *Elcock* v. *Thomson*[17] the assured suffered a 30 per cent. loss to his mansion and was held to be entitled to 30 per cent. of the agreed value, even though the agreed value was some six times greater than the actual value. This rule is modified in marine insurance in the event of damage to a vessel: the agreed value is disregarded and recovery is based upon the reasonable cost of repairs.[18]

Unvalued policies   **8–05**

Non-marine insurance. The general rule is that the measure of indemnity in respect of the total loss of any property is determined not by its cost but by its value at the date[19] and place of the loss.[20] If the value has increased during the currency of the policy, the assured is therefore entitled to an indemnity on the basis of the increased value.[21]

In assessing the amount of the value, no allowance is to be made for loss of prospective profits or other consequential loss,[22] or for mere sentimental value.[23] Thus, if a partially completed film is destroyed, the assured is entitled to recover only the difference between the market value of the completed film and the costs of completion.[24]

The pre-loss value of the insured subject matter which forms the basis of the measure of indemnity for total loss will in the case of properly insurance commonly be the reinstatement value of the property in precisely its pre-loss form.[25] However, if it can be shown that the assured's actual loss was some lesser sum, for example because his needs would be satisfied by a cheaper modern equivalent building.[26] or because he had prior to the loss sought to see the property at its market rather than reinstatement value,[27] that lesser sum will be the proper measure of his loss.

---

[14] Marine Insruance Act 1906, ss.27, 28.
[15] See generally § 1–12, *supra*, for this principle and its exceptions.
[16] Marine Insurance Act 1906, ss.67(1), 68(1).
[17] [1949] 2 K.B. 755.
[18] M.I.A. 1906, s.69.
[19] *Hercules Insurance* v. *Hunter* (1836) 14 Sh. (Ct. of Sess.) 1137; *Chapman* v. *Pole* (1870) 22 L.T. 306; *Vance* v. *Forster* (1841) Ir.Circ.Rep. 47; *Re Wilson and Scottish Insurance* [1920] 2 Ch. 28.
[20] Bramwell B. in *Rice* v. *Baxendale* (1861) 7 H. & N. 96, 101.
[21] *Re Wilson and Scottish Insurance, supra.*
[22] *Re Wright and Pole* (1834) 1 Ad. & El. 621.
[23] *Re Egmont's Trusts* [1908] 1 Ch. 821, 826, *per* Warrington J.
[24] *Aubrey Film Productions* v. *Graham* [1960] 2 Lloyd's Rep. 101.
[25] *Reynolds* v. *Phoenix* [1978] 2 Lloyd's Rep. 440; *Pleasurama* v. *Sun Alliance* [1979] 1 Lloyd's Rep. 389.
[26] *Exchange Theatre* v. *Iron Trades Mutual* [1983] 1 Lloyd's Rep. 674.
[27] *Leppard* v. *Excess* [1979] 2 All E.R. 668; *McClean* v. *Ecclesiastical Insurance* [1986] 2 Lloyd's Rep. 416.

8–06   In the case of a partial loss, the cost of restoration provides the basis of the measure of indemnity.[28] Where fixtures are destroyed the cost of refixing new ones is necessarily to be taken into account.[29]

8–07   *Marine insurance.* Most marine policies are valued, so that a dispute rarely arises as to the amount recoverable under an unvalued marine policy. Where the point is relevant, marine insurance, unlike non-marine insurance, uses as the basis for the measure of indemnity (the "insurable value") the value of the subject matter *at the commencement of the risk*,[30] although some other basis may be used if the intention of the parties so indicates.[31]

In the case of a total loss, the amount recoverable as the insurable value is the value of the subject matter at the commencement of the risk.[32] The amount recoverable for a partial loss depends upon the subject matter insured. In the case or a vessel the measure of indemnity is the reasonable cost of repairs,[33] although if the vessel has not been fully repaired the measure of indemnity is reasonable depreciation.[34] In the case of goods which are delivered damaged, the assured may recover the proportion of the insurable value as the difference between the gross sound and damaged values at the place of arrival bears to the gross sound value.[35]

8–08 Allowance "new for old"

Where the cost of restoration is adopted as the measure of loss, some allowance may have to be made "new for old." In marine insurance this allowance is fixed by custom,[36] one-third new for old being deductible in the case of repairs to a wooden vessel.[37] There is, however, no fixed standard for this allowance in non-marine insurance. Thus Pennefather B. said in an Irish case[38] that no settled rule of deduction, of one-third or one-fourth, or of any other proportion, existed in the case of old premises or property insured against fire, but that the injury might, as a criterion of the actual damage, see what would be the expense of placing new machinery, such as was in the premises before the fire, and deduct from that sum the difference in value between the new and the old. There is no modern authority on the point.[39]

---

[28] Lord Selborne in *Westminster Fire* v. *Glasgow Provident* (1883) 13 App.Cas. 669, 713; Palles C.B. in *Andrews* v. *Patriotic Assurance* (*No.* 2) (1886) L.R.Ir. 355, 366; *Scottish Amicable* v. *Northern Assurance* (1883) 11 R. (Ct. of Sess.) 287, 295 *per* Lord Craighill.

[29] *Vance* v. *Forster* (1841) Ir.Circ.Rep. 47.

[30] M.I.A. 1906, s.16. In the case of goods, this is their "prime cost," (*i.e.* their original cost). In fact, however, prime cost has often been ignored, and the courts have applied the test of the true value at the commencement of the adventure: *Williams* v. *Atlantic Assurance* [1933] 1 K.B. 81. "Where the assured is not the manufacturer and has bought the goods some time before the insured adventure commence, their original cost may not give any reliable guidance to their value at the relevant time": *per* Kerr J. in *Berger* v. *Pollock* [1973] 2 Lloyd's Rep. 442, 455.

[31] *Continental Alliance* v. *Bathurst, The Captain Panagos* [1985] 1 Lloyd's Rep. 435.

[32] M.I.A. 1906, s.68(2).

[33] M.I.A. 1906, s.69(1).

[34] M.I.A. 1906, s.69(2)–(3).

[35] M.I.A. 1906, s.71(3)–(4).

[36] M.I.A. 1906, s.69(1).

[37] *Pitman* v. *Universal Marine* (1882) 9 Q.B.D. 192, 215. Marine insurance policies written in England no longer incorporate the customary deduction.

[38] *Vance* v. *Forster* (1841) Ir.Circ.Rep. 47.

[39] In *Reynolds* v. *Phoenix* [1978] 2 Lloyd's Rep. nevertheless regarded the principle of deduction for betterment as well established.

3. SUBROGATION

Closely analogous to the salvage concept and the doctrine of abandon- **8–09**
ment is the more important doctrine of subrogation. Salvage is primarily a
matter of salvage of physical things; subrogation is primarily concerned
with the legal rights of the assured against third parties. By virtue of this
doctrine the insurer can also recover from the assured the value of any
benefits received by him incidental to the loss. The assured cannot take
with both hands. Any sums received by him which diminish his loss must be
held by him on trust for his insurer, who has an equitable proprietary interest in such sums.[40] If he has any ways and means open to him to repair his
loss, otherwise than at his own expense or at the cost of his insurer, he must
either cede such ways and means to the insurer, on being paid in full the
amount of his loss, or he must exercise such ways and means for the benefit
of the insurer.[41] The effect of the doctrine is concisely stated in section 79
(*right of subrogation*) of the Marine Insurance Act 1906:

> (1) where the insurer pays for a total loss, either of the whole, or in the case
> of goods of any apportionable part, of the subject-matter insured, he there-
> upon becomes entitled to take over the interest of the assured in whatever
> may remain of the subject-matter so paid for, and he is thereby subrogated to
> all the rights and remedies of the assured in and in respect of that subject-
> matter as from the time of the casualty causing the loss.

Right of action by assured against third party   **8–10**
The principle that the assured must recover no more than his loss does
not mean that, where the loss is caused by the fault of another, or where
by contract another is liable to bear the risk insured against, the assured
is precluded from recovering from his insurers on the ground that he has
a remedy against someone else. In such a case the insurers are liable to
pay the claim against them irrespective of any rights the assured may
have against third parties, in respect of the loss.[42] Where a third party is
liable to the assured in tort in respect of the loss, the defence that the
insurers have paid, or are liable to pay, the assured in respect of it
affords him no defence, and cannot be pleaded by him in mitigation of
damages.[43] A third party who has contracted with the assured to bear
the loss can claim no rights under the policy unless it was made on his
behalf,[44] or it is an express or implied term of the contract that his liability to the assured should be extinguished or reduced in the event of the
assured recovering under a policy of insurance.

It follows from these rules that, where the assured has rights both **8–11**
against his insurers and against a third party in respect of a loss, he may
recover from them an aggregate sum substantially in excess of his loss. It

---

[40] *Re Miller, Gibb* [1957] 1 W.L.R. 703.
[41] *Castellain* v. *Preston* (1883) 11 Q.B.D. 380.
[42] *Cullen* v. *Butler* (1816) 5 M. & S. 461; *Quebec Fire* v. *Louis* (1851) 7 Moo.P.C. 286; *Dickenson* v.
Jardine (1868) L.R. 3 C.P. 639, 644; *North British* v. *London, Liverpool & Globe* (1877) 5 Ch.D. 569,
575; *Collingridge* v. *Royal Exchange Assurance* (1877) 3 Q.B.D. 173, 176, 177.
[43] *Mason* v. *Sainsbury* (1782) 3 Doug. 61; *Clark* v. *Blything* (1823) 2 B. & C. 254; *Yates* v. *Whyte*
(1838) 4 Bing.N.C. 272; *Bradburn* v. *G. W. Ry.* (1874) L.R. 10 Ex. 1; *King* v. *Victoria Insurance* [1896]
A.C. 250.
[44] *Hobbs* v. *Marlowe* [1978] A.C. 16; *Nichols* v. *Scottish Union* (1885) 2 T.L.R. 190.

is here that the doctrine of "subrogation" comes into operation. If, after satisfaction from the insurers, the assured receives any further compensation in respect of his loss, he must hold it as a trustee for his insurer.[45] In this way principles of equity[46] have come to the assistance of the common law in preventing the assured from profiting from his loss. If, in such a case, the assured declined to enforce his rights against a third party after payment by his insurers, the insurers were allowed to sue the third party "in his shoes" and in 1782 Lord Mansfield could say: "Every day the insurer is put in the place of the insured."[47] The common law was able to apply equitable principles in this respect, by regarding the right of subrogation as an implied term of the contract.[48] This right of "subrogation" rests upon the ground that the insurer's contract is in the nature of a contract of indemnity and that he is therefore entitled, upon paying a sum for which others are primarily liable to the assured, to be proportionately subrogated to the right of action of the assured against them.[49]

Thus, if the liability of an employer for his employee's negligence is insured, the insurer is entitled to sue the employee in the employer's name for the amount of the liability.[50] However, although the right of subrogation will normally attach to a contract of indemnity there are circumstances in which the right will not apply.[51]

8–12 Sums received by the assured from a third party

It is to be noted that the doctrine does not apply only where there is a right of action, but also affects sums received by the assured which have been paid to him by the third party. In *Castellain* v. *Preston*[52] the contractual right of the assured was against a purchaser who had agreed unconditionally to purchase his house. The house was destroyed by fire and the assured was paid by his insurers. He was also paid the purchase price, and it was held that the insurers were thereupon entitled to recover from him a sum equal to the insurance money.

> "As between the underwriter and the assured the underwriter is entitled to the advantage of every right of the assured, whether such right consists in contract fulfilled or unfulfilled, or in remedy for tort capable of being insisted on, or any other right, whether by way of condition or otherwise, legal or equitable, which can be, or has been exercised or has accrued, and

---

[45] *Per* Lord Hardwicke in *Randal* v. *Cockran* (1748) 1 Ves.Sen. 98, 99; *Blaauwpot* v. *Da Costa* (1758) 1 Eden 130. "Although often referred to as an 'equity,' [subrogation] is not an exclusively equitable doctrine. It was applied by the common law courts in insurance cases long before the fusion of law and equity, although the powers of the common law courts might in some cases require to be supplemented by those of a court of equity in order to give full effect to the doctrine; for example, in compelling an assured to allow his name to be used by the insurer for the purpose of enforcing the assured's remedies against third parties in respect of the subject-matter of the loss." *Per* Diplock J. in *Yorkshire Ins. Co.* v. *Nisbet Shipping Co.* [1962] 2 Q.B. 330, 339.

[46] See *per* Diplock J. in *Yorkshire Ins. Co.* v. *Nisbet, supra*, at p. 339, 341.

[47] *Mason* v. *Sainsbury* (1782) 3 Doug. 61, 64.

[48] Cotton L.J. in *Darrell* v. *Tibbitts* (1880) 5 Q.B.D. 560, 565. The "implied term," basis of subrogation, suggested by Diplock J. in *Yorkshire* v. *Nisbet, supra*, was adopted by him in the House of Lords in *Orakpo* v. *Manson Investments* [1978] A.C. 95 and *Hobbs* v. *Marlowe, supra*.

[49] This passage was quoted with approval by McCardie J. in *Edwards* v. *Motor Union* [1922] 2 K.B. 249, 253.

[50] See *Lister* v. *Romford* [1957] A.C. 555; [1956] 2 Q.B. 180 (C.A.).

[51] *Morris* v. *Ford Motor Co. Ltd.*; *Cameron Industrial Services Ltd. (Third Party), Roberts (Fourth Party)* [1973] 1 Q.B. 792. See *infra*.

[52] (1883) 11 Q.B.D. 380.

whether such right could or could not be enforced by the insurer in the name of the assured, by the exercise or acquiring of which right or condition the loss against which the assured is insured, can be, or has been, diminished."[53]

Its scope where the insurers do not sue in the place of the assured is perhaps best summed up by Lord Blackburn in *Burnand* v. *Rodocanachi*[54]:

"Where there is a contract of indemnity . . . and a loss happens, anything which reduces or diminishes that loss reduces or diminishes the amount which the indemnifier is bound to pay; and if the indemnifier has already paid it, then, if anything which diminishes the loss comes into the hands of the person to whom he has paid it, it becomes an equity that the person who has already paid the full indemnity is entitled to be recouped by having that amount back."

Or put another way:

"A person who wishes to recover from and is paid by the insurers for a total loss, cannot take with both hands. If he has a means of diminishing the loss, the result of the use of those means belongs to the underwriters."[55]

Payments to which subrogation rights attach   8–13
The general principle is that the insurer is entitled to be subrogated to any right owing, or payment made, to the assured by a third party which diminishes the assured's loss. However, certain rights and payments may be personal to the assured and not be the subject of subrogation.

Gifts. If the assured has received an *ex gratia* payment from a third **8–14** party, the insurer will be able to claim it only if the third party intended that payment to go toward the diminution of the assured's loss, as opposed, for example, to taking effect as personal compensation. Thus where the assured's property has been seized, and payment has been made to him by the person seizing that property, the assured will normally be liable to account for it to his insurer by way of subrogation,[56] but a different conclusion will be reached where the money is bestowed upon the assured not as a right but as a gift which is intended to benefit the assured beyond the amount of any insurance money.[57] The insurer will be entitled to be subrogated to an *ex gratia* payment by another insurance company, even though the assured had no right of action for it, provided that it is incidental to the subject matter of the loss.[58]

Non-incidental benefits. The benefit to which the insurers seek to be **8–15** subrogated must be incidental to the subject matter of the loss. Thus, on payment for the loss of a vessel, the underwriters are not subrogated to the owners' right of action against the wrongdoing vessel for loss of

---

[53] *Ibid. per* Brett L.J. at 388.
[54] (1882) 7 App.Cas. 333, 339.
[55] *Per* Bowen L.J. in *Castellain* v. *Preston* (1883) 11 Q.B.D. 380, 402.
[56] *Stearns* v. *Village Gold Mining Co.* (1905) 10 Com.Cas. 89, following *Randal* v. *Cockran* (1748) 1 Ves.Sen. 98.
[57] *Burnand* v. *Rodocanachi* (1882) 7 App.Cas. 333.
[58] See Tucker J. in *Austin* v. *Zurich* [1944] 2 All E.R. 243, 246; not disapproved [1945] 1 All E.R. 316.

freight, as such loss is uninsured consequential loss.[59] Similarly, if an insurer is liable to its assured for total loss of a hull and also for collision liability, but is reinsured only in respect of its hull liability, the reinsurer cannot claim the benefit of any limitation on the insurer's collision liability,[60] although if the reinsured discovers that the assured's claim was fraudulent and recovers damages from the assured, the reinsurer is entitled to be subrogated to the damages payable by the assured as such sum is sufficiently incidental to the reinsured's loss.[61] Again,

> "if one of two unique china vases is insured and destroyed, it does not avail the underwriter that by the destruction the second vase has become more unique and more valuable."[62]

8–16 Assured may not renounce his rights

Rights of the insurer against the third party. The assured may not renounce or compromise any right of action he has against a third party by the exercise of which he can diminish his rights. Before the assured has received an indemnity from the insurer the right to control the action against the third party remains under the sole control of the assured,[63] so that any binding agreement with the third party reducing or eliminating the latter's liability will be binding on the insurer; on principle, given that subrogation rights are exercisable only in the name of the assured, the same should follow even if the agreement is reached between assured and third party after the assured has been fully indemnified and has thus lost the control of the action to the insurer.[64]

8–17   *Rights of the insurer against the assured.* Where the insurer's rights are defeated by an agreement of this nature, the insurer will be entitled to bring proceedings against the assured for the loss of its subrogation rights.[65] Thus, where buildings were destroyed by fire, and the assured agreed to reduce a claim for compensation she had against Plymouth Corporation by the amount she had received from her insurers, the insurers were entitled to recover this amount from her.[66] It has also been held that where a third party renounces rights against the assured incidental to the loss, this is also a loss of benefit for which the assured must compensate his insurers. Thus where a tenant responsible under his lease for loss by fire made an advantageous settlement with his lessor in respect of a fire, it was held that his insurers were entitled to benefit accordingly.[67]

But, while the assured may not renounce or compromise any rights he has, the insurers have no right to call upon him to exercise a possible

---

[59] *Sea Insurance* v. *Hadden* (1884) 13 Q.B.D. 706; *Attorney General* v. *Glen Line* (1930) 36 Com.Cas. 1, 14, 16.

[60] *Young* v. *Merchants Marine* [1932] 2 K.B. 705.

[61] *Assicurazioni Generali* v. *Empress Assurance* [1907] 2 K.B. 814.

[62] Scrutton J. in *City Tailors* v. *Evans* (1921) 91 L.J.K.B. 379, 385.

[63] *Commercial Union* v. *Lister* (1874) 9 Ch.App. 483.

[64] The contrary was, it is submitted, incorrectly, assumed in *Haigh* v. *Lawford* (1964) 114 N.L.J. 208 (county court).

[65] *Commercial Union* v. *Lister* (1874) 9 Ch.App. 483; *Dufourcet* v. *Bishop* (1886) 18 Q.B.D. 373; *Horse Carriage Insurance* v. *Petch* (1916) 33 T.L.R. 131; *Boag* v. *Standard Marine* [1937] 2 K.B. 113.

[66] *Phoenix Assurance* v. *Spooner* [1905] 2 K.B. 753.

[67] *West of England Fire* v. *Isaacs* [1897] 1 Q.B. 226.

option to be released from a contract under circumstances in which no honourable man would exercise it.[68]

On the other hand, if the settlement reached by the assured with the third party is a bona fide compromise, it may be difficult for the insurer to prove that he has suffered any loss.[69]

Limitations on the doctrine   **8–18**

(i) *Policy must be one of indemnity.* An insurer under a life[70] or personal accident[71] policy has no subrogation rights. This is so because such policies are not indemnity policies, so that the rationale for subrogation does not come into operation.

(ii) *Insurer must first pay.* No right of subrogation accrues to the **8–19** insurers until they have paid under the policy.[72] Nor will the fact that they have paid before the trial of an action in which they claim to be subrogated avail them, unless they have paid before issue of the writ.[73] It is from actual payment under a contract of indemnity that the right of subrogation springs.[74] If the assured is underinsured, the insurer does not, however, acquire the right to control any action which the assured might bring against the third party.[75]

There is, however, authority for the proposition that the making of the policy confers a contingent right of subrogation upon the insurer,[76] so that the assured may well face liability to the insurer for failing to take reasonable steps to preserve the insurer's rights—for example, by the issue of a writ within the relevant limitation period—pending indemnification by the insurer. This matter is generally dealt with by express provision, requiring the assured to take all reasonable steps to preserve the insurer's right of action.

(iii) *Ex gratia payments by the insurer.* There can be no right of subro- **8–20** gation under an honour policy, for it is not a contract of indemnity.[77] But where the insurer pays under a valid policy of indemnity and seeks to exercise subrogation rights, it is no defence to the third party to say that the insurer was not legally bound to pay under the terms of the policy.[78]

(iv) *Assured must have been able to bring action.* The insurers can be **8–21** subrogated only to actions which the assured could have himself brought.

(a) The assured cannot sue himself. Thus where two ships owned by

---

[68] *Sparkes* v. *Marshall* (1836) 2 Bing N.C. 761; *Inglis* v. *Stock* (1885) 10 App.Cas. 263.

[69] *Globe & Rutgers Fire* v. *Truedell* [1927] 2 D.L.R. 659; *Willumsen* v. *Royal Exchange* 63 D.L.R. (3d.) 112, (1975).

[70] *Solicitors and General* v. *Lamb* (1864) 1 De G.J. & Sm. 251.

[71] *Theobald* v. *Railway Passengers Assurance* (1854) 10 Ex. 45.

[72] *City Tailors* v. *Evans* (1921) 91 L.J.K.B. 379, 385 *per* Scrutton L.J.; *Scottish Union* v. *Davis* [1970] 1 Lloyd's Rep. 1.

[73] *Page* v. *Scottish Insurance* (1929) 98 L.J.K.B. 308.

[74] *Edwards* v. *Motor Union* [1922] 2 K.B. 249, 254, 255, *per* McCardie J.

[75] *Commercial Union* v. *Lister, supra.*

[76] *Boag* v. *Standard Marine* [1937] 2 K.B. 113.

[77] *Edwards* v. *Motor Union, supra.*

[78] *King* v. *Victoria Insurance* [1896] A.C. 250. A similar result was reached by indirect means in *Naumann* v. *Ford* [1985] 2 E.G.L.R. 70.

the same man collide by the fault of one of them, the insurers of the ship not at fault have been held not to be entitled to make any claim on the owner for the act of the other ship, though the insurers of the cargo owned by a third party would have had a claim against him.[79]

(b) The assured may be prevented from suing the wrongdoer by operation of law or by virtue of a contract between the assured and the wrongdoer. So, where the assured's wife set fire to his house, and the insurers paid, they could not recover the insurance money as the assured had no right of action against his wife.[80] Again, where the assured has agreed that a third party is not to bear responsibility in the event of a loss caused by him and the assured will look to his insurer, the insurer is bound by that agreement to the same extent as the assured,[81] although if the agreement exempting the third party was entered into prior to the making of the contract of insurance the insurer may, in exceptional cases, be able to avoid the policy for the assured's failure to disclose the nature of his bargain.[82]

(c) Where the assured and the wrongdoer are co-assureds under the same policy, subrogation rights are not available. This was decided in *Petrofina* v. *Magnaload*,[83] where contract works were insured by the head contractor in his own name and the names of the employer and all sub-contractors. Property on site was damaged by the negligence of a sub-contractor, and the insurer—having paid the owners claimed subrogation rights against the sub-contractor. Lloyd J. ruled that each of the named parties was co-assured for the entire contract works, and that it was not open to the insurer to exercise subrogation rights against its own assured.

(d) Where the wrongdoer is not a party to the insurance contract, but it is explicit in the arrangements between assured and wrongdoer that the policy is at least in part for the wrongdoer's benefit, the *Petrofina* principle will apply. Thus in *Mark Rowlands* v. *Berni Inns*[84] the fire insurer of a landlord was held not to have subrogation rights against the tenant who had negligently caused a fire, as the lease obliged the tenant to pay insurance premiums to the landlord who was to insure the premises in its own name but for their respective interests.

(e) It may, in the absence of express agreement, be possible to imply into the contract between the assured and wrongdoer an obligation on the assured to indemnify the wrongdoer. Such an argument was presented to the House of Lords in *Lister* v. *Romford Ice*,[85] although it failed in the circumstances. Here the assured

---

[79] *Simpson* v. *Thompson* (1877) 3 App.Cas. 279.
[80] *Midland Insurance* v. *Smith* (1881) 6 Q.B.D. 561.
[81] *Thomas* v. *Brown* (1891) 4 Com.Cas. 186; *Canadian Transport* v. *Court Line* [1940] A.C. 934; *Coupar Transport* v. *Smith's* [1959] 1 Lloyd's Rep. 369.
[82] *Tate* v. *Hyslop* (1885) 15 Q.B.D. 368.
[83] [1983] 2 Lloyd's Rep. 91.
[84] [1985] 3 All E.R. 473.
[85] [1957] A.C. 555.

employer was found to be vicariously liable for a tort committed by one employee against a fellow employee, who happened to be his father. The insurer, having indemnified the employer in respect of his liability to the father, exercised subrogation rights against the son. The son's argument—that the contract of employment contained an implied term whereby the employer would indemnify his employee for the consequence of his negligence was rejected. Subsequently, insurers agreed with government that subrogation rights would not be exercised in these circumstances. An attempt was made to circumvent this agreement in *Morris* v. *Ford Motor Co.*,[86] where the liability insurers of employer A sought an indemnity from the employee of employer B in respect of an act of negligence on employer A's premises. The Court of Appeal, by a majority, ruled that subrogation was not available as the liability of B's employees had been implicitly excluded in the agreement between the employers.

Action to be brought in the assured's name   8–22

It is well established that the insurer is not directly a party to the proceedings against the third party, but must sue in the name of the assured.[87] It is for this reason that the insurer's rights can be no better than those of the assured. This rule has a number of consequences. Thus, the third party cannot obtain discovery in the subrogation action from the insurer as such.[88] If the assured has allowed the action to become time-barred, the limitation period may be pleaded against the insurer,[89] although it is possible that the insurer might have some recourse to the assured in these circumstances.[90] If the assured is a company which has gone into liquidation and has been removed from the register of companies, it has ceased to exist and its name cannot be used in subrogation proceedings.[91] The rule of the county courts, that in the small claims procedure each side bears its own legal costs, will not be waived simply because the true parties are the insurers of the nominal plaintiff and defendant.[92] Finally, if the insurer reaches a settlement with the third party, such settlement must be in the name of the assured and not merely in the name of the insurer, as the insurer strictly speaking is not a party to the dispute giving rise to the settlement.[93]

Extent of subrogation rights   8–23

Insurers are entitled to recoupment only for a loss which they have paid, and to the extent of their payment. "Subrogation will only give the insurer

[86] [1973] Q.B. 792.
[87] *London Assurance* v. *Sainsbury* (1783) 3 Doug. 245; *Esso* v. *Hall Russell* [1988] 3 W.L.R. 730.
[88] *James Nelson* v. *Nelson Line* [1906] 2 K.B. 217.
[89] *London Assurance* v. *Johnson* (1737) Hardw. 269.
[90] On the principle of *Boag* v. *Standard Marine*, *supra*.
[91] *Smith Ltd.* v. *Mainwaring* [1986] 2 Lloyd's Rep. 244.
[92] *Russell* v. *Wilson* (1989), unreported.
[93] *Kitchen Design* v. *Lea Valley Water* [1989] 2 Lloyd's Rep. 221, where Phillips J. was able to construe the settlement as binding the insurer not to exercise subrogation rights, as well as binding the assured to abandon all further claims.

rights up to 20 shillings in the pound on what has been paid."[94] If the assured is not fully insured, he is entitled to make up the shortfall from damages received from the third party before the insurer can exercise subrogation rights, so that if the sum received from the third party is not sufficient to cover the full loss, the insurer will bear any deficit.[95] But the insurer under a valued policy is entitled to damages received by the assured in respect of loss to that, even though the agreed valuation is less than the true value of the thing lost, as the valuation is conclusive as between the parties. Thus, where a ship at a low valuation was lost in a collision, the insurers were held entitled to the collision damages recovered by the assured up to the value of the sum insured.[96] And where damages less than the agreed valuation are recovered in respect of a partial loss, the insurer may retain them notwithstanding that the actual cost of repairs exceeds the agreed valuation.[97] But he cannot retain any damages in excess of the sum insured,[98] so that where currency fluctuations permitted recovery from the third party for a nominal sum in excess of the market value of the subject matter, the surplus belonged to the assured and not to the insurer.[99]

8–24   Any sums recovered by the assured to which the insurer has a claim by way of subrogation are held on trust by the assured[1] or his agent.[2] The court will in a subrogation action award interest in the usual way, that is, from the date at which the plaintiff's cause of action accrued.[3]

8–25 Assignment to insurer of assured's claim

Where the assured assigns his rights against the third party to the insurer, under a legal assignment under section 136 of the Law of Property Act 1925, the insurer's position is somewhat different. First, the insurer who takes an assignment is entitled to use its own name to sue the third party. Secondly, the third party can be sued *before* the insurer has provided an indemnity. Thirdly, in the event of recovery from the third party, the insurer is entitled to retain sums in excess of those which he has actually paid to the assured.[4]

8–26 Procedural matters

It is usual for insurers to pay the assured and then to commence proceedings against the third party in the assured's name. If the assured

---

[94] *Per* Lord Atkin in *Glen Line* v. *Attorney General* (1930) 6 Com.Cas. 1, 14. In *Scottish Union* v. *Davis* [1970] 1 Lloyd's Rep. 1, insurers claimed by way of subrogation £350 received by the assured from the third party for damage to a motor car, on the grounds that they had paid £409 for repairs. They had no satisfaction note from the assured, and the repairs were useless. The Court of Appeal held that the insurers were entitled to nothing. So far as the assured was concerned, they might as well have thrown the bank notes into the Thames: *per* Russell L.J. at p. 4.

[95] *Hobbs* v. *Marlowe* [1978] A.C. 16.

[96] *Thames & Mersey Marine Insurance* v. *British & Chilian Steamship Co.* [1916] 1 K.B. 30.

[97] *Goole & Hull Steam Towing Co.* v. *Ocean Marine* [1928] 1 K.B. 589.

[98] *Ibid. per* MacKinnon J. at p. 598.

[99] *Yorkshire Insurance* v. *Nisbet Shipping* [1962] 2 Q.B. 330, disapproving earlier suggestions to the contrary in *North of England* v. *Armstrong* (1870) L.R. 5 Q.B. 244, 249. This decision was similarly criticised in *Burnand* v. *Rodocanachi*, (1882) 7 App.Cas. 333.

[1] *Re Miller, Gibb & Co.* [1957] 2 All E.R. 266.

[2] *Elgood* v. *Harris* [1896] 2 Q.B. 491.

[3] *Cousins* v. *D. & C. Carriers* [1971] 2 Q.B. 230. It had previously been held that interest was awardable only from the date at which the insurer made payment to the assured—*Harbutts "Plasticine"* v. *Wayne Tank and Pump Co.* [1970] 1 Q.B. 447—but it was recognised in the later case that the effect of this was to deny the insurer its proper interest entitlement.

[4] *Compania Colombiana de Seguros* v. *Pacific Steam Navigation Co.* [1965] 1 Q.B. 101.

upon tender of a proper indemnity as to costs refuses the use of his name, the insurers can by proceedings in equity compel him to give it,[5] but they cannot insist on the assured taking any steps against the third party until they have paid him.[6] Should the assured himself recover damages without assistance from the insurer, where for instance the insurers are only entitled to a part of them, he is entitled to deduct the reasonable expenses of recovery from the amount he hands over to the insurers.[7]

Once the assured has received a full indemnity, so that the control of the action has passed to the insurer, it is seemingly the case that the insurer can instruct the assured to discontinue proceedings against the third party[8]; motor polices normally contain express provisions to this effect.[9] The insurer may well wish to exercise this right where there exist between insurers agreements not to sue each other in respect of particular forms of loss; motor "knock-for-knock" agreements are the most important type here.

Where the assured is underinsured, for example because he bears an excess or other retention under the policy, he retains control of the action against the third party, despite full payment under the policy by the insurer. Insurers must in this situation be alert to the possibility that the assured may bring an action against the third party for the uninsured sum only. The insurer is entitled to apply for the amendment of the assured's writ to cover the full amount of the loss, both insured and uninsured, before the assured's action has proceeded to judgment,[10] although once judgment has been given the insurer will be able to set that judgment aside only where it can be shown that the defendant or his insurers have acted unconscionably in their defence of the action for the uninsured loss.[11] If, however, the assured and the third party have reached a settlement in respect of the uninsured sum only, the insurer will not be precluded from bringing proceedings in the assured's name for a sum representing the assured's loss.[12]

4. DOUBLE INSURANCE: CONTRIBUTION

Double insurance   8–27
The general rule is that any person may take out as many policies as he chooses against the same risk, and that he is free to claim payment from his insurers in such order as he thinks fit, although the assured cannot by any combination of claims recover more than an indemnity.

But, until the assured has received the full amount of his loss, he is entitled to call upon any of his insurers to pay him in full, and the fact that others are also liable will afford that insurer no defence. This principle

---

[5] *Commercial Union* v. *Lister, supra*; McCardie J. in *Edwards* v. *Motor Union* [1922] 2 K.B. 249, 254.
[6] *Andrews* v. *Patriotic* (1886) 18 L.R.Ir. 355.
[7] *Assicurazioni* v. *Empress Assurance* [1907] 2 K.B. 814.
[8] *Hobbs* v. *Marlowe* [1978] A.C. 16 casts doubt upon the decision in *Morley* v. *Moore* [1936] 2 K.B. 359, which is to the contrary.
[9] *Hobbs* v. *Marlowe, supra*.
[10] *Buckland* v. *Palmer* [1984] 3 All E.R., which demonstrates that the insurer cannot issue a further writ in the assured's name in respect of the same incident.
[11] *Hayler* v. *Chapman* [1989] 1 Lloyd's Rep. 490, distinguishing *Cotton* v. *Burns* (1988), unreported.
[12] *Taylor* v. *O'Wray* [1971] 1 Lloyd's Rep. 497.

appeared in a case as early as 1758,[13] in which a custom was proved to the contrary. It was applied early in marine decisions,[14] and has general application.[15]

8–28 Section 32 of the Marine Insurance Act 1906 is representative of both marine and non-marine law:

(1) Where two or more policies are effected by or on behalf of the assured on the same adventure and interest or any part thereof, and the sums insured exceed the indemnity allowed by this Act, the assured is said to be over-insured by double insurance.

(2) Where the assured is over-insured by double insurance—

(a) The assured, unless the policy otherwise provides, may claim payment from the insurers in such order as he may think fit, provided that he is not entitled to receive any sum in excess of the indemnity allowed by this Act;

(b) Where the policy under which the assured claims is a valued policy, the assured must give credit as against the valuation for any sum received by him under any other policy without regard to the actual value of the subject-matter insured;

(c) Where the policy under which the assured claims is an unvalued policy he must give credit, as against the full insurable value, for any sum received by him under any other policy;

(d) Where the assured receives any sum in excess of the indemnity allowed by this Act, he is deemed to hold such sum in trust for the insurers, according to their right of contribution among themselves.

Continental law makes successive insurers liable in order of date, and American policies generally adopt that rule, but the rule that the assured has a free choice upon which insurer he shall call to pay him is well established in English law.[16] In the case of valued policies his order of choice may substantially affect the amount he can recover. Thus when property is valued at £9,000 and insured for £2,000 with one insurer, and valued at £8,000 and insured for £8,000 with another, if the assured claims £2,000 first from the first insurer, he will be entitled to no more than £6,000, the balance of £8,000, from the second, but if he claims £8,000 from the second first, he will be entitled to £1,000, the balance of £9,000, from the first insurer.[17]

8–29 Although one assured cannot, by double insurance, recover more than the amount of his loss, a number of persons, interested in the same subject-matter, may take out insurances of their separate interests and recover, in all, a sum exceeding the value of that subject-matter. In a Scottish case the pursuers, having a hereditable security by bond on certain premises, insured them against fire in the defender's office for £900. Prior securities had been given by the owner upon the same premises to other creditors who had insured in other offices. The premises having been in part destroyed by fire, the prior incumbrances were paid by their

---

[13] *Godin* v. *London Assurance* (1758) 1 Burr. 489.

[14] *Newby* v. *Reed* (1763) 1 Wm.Bl. 416; *Rogers* v. *Davis* (1777) 2 Park (8th ed.) 601; see now M.I.A. 1906, s.32(2)(a), *infra*, § 8–28.

[15] See *North British* v. *London, Liverpool & Globe* (1877) 5 Ch.D. 569, 583, *per* Mellish L.J. and p. 587, *per* Baggallay L.J.

[16] It was also the law in Canada; *Bank of British North America* v. *Western* (1884) 7 Ont.App. 166.

[17] *Bruce* v. *Jones* (1863) 1 H. & C. 769.

insurers an amount sufficient to reinstate the premises, and to pay the rent during the period of reinstatement, but the premises were not in fact reinstated. Before the fire the value of the premises was sufficient to cover the prior bonds and that of the pursuers, but after the fire the value of the premises was so reduced as to be inadequate to meet the balance due to the prior creditors, and the pursuers' bond was left entirely uncovered. The House of Lords decided that the pursuers were entitled, notwithstanding the amount paid to the other creditors, to recover their loss.[18]

Contribution 8–30

By the operation of the principle of indemnity, payment by one insurer of the full amount of the assured's loss will, in effect, discharge any other insurer of the same interest against the same risk of his liability. But the insurer who has paid can nevertheless call upon any others to contribute their share of the loss on equitable principles. This was an old principle of marine insurance law,[19] and it is now well established that it applies generally, to fire,[20] liability,[21] fidelity[22] and other indemnity insurance.

The rules are codified in the Marine Insurance Act 1906. By section 80 (*right of contribution*)[23]:

> (1) Where the assured is over-insured by double insurance, each insurer is bound, as between himself and the other insurers, to contribute rateably to the loss in proportion to the amount for which he is liable under his contract.
>
> (2) If any insurer pays more than his proportion of the loss, he is entitled to maintain an action for contribution against the other insurers, and is entitled to the like remedies as a surety who has paid more than his proportion of the debt.

The right of contribution amongst co-insurers, is, like the right of contribution between co-sureties, independent of contract.[24] It is an equitable right depending on the maxim "equality is equity."

Subrogation contrasted 8–31

Contribution is quite distinct from subrogation. Since contribution implies more than one contract of insurance it is only where there are two or more policies involved that there can be any confusion between the two. But suppose A insures goods with company X and B insures the same goods with company Y. If company X pays A they may have a remedy either by subrogation or contribution. If B is liable to A in respect of the loss, company X will be subrogated to A's right against B, and will eventually recover the whole amount paid from company Y. If A is liable to B, company X will be entitled to recover nothing, unless B

---

[18] *Westminster Fire Office* v. *Glasgow Provident* (1888) 13 App.Cas. 699.

[19] *Newby* v. *Reed* (1763) 1 Wm.Bl. 416; see now M.I.A. 1906, s.80, *infra.*

[20] *North British* v. *London, Liverpool & Globe* (1877) 5 Ch.D. 569, 583, 587.

[21] *Sickness & Accident* v. *General Accident* (1892) 19 R. (Ct. of Sess.) 977, *per* Lord Low.

[22] *American Surety Co.* v. *Wrightson* (1910) 27 T.L.R. 91.

[23] s.80(1) has been criticised as ambiguous in the Court of Appeal; *Commercial Union* v. *Hayden* [1977] 1 Lloyd's Rep. 1, *per* Cairns L.J. at p. 10 and Stephenson L.J. at p. 14. It might refer to the liability for which a co-insurer is liable *either actually or potentially.* But, with respect it is difficult to see how "*is liable*" can mean *might* be liable. See *infra.* n. 39.

[24] Hamilton J. in *American Surety Co.* v. *Wrightson* (1910) 27 T.L.R. 91, 93.

has also recovered A's interest, in which case company X will be entitled to contribution from company Y.[25] Subrogation ensures that the assured shall receive no more than an indemnity; contribution ensures that the insurers shall not indirectly suffer injustice *inter se* because of that rule. Unlike a claim for subrogation a contribution action must be brought in the insurer's own name.[26]

Sometimes both principles are applicable in the same case. Thus, if the owner of premises insures them with two insurers, both of whom pay him in respect of a loss, they will be entitled to contribution between each other with regard to any subrogation rights against a tenant in respect of repairs. One insurer cannot proceed against the tenant in the assured's name and retain the whole of the proceeds.[27] Contribution, in fact, applies not only to the liabilities, but also to the benefits to which an insurer is entitled under a policy.

8–32 Pre-requisites to right of contribution

To give rise to a right of contribution the following conditions must be satisfied:

(i) *The insurances must have a common subject-matter.* Generally this will be some property, *e.g.* a ship or building or goods,[28] covered by more than one insurance. But the principle is not limited to property insurance. In *American Surety Co.* v. *Wrightson*[29] a bank insured—

(a) against loss or damage caused by the dishonesty of employee X up to $2,500, and against other such losses, and
(b) by another policy, for £40,000 against a great variety of losses including fire, burglary and losses through the dishonesty of employees,

and it was not disputed that, X having made defalcations to the extent of $2,680, contribution applied. It is not necessary in fact that the whole subject-matter of each insurance should be identical. It is sufficient if the loss which has occurred (in that case loss of $2,680) is covered by both policies.

An example of an insurance upon the same property which, nevertheless, has not the same subject-matter is afforded by increased value policies. The insurers under a valued policy have no right of contribution as against subsequent insurers under an increased value policy,[30] the increased value of the property rather than the property itself being the subject-matter of the second insurance.

8–33 (ii) *The loss must be due to a peril which is common to both policies.* *American Surety Co.* v. *Wrightson*[31] again affords a good illustration of this principle. In that case X's dishonesty was the common peril and it

[25] *North British* v. *London, Liverpool & Globe* (1877) 5 Ch.D. 569; *Zurich Insurance* v. *Shield Insurance* [1988] I.R. 174.
[26] *Austin* v. *Zurich* [1945] 1 K.B. 250.
[27] See Lord Wright M.R. in *Boag* v. *Standard Marine* [1937] 2 K.B. 113, 123.
[28] See James L.J. in *North British* v. *London, Liverpool & Globe* (1877) 5 Ch.D. 569, 581.
[29] (1910) 27 T.L.R. 91. See also *Boag* v. *Economic Insurance* [1954] 2 Lloyd's Rep. 581.
[30] *Boag* v. *Standard Marine* [1937] 2 K.B. 113.
[31] (1910) 27 T.L.R. 91.

did not matter that a number of other perils were also included in the respective policies.

With regard to both these requirements of common subject-matter and common risk it may still, however, be arguable that the right of contribution does not apply if the policies differ sufficiently in their scope.[32]

(iii) *The same interests must be covered by both policies.*[33] Again, it **8–34** does not matter if other interests are covered by one of the policies, provided one interest covered by both is identical. Thus, if a mortgagor takes out a policy covering his interest alone, and his mortgagee takes out another policy covering both their interests, their respective insurers will have a right of contribution as against each other,[34] but it is otherwise where a mortgagor and mortgagee insure their own interests alone by separate insurances.[35] The same rule applies to policies taken out by landlord and tenant.[36] In any event the principle only applies where the actual loss falls on the common interest. If a bailee insures his own interest in goods and the interest of the owner, and the owner also insures his interest, and the goods are lost by a peril in respect of which the bailee is liable to his bailor, there will be no right of contribution between their insurers.[37] In such a case the bailor's insurer, upon payment, is subrogated to his rights against the bailee, and no question of contribution arises. But it would be otherwise if the loss were caused by a fire for which the bailee was not responsible.

(iv) *Both policies must be enforceable.* A policy which is not legally **8–35** binding cannot give rise to a claim for contribution,[38] nor can one which is unenforceable for breach of a condition.[39] Both insurances must be such that the assured is entitled to call upon either insurer to pay in respect of the loss,[40] and both insurances must of course be enforceable at the time of the loss.[41]

Contractual restrictions on contribution   **8–36**

While the above principles are well recognised, it is common for insurers to seek to contract out of contribution and instead to cast the burden of full payment on the other insurer or insurers. This may be

---

[32] *Ibid.* at p. 93, *per* Hamilton, J. See also *Australian Agricultural Co.* v. *Saunders* (1875) L.R. 10 C.P. 668 and *Zurich Insurance* v. *Shield Insurance* [1988] I.R. 174.

[33] *Andrews* v. *Patriotic Assurance of Ireland* (1886) 18 L.R.Ir. 355.

[34] *Nichols* v. *Scottish Union* (1885) 2 T.L.R. 190, See § 14–27, *et seq infra.*

[35] *Scottish Amicable* v. *Northern Assurance* (1883) 11 R. (Ct. of Sees.) 287.

[36] *Portavon Cinema* v. *Price* (1939) 161 L.T. 417.

[37] *North British* v. *London, Liverpool & Globe* (1877) 5 Ch.D. 569.

[38] See *Woods* v. *Co-operative Insurance*, 1924, S.C. 692.

[39] *Austin* v. *Zurich* [1945] 1 K.B. 250. However, if the condition broken is a failure to notify a loss, such breach will not prevent contribution. Thus in *Legal and General Assurance* v. *Drake Insurance* [1989] 3 All E.R. 923 the assured made a full claim against insurer A, but did not claim against insurer B. When insurer A sought contribution from insurer B, insurer B argued that the assured had failed to notify his loss, in breach of condition, so that B was not liable. *Held*, not following *Monksfield* v. *Vehicle & General* [1971] 1 Lloyd's Rep. 139, that this was no defence to B as against A in contribution proceedings. *Quaere* how this sensible result can be reconciled with s.80(1) of the M.I.A. 1906. *Cf.* n. 23, *supra.*

[40] Goddard J. in *Jenkins* v. *Deane* (1933) 103 L.J.K.B. 250 254, 255.

[41] *Sickness & Accident* v. *General Accident* (1892) 19 R. (Ct. of Sess.) 977; *Equitable Fire* v. *Ching* [1907] A.C. 96; *Home Insurance* v. *Gavel* (1928) 30 Ll.L.R. 139.

done by a variety of clauses. Some policies contain non-contribution clauses, the effect of which is to exempt the insurer from liability if the assured is entitled to an indemnity under any other policy. Other policies contain rateable proportion clauses, whereby the insurer is only liable for his rateable proportion of the loss; such a clause prevents the assured from claiming the full amount from that insurer and leaving it to the insurer to seek to recover from the others by way of contribution. Clauses of these types, like contribution itself, only extend to the case where both policies cover the same interest and not where, for example, tenant for life and remainderman, or first and second mortgagee, both insure their separate interest in the same goods.[42] Like the right to contribution also, the clause does not apply where the assured has no legal right to recover under one of the policies.[43]

The courts do not favour clauses which seek to exempt the insurer from all liability where other insurance exists, and where such a clause appeared in a motor vehicle policy in conjunction with a rateable proportion clause Roche J. held the former to be qualified by the latter.[44] Where two policies covering the same accident both contained such an exemption, Rowlatt J. held that both insurers were liable under their respective policies.[45]

> "The reasonable construction is to exclude from the category of co-existing cover any cover which is expressed to be cancelled by such co-existence."[46]

However, it was subsequently held in a case involving consecutive liability insurances that a clause in the later policy excluding the insurer's liability in respect of claims notified under any earlier policy was effective to cast the entire burden upon the first insurer.[47]

8–37 Extent of insurer's liability

While the principles as to when an insurer is liable for contribution or protected by a rateable proportion clause are fairly clear, it is not always so clear what sum amounts to his rateable share. Where both insurances are unlimited, as in the case of most motor-vehicle policies, the total liability will be divided equally between them.[48] Where both insurances are limited to a fixed sum, each insurer will be liable to contribute in proportion to the amount for which he is liable under his contract.[49] Thus, if a house is insured with company X for £1,000 and with company Y for £2,000, and the damage amounts to £600, company X will apparently be liable to contribute £200 and company Y to contribute £400.[50]

---

[42] *North British* v. *London, Liverpool & Globe* (1877) 5 Ch.D. 569, 577, *per* Jessel M.R.; *Scottish Amicable* v. *Northern Assurance* (1883) 11 R. (Ct. of Sess.) 287. See also the authorities cited in para. 8–34, *supra*.

[43] Goddard J. in *Jenkins* v. *Deane* (1933) L.J.K.B. 250. See also *Woods* v. *Co-operative Insurance* 1924 S.C. 692, *Portavon Cinema* v. *Price* (1939) 161 L.T. 417 and the authorities cited in para. 8–35, *supra*.

[44] *Gale* v. *Motor Union* [1928] 1 K.B. 359.

[45] *Weddell* v. *Road Transport & General* [1932] 2 K.B. 563.

[46] *Ibid.* at p. 567.

[47] *National Employers Mutual* v. *Haydon* [1980] 2 Lloyd's Rep. 149.

[48] See *Weddell* v. *Road Transport & General* [1932] 2 K.B. 563; *Austin* v. *Zurich* [1945] 1 K.B. 250.

[49] See M.I.A. 1906, s.80(1).

[50] *Unitarian Congregation of Toronto* v. *Western* (1866) 26 U.C.Q.B. 175.

But contribution depends on equitable principles, and such a distribution would be inequitable where, for instance, one only of the insurances was subject to average. No general principles can, in fact, be laid down as to the assessment of each insurer's share, and there is hardly any English case law on the matter, while American decisions cannot be relied on.[51] Where, in *American Surety Co.* v. *Wrightson*[52] the insurances covered widely different risks, Hamilton J. held that the insurers were liable to contribute in proportion to the amounts for which each would have been liable had there been no other insurance. Thus, since one was liable for $2,500 only, and the sum insured in the case of the other was £40,000, but the loss only amounted to $2,680, it was held that they should each share this loss in the proportion, 2,500:2,680. This is referred to as the "in dependent liability" basis of calculation.

In *Commercial Union* v. *Hayden*[53] the calculation of contribution in **8–38** the context of *liability* insurance arose for decision. The assured were insured in the sum of £10,000 under a Lloyd's Public Liability Policy and in the sum of £100,000 under a compact policy of the plaintiffs, containing fire, money and public liability sections. By condition 3 of the Lloyd's policy: "*Other Insurance.* 3. If any claim covered by this Policy is also covered in whole or in part by any other insurance, the liability of the Underwriters shall be limited to their *rateable proportion* of such claim." The Compact policy contained a clause to the same effect. A man suffered an injury on the assured's premises. The plaintiffs settled this claim for £4,425.45 and claimed half of that (£2,212.72) from Lloyd's underwriters. Lloyd's underwriters paid only £402.31 (1/11th) to the plaintiffs who sued them for the balance. Donaldson J. gave judgment for the underwriters, but the Court of Appeal reversed his decision, granting leave to appeal to the Lords.

The contest was between the maximum liability ratio—each insurer bears that proportion of the loss which the sum insured by his policy bears to the aggregate of the sum insured by all the policies—and the independent liability ratio (applied by Viscount Sumner as Hamilton J. in the *Wrightson* case above)—each insurer bears that proportion of the loss which the sum for which he is liable under his policy bears to the aggregate of the liability under all the policies.

Donaldson J. had potent reasons for adopting the maximum liability basis: it was universally adopted in North America[54] and in England in relation to sureties.[55]

The Court of Appeal held, notwithstanding, that such clauses in liability policies[56] were to be construed on the independent liability basis; "The obvious purpose of having a limit of liability under an insurance policy is to protect the insurer from the effect of exceptionally large claims: it seems to me artificial to use the limits under two policies to

---

[51] Hamilton J. in *American Surety Co.* v. *Wrightson* (1910) 27 T.L.R. 91.
[52] (1910) 27 T.L.R. 91.
[53] [1977] 1 Lloyd's Rep. 1.
[54] [1977] 1 Lloyd's Rep. 1, 4.
[55] *Ibid.* at p. 5.
[56] The court refrained from determining the property insurance position.

adjust liability in respect of claims which are within the limits of either policy."[57]

Further, in the submission of this work, "*is liable*" in section 80(1) of the Marine Insurance Act 1906 cannot mean "might be liable" and is referable only to an independent liability basis. Marine insurance is property insurance. *Ergo*, that basis applies to an important part of property insurance, and to make exceptions to this rule on the basis of *Commercial Union* v. *Hayden* would be confusing and unnecessary.

---

[57] *Per* Cairns L.J. at p. 12.

CHAPTER 9

CLAIMS AND ARBITRATION

1. NOTICE AND PROOF

9–01 THE right of a claimant to demand payment cannot be enforced until he has done all the things which, by terms of the policy under which the right is asserted, are made conditions precedent to the liability of the insurers. If the undertaking is only to pay an amount which shall be fixed in a particular way the claimant will have no cause of action until after this has been done. If the undertaking is to pay a sum of money to some person chosen, either by the insurers themselves or by someone else, as being the one who is entitled to receive it, the claimant must prove that he is the person so chosen; in such a case, payment to a beneficiary chosen in good faith and according to the prescribed manner will be a good defence to claims made by other persons.[1]

9–02 Notice of loss[2]

Although by the principles of marine insurance law the assured is bound to give notice of abandonment to his insurers with reasonable diligence after a constructive total loss,[3] there is no duty upon him, apart from the express terms of the policy, to give immediate notice of an ordinary loss,[4] and the latter principle applies generally throughout insurance law. Except in the case of marine, life and certain Lloyd's policies, an express stipulation was nearly always inserted in policies of insurance which laid an obligation on the assured to give notice of a loss within a specified time. Such time might be limited in days,[5] or such words as "forthwith"[6] or "as soon as possible"[7] might be used.

Like other terms of the policy it is a matter of construction whether such provisions are conditions precedent to the assured's right of recovery, or mere collateral agreements, in which case the insurer's only remedy in the event of breach is a claim for damages to cover extra expense incurred by him owing to the assured's failure to give due notice.[8]

---

[1] *Law* v. *George Newnes Ltd.* (1894) 21 R. (Ct. of Sess.) 1027; *Hunter* v. *Hunter* (1904) 7 F. (Ct. of Sess.) 136; *O'Reilly* v. *Prudential Assurance* [1934] Ch. 519.

[2] Insurers' representative bodies, in their 1977 Statements of Practice, as subsequently revised, state that policy holders should not be asked to do more than report a claim and subsequent developments as soon as reasonably possible (except, in the case of non-life insurances, where there are legal processes and claims which a third party requires the policy holder to notify within a fixed time, and immediate advice may be required). The law stated in the text remains good law subject to the implementation of such statements by individual insurers.

[3] *Rankin* v. *Potter* (1873) L.R. 6 H.L. 83; M.I.A. 1906, s.62. If no notice of abandonment is given, the assured may treat a constructive total loss as a partial loss only.

[4] *Rankin* v. *Potter, supra, per* Brett J. at p. 103.

[5] *Cowley* v. *National Employers' Accident* (1885) Cab. & El. 597.

[6] *Trask* v. *State Fire* (1858) 29 Penn. 198; *Edwards* v. *Lycoming County Mutual* (1874) 75 Penn. 378; *Griffey* v. *New York Central* (1885) 53 Am.Rep. 202.

[7] *Verelst's Administratrix* v. *Motor Union* [1925] 2 K.B. 137.

[8] *Stoneham* v. *Ocean Accident* (1887) 19 Q.B.D. 237; *Re Coleman's Depositories* [1907] 2 K.B. 798; *Re Bradley and Essex & Suffolk Accident* [1912] 1 K.B. 415.

Where the policy provides that the notice is to be given "as soon as possible" all existing circumstances must be taken into account, including the available means of knowledge of the assured's personal representative, where the claim is in respect of the assured's death, of the existence of the policy and the identity of the insurance company.[9] Where notice is required to be given "immediately" or "forthwith" it is taken to mean within a reasonable time and without any unjustifiable delay.[10] In America notices given 11, or 18,[11] days after a fire have been held too late, but one given five days, including a Sunday, after the fire has been held in time.[12] In liability insurance the assured is generally required to give notice of an occurrence or event likely to give rise to a claim.[13]

9–03   *Condition applies even where notice impossible.* Where a clause requiring notice is a condition precedent the insurers may be entitled to rely on it even where no immediate ill resulted from an occurrence which afterwards gave rise to a claim. Thus, in *Cassel* v. *Lancashire and Yorkshire Accident*[14] the assured under an accident policy suffered a mishap while paddling a canoe, but the injury did not develop until eight months afterwards. He thereupon gave notice, but it was held that this notice did not comply with an obligation to give notice within 14 days after the date of the accident. It follows from this decision that where the policy lays down a fixed time for giving notice, the obligation on the assured or his representative is an absolute one, and no excuse, *e.g.* that the assured was in prison during the relevant period,[15] or that his representative did not know of the policy's existence,[16] that he did not know cash had been embezzled by his servant,[17] or that the claimant was the statutory assignee of the assured's rights under the policy, in accordance with the Third Parties (Rights against Insurers) Act 1930 and that a claim in time by him was impractical,[18] will avail. Nor did the fact that an accident caused the instantaneous death of the assured excuse his representatives from complying with a condition in an accident policy that, in the event of any accident to the assured, he or his representatives should give notice thereof in writing to the company with 10 days after its occurrence.[19] Moreover, in such cases it is no defence to the

---

[9] *Verelst's Administratrix* v. *Motor Union Ins. Co.* [1925] 2 K.B. 137.

[10] *Williams* v. *Lancashire & Yorkshire Accident* (1902) 19 T.L.R. 82; *Farrell* v. *Federated Employers Assurance* [1970] 3 All E.R. 632.

[11] *Trask* v. *State Fire, supra; Edwards* v. *Lycoming, supra.*

[12] *Griffey* v. *New York Central, supra.*

[13] *Thorman* v. *New Hampshire* [1988] 1 F.T.L.R. 30, holding that the issue of a writ is such an "occurrence."

[14] (1885) 1 T.L.R. 495. In *Browning* v. *Provincial Insurance of Canada* (1873) L.R. 5 P.C. 263 a policy on cargo provided that no action should be brought on it unless within 12 months "after any loss or damage shall occur." The vessel was lost with all hands. Some months later the wreck was found and part of the cargo sold. The Privy Council held that it was only then that time began to run "for not until that time were the facts constituting a total loss ascertained," and the condition "must receive a reasonable interpretation." *Quaere* whether this decision is sound in English law; the "Canadian Code," *inter alia*, was relied on. It may be noted, as the judgment observed, that there was "no defence whatever on the merits."

[15] *Tailman* v. *Mutual Fire of Clinton* (1867) 27 U.C.Q.B. 100.

[16] See n. 9.

[17] *Adamson* v. *Liverpool & London and Globe Ins.* [1953] 2 Lloyd's Rep. 355.

[18] *Farrell* v. *Federated Employers, supra; Pioneer Concrete* v. *National Employers Mutual* [1985] 2 All E.R. 395.

[19] *Patton* v. *Employers' Liability Assurance* (1887) 20 L.R.Ir. 93.

assured to argue that the insurer has not been prejudiced by the lateness of the claim.[20]

Where, however, an accident occurred before the policy was delivered to the assured, he being covered meanwhile by a cover note neither containing a condition as to notice nor referring to the conditions in the policy, it was held that the insurers could not take advantage of a condition in the policy requiring immediate notice.[21]

How notice should be given. Unless notice in writing is expressly **9–04** required by the policy[22] an oral notice will be sufficient.[23] It must be given, however, to an agent of the insurers who has authority to receive it; notice to a local agent is not necessarily sufficient.[24] But it is only necessary that he should have ostensible authority; the fact that, without the knowledge of the assured, he has ceased to represent the insurers, is not fatal.[25] The policy may require notice at the company's head office in which case notice to a local agent will rarely suffice.[26]

Notice need not be given by the assured (or his personal representative)[27] personally, even where the condition requires notice from him. It may be given by an agent,[28] by any person purporting to act on his behalf,[29] and it may even suffice that the insurer has otherwise become aware of the loss.[30]

Meaning of "notice." The meaning of "notice" in various enactments **9–05** has often been considered by the courts. Whether actual knowledge, however acquired, always amounts to notice is questionable.[31] "Notice" certainly means more than vague information which, if followed up, would lead to notice, and has been held to mean such notice as "brings home to the mind of a reasonable intelligent and careful recipient such knowledge as fairly, and in a business sense, amounts to notice of" the subject-matter in question.[32] But no general rule can be laid down: it depends on the interpretation of each individual statute. A casual conversation with an agent of an insurance company that did not indicate to him that formal notice was being given has been held insufficient notice of proceedings by a third party against the assured for the purposes of what is now section 149(2)(a) of the Road Traffic Act 1988[33]; so also where notice was given only that proceedings might be brought.[34] The Privy Council held,[35] in respect of a similar provision in a Ceylon Ordi-

---

[20] *Pioneer Concrete* v. *National Employers Mutual, supra.*
[21] *Re Coleman's Depositories* [1907] 2 K.B. 798.
[22] *Brook* v. *Trafalgar* (1947) 79 Ll.L.R. 365.
[23] See *Re Solvency Mutual; Hawthorn's Case* (1862) 31 L.J.Ch. 625.
[24] *Patton* v. *Employers' Liability Assurance* (1887) 20 L.R.Ir. 93.
[25] *Marsden* v. *City & County Insurance* (1865) L.R. 1 C.P. 232.
[26] *Marsden* v. *City & County Assurance* (1865) L.R. 1 C.P. 232; *Brook* v. *Trafalgar* (1947) 79 Ll.L.R. 365.
[27] See n. 24.
[28] *Davies* v. *National Fire of New Zealand* [1891] A.C. 485, 489 (P.C.).
[29] Murphy J. in *Patton* v. *Employers' Liability Assurance, supra,* at p. 100.
[30] *Barret Bros.* v. *Davies* [1966] 1 W.L.R. 1334.
[31] Lord Blackburn in *Mildred* v. *Maspons* (1883) 8 App.Cas. 874, 888. But see *per* Earl Selborne L.C. at p. 888.
[32] Lindley M.R. in *Greenwood* v. *Leather Shod Wheel Co.* [1900] 1 Ch. 421, 436.
[33] *Herbert* v. *Railway Passengers Ass.* [1938] 1 All E.R. 650.
[34] *Weldrick* v. *Essex* (1949) 83 Ll.L.R. 91; *Harrington* v. *Link Motor Policies* [1989] 2 Lloyd's Rep. 310.
[35] *Ceylon Motor Ins.* v. *Thambulaga* [1953] A.C. 584.

nance requiring "notice of the action," that it was unnecessary to give the name of the court—but that provision, like section 149(2)(a), contemplated the possibility of giving notice before the proceedings began.

In the case of a policy insuring against workmen's compensation risks a condition was inserted requiring the assured to forward "any written notice or information as to any verbal notice of claim arising through any accident." The assured forwarded the notice of claim but not a request for arbitration, but it was held that the office was liable, for the request for arbitration was but a step in procedure, and was not a written notice of claim within the meaning of the policy.[36]

9–06   *Waiver.* If the insurers know all the relevant facts, they may, by accepting that a claim has been made, be estopped from relying on the assured's failure to give notice which otherwise would have been requisite.[37] Mere delay by the insurer does not however, suffice.[38]

9–07   *Deemed abandonment of claim.* Policies sometimes provide that if a claim has been made by the assured and rejected by the insurer, the claim is deemed to have been abandoned unless proceedings are commenced by the assured within a stated period (normally 12 months from the date of rejection). Such clauses are enforceable even though compliance by the assured is impracticable. In *Walker* v. *Penine Insurance*[39] the assured notified his insurers of a possible claim against him under his motor liability policy, and the insurers replied by stating that they would not provide an indemnity. Judgment was not given against the assured for a further five years, at which point he instituted proceedings against the insurer. The Court of Appeal held that the clause barred the action, and that the assured's proper approach would have been to seek declaratory relief against the insurer within the period specified.

9–08 Particulars and proof of loss

It was the practice[40] of insurers to incorporate a provision in their policies making delivery of particulars or proof of loss in a stipulated way or in a stipulated time a condition precedent to recovery[41] and it has been held as long ago as 1796[42] that such provisions must be complied with, and that until they are the assured has no cause of action.[43] They have been reasonably construed[44] but the courts were in no way adverse to their enforcement.[45]

It may be a difficult question of construction as to how far such a pro-

---

[36] *Wilkinson* v. *Car & General Insurance* (1913) 110 L.T. 468.
[37] *Barrett* v. *Davies* [1966] 1 W.L.R. 1334.
[38] *Allen* v. *Robles* [1969] 3 All E.R. 154.
[39] [1980] 2 Lloyd's Rep. 156.
[40] It may be presumed, that this practice has ceased to be the practice after the 1977 Statements of Practice. "Particulars of loss" should surely be read as included in "a claim and subsequent developments."
[41] Lord Blackburn in *London Guarantee* v. *Fearnley* (1880) 5 App.Cas. 911, 916.
[42] *Worsley* v. *Wood* (1796) 6 T.R. 710.
[43] Bramwell B. in *Elliott* v. *Royal Exchange* (1867) L.R. 2 Ex. 237, 245.
[44] *Mason* v. *Harvey* (1853) 8 Ex. 819.
[45] *Welch* v. *Royal Exchange* [1939] 1 K.B. 294. This was then the standard form for a fire policy in this country.

vision should be construed as a condition precedent. Thus, in an Irish case, *Weir* v. *Northern Counties Insurance*,[46] it was held that where the time for an account of the loss was limited and the provision stipulated that "no claim was payable *until* such account" was given, the word *until* operated so that an account was only a condition precedent to a claim if it was never given. This case was distinguished in *Welch* v. *Royal Exchange*.[47] The provision in that case stipulated that the required particulars were to be given within a reasonable time and that no claim should be payable *unless* this were done. It was held that production of such particulars *within a reasonable time* was a condition precedent to recovery, and it did not avail the assured that he had ultimately produced them. Questions of construction may also arise where a clause expressed as a condition precedent to liability combines notice requirements and provision of proofs.[48]

Particulars required. The mere fact that such particulars are not completely accurate will not bar the assured's right of recovery[49] or estop him from later claiming the true amount of a loss.[50] But sufficient particulars must be given by the assured to enable the insurers to ascertain the nature, extent and character of the loss. "Full particulars" required by a condition means "the best particulars which the assured can reasonably give."[51] Although inadvertent omissions on the part of the assured will not be fatal, the fact that the assured could have more fully complied with a condition as to giving, within 15 days, such a detailed account of their loss "as the nature and circumstances of the case will permit," has been held to preclude him from recovery.[52]   **9–09**

The time for giving particulars might be limited in days or months,[53] or a reasonable time might be stipulated, in which case the court would allow the assured a longer time than they would for giving notice of loss.[54]

Proof required. Where proof satisfactory to the insurers is stipulated, proof that is reasonably satisfactory will be sufficient,[55] unless the insurers are bona fide dissatisfied.[56] It would not be reasonable were the insurers to demand a post-mortem of a person over whom the assured had no control, where it appeared on the whole evidence that the assured had died from an accident insured against.[57] Canadian authorities illustrate in some detail the proof that insurers may reasonably require. Thus, it has been held, they are entitled to call for the produc-   **9–10**

---

[46] (1879) 4 L.R.Ir. 689. See also *Oldham* v. *Bewicke* (1786) 2 H.Bl. 577 (note); *Western Australian Bank* v. *Royal* (1908) 5 C.L.R. 533.
[47] [1939] 1 K.B. 294.
[48] *Pioneer Concrete* v. *National Employers Mutual* [1985] 2 All E.R. 395.
[49] *Mason* v. *Harvey, supra.*
[50] *Vance* v. *Forster* (1841) Ir.Circ.Rep. 47; *Smiley* v. *Citizens* 14 West Virginia 33 (1878).
[51] Pollock C.B. in *Mason* v. *Harvey, supra,* at p. 821.
[52] *Hiddle* v. *National Fire of New Zealand* [1896] A.C. 372.
[53] See n. 44.
[54] *Re Carr* (1897) 13 T.L.R. 186.
[55] *Braunstein* v. *Accidental Death* (1861) 1 B. & S. 782. See *Manby* v. *Gresham Life* (1861) 4 L.T. 347.
[56] *London Guarantee* v. *Fearnley, supra; Welch* v. *Royal Exchange* [1939] 11 K.B. 294.
[57] *Ballantine* v. *Employers' Insurance* (1893) 31 S.L.R. 230.

tion of any relevant vouchers or accounts,[58] or for a builder's certificate of the value of a house at the time of a fire,[59] and a mere affidavit of the value of goods lost sworn by the assured has been held to be insufficient.[60]

Where the insurers do not insist on the proof of loss stipulated as a condition precedent in the policy, but conduct themselves so as to lead the assured to incur expense on another method of proof, they will not afterwards be entitled to rely on the condition.[61]

9–11　*Proof of death.* As to proof of death, evidence on which the court may deem a tenant for life to be dead is not necessarily satisfactory proof of his death to an insurance company with whom his life is insured,[62] but where the assured has disappeared and has not been seen or heard of for seven years by those, who, if he were alive, would be likely to hear of him, his death will be presumed.[63]

9–12　*Lost policy.* Apart from any express conditions in the policy no more evidence is necessary to sustain an action on a contract of insurance than any other similar action. Thus, if the policy is lost or destroyed, an action will nevertheless lie to recover the insurance money provided secondary evidence of its terms is available, and the order or judgment of the court directing the office to pay will be a sufficient indemnity against subsequent claims.[64]

9–13　*Condition as to ascertainment of amount of loss.* Ascertainment of the amount of the loss may also be made a condition precedent to recovery.[65] If the policy provides that the loss of profits due to fire should be assessed by the assured's auditors, the assessment of the auditors is conclusive of the quantum of the loss unless it is shown that the auditors had misdirected themselves in point of law, or had failed to take into account some material fact.[66]

9–14　*Proof of interest.* Similarly, provision may be made in a policy for proof of interest. Where a policy on the life of a third person stated that the proposer alleged that he was interested in the life of the assured "of which allegation satisfactory proof has to be furnished to the directors of the company," and went on to provide that should any difference or dispute arise between the proposer and the company the difference was to be decided by the judge of the county court, who should alone have jurisdiction to hear and determine it, it was held that proof of insurable

---

[58] *Cinqmars* v. *Equitable Insurance* (1857) 15 U.C.R. 143, 246; *Banting* v. *Niagara District Mutual Fire* (1866) 25 U.C.R. 431; *Carter* v. *Niagara Fire* (1868) 19 U.C.C.P. 143.

[59] *Fawcett* v. *London, Liverpool & Globe* (1868) 27 U.C.R. 225.

[60] *Mulvey* v. *Gore District Mutual Fire* (1866) 25 U.C.Q.B. 424.

[61] *Toronto Railway* v. *National British* (1914) 111 L.T. 555. See also *Yorkshire Insurance* v. *Craine* [1922] 2 A.C. 541.

[62] *Doyle* v. *City of Glasgow Ass.* (1883) 53 L.J.Ch. 527.

[63] *Willyams* v. *Scottish Widows' Fund, Law Assurance Society* (1888) 4 T.L.R. 489; *Prudential* v. *Edmonds* (1877) 2 App.Cas. 487, 509, *per* Lord Blackburn. *Cf. Thompson* v. *Thompson* [1956] P. 414.

[64] *Crokatt* v. *Ford* (1856) 25 L.J.Ch. 552; *England* v. *Tredegar* (1886) L.R. 1 Eq. 344.

[65] *Elliot* v. *Royal Exchange* (1867) L.R. 2 Ex. 237. See also *Johnston* v. *Western Assurance Co.* (1879) 4 U.C.App. 281; *Lampkin* v. *Western Assurance Co.* (1856) 13 U.C.Q.B. 237; *London and Lancashire Ins. Co.* v. *Honey* (1876) 2 Vict.L.R. 7.

[66] *Recher* v. *North British* [1915] 3 K.B. 277.

interest was not a condition precedent to the company's liability, and that the matter in dispute might be tried by a county court judge.[67]

Limitation Act 1980. Apart from such conditions an action on any **9–15** contract, including one of insurance, must by the Limitation Act 1980, be begun within six years from the date on which the cause of action accrued[68] unless the contract is under seal, in which case the period is 12 years.[69] Where the action is based on fraud or mistake, as where rescission or rectification of a life insurance policy is sought, the period of limitation only begins to run when the fraud or mistake is discovered, or could with reasonable diligence have been discovered.[70] This provision does not apply however where the policy has been assigned to a bona fide assignee for value.[71]

Where the policy contains a condition precedent to the assured's right to payment, the period will not begin to run until this condition has been fulfilled.[72] This principle used to apply where an award by arbitrators was a condition precedent to recovery,[72] but now a right of action under an agreement containing an arbitration clause is to accrue as it would but for that clause.[73]

These periods of limitation now apply to arbitrations as they do to actions, notice to appoint an arbitrator or to submit being replaced for issue of a writ.

Limitation for time of action by condition. The time laid down by the **9–16** Limitation Act in which an action or arbitration on a policy may be commenced is usually cut down, however, by an express clause in the policy, to some such period as 12 months.[74] The court may, in the case of arbitrations, extend such time "on such terms, if any, as the justice of the case may require . . . for such period as it thinks proper," but not beyond the time prescribed by the Limitation Act.[75]

2. SETTLEMENT OF CLAIMS

Binding settlements **9–17**

The adjustment and settlement of a claim under a contract of indemnity is usually a matter of negotiation, conducted between the insurers and their assessor on one side and the assured, advised possibly by a valuer or claim maker, on the other. A binding settlement can only be made, like any other contract, by the unconditional acceptance of an

---

[67] *Cowell* v. *Yorkshire Provident Life* (1901) 17 T.L.R. 452.

[68] Limitation Act 1980, s.5. *Quaere* when an action accrues under a policy of insurance. It is submitted that the action only accrues when the insurer rejects the assured's claim, and not at any earlier date.

[69] *Ibid.* s.8.

[70] *Ibid.* s.32. But where, *e.g.* a stolen car cannot be found, time will run, and insurers who have paid in respect of its loss will lose their subrogation rights if they cannot discover its whereabouts for six years: *R. B. Policies* v. *Butler* (1949) 65 T.L.R. 436.

[71] *Ibid.* s.32, proviso.

[72] *Cayzer Irvine* v. *Board of Trade* [1927] 1 K.B. 269.

[73] Limitation Act 1980, s.34.

[74] *Browning* v. *Provincial Insurance of Canada* (1873) L.R. 5 P.C. 263. See also *Walker* v. *Penine Insurance Co.* [1980] 2 Lloyd's Rep. 156.

[75] Arbitration Act 1950, s.27. The power to extend time is not confined to exceptional circumstances, and is exercisable despite the fact that the arbitration clause itself confers a power on the arbitrators to extend time: *Comdel* v. *Siporex* [1989] 2 Lloyd's Rep. 13.

offer,[76] and such a settlement replaces the insurers' obligations under the policy.[77] By such a settlement the insurers may even lose their rights of subrogation, as in a case in which the insurers only agreed to pay for a partial loss in respect of cotton seized and it was held that they were not entitled to the compensation the assured ultimately received in respect of the seizure.[78]

9–18 Simple adjustments

Such an agreement should be distinguished from a simple promise to pay on the part of the insurers, which will not be binding unless founded on previous liability.[79] Thus it has long been held that an adjustment of a marine insurance claim signed by an underwriter, though evidence against him,[80] is not conclusive,[81] where he is ignorant as to the true facts[82] or law[83] of the case and that in no case in such an adjustment any more than evidence of his liability.[84]

9–19 Payment irrecoverable unless made under mistake of fact

While a mere promise by the insurers to pay, apart from agreement, confers no right on the assured, whether or not the word "adjustment" is used,[85] payment once made by the insurers is irrecoverable unless it is made under a mistake of fact: *Kelly* v. *Solari*.[86] Thus where the insurers paid in ignorance that a warranty had been broken, it was held in an Irish case that the moneys were recoverable,[87] but where they paid in ignorance that since the policies were not stamped they were not legally liable, this was held to be a mistake of law and the moneys were therefore held irrecoverable, although they had not in fact been aware that the policies were not stamped.[88] Where the insurers, having paid, discovered that the assured being a mortgagee, his interest was not coextensive with the value of the ship insured, it was held that they were entitled to recover the balance.[89] So if the insurers pay in the mistaken belief that the loss was caused by perils insured against, they will be entitled to recover if their mistake was one of fact, but not if it was one as to the legal effect of the policy.[90] In a Scottish case it was held that moneys paid on a life policy in ignorance that the "life" assured had not expired were recoverable.[91] On the same principles money paid on account has been held recoverable, when it ultimately transpired that the insurers were under no liability.[92] It is unclear whether an insurer

---

[76] *Re Norske Lloyd* [1928] W.N. 99; *Chandler* v. *Poland* (1932) 44 Ll.L.R. 349. Contrast *Adams* v. *Saunders* (1829) 4 C. & P. 25, with *Herbert* v. *Champion* (1807) 1 Camp. 134.
[77] *Holmes* v. *Payne* [1930] 2 K.B. 301.
[78] *Brooks* v. *MacDonnell* (1835) 1 Y. & C. 500.
[79] *Herbert* v. *Champion* (1807) 1 Camp. 134.
[80] *Hogg* v. *Gouldney* (1745) Beawes 460; *Hewit* v. *Flexney* (1746) Beawes 458 (6th ed.).
[81] See cases cited 1 Park Ins. 267; *Christian* v. *Coombe* (1796) 2 Esp. 487.
[82] *Sheriff* v. *Potts* (1803) 5 Esp. 96.
[83] See n. 79.
[84] *Luckie* v. *Bushby* (1853) 13 C.B. 864.
[85] *Herbert* v. *Champion* (1807) 1 Camp. 134.
[86] (1841) 9 M. & W. 54, 58; *Pennsylvania Co.* v. *Mumford* [1920] 2 K.B. 537.
[87] *M'Entire* v. *Sun Fire* (1895) 29 Ir.L.T. 103.
[88] *Home & Colonial* v. *London Guarantee* (1928) 34 Com.Cas. 163.
[89] *Irving* v. *Richardson* (1831) 2 B. & Ald. 193.
[90] *Norwich Union* v. *Price* [1934] A.C. 455 (P.C.).
[91] *North British* v. *Stewart* (1871) 9 M. (Ct. of Sess.) 534.
[92] *The Dora Forester* [1900] P. 241.

who settles without realising that the policy is voidable for misrepresentation is under a mistake of fact[93] or law.[94]

Fraud 9–20

Neither a settlement,[95] even if sanctioned by the court,[96] nor a payment will be allowed to stand if it has been obtained by fraud, or if the payee has taken an unfair advantage of a mistake made by the payer.[97]

3. ARBITRATION

Clauses providing for the reference of disputes to arbitration are gener- 9–21
ally included in policies of assurance to prevent the delay and expense of litigation.[98] Quarrels on policies can thus be kept from the public eye, and discussion in public avoided, which might be painful and injurious even to a successful litigant.[99]

Like much of insurance law, a considerable part of the law relating to the enforcement of such clauses by insurers is now largely academic, consequent on the high standards set for themselves by most British insurers. The Association of British Insurers and Lloyd's made it known in 1956[1] that their members had agreed in general to refrain from insisting upon the enforcement of arbitration clauses in cases where the assured preferred to have the question of liability, as distinct from amount, determined by a court in the United Kingdom. It is understood that this does not apply to marine or aircraft insurance or reinsurance, or in cases where the terms of a policy including an arbitration clause have been specially negotiated.

Scott v. Avery clause 9–22

It was held in *Scott* v. *Avery*,[2] reversing old decisions to the contrary,[3] that it was a defence to a claim on an insurance policy that the parties had agreed to make submission of their disputes to arbitration a condition precedent to the enforcement of a claim. Though the parties cannot, by agreeing that no action shall be brought, oust the jurisdiction of the courts, they may agree that no action shall be brought until an award is made.[4]

Where an award is made a condition precedent to payment it does not

---

[93] *Magee* v. *Pennine Insurance* [1969] 2 Q.B. 507.
[94] *Bilbie* v. *Lumley* (1802) 2 East. 469.
[95] *Cook* v. *Wright* (1861) 1 B. & S. 559.
[96] *Stainton* v. *Carron Co*. (1854) 23 L.J.Ch. 299.
[97] *Ward* v. *Wallis* [1900] 1 Q.B. 675; *Saunders* v. *Ford Motor Co*. [1970] 1 Lloyd's Rep. 379; *Horry* v. *Tate & Lyle* [1982] 2 Lloyd's Rep. 416.
[98] *Per* Jessel M.R. in *Piercy* v. *Young* (1879) 14 Ch.D. 200, 208.
[99] Jessel M.R. in *Russell* v. *Russell* (1880) 14 Ch.D. 471, 477.
[1] See Law Reform Committee Fifth Report (Conditions and Exceptions in Insurance Policies) 1957, Cmnd. 62.
[2] (1856) 5 H.L.C. 811.
[3] *Kill* v. *Hollister* (1746) 1 Wils. 129; *Thompson* v. *Charnock* (1779) 8 T.R. 139.
[4] *Jureidini* v. *National British Insurance* [1915] A.C. 499, 504, *per* Viscount Haldane; Lord Dunedin in *Atlantic* v. *Louis Dreyfus* [1922] 2 A.C. 250, 255; Scrutton L.J. in *Czarnikow* v. *Roth, Schmidt* [1922] 2 K.B. 478, 488.

matter whether only the amount of such payment is left to arbitrators,[5] or whether the question of liability is left to them as well.[6]

Similarly it has been held in Scottish law, by which a reference to unnamed arbiters cannot usually be enforced, that where such reference is made a condition precedent to the bringing of any action upon a policy, the policy is unenforceable until an award has been made.[7]

9–23 Collateral agreements for arbitration

Such clauses should be distinguished from those by which, though there is a collateral agreement to refer a dispute to arbitration, such submission is not a condition precedent to bringing an action.[8] Thus, in *Collins* v. *Locke*,[9] a clause stipulating that all matters in difference should be submitted to arbitration, and prohibiting any action from being brought in respect of the matters actually submitted, was held to be a mere collateral agreement, and therefore no defence to an action. The question whether such a provision is a condition precedent or a collateral promise is a question of the construction of the particular policy in question.[10] Sometimes the policy expressly provides which clauses are to be read as conditions precedent[11]; in other cases it may be a question as to whether the parties have used sufficiently emphatic words.[12] Where it expressly states there can be no right of suit until arbitration, then arbitration is clearly a condition precedent.[13] The fact that the policy provides that disputes are to be referred to arbitration only if the insurers so require does not prevent the provision from being a condition.[14]

Where the arbitration clause is a mere collateral agreement the only remedy at common law against a party who refuses to arbitrate is an action for damages,[15] and such damages will probably be only nominal.

9–24 Stay of proceedings

But whatever the nature of the provision for arbitration, if legal proceedings are brought in any court in respect of any matter agreed to be referred to arbitration, an application may be made to the court to stay the proceedings. The decision of the Court whether or not to stay will depend on whether the arbitration agreement is "domestic" or non-domestic: in the former case the court has a discretion to stay the proceedings under section 4(1) of the Arbitration Act 1950, whereas in the latter case the court must grant a stay, in accordance with the provisions of the Arbitration Act 1975. An arbitration agreement is "domestic" if (1) it does not provide for arbitration in any state other than the United

---

[5] *Viney* v. *Bignold* (1887) 20 Q.B.D. 172.

[6] *Trainor* v. *Phoenix* (1891) 65 L.T. 825; Lord Lindley in *Spurrier* v. *La Cloche* [1902] A.C. 446, 451 (P.C.); *Lock* v. *Army Navy & General Assurance* (1915) 31 T.L.R. 297, 298, *per* Astbury J.

[7] *Caledonian Insurance* v. *Gilmour* [1893] A.C. 85.

[8] Contrast *Roper* v. *Lendon* (1859) 1 E. & E. 825 with *Elliot* v. *Royal Exchange* (1867) L.R. 2 Ex. 237.

[9] (1879) 4 App.Cas. 674.

[10] *Ibid.* at p. 689, *per* Sir Montague Smith.

[11] *Stoneham* v. *Ocean Accident* (1887) 19 Q.B.D. 237.

[12] *Braunstein* v. *Accidental Death* (1861) 1 B. & S. 782.

[13] *Viney* v. *Bignold* (1887) 20 Q.B.D. 172.

[14] *Woodall* v. *Pearl Assurance* [1919] 1 K.B. 593.

[15] See Lord Watson in *Caledonian Insurance* v. *Gilmour* [1893] A.C. 85, 96.

Kingdom *and* (2) neither party is: (a) an individual who is a national of or habitually resident in any state other than the United Kingdom; nor (b) a body corporate incorporated in, or where the central management or control is exercised in, any state other than the United Kingdom.[16] Consequently, if the agreement has any domestic flavour whatsoever, it will fall outside the 1975 Act.

Mandatory stay of proceedings in non-domestic cases[17]

In the case of a non-domestic agreement, the court is generally **9–25** required to grant a stay of the judicial proceedings under section 1 of the 1975 Act on the application of either of the parties. The court may refuse a stay only where it is satisfied that the arbitration agreement is void or does not cover the dispute between the parties, or where the person applying for the stay has taken a step in the judical proceedings.[18]

Discretionary stay of proceedings in domestic cases

The power to stay judicial proceedings is conferred upon the court by **9–26** section 4(1) of the Arbitration Act 1950. The section applies wherever there has been a "submission", defined in section 32 as a "written agreement to submit present or future differences to arbitration," and it has been held that a policy of insurance containing a clause that differences arising under it should be referred to arbitration, amounts to such a submission although it has not been signed by the assured.[19] An agreement to refer a question to valuers is not such a submission, but an agreement to refer it to any particular British or foreign court is.

The court's power to stay the action is purely discretionary.[20] Where the arbitration is a condition precedent to the claim it ought generally to stay an action which could not succeed,[21] but a stay may be refused where difficult questions of law are involved.[22] A stay will normally be refused where questions of law only are in dispute,[23] but where questions both of law and fact are in dispute a stay will not be refused on the sole ground that a question of law is involved.[24]

The fact that the dispute mainly covers matters not within the arbi- **9–27** tration clause is a ground for refusing a stay[25] as is the fact that the applicant for the stay has taken a step in the judicial proceedings other than merely appearing to contest the jurisdiction of the court.[26]

---

[16] Arbitration Act 1975, s.1(4).

[17] The provisions of the Arbitration Act 1975 bring into effect in English law the New York Convention on the Recognition and Enforcement of Foreign Arbitral Awards, 1958.

[18] See *infra*, § 9–27.

[19] *Baker* v. *Yorkshire Fire and Life* [1892] 1 Q.B. 144; *Austrian Lloyd Steamship Co.* v. *Gresham Life* [1903] 1 K.B. 249, 252.

[20] Astbury J. in *Lock* v. *Army, Navy & General Insurance* (1915) 31 T.L.R. 297, 298.

[21] *Freshwater* v. *Western Australian Assurance* [1933] 1 K.B. 515, 528, *per* Romer L.J. See also Collins M.R. in *Hodson* v. *Railway Passengers' Assurance* [1904] 2 K.B. 833, 837; Scrutton L.J. in *Jones* v. *Birch* [1933] 2 K.B. 597, 604.

[22] *Clough* v. *County Live Stock Insurance* (1916) 85 L.J.K.B. 1185.

[23] *Re Carlisle* (1890) 44 Ch.D. 200; *Montagu* v. *Provident Accident* (1935) 51 Ll.L.R. 153; but see *Lock* v. *Army, Navy & General Insurance* (1915) 31 T.L.R. 297.

[24] *Rowe Bros.* v. *Crossley* (1912) 108 L.T. 11, 13, 14, 15; *Valle Jones* v. *Liverpool & London & Globe* (1933) 46 Ll.L.R. 313.

[25] *Turnock* v. *Sartoris* (1889) 43 Ch.D. 150; contrast *Ives* v. *Barker & Williams* [1894] 2 Ch. 478.

[26] *Eagle Star* v. *Yuval* [1978] 1 Lloyd's Rep. 357.

An allegation of fraud, especially if made by the applicant,[27] was always a good ground for refusing a stay[28] where the arbitration clause was not a condition precedent to liability.[29] Now, by section 24(2) of the Arbitration Act 1950, the court may order that an agreement to refer shall cease to have effect where the question whether any party has been guilty of fraud arises, and by section 14(3) the court may also refuse to stay an action brought in such circumstances in breach of the agreement. Fraud has thus become a good ground for refusing a stay in all cases.

The fact that someone has begun proceedings against the assured is no ground for refusing the insurers a stay in third party proceedings brought against them by the assured.[30] The poverty of the assured is not a ground for refusing a stay.[31]

9–28 Burden of proof

The applicant for a stay must adduce evidence that he is ready and willing to refer the dispute to arbitration,[32] but having done so the onus will shift to the plaintiff in the action to show reason why it should not be referred.[33] It is essential that the person opposing the application should show some special circumstances by reason of which the court should allow him to depart from his contractual engagement to arbitrate.[34] Partiality of the arbitrator is such a circumstance.[35]

9–29 Disputes not covered by clauses

A party to a contract cannot deny its validity and also rely on an arbitration clause in it, but he will not be held to have elected to affirm the contract where he seeks to rely on the arbitration clause and also to rescind the contract for breach of condition by the other party to it: *Heyman* v. *Darwins*.[36] The issue of his right to rescind will be covered by a sufficiently wide clause. "In a situation where the parties are at one in asserting that they entered into a binding contract, but a difference has arisen between them whether there has been a breach by one side or the other, or whether circumstances have arisen which have discharged one or both parties from further performance, such differences should be regarded as differences which have arisen "in respect of," or "with regard to," or "under" the contract, and an arbitration clause which uses these, or similar, expressions should be construed accordingly."[37]

---

[27] *Russell* v. *Russell* (1880) 14 Ch.D. 471, 476–477, *per* Jessel M.R.

[28] *Trainor* v. *Phoenix Assurance* (1891) 65 L.T. 825, 828, *per* Coleridge L.C.J.; *Vawdrey* v. *Simpson* [1896] 1 Ch. 166, *per* Chitty J.

[29] Romer L.J. in *Stevens* v. *Timber Accident* (1933) 102 L.J.K.B. 337, 341; *Scott* v. *Mercantile Accident* (1892) 66 L.T. 811.

[30] *Gowar* v. *Hales* [1928] 1 K.B. 191.

[31] *Smith* v. *Pearl* (1939) 55 T.L.R. 335. See also *Fakes* v. *Taylor Woodrow* [1973] 1 Q.B. 436 and *Goodman* v. *Winchester and Alton Railway* [1984] 3 All E.R. 594.

[32] Jessel M.R. in *Piercy* v. *Young* (1879) 14 Ch.D. 200, 209; and see *Hodson* v. *Railway Passengers' Assurance, supra.*

[33] Jessel M.R. in *Hodson* v. *Railway Passengers' Assurance* (1882) 9 Q.B.D. 188, 190; Chitty J. in *Vawdrey* v. *Simpson* [1896] 1 Ch. 166; Eve J. in *Skinner* v. *Uzielli* (1908) 24 T.L.R. 266–267.

[34] Scrutton L.J. in *Gowar* v. *Hales* [1928] 1 K.B. 191, 198–199, and in *Valle Jones* v. *Liverpool, London & Globe* (1933) 46 Ll.L.R. 313.

[35] *Edwards* v. *Aberayron Mutual Ship* (1876) 1 Q.B.D. 563; Cozens-Hardy M.R. in *Rowe Bros.* v. *Crossley* (1912) 108 L.T. 11, 14.

[36] [1942] A.C. 356, 366. See also Greene L.J.'s judgment in *Toller* v. *Law Accident* [1936] 2 All E.R. 952, 955–957; *Woolf* v. *Collis Removal Service* [1948] 1 K.B. 11. See also § 9–32 *infra*.

[37] *Per* Viscount Simon in *Heyman* v. *Darwins* [1942] A.C. 356, 366.

An arbitration clause will rarely be drawn in terms sufficiently wide to **9–30** cover any disputes except those arising under the contract. It will not usually cover disputes under subsequent agreements. Thus, an arbitration clause in a policy has been held not to cover an agreement to compromise after a loss, and not to preclude, therefore, in any way, an action based on such compromise.[38] However, an arbitration clause may cover a claim by one party for rectification of the policy, even though a claim does not arise out of the particular written agreement in question, but seeks to substitute another agreement for it.[39]

It follows from these principles that the insurers under a policy of insurance cannot both rely on a clause providing for arbitration and also:

(a) deny that any binding contract of insurance was ever completed,[40]

(b) claim that the policy is void on the ground that the assured has not the necessary insurable interest required by statute,[41]

(c) avoid the policy for non-disclosure or misrepresentation.[42]

Issue of fraud   **9–31**

In the much discussed case of *Jureidini* v. *National British and Irish Millers Insurance*[43] the insurers repudiated a claim for loss by fire on the ground of arson by the assured. The policy provided that if any difference arose as to the *amount* of any loss such difference should be referred to arbitration, and that it should be a condition precedent to any right of action upon the policy that the award of the arbitrator as to the amount of the loss, if disputed, should be first obtained. It was held that this latter clause did not preclude the assured from bringing an action to enforce his claim. The majority of the House of Lords came to this conclusion on the ground that no difference as to amount had arisen and that the clause had therefore no application.[44] Viscount Haldane, however, appeared to decide the case on the ground that the insurers' objection to payment was based on a charge of fraud, which went to the substance of the whole contract. The better view, however, is that fraud is merely a breach of contract which does not normally permit rescission *ab initio* but merely termination for breach. It is in any event clear from subsequent cases that *Jureidini's* case does not decide that where the insurers do no more than make allegations which, if established, would relieve them from liability under the terms of the policy, they cannot also rely on an arbitration clause in it.[45]

---

[38] *Taylor* v. *Warden Insurance* (1933) 45 Ll.L.R. 218.

[39] All depends upon the wording. A narrow view was taken by Greene M.R. in *Crane* v. *Hegeman-Harris* [1939] 4 All E.R. 68, 72 and by Warrington J. in *Printing Machinery* v. *Linotype* [1912] 1 Ch. 566, 572. Cf. *Fillite (Runcorn) Ltd.* v. *Aqaulift* (1989) *The Times*, February 28. But see *Ashville* v. *Elmer* [1988] 2 All E.R. 577; *Ethiopian Oilseeds* v. *Rio del Mar Foods* (1989) *The Financial Times*, August 8.

[40] *Toller* v. *Law Accident* [1936] 2 All E.R. 952. See Greene L.J. at pp. 955–957.

[41] *Macaura* v. *Northern Assurance* [1925] A.C. 619.

[42] *Ashville* v. *Elmer*, *supra*.

[43] [1915] A.C. 499.

[44] Viscount Simon in *Heyman* v. *Darwins* [1942] A.C. 356, 365.

[45] See Lord Wright in *Heyman* v. *Darwins* [1942] A.C. 356, 387.

9–32 Repudiation in lieu of avoidance

It frequently happens that it will benefit the insurers not to avoid a policy, even where there has been a material misrepresentation on the part of the assured, but to rely solely on the condition usually to be found in a policy that all answers in the proposal form shall be true. It has been held time and again that where they repudiate liability only on this ground they can also rely on an arbitration clause in the policy.[46] It will not necessarily matter even that the insurers have previously alleged non-disclosure and have claimed to avoid the contract on that ground, providing that their avoidance is incomplete[47] or duly withdrawn.[48] So where the insurers agree not to rely on a suggested non-disclosure a stay will be refused.[49]

The Irish cases *Ballasty* v. *Army, Navy*[50] and *Finey* v. *Eagle Star*[51] can only now be considered authorities in that country for the proposition that the insurers cannot avoid for non-disclosure or misrepresentation and also rely on an arbitration clause. The truth of statements made was warranted in the policies, and yet the insurers were held not to be able to rely on these warranties and on the arbitration clauses, but the decisions were in this respect in conflict with the English cases cited above.

9–33 Persons standing in assured's shoes bound by clause

Persons who have, by Act of Parliament, been given the same rights under the policy as the assured will, like him, be bound by an arbitration clause in the policy. This was decided in respect of third parties' rights under the Road Traffic Act now of 1972[52] and in respect of the Third Parties (Rights against Insurers) Act 1930.[53]

4. FRAUDULENT CLAIMS

9–34 Where the assured makes a fraudulent claim the insurer apparently has the right either to reject the claim or to regard the policy as having been repudiated by the assured's breach.[54] There is some authority for the proposition that the fact that the policy is one of utmost good faith entitles the insurer to avoid the contract *ab initio*, but this would appear to be a doubtful proposition.[55] What is clear, however, is that if the assured makes a fraudulent claim he cannot recover at all,[56] and con-

---

[46] *Stebbing* v. *Liverpool & London & Globe* [1917] 2 K.B. 433; *Woodall* v. *Pearl* [1919] 1 K.B. 593; *Golding* v. *London & Edinburgh* (1932) 43 Ll.L.R. 487; *Stevens* v. *Timber Accident* (1933) 49 T.L.R. 224; *Freshwater* v. *Western Australian Assurance* [1933] 1 K.B. 515.

[47] *Golding* v. *London & Edinburgh, supra.*

[48] *Stevens* v. *Timber Accident, supra.*

[49] *Metal Products Ltd.* v. *Phoenix Assurance* (1925) 23 Ll.L.R. 87.

[50] (1916) 50 Ir.L.T. 114.

[51] (1922) 56 Ir.L.T. 23.

[52] *Freshwater* v. *Western Australian Assurance* [1933] 1 K.B. 515; *Jones* v. *Birch Bros.* [1933] 2 K.B. 597.

[53] *The Padre Island* (No. 1) [1984] 2 Lloyd's Rep. 408.

[54] *Britton* v. *Royal Insurance* (1866) 4 F. & F. 905.

[55] See the speech of Viscount Haldane in *Jureidini* v. *National British* [1915] A.C. 499. *Cf. Black King Shipping* v. *Massie, The Litsion Pride* [1985] 1 Lloyd's Rep. 437 and *Continental Illinois National Bank* v. *Alliance Insurance* [1986] 2 Lloyd's Rep. 470. These cases rest upon the questionable proposition that the duty of utmost good faith continues beyond the formation of the contract: see *supra.*, 5.05.

[56] *Britton* v. *Royal, supra.*; Pollock C.B. in *Goulstone* v. *Royal* (1858) 1 F. & F. 276; *Norton* v. *Royal* (1885) 1 T.L.R. 460.

ditions in the policy to this effect[57] are declaratory of the legal position without them.[58]

A statement made by the assured is fraudulent if he knows it to be false and makes it in order that the insurers may act upon it. The most common examples are claims made by an assured who has himself destroyed the property insured, or grossly exaggerated claims. Mere exaggeration, however, is not conclusive evidence of fraud,[59] for value is often a matter of opinion, though such exaggeration will amount to fraud if it is dishonestly made, or so greatly in excess of the true amount as to be incompatible with good faith.[60] It has been said that twice the actual amount would be evidence of fraud.[61] The question whether, despite an exaggerated claim, the assured can recover the real amount of his loss, or whether, the claim being fraudulent, he can recover nothing[62] is a question of fact depending on the circumstances of each case,[63] and juries have come to some odd decisions, having allowed £87 in a claim for £274[64] and £150 in a claim for £507[65] without finding fraud.

Other forms of fraud include deliberate destruction by the assured[66] and misstatement as to the circumstances of the loss.[67] Where the assured is shown to have made a fraudulent claim, neither he nor anyone else can recover under his policy. Thus, his trustee in bankruptcy has also been held to be precluded from recovery.[68]

Fraud may be inferred from gross negligence,[69] or from forbearance to use reasonable exertions and means at hand to arrest the development of a fire or other casualty.[70]

Fraud of one assured only 9–35

Where a policy is taken out by two persons jointly interested in property, and one puts in a fraudulent claim, both are precluded from recovering on the policy, but where a composite policy is taken out covering the interests of several persons, a fraudulent claim by one will in no way prejudice proper claims by the others if they are not tainted by the fraud.[71]

---

[57] As in *Jureidini* v. *National British*, *supra*.
[58] *Britton* v. *Royal*, *supra*.
[59] Goddard J. in *London Assurance* v. *Clare* (1937) 57 Ll.L.R. 254, 268.
[60] *Chapman* v. *Pole* (1870) 22 L.T. 306; *Herman* v. *Phoenix* (1924) 18 Ll.L.R. 371; *Dome Mining Corporation* v. *Drysdale* (1931) 41 Ll.L.R. 109; *Central Bank of India* v. *Guardian* (1936) 54 Ll.L.R. 247; *Shoot* v. *Hill* (1936) 55 Ll.L.R. 29.
[61] *Britton* v. *Royal*, *supra*.
[62] *Jureidini* v. *National British*, *supra*.
[63] See n. 60.
[64] *Norton* v. *Royal*, *supra*.
[65] *Hodgkins* v. *Wrightson* (1910) *The Times*, March 24.
[66] M.I.A. 1906, s.55(2)(a): see 4.03 *et seq.*
[67] *Lek* v. *Mathews* (1927) 22 W.L.R. 141; *Cox* v. *Orion* [1982] R.T.R. 1; *The Litsion Pride* [1985] 1 Lloyd's Rep. 437.
[68] *Re Carr and Sun Insurance* (1897) 13 T.L.R. 186.
[69] *Goodman* v. *Harvey* (1836) 4 A. & E. 870, 876.
[70] *Gove* v. *Farmers' Mutual Fire Ins. Co.* (1868) 2 Am.Rep. 168; 48 N.H. 41; *Huckins* v. *People's Ins. Co.* (1855) 3 N.H. 238, 248; *Chandler* v. *Worcester Mutual* (1849) 57 Mass. 328; *Devlin* v. *Queen Insurance* (1882) 46 U.C.R. 611, 621–623.
[71] *General Accident, Fire & Life* v. *Midland Bank* [1940] 2 K.B. 388. See also *Small* v. *United Kingdom Marine* [1897] 2 Q.B. 42.

CHAPTER 10

PROPERTY IN POLICIES

1. POLICIES AS A FORM OF PROPERTY

A POLICY of insurance constitutes not only a contract *inter partes*; it is **10–01** also a species of property. In cases, for instance, such as *Waters* v. *Monarch Life*,[1] an assured who has only a limited interest in the subject-matter insured will be obliged, if he has insured with the intention of covering the interest of the owner, to hold his share of any moneys paid under the policy as trustee for him. In such a case the owner of the subject-matter has a proprietary interest in the policy moneys.

So it is necessary generally to consider:

(a) the extent to which the assured may assign his rights under a policy to third parties;

(b) how far third parties, notwithstanding the fact that they are strangers to the contract of insurance, may have equitable rights of a proprietary nature, either as beneficiaries under a trust or otherwise apart from assignment, in a policy or in moneys paid under it; and

(c) common law liens (dependent on possession) and equitable liens on policies.

2. ASSIGNMENT OF POLICIES

Since practically all the decided cases on the assignment of insurance **10–02** policies have been decisions on life policies and the matter is one of some difficulty, detailed consideration of it has been reserved for Chapter 16. The fundamental principles of assignment are common to all policies.

The old common law rule was that things in action, such as a debt due under a contract, could not be assigned to another without the assent of the debtor. A novation of the debt by the consent of all three parties was necessary. Assignments were always valid in equity, however, and courts of equity enabled the assignee even of a legal thing in action to bring an action at law against the debtor in the assignor's name, by restraining the assignor from objecting to his use of it on being given a proper indemnity against costs.[2] "A policy certainly must be transferred: for though a *chose in action* cannot in law be assigned, yet in equity it may; therefore we will permit the action to be brought by

---

[1] (1856) 5 E. & B. 870.
[2] *Row* v. *Dawson* (1749) White and Tudor's *Equity Cases*, Vol. I, p. 105; *Ashley* v. *Ashley* (1829) 3 Sim. 149; *Pearson* v. *Amicable Assurance* (1859) 27 Beav. 229.

trustees."[3] The Policies of Assurance Act 1867, and the Policies of Marine Assurance Act 1868,[4] made life and marine insurance policies respectively assignable at law, and section 25(6) of the Judicature Act 1873 made all debts and other things in action thus assignable. Section 136 of the Law of Property Act 1925 now replaces this general provision, and covers absolute assignments in writing of things in action. An assignment which does not comply with section 136 may nevertheless take effect in equity.

10–03   *Section 136 of the Law of Property Act 1925 (Legal assignment of things in action)* provides:

> (1) Any absolute assignment by writing under the hand of the assignor (not purporting to be by way of charge only) of any debt or other legal thing in action, of which express notice in writing has been given to the debtor, trustee or other person from whom the assignor would have been entitled to claim such debt or thing in action, is effectual in law (subject to equities having priority over the right of the assignee) to pass and transfer from the date of such notice—
>
> > (*a*)   the legal right to such debt or thing in action;
> >
> > (*b*)   all legal and other remedies for the same; and
> >
> > (*c*)   the power to give a good discharge for the same without the concurrence of the assignor:
> >
> > Provided that, if the debtor, trustee or other person liable in respect of such debt or thing in action has notice—
> >
> > (*a*)   that the assignment is disputed by the assignor or any person claiming under him; or
> >
> > (*b*)   of any other opposing or conflicting claims to such debt or thing in action;
>
> he may, if he thinks fit, either call upon the persons making claim thereto to interplead concerning the same, or pay the debt or other thing in action into court under the provisions of the Trustee Act 1925.

10–04 Life policies

Life policies are to be considered something more than a contract. They are treated as securities for money[5] payable at an uncertain but future date which is bound to occur. Apart from the operation of excepted peril, the insurers will be bound to pay the sum insured at some date, and the original contract is therefore to be considered as the purchase of a reversionary sum in consideration of the payment of an annuity.[6] Even the present "surrender" value of the policy is computable actuarially. Insurance offices will usually accept surrender for such a consideration, and banks will therefore lend money on it to this amount. If a life policy is in the possession of a third party on the death of the assured, his personal representatives can maintain an action of trover against the third party in respect of it.[7] If the insurance is upon the assured's own life, the right to the policy moneys will devolve on his

---

[3] Ashhurst J. in *Delaney* v. *Stoddart* (1785) 1 T.R. 22, 26.

[4] See now Marine Insurance Act 1906, s.50.

[5] Romilly M.R. in *Stokoe* v. *Cowan* (1861) 4 L.T. 675, 685.

[6] Jessel M.R. in *Fryer* v. *Morland* (1876) 3 Ch.D. 675, 685. See also *Re Harrison and Ingram, ex p. Whinney* [1900] 2 Q.B. 710, 718.

[7] *Rummens* v. *Hare* (1876) 1 Ex.D. 169.

personal representatives on his death, who will be bound to treat it as money owing to him and forming part of his estate[8] just as much as money due to him under a promissory note.[9]

Life policies are things in action[10] and are freely assignable whether **10–05** they are expressed to be payable to the assigns of the assured[11] or not,[12] provided that the assignment complies with s.136 of the Law of Property Act 1925 or the Policies of Assurance Act 1867.[13] The assignment may take the form of sale, mortgage, settlement or gift. He may leave it by will, or make it, without anything in writing, the subject of a *donatio mortis causa*.[14] On the other hand an assured's creditors may be entitled to take his life policy, like other property, in execution.[15]

An assignment passes a right to the insurance moneys whether or not the assignor[16] or the assignee[17] has an insurable interest in the life assured, provided that the assurance was valid in the first place. A life policy will not be valid in its inception if the *ab initio* intention of the assured was to assign it to a person without interest.[18]

Conditions forbidding assignment. However, the right of the assured **10–06** to deal with the policy as he chooses only exists subject to any condition in the policy to the contrary. Thus a condition forbidding assignment has been held to make a policy non-assignable at law.[19] A court would be slow, however, to construe such a condition in such a way as to prevent an assignee's interest from being enforceable in equity, nor will it affect the interest of a beneficiary under a declaration of trust.[20] Nor is the assignment of a claim on a policy after loss a breach of a condition against alienation of the property insured.[21]

Indemnity policies 10–07

Assignment of the policy. Indemnity policies are things in action in the same was as life policies,[22] and may be assigned at law in accordance with section 136 of the Law of Property Act 1925, although the assignment is subject to equities, so that any defences which the insurer possessed against the assured will be available against the assignee. There are nevertheless two restrictions on assignability. First, as indemnity policies are personal to the assured, it is necessary—subject to any con-

---

[8] *Petty* v. *Wilson* (1869) L.R. 4 Ch. 574.
[9] *Ibid.* at p. 575, *per* Selwyn L.J.
[10] *Re Moore* (1878) 8 Ch.D. 519.
[11] *Williams* v. *Thorp* (1828) 2 Sim. 257.
[12] *Haas* v. *Atlas Insurance* [1913] 2 K.B. 209.
[13] See § 16.35 *et seq.*
[14] *Witt* v. *Amis* (1861) 1 B. & S. 109.
[15] *Stokoe* v. *Cowan* (1861) 29 Beav. 637; but see *contra* the Irish decisions, *Alleyne* v. *Darcy* (1855) 5 Ir.Ch.R. 56 and *Re Sargent's Policy* (1879) 7 L.R.Ir. 66.
[16] *Dalby* v. *India & London Life* (1854) 15 C.B. 365; *Law* v. *London Indisputable Life* (1855) 1 K. & J. 223.
[17] *Ashley* v. *Ashley* (1829) 3 Sim. 149.
[18] *M'Farlane* v. *Royal London Friendly Society* (1886) 2 T.L.R. 755.
[19] *Re Turcan* (1888) 40 Ch.D. 5.
[20] *Ibid. per* Cotton L.J. at pp. 9, 10.
[21] *Garden* v. *Ingram* (1852) 23 L.J. Ch. 478; see also *Randall* v. *Lithgow* (1884) 12 Q.B.D. 525.
[22] Lord Hanworth M.R. in *Hood's Trustees* v. *Southern Union* [1928] Ch. 793, 803.

tractual waiver by the insurer—to obtain the consent of the insurer to any assignment.[23] It has been held that any purported assignment without consent operates as an automatically determining factor.[24] Thus, a valid assignment operates as a novation, with a change of assured.

The second restriction is imposed by the rules of insurable interest, and requires that there is a contemporaneous assignment of the policy and the subject matter insured by the policy. If the insured subject matter is assigned but the policy is not assigned, the policy will lapse automatically as a matter of law for the assured has lost his insurable interest[25]; policies often expressly provide for lapse in such circumstances.[26] This rule operates only where the assured parts with the entirety of his interest, so that if he has merely agreed to sell property and has retained legal title the policy will not lapse.[27]

Conversely, if the assured has assigned the policy without assigning the underlying insured subject matter, the assignee has no insurable interest to support the policy and thus will not be able to recover.[28]

10–08   *Assignment of the proceeds of the policy.* The proceeds of a policy of insurance are a chose in action and the assured can grant a valid assignment of the right to recover under any policy without the consent of the insurer or the assignment of the insured subject matter. If it complies with the relevant Acts the assignment will be valid in law and the assignee may sue the company in his own name. If it does not, it may nevertheless be effective in equity, and the assignee may only sue the company in his own name if the assignor has been joined in the action, as plaintiff if he consents, or otherwise as defendant.[29]

Although the right to recover under a policy of indemnity is a thing in action it is not regarded as a debt but as a right to unliquidated damages.[30]

On the liquidation[31] or bankruptcy[32] of the assured the right to claim under the policy is assigned by operation of law to the liquidator or trustee in bankruptcy.

It is immaterial whether the proceeds of the policy are assigned to one interested in the subject matter insured or not, or whether it is made before or after the loss.[33]

---

[23] *Lynch* v. *Dalzell* (1729) 4 Bro. 431; *Sadler's Company* v. *Badcock* (1743) 2 Atk. 554. Marine policies are an exception to this rule: M.I.A. 1906, s.50. However, policies on hulls may on occasion expressly require the insurer's consent to assignment.

[24] *Peters* v. *General Accident* [1938] 2 All E.R. 267.

[25] *Ecclesiastical Commissioners* v. *Royal Exchange* (1895) 11 T.L.R. 476; *Rogerson* v. *Scottish Automobile Insurance* [1931] 1 All E.R. Rep. 606; *Tattersall* v. *Drysdale* [1935] 2 K.B. 174. The marine rule is the same: M.I.A. 1906, s.51, codifying *Powles* v. *Innes* (1843) 11 M. & W. 10 and *North of England Oil Cake Co.* v. *Archangel Insurance* (1875) L.R. 10 Q.B. 249. There is no rule of law to the effect that the assignment of insured subject matter carries with it the policy: M.I.A. 1906, s.15.

[26] *Boss* v. *Kingston* [1962] 2 Lloyd's Rep. 431.

[27] *Collingridge* v. *Royal Exchange* (1877) 3 Q.B.D. 173; *Rayner* v. *Preston* (1881) 18 Ch.D. 1.

[28] *Lloyd* v. *Fleming* (1872) L.R. 7 Q.B. 299.

[29] *Performing Right Society* v. *London Theatre of Varieties* [1924] A.C. 1. *Cf. Brandt* v. *Dunlop* [1905] A.C. 454.

[30] Pearson J. in *Jabbour* v. *Custodian of Israeli Absentee Property* [1954] 1 W.L.R. 139, 143 *et seq.* and cases there cited; *Edmunds* v. *Lloyd Italico* [1986] 1 All E.R. 249.

[31] *Re Harrington Motor Co.* [1928] Ch. 105.

[32] *Hood's Trustees* v. *Southern Union* [1928] Ch. 793.

[33] *Brice* v. *Bannister* (1878) 3 Q.B.D. 569; *English & Scottish Investment Co.* v. *Brunton* [1892] 2 Q.B. 700; *Bank of Toronto* v. *St. Lawrence Fire* [1903] A.C. 59.

The right that is assignable in the case of a contract of indemnity is the **10–09** right to recover in respect of a loss suffered *only* by the assured and not in respect of any loss that may be suffered by the assignee. The assignment cannot operate to alter the terms of the original contract in this crucial respect. If the assignor divests himself of his interest in the subject matter insured (whether or not to the assignee of the proceeds of the policy) he will have no rights which he can assign, and if after assignment he parts with his interest the assignment will be valueless.

The assignment is subject to equities in the usual way, so that any defences open to the insurer against the assured will defeat the assignee's claim against the insurer.[34] Thus the assignee has no claim if the assured is an enemy alien,[35] has a broken warranty[36] or his duty of utmost good faith,[37] has made a fraudulent claim,[38] or has deliberately cast away the insured subject matter.[39] The insurer may, to assist the assignee, issue a letter of undertaking to the assignee whereby the insurer undertakes to pay the proceeds directly to the assignee and to inform him in the event that the policy ceases. Such a letter of undertaking, while contractual, does not impose a duty of utmost good faith on the insurer and thus cannot oblige the insurer to disclose to the assignee any breaches of duty by the assured of which the insurer is aware and which might give the insurer the right to reject a claim.[40]

The policy may in terms cover the interests of others as well as that of **10–10** the assured, and in this case an assignment by the assured to such persons would be effective, whether or not he has parted with his interest at the time of the loss. But in the absence of such a clause, or at any rate of an implied intention to cover others,[41] no assignee, whether so by contract or by operation of law, can recover once the assured has parted with his interest. Thus, while claims occurring before the assured's death will be enforceable by his personal representatives, they will be unable to recover under a policy of indemnity where the loss occurs after his death,[42] unless they can rely on an express provision in the policy. Mere recognition of the assured's right to assign in a term of the policy is not sufficient,[42] the policy must be one which was taken out as an indemnity not to the assured only, but also to his assigns.

Conditions against assignment. Although it is apprehended that the **10–11** law as to the assignment of policies of indemnity is correctly set out in these pages, there has been some confusion in the matter,[43] and it has therefore been common to include a condition in the policy making it clear that where the assured parts with his interest no one else may recover unless the insurers have assented to an assignment of the

---

[34] M.I.A. 1906, s.50(3).
[35] *Bank of New South Wales* v. *South British Insurance* (1920) 4 Ll.L.R. 266.
[36] *Bank of Nova Scotia* v. *Hellenic Mutual, The Good Luck* [1989] 2 Lloyd's Rep. 238.
[37] *Pickersgill* v. *London and Provincial* (1912) 107 L.T. 305.
[38] *Black King Shipping* v. *Massie, The Litsion Pride* [1985] 1 Lloyd's Rep. 437.
[39] *Graham* v. *Merchants Marine* [1924] A.C. 294.
[40] *The Good Luck, supra.*
[41] See *Castellain* v. *Preston* (1883) 11 Q.B.D. 380, 406, and § 3–34, *supra.*
[42] *Mildmay* v. *Folgham* (1797) 3 Ves. 471.
[43] See, for instance, Brett L.J. in *Rayner* v. *Preston* (1881) 18 Ch.D. 1, 10, and Sir Wilfrid Green M.R. in *Peters* v. *General Fire* [1938] 2 All E.R. 267, 269.

policy.[44] Where the insurers do so consent, a new contract of insurance is formed between them and the assignees, and it is then under this new contract that the assignee is entitled to recover in the event of a loss.

10–12   *Fire insurance.* Thus, if an assignment of property insured against fire be total, the assignor cannot recover on the policy for himself, as his interest in the property will have ceased. If the assignment be partial, he can recover for his own benefit only to the extent of his remaining interest.

The assignee of property insured against fire can recover nothing under a policy effected by the assignor unless—

(1) It was part of the contract between the insurer and assignee that the latter should have the benefit of the policy as between assignor and himself; and (2) the office consented to hold covered the assignee assured either by the terms of the policy, or on notice of the intention to assign before transfer of the property. If the policy expresses that the consent of the office shall be given in any particular form, that form must be strictly complied with. The position may be affected by section 47 of the Law of Property Act 1925.[45]

10–13   *Change of partners.* There is no direct English authority as to the effect of a change of partners in a business firm on policies on the firm's property taken out by the firm, *i.e.* by the partners in it. "Bearing in mind that a contract of insurance is essentially a personal contract,"[46] it has been said,[47] where such property is lost "it would be a good defence to the insurers to prove that a new partner had been admitted without their consent." But, it has been held,[47] such a new admission will not excuse the insurers from indemnifying the original partners under a liability policy in respect of third-party claims, on the ground that, since those partners might be called on to pay the whole loss, the admission of the new partner could make no difference to the insurers. And there seems to be no sufficient reason why, where a partner retires, the remaining partners should not be entitled to recover on any class of policy.[48] But it was held in New Zealand, where two partners had effected an insurance on the partnership goods and, before a fire occurred, the partnership had been dissolved and one partner had become owner of the partnership goods without notice to the insurance company, that that constituted a breach of the covenant against assignment contained in the policy.[49] No such difficulties arise in the case of insurance by an incorporated company, as it has a legal existence separate from that of its members.

10–14   *Death of assured.* Apart from the question whether the personal representatives of the assured are entitled to claim upon a policy of indemnity taken out by the assured, the question rises to whom are any

---

[44] See *Lynch* v. *Dalzell* (1729) 4 Bro.P.C. 431.

[45] See § 14–39 *et seq., infra.*

[46] See *Lynch* v. *Dalzell, supra.*

[47] *Per* Goddard J. in *Jenkins* v. *Deane* (1933) 103 L.J.K.B. 250, 255. See also *Maxwell* v. *Price* [1960] 2 Lloyd's Rep. 155 (Aust. High Ct.) Lloyd's solicitor's liability policy.

[48] *Ibid.* at p. 256.

[49] *McKay* v. *Eagle, Star & British Dominions Ins. Co.* (1879) 18 M.C.R. (N.Z.) 83.

benefits they may receive payable? Do they belong to the legatee of the subject-matter insured, or to the residuary estate? The answer appears to be that where the loss occurs before or at the time of the death of the assured, then any claims will be for the benefit of the residuary estate,[50] but if the loss occurs afterwards, then it will be the legatees of the subject-matter insured who will be entitled to benefit.[51]

3. DECLARATION OF TRUST

Apart from assignment, a policy holder can pass the beneficial interest **10–15** in the policy by a declaration that he holds it as trustee for a named beneficiary. Such a declaration may be made at the time of taking out the policy,[52] or may be made afterwards.[53] Such trusts may be made in a will, or declared in it by reference to some document already in existence: but they cannot be so declared by reference to a document which is to be executed afterwards.[54] In such a case there would be a resulting trust in favour of the deceased's personal representatives. A declaration of trust made after the policy is effected cannot by itself, any more than an assignment, give the beneficiary any rights under a policy of indemnity unless the assured himself suffers a loss. One cannot pass the benefit of a fire insurance policy to the purchaser of one's property simply by declaring that one holds it on trust for him. But it is otherwise if one has the legal title or possession of such property and make the declaration on effecting the insurance. In such a case the principles applicable where an assured takes out a policy covering other interests also apply.[55] In the case of life insurance policies no such difficulties arise, and the benefit of them can freely be disposed of in this way.[56]

Resulting trusts   **10–16**
    Should A take out a policy and afterwards execute a legal assignment in favour of a donee, B, continuing however to pay the premiums, it may be that a resulting trust arises by virtue of which B is bound to hold the policy as trustee for A.[57] At any rate no such trust would arise were B the wife or child of A, for in such a case the presumption of advancement would displace the presumption that a resulting trust was intended.[58]
    Re Scottish Equitable Life Policy 6402[59] was another type of case in which a resulting trust was apparently held to arise. A took out a policy as agent for B, his wife's sister, and paid the premiums. The legal property in the policy was therefore in B, but since A had paid the premiums

---

[50] *Durrant* v. *Friend* (1852) 5 De G. & S. 343.
[51] *Parry* v. *Ashey* (1829) 3 Sim. 97, 134, 135; *Durrant* v. *Friend, supra*, but see Cotton L.J. in *Rayner* v. *Preston* (1881) 18 Ch.D. 1, 8.
[52] *Re Webb* [1941] Ch. 225.
[53] *Pedder* v. *Mosley* (1862) 31 Beav. 159.
[54] *Johnson* v. *Ball* (1851) 5 De G. & Sm. 85; *Re Keen's Estate* [1937] 1 Ch. 236; see Holdsworth 53 L.Q.R. 501, 507.
[55] See §§ 3–34 *et seq.*, *supra.*
[56] See §§ 16–35 *et seq.*, *infra.*
[57] See Cotton L.J. in *Standing* v. *Bowring* (1885) 31 Ch.D. 282, 287.
[58] Romer J. in *Re Engelbach's Estate* [1924] 2 Ch. 348, 351. (Doubted on other grounds in *Beswick* v. *Beswick* [1968] A.C. 50.)
[59] [1902] 1 Ch. 282.

Joyce J. held that his representatives were entitled, in equity, to receive the policy moneys. *Re Richardson*[60] was a similar case, but here B was A's daughter. It was held therefore that a presumption of advancement arose, and that both the legal and equitable interests in the policy were vested in her, although he had retained possession of the policy.

Trusts of life policies also arise under the Married Women's Property Acts.[61]

4. LIEN

10–17 Besides rights to or in policies accruing to persons (other than the person taking out the same) by way of assignment, charge or trust, numerous questions arise as to liens on policies. A lien at common law is a personal and untransferable right[62] which only arises where a person is in possession of a property, and entitles him to hold it as against the true owner, until some debt is discharged.[63] An equitable lien is a similar right, but is not, unlike a common law lien, dependent for its existence on the possession of the subject-matter.[64] Thus, a person may have in equity a lien upon policy moneys that have been paid to another, whether or not he has possession of the policy. A lien can exist no longer than the policy, and when a policy drops, the lien drops with it.[65]

From payment of premiums

10–18 An equitable lien may be created upon the moneys payable under a policy by payment of premiums where the payment is made:

(i) *By contract* with the beneficial owner of the policy.

(ii) *By trustees*, on the ground of their right to an indemnity out of the trust property for money expended by them in its preservation.

(iii) *By persons subrogated to the rights of trustees* (having paid premiums at their request).

(iv) *By mortgagees*, or other persons having a charge upon the policy, on the ground of their right to add to their charge any moneys which have been paid by them to preserve the property mortgaged.[66]

A lien may also possibly be created where the owner of onerous property agrees to indemnify another from the burdens on it which may fall on that other or on his property, and where the owner makes default and that other on his property has to bear these burdens.[67]

---

[60] (1882) 47 L.T. 514.

[61] Such trusts, and other similar interests in life policies are considered below, §§ 16–79 *et seq.*

[62] *Legg* v. *Evans* (1840) 6 M. & W. 36; *Thompson* v. *Farmer* (1827) 1 Moo. & Mal. 48.

[63] See *Bibby* v. *Woods* [1949] W.N. 244.

[64] *Burgess* v. *Wheate* (1759) 1 W.Bl. 123.

[65] *Busteed* v. *West of England Fire & Life* (1856) 5 Ir.Ch.R. 553; *Norris* v. *Caledonian Insurance* (1869) L.R. 8 Eq. 127.

[66] *Per* Fry J. in *Re Leslie*, *Leslie* v. *French* (1883) 23 Ch.D. 552, 561; *Falcke* v. *Scottish Insurance* (1886) 34 Ch.D. 234.

[67] Lindley L.J. in *Strutt* v. *Tippett* (1890) 62 L.T. 475, 477.

Except under these circumstances[68] no lien is created by the payment of the premiums by a mere stranger, as where a husband paid the premiums on a policy on the life of his wife taken out by her before her marriage,[69] or by a part owner.

(i) *Lien by contract.* A contract by a stranger to a policy with the **10–19** beneficial owner to pay the premiums will give him a lien upon it for their repayment.[70] Thus where sureties had covenanted to pay the premiums on certain policies on the default of the mortgagor of the policies, and did so, it was held that they had a lien upon the policy moneys, and that the mortgagees of the policies were not entitled to take the proceeds of the policies without repaying the premiums to the sureties.[71]

A contract will however be readily inferred, as where someone not responsible for payment of the premiums pays them with the knowledge and acquiescence of the person who is responsible.[72] *A fortiori* where the person responsible requests another to pay the premiums, that other acquires a lien on the policy.[73]

Thus, where A, with an interest in a policy, had written to B, the person responsible for payment of the premiums, offering to pay them in order to keep up the policy, B being unable to do so, and B had not replied, A was held to have a lien on the policy in respect of any premiums subsequently paid by him.[74]

But this principle will not apply where someone interested in the policy, but not responsible for payment of the premiums, requests a stranger to pay them on the default of the person liable. Thus, in *Strutt* v. *Tippett*[75] the mortgagor of a policy who was liable for payment of the premiums failed, whereupon the mortgagees called on a stranger to pay them, threatening to call in another mortgage if he did not. He did so. It was held that he had no lien on the policy.

If a mortgagor after his bankruptcy pays premiums to keep up a mortgaged policy, he is not entitled, in the absence of special agreement, to a lien on the policy for the amount so paid.[76]

(ii) *Trustees' lien.* A trustee has a lien on moneys payable under a **10–20** policy which forms part of the trust property for any money expended by him on the preservation of the trust property, including premiums paid out of his own pocket on such a policy which would otherwise have lapsed. But where he pays premiums on a policy which does not form part of the trust fund, no such lien arises.[77] The duty of a trustee of a

---

[68] North J. in *Re Winchilsea's Policy Trusts* (1888) 39 Ch.D. 168, 172, 173; Chitty J. in *Strutt* v. *Tippett* (1889) 61 L.T. 460, 463.

[69] See n. 66.

[70] See Knight-Bruce L.J. in *Burridge* v. *Row* (1842) 1 Y. & C.C.C. 183.

[71] *Aylwin* v. *Witty* (1861) 30 L.J.Ch. 860.

[72] *West* v. *Reid* (1843) 2 Hare 249, discussed by Cotton L.J. in *Falcke* v. *Scottish* (1886) 34 Ch.D. 234, 244; *Re Power's Policies* [1899] 1 Ir.R. 6. See also *Re Tyler* [1907] 1 K.B. 865.

[73] *Falcke* v. *Scottish Imperial Insurance* (1886) 34 Ch.D. 234; *Re McKerrell, McKerrell* v. *Gowans* [1912] 2 Ch. 648, 652, 653.

[74] *West* v. *Reid, Re Power's Policies, supra.*

[75] (1889) 62 L.T. 475.

[76] See *Saunders* v. *Dunman* (1878) 7 Ch.D. 825; *Falcke* v. *Scottish Imperial Insurance* (1886) 34 Ch.D. 234. These cases explain *Shearman* v. *British Empire Mutual Insurance* (1872) L.R. 14 Eq. 4.

[77] *Re Earl of Winchilsea's Policy Trusts* (1888) 39 Ch.D. 168.

policy is, unless the settlor is liable and able to pay the premiums, to pay them out of the trust funds,[78] and if with such funds at his disposal he pays them out of his own pocket this gives him no lien upon the policy moneys.[79] But the mere fact that a trustee, with no such funds at his disposal, might possibly have taken some other course to preserve the policy, will not prevent a lien from arising.[80]

In *Re Roberts*[81] a father took out a policy as trustee for his son and paid the premiums. In this case, it was held that the relation of father and son predominated over that of trustee and *cestui que trust*, and the presumption that he intended to advance the premiums operated in the son's favour. No such presumption arose, however, in the case of premiums subsequently paid by the father's executors, and it was held, therefore, that the residuary legatees were entitled to a lien on the policy moneys for those payments. And a similar principle applies where the child or wife of the trustee dies and he continues to pay the premiums, for in this case the presumption of advancement ceases.[82]

10–21   (iii) *Subrogation to trustees' lien*. Anyone subrogated to the rights of the trustees would have a similar lien.[83] It appears from the decisions that if trustees, who would, by the payment of premiums, have acquired a lien upon moneys paid under a policy, request another to pay such premiums, that other is in equity subrogated to their rights including their equitable lien.[84] But a request or authorisation is essential, otherwise the person paying the premiums is simply in the position of a stranger.[85] And trustees cannot confer a lien on a third person advancing the policy moneys unless they themselves, by paying the premiums, would have acquired such a lien.[86]

10–22   (iv) *Mortgagees' lien Gill* v. *Downing*,[87] in which the mortgagees of a married woman's power of appointment after her life estate in a policy paid premiums on the policy, and where by a clause in the mortgage deed such sums were included in the debt secured, was a case in which mortgagees had a lien on the policy moneys in question.[88]

10–23 Lien and salvage
Payments of premiums under these heads have been described as "salvage payments,"[89] especially in Ireland,[90] but whatever the nomenclature used, it is clear that there is no equitable doctrine similar to the maritime doctrine of salvage by which a complete stranger may,

---

[78] See § 14–03, *infra*.
[79] *Clack* v. *Holland* (1854) 19 Beav. 262.
[80] *Todd* v. *Moorhouse* (1874) L.R. 19 Eq. 69.
[81] [1946] 1 Ch. 1.
[82] *Re Smith's Estate* [1937] Ch. 636, 640.
[83] *Todd* v. *Moorhouse, supra*; Fry J. in *Re Leslie, Leslie* v. *French* (1883) 23 Ch.D. 552, 561.
[84] *Todd* v. *Moorhouse, supra*; *Falcke* v. *Scottish Imperial Insurance* (1886) 34 Ch.D. 234. See also *Gill* v. *Downing* (1874) L.R. 17 Eq. 316.
[85] *Falcke* v. *Scottish, supra*.
[86] *Clack* v. *Holland* (1854) 19 Beav. 262.
[87] (1874) L.R. 17 Eq. 316.
[88] See Cotton L.J. in *Falcke* v. *Scottish Imperial Insurance* (1886) 34 Ch.D. 234, 246, 247.
[89] *Re Tharpe* (1852) 2 Sm. & G. 578n.
[90] *Re Power's Policies* [1899] 1 Ir.R. 6; Fry J. in *Falcke* v. *Scottish* (1886) 34 Ch.D. 234, 254.

owing to the exigencies of public policy and for the advantage of trade, acquire a lien upon a ship of goods by the voluntary expenditure of labour or money.[91]

Payment of premiums by stranger

10–24

Except under the above circumstances no lien is created by the payment of the premiums by a stranger to the policy, or even by a part owner beneficially interested in it.[92] Thus, where a husband pays premiums on a policy taken out by his wife before marriage,[93] or the assignor of a policy continues to pay the premiums,[94] such payments confer no lien upon the payor.

It does not matter what the object of the stranger is in paying the premiums, whether it be the preservation of the policy or of other property,[95] or whether he pays under a mistaken belief that he has an interest in the policy,[96] provided the beneficial owner does not know of this mistaken belief.[97] But where a person paid premiums in the mistaken belief, shared by all parties, that he was the owner of the policy, it was held that he acquired a lien.[98]

Where, however, a bankrupt had two policies of assurance on his own life, and his wife, to the knowledge of the trustee in bankruptcy, paid the premiums until her husband's death, the court ordered the trustee, as a matter of honesty and fair dealing, to repay her, out of the policy moneys, the amount so paid by her to keep the policies on foot, without regard to the question whether she had any equitable lien.[99] Such cases, however, turn on special principles to be considered below.[1]

Payment by part owner

10–25

Similarly, payments of premiums by a part owner, except under a contract[2], give him no title as against the other part owners of a policy[2]; to give him a lien on the policy there must be something in the nature of a request to pay them by another part owner.[3] Thus, payments by a mortgagor create no lien as against a mortgagee,[4] and payments by a tenant for life create no lien against a remainderman.[5] Even where the part owners are tenants in common, and therefore entitled to contribution between themselves, this right is a purely personal right, and will not of itself confer a lien.[6]

---

[91] *Ibid. per* Bowen L.J. at pp. 248 and 249.

[92] Fry J. in *Re Leslie, Leslie* v. *French* (1883) 23 Ch.D. 552, 561; North J. in *Re Winchilsea's Policy* (1888) 39 Ch.D. 168, 172, 173; Chitty J. in *Strutt* v. *Tippett* (1889) 61 L.T. 460, 463. See § 10–18, *supra*.

[93] *Re Leslie, Leslie* v. *French, supra*.

[94] *Re Winn, Reed* v. *Winn* (1887) 57 L.T. 382.

[95] *Strutt* v. *Tippett* (1889) 61 L.T. 460, 463.

[96] *Falcke* v. *Scottish Imperial Insurance* (1886) 34 Ch.D. 234; *Urquhart* v. *Butterfield* (1887) 37 Ch.D. 357, 377.

[97] Cotton L.J. in *Falcke's* case, *supra*, at pp. 242, 243.

[98] *Re Foster (No. 2)* (1938) 159 L.T. 279.

[99] *Re Tyler* [1907] K.B. 865.

[1] See § 16–98, *infra*.

[2] Fry J. in *Re Leslie, Leslie* v. *French, supra*.

[3] See *Re McKerrell* [1912] 2 Ch. 648, 652.

[4] *Norris* v. *Caledonian Insurance* (1869) L.R. 8 Eq. 127, 132, *per* Romilly M.R.; Fry J. in *Re Leslie, Leslie* v. *French* (1883) 23 Ch.D. 552, 563.

[5] *Re Waugh's Trusts* (1877) 46 L.J.Ch. 629; Fry J. in *Re Leslie, supra*; *Re Jones, Stunt* v. *Jones* [1915] 1 Ch. 373.

[6] *Ex p. Young* (1813) 2 Ves. & B. 242; Fry in *Re Leslie, supra*; at pp. 563, 564.

Possessory liens

10–26 Broker's lien

The best example of a lien at common law on a policy of insurance is afforded by the case where an insurance broker is commissioned to effect a policy. On effecting it he has, at common law, a lien upon it for his commission and also for the premium, if he has paid it. But such a lien amounts to no more than the right to retain the actual policy until he is paid[7]; once he parts with the possession of the policy his lien is lost, and he has no rights at law against the policy moneys if and when they become payable, although he will have an equitable lien in respect of any premium that he may have paid.

An insurance broker engaged to effect policies will have a lien upon all policies in his possession for the balance of his account in respect of all of them,[8] but he is not entitled to a general lien upon such policies for moneys due in respect of other services, *e.g.* where he has formerly been employed by the same principal to sell goods on commission,[9] unless he was employed as a general agent. So the mere deposit of a policy with an agent will not give him a lien upon it, but where it is deposited with him as a security for his advances he will have a lien upon it by special contract.[10] If one broker is employed by another broker to effect a policy for that other's principal, the sub-agent has still a lien on the policy for premiums due from the broker who employed him.[11]

10–27 Solicitor's lien

A solicitor has a general lien upon his client's papers, including policies of insurance which are in his hands for professional purposes, for his costs.[12] This lien covers all his costs and not merely those arising out of his services in respect of the document in question,[13] but does not extend to general debts.[14] Until his lien is satisfied he cannot be made to part with such documents except by order of the court, and such order will only be given where the document is necessary to secure the property to which it relates and suitable security can be given.[15] This lien is simply a right of continued possession: it is only a passive remedy that cannot normally be enforced by suit.[16] Notice to the insurers is not therefore necessary to complete the right.[17]

10–28 Subrogation to lien

Although a common law lien is inalienable, the insurers may be subrogated to a possessory lien of the assured as against a third party; so

---

[7] Lord Penzance in *Fisher* v. *Smith* (1878) 4 App.Cas. 1, 7, 8.

[8] *Castling* v. *Aubert* (1802) 2 East 325. See also s.53(2) of the M.I.A. 1906.

[9] *Dixon* v. *Stansfield* (1850) 10 C.B. 398.

[10] *Muir* v. *Fleming* (1822) 1 Dow. & Ry.N.P. 29.

[11] *Fisher* v. *Smith* (1878) 4 App.Cas. 1.

[12] *Richards* v. *Platel* (1841) Cr. & Ph. 79; 10 L.J.Ch. 375; *West of England Bank* v. *Batchelor* (1882) 51 L.J.Ch. 199; *Hughes* v. *Hughes* [1958] P. 224.

[13] *Worral* v. *Johnson* (1820) 2 Jac. & Walk. 214, as explained by Cottenham L.J. in *Stedman* v. *Webb* (1839) 4 Myl. & Cr. 346, 352.

[14] *Stedman* v. *Webb, supra.*

[15] *Richards* v. *Platel, supra.*

[16] *Stedman* v. *Webb, supra.*

[17] Fry J. in *West of England Bank* v. *Batchelor* (1882) 51 L.J.Ch. 199, 200.

where an unpaid vendor still in possession recovers from the insurers, they are entitled to the advantage of his lien on the property sold.[18]

A surety may be subrogated to a lien of the creditor upon a policy by payment of the guaranteed debt, but only where the creditor's lien is in respect of the debt so paid.[19]

---

[18] Brown L.J. in *Castellain* v. *Preston* (1883) 11 Q.B.D. 380.
[19] *Farebrother* v. *Wodehouse* (1856) 23 Beav. 18; *Re Jeffrey's Policy* (1872) 20 W.R. 857.

CHAPTER 11

REINSTATEMENT

1. KINDS OF RESTORATION

THE word "reinstate," in a policy of insurance refers to buildings or **11–01**
chattels which have been damaged, and the word "replace" refers to
those which have been destroyed.[1] "Restoration" is a convenient term
to cover both reinstatement and replacement.

The normal liability of the insurers under a policy is the payment of
money, although they may, in certain circumstances only, have an
option to spend the money in rebuilding damaged premises,[2] or in replacing goods lost.

The only circumstances in which the assured will be bound to accept
reinstatement or replacement in place of a money payment are:

(a) where there is a clause in the contract of insurance giving the
insurers an option either to pay or to restore, and they exercise
this option in favour of restoration; or
(b) where the insurers are bound to reinstate under section 83 of the
Fire Prevention (Metropolis) Act 1774.

2. REINSTATEMENT UNDER CONTRACT

Clauses in the contract of insurance giving the insurers an option either **11–02**
to pay or to reinstate or replace have been common in fire policies[3] for
centuries, since such an option gives the insurers valuable protection
against fraud and excessive demands.[4]

The clause, it is noted, is for the benefit of the insurers alone,[5] even
where their liability is expressed as a bare promise to pay *or make good*,
and, if they elect to pay, the assured cannot insist upon restoration
under the clause or to argue that the presence of a reinstatment clause
fixes his measure of indemnity as the reinstatement value when his
actual loss is a lesser sum.[6] The assured, on the other hand, is not bound
to lay out the money so paid in reinstatement, but so far as the insurers
are concerned, can spend it how he chooses.[7]

---

[1] Bowen L.J. in *Anderson* v. *Commercial Union* (1885) 55 L.J.Q.B. 146, 149.
[2] Brett L.J. in *Rayner* v. *Preston* (1881) 18 Ch.D. 1.
[3] See *Sadlers Company* v. *Badcock* (1743) 2 Atk. 554; Robinson C.J. in *Home District Mutual* v.
Thompson (1847) 1 U.C. Err. & App. 247.
[4] Pennefather B. in *Vance* v. *Forster* (1841) Ir.Circ.Rep. 47, 51.
[5] Bowen L.J. in *Anderson* v. *Commercial Union, supra*, p. 149.
[6] *Leppard* v. *Excess* [1979] 2 All E.R. 668.
[7] *Queen Insurance* v. *Vey* 16 L.T. 239; *Rayner* v. *Preston* (1881) 18 Ch.D. 1. If the assured expressly
agrees with the insurer to reinstate, the policy moneys cannot be withheld until he has done so: *Mac-
lean* v. *Ecclesiastical Insurance* [1986] 2 Lloyd's Rep. 416.

11–03 Effect of election to reinstate

But although the insurer is free to elect whether he will pay or restore, once he has exercised his election one way or the other, he will be bound by it; he will not then be entitled to change his mind because he finds his choice to be an unwise one. The selection of one alternative necessarily constitutes an abandonment of the other.[8]

Thus, where he elects to reinstate, the case stands as if the policy had been simply to reinstate in the first place.[9] The election relates back, and the case is the same as if he had originally contracted absolutely to reinstate.[10] The contract of insurance becomes enforceable, in fact, as a building contract,[11] or, in the case of a chattel such as a motor-vehicle, as a contract of repair.[12] On this basis it would seem that any exclusion clauses limiting the insurer's liability for defective work are subject to the Unfair Contract Terms Act 1977 despite the exclusion in that Act of contracts of insurance.

11–04   The election of the insurers to reinstate and thus having changed the nature of their obligation the following consequences ensue:

(a) They will not be entitled to limit their expenditure to the sum insured, unless the contract of insurance clearly gives them the right to do so.[13]

(b) The insurers will be liable in damages for breach of contract if they fail to restore the building substantially *in statu quo*, even though such restoration turns out to be more expensive than they had anticipated owing to the defective state of part of the property unaffected by the fire.[14]

(c) The insurers are bound to carry out the work of restoration within a reasonable time, and, if they do not do so, after electing to reinstate, they will be liable to the assured in damages for the delay.[15]

(d) The insurers, being in the position of building contractors, must bear any loss or damage which may happen to the property while they are in possession of it for the purpose of reinstatement.[16]

Thus, if a second fire occurs during reinstatement, they must com-

---

[8] *Times Fire* v. *Hawke* (1858) 1 F. & F. 406.
[9] Lord Campbell C.J. in *Brown* v. *Royal* (1859) 1 El. & El. 853, 858.
[10] Richmond J. in *Bank of New South Wales* v. *Royal* (1880) 2 N.Z.L.R. 337.
[11] Davies J. in *Morrell* v. *Irving Fire* (1865) 33 N.Y. 429.
[12] *Maher* v. *Lumbermen's Mutual* [1932] 2 D.L.R. 593, 601.
[13] See *Home Mutual Fire* v. *Garfield* (1871) 14 Am.Rep. 27.
[14] *Brown* v. *Royal* (1859) 1 El. & El. 853, 860, Hill J. Lord Campbell C.J. said (p. 859) that the fact that reinstatement "has become impossible is no legal reason for their not performing it; and they are liable in damages" if they do not. But that was before the development of the doctrine of frustration based on *Taylor* v. *Caldwell* (1863) 3 B. & S. 826. If re-instatement or restoration is or becomes impossible (in the sense that a contract to effect it would be frustrated) it is now clear on principle, and from the judgments in *Anderson* v. *Commercial Union* (1885) 55 L.J.Q.B. 146, that the insurer must elect to pay or make a fresh election to pay; he is neither liable in damages for not reinstating nor discharging wholly from his obligations. Thus where reinstatement is illegal, the election to reinstate is a nullity: *Alchorne* v. *Favill* (1825) 4 L.J.(o.s.) 47. See as to these principles [1960] *Journal of Business Law*, pp. 236–239.
[15] *Home Mutual Fire* v. *Garfield* (1871) 14 Am.Rep. 27; *Davidson* v. *Guardian Royal Excahnge* [1979] 1 Lloyd's Rep. 406. As to the allocation of damages between the assured and persons interested in the subject matter, see *Re King* [1963] Ch. 459 and *Beacon Carpets* v. *Kirby* [1984] 2 All E.R. 726.
[16] *Waring & Gillow* v. *Doughty*, *The Times*, February 21 (1922).

mence reinstating anew, and cannot charge the assured with the cost of the second fire.[17]

(e) The assured, on his part, is bound to allow the insurers to enter his land to carry out the work, and the court will not grant him an injunction to restrain them.[18]

If the work is not carried out properly his proper remedy is an action for damages.[19] His affirmation of his right to payment amounts to an affirmation of the policy entitling the insurers to enter.[20] If the assured does not allow the insurers to reinstate but carries out the work himself he leaves himself without any remedy under the policy.[21]

(f) Even the finding of a lost chattel will not excuse the insurer if he has elected or agreed to replace it,[22] although he will be entitled to the chattel so found as salvage.[23]

Exercise of election   11–05

Where the insurers negotiated with the assured on the footing that a money payment, to be fixed by arbitration, was to be made by them, it was held that they had lost their option to reinstate,[24] but it was held otherwise where, although negotiations as to payment were pending with the assured, and notice had been served on him requiring him to join in referring the dispute to arbitration, the insurers had done nothing to abandon their right of reinstatement.[25] In an American case it was held that the acceptance by the insurers of an order by the assured to pay a third party did not amount to an election to pay, but merely operated as a notice of assignment of the assured's right.[26]

If no time limit is set by the contract, the insurers must exercise their option to reinstate *within a reasonable time*; otherwise they will be obliged to pay, it was held in America.[27] But the insurers are entitled to examine the matter, and to consider it in the ordinary course of business.[28]

Right of insurers to combine in reinstatement   11–06

When two or more insurers who have granted insurances on the same subject-matter elect, under their respective policies, to reinstate, the assured cannot prevent them from joining to do the work, and, when it has been done, their liabilities under the policies will be discharged.[29] This right of the insurers may be a valuable one where the policies relate

---

[17] *Smith* v. *Colonial Mutual Fire* (1880) 6 Vict.L.R. 200.
[18] *Bisset* v. *Royal Exchange* (1821) 1 Sh. (Ct. of Sess.) 174.
[19] *Home District Mutual* v. *Thompson* (1847) 1 U.C.Err. & App. 247.
[20] Coleridge L.C.J. in *Baker* v. *Yorkshire Fire* [1892] 1 Q.B. 144, 145, 146.
[21] *Beals* v. *Home Insurance* (1867) 36 N.Y. 522.
[22] *Holmes* v. *Payne* [1930] 2 K.B. 301.
[23] *Ibid.* at p. 311.
[24] *Scottish Amicable* v. *Northern Assurance* (1883) 11 R. (Ct. of Sess.) 287.
[25] *Sutherland* v. *Sun Fire Office* (1852) 14 D. (Ct. of Sess.) 775.
[26] *Tolman* v. *Manufacturers Insurance* 55 Mass. (15 Cush.) 73 (1848).
[27] *Insurance of North America* v. *Hope* 11 Am.Rep. 48, 49 (1871).
[28] *Sutherland* v. *Sun Fire Office* (1852) 14 D. (Ct. of Sess.) 775, 778, 779.
[29] *Scottish Amicable* v. *Northern* (1883) 11 R. (Ct. of Sess.) 287.

to separate interests, because the cost of reinstatement may then be very much less than the measure of the loss.[30]

3. FIRE PREVENTION (METROPOLIS) ACT 1774, s.83[31]

11–07 Under this section, companies insuring buildings against loss by fire are bound to lay out the insurance money,[32] as far as it will go, towards rebuilding or reinstating buildings burnt down or damaged by fire,

(i) upon the request of any person or persons interested in such buildings, *or*

(ii) upon any grounds of suspicion that the assured has been guilty of fraud, or of wilfully setting fire to such buildings, *unless*

(a) the assured shall, within 60 days of the claim being adjusted, give a sufficient security to such company that the insurance money will be so laid out, *or*

(b) the said insurance money shall be in that time settled and disposed of to and amongst all the contending parties, to the satisfaction and approbation of the governors or directors of such company.

11–08 It was for long thought that section 83 of the Act of 1774 applied only to property within the metropolitan area, but in 1864 Lord Chancellor Westbury held that it was of general and not merely of local application.[33] This decision, however, is of doubtful authority both as regards Scotland and Ireland.[34] The whole of the Act except sections 83 and 86[35] (dealing with liability in tort for accidental fires) has been repealed by subsequent statutes.

11–09 The following points should be noted in regard to section 83:

(a) It only applies in the case of fire of buildings. Thus it applies to such fixtures as would pass by a conveyance, but not to trade fixtures removable by the tenant[36] or other fixtures not attached to the freehold.[37]

(b) It does not apply where the insurance is by Lloyd's underwriters.[38]

(c) Unlike an election to restore, restoration need not be complete, but only complete so far as the insurance money will allow. But the insurers are bound to lay out this money judiciously, and bear the burden of showing they have done so.[39]

---

[30] *Westminster Fire Office* v. *Glasgow Provident Investment Society* (1888) 13 App.Cas. 699.

[31] For the full text, see Appendix.

[32] Compensation paid under the Compensation Defence Act 1939, s.2(1)(*b*), in respect of a burnt-out pier was held not to be insurance money for this purpose: *Radnor* v. *Folkestone Pier* (1950) 66 T.L.R. (Pt. 2) 722.

[33] *Ex p. Gorely* (1864) 4 De G.J. & S. 477; followed in *Re Quicke's Trusts* [1908] 1 Ch. 887; *Sinnott* v. *Bowden* [1912] 2 Ch. 414.

[34] *Westminster Fire Office* v. *Glasgow Provident* (1888) 13 App.Cas. 699, 716; *Andrews* v. *Patriotic Assurance of Ireland* (1886) 18 L.R.Ir. 355.

[35] See § 14–12, *infra.*

[36] *Ex p. Gorely* (1864) 4 De G.J. & S. 477.

[37] *Re Quicke's Trusts* [1908] 1 Ch. 887, 894.

[38] *Portavon Cinema* v. *Price* (1939) 161 L.T. 417.

[39] *Simpson* v. *Scottish* (1863) 1 H. & M. 615, 629, *per* Page-Wood V.-C.

(d) Unless the insurers have grounds to suspect fraud, a distinct request from an interested party[40] is necessary to bring the section into operation.[41] The assured himself is not an "interested party" for this purpose.[42]

(e) A positive duty, not a mere option, is conferred on the insurers to restore under either set of circumstances.

(f) The assured may undertake to carry out the restoration in the insurers' place.

(g) Settlement between all the interested parties absolves the insurers from their duty under this section.

The insurers cannot be forced to fulfil their statutory duty to restore **11–10** under this section by writ of mandamus.[43] The remedy of an interested third party against them is to apply for an injunction to restrain them from paying over the insurance money to the assured, without obtaining sufficient security from him that it will be laid out in reinstatement. Once the money has been paid over to the assured the third party's remedy is lost.[44]

Third party not an assured   **11–11**

The effect of the statute is not to give the third party an interest in the insurance itself, and his right does not therefore amount to an insurance for the purposes of conditions relating to double insurance.[45] "There is all the difference in the world between giving A, who is interested in the premises upon which B has taken out a policy, a right to call upon B's insurers to expend those policy moneys upon the property, and saying that the statute has invested A with an insurance upon those properties. One is a statutory right and the other is a right arising *ex contractu*, and I think that it is quite wrong to say that the effect of the Fire Prevention (Metropolis) Act 1774, s.83, is to make anybody an insured."[46] The third party cannot, therefore, give notice to the insurers until the assured has actually made a claim under the policy, although if the assured has contracted with the third party to apply policy moneys to reinstatement the courts will imply a term into their contract requiring the assured to make a claim on the insurers.[47]

"Persons interested"   **11–12**

Persons entitled to give notice under section 83 include mortgagor and mortgagee,[48] landlord and tenant[49] and purchaser prior to completion.[50] In all of these cases, however, the party giving notice cannot be an assured under the policy.[51]

---

[40] Grant M.R. in *Paris* v. *Gilham* (1813) Coop.G. 56.
[41] *Simpson* v. *Scottish Insurance* (1863) 1 H. & M. 615; *Wimbledon Golf Club* v. *Imperial* (1902) 18 T.L.R. 815.
[42] *Reynolds* v. *Phoenix Assurance* [1978] 2 Lloyd's Rep 440.
[43] *Wimbledon Golf Club* v. *Imperial* (1902) 18 T.L.R. 815.
[44] *Simpson* v. *Scottish Insurance* (1863) 1 H. & M. 615.
[45] *Portavon Cinema* v. *Price* (1939) 161 L.T. 417.
[46] *Portavon Cinema* v. *Price* (1939) 161 L.T. 417, 419, *per* Branson J.
[47] *Vural* v. *Security Archives* (1989) E.G. Leg. Supp. 2.
[48] *Wimbledon Golf Club* v. *Imperial*, n. 43 *supra*.
[49] *Re Quicke's Trusts*, n. 37 *supra*.
[50] *Rayner* v. *Preston* (1881) 18 Ch.D. 1. For practical difficulties faced by a purchaser, see *Keen* v. *Reid* [1987] C.L.R. 164.
[51] *Supra*, n. 42.

CHAPTER 12

REINSURANCE

1. GENERAL

INSURERS rely on the principle that by the operation of the laws of **12–01** chance the premiums received for a large number of risks will, in any given period of time, and coupled with the interest which is earned on premium income, be more than enough to meet the liabilities incurred. The acceptance of an insurance for an unduly large sum against one event, though potentially profitable, endangers this principle, as indeed does the general risk of an unusually large series of claims affecting a particular class of policy. For these reasons it is usual for insurers to reinsure at least a part of the risk with another company or with underwriters.[1]

Reinsurance in fact consists of a new insurance, effected by a new policy to indemnify the insurer, in whole or in part, against his previous liability,[2] although the perils covered by the reinsurance agreement may be narrower than those insured under the original or underlying policy.[3] The original policy and the reinsurance may, however, be framed in identical terms, for example, by the attaching of the insurance agreement to a reinsurance slip or by using words of incorporation in the reinsurance agreement; in these circumstances the courts will, as far as is appropriate, construe the two agreements as having the same meaning so that the cover provided by the reinsurance matches that offered by the original insurer.[4] It is common practice on the London market for reinsurance to be arranged before the original policy has been incepted, in order to make original insurance more attractive to potential insurers: the English courts have not regarded this procedure as bringing the validity of the reinsurance into question, and have also accepted that a broker who arranges reinsurance in this way acts on behalf of the ultimate insurer even though that insurer had not been identified at the date of the reinsurance agreement.[5]

Types of reinsurance **12–02**

A reinsurance agreement may reinsure liability under a single policy, in which case it is referred to as "facultative," or it may reinsure a class of policies, in which case it will take the form of a treaty. In addition, the power to reinsure may be delegated by a reinsurer to a broker, by means of a brokers' open cover (obligatory facultative reinsurance), by virtue

---

[1] See Kay J. in *Re Norwich Equitable Fire* (1887) 3 T.L.R. 781.
[2] *Per* Mansfield C.J. in *Delver* v. *Barnes* (1807) 1 Taunt. 48, 51.
[3] *Imperial Marine* v. *Fire Insurance Corporation* (1879) 4 C.P.D. 166; *Traders & General* v. *Bankers & General Insurance* (1921) 38 T.L.R. 94. Thus a marine insurer may reinsure against fire only, or against total rather than partial losses.
[4] *Forsikringsaktieselskapet Vesta* v. *Butcher* [1989] 1 All E.R. 402. See *infra.* para. 12–16.
[5] *General Accident* v. *Tanter* [1985] 2 Lloyd's Rep. 529.

of which the reinsurer binds itself to take any reinsurance proposals of a specified description accepted by authorised brokers.

Reinsurance treaties may be proportional or non-proportional. Under a proportional treaty the reinsurer offers to reinsure an agreed proportion of any risk accepted by the reinsured and falling within the terms of the treaty. Proportional treaties are normally in surplus form, whereby the reinsured cedes to the reinsurer in the agreed proportions the excess of any liability over the maximum which the reinsured is willing to bear without reinsurance. A variation of this is the quota share treaty, under which the reinsured has no discretion to retain risks for himself and the agreed proportion of any risk accepted by him is automatically ceded to the reinsurer.

Non-proportional treaties are characterised by the absence of any predetermined fixed share. Under an excess of loss treaty the reinsurer agrees to provide an indemnity in respect of all sums paid by the reinsured in excess of its retention (also referred to as its deductible, excess or priority). A stop loss treaty, by contrast, is concerned with aggregate losses suffered by the reinsured, and will come into operation where the reinsured's losses reach a given level.

In the case of a treaty, particularly in proportional form, there is undoubtedly a close relationship between reinsurer and reinsured. However, it has been decided that the parties are not in a partnership, nor is the reinsured the agent of the reinsurer in accepting risks.[6] It follows that there is no contractual relationship between the original assured and the reinsurer, so that in the event of the reinsured's default the assured has no right of action against the reinsurer unless the reinsurance policy otherwise provides.[7]

12–03 Nature of reinsurance

There is some uncertainty as to the status of reinsurance as insurance. A facultative policy is undoubtedly insurance, as it is a simple promise to indemnify the reinsured for its liability under a specific original policy.[8] Treaty reinsurances and open covers give rise to more difficulty in that they do not share the generally accepted characteristics of insurance: it is impossible for the reinsurer to know in advance, for example, exactly which risks are to be covered by him. Nevertheless, the courts have generally operated on the assumption that these forms of reinsurance are contracts of insurance proper and, most importantly, attract the duty of utmost good faith.[9]

---

[6] *Re Norwich Equitable Fire* (1887) 57 L.T. 241; *Glasgow Assurance* v. *Welsh Insurance* 1914 S.C. 320; *English Insurance* v. *National Benefit Assurance* [1929] A.C. 114; *Motor Union Insurance* v. *Mannheimer* [1933] 1 K.B. 812.

[7] M.I.A. 1906, s.9(2). Some reinsurance agreements do contain "cut-through" clauses, which seek to confer a cause of action on the assured against the reinsurer, normally in the event of the reinsured's insolvency. However, the assured is not a party to the reinsurance agreement and it is thought that the doctrine of privity of contract would prevent the assured from seeking to take advantage of the clause. For other possible devices, see *infra* § 12–14.

[8] *Delver* v. *Barnes* (1807) 1 Taunt. 48; *Australian Widows Fund* v. *National Mutual Life* [1914] A.C. 634; *Re London County Commercial Reinsurance Office* [1922] Ch. 67.

[9] *Glasgow Assurance* v. *Symondson* (1911) 104 L.T. 254. See also *Law Guarantee Trust* v. *Munich Reinsurance* [1912] 1 Ch. 138; *First Russian Insurance* v. *London and Lancashire Insurance* [1928] 1 Ch. 922; *Forsikringsaktieselskapet National* v. *Attorney-General* [1925] A.C. 639.

Early reinsurance cases classified a reinsurance policy as a further policy on the subject matter insured under the original policy, as opposed to a distinct insurance on the reinsured's liability,[10] and this reasoning was approved by the House of Lords in *Forsikringsaktiesels-kapet National* v. *Attorney General*.[11] However, it was assumed by the draftsman of the Marine Insurance Act that reinsurance is liability insurance and not fresh insurance on the original subject matter,[12] and much will depend upon the wording used. Thus, while facultative reinsurances and proportional treaties are normally drafted as constituting a new insurance on the original subject matter,[13] non-proportional treaties can rarely be construed as anything other than liability insurances. This point is important in relation to the Insurance Companies Act 1982, which requires insurers to be authorised separately to carry on long-term and general business, and in the latter case in respect of business falling within each of the 18 classes laid down by the Act.[14] This raises the question whether a reinsurer has to be authorised individually in respect of each class of business which it wishes to reinsure, or whether it suffices that the reinsurer is authorised to carry on liability insurance business. The point has arisen in only one case, *Stewart* v. *Oriental Fire*,[15] in which it was assumed without argument that a facultative policy reinsures the original subject matter.

Reinsured's insurable interest   12–04

A contract to insure gives the insurer an insurable interest which will support a reinsurance to the full amount of the insurer's liability on the original policy.[16] If the original assured has no insurable interest, it follows that the insurer faces no liability and thus himself has no insurable interest with which to support a reinsurance.[17]

Where the reinsurance constitutes an insurance on the reinsured's liability, it will be governed by the usual insurable interest rules applicable to liability policies. Where, however, it constitutes a fresh insurance on the subject matter originally insured,[18] the reinsurance must comply with the insurable interest rules affecting original insurances of that class.[19] Thus, if a life insurer procures reinsurance under a policy of the latter type, the policy is not to be construed as an indemnity policy and in accordance with the Life Assurance Act 1774 the insurer can recover from the reinsurer despite the fact that its own interest has lapsed during the currency of the reinsurance agreement.[20]

---

[10] *Delver* v. *Barnes* (1807) 1 Taunt. 48; *Mackenzie* v. *Whitworth* (1875) 1 Ex.D. 36; *Uzielli* v. *Boston Marine* (1884) 15 Q.B.D. 11; *Nelson* v. *Empress Assurance* [1905] 2 K.B. 281.

[11] [1925] A.C. 639.

[12] s.9(1) refers to the insurer reinsuring "his risk."

[13] But see *Forsikringsaktieselskapet Vesta* v. *Butcher* [1989] 1 All E.R. 402.

[14] See generally Chap. 13.

[15] [1984] 3 All E.R. 777.

[16] *Mackenzie* v. *Whitworth* (1875) 1 Ex.D. 36; M.I.A. 1906, s.9(1).

[17] *Colonial Insurance Co. of New Zealand* v. *Adelaide Marine Insurane* (1886) 12 App.Cas. 128; *Hewitt* v. *London General Insurance* (1925) 23 Ll.L.R. 243; *Re Overseas Marine Insurance* (1930) 36 Ll.L.R. 183; *General Reinsurance Corporation* v. *Fennia* [1982] 1 Lloyd's Rep. 87, reversed on another point [1983] 2 Lloyd's Rep. 287.

[18] For this distinction, see *supra* § 12–03.

[19] Insurable interest is discussed in Chap. 3.

[20] *Dalby* v. *India and London Life* (1854) 15 C.B. 365.

2. CONTRACTUAL PRINCIPLES

12–05 Reinsurance contracts, as contracts of insurance, are for the most part governed by principles common to those which govern original insurances. A marine reinsurance is thus subject to the Marine Insurance Act 1906.[21] The precise manner in which the ordinary principles of insurance apply to reinsurances will, nevertheless, reflect the special nature of reinsurance agreements.

Misrepresentation and non-disclosure

12–06 *Applicability of utmost good faith.* Contracts of reinsurance, whether in facultative, treaty or open cover form, are contracts of utmost good faith, so that full disclosure must be made prior to the making of the contract.[22] However, in the case of treaties and open covers, the reinsured, by issuing new contracts, is capable of extending the liability of reinsurer, and the question arises whether the duty of utmost good faith applies to each cession under a treaty or new risk under an open cover, or whether the duty is exhausted as soon as the treaty or open cover comes into force. Where the reinsurance cover automatically operates on the reinsured accepting a risk, or where the reinsurer is otherwise obliged to provide reinsurance on demand, there is seemingly no room for the duty of utmost good faith to operate,[23] for acceptance and the premium have been predetermined and consequently materiality has been exhausted. By contrast, where the reinsurer has a right to consider and to reject a particular risk offered by the reinsured,[24] or where the reinsured puts forward a risk which falls outside the limits of the treaty or open cover,[25] the duty of utmost good faith operates in respect of that risk and the reinsurer may refuse liability in respect of it.

12–07 *Breach of duty.* If the assured makes false statements to the reinsured, and the reinsured passes on those false statements to the reinsurer under a facultative policy,[26] either expressly[27] or indirectly by means of a provision incorporating the assured's proposal into the reinsurance agreement,[28] the reinsurer will normally be able to avoid the reinsurance agreement even if the reinsured wishes to make payment. However, this right may be overridden by a "follow the settlements" or similar clause,[29] but not by an "errors and omissions" clause.[30]

---

[21] *Imperial Marine* v. *Fire Insurance Corporation* (1879) 4 C.P.D. 166; *North British Fishing Boat Insurance* v. *Starr* (1922) 13 Ll.L.R. 206.

[22] *Brownlie* v. *Campbell* (1880) 5 App.Cas. 925, 924; *Glasgow Assurance* v. *Symondson* (1911) 104 L.T. 254; *Everett* v. *Hogg Robinson* [1973] 2 Lloyd's Rep. 217.

[23] *Law Guarantee Trust* v. *Munich Reinsurance* (1915) 31 T.L.R. 572.

[24] *Berger* v. *Pollock* [1973] 2 Lloyd's Rep. 442, a case involving a brokers' open cover. As the reinsured was not a party to the reinsurer's promise to issue reinsurance to the broker's clients, a duty of utmost good faith was owed by the reinsured.

[25] *Inversiones Manria* v. *Sphere Drake Insurance* [1989] 1 Lloyd's Rep. 69 (original risk rather than reinsurance risk offered to reinsurers).

[26] The point is unlikely to arise in the case of a treaty.

[27] *Equitable Life Assurance* v. *General Accident Insurance* 1904 12 S.L.T. 348; *Highlands Insurance* v. *Continental Insurance* [1987] 1 Lloyd's Rep. 109.

[28] *Foster* v. *Mentor Life* (1854) 3 E. & B. 48; *Australian Widows Fund* v. *National Mutual Life* [1914] A.C. 634.

[29] See *infra*, § 12–12.

[30] *Highlands* v. *Continental, supra* n. 27.

Materiality in reinsurance cases. What is material will depend upon **12–08** the nature of the reinsurance agreement. There is no authority on the scope of materiality as regards a reinsurance treaty, although factors which affect the premium demanded by a reinsurer will include the nature of the insurances to be ceded, the amount of the reinsured's net retention and the insured's claims history. Facts held to be material to a facultative reinsurance include the amount of the assured's net retention,[31] the extent of the reinsured's previous losses[32] and the inclusion in the original insurance of terms which extend the insurer's liability to an unusual extent and in respect of which the reinsurer will be obliged to provide an indemnity.[33] The fact that a policy is one of reinsurance rather than of insurance is not a material fact.[34]

Warranties **12–09**
Warranties have the same effect in a contract of reinsurance as in the original policy.[35] Thus where the insurer is, under the governing law of the contract of insurance, obliged to make payment despite a breach of warranty, the reinsurer is bound to provide an indemnity under a reinsurance contract governed by English law even though the breach of warranty by the assured would have provided a defence under English law.[36]

Whether treaty binding other than in honour **12–10**
Arbitration clauses in reinsurance treaties are commonly in "honourable engagement" form, typically:

> "The arbitrators and umpire shall interpret this reinsurance as an honourable engagement and they shall make their award with a view to effecting the general purpose of this reinsurance in a reasonable manner rather than in accordance with a literal interpretation of the language."

The modern trend is not to regard honourable engagement clauses as rendering the entire reinsurance treaty void for uncertainty,[37] or to treat the arbitration clause itself as void on the ground that it ousts the jurisdiction of the courts,[38] but to treat them as binding.[39] The precise latitude allowed to arbitrators under an honourable engagement clause is not, however, clear, and it may be that the arbitrators are not empowered to ignore strict rules of law but are merely entitled to construe the

---

[31] *Foster* v. *Mentor Life* (1854) 3 E. & B. 48; *Traill* v. *Baring* (1864) 33 L.J.Ch. 521; *Irish National Insurance* v. *Oman Insurance* [1983] 2 Lloyd's Rep. 453. *Cf. Great Atlantic* v. *Home Insurance* [1981] 2 Lloyd's Rep. 219, where the matter turned upon the construction of a warranty.
[32] *General Accident* v. *Campbell* (1925) 21 Ll.L.R. 151; *Everett* v. *Hogg Robinson* [1973] 2 Lloyd's Rep. 217.
[33] *Charlesworth* v. *Faber* (1900) 5 Com.Cas. 408; *Property Insurance* v. *National Protector Insurance* (1913) 108 L.T. 104.
[34] *Crowley* v. *Cohen* (1832) 3 B. & Ad. 478; *Mackenzie* v. *Whitworth* (1875) 1 Ex.D. 36; *Imperial Marine* v. *Fire Insurance Corporation* (1879) 4 C.P.D. 166; *Re London County Commercial Reinsurance Office* [1922] 2 Ch. 67.
[35] *Duckett* v. *Williams* (1834) 2 Cr. & M. 348; *Life Association of Scotland* v. *Forster* (1873) 11 M. 351. See also the cases cited *supra* in n. 28.
[36] *Forsikrinsaktieselskapet Vesta* v. *Butcher* [1989] 1 All E.R. 402.
[37] As was apparently done by Goddard J. in *Maritime Insurance* v. *Assecuranz Union* (1935) 52 Ll.L.R. 16, where, however, the wording sought to oust strict rules of law.
[38] This was the approach adopted by Megaw J. in *Orion* v. *Belfort* [1962] 2 Lloyd's Rep. 257, when faced with a clause which sought to substitute discretion for the strict rules of law.
[39] *Eagle Star* v. *Yuval Insurance* [1978] 1 Lloyd's Rep. 357; *Home Insurance* v. *Administratia Asiguraricor de Stat* [1983] 2 Lloyd's Rep. 674.

wording of the reinsurance agreement in a purposive rather than purely literal fashion.[40]

3. LOSS AND INDEMNITY

12–11 Incorporating the terms of the original policy

Reinsurance agreements commonly contain the wording: "being a reinsurance of and warranted same gross rate and terms and conditions" as the original policy. The purpose of such wording is to ensure that the insurance and reinsurance agreements are back-to-back so that the liability of the reinsured is matched by that of the reinsurer.[41] There are inherent dangers with incorporation, however, for the terms of the original policy may be inappropriate in a reinsurance agreement or, alternatively, there may be a direct conflict between the express terms of the reinsurance and the terms of the original policy incorporated into it. In such circumstances the courts have refused full incorporation. Thus, in *Home Insurance of New York* v. *Victoria-Montreal Fire*[42] the Privy Council held that a condition in the original fire policy limiting claims to those begun within 12 months of the fire did not apply to the reinsurance agreement, for the reinsured could not move until the actual loss had been ascertained and compliance with such a limit would not have been practicable. Again, in *Pine Top Insurance* v. *Unione Italiana Anglo Saxon Reinsurance*[43] Gatehouse J. held that the words "all terms and conditions as original" were not appropriate to incorporate into a retrocession agreement[44] an arbitration clause which appeared in the original policy, as that clause was quite inappropriate to the retrocession. There are, therefore, limits to exactly what will be incorporated into a reinsurance agreement by a "same terms and conditions as original" clause, and the House of Lords has recently frowned upon incorporation as a "highly unsatisfactory" manner of conducting reinsurance business.[45]

12–12 "Follow the settlements"

Reinsurance agreements generally require the reinsurer to follow the settlements of the reinsured.[46] It was established by the Court of Appeal in *Insurance Co. of Africa* v. *Scor (U.K.) Reinsurance*[47] that the "follow

---

[40] This was the view of the Court of Appeal in *Home and Overseas Insurance* v. *Mentor Insurance* [1989] 1 Lloyd's Rep. 473, impliedly disapproving the opinion of Evans J. in *Overseas Union* v. *A.A. Mutual International* [1988] 1 F.T.L.R. 421, where the learned judge held that an honourable engagement clause merely relaxed the rules of evidence and allowed the arbitrators to rely upon their own knowledge and experience.

[41] *Re Eddystone Marine Insurance* [1892] 2 Ch. 423, 425.

[42] [1907] A.C. 59.

[43] [1987] 1 Lloyd's Rep. 476.

[44] *I.e.* a reinsurance of a reinsurance.

[45] Lord Griffiths in *Forsakringsiktieselskapet Vesta* v. *Butcher* [1989] 1 All E.R. 402, 407. *Cf.* Lord Lowry at p. 420. The House of Lords was in this case unable to pronounce directly upon the issue, as incorporation had been ruled to have taken place by the trial judge and this assumption had not been challenged on appeal.

[46] Earlier wording replaced by this formulation was "to pay as may be paid thereon." The effect of this was to bind the reinsurer to honour a reasonable compromise by the reinsured with the reinsurer unless it had been effected dishonestly or carelessly: *Chippendale* v. *Holt* (1895) 65 L.J.Q.B. 104; *Western Assurance of Toronto* v. *Poole* [1903] 1 K.B. 376; *Excess Insurance* v. *Matthews* (1925) 21 Com.Cas. 43; *Traders* v. *Bankers and General Insurance* (1921) 38 T.L.R. 94; *Gurney* v. *Grimmer* (1932) 44 Ll.L.R. 189.

[47] [1985] 1 Lloyd's Rep. 312, following *Excess Insurance* v. *Matthews* (1925) 21 Com.Cas. 43.

the settlements" wording obliges the reinsurer to indemnify the reinsured in respect of any settlement reached by the assured honestly and with all proper and businesslike steps. Consequently, it is possible for a reinsurer to incur liability even though the settlement reached by the reinsured is subsequently shown to have been unjustified, as long as it was reached honestly and in a businesslike fashion. However, the reinsurer will not be liable in respect of *ex gratia* payments made by the reinsured in the knowledge that it did not face legal liability to the assured. The reinsurer bears the burden of proving that the reinsured's payment was in some way improper.[47A] Moreover, in accordance with the *Scor* decision, the "follow the settlements" clause will not oblige the reinsurer to meet any of the following payments by the reinsured:

(a) liabilities incurred by the reinsured which are not covered by the reinsurance agreement;

(b) costs incurred by the reinsured in reaching a settlement with the assured[48] or in establishing its non-liability to the assured[49]; and

(c) punitive or other extra-contractual damages awarded against the reinsured for failing to reach a proper settlement with the assured.

In the absence of a provision obliging the reinsurer to follow the settlements or fortunes of the reinsured, it is necessary for the reinsured to prove its loss, *i.e.* to establish that its payment to the assured was based upon an actual legal liability to the assured and otherwise fell within the terms of the reinsurance agreement. The fact that the reinsured has made payment under the original policy will not suffice.[50]

Claims control and claims co-operation provisions   12–13
Reinsurers today are less willing than was once the case to follow unconditionally any settlements reached by their reinsureds, and use claims control and claims co-operation provisions to regulate liability towards reinsureds. Under a claims control clause the reinsurer asserts the right to take over and control all negotiations with the original assured, and under a claims co-operation clause the reinsured will be precluded from reaching a settlement with the assured unless the reinsurer first approves it. Generally such clauses are stated to be conditions precedent to the reinsurer's liability. It was held by the Court of Appeal in *Scor* that the reinsurer is liable despite the presence of a claims control or co-operation provision if the reinsured is able to prove its loss under the reinsurance, by demonstrating legal liability to the original assured; in *Scor* itself, the reinsured's failure to comply with a claims control provision was excused by the fact that judgment had been given

---

[47A] *Insurance Co. of Pennsylvania* v. *Grand Union Insurance* [1990] 1 Lloyd's Rep. 208 (Hong Kong C.A.).

[48] The costs of reaching a settlement with the assured incurred by a reinsured were allowed in *British Dominion General Insurance* v. *Duder* [1915] 2 K.B. 394. This is difficult to reconcile with *Scor*. The question of costs may be governed by express provision: *British General* v. *Mountain* (1919) 36 T.L.R. 171.

[49] *Scottish Metropolitan Association* v. *Groom* (1924) 41 L.T. 35.

[50] Mathew L.J. in *Nelson* v. *Empress Assurance* [1905] 2 K.B. 281, 285; Kennedy J. in *St. Paul Fire* v. *Morice* (1906) 11 Com.Cas. 153, 164–165.

against it in the assured's favour, so that its loss under the reinsurance agreement had been demonstrated.

It was further decided in *Scor* that where a "follow the settlements" clause and a claims control clause appear in the same contract, the former is to be read subject to—and is to be regarded as emasculated by— the latter. Some doubt was cast upon this position *in arguendo* by the House of Lords in *Forsikringsaktieselskapet Vesta* v. *Butcher*,[51] and further determination of this issue is awaited.

12–14 Reinsured's loss

The reinsurer may, depending upon the wording of the reinsurance policy, be liable either for losses suffered by the reinsured during the currency of the reinsurance agreement or for losses flowing from events occurring during the currency of the reinsurance policy. In both cases the reinsurer will not itself face liability until the amount due to the assured under the original policy has been ascertained.[52] The measure of indemnity under the reinsurance must be fixed as at that date, which is the effective date of the reinsured's loss.

It has been said that there must not only be liability but also payment to support a claim under a contract of reinsurance.[53] The true principle, however, is that the matter is one to be determined according to the proper construction of the reinsurance agreement, although there is a presumption that actual payment need not be made by the reinsured. Thus if the reinsurance provides "to pay as may be paid thereon," the reinsurer is liable as soon as the reinsured has established its liability[54] whereas if the agreement states that the reinsurers are to be liable only for sums actually paid then actual payment must be made by the reinsured.[55] If there is any ambiguity, however, actual payment may not be required: in *Home* v. *Mentor*[56] the words "sums actually paid" were held by the Court of Appeal not to be conclusive of the reinsurer's right to withhold payment until payment by the reinsured, as other terms of the contract were not fully consistent with this approach, and the resolution of the dispute was remitted to the arbitrators.

The prepayment issue is most likely to arise in the event of the reinsured's insolvency. The general principle here is that if the reinsurer is not liable to the reinsured's liquidator because the reinsured has not made payment to the assured,[57] the assured cannot seek payment directly from the reinsurer,[58] nor can he make a claim against the reinsurer under the Third Parties (Rights against Insurers) Act 1930.[59] Amounts paid by the reinsurer only go to swell the general assets of the reinsured, and the original assured's right against these assets is merely

---

[51] [1989] 1 All E.R. 402.

[52] *Verischerungs* v. *Henderson* (1934) 49 Ll.L.R. 252.

[53] Bateson J. in *Fireman's Fund* v. *Western Australian Insurance* (1927) 138 L.T. 108, 110.

[54] *Re Eddystone Marine* [1892] 2 Ch. 423; *Re Law Guarantee Trust* [1914] 2 Ch. 617.

[55] *Nepean* v. *Marten* (1895) 11 T.L.R. 256.

[56] [1989] 1 Lloyd's Rep. 473.

[57] Hirst J. at first instance in *Home* v. *Mentor* stated that such a conclusion would be "unjust and discordant with commercial good sense."

[58] M.I.A. 1906, s.9(2): see *supra*, § 12–02.

[59] Reinsurance is excluded by s.1(5) of the 1930 Act.

to prove as an ordinary creditor for his share.[60] Underwriters, therefore, at one time engaged in the original policy to reinsure the amount underwritten and to give the assured a charge upon the policy of reinsurance so effected, in which case the original assured could recover the whole amount payable by the reinsurer on the bankruptcy of the underwriter.[61] The validity of such a clause is, however, doubtful, as it may require registration as a charge under section 395 of the Companies Act 1985, and these clauses are no longer used. More common are cut-through clauses contained in reinsurance, which confer a direct right of action upon the assured in the event of the reinsured's insolvency, but as the assured is not privy to the agreement it is doubtful whether a cut-through clause is enforceable.

Variation of original policy   12–15
Variation in the terms of the original policy discharges the reinsurer from liability under the reinsurance policy.[62] "It is one thing for the reinsurer to trust to the policies which the reinsured had made and another to trust to those he might make in the future."[63]

Conflict of laws   12–16
Reinsurance is an international business and it is quite common for reinsurance and insurance agreements to be governed by different proper laws and, indeed, written in different languages. Where possible, the courts will seek to hold that the proper law of a reinsurance agreement is the same as that of underlying insurance, as the general intention of the parties is that such agreements are to be back-to-back. However, a court will not distort the true situation: thus, in *Forsikringsaktieselskapet Vesta* v. *Butcher*[64] the original policy was governed by Norwegian law, but the House of Lords refused to countenance the argument that the reinsurance agreement, or any part of it, was itself governed by Norwegian law when it had been drafted, broked, executed and administered in England. The precise problem in *Vesta* was a warranty in the original policy (governed by Norwegian law) requiring the assured fish farmer to maintain a 24-hour watch over his fish farm, but he failed to do so. This breach of warranty did not, however, discharge the Norwegian insurers, as in Norwegian law as a warranty is operative only where causative of the loss. The terms of the Norwegian policy had been incorporated into a reinsurance governed by English law, and the reinsurers argued that the assured's breach of warranty allowed them to terminate the reinsurance agreement for breach even though the insurers themselves faced liability. The House of Lords, faced with the concession that incorporation had taken place,[65] held that while the proper law of the reinsurance agreement was English law, the fact that it had the same terms as the original policy meant that the warranty was to

---

[60] *Re Law Guarantee Trust* [1915] 1 Ch. 340; *Re Harrington Motor Co.* [1928] Ch. 105.
[61] *General Insurance of Trieste* v. *Miller* (1896) 12 T.L.R. 395; *Leo Steamship* v. *Corderoy* (1896) 1 Com.Cas. 300.
[62] *Norwich Union* v. *Colonial Mutual Fire* [1922] 2 K.B. 461.
[63] *Lower Rhine Insurance* v. *Sedgwick* [1899] 1 Q.B. 179.
[64] [1989] 1 All E.R. 402.
[65] See *supra* § 12–11.

be given its Norwegian construction, namely that its breach did not give rise to a defence in the circumstances.

The *Vesta* decision related to a case in which the insurance and reinsurance agreements had a common origin and were framed in the same terms. It does not necessarily follow from *Vesta* that the English courts will adopt a similar approach where two policies governed by different proper laws and framed in different terms share some common expressions. Thus in *St. Paul Insurance* v. *Morice*[66] it was held that the phrase "risks of mortality" had a wider meaning in American law than in English law, and that English reinsurers were not bound to pay under the English reinsurance even though the insurers were bound to pay under the American reinsurance. Nevertheless, the *Vesta* decision casts doubt upon this sort of reasoning.

---

[66] (1906) 22 T.L.R. 449.

Part Two

PARTIES TO INSURANCE CONTRACTS

CHAPTER 13

THE INSURER

1. THE REGULATION OF INSURERS

Types of insurer   13–01

Insurers of various types are permitted to carry on insurance business in the United Kingdom. Insurers fall under the following heads:

(a) insurance companies authorised to carry on insurance business under the Insurance Companies Act 1982;
(b) Lloyd's underwriters;
(c) friendly societies and similar bodies.

There will in due course be a fourth category when the internal market of the European Communities is completed, namely, insurers located in some other member state but authorised to carry on insurance business in their home territories. The present law is in a state of transition and discussion of the manner in which E.C. insurers are to be authorised remains ongoing at time of writing.

Insurers are subject to various forms of regulation. Lloyd's underwriters and friendly societies are governed by their own statutory schemes, while insurance companies and mutual insurers must comply with the complex provisions of the Insurance Companies Act 1982. In addition, any insurer offering life policies falls within the Financial Services Act 1986 and is subject to controls affecting investment businesses; detailed provision is made to mitigate the overlaps between the primary insurance legislation and the Financial Services Act 1986.

The following paragraphs outline the situation of Lloyd's underwriters and friendly societies, and briefly mention two specific forms of insurance, namely industrial assurance and mutual insurance. The impact of the Insurance Companies Act 1982, the Financial Services Act 1986 and the European position are discussed in the remaining parts of this chapter.

Lloyd's underwriters   13–02

History. "Lloyd's" is, or was, the name of a coffee-shop owned by one Edward Lloyd. When it was first opened is uncertain, but the *London Gazette* of February 21, 1688, records its existence at that time by an advertisement offering a reward, claimable at Lloyd's Coffee House, for watches stolen from an Edward Bramsby. Lloyd's became established as the centre of marine underwriting, although much marine insurance was underwritten in counting houses belonging to individuals, and also in the Jamaica and Jerusalem coffee houses and at the Coal Exchange.

There is no evidence to suggest that Lloyd's was better appointed, more attentively served or had greater brilliance of conversation or debate[1] than the majority of its coffee house contemporaries; it had the advantage, however, of being near the River Thames and thus attracting the patronage of merchants willing to accept insurances on ships and their cargoes.

Lloyd's prospered, and the house became recognised as a likely place for persons wanting to find underwriters to write their names beneath the wording of insurance policies, to guarantee commercial ventures on a personal basis. Edward Lloyd prompted the trend towards business by providing his customers with shipping information provided from the waterfront by runners. In 1696 he published a newsheet, *Lloyd's News*, and although this was discontinued it may be regarded as the forerunner of *Lloyd's List and Shipping Gazette*, London's oldest daily newspaper, which first appeared in 1734, 21 years after Lloyd's death.

Requirements for more space caused Lloyd's to move to the Royal Exchange in 1774, the move being funded by the first Committee of Lloyd's which had been established in 1771. For the next century the private club characteristic of Lloyd's was further moulded by restricting membership, introducing subscriptions, giving the elected committee increased authority, and regulating the basis on which Committee members served. Lloyd's finally moved to Lime Street in 1957.

13–03 *Organisation.* Lloyd's is a society, incorporated by the Lloyd's Act 1871, whose members, known as "underwriting members of Lloyd's," transact insurance for their own account. The Corporation of Lloyd's does not accept insurance, nor does it assume liability for the insurance business transacted by its members. Nevertheless, it provides the premises, lays down through a committee strict financial and other regulations regarding membership, and administers the Corporation's activities.

13–04 The Lloyd's market is administered by a Committee, comprising 16 elected members. The Committee does not, other than in a very few instances, dictate the type of business accepted at Lloyd's or interfere in the day-to-day conduct of underwriting, but rather is concerned with the election of new members and the financial stability of those doing business at Lloyd's. It administers the affairs of the Corporation, including the provision of claims offices, shipping intelligence and publications, an aviation department, the agency network and the Lloyd's policy signing office.

13–05 *Membership.* Insurance can only be accepted at Lloyd's by elected underwriting members, who must satisfy the most stringent conditions in order to qualify. They must:

(a) be nominated by one and supported by five other members;
(b) transact business with unlimited and personal liability;
(c) furnish security of a specified minimum amount, to be held in trust by Lloyd's;
(d) pay all premiums into Premium Trust Funds under Deeds of

---

[1] The early London coffee houses were also centres of debate, and had some political influence. Charles II attempted, unsuccessfully, to suppress them as "nurseries of sedition and rebellion."

Trust, from which claims, expenses and ascertained profits only may be paid. Every member on election must pay a substantial sum (independent of the deposit) as an initial contribution to this Fund;

(e) furnish a guarantee policy each year based on the member's premium income; and

(f) contribute by means of a levy on premium income to a Central Fund intended to meet the underwriting liabilities of any member in the unlikely event of his security and personal assets proving to be insufficient to meet underwriting liabilities.

The Audit. A main link in the chain of security around the Lloyd's **13–06** policy is the Annual Audit to which all underwriting members must submit. Each member is required to show that the value of his underwriting assets is sufficient to meet his liabilities. The Audit is designed to detect any weakness in the underwriter's position at the earliest moment and to ensure that provision is made to remedy any adverse trend. The Audit was first introduced voluntarily in 1908 but was subsequently given statutory authority.

Syndicates. Though Lloyd's underwriters still transact business as **13–07** individuals, the complexity of modern commerce and the enormous insured values involved necessitated change. Underwriters now group into syndicates of a few hundred members, and it is the underwriting agents who accept risks on behalf of the "names" on the syndicates. Thus, when a syndicate underwriter accepts a risk he can do so for a very much larger amount than if he were acting on his own behalf; the personal and individual liability of the members on whose behalf he acts is not altered in any way.

Placing business. Insurance may be placed with Lloyd's underwriters **13–08** only through Lloyd's brokers, although such brokers may also place business with non-Lloyd's insurers. The role of brokers is considered in Chapter 15. Insurance contracts are made at Lloyd's by means of slip; the legal issues arising from this procedure were examined in Chapter 1.

Statutory framework 13–09

Lloyd's Acts 1871–1982. The earliest legislation was the Lloyd's Act 1871, which gave Lloyd's corporate status and gave statutory status to the bye-laws which governed the operation of Lloyd's. This was amended by the Lloyd's Act 1911, which extended the purposes of Lloyd's and conferred upon it greater disciplinary powers over members. Further amendments took place by virtue of the Lloyd's Acts 1925 and 1951, the latter extending Lloyd's borrowing and trustee powers. The main governing legislation is now the Lloyd's Act 1982, which established a new constitutional structure. Lloyd's is now governed by a Council consisting of 16 elected members of Lloyd's, eight external members and three nominated members (section 3). The Council in turn elects a Chairman and Deputy Chairman of Lloyd's (section 4). The working members of the Council constitute the Committee of Lloyd's (section 5). Constitutionally, the Council is the legislative arm of Lloyd's, charged with the making of bye-laws, although this function may be delegated to the Committee (section 6). Discipline is in the hands of a Disciplinary Committee and an Appeal Tribunal (section 7).[2] Members are to be personally liable on contracts, may contract only through underwriting agencies and membership terminates on bankruptcy (sections 8–9). Finally, there is a strict separation of the functions of underwriters and brokers (sections 11–12).

13–10 *Insurance Companies Act 1982.* Lloyd's underwriters are exempted from the normal requirement of authorisation by the Secretary of State to carry on insurance business[3] and from the regulatory provisions applicable to insurance companies contained in Part II of the 1982 Act.[4] In their place, Lloyd's must comply with sections 83–86 of the Act. Section 83 imposes the obligations for all premiums to be paid into a trust fund and for an annual audit; section 84 obliges Lloyd's as a whole to maintain a solvency margin[5]; section 85 imposes the restrictions on transfer of business (contained in sections 49–52)[6] on Lloyd's, but only if one of the parties to the transfer is not a Lloyd's underwriter; and section 86 requires the Committee of Lloyd's to deposit with the Secretary of State an annual statement summarising the extent and character of the business done by Lloyd's members in the preceding 12 months.[7]

13–11 *Representative proceedings against Lloyd's underwriters.* The practice at Lloyd's is for one underwriter to be nominated as the "leading underwriter" in respect of any risk; in the case of large risks this nomination may extend beyond Lloyd's underwriters and may relate to insurance companies and to overseas insurers. Under Order 15, rule 12(1) of the Rules of the Supreme Court, a representative action may be brought by or against one person representing other persons "where there are numerous persons having the same interest in proceedings." It has been held that such an action may be brought against a leading underwriter as representing all of the subscribing insurers and underwriters under a policy, and that this is so even if some of those insurers would not otherwise be subject to the jurisdiction of the English courts under Order 11 of the Rules of the Supreme Court.[8]

13–12 Friendly Societies

Nature. Friendly societies provide a variety of benefits for their members, including limited forms of insurance. A registered friendly society is exempted from the authorisation requirement contained in the 1982

---

[2] Questions of fact, such as guilt or innocence of discreditable conduct, and whether the member should be excluded from membership, are not subject to judicial review: *R.* v. *Committee of Lloyd's, ex parte Moran* (1983), *The Times*, June 24. However, the court has jurisdiction over the disciplinary process generally, and may declare any order to be *ultra vires* (*e.g.*, suspension of a member): *R.* v. *Committee of Lloyd's, ex parte Posgate* (1983), *The Times*, January 12.

[3] Insurance Companies Act 1982, s.2(2)(a).

[4] s.15(4).

[5] See *infra*.

[6] See *infra*.

[7] For the prescribed form of this statement, and for other matters relating to Lloyd's, see the Insurance (Lloyd's) Regulations 1983, S.I. 1983 No. 224.

[8] *Irish Shipping* v. *Commercial Union, The Irish Rowan* [1989] 2 Lloyd's Rep. 44. The leading underwriter here was not a Lloyd's underwriter, but the principle is clear.

Act.[9] The relevant legislation is now consolidated in the Friendly Societies Act 1974, as amended by the Friendly Societies Act 1984. The forms of societies which may be registered are listed in section 7 of the Friendly Societies Act 1974, as amended, and consist of:

(a) friendly societies proper, which have amongst their objects the relief of or maintenance of society members and their dependants, and insurance on life, funeral expenses and birth;

(b) cattle insurance societies, which provide various forms of livestock insurance;

(c) benevolent societies, established for benevolent or charitable purposes;

(d) working men's clubs;

(e) old people's home societies; and

(f) specially authorised societies for a purpose authorised by the Treasury.

Members' rights to insure. The principal provisions regarding insur- **13–13** ance are contained in sections 64 *et seq.* of the 1974 Act. Section 64 sets out maximum permitted benefits: under *tax exempt* life or endowment business £500 gross or £104 a year by way of annuity; under life or endowment business not exempt from tax £10,000 gross (whether or not the entitlement is under any mortgage protection policy) or £1,000 a year by way of annuity.

Industrial assurance   13–14

Industrial assurance is governed by the Industrial Assurance Act 1923, as amended most importantly by the Friendly Societies Act 1948. Industrial assurance is in essence life insurance for very small sums where the premiums are received by means of collectors, generally monthly (see Industrial Assurance Act 1923, s.1). This type of insurance falls within the Insurance Companies Act 1982, although where conducted by a friendly society it is governed by the friendly societies legislation rather than by the 1982 Act.[10]

Mutual insurance   13–15

This type of insurance has been associated historically with marine insurance,[11] but in recent years has been adopted by an increasing number of professions. Mutual associations provide membership to a group of persons bearing common risks, and each person contributes to the association's funds; the terms of the insurance are contained in the contract of membership of the association. Mutual insurers are regulated as insurance companies by the Insurance Companies Act 1982, although a number of marine mutual insurers arrange their affairs so that they do not carry on business in the U.K. and thus fall outside the 1982 Act.

---

[9] Insurance Companies Act 1982, s.2(2)(*b*), (3).
[10] Insurance Companies Act 1982, s.2(3).
[11] See § 23–86 *infra.*

2. INSURANCE COMPANIES ACT 1982

13–16 History

Reasons for regulation. Although the general principle of the common law is that anyone with normal contractual capacity may enter into a contract, Parliament has, by a succession of enactments culminating in the Insurance Companies Act 1982, restricted the classes of persons who may engage in insurance business, and has regulated insurance business generally.

The justification for such legislation may be summed up by the words of Maugham J. in *Re North and South Insurance.* [12]

> "An insurance company differs in its nature from almost every other trading concern. It starts, in the first instance, without liabilities. It obtains premiums sometimes to very large amounts . . . inasmuch as the claim comes in in every case after the premiums have been secured, there is always a risk that an insurance company may, by offering what look like very advantageous terms to the public, obtain a very large premium income which, as the result of the practical working of the company, proves to be an insufficient income for the purpose of meeting claims."

The history of insurance regulation has indeed been *ad hoc* response to successive insurance failures; a comprehensive approach was not adopted until the 1980s.

13–17 *Legislative history.* Insurance companies have always been subject to the ordinary provisions of the companies legislation. Specific insurance legislation commenced with the Life Assurance Companies Act 1870. [13] Under this Act all new life companies were required to deposit £20,000 in court, special provision was made for their amalgamation and winding up, and certain provisions of the Companies Acts were applied to non-incorporated life offices. The scheme was extended to employers' liability insurance by the Employers' Liability Insurance Companies Act 1907.

The Assurance Companies Act 1909, replacing the 1870 and 1907 Acts, applied the principle of control to fire and accident insurance and bond investment business. Motor insurance business was added by section 42(1) of the Road Traffic Act 1930, and aircraft insurance by section 20 of the Air Navigation Act 1936. Marine and transit insurance, which remained the chief forms of unregulated business, were brought within the legislation by the Assurance Companies Act 1946.

13–18 *The replacement of deposits.* Until 1946 the legislation proceeded on the principle of applying the requirement of deposits in court to a successively larger range of insurance companies. The normal deposit for each class of business was £20,000, and these deposits were available to meet claims in the event of the insurer's insolvency. The Assurance Companies Act 1946 substituted for the deposit system a system designed to secure that the assets of companies carrying on *general* (*i.e.*, non-life) business should always exceed their liabilities by £50,000 or one-tenth of their annual premium income, whichever sum was greater.

---

[12] (1933) 47 Ll.L.R. 356–358.
[13] This Act was inspired by the failure of the Albert and European Assurance companies in 1868.

This scheme was retained by a consolidating and amending Act, the Insurance Companies Act 1958. The 1958 Act was itself amended by Part II of the Companies Act 1967, which introduced more drastic provisions to ensure solvency. The Insurance Companies Amendment Act 1973 continued this process, and the entire legislation was consolidated by the Insurance Companies Act 1974.[14]

The modern system. Further reform became inevitable by the **13–19** accession of the United Kingdom to the European Communities in 1973, as E.C. law differed in a number of significant respects from the existing system, particularly in calculating the margin of solvency and in laying down classes of insurance business. United Kingdom law was brought fully into line by the Insurance Companies Act 1982, consolidating United Kingdom and E.C. principles. This Act is now the governing provision, although it has been amended in respect of life assurance by the Financial Services Act 1986[15] and will be subjected to further amendments as E.C. law continues to develop.[16]

Classes of insurance business **13–20**
The 1982 Act divides insurance business into "long term" business and "general"business,[17] and thereafter requires insurers to treat these two broad types of business as distinct operations. Each type consists of a large number of classes, and in all cases insurance business of any class is conducted by effecting and carrying out contracts of that class.[18] Where insurance business falls within two classes, it is deemed to be of the class consistent with the principal object of the business.[19]

Long term business is set out in Schedule 1, and consists of seven classes: life and annuity; marriage and birth; linked long term; permanent health; tontines; capital redemption; and pension fund management.

General business is set out in Schedule 2, and consists of 18 classes: accident; sickness; land vehicles; railway rolling stock; aircraft; ships; goods in transit; fire and natural forces; damage to property; motor vehicle liability; aircraft liability; liability for ships; general liability; credit; suretyship; miscellaneous financial loss; legal expenses; and assistance. These various classes are grouped into eight groups, for the purpose of authorisation by the Secretary of State.

Authorisation **13–21**
By section 2, no person may carry on any insurance business in the United Kingdom unless authorised by the Secretary of State, although general exceptions are provided for Lloyd's and friendly societies, and

---

[14] The legislation in the 1970s was inspired by the spectacular activities of Dr. Savundra.
[15] See *infra*.
[16] Changes will be implemented by secondary legislation, made under the European Communities Act 1972, bringing into force various outstanding Council Regulations. See *infra*.
[17] s.1(1).
[18] This phrase is important, for any person effecting and carrying out insurance business in the U.K. must be authorised. It would seem that business is carried on in the U.K. either by the acceptance of risks or by the paying of claims: *Stewart* v. *Oriental Fire* [1984] 2 Lloyd's Rep. 109.
[19] s.1(2)–(4).

limited exceptions are provided for trade unions, employers' associations and banks. In addition, policies providing benefits in kind may be exempted.[20] If an insurer is not authorised, the contract is voidable at the instance of the assured and the premiums recoverable, although the court may refuse to allow the assured to avoid the contract if the insurer had acted in good faith and that avoidance would be inequitable.[21]

Authorisation is granted on a class by class basis by the Secretary of State under section 3 (existing authorisations are continued by section 4). Application for authorisation must contain specified information[22]; and reasons must be given by the Secretary of State for his decision (section 5(2)) so that judicial review is available. New authorisations will not, under section 6, be given in respect of both long term and general business. Authorisation will not be granted to an applicant with its head office in the United Kingdom unless it is a company and its directors, controllers, managers or main agent are all fit and proper persons.[23] Applications from other member states of the E.C. are subject to similar requirements, but any applicant must in addition have a representative resident in the United Kingdom who is authorised to act generally and to receive service on the company's behalf.[24] Overseas applicants from outside the E.C. are treated in much the same way, but must also be authorised in their home state.[25] Authorisations, once granted, may be withdrawn.[26]

13–22 Regulation of insurance companies

Scope. Part II of the 1982 Act sets out a series of controls on the operation of insurance businesses, applicable to all insurance companies, wherever established, which carry on insurance business in the United Kingdom, but subject to similar exceptions to those operating in respect of authorisation.[27] The relevant sections, which are supplemented by the Insurance Companies Regulations 1981 as amended, and many of which have been introduced to comply with E.C. law, are summarised below.[28]

13–23 *Restriction on other business.* An insurance company is not permitted to carry on any other form of business.[29] This ensures that assets are not dissipated on speculative ventures.

---

[20] s.2(5), under which the Insurance Companies Regulations 1981, S.I. 1981 No. 1654, reg. 23, excludes motor breakdown assistance business from the need for authorisation.

[21] Financial Services Act 1986, s.132. This section applies only to contracts made after the passing of the 1986 Act: in the case of contracts made earlier, it had after some earlier disagreement been established that such a contract was illegal (*Phoenix General* v. *A.D.A.S.* [1986] 2 Lloyd's Rep. 552), although the assured was entitled to recover the premiums despite the illegality (*Re Cavalier Insurance* [1989] 2 Lloyd's Rep. 430). Effecting and carrying on insurance business without authorisation is a criminal offence: s.14.

[22] s.5(1), supplemented by the Insurance Companies Regulations 1981, reg. 29 and Sched. 4.

[23] s.7.

[24] ss.8, 10.

[25] ss.9–10.

[26] ss.11–13.

[27] s.15.

[28] The relevant regulations, along with the full annotated text of the 1982 Act, are contained in the companion looseleaf work *Encyclopedia of Insurance Law*, Sweet & Maxwell.

[29] s.16.

Accounts and statements. Sections 17–27 set out the framework for the **13–24** complex accounting requirements[30] affecting insurance companies. Every company must prepare a revenue account for each year, a balance sheet as at the end of the year, and an income and expenditure account for the year.[31] These must be deposited with the Secretary of State[32] and are to be made available to shareholders and policyholders.[33] Annual statements of each class of long term and general business are also to be prepared.[34] The balance sheet and accounts are to be audited.[35]

Separation of assets. Sections 28–31A provide for a strict separation of **13–25** assets in respect of long term business and general business; the purpose of this is to protect the funds available for long term policyholders. A distinct long term fund must be established,[36] and assets representing a company's long term business are to be applicable only for the purpose of that business and may not be transferred so as to be available for other purposes.[37] Where a company issues "with-profits" policies, which allow policyholders to participate in any surplus in the long term fund, a statutory formula establishes the minimum participation available to those policyholders.[38] Finally, the Act restricts the proportion of an insurance company's long term funds which may be invested in shares in subordinate companies, or loans to such companies or their controllers. Only five per cent. of the long term funds can be used for these purposes.[39]

Solvency margins. By section 32(1), implementing E.C. principles, **13–26** every insurance company with its head office in the United Kingdom or whose business in the United Kingdom is restricted to reinsurance is required to maintain a margin of solvency as prescribed. The Insurance Companies Regulations 1981 contain the details of this, setting out different calculations of long term and general business and laying down the means of valuing the assets of the company. While the solvency margin system has superseded the old deposit system, deposits remain relevant in that a deposit must be made as a condition of initial authorisation,[40] again to be calculated in accordance with the 1981 Regulations.

---

[30] Contained in the Insurance Companies (Accounts and Statements) Regulations 1983, S.I. 1983 No. 1811, as amended.

[31] s.17. Companies from outside the E.C. must keep in the U.K. proper accounts and records relating to insurance business carried on in the U.K.: s.27.

[32] s.22. For the position of societies registered as industrial and provident societies, see s.24. s.26 authorises the Secretary of State to prescribe classes of transactions thought to be undesirable in the interests of policy holders: details of such transactions must also be given to the Secretary of State (s.26).

[33] s.23.

[34] s.20.

[35] s.21. The auditor is entitled to communicate relevant information to the Secretary of State: s.21A. In the case of a company carrying on long term business, periodic actuarial investigation is required: ss.18–19.

[36] s.28.

[37] s.29. S.31A, inserted by the Financial Services Act 1986, lays down a general rule that a company carrying on long term business must ensure that transactions affecting the assets of the company do not operate unfairly as between the long term fund and the company's other assets.

[38] s.30.

[39] s.31.

[40] s.9(1)(c).

An insurance company whose head office is not in the United Kingdom or an E.C. member state must similarly maintain a margin of solvency in respect of its United Kingdom business (unless that business is limited to reinsurance).[41]

If the solvency margin is not maintained, the Secretary of State may require the company to submit a plan under which the margin is to be restored; if agreed to by the Secretary of State, the plan becomes a binding obligation on the company.[42] Alternatively, the Secretary of State can request that a short-term financial scheme is submitted to him for approval; non-compliance with any approved plan is a criminal offence.[43] Section 35 confers upon the Secretary of State the power to make regulations governing the form and situation of assets: the relevant regulations deal with matters such as the currency in which assets are to be represented (1981 Regulations, regs. 25–27).

The United Kingdom solvency margin does not apply to insurers with their head offices in other E.C. member states, as each member state will itself impose such a margin in accordance with E.C. law. Instead, section 34 requires that such a company shall secure that the value of the assets of the business carried on by it in the United Kingdom does not fall below the amount of the liabilities of that business, values being determined in accordance with the 1981 Regulations.

13–27   *Liabilities of unlimited amount.* Section 36 avoids contracts of insurance by which the insurer undertakes to pay an amount or maximum amount which is uncertain when the contract is made, although this provision has yet to be brought into force.

13–28   *Powers of intervention.* Sections 37 to 48 confer detailed powers of intervention on the Secretary of State. The grounds upon which these powers can be exercised are widely cast, discretionary and set out in section 37. Exercise is possible when:

(a) the Secretary of State considers the exercise of the power to be desirable for protecting actual or potential policy holders as regards solvency or (in the case of long term policies) reasonable expectations;

(b) it appears to the Secretary of State that the company or an associated company has failed to comply with a requirement of the insurance companies' legislation;

(c) it appears to him that the company has furnished misleading information under the legislation;

(d) he is not satisfied that adequate arrangements are in force for reinsurance;

(e) there exists a ground upon which authorisation would have been prohibited;

(f) it appears to him that there has been a substantial departure from any forecast submitted for authorisation purposes;

---

[41] s.32(2)–(3).
[42] s.32(4).
[43] s.33.

(g) the authorisation of the company has been withdrawn in the member state hosting its head office.

Where any power of intervention is to be exercised on the ground that authorisation would have been refused on the ground of the unfitness of any person to be involved in an insurance company, section 46 requires the Secretary of State to serve a preliminary notice on that person, giving him the right to make representations.

The powers of intervention vested in the Secretary of State and set **13–29** out in the 1982 Act may be summarised as follows:

(a) The investment policy of a company may be regulated.[44]
(b) Assets equalling the whole of the company's domestic liabilities may be required to be maintained in the United Kingdom. Where such an order is made the whole or any proportion of those assets may be required to be held by a trustee approved by the Secretary of State.[45]
(c) Premium income may be limited.[46]
(d) A company which carries on long term business may be subjected to an actuarial investigation at any time, in advance of the periods required under section 18.[47]
(e) The deposit of accounting documents required by section 22 may be accelerated, and the Secretary of State has power to obtain or require the production of books, papers and information in any form.[48]
(f) The Secretary of State has a residual power to require an insurance company to take such action as appears to him to be appropriate to protect the interests of actual and potential policy holders.[49]

The exercise of any of these powers may be rescinded or varied.[50]

The Secretary of State is, finally under this head, authorised by section 48 to bring civil proceedings in the name of the company. This power exists in relation to all companies under section 438 of the Companies Act 1985.

Transfers of insurance business. The 1982 Act makes separate pro- **13–30** vision for supervision of transfers of long term and general business. Transfers of long term business must be approved by the court on application by petition; an order made by the court may authorise the transfer of all or any part of the transferor's undertaking, property or liabilities, and its shares, debentures and policies. The transferor may be

---

[44] s.38.
[45] ss.39–40.
[46] s.41.
[47] s.42.
[48] ss.43–44, the latter as amended by the Companies Act 1989, s.77(2). A new s.44A, inserted by s.77(3) of the Companies Act 1989, permits the issue of search warrants by magistrates to obtain information wrongly withheld. Any information obtained under s.44 may not be disclosed to any third party other than the relevant authorities administering the Companies Act 1985 and the Financial Services Act 1986: s.47A. In addition, seizure may be resisted on the ground of legal privilege: s.47B.
[49] s.45. This is a last resort measure, and cannot be used unless the Secretary of State is of the view that the powers under ss.38–44 would not be sufficient: s.37(6).
[50] s.47.

wound up by the court if appropriate.[51] This procedure does away with the equitable principle that the consent of each individual policy holder would have been required for any assignment of rights of this nature; the consent of the court is substituted for this.

The transfer of general business is less complex; it requires the approval of the Secretary of State rather than that of the court.[52]

13–31 *Winding up.* The ordinary winding up provisions of the Insolvency Act 1986 are applicable to the winding up of an insurance company,[53] with the following modifications:

(a) the Secretary of State is under section 54 additionally entitled to petition the court for a winding up order, on the ground that the company is insolvent, has failed to satisfy any condition under the insurance companies legislation or has failed to keep proper accounting records in accordance with sections 221 and 222 of the Companies Act 1985;

(b) an insurance company with long term business may not be wound up voluntarily, and when a winding up takes effect by order of the court assets in the long term fund are only available for meeting long term liabilities[54];

(c) on the winding up of a company with long term business, the liquidator must arrange for the continuation of that business pending its transfer to another insurer[55];

(d) on the winding up of an insurance company, the court will also order the winding up of a "subsidiary" company[56];

(e) supplementary winding up rules govern the detail of the winding up of insurance companies.[57]

Where the court has the jurisdiction to wind up an insurance company on the ground that it is insolvent, it may, as an alternative, order a reduction in the amount payable under its contracts of insurance.[58] Any such reduction must achieve broad equity amongst the policy holders, and cannot in any event affect *accrued* liabilities (*i.e.*, outstanding claims).[59]

13–32 *Changes of director, controller, or manager.* A condition of initial authorisation, as noted earlier, is that the managers or representative agents of the insurer are fit and proper persons. Sections 60–64 ensure that the identity of managers cannot change without the scrutiny of the Secretary of State. Sections 60 and 61 contain the general provision that any change in managing director, chief executive or other controller of

---

[51] ss.49–50.

[52] ss.51–52.

[53] s.53, which gives the right to petition to 10 or more policy holders owning policies to an aggregate value of not less than £10,000.

[54] s.55.

[55] s.56. The Policyholders Protection Act 1975 provides the mechanism for transfer or other continuation of long term business: see Chap. 22.

[56] s.57. A subsidiary company is a transferee of any part of the principal company's business on terms that the subsidiary is liable to the principal's creditors.

[57] See the Insurance Companies (Winding Up) Rules 1985, S.I. 1985 No. 95, made under s.58. The Rules contain, in particular, rules for the valuation of insurance policies in a winding up.

[58] s.58.

[59] See generally *Re Capital Annuities* [1979] 1 W.L.R. 170.

an insurance company must be approved by the Secretary of State, following notice of the changes given under section 62. These provisions are extended to overseas companies, whether inside or outside the E.C., by sections 63 and 64.

Miscellaneous provisions. The concluding sections of Part II of the **13–33** 1982 Act, sections 65–71, deal with matters such as the deposit of documents with the registrar of companies, address for service, powers of modification of Part II, and offences under Part II.

Conduct of insurance business   13–34

Advertisements. Section 72 authorises the making of regulations governing the form and content of insurance advertisements. This provision is supplemented by section 75, which requires intermediaries to disclose prescribed information to potential assureds. Where an insurer of long term business is not authorised to carry on business of that nature, the Insurance Companies Regulations 1981 require disclosure of that fact, and, where a statement of authorised capital is made in an advertisement, it must also state the amount of capital paid up and subscribed.[60]

Misleading statements. The Financial Services Act 1986, sections 47 **13–35** and 133, repealing and replacing section 73 of the Insurance Companies Act 1982, create offences where misleading statements are made during the pre-contractual negotiations for insurance.[61]

"Cooling-off" period for long term policies. Sections 75–77 of the **13–36** 1982 Act make special provision for long term policies whereby an assured is given a 10 day period to consider whether the contract should be cancelled. Detailed provision is made by these sections and under supplementary regulations[62] for the service of notices by the insurer and for the service of the notice of cancellation by the assured. Briefly, a notice in statutory form must be served on the assured either when the contract is made or by post before the contract is made, and the assured has 10 days during which to cancel, running from either the receipt of the notice or from the earliest date on which the assured was aware that the contract had been made and the first premium paid, whichever date is the later. On cancellation, which need not be in the form required to be annexed to the insurer's statutory notice, any premium paid is recoverable as a simple debt. These provisions are to be superseded by the equivalent provisions of the Financial Services Act 1986.

3. FINANCIAL SERVICES ACT 1986

The 1986 Act and insurance   13–37

The purpose of the Financial Services Act 1986 is to provide a unified framework for the regulation of all forms of investment business, mainly

---

[60] 1981 Regulations, regs. 65A-C and 66. Additional controls are imposed in respect of long term business governed by the Financial Services Act 1986. See *infra.*

[61] See § 15–09, *infra.*

[62] 1981 Regulations, regs. 70–71.

as a measure of investor protection and partly at least in order to allow investors to be able to assess the comparative merit of the variety of available investments. General insurance business is unaffected by the Act, but long term insurance within the meaning of the Insurance Companies Act 1982 is deemed to be investment business.[63] However, long term insurance is excluded from the 1986 Act if:

    (a) the benefits under the contract are payable only on death or in respect of incapacity due to injury, sickness or infirmity;

    (b) no benefits are payable under the contract on a death (other than a death due to accident) unless it occurs within 10 years of the date on which the life of the person in question was first insured under the contract or before that person attains a specified age not exceeding 70 years;

    (c) the contract has no surrender value or the consideration consists of a single premium and the surrender value does not exceed that premium; and

    (d) the contract does not make provision for its conversion or extension in such a manner that would result in its ceasing to comply with paragraphs (a), (b) and (c) above.

13–38 Authorisation

No person is entitled to carry on investment business unless he is either authorised by the Secretary of State or is an exempted person.[64] If investment business is carried on without authorisation an offence is committed and the contracts themselves are unenforceable against the investor.[65] Insurers authorised to carry on long term business under the Insurance Companies Act 1982 receive automatic authorisation under the Financial Services Act 1986 to carry on investment business.[66] Lloyd's is an exempted person for authorisation purposes.[67]

Authorisation under the 1986 Act may be withdrawn where the authorised person fails to comply with the requirements of the Act.[68] In the case of an authorised insurer, breach of the rules under the 1986 Act may lead to a withdrawal of authorisation under the Insurance Companies Act 1982,[69] thereby automatically rendering the insurer unauthorised for the purposes of the 1986 Act.

13–39 Conduct of investment business

General principles. The Financial Services Act 1986 creates two parallel forms of regulation of the conduct of investment businesses. First, the Securities and Investment Board (S.I.B.), under powers dele-

---

[63] Financial Services Act, s.1 and Sched. 1 para. 10. References in the following paragraphs to section numbers refer to this Act unless otherwise stated.

[64] s.3.

[65] ss.4–5.

[66] s.22. Long term insurers authorised in other E.C. member states similarly receive automatic exemption, although notice of intention to commence business in the U.K. must be given to the Secretary of State: ss.31–32 and Sched. 10, § 8.

[67] s.42.

[68] s.19.

[69] Insurance Companies Act 1982, s.13(2A)–(2B), as inserted by the Financial Services Act 1986.

gated by the Secretary of State,[70] is authorised to make rules on the following matters: general conduct of business rules, governing advertising, commissions, accounting procedures, and related matters[71]; financial resources rules[72]; rules governing the rights of investors to cancel investment contracts[73]; notification regulations, specifying the circumstances in which the Secretary of State is to receive information from an authorised person[74]; rules concerning the indemnification of investors where the person carrying on the business incurs civil liability, including the establishment of a compensation fund and rules governing the manner in which[75] clients' money is held.[76] Authorised persons are required to adhere to these rules, failing which authorisation may be withdrawn.

Secondly, and alternatively, the S.I.B. rules do not apply to any person who becomes a member of a Self Regulating Organisation (S.R.O.); membership of an S.R.O. of itself constitutes authorisation to carry on investment business. To qualify as an S.R.O., a body must be recognised by the Secretary of State, and stringent requirements are laid down for recognition.[77] Most importantly, the rules of every S.R.O. must be equivalent to those rules laid down by the S.I.B. under its delegated powers. Failure of a member to comply with the rules of its S.R.O. are potentially as severe as failure of a non-member authorised person to comply with the rules of the S.I.B.: after appropriate disciplinary procedures, if a member is expelled its automatic authorisation gained by virtue of its membership will be lost, and fresh authorisation—either directly or by membership of another S.R.O.—must be sought.

In the result, therefore, the rules governing authorised persons will be in general terms the same whether or not they are members of an S.R.O.

Application to authorised insurers. Insurers authorised to carry on **13–40** long term insurance business under the Insurance Companies Act 1982 have for the most part joined the Life Assurance and Unit Trusts Regulatory Organisation (LAUTRO), which is a recognised S.R.O. They must, therefore, comply with its rules. However, given the controls imposed upon insurers by the Insurance Companies Act 1982, various exemptions from the investment businesses rules are conferred upon insurers as S.R.O. members.[78] Conversely, the intermediaries and cooling-off rules contained in sections 74–77 of the Insurance Companies Act 1982 do not apply where the 1986 Act is itself applicable.[79]

---

[70] By the Financial Services Act 1986 (Delegation of Functions) Order 1987, S.I. 1987 No. 942, made under the power to delegate in s.114.

[71] s.48.

[72] ss.49–50.

[73] s.51.

[74] s.52.

[75] s.53–54. The authority to make indemnity rules under s.53 has not been delegated to the S.I.B. but has been retained by the Secretary of State.

[76] s.55.

[77] s.10 and Sched. 2. Where the S.R.O. has life offices amongst its members, its rules must require them to adhere to Part II of the Insurance Companies Act 1982: Financial Services Act 1986, Sched. 10, para. 3.

[78] Sched. 10, § 4.

[79] Sched. 10, § 5.

13–41   *Other rules.* The 1986 Act also establishes various rules applicable to all persons carrying on investment business, whether or not members of an S.R.O.

   (a) It is a criminal offence, in relation to the making of an investment contract, for a person to make a statement, promise or forecast which he knows to be misleading, false or deceptive, to dishonestly conceal any material facts, or recklessly to make a statement, promise or forecast which is misleading, false or deceptive.[80]
   (b) Unsolicited calls are, subject to exemptions contained in subordinate legislation, prohibited.[81]
   (c) Advertisements cannot be issued unless they have been approved by an authorised person.[82]

13–42 Supervisory powers

Impact on authorised insurers. The Secretary of State has a series of powers of intervention, contained in sections 64–71 and exercisable where it appears to the Secretary of State: that such exercise is desirable to protect investors; that an authorised person is not a fit and proper person to carry on investment business; or that an authorised person has failed to comply with rules made in or under the 1986 Act. The Financial Services Act powers are broadly equivalent to the powers of intervention available to the Secretary of State under the Insurance Companies Act 1982 and are thus in general not exercisable against an authorised insurer. Similarly, the power of the Secretary of State to present a winding up petition against a person authorised to carry on investment business, conferred by sections 72–73 of the 1986 Act, are not applicable to life offices.[83]

13–43   *The Financial Services Tribunal.* This Tribunal, established under the 1986 Act, is an appeal body. Its jurisdiction includes appeals against refusal to grant authorisation, withdrawal of authorisation, and exercise of certain powers of intervention.[84] In the context of the long term business of insurance companies, the Tribunal has jurisdiction to hear appeals against loss of authorisation under the Insurance Companies Act 1982 by virtue of loss of authorisation under the 1986 Act.[85]

4. THE EUROPEAN COMMUNITY DIMENSION

13–44 Insurance in the internal market

Completing the internal market. European Community law now contains detailed provision for the harmonisation of insurance regulation

---

[80] s.47, echoed in relation to general insurance business by s.133; these sections replace the more limited s.73 of the Insurance Companies Act 1982.
[81] s.56. The power to make exempting regulations is delegated to the S.I.B.
[82] s.57. This and the other advertising rules established by the 1986 Act supersede the advertising regulations made under s.72 of the Insurance Companies Act 1982 as far as long term insurance is concerned: Financial Services Act 1986, Sched. 10, para. 5.
[83] Sched. 10, para. 6.
[84] The Tribunal's constitution and powers are set out in ss.96–101.
[85] Financial Services Act 1986, Sched. 10, paras. 7, 9.

throughout the E.C., much of this dating back some years. The harmonisation is, at time of writing, far from complete, and is unlikely to be so until some time in 1992 or 1993. Insurance nevertheless plays a central role in the completion of the European internal market; the objective is that insurance services, in common with all other forms of financial services, should be available across national boundaries and without discrimination by regulatory authorities on the ground of the national origin or nationality of the insurer.

Difficulty has arisen in determining the precise manner in which the **13–45** market should be opened. The E.C. rules on services are based on twin principles contained in the Treaty of Rome: freedom of establishment, whereby an undertaking with its head office in one member state is free to operate in any other member state; and freedom to provide services, whereby an undertaking is free to provide services across national boundaries. In the context of insurance there has been uncertainty as to whether the right to provide services should be based on establishment, and, irrespective of that, whether each member state should be free to apply its own regulatory rules to an insurer primarily established elsewhere but seeking to do business within its territory.

The general approach adopted to date is that each member state is to **13–46** permit insurance services to be offered by an insurer established in some other member state, but that in certain circumstances authorisation may be required by the member state in which services are being provided. This approach may, however, well be modified, detailed consideration having been given by the Community's institutions to the concept of a single European licence. The United Kingdom, by virtue of section 8 of the Insurance Companies Act 1982, has taken a liberal approach to this issue going beyond what has thus far been required by E.C. law: as long as an insurer with its head office, and authorisation, elsewhere in the E.C. has some form of permanent presence in the United Kingdom by means of a resident person with authority to bind the insurer generally, that insurer will not require United Kingdom authorisation.

Existing provisions. E.C. Directives on insurance law govern the fol- **13–47** lowing matters:

(a) motor insurance;
(b) reinsurance;
(c) co-insurance;
(d) non-life insurance;
(e) life insurance;
(f) legal expenses insurance;
(g) winding up;
(h) miscellaneous matters.

Categories (a), (b), (g) and (h) may be discussed briefly here, the other categories being given lengthier consideration in subsequent paragraphs.

13–48　　*Motor vehicle insurance*[86] has been the subject of two Directives. The First Directive, in 1972,[87] established the "Green Card" scheme, whereby compulsory motor insurance in one member state will be effective in other member states. The Second Directive, of 1985,[88] extended compulsory insurance to property damage and to persons driving without the assured's authorisation. Both Directives were implemented in the United Kingdom by statutory instrument, and now form a part of the consolidated motor insurance provisions contained in the Road Traffic Act 1988. A proposal for a Third Directive, published originally in December 1988 and adopted in an amended form in May 1990, will create the position whereby the payment of a single premium will provide compulsory cover in all member states, and will permit an action against the Motor Insurers Bureau (and its equivalent bodies in other member states) without the need first to prove that the defendant was unwilling or unable to pay. The Commission announced in February 1990 that a Fourth Directive was under consideration.

13–49　　*Reinsurance* has been the subject of a single Directive, in 1964.[89] The Directive required member states to abolish restrictions based on nationality on the rights of reinsurers to provide reinsurance services. No specific implementation of this Directive was necessary under United Kingdom law on the accession of the United Kingdom to the E.C. in 1973.

13–50　　Proposals for a Directive on *winding up* were first made in March 1987, but were revised in October 1989. The proposals seek to co-ordinate the position where an insurer operating in a number of member states is wound up in one of them.

13–51　　A number of matters fall within the *miscellaneous* category. Proposals for the co-ordination of various aspects of insurance contract law, namely utmost good faith and warranties, were made by the European Commission in 1978 but agreement on them was not forthcoming in the Council of Ministers. These proposals are likely to be revived early in the 1990s. Their effect in the United Kingdom, if implemented will be to remove much of the generally accepted harshness from these areas of law. Other aspects which may be mentioned include: *reform of accounting procedures* (proposals published in February 1990); *reciprocal arrangements* with nations outside the Communities; and the *regulation of intermediaries* (implemented in the U.K. by the Insurance Brokers (Registration) Act 1977).

13–52 Co-insurance

The Directive. The Co-Insurance Directive of 1978[90] seeks to remove national restrictions by which a member state prevents insurance of risks

---

[86] For further discussion, see Chap. 20, *infra*.
[87] 72/166/E.C., as amended by Directive 72/430/E.C.
[88] 84/5/E.C.
[89] 64/225/E.C.
[90] 78/473/E.C.

located within it by an insurer established and authorised in another
member state; participation in the insurance of such risks is allowed by
means of co-insurance. The Directive applies where the risk is situated
in the Community, where the leading underwriter is authorised, and
where one of the co-insurers is established in a member state different
from that in which the leading underwriter is authorised.

The insurance cases. The scope of this Directive was tested before the **13–53**
European Court of Justice in a series of cases reported in 1987. The
cases are important in the present context and also in that they have dic-
tated the principles underlying the Life and Non-Life Directives
adopted subsequently. In *Commission* v. *Germany*[91] German law specified that: (a) only an insurer established and authorised in Germany
could be the leading insurer under a co-insurance arrangement in
respect of a risk situated in Germany; and (b) brokers in Germany could
arrange the insurance of risks situated in Germany only with insurers
established and authorised in Germany. The Court held that both
restrictions were unjustified.

As to (a), the Court took the view that the proper construction of the
Directive (which was admittedly ambiguous) was that it was sufficient
for the leading insurer to be authorised in *any* member state, and not
necessarily in the member state where the risk was located. This was so
because authorisation, while a necessary requirement for the protection
of domestic policyholders, was not justified in the case of the large commercial risks covered by co-insurance. The Court went on to hold that
the requirement that the leading insurer be established in the member
state in which the risk was located was contrary to the free movement of
services provisions of the Treaty of Rome.[92]

As to (b), the Court laid down the following principles. (i) If an
insurer is established in a member state, it must abide by the domestic
rules of that member state; it must, therefore, be authorised if that is
required by the host member state irrespective of establishment and
authorisation elsewhere in the E.C. (ii) Where an insurer is established
and authorised in member state A, but wishes to provide insurance services in member state B without being authorised in member state B,
authorisation can be demanded by member state B only where the public interest demands it because of the insufficiency of the regulatory provisions of member state A. As will be seen below, the Life and Non-Life
Directives have followed this reasoning, and are drafted on the basis
that authorisation is required only where necessary to protect the consumer. (iii) Where an insurer is established and authorised in member
state A, but wishes to provide insurance services in member state B
without being *established* in member state B, it should normally be free
to do so. In pursuance of this ruling, the Life and Non-Life Directives
now adopt the principle that any form of permanent presence within a
member state, including the use of an independent person with auth-

[91] Case 205/84 [1987] 2 C.M.L.R. 69.
[92] The reasoning in this part of the judgment was echoed in *Commission* v. *France* Case 220/83 [1987]
2 C.M.L.R. 113, *Commission* v. *Ireland* Case 206/84 [1987] 2 C.M.L.R. 150 and *Commission* v. *Denmark* Case 252/83 [1987] 2 C.M.L.R. 169.

ority to act on behalf of the insurer, is a sufficient basis for its provision of services there, so that establishment is no longer a serious obstacle.

13–54   A further issue arose in *Commission* v. *France*.[93] The relevant French domestic law prevented participation in co-insurance for risks below certain thresholds, with the effect that co-insurance operations were prohibited below specified financial limits. The Court, rejecting the Commission's argument that all thresholds were void, held that such thresholds were permissible, although the Court did not seek to determine the levels at which thresholds might be set. Following this ruling, the Co-Insurance Directive was amended, to make it clear that it is applicable only to "large risks."[94]

13–55   In *Commission* v. *Denmark*[95] the Court also upheld a domestic Danish rule whereby an insurer established in Denmark, or merely having branches in Denmark, required authorisation from the Danish authorities to conduct business in other member states. The Court held that there was nothing discriminatory or restrictive in this rule.

13–56   *Impact on the United Kingdom.* The Insurance Companies Act 1982 does not place restrictions on participation in co-insurance operations, so that the Directive did not require distinct implementation in the United Kingdom.

13–57 Non-life insurance

The First Directive. The First Directive on Direct Non-Life Insurance was published in 1973.[96] This set out, *inter alia*, the need for authorisation, the solvency margin principle, the division of insurance into classes, and the right of an insurer to offer services across national boundaries by becoming established in other member states. The First Directive is fully implemented in the Insurance Companies Act 1982, discussed above.

13–58   *The Second Directive.* The Second Directive on Direct Non-Life Insurance[97] was published in June 1988, and is to be implemented by member states by June 1990. This makes a number of significant changes to the First Directive, many of which require amendments to the Insurance Companies Act 1982. The most important aspects of the Second Directive are as follows:

    (a) A distinction is drawn between "large" risks and "mass" risks. Where an insurer with its head office in member state A wishes to

---

[93] *Supra* n. 92. The same point also arose in *Commission* v. *Ireland*, *supra* n. 92, and *Commission* v. *Denmark*, *supra* n. 92.

[94] As defined in the Second Directive on Direct Non-Life Insurance, art. 5, *infra*, § 13–58. The amendment to the Co-Insurance Directive was made by art. 26 of the Second Non-Life Directive.

[95] *Supra*, n. 92.

[96] 73/239/E.C., amended in various respects by the following Directives: 76/580/E.C. (redefining currency conversions); 84/641/E.C. (adding tourist assistance assurance); 87/343/E.C. (adding credit insurance).

[97] 88/357/E.C. Amendments designed to bring compulsory motor insurance within the ambit of this Directive were published by the European Commission in January 1989.

provide insurance for a large risk located in member state B, it may do so by becoming established in member state B (by creating a branch, agency or some permanent presence) but does not require authorisation in member state B as long as it is authorised in member state A. In the case of other (mass) risks, an authorisation requirement may be imposed by member state B. This change, which adopts the reasoning in the insurance cases discussed above, will not affect the United Kingdom's position, as section 8 of the Insurance Companies Act 1982 will not require domestic authorisation for any class of risk as long as the insurer is established in the United Kingdom and is authorised and established in some other member state. A definition of large risks will, however, be added to the 1982 Act, for classification and accounting purposes.

(b) Services may be provided in a member state as long as the insurer has some form of permanent presence there, whether by branch, agency or even the use of an independent authorised intermediary. This is already provided for by sections 8 and 10 of the Insurance Companies Act 1982: an insurer authorised and established in another member state must have a general representative in the United Kingdom, but this requirement is fulfilled if the representative is resident in the United Kingdom and authorised generally to act on the insurer's behalf.

(c) Rules for determining the law applicable to a contract are to be introduced; the Second Directive's principles do not comply to those operated by the United Kingdom courts,[98] and implementing legislation will be needed.

(d) Compulsory insurance may under the Directive be offered by insurers not authorised in the host member state. Minor amendments to English law will be needed to implement this principle, as compulsory insurance is at present limited to authorised insurers.

(e) Authorising member states are to be permitted to exercise control over the activities of their authorised insurers in other member states; the powers of the Secretary of State under the 1982 Act are to be extended accordingly.

(f) A series of accounting and procedural changes are also introduced by the Directive, most of which will require legislation in the United Kingdom.

Life insurance   13–59

The First Directive. The First Directive on Direct Life Insurance[99] was adopted in 1979, and was implemented in the United Kingdom by the Insurance Companies Act 1982. The principles of the First Directive are familiar, namely, authorisation procedures, the separation of long term

---

[98] See generally Chap. 1, *supra*, for the existing English law. Any changes to the conflicts of laws rules will necessarily affect only E.C. contracts.
[99] 79/267/E.C.

from general assets, and the margin of solvency with its attendant accounting requirements.

13–60   *The Second Draft Directive.* A proposal for a Second Directive was first published by the European Commission in June 1988, and was published in an amended form in March 1990. This sets out provisions similar to those contained in the Second Non-Life Directive in that conflicts of laws rules for life policies are laid down, and permanent presence within a member state is treated as establishment within that member state. The proposals also contain new procedures for the transfer of life business as between insurers established in different member states and increase the powers of national authorities to obtain information from an insurer providing insurance services within their territory.

13–61   The most important change proposed in the draft Directive is a significant increase in the freedom to provide services across national boundaries. A member state *may*, as is the case with the Second Non-Life Directive, impose an authorisation requirement in respect of long term business (it will be recalled that United Kingdom law will not do so). However, the need for authorisation and establishment is dispensed with where a policy is issued by an establishment in a different member state if this occurred at the instigation of the policy holder; an assured is, therefore, entitled to seek life assurance from an insurer established and authorised in any other member state. However, advertising for such business is not permitted by either insurers or brokers, the insurer must inform the member state in question of its intention to supply services within its territory in this way, and any policy made in this way may be cancelled within at least 30 days by the assured. Where a contract is made under these provisions, the authorities of the "host" member state may demand documents as in the case of an established insurer, and domestic legislation protecting assureds in the event of their insurer's insolvency is to apply despite the insurer's want of authorisation.[1]

It remains to be seen whether this approach will be retained in the final version of this proposed Directive.

13–62 Legal expenses insurance

The Legal Expenses Insurance Directive[2] was adopted in 1987. Its principles are as follows:

    (a) The Directive requires a distinct policy, or at least a special section in some other form of policy, for this type of insurance.

    (b) An attempt is made to prevent conflicts of interest where the assured's legal expenses insurer is also the insurer, in some other capacity, of the other party.

    (c) The assured is entitled to choose his own lawyer.

    (d) Disputes between insurer and assured are to be resolved by arbitration.

---

[1] *Cf.* the Second Non-Life Directive on this point. In the U.K., the relevant legislation is the Policyholders Protection Act 1975; see *infra*, 22–01 *et seq.* This result is already achieved under that Act.

[2] 87/394/E.C. This is to be implemented in the U.K. with effect from July 1, 1990.

Competition policy   **13–63**

It should not be forgotten that the insurance sector is subject to the competition rules contained in Articles 85 and 86 of the Treaty of Rome. Matters such as agreements for standard terms and premiums,[3] mergers,[4] and mutual retrocession arrangements[5] have been found to fall within these rules.

---

[3] *V.D.S.* v. *Commission* Case 45/85, unreported; *Re Concordato Italiano Incendio Rischi Industriali* [1990] 4 C.M.L.R. 179. A block exemption is proposed for such agreements.
[4] *Re the Agreements between A.M.B. and La Fondaria* [1990] 4 C.M.L.R. 23.
[5] *TEKO* O.J. 1990 L13/34.

CHAPTER 14

THE ASSURED

1. CONTRACTUAL CAPACITY

The principle of capacity   14–01

The general rule is that anyone may, as an assured, enter into a contract of insurance provided that he has the requisite insurable interest. This rule is subject to the limitations on the contractual capacity of certain classes of persons that apply throughout the law of contract. Enemy aliens thus have no capacity to contract with UK insurers, and the ordinary rules affecting persons suffering from drunkenness and mental incapacity at the date of the contract will apply. Corporations were at one time subject to the doctrine of *ultra vires*, but this was finally abolished by section 35 of the Companies Act 1985 (in the form inserted by the Companies Act 1989).

Minors   14–02

Minors, that is persons under 18 years of age,[1] do not have the full capacity of their persons. But this disability is given them for their own protection, and insurers who grant policies to them will be liable for losses, the only question to be considered being whether the assured minor is also bound by the obligations he undertakes. Usually, other than in the case of contracts for necessary goods or services, contracts by a minor are voidable at his election[2] or unenforceable against him unless he chooses to adopt them.[3] However, a minor will usually be bound by a contract of insurance if it is necessarily for his benefit, having regard to his station in life. Thus a minor who joined a mutual society against accident on entering the service of a railway company was held to be bound by its rules.[4]

The question sometimes arises whether premiums paid by a minor, under a policy which is not necessary for his benefit and is unenforceable against him because he has not adopted it, are recoverable. The general rule is that the minor cannot recover back money paid by him under a contract from which he has had some advantage, however small, unless the other party can be put back into the position in which he would have been had the transaction never taken place.[5] Thus an assured minor

---

[1] Family Law Reform Act 1969.

[2] In that, on reaching his majority, the infant is entitled to disaffirm them. Various forms of long-term contracts, such as contracts of partnership or for interests in land or shares, fall into this category.

[3] All contracts other than for necessaries or which are voidable fall into this category. Under the Minors Contracts Act 1987, s.1, a contract of this type is not binding upon the infant unless he expressly affirms it on reaching his majority; fresh consideration is not required. This section repeals the Infants Relief Act 1874, which rendered these contracts absolutely void so that a fresh contract was required on the minor reaching his majority.

[4] *Clements* v. *London, North-Western Ry.* [1894] 2 Q.B. 482.

[5] *Steinberg* v. *Scala* [1923] 2 Ch. 452.

231

cannot normally recover a premium he has paid once the risk has began to run.[6]

Insurances on the property of a minor may be taken out by his guardian,[7] but there is nothing to prevent him taking out an insurance on it himself. In fact insurances by infants are common both under the Friendly Societies Acts and by minor drivers of motor vehicles.[8]

Thus an infant may be a member of a friendly society, whatever his age,[9] but if he is under 16 his parent or guardian shall execute all instruments and give all acquittances necessary.[10] This right is a useful one, for whereas a minor is generally unable to execute a valid will[11] he can make an effective nomination under the Friendly Societies Acts.[12]

2. TRUSTEES AND PERSONAL REPRESENTATIVES

14–03 Trustees

Trustees have an insurable interest in the subject-matter of a trust. They are empowered, but not directed, by statute to insure against fire to the extent of three-fourths of the full value of buildings or chattels.[13] The premiums on insurances thus taken out or renewed are payable out of the income arising from the whole of the funds comprised in the same trust: thus where the trust comprises heirlooms and other property bearing income the trustees are entitled, without the consent of all or any of the beneficiaries, to insure the heirlooms out of this income.[14]

Money recovered, however, for losses occurring under such policies will be capital money for the benefit of all those entitled under the trust,[15] and will not belong to the person at present entitled to the income out of which the premiums have been paid.

14–04 Personal representatives

The personal representatives of a deceased person, be they executors or administrators, have, like trustees, an insurable interest in property comprised in his estate. They may take out new insurances, or renew old ones.[16]

They have also a sufficient interest to insure in their own name the life of a person who has granted an annuity to the deceased, and which the deceased has bequeathed to persons not parties to the insurance.[17]

14–05 *Duty to insure.* Personal representatives, while they may not allow existing insurances to expire, cannot be called to account for failing to insure against fire property not insured by the deceased.[18] Where the

---

[6] *Ritchie* v. *Salvation Army Assurance* [1930] I.A.C. Rep. 31. This rule is not affected by the Minors Contracts Act 1987.

[7] *Warwicker* v. *Bretnall* (1882) 23 Ch.D. 188.

[8] See, *e.g. English* v. *Weston* [1940] 1 K.B. 145.

[9] Friendly Societies Act 1974, s.60(1).

[10] *Ibid.* s.60(2).

[11] Wills Act 1837, s.7.

[12] See § 16–88, *infra.*

[13] Settled Land Act 1925, s.102; Trustee Act 1925, s.19.

[14] Trustee Act 1925, s.19; *Re Egmont's Trusts* [1908] 1 Ch. 821.

[15] *Ibid.* s.20; see Settled Land Act 1925, s.102; *Re Bladon* [1911] 2 Ch. 350, 354.

[16] *Parry* v. *Ashley* (1829) 3 Sim. 97.

[17] *Tidswell* v. *Ankerstein* (1792) Peake 204.

[18] *Croft* v. *Lyndsey* (1676) Freeman Ch. 1; *Fry* v. *Fry* (1859) 27 Beav. 144; *Re McEacharn* (1911) 103 L.T. 900.

deceased lessee was bound to insure, but allowed the insurance to expire, his executors were held not liable for failing to renew it.[19] So also where the deceased left a business partner who failed to renew the insurance on the business premises it was held that the deceased's executors were not chargeable as for wilful default for not having done so.[20] But while they may be under no legal obligation to insure they ought normally to do so at the expense and for the benefit of the estate,[21] and they will be entitled to recover the premiums from that part of the estate which is protected by the insurance.[22] Moreover, an obligation to insure may be expressly laid upon them by the terms of the deceased's will. And once an executor takes out a policy, a life policy for instance to secure a debt owing to the estate, he may be called to account if he drops it without good reason.[23]

To whom policy moneys are payable. Money paid under a policy **14–06** effected or renewed by an executor is payable to the parties interested in the property insured: it does not form part of the testator's general personal estate.[24]

3. LANDLORD AND TENANT

Insurance arrangements   **14–07**
Premises may be insured by the landlord on his own behalf, by the tenant on his own behalf, and by either party on behalf of himself and the other. This will be determined by the terms of the lease. The last-mentioned arrangement is increasingly common: the insuring party will often be the landlord, although the tenant will contribute to the insurance premium by an additional element in his rent. It is important for insurance to be settled by the lease, for if the landlord voluntarily procures a policy but does not maintain it, the tenant will have no action against him.[25]

Where the landlord insures on behalf of himself and the tenant (or vice versa), it is sometimes the case that both parties are named as assureds for their respective rights and interests. Here, the policy is a composite one, and each party—as an independent assured—has independent rights against the insurer. If the tenant is not a named party in his own right, but either his interest is noted on the policy or he is not referred to at all, then while he cannot sue on the policy due to want of privity he will be regarded as having sufficient interest in the policy, by virtue of having contributed to the premiums, to avoid a subrogation action by the insurer in the landlord's name if the loss is due to the ten-

---

[19] *Tidswell* v. *Ankerstein* (1792) Peake 204.
[20] *Bailey* v. *Gould* (1840) 4 Y. & C. 221.
[21] North J. in *Re Betty* [1899] 1 Ch. 821, 829.
[22] *Re Smith's estate* [1937] Ch. 636.
[23] *Garner* v. *Moore* (1855) 3 Drew. 277.
[24] *Parry* v. *Ashley* (1829) 3 Sim. 97.
[25] *Argy Trading* v. *Lapid Developments* [1977] 1 W.L.R. 444.

ant's negligence.[26] The noting of the interest of an unnamed party, while common, is legally not necessary.[27]

14–08 Insurable interest of landlord

The landlord has an insurable interest in his reversion. Moreover, he may have agreed to keep the premises in repair.[28] In such cases he can recover in full under an insurance for his own benefit only, and his claim will not be limited by the principle of indemnity to the value of the reversion. But where the tenant is responsible for repairs, although the landlord may, by virtue of his legal estate, recover the whole value of the premises under his own insurance,[29] the insurers will be subrogated to his claim for repairs as against the tenant.[30]

14–09 Insurance by landlord

A tenant can recover nothing under an insurance by the landlord alone even if he is not bound to repair and the tenant's liability for rent continues,[31] although the tenant may have a statutory right to reinstatement.[32] He has no equity otherwise to compel the landlord to repair the damage.[33]

But where a landlord's obligation under a lease to insure was intended to enure for the benefit of both landlord and tenant, it was held that the landlord was obliged under the lease to use the insurance money towards reinstatement of the property, although there was no covenant in the lease to reinstate. The lease was held, *inter alia*, to enure for the benefit of both because the tenant had covenanted to pay "a yearly insurance rent equal to the premium."[34]

But where the tenant covenants to insure both their interests, and the lessor also takes out an insurance, and thus reduces the amount to which the tenant is entitled on a loss, due to an apportionment by the insurers between the two policies, the lessor must account to the tenant for the difference.[35] He is not entitled both to the retention of this amount and to the repair of the premises.

Where the tenant covenants to insure in the landlord's name he is not entitled to receive the policy moneys in case of a fire, or to reinstate and then demand the policy moneys.[36] His remedy is to serve a notice to

---

[26] *Mark Rowlands Ltd.* v. *Berni Inns Ltd.* [1985] 3 W.L.R. 964.

[27] "Noting" is traditionally thought to have three effects: (a) it preserves the legality of the policy under s.2 of the Life Assurance Act 1774, which requires all interested parties to be identified; (b) it prevents the exercise of subrogation rights by the insurer; (c) it allows the tenant to require the insurer to reinstate the premises in accordance with s.83 of the Fires Prevention (Metropolis) Act 1774. The *Mark Rowlands* decision makes it clear that the Life Assurance Act 1774 does not apply to policies on buildings, and that the landlord's insurers have no subrogation rights irrespective of noting. Further, there is nothing in s.83 of the Fires Prevention (Metropolis) Act 1774 to indicate that noting is a prerequisite to its operation.

[28] *Tredway* v. *Machin* (1904) 91 L.T. 310.

[29] *Collingridge* v. *Royal Exchange* (1877) 3 Q.B.D. 173.

[30] *Darrell* v. *Tibbitts* (1880) 5 Q.B.D. 560.

[31] *Belfour* v. *Weston* (1786) 1 T.R. 310; *Hare* v. *Groves* (1796) 3 Anstr. 687.

[32] Under the Fires Prevention (Metropolis) Act 1774.

[33] Leach M.R. in *Leeds* v. *Cheetham* (1827) 1 Sim. 146, 150; *Lofft* v. *Dennis* (1859) 28 L.J. Q.B. 168; *Edwards* v. *West* (1878) 7 Ch.D. 858. See also *Andrews* v. *Patriotic* (*No.* 2) (1886) 18 L.R.Ir. 355.

[34] *Mumford Hotels* v. *Wheler* [1964] Ch. 117.

[35] *Reynard* v. *Arnold* (1875) L.R. 10 Ch. 386.

[36] Lord St. Leonards in *Garden* v. *Ingram* (1852) 23 L.J. Ch. 478, 479.

reinstate upon the insurer under the Fires Prevention (Metropolis) Act 1774.

Where the landlord insures in his own name but in part for the tenant's benefit, and covenants to lay out any insurance moneys in reinstatement, the landlord is under an implied obligation to pursue his claim against the insurer with all reasonable speed.[37] The tenant has, moreover, a statutory right under the Landlord and Tenant Act 1987 to preserve the validity of the landlord's claim under the policy where the landlord has not himself pursued the claim: the tenant, though not a party to the policy, may serve a notice on the insurer, with the effect that in that period the insurer cannot plead that the landlord's claim is late under the terms of the policy and the tenant can seek an appropriate order against the landlord forcing him to claim under the policy.[38]

Breach of landlord's covenant to insure   **14–10**

If the landlord, in breach of an insuring covenant, fails to insure, he is liable in damages to the tenant. In *Naumann* v. *Ford*[39] the landlord failed to renew a policy, in breach of covenant, but the insurer reached an agreement with the tenant whereby the tenant was to be paid the cost of repairs in consideration for his bringing an action for breach of covenant against the landlord and holding the proceeds on trust for the insurers. It was held that the landlord could not resist the tenant's action by pleading that the tenant had received an indemnity from the insurers.

Insurance interest of tenant   **14–11**

The tenant has an insurable interest, by virtue of his possession, in the premises leased, and he may insure them for his own benefit and for the benefit of his landlord to the full extent of their value. But if he insures for his own benefit only, by the principle of indemnity he will be able to recover no more than he has personally lost, and unless either by virtue of his liability by obligation of law, or by a covenant to repair, on his part, in the lease, he is liable to his landlord in respect of the whole value of the loss, he will be unable to recover it.[40] Nor will the right to claim reinstatement under the Fires Prevention (Metropolis) Act 1774 aid either the landlord or the tenant in such a case, since this only requires the insurers to lay out "the insurance money . . . as far as the same will go"[41] and does not authorise the assured to claim more than an indemnity.[42]

But a tenant who is liable to his landlord in the event of the destruction of the premises leased, under a covenant to repair for instance, and insures them, will not be limited in a claim against his insurers to the marketable value of his lease,[43] even if he only insures his own interest.

---

[37] *Vural* v. *Security Archives* (1989) 2 E.T. 36.
[38] 1987 Act, Sched. 3, para. 7. The 1987 Act further allows a tenant for whose benefit a policy is procured by the landlord under the lease to receive a summary of the policy, to check that premiums have been paid by the landlord and to object to the insurer or the policy.
[39] [1985] 2 E.G.L.R. 70.
[40] Bowen L.J. in *Castellain* v. *Preston* (1883) 11 Q.B.D. 380, 400, 401.
[41] s.83.
[42] Younger L.J. in *Matthey* v. *Curling* [1922] 2 A.C. 180, 219.
[43] See *Simpson* v. *Scottish Union* (1863) 1 H. & M. 618, 628, and Bowen L.J. in *Castellain* v. *Preston* (1883) 11 Q.B.D. 380, 400.

In any event a tenant has usually an insurable interest in the premises commensurate with his liability for rent. In the absence of an express stipulation on the matter this liability continues even after the total destruction of the premises, however it may occur.[44] Even a covenant excluding the liability to repair in case of casualties by fire will not remove this liability for rent, whether or not the landlord has insured the premises,[45] and even though the landlord has covenanted to repair the part burnt down the tenant must pay the rent meanwhile.[46]

Scottish law is more favourable to a tenant in this respect: once an essential part of the premises is so damaged as to be no longer fit for the purpose for which it is let, the tenant's liability in Scotland ceases.[47]

14–12 Contract apart, a tenant is not liable to anyone for loss due to an accidental fire,[48] but he is liable in tort at common law for damage done by a fire caused by his own negligence or that of his servants, to the property of his neighbours[49] or his landlord. He will even be liable where the negligence is that of a third party whom he has allowed onto his land.[50] By virtue of this liability alone he has an insurable interest in the premises occupied by him,[51] and he will be able to recover in full under a fire policy in respect of such losses caused by negligence. This principle applies in fact to all occupiers of land, and there is nothing to prevent them insuring against any other common law liability imposed upon them, such as liability for the escape of dangerous things under the rule in *Rylands* v. *Fletcher*.[52] Thus a tenant's common law liability for waste[53] may be so recovered.

Apart from such liability at common law it is usual for tenants under a lease to covenant to repair the premises in event of loss.[54] Such a covenant constitutes an absolute undertaking to deliver the premises up in good repair,[55] unless by its terms the covenant is expressly limited in its operation.[56]

14–13 Tenant's covenant to insure

Since such covenants to repair afford no security to the landlord in the event of the insolvency of the tenant the lease may require the tenant to insure the premises. Apart from such a covenant, tenants for years are not at common law obliged to do so.

Frequently, moreover, the case of loss or damage by fire is excluded from the covenant to repair, and a covenant by the tenant to insure the

---

[44] *Paradine* v. *Jane* (1647) Aleyn 26; *Matthey* v. *Curling* [1922] 2 A.C. 180; *Cricklewood Property* v. *Leighton* [1945] A.C. 221.

[45] *Belfour* v. *Weston* (1786) 1 T.R. 310, and *Pindar* v. *Ainsley* (1767) therein cited, at p.312.

[46] *Leeds* v. *Cheetham* (1827) 1 Sim. 146.

[47] *Allan* v. *Markland* (1882) 20 S.L.R. 267, 268.

[48] Fires Prevention (Metropolis) Act 1774, s.86.

[49] *Filliter* v. *Phippard* (1847) 11 Q.B. 347; *Musgrove* v. *Pandelis* [1919] 2 K.B. 43.

[50] *Black* v. *Christchurch Finance Co.* [1894] A.C. 48; see *Collingwood* v. *Home & Colonial Stores* (1936) 155 L.T. 550.

[51] See Tenterden C.J. in *Dobson* v. *Sotheby* (1827) 1 Moo. & M. 90, 93.

[52] (1866) L.R. 1 Ex. 265; (1868) L.R. 3 H.L. 330.

[53] *Wedd* v. *Porter* [1916] 2 K.B. 91.

[54] *Sharp* v. *Milligan* (1857) 23 Beav. 419.

[55] *Leeds* v. *Cheetham* (1827) 1 Sim. 146; *Tucker* v. *Linger* (1882) 21 Ch.D. 18; *Matthey* v. *Curling* [1922] 2 A.C. 180.

[56] *Davies* v. *Underwood* (1857) 2 H. & N. 570; *Darrell* v. *Tibbitts* (1880) 5 Q.B.D. 560.

landlord's interest is then necessary to protect the landlord from such loss or damage.[57]

The covenant to repair, in effect, makes the tenant an insurer to the full value of the premises, even if he also covenants to insure for a fixed sum. The latter covenant is a collateral security to the landlord. It supplies a fund out of which the tenant may, in whole or in part, recoup himself in respect of liability under a covenant to repair but in no way limits his liability under that covenant.[58] Thus if he does not insure for the full amount, or if the loss is due to an excepted peril, he will have to pay the balance, or the whole, of the loss himself.

Covenants to insure run with the land, and an assignee of the landlord **14-14** is entitled to enforce them.[59] Even though the landlord has assented to a breach of such covenant by the lessee, this will not protect the lessee against an assignee of the landlord,[60] and he should always, therefore, strictly comply with its terms. Such a covenant is, however, to be construed reasonably.[61]

But while such covenants are enforceable by the landlord's assignee, as a cause of forfeiture, for instance, he will not be able to benefit or control the policy moneys under an insurance made for the benefit of the original landlord and tenant only, unless either he exercises his statutory right of requiring reinstatement, or there is a provision in the lease that such moneys are to be laid out in restoring premises.[62] While a covenant to insure may run with the land, the benefit of insurance does not normally do so.[63] Thus, covenants apart, the landlord's assignee could not benefit under a policy taken out by the tenant and covering the landlord's interest.

The landlord is not entitled to benefit under an insurance made by the tenant alone,[64] either voluntarily[65] or in pursuance of a simple covenant to insure, unless it was made for his benefit, or he exercises his statutory right to reinstatement.[66]

Compliance with covenant to insure **14-15**

The covenant to insure may stipulate a named insurer,[67] and the risk to be insured against. If not, an insurance against fire with a company which normally accepts such risks will satisfy it,[68] but the covenantor must choose an office which will give him full protection, not, for example, an office which excludes losses due to enemy action,[69] unless

---

[57] See *Weigall* v. *Waters* (1795) 6 T.R. 488; *Darrell* v. *Tibbitts* (1880) 5 Q.B.D. 560.

[58] *Digby* v. *Atkinson* (1815) 4 Camp. 275, 278, *per* Lord Ellenborough C.J.

[59] *Bullock* v. *Domitt* (1796) 6 T.R. 650; *Vernon* v. *Smith* (1821) 5 B. & Ald. 1; see now Law of Property Act 1925, s.141.

[60] *Doe* d. *Muston* v. *Gladwin* (1845) 6 Q.B. 953.

[61] *Doe* d. *Pittman* v. *Sutton* (1841) 9 Car. & P. 706.

[62] *Garden* v. *Ingram* (1852) 23 L.J.Ch. 478; *Rayner* v. *Preston* (1881) 18 Ch.D. 1, 7, 8, *per* Cotton L.J.

[63] *Rayner* v. *Preston, supra.*

[64] *Lees* v. *Whiteley* (1866) L.R. 2 Eq. 143.

[65] *Leeds* v. *Cheetham* (1827) 1 Sim. 146.

[66] Under Fires Prevention (Metropolis) Act 1774. See *Reynard* v. *Arnold* (1875) L.R. 10 Ch. 386; *Andrews* v. *Patriotic Assurance (No. 2)* (1886) 18 L.R.Ir. 355.

[67] *Tredegar* v. *Harwood* [1929] A.C. 72.

[68] *Doe* d. *Pitt* v. *Shewin* (1811) 3 Camp 134.

[69] *Enlayde* v. *Roberts* [1917] 1 Ch. 109.

the covenant expressly stipulates offices approved by the lessor and he has approved the office in question.[70] Where the covenant is to insure in a named office, or in some other responsible office to be approved by the lessor, the primary obligation on the tenant is to insure in the named office and the landlord has an absolute right to withhold his approval of an alternative office, without giving any reason.[71]

Neither the fact that a covenant to insure omits the words "against fire" nor the name of any office makes it void for uncertainty.[72]

14–16 Name

The covenant to insure generally stipulates in whose name the tenant is bound to insure. Where he covenants to insure jointly in the names of himself and his landlord he is entitled to insure in the name of his landlord only.[73] But he is not entitled, on the other hand, to insure jointly in the names of himself, his landlord and another, for such other would be entitled to give the insurers a good discharge for the insurance moneys and would have a control over them.[74] Thus, if he mortgages his lease, and binds himself to insure in the mortgagee's name, he will be bound to make a separate insurance. The difficulty may be avoided by his assigning to the mortgagee his interest in the policy which he has promised his landlord to take out, provided the mortgagee assents to this arrangement in place of an insurance in his name.

14–17 Time

Insurance must normally be made immediately on the commencement of the term,[75] and failure to pay a renewal premium is a breach of the covenant to keep insured, once the days of grace have run out and any extension granted by the insurers has expired. Payment afterwards will not mend the breach,[76] nor does the fact that the insurers antedate the receipt affect the position.[77]

14–18 Amount

Where the covenant fixes the amount of the insurance it will not be affected by a change in the value of the premises. Thus, where the covenant was to insure for £2,000, and the lease excluded part of the premises after six years, it was held that the tenant was nevertheless obliged to keep the remainder insured for £2,000.[78] Conversely an increase in the market value of the subject-matter will not oblige the covenantor to insure for more than the named sum.[79]

Nor will the tenant be excused wholly or partly from performing his

---

[70] *Upjohn* v. *Hitchins* [1918] 1 K.B. 171; [1918] 2 K.B. 48.
[71] See n. 67, *supra.*
[72] *Doe* d. *Pitt* v. *Shewin* (1811) 3 Camp. 134.
[73] *Havens* v. *Middleton* (1853) 10 Hare 641.
[74] *Penniall* v. *Harborne* (1848) 11 Q.B. 368.
[75] *Doe* d. *Darlington* v. *Ulph* (1849) 18 L.J.Q.B. 106, but see *Doe* d. *Pittman* v. *Sutton* (1841) 9 Car. & P. 706.
[76] *Wilson* v. *Wilson* (1854) 14 C.B. 616.
[77] *Howell* v. *Kightley* (1856) 21 Beav. 331.
[78] *Heckman* v. *Isaac* (1862) 6 L.T. 383.
[79] See *Carreras* v. *Cunard* [1918] 1 K.B. 118, an agreement to insure goods.

covenant to insure if the landlord makes such use of the adjacent land as to increase the risk and bring about an increase of the premium.[80]

Landlord's remedies for breach of covenant to insure 14–19

In the event of a breach by the tenant of his covenant to insure, the landlord may have two remedies:

(a) an action for damages; and
(b) if there is a provision in the lease reserving him a right of re-entry in the event of breach of covenant, forfeiture of the lease.

A landlord has no right of forfeiture in the absence of such a stipulation; in such a case his only remedy for a breach of the covenant is an action for damages.

(i) *Action for damages.* Such an action is always open to the landlord 14–20 in the event of the breach of a covenant to insure by the tenant. Where a loss has occurred the damage done by fire, not exceeding the specific amount, if any, for which the insurance should have been made, will afford the measure of damages.[81] Where no loss has occurred, the landlord may only be entitled to nominal damages, but he will usually be entitled, by way of damages, to any premiums which he has had to pay to insure himself and thus put himself into the position in which he would have been but for the omission of the tenant.[82]

(ii) *Forfeiture.* Where once the covenant had been broken, for how- 14–21 ever short a period, the landlord could, at common law, exercise a right of forfeiture,[83] but the High Court now has wide powers of relief against forfeiture in the case of the breach of any covenant by a tenant on such terms as seem just.[84] Not even the gross negligence of the tenant in failing to insure now bars him from relief.[85] Moreover, a right of forfeiture is only now enforceable after service by the lessor on the lessee of a notice specifying the breach complained of, requiring it, if possible, to be remedied and requiring a money compensation for it.[86]

Landlord may be estopped 14–22

The landlord may, by his conduct, be estopped from enforcing the penalty for the breach of a covenant to insure, as where the landlord led the tenant to believe that he had made the requisite insurance.[87] So where a landlord led his tenant into believing that he had insured in a sufficient sum, that being the sum in which the landlord had previously insured the premises, he was held to be estopped from relying on a covenant to insure for two-thirds of the value of the premises.[88] So also

---

[80] *O'Cedar Ltd.* v. *Slough Trading Co.* [1927] 2 K.B. 123.
[81] See *Yates* v. *Dunster* (1855) 11 Ex. 15; *Charles* v. *Atlin* (1854) 15 C.B. 46.
[82] See *Hey* v. *Wyche* (1842) 2 Gale & D. 569; *Browne* v. *Price* (1858) 4 C.B.(N.S.) 598; *Douglas* v. *Murphy* (1858) 16 U.C.Q.B. 116.
[83] *Hey* v. *Wyche* (1842) 2 Gale & D. 569; *Doe* d. *Darlington* v. *Ulph* (1849) 18 L.J.Q.B. 106.
[84] Law of Property Act 1925, s.146.
[85] *Quilter* v. *Mapleson* (1882) 9 Q.B.D. 672; Parker J. in *Matthews* v. *Smallwood* [1910] 1 Ch. 777, 793.
[86] Law of Property Act 1925, s.146(1).
[87] *Doe* d. *Pittman* v. *Sutton* (1841) 9 C. & P. 706.
[88] *Doe* d. *Pitt* v. *Rowe* (1826) 1 Ry. & M. 343.

where he had accepted rent after knowledge of the breach,[89] or where he had distrained for rent[90] after such knowledge, he could not afterwards eject the tenant unless the breach continued after such acceptance or distraint, in which case the estoppel only operated as to the portion of time before it.[91]

14–23 Tenant's liability for increase of risk

In the absence of any covenant by the tenant to insure, a landlord who wishes so to be protected must bear the cost of insurance himself. At common law, even if the tenant did something to increase the premium, as by storing matches on premises, he could not be called upon to breach the additional premium unless he was in breach of the lease in so doing,[92] or the lease expressly provided that he should do so.[93] But now, where the landlord has undertaken to pay the premiums on a fire policy on the premises, the tenant is liable to him for any increase in the rate of premium due to any improvements executed by him on the premises.[94]

14–24 Reinstatement

Where the policy is taken out by the landlord or the tenant in his own name, and the insurance moneys are paid over to him, he may apply them as he thinks fit in the absence of any agreement binding him to use them to reinstate the premises.[95] Where, however, a landlord insures in his own name under a policy for which the tenant has paid the premium, the landlord will be under an implied obligation to apply the proceeds towards reinstatement.[96]

In the case of a single name policy by the landlord or the tenant where there is no contractual obligation by the assured to reinstate, the other party may give notice to the insurer, before the insurance moneys have been paid to the assured, requiring the insurer to use the policy moneys to reinstate the premises.[97]

Difficulties may be encountered where the policy moneys are to be applied for the purposes of reinstatement either by contract or under statute but where reinstatement is impossible as a matter of practice or law. It here falls to be decided how the policy moneys are to be allocated between the parties. In *Re King*[98] the tenant insured the premises under a policy in the joint names of himself and the landlord; the insuring covenant in the lease required the tenant to lay out the policy sums towards reinstatement in the event of a loss. Following a fire the premises became subject to a compulsory purchase order, and the Court of Appeal, Lord Denning dissenting, held that the tenant was entitled to retain the policy moneys. However, in *Beacon Carpets* v. *Kirby*,[99] a case

---

[89] *Doe* d. *Muston* v. *Gladwin* (1845) 6 Q.B. 953.
[90] *Doe* d. *Flower* v. *Peck* (1830) 1 B. & Ad. 428.
[91] *Doe* d. *Flower* v. *Peck, supra; Price* v. *Worwood* (1859) 4 H. & N. 512.
[92] *Heckman* v. *Isaac* (1861) 4 L.T. 825; (1862) 6 L.T. 383.
[93] *Duke of Hamilton's Trustees* v. *Fleming* (1870) 9 M. (Ct. of Sess.) 329.
[94] Landlord and Tenant Act 1927, s.16.
[95] *Lees* v. *Whiteley* (1866) L.R. 2 Eq. 143.
[96] *Mumford Hotels* v. *Wheler* [1964] Ch. 117.
[97] Fires Prevention (Metropolis) Act 1774, s.83. See Chap. 11.
[98] [1963] Ch. 459.
[99] [1984] 2 All E.R. 726.

in which the landlord insured in the joint names of himself and the tenant, with the tenant contributing to the premium, the Court of Appeal held in similar circumstances that the policy moneys received by the landlord were to be apportioned between him and the tenant in accordance with their respective interests in the property. In the light of this, it is doubtful whether *Re King* can any longer safely be relied on.

4. TENANT FOR LIFE

Insurable interest   **14–25**
The insurable interest of a tenant for life is similar to that of a tenant for years, except that, while a tenant for years is generally, as a condition of his lease, liable to render up the premises in good repair, a tenant for life is liable for voluntary, but not mere permissive,[1] waste to those premises. Subject to the terms of the settlement under which he derives his title,[2] he is not liable for allowing the premises to fall into disrepair, and the amount he claims under an insurance of his own interest only would therefore be less than the whole value of the premises.[3]

To whom insurance moneys are payable   **14–26**
In the absence of any provision in the settlement regarding insurance, a tenant for life of buildings is under no obligation to insure them.[4] He will generally do so, however, and the question then arises to whom, in the event of a loss, are the insurance moneys payable: do they, like the buildings in respect of which they are paid, represent capital for the benefit of the persons successively entitled to the buildings, or is the tenant for life absolutely entitled to them? The principle on which this question is to be decided is laid down by Bowen L.J. in *Castellain* v. *Preston*[5]: "A person with a limited interest may insure either for himself and to cover his own interest only, or he may insure so as to cover not merely his own limited interest, but the interest of all others who are interested in the property. It is a question of fact what is his intention when he obtains a policy." Such is not quite the law. It depends on the construction of the contract of insurance. But since, as regards tenants for life, this question is determined by a judge of the Chancery Division, it is decided according to judicial precedent, and where a tenant for life insures voluntarily, with nothing to show whose interest he intends to protect, it is well settled that he is taken to insure for his own benefit only.[6] Thus in the event of a loss he alone will be entitled to the insurance moneys, and the remainderman will have no interest in them, beyond his statutory right to demand reinstatement of the premises.[7] Technically the tenant for life can recover from the insurers no more

---

[1] *Re Cartwright* (1889) 41 Ch.D. 532; *Re Parry and Hopkin* [1900] 1 Ch. 160.
[2] *Gregg* v. *Coates* (1856) 23 Beav. 33, 38; *Re Skingley* (1851) 3 Mac. & G. 221.
[3] Bowen L.J. in *Castellain* v. *Preston* (1883) 11 Q.B.D. 380, 401.
[4] *Re Betty* [1899] 1 Ch. 821; *Re Egmont's Trusts* [1908] 1 Ch. 821.
[5] (1883) 11 Q.B.D. 380, 398.
[6] *Seymour* v. *Vernon* (1852) 21 L.J.Ch. 433; *Warwicker* v. *Bretnall* (1882) 23 Ch.D. 188; *Gaussen* v. *Whatman* (1905) 93 L.T. 101. These decisions may not be applicable, however, where the whole legal estate is vested in the tenant for life under the Settled Land Act 1925.
[7] See §§ 11–07 *et seq., supra; Re Quicke's Trusts* [1908] 1 Ch. 887; *Re Bladon* [1911] 2 Ch. 350, 354, *per* Neville J.

than the value of his interest, but if he is paid in full he will be entitled, as against the remainderman, to the whole.[8]

Where, on the other hand, the tenant for life is bound by the settlement to insure, the insurance is taken to be for the benefit of the persons successively entitled.[9]

5. MORTGAGOR AND MORTGAGEE

14–27 Mortgagor's interest

A mortgagor has an insurable interest in property mortgaged[10] to its full value, even though he parts with the legal title,[11] because: (a) an equitable interest, the equity of redemption, that is to say the right to regain his whole interest in the property on repayment of the debt, is still vested in him,[12] and (b) even if the property is destroyed, he is still liable to pay the debt.[13]

It follows, therefore, that if the owner of property, after insuring it, charges it by way of mortgage, the liability of the insurers will not be diminished.[14]

The mortgagor's interest ceases on sale or foreclosure by the mortgagee.

14–28 Mortgagee's interest

The mortgagee also has an insurable interest in the property mortgaged, for the security upon which he relies will be diminished by its loss,[15] but if he insures for his own benefit only the amount of the mortgage debt owing to him at the time of the loss is all he can recover.[16] Moreover the insurers will be entitled to be subrogated to the mortgagee's right to be repaid the mortgage debt, to the full extent of moneys paid by them.[17] Where the mortgagor reinstates the mortgagee can recover nothing since his security has not been impaired.[18]

14–29 Separate insurances

It follows from these principles that both mortgagor and mortgagee can take out separate insurances on the same property. Unless one of them reinstates, both can recover in full from their insurers, subject to the right of the mortgagee's insurers to subrogation. In such a case the insurers are not entitled to contribution between themselves, provided the policies cover only the limit of the interests of each assured.[19] But it

---

[8] See n. 5, *supra.*

[9] Neville J. in *Re Bladon, supra.*

[10] *Smith* v. *Lascelles* (1788) 2 T.R. 187.

[11] *Alston* v. *Campbell* (1779) 4 Bro.P.C. 476; *Hutchinson* v. *Wright* (1858) 25 Beav. 444.

[12] *Glover* v. *Black* (1763) 1 Wm.Bl. 396; *Lees* v. *Whiteley* (1866) L.R. 2 Eq. 143.

[13] *Provincial Insurance of Canada* v. *Leduc* (1874) L.R. 6 P.C. 224, 244.

[14] Lord St. Leonards in *Garden* v. *Ingram* (1852) 23 L.J.Ch. 478.

[15] Lord Mansfield in *Glover* v. *Black* (1763) 1 Wm.Bl. 396; Bovill C.J. in *Ebsworth* v. *Alliance Marine* (1873) L.R. 8 C.P. 596, 608; *Westminster Fire* v. *Glasgow Provident Society* (1888) 13 App.Cas. 699; *Samuel* v. *Dumas* [1924] A.C. 431.

[16] *Ebsworth* v. *Alliance Marine, supra; Castellain* v. *Preston* (1883) 11 Q.B.D. 380, 398, *per* Bowen L.J.

[17] See Bowen L.J. in *Castellain* v. *Preston, supra,* at p.405; Jessel M.R. in *Commercial Union* v. *Lister* (1874) 9 Ch.App. 483, 484; Mellish L.J. in *North British* v. *London, Liverpool & Globe* (1877) 5 Ch.D. 569, 583.

[18] *Darrell* v. *Tibbitts* (1880) 5 Q.B.D. 560.

[19] See Chap. 8, *supra.*

is otherwise where one of the two policies covers the interest of both. Thus, where buildings were insured (a) by the mortgagor and (b) by a policy taken out by the mortgagees but covering the mortgagor's interest, and there was a provision in the latter policy that where the buildings were insured elsewhere the insurers were only to be liable for their rateable proportion of any loss, it was held that both insurances had to be taken into account in assessing this proportion.[20]

Successive mortgagees can insure their respective interests to their full value, and it will be no defence to their insurers that claims made by them together amount to more than the value of the property destroyed.[21]

Insurance in joint names   14–30
Where the policy is taken out in the joint names of mortgagor and mortgagee either of them can give the insurers a good discharge for the insurance money,[22] but the court will not allow him to apply it in disregard of the rights of the other.[23]

As under a joint names policy each party is insured for his own rights and interests, the ability of each party to make a claim is independent. Thus if the mortgagor has failed to disclose a material fact to the insurer, the mortgagee's claim is not affected.[24]

Rule in Lees v. Whiteley   14–31
It was held in *Lees* v. *Whiteley*[25] that the assignee under a bill of sale of certain chattels had no claim to the benefit of a policy against fire effected by the mortgagor, even though the bill of sale contained a covenant by him to insure. The principle is clear that apart from special contract or statutory provisions a mortgagee has no rights under a policy taken out by the mortgagor for his own benefit.[26] The mortgagor is in no sense a trustee of the insurance moneys for the mortgagee.[27]

Fires Prevention (Metropolis) Act 1774   14–32
An exception to this rule is provided by section 83 of the Fires Prevention (Metropolis) Act.[28] By this section insurance companies are required upon the request[29] of any person or persons, including mortgagees,[30] interested in buildings destroyed or damaged by fire to cause the insurance money to be laid out in restoring the building. By exercising his right under this section the mortgagee can always ensure that his security shall not at any rate be wholly lost where it is destroyed by fire

---

[20] *Nichols* v. *Scottish Union* (1885) 2 T.L.R. 190.
[21] *Westminster Fire* v. *Glasgow Provident* (1888) 13 App.Cas. 699.
[22] 2 Rol.Abr. 410 (D), pt. 1, 5; *Penniall* v. *Harbourne* (1848) 11 Q.B. 368; *General Accident* v. *Midland Bank* [1940] 2 K.B. 388.
[23] *Rogers* v. *Grazebrooke* (1842) 12 Sim. 557.
[24] One exception arises where the assured under a marine policy deliberately scuttles the insured vessel, for here there is no insured peril (wilful misconduct not constituting a "peril of the sea") and the mortgagee has no claim: *Samuel* v. *Dumas* [1924] A.C. 431. For this reason the mortgagees of vessels will generally take out a fall-back policy in the form of a mortgagees' interest policy.
[25] (1866) L.R. 2 Eq. 143.
[26] Parker J. in *Sinnott* v. *Bowden* [1912] 2 Ch. 414, 419.
[27] Wright J. in *Halifax Building Society* v. *Keighley* [1931] 2 K.B. 248, 255.
[28] See Chap. 11, *supra*.
[29] *Simpson* v. *Scottish Insurance* (1863) 32 L.J.Ch. 329.
[30] *Sinnott* v. *Bowden* [1912] 2 Ch. 414.

and it has been insured against this risk. But he cannot demand the money from the company; if he fails to require them to reinstate before settlement, his remedy is lost.[31]

14–33 Law of Property Act 1925

Since, where property is mortgaged, a mortgagee has no inherent right to effect any insurances upon it at the borrower's expense,[32] nor, as we have seen, will he necessarily be able to take advantage of insurances taken out by the mortgagor, it is important that he should ensure that his interests in this respect are safeguarded in the mortgage instrument. By the Law of Property Act 1925, s.101(1)(ii), a mortgagee has certain limited rights to effect insurances and charge the property mortgaged with the premiums. Apart from these provisions it is important that appropriate covenants should be inserted in the mortgage deed as to the insurance of the property either by the mortgagor or by the mortgagee at his expense.[32] If the mortgagor expressly covenants to insure, not even the impossibility of effecting such insurance will excuse him for failure to effect it.[33]

The power given by section 101(1)(ii) of the Law of Property Act applies only to cases where the mortgage is by deed, and is limited to insurance against fire. It is not to exceed two-thirds of the cost of restoration in the event of a total loss, or if an amount is specified in the mortgage deed, the amount specified.[34] It does not apply where the mortgage deed deals with insurance[35] or where the mortgagor already keeps up an insurance with the mortgagee's consent to the authorised amount.[36]

14–34   Section 108(3) and (4) of the Law of Property Act 1925 are important provisions. They apply to all insurances under the Act, including insurance against fire under section 101(1)(ii) and to insurances for the maintenance of which the mortgagor is liable under the mortgage deed. But such insurances must be insurances by the mortgagee. The subsections do not apply to an ordinary Lees v. Whiteley covenant to insure.[37]

In these cases the mortgagee may insist either on reinstatement by the mortgagor in the event of a loss, section 108(3), or that the insurance money be applied in paying off or reducing the mortgage debt, section 108(4).

Section 109(7) provides that the mortgagee may by writing direct a receiver to exercise his powers of insurance under the Act out of rents, etc., received by him.

Where a mortgagor compels a mortgagee to transfer his mortgage to a third person under section 95(1) of the Law of Property Act 1925, he would no doubt be entitled to require him to assign any insurance he had made under the Act if the insurers agreed, since the premiums are

---

[31] See n. 27, *supra*.
[32] *Bellamy* v. *Brickenden* (1861) 2 J. & H. 137; *Dobson* v. *Land* (1850) 8 Hare 216.
[33] *Re Moorgate Estates* [1942] Ch. 321.
[34] s.108(1).
[35] s.108(2)(i) and (ii).
[36] s.108(2)(iii).
[37] *Halifax Building Society* v. *Keighley* [1931] 2 K.B. 248.

chargeable on the mortgage property and the policy forms part of his security.

Mortgagee of leasehold property   14–35
The mortgagee of leasehold property may, by exercising his statutory right to reinstatement,[38] to that extent rely on an insurance made either by the lessor or the lessee against fire. His rights under any covenants in the lease depend on the extent to which they, and the benefit of any policies made in pursuance of them, run with the land.[39]

6. VENDOR AND PURCHASER OF LAND

Purchaser's interest   14–36
A purchaser of land has an insurable interest in the premises purchased from the signing of the contract and before completion, since:

(a) he has the equitable interest in it, being generally entitled to specific performance of the contract, and
(b) the property is at his risk; and if it is burnt down he must still pay for it.[40]

After completion, of course, he has an insurable interest as legal owner of the land.

Vendor's interest   14–37
An unpaid vendor of land who is still in possession has an insurable interest in it and can recover to the full extent of its value under a policy of fire insurance; for until he is paid he cannot tell for certain whether he will ultimately receive the purchase money or not. If it were otherwise he would have to rely entirely on the solvency of the purchaser if the property were destroyed by fire.[41] But once the transfer is complete he will be unable to recover on a policy insuring his own interest alone.[42]

Insurance by vendor   14–38
The position at common law where the vendor alone insured was that if a loss occurred after the contract for sale was executed the insurers would eventually escape all responsibility for it, unless the buyer was insolvent or the vendor's title proved defective. For while the vendor, as legal owner, could, in the first place, recover from his insurers the entire amount of the purchase money,[43] the insurers would become subrogaged to his right to the purchase money as against the purchase.[44] And, as to the purchaser, he had no right to benefit under the vendor's

---

[38] See § 14–32, *supra*.
[39] See § 14–14, *supra*, and *Garden* v. *Ingram* (1852) 23 L.J.Ch. 478.
[40] *Paine* v. *Meller* (1801) 6 Ves. 349; *Sutherland* v. *Pratt* (1843) 11 M. & W. 296.
[41] *Collingridge* v. *Royal Exchange* (1877) 3 Q.B.D. 173, 177.
[42] *Ecclesiastical Commissioners* v. *Royal Exchange* (1895) 11 T.L.R. 476; Lush J. in *Collingridge's case, supra*, at p.177.
[43] *Collingridge* v. *Royal Exchange* (1877) 3 Q.B.D. 173.
[44] *Castellain* v. *Preston* (1883) 11 Q.B.D. 380.

policy,[45] for the benefit of such policies does not run with the land.[46] The vendor might assign the policy to the purchaser, on executing the contract of sale, but such an assignment would require the assent of the insurers in order to confer on the purchaser the right to benefit under it. Should that assent be refused, the policy would become virtually worthless, and the purchaser's only remedy would be to effect an insurance of his own. Not even a condition in the contract of sale that the purchaser was to have the benefit of the vendor's policy could take away from the insurers their right of subrogation.[47] Nor could the exercise by the purchaser of his rights under the Fires Prevention (Metropolis) Act 1774, s.83,[48] materially assist him.[49] Though he might require the insurers to lay out the money in reinstatement of the property under that Act, there would be no reason why they should not thereupon be subrogated to the vendor's right to payment against him.[50] Moreover, if the purchaser has actually paid the purchase price, the vendor suffers no loss and are thus in any event discharged.

These principles apply in the case of compulsory purchase of land under a statute; once the transfer is complete neither party can recover under a policy taken out by the original owner.[51]

14–39 Law of Property Act 1925, s.47

This unsatisfactory state of the law was remedied a little by section 47(1) of the Law of Property Act 1925, whereby insurance money that becomes payable to the vendor after the date of the contract for sale or exchange of any property, under a policy maintained by him against damage to or destruction of that property, shall, "on completion of the contract, be held or receivable by the vendor on behalf of the purchaser and paid by the vendor to the purchaser on completion of the sale or exchange, or so soon thereafter as the same shall be received by the vendor." Thus, this subsection reverses the decision in *Rayner* v. *Preston*,[52] but since by section 47(2) it has effect subject to:

(a) any stipulation to the contrary contained in the contract,
(b) *any requisite consents of the insurers*,
(c) the payment by the purchaser of the proportionate part of the premium from the date of the contract,

it merely saves introducing a condition into the contract that the purchaser is to have the benefit of the vendor's policy, and the consent of the insurers is always necessary in order to give the purchaser any rights under it, unless there is a condition in the policy giving the benefit of it to any purchaser, or unless it was taken out with that intent.[53] The sec-

---

[45] *Poole* v. *Adams* (1864) 10 L.T. 287.
[46] *Rayner* v. *Preston* (1881) 18 Ch.D. 1. Further, many modern householders' comprehensive policies do not cover against risks where a house is left unfurnished, and an additional premium is usually required to cover them.
[47] *Phoenix Assurance* v. *Spooner* [1905] 2 K.B. 753; see § 8–16, *et seq.*, *supra*.
[48] See §§ 11–07 *et seq.*, *supra*.
[49] This follows from Younger L.J.'s dictum in *Matthey* v. *Curling* [1922] 2 A.C. 180, 219.
[50] See Cotton L.J. in *Rayner* v. *Preston, supra*, at p. 7. As to James L.J.'s dictum at p.15, see Bowen L.J. in *Castellain* v. *Preston* (1883) 11 Q.B.D. 380, 400.
[51] *Ecclesiastical Commissioners* v. *Royal Exchange* (1895) 11 T.L.R. 476.
[52] See n. 45, *supra*.
[53] See Bowen L.J. in *Castellain* v. *Preston, supra*, at p.406.

tion applies to sales or exchange by an order of the court.[54] In practice section 47 is rarely relied upon, for its operation is defeated by the doctrine of subrogation: if the purchaser pays the purchase price the insurer is discharged from liability to the vendor as the vendor has suffered no loss, so that there are no proceeds to which section 47 can attach; if the purchaser does not pay, any benefit he receives under section 47 will be lost if the insurer exercises the vendor's subrogation rights in respect of the price. The solution adopted in practice—under the Law Society's National Conditions of Sale (operative from March 1990)—is to vest the risk of damage pending completion in the vendor, so that only the vendor need insure. A prudent purchaser will nevertheless continue to insure to overcome the vendor's refusal to make good any loss.

7. VENDOR AND PURCHASER OF GOODS

Floating and declaration policies   14–40

As insurances of goods are not covered by the Life Assurance Act 1774,[55] the only insurable interest that has to be considered is the interest in them at the time of their loss. Thus, a buyer may insure goods before he has bought them; he may take out a 'floating" policy[56] to cover all the goods in his warehouse, or otherwise ascertainable at the time of loss, up to a named amount, or a "declaration" policy covering goods declared from time to time.[57] In certain businesses in this country it is the practice to take out an open policy against all risks by sea and land, and to provide that the assured may declare thereon so soon as he learns that property at his risk of the class insured is in transit to him and whether such property is at the time lost or not. Firms which have to transmit valuable property or securities through the post insure them thus; and even when they are simultaneously advised of transmission and loss, they can still declare their loss under such a policy, provided only that they observe good faith in the transaction.[58] Certificates for assignment to a buyer are sometimes issued by insurers under a floating policy already taken out by the seller covering the goods sold. Such certificates themselves usually constitute contracts of insurance, and the terms of the floating policy are not necessarily incorporated in them.[59]

Insurable interest   14–41

The respective insurance interests of buyer and seller depend principally on when the risk passes.[60] Once the risk has passed to the buyer the seller, although he may retain a legal title sufficient to support a

---

[54] Law of Property Act 1925, s.47(3).

[55] See § 3–03, *supra.*

[56] *Crowley* v. *Cohen* (1832) 3 B. & Ad. 478; *Joyce* v. *Kennard* (1871) L.R. 7 Q.B. 78; *Ewing* v. *Sicklemore* (1918) 35 T.L.R. 55.

[57] *Rivaz* v. *Gerussi* (1880) 6 Q.B.D. 222.

[58] With regard to declaration on an open policy, see *Davies* v. *National Fire & Marine Ins. Co.* [1891] A.C. 485.

[59] *MacLeod Ross* v. *Compagnie d'Assurances* [1952] 1 T.L.R. 314; *Phoenix Ins.* v. *De Monchy* (1929) 35 Com.Cas. 67 (H.L.).

[60] *Anderson* v. *Morice* (1875) L.R. 10 C.P. 609; (1876) 1 App.Cas. 713.

claim against his insurers, would have to cede to his insurers by way of subrogation his rights against the seller in respect of a loss.[61]

Once the risk has passed to the buyer he will have an insurable interest, even though the property has not passed to him.[62] Normally property and risk pass together,[63] but this depends entirely on the contract of sale.[64] The two are not inseparable.[64] And in any case the buyer has a good claim against his insurers (subject to their right of subrogation as against the seller) where the property alone has passed.[65]

Where both property and risk pass to the buyer, even where the seller remains in possession, the seller, his lien apart, no longer has any interest in the goods though his possession entitles him to make an insurance covering the buyer's interest if he so intends and provided there is nothing in the policy to preclude him from doing so.[66]

14–42   Where the buyer becomes insolvent, or unwilling for some other reason to pay the price, the seller has a special interest in the goods, even though the risk has passed to the buyer. If he is still in possession, he will have a lien on the goods for the purchase price[67]; if he has parted with the possession of the goods, he has a right to regain it provided the goods are still in transit,[68] and either of these interests may support an insurance by him. But the fact that he retains a lien in no way affects an insurance by the buyer, if the risk has passed to him,[69] nor do the seller's lien or his right to stop in transit entitle him to benefit under policies by the buyer.[70]

The buyer's interest in the goods ceases if he exercises a right to reject them, provided, by redelivering them to the seller, he is no longer responsible for their safety.[71]

Apart from these special considerations the rules applicable to insurances by the buyers and sellers of goods are those applicable to the vendors and purchasers of land. Thus the buyer will be unable to benefit from an insurance by the seller unless it is taken out for his benefit,[72] as is the case where a shipper of goods insures them under a c.i.f.—"cost, insurance, freight"—contract for the benefit of his consignee. Section 47 of the Law of Property Act 1925 in principle applies to insurance of goods.

---

[61] On the analogy of *Collingridge* v. *Royal Exchange* and *Castellain* v. *Preston, supra.*

[62] *Joyce* v. *Swann* (1864) 17 C.B.(N.S.) 84, 103, 104, *per* Willes J.; *Colonial Insurance* v. *Adelaide Marine Insurance* (1886) 12 App.Cas. 128. See *Anderson* v. *Morice, supra,* for a case in which the risk had not passed to the buyer.

[63] Sale of Goods Act 1979, s.20. See *Rugg* v. *Minett* (1809) 11 East 210; Lord Blackburn in *Anderson* v. *Morice* (1875) L.R. 10 C.P. 609, 619.

[64] Blackburn J. in *Martineau* v. *Kitching* (1872) L.R. 7 Q.B. 436, 454. See *Inglis* v. *Stock* (1885) 10 App. Cas. 263.

[65] *Sparkes* v. *Marshall* (1836) 2 Bing.N.C. 761.

[66] *North British* v. *Moffatt* (1871) L.R. 7 C.P. 25, 30, 31.

[67] Sale of Goods Act 1979, s.41.

[68] *Kendall* v. *Marshall Stevens* (1883) 11 Q.B.D. 356, 364; Sale of Goods Act 1979, s.44.

[69] Blackburn J. in *Anderson* v. *Morice* (1875) L.R. 10 C.P. 609, 619.

[70] *Berndtson* v. *Strang* (1868) L.R. 3 Ch.App. 588, *per* Cairns L.C. at p. 591.

[71] *Colonial Insurance* v. *Adelaide Marine Insurance* (1886) 12 App.Cas. 128.

[72] *Martineau* v. *Kitching, supra; Dalgleish* v. *Buchanan* (1854) 16 D.(Ct. of Sess.) 332.

CHAPTER 15

AGENTS

1. GENERAL ISSUES

Liabilty of principal for acts of agent   15–01

A principal is liable in respect of all acts done by his authorised agent on his behalf. If the agent does not possess the requisite authority but is held out as doing so, no private instructions can prevent his acts within the scope of that apparent authority from binding his principal,[1] but where his authority depends, and is known by those dealing with him to depend, upon written mandate, it may be necessary to produce or account for the non-production of that writing in order to prove what was the scope of the agent's authority.[2] In the case of a company, however, the powers of the directors are deemed to be free of any limitations, even in favour of a person who is aware of those limitations.[3]

Except in such rare cases where the question of written authority arises, it will be the agent's ostensible, not his actual, authority that will determine the extent to which he may bind his principal. Thus, where an insurance agent had been in the habit of giving temporary cover with the knowledge and consent of the insurers, it was held that a temporary cover given by him, pending the company's decision on a proposal, was binding on the company, though he had no express authority to give it.[4]

The basis of this rule is that where a third party deals in good faith with an agent in reliance upon the credentials with which he has been entrusted by his principal,[5] his principal is estopped from denying his authority.[6] The assured is not bound by unusual limitations on an insurance agent's authority unless he knows of them.[7]

So it has been held that where an agent has authority to grant a policy 15–02 he also has authority to receive a notice terminating it, and the fact that the society for which he acts has not given him instructions on the passing on of such notices will not protect them.[8]

On this ground an underwriter has even been held liable on policies made on his behalf by one who had ceased to be his agent, where he had failed to give notice to the assured that the agency had terminated.[9]

Ostensible authority may extend to a sub-agent even though the agent had no authority to appoint him.[10]

---

[1] *Pickering* v. *Busk* (1812) 15 East 38.
[2] Lord Blackburn in *National Bolivian Navigation Co.* v. *Wilson* (1880) 5 App.Cas. 176, 209.
[3] Companies Act 1985, s.35A, inserted by the Companies Act 1989, s.108.
[4] *Murfitt* v. *Royal* (1922) 38 T.L.R. 334.
[5] Lord Selborne in *Houldsworth* v. *City of Glasgow Bank* (1880) 5 App.Cas. 317, 327.
[6] Erle C.J. in *Brady* v. *Todd* (1861) 9 C.B.(N.S.) 592, 604.
[7] Malins V.-C. in *Mackie* v. *European Assurance* (1869) 21 L.T. 102, 105.
[8] *Re Solvency Mutual* (1862) 31 L.J.Ch. 625.
[9] *Willis, Faber* v. *Joyce* (1911) 27 T.L.R. 388.
[10] *Rossiter* v. *Trafalgar* (1859) 27 Beav. 377.

15–03   On the same ground[11] a principal is liable for the fraud, concealment, misrepresentation or wrong[12] of his agent where the agent is acting, or purporting to act, in the course of business such as he was authorised, or held out as authorised, to transact on behalf of his principal.[13] It does not matter whether the act was intended for his principal's benefit or his own,[14] but his principal will not be bound by fraudulent acts wholly outside the agent's authority.[15]

Thus the representations of an agent having authority to solicit assurances and receive proposals bind the company,[16] and misrepresentation by the assured's agent is fatal whether made with the assured's knowledge and consent or not.[17]

Though the fraud is not even within the apparent authority of the agent, the principal cannot retain the benefit of it,[18] for by keeping the benefit he must be taken to have adopted the act of his agent.[19]

But where the assured has notice,[20] by a condition in a proposal form,[21] receipt[22] or policy[23] for instance, of a limitation of the agent's authority, he cannot afterwards make the principal answerable.[24] So also where it is usual for underwriters to limit the authority of agents, the assured cannot claim that the apparent authority of the agent was wider than his actual authority.[25]

An assurance company will be bound by the contract of their authorised agent, even where the assured is under the misapprehension that he is contracting with another company.[26]

15–04 Ratification

Where the act is not even within the apparent authority of the agent, it will only bind the principal if he afterwards ratifies it. An insurance company can adopt any acts of its agents by subsequent ratification provided they are within its own powers.[27]

So also a policy taken out without authority by the agent of the assured may afterwards be adopted by him,[28] and a policy made by one without interest for the benefit of all concerned may be subsequently adopted by one with interest.[29]

---

[11] Lord Selborne in *Houldsworth* v. *City of Glasgow Bank* (1880) 5 App.Cas. 317, 327.

[12] *Barwick* v. *English Joint Stock Bank* (1867) L.R. 2 Ex. 259.

[13] Loreburn L.C. in *Lloyd* v. *Grace, Smith* [1912] A.C. 716, 725.

[14] *Lloyd* v. *Grace, Smith, supra*; Greer L.J. in *Algemeene Bankvereeniging* v. *Langton* (1935) 40 Com.Cas. 247, 258.

[15] *McGowan* v. *Dyer* (1873) L.R. 8 Q.B. 141; *Ruben* v. *Great Fingall Consolidated* [1906] A.C. 439; Lord Shaw in *Lloyd* v. *Grace, Smith, supra*, at p.741; *Newsholme* v. *Road Transport Insurance* [1929] 2 K.B. 356.

[16] *Splents* v. *Lefevre* (1863) 11 L.T. 114; *Kettlewell* v. *Refuge Insurance* [1908] 1 K.B. 545; [1909] A.C. 243.

[17] *Fitzherbert* v. *Mather* (1785) 1 Term.Rep. 12.

[18] *Refuge Assurance* v. *Kettlewell* [1909] A.C. 243.

[19] Lord Macnaghten in *Lloyd* v. *Grace, Smith* [1912] A.C. 716, 738.

[20] See Lord Finlay in *Hood* v. *Anchor Line* [1918] A.C. 837, 842–843.

[21] *Levy* v. *Scottish Employers* (1901) 17 T.L.R. 229.

[22] *Acey* v. *Fernie* (1840) 7 M. & W. 151.

[23] *Biggar* v. *Rock Life* [1902] 1 K.B. 516; *M'Millan* v. *Accident Insurance*, 1907 S.C. 484.

[24] *Horncastle* v. *Equitable Life* (1906) 22 T.L.R. 735; *Comerford* v. *Britannic* (1908) 24 T.L.R. 593.

[25] *Willis, Faber* v. *Joyce* (1911) 27 T.L.R. 388; *Baines* v. *Ewing* (1866) L.R. 1 Ex. 320.

[26] *Mackie* v. *European* (1869) 21 L.T. 102.

[27] *Re Phoenix Life* (1862) 2 J. & H. 441; *Re Era* (1862) 1 Hem. & M. 672.

[28] *Lucena* v. *Craufurd* (1808) 1 Taunt. 325; *Stirling* v. *Vaughan* (1809) 11 East 619.

[29] *Routh* v. *Thompson* (1811) 13 East 274.

The general principle is that ratification can only be effectual when he who ratifies could, at the time when he so ratified, have made the original contract. Nevertheless it has been held in marine insurance cases that where a policy has been effected by an agent without authority it may be ratified by the principals even after a loss has happened.[30] This rule has been applied to insurance law generally in Canadian and American cases,[31] but in Great Britain it has been restricted to marine insurance law, and has not been extended to fire; or other kinds of insurance. So it has been held that an insurance of premises against fire by an agent without his principal's authority cannot be ratified by the principal after a fire has occurred.[32]

The effect of taking out a policy on the chance of its being adopted by **15–05** someone interested is that it is purely optional whether the person interested adopts it or not. If he does he becomes privy to the policy and can sue upon it. The man who effects the insurance and pays the premiums takes the risk of losing them, as he is acting outside the scope of his agency, nor can he at any time before the risk ends recover his premiums, as the insurer may answer that the persons beneficially interested are still entitled to adopt the policy.[33]

Liability of agent to third party   **15–06**
In the general law, where an agent makes a contract that is expressed to be on behalf of his principal he will not be personally liable upon it, although if he makes himself a party to it he may sue and be sued on it accordingly.

However, an insurance broker may sue or be sued on behalf of the assured in the absence of wording making it clear that he is *not* a party to contract, although any sums recovered by the broker from the insurer are to be held on trust for the assured.[34]

If the agent purports to contract as another's agent, but exceeds his authority so that the other is not liable, he will be deemed to have warranted his authority and will be liable to an action for damages for breach of warranty of authority.[35]

In exceptional cases the broker may be found to owe a duty of care to the third party and thus to face liability independently of the contract of insurance. Thus if a broker undertakes to an underwriter that he will use his best endeavours to obtain a stated level of subscription to the slip from other underwriters, but fails to use best endeavours, he will be liable to the underwriter under a collateral contract.[36] Again, if a broker

[30] See *Williams* v. *North China Insurance* (1876) 1 C.P.D. 757; and M.I.A. 1906, s.86.
[31] *Ogden* v. *Montreal Fire* (1853) 3 U.C.C.P. 497; *Giffard* v. *Queen Insurance* (1869) 12 N.B.R. (1 Han.) 432; *Home Insurance* v. *Baltimore Co.* (1876) 93 U.S. 527; *Snow* v. *Carr* (1878) 32 Am.Rep. 3; but the Saskatchewan Court of Appeal was equally divided on the question in *Goulding* v. *Norwich Union* [1948] 1 D.L.R. 526.
[32] *Grover* v. *Mathews* [1910] 2 K.B. 401; *Ferguson* v. *Aberdeen Parish Council*, 1916 S.C. 715.
[33] *Hagedorn* v. *Oliverson* (1814) 2 M. & S. 485, 490, 492, 493; *Cory* v. *Patton* (1874) L.R. 9 Q.B. 577.
[34] *Provincial Insurance of Canada* v. *Leduc* (1874) L.R. 6 P.C. 224; *Transcontinental Underwriting* v. *Grand Union* [1987] 2 F.T.L.R. 35; *Pan Atlantic* v. *Pine Top* [1989] 1 Lloyd's Rep. 568.
[35] *Albion Fire* v. *Mills* (1828) 3 Wills. & S. 218.
[36] *General Accident* v. *Tanter, The Zephyr* [1985] 2 Lloyd's Rep. 529, disapproving the first instance view of Hobhouse J., at [1984] 1 Lloyd's Rep. 58, that a tortious duty of care to achieve the stated level of subscription might be imposed.

promises to procure the transfer of a policy, but fails to do so, he will face an action by the intended transferee of the policy.[37] However, if a broker acts negligently and fails to obtain binding liability insurance for the assured, he will not face liability to a third party who is unable to recover an indemnity from the assured due to the absence of a valid liability policy, as such loss is too remote to be recovered in a tort action.[38]

15–07 Dual capacity of agents

Insurance agents fall broadly into the agents of insurers, who may be employed or occasional, and the agents of assureds, who will normally be brokers. An agent of one party to a transaction may, with his principal's consent, act on behalf of the other in respect of the same transaction.[39] Thus, where a solicitor of the assured was also the authorised agent of the insurers to receive notice of assignment of a policy, and he had received the notice in the capacity of solicitor and had not transmitted it, it was held that the company was bound.[40] Insurance brokers commonly perform functions on behalf of insurers and may in particular be authorised to issue cover notes or full insurances.[41] If, however, an agent, by acting in a dual capacity without consent, prejudices the interests of his principal, he will be liable to the principal.[42]

Regulation of insurance agents

15–08 *The general scheme.* There is no unified system for the regulation of insurance agents. Agents who wish to act as brokers, and to do so under the title "insurance broker," must be registered in accordance with the Insurance Brokers Registration Act 1977; the right to become and remain registered depends upon the attainment of recognised professional qualifications and compliance with the Code of Conduct issued by the Insurance Brokers Registration Council under the 1977 Act.[43] Agents of all classes who deal with life policies are regulated by and under the Financial Services Act 1986, the main object of which is to ensure that full information is given to prospective assureds and other investors.[44] The residuary class—consisting of agents dealing with general (*i.e.*, non-life) business, other than registered insurance brokers and agents handling only reinsurance business—are regulated by the Association of British Insurers' Code of Conduct, issued at the beginning of 1989 and fully operative from July 1, 1989.

The 1989 Code is similar in its aims to the 1977 and 1986 Acts, in that it seeks to ensure that potential assureds are given as much information as possible when entering into the contract. In particular the Code requires an agent to avoid making calls without appointment, to disclose

---

[37] *Bromley L.B.C.* v. *Ellis* [1971] 1 Lloyd's Rep. 97.
[38] *Federation General* v. *Knott Becker* [1990] 1 Lloyd's Rep. 98.
[39] Webster J. in *Excess Life* v. *Fireman's Fund Insurance* [1982] 2 Lloyd's Rep. 599, 619.
[40] *Gale* v. *Lewis* (1846) 9 Q.B. 730. But see *Edwards* v. *Martin* (1865) L.R. 1 Eq. 121; *North British* v. *Hallett* (1861) 7 Jur. (N.S.) 1263.
[41] See *Stockton* v. *Mason* [1978] 2 Lloyd's Rep. 430.
[42] *North & South Trust* v. *Berkeley* [1971] 1 All E.R. 980 (broker acting for underwriter in assessing loss); *Forsakringsiktieselskapet Vesta* v. *Butcher* [1989] 1 All E.R. 402 (broker creating a conflict of interest by drafting the terms of the insurance for underwriters).
[43] See *infra*, § 15–25.
[44] See generally Chap. 14, *supra*.

whether he is independent or tied to one or more insurers, to explain the terms of any policy being recommended to the assured, to warn the assured of the need to disclose all material facts, and, following the making of the contract, to keep proper accounting records. Each agent is required to procure and maintain liability insurance for a minimum of £250,000, thereby guaranteeing a fund to the assured in the event of the agent's negligence.

Offences. It is a criminal offence if any person, for the purposes of **15–09** inducing a contract of insurance, (a) makes a statement, promise or forecast which he knows to be misleading, false or deceptive, or dishonestly conceals relevant facts, or (b) recklessly makes a statement, promise or forecast which is misleading or deceptive.[45] Moreover, any person connected with an insurance company, whether by way of employment, exclusive agency or in any other manner, must disclose that fact to the assured when inviting the assured to enter into a contract of insurance.[46]

2. IMPUTATION OF AGENT'S KNOWLEDGE TO PRINCIPAL

There is no general principle in insurance law that the knowledge of an **15–10** agent *is* the knowledge of his principal, and the mere fact that an agent has received notice of a matter involves no implication of law that his principal also has had notice of it. Commercial law does not favour any such doctrine of constructive notice.[47]

Thus, in *Blackburn* v. *Vigors*[48] a vessel was reinsured and while effecting the reinsurance the reinsured's broker received information material to the risk, which he did not communicate to the reinsured. It was held that this information did not preclude the reinsured from recovering on a separate subsequent reinsurance through another broker.

Estoppel   **15–11**

But an insurance company may be estopped from denying that an agent has passed on information to them. Thus, in *Wing* v. *Harvey*[49] an agent, who had authority to do so, accepted premiums on his company's behalf and paid them to his directors. He knew at the time that the assured had broken a condition of the policy. It was held that the assured was entitled to rely on the agent passing on his knowledge to the directors, and that by accepting the premium through their authorised agent the company had therefore to be taken to have affirmed the

---

[45] Financial Services Act 1986, s. 47 (long-term policies) and s.133 (general business).

[46] Insurance Companies Act 1982, s.74, supplemented by the Insurance Companies Regulations 1981 (S.I. 1981 No. 1654), regs. 67–69, governs this matter in respect of general business. As far as long-term business is concerned, the Financial Services Act 1986 is of the same general effect: see Chap. 14, *supra*.

[47] Lindley L.J. in *Manchester Trust* v. *Furness* [1895] 2 Q.B. 539, 545; Scrutton L.J. in *Newsholme* v. *Road Transport* [1929] 2 K.B. 356, 374.

[48] (1887) 12 App.Cas. 531. Contrast *Blackburn* v. *Haslam* (1881) 21 Q.B.D. 144, where the broker was under a duty to communicate the information to the reinsured, and it was held that the reinsured was deemed to be aware of the information.

[49] (1854) 5 De G.M. & G. 265.

policy. Those who deal in good faith with an agent are entitled to take it for granted that he does his duty.[50] In *Evans* v. *Employers Mutual*[51] it was held that, where it must have been clear to a clerk of the insurers, from perusing a claim, that an answer in the proposal was untrue, his knowledge amounted to knowledge by the company and that they had then to elect whether to continue with the contract. In a sense,[52] where knowledge is to be attributed to a company it must be the knowledge of its agents.[53]

And where the assured orally volunteered material information to an agent, the company could not be heard to say that the assured concealed the matter even though no mention was made of it in his written proposal.[54] So also where an agent filled in erroneous answers in a proposal form to save the assured trouble, and the assured later pointed out his mistake, and the agent undertook to have the matter put right, the company could not be heard to say that the assured had made a misrepresentation.[55] Similar decisions have been reached in respect of notifications of assignment, termination and loss.[56]

15–12   All such cases are based on the doctrine of estoppel. The company by some act, such as the acceptance of a premium or of a proposal, are estopped from denying that they were already in possession of certain information. But some act of the company on which the assured relies is essential to found such an estoppel. Where an agent accepted an overdue premium without authority, and the company debited his account with the amount on the assumption that it had been duly paid, it was held that the mere debiting of the agent with the premium could not be considered as a payment to the company by the assured on which the assured could rely.[57]

Similarly in a Scottish case, *Cruikshank* v. *Northern Accident Assurance*,[58] the assured answered, in a proposal for an accident policy, to the question, "Are there any circumstances which render you peculiarly liable to accident?" "Slight lameness from birth," and that he had not had paralysis or a fit of any kind, and had no physical infirmity. His answers being warranted, the company alleged that his declaration was untrue and that the policy was void on the ground that he had had local paralysis resulting in lameness caused by a fall. But he was held to be entitled to recover, because, amongst other reasons, his lameness had been seen by the agent of the company, who had concurred in its being described as "slight."

---

[50] Lord Shaw in *Lloyd* v. *Grace, Smith* [1912] A.C. 716, 740–741.

[51] [1936] 1 K.B. 505.

[52] See *Lennard's Co.* v. *Asiatic Petroleum* [1915] A.C. 705 and *Houghton* v. *Nothard, Lowe* [1928] A.C. 1.

[53] *Per* Greer L.J. in *Evans* v. *Employers Mutual* [1936] 1 K.B. 505, 515.

[54] *Ayrey* v. *British Legal Assurance* [1918] 1 K.B. 136, explained by Greer L.J. in *Newsholme* v. *Road Transport* [1929] 2 K.B. 356, 384. See also *Holdsworth* v. *Lancs. and Yorks. Insurance* (1907) 23 T.L.R. 521 and *Blackley* v. *National Mutual Life Association of Australasia Ltd.* [1972] N.Z.L.R. 1038.

[55] *Golding* v. *Royal London* (1914) 30 T.L.R. 350.

[56] *Gale* v. *Lewis* (1846) 9 Q.B. 730; *Re Solvency Mutual* (1862) 31 L.J. Ch. 625; *Brook* v. *Trafalgar* (1946) 79 Ll.L.R. 365.

[57] *Acey* v. *Fernie* (1840) 7 M. & W. 151.

[58] (1895) 33 S.L.R. 134.

Proposals filled in by insurer's agent[59]   **15–13**

It would seem clear on principle that where an insurance agent and the assured join together to defraud the company, no question of estoppel can arise, as the agent merely acts as the assured's amenuensis.[60] Th position where the assured has honestly disclosed information to the agent, but the agent has failed to add it to the proposal, is uncertain. In *Bawden* v. *London, Edinburgh and Glasgow Assurance*[61] the local agent of the insurers filled in a proposal form for a one-eyed man who, although he signed the form, was almost illiterate. The form contained a printed declaration that the applicant had no physical infirmity. The Court of Appeal held that the knowledge of the agent was the knowledge of the company and that the declaration was therefore no defence to a claim by the assured. In *Newsholme* v. *Road Transport Insurance*[62] the Court of Appeal came to a contrary conclusion where an agent intentionally filled in untrue answers in the applicant's proposal form and the applicant signed it. The Court of Appeal held that the agent was merely the assured's amenuensis so that questions of agency did not arise, that the parol evidence rule prevented the assured from aguing that information not appearing on the proposal was known to the insurers via their agent, and that the assured was estopped by its signature from denying that the proposal represented the entirety of the information disclosed to the insurer. The *Bawden* and *Newsholme* approaches are plainly inconsistent, and it remains uncertain which of them represents the law. Similar confusion prevails in those common law jurisdictions in which the matter has not been resolved by statute.

The English courts have taken an approach more generous to the **15–14** assured where the agent has failed to warn the assured of his duty to disclose material facts and the proposal form as a result omits such facts known to the assured. In *Stone* v. *Reliance Mutual*[63] an inspector employed by the insurers visited the assured in order to reinstate a lapsed policy. Various material facts were not disclosed to the insurers, although the relevant information had not been requested by the inspector when completing the form, which was signed by the assured's wife without reading it. It was held by the Court of Appeal that the insurers were liable, apparently on the basis that they had impliedly waived disclosure of information not specifically requested from the assured. The same result would not follow, however, where the agent is not of sufficient seniority to be authorised to waive such disclosure.[64]

---

[59] As to where it is filled in by the assured's agent, see *infra*, § 15–21.
[60] *Newsholme* v. *Road Transport* [1929] 2 K.B. 356, 364; *St Margaret's Trust* v. *Navigators* (1949) 82 Ll.L.R. 752.
[61] [1892] 2 Q.B. 534; *cf. Brewster* v. *National Life* (1892) 8 T.L.R. 648. *Bawden* was followed in: *Holdsworth* v. *Lancashire and Yorkshire Insurance* (1907) 23 T.L.R. 521; *Thornton-Smith* v. *Motor Union* (1913) 30 T.L.R. 139; *Golding* v. *Royal London* (1914) 30 T.L.R. 350; *Keeling* v. *Pearl* (1923) 129 L.T. 573; *Kaufmann* v. *British Surety* (1929) 45 T.L.R. 399.
[62] [1929] 2 K.B. 356, following *Biggar* v. *Rock Life* [1902] 1 K.B. 516. See also: *Hough* v. *Guardian Fire* (1902) 18 T.L.R. 273; *Paxman* v. *Union Assurance* (1923) 39 T.L.R. 424. The *Newsholme* decision was followed in *Dunn* v. *Ocean Accident* (1933) 50 T.L.R. 32 and *Facer* v. *Vehicle & General* [1956] 1 Lloyd's Rep. 113.
[63] [1972] 1 Lloyd's Rep. 469.
[64] *Arterial Caravans* v. *Yorkshire Insurance* [1973] 1 Lloyd's Rep. 169.

15–15   Where the agent signs the proposal form on behalf of the assured,[65] or where the agent fills in incorrect answers in the proposal form after the assured has signed it and without his knowledge, the policy is enforceable against the company.[66]

3. AGENTS OF INSURERS

15–16 General agents

All artificial persons can act only through agents,[67] and insurance companies are no exception to this rule. Their chief agents are their directors, elected or appointed by the members, whose powers cannot be greater, but may be less than those of the company itself. Since the passing of the Companies Act 1989 the directors will bind their company whether or not they act within their powers.[68]

15–17 Special or local agents

Besides such general agents and their clerical staff, assurance companies employ a great number of special or local agents to solicit applications for insurance and collect premiums. The powers of such agents vary widely, and their ostensible authority is a question of fact in each case. The following illustrations may, however, serve as a guide.

It is not within the ordinary duty of an insurance agent to undertake to grant a policy, and such an undertaking will not usually bind the company unless the agent was specially authorised.[69] His duties are generally limited to receiving and submitting proposals made.

Agents may, however, have implied authority to give temporary cover pending the company's decision on a proposal.[70] Thus where a company supplied its agent with a book of printed forms it was held that he was authorised to make contracts on their behalf in accordance with the terms of those forms.[71]

15–18   Local agents have been held to have no ostensible authority to vary the terms of the company's policies.[72] Such agents cannot waive a condition requiring notice of loss in writing at the company's head office.[73]

An agent negotiating contracts of insurance has been held to have authority, on the other hand, to fill in blanks in an illustration setting out the benefits the assured would receive.[74]

---

[65] *Pearl Life* v. *Johnson* [1909] 2 K.B. 288.
[66] Keeling v. *Pearl* (1923) 129 L.T. 573; *Western Australian Insurance* v. *Dayton* (1924) 35 C.L.R. 355; *Blanchette* v. *C.I.S.* 36 D.L.R. (3d) 561 (1973).
[67] Lord Cranworth in *Ranger* v. *G.W.R.* (1854) 5 H.L.C. 72, 86. Lord Sumner in *Houghton* v. *Northard, Lowe* [1928] A.C. 1, 18.
[68] See n. 3, *supra.*
[69] *Linford* v. *Provincial Horse & Cattle Insurance* (1864) 34 Beav. 291; *Gale* v. *Lewis* (1846) 9 Q.B. 730.
[70] *Murfitt* v. *Royal* (1922) 38 T.L.R. 334.
[71] *Mackie* v. *European* (1869) 21 L.T. 102. *Mackie* v. and *Murfitt* were distinguished in *World Marine* v. *Leger* [1952] 1 D.L.R. 755.
[72] *London and Lancashire Life* v. *Fleming* [1897] A.C. 499 (P.C.); *Comerford* v. *Britannic Assurance* (1908) 24 T.L.R. 593; *Gliksten* v. *State* (1922) 10 Ll.L.R. 604, 606 (contract made by agent).
[73] *Brook* v. *Trafalgar* (1947) 79 Ll.L.R. 365.
[74] *Sun Life of Canada* v. *Jervis* (1943) 113 L.J.K.B. 174.

Whether a local agent has authority to receive premiums will depend on the circumstances of each case.[75]

Authority to receive premiums does not necessarily imply authority to give credit or receive premiums overdue[76] and the burden is on the assured to prove, if he can, that an agent has such authority.[77] But by giving their agent authority to sign receipts a company will be estopped as against an innocent third party from denying that a premium has been paid.[78]

It has been held in American cases that an agent's authority does not extend to granting insurances in his own favour,[79] or on property in which he has an interest.[80]

4. AGENTS OF ASSUREDS

Brokers and other agents   **15–19**

Anyone who undertakes to make, or whose duty it is to make, a contract of insurance for the assured is his agent. Insurance brokers, solicitors acting for their clients, correspondents in this country of merchants abroad[81] and shippers selling under c.i.f. contracts provide such examples. It may, however, be less easy to imply a duty to insure where no express obligation is undertaken. Thus, while a driving school is under an implied duty to provide complete insurance cover for its pupils,[82] an employer is not obliged to take out accident insurance for employees working abroad[83] and a school is not required to take out accident insurance in respect of personal injuries suffered by pupils.[84] Where a duty to insure does exist, the agent, even if gratuitous, is under a duty to the assured to act carefully[85] and is liable to him in damages for breach of duty if he fails to do so.[86]

Where the assured solicitor employed an auditor to certify his gross profits for the purpose of enabling him adequately to insure them against consequential loss, the auditor was held liable for breach of duty for failing to assess the profits accurately and thereby causing the assured to underinsure.[87]

Insurance brokers form the single most important class of agent for **15–20** assureds. Lloyd's brokers in particular hold a special position, since contracts of insurance with Lloyd's underwriters cannot be made except

---

[75] *Rossiter* v. *Trafalgar Life* (1879) 27 Beav. 377; *Linford* v. *Provincial Horse & Cattle Insurance* (1864) 34 Beav. 291.

[76] *Acey* v. *Fernie* (1840) 7 M. & W. 151; *London & Lancashire Life* v. *Fleming* [1897] A.C. 499 (P.C.).

[77] *British Industry Life* v. *Ward* (1856) 17 C.B. 644, 649.

[78] *Re Economic Fire Office* (1876) 12 T.L.R. 142.

[79] *White* v. *Lancashire* (1879) 27 Grant (U.C.) 61.

[80] *Ritt* v. *Washington Marine* (1865), 41 Barb.(N.Y.) 353.

[81] *Smith* v. *Lascelles* (1788) 2 T.R. 187.

[82] *British School of Motoring* v. *Simms* [1971] R.T.R. 190.

[83] *Reid* v. *Rush & Tompkins* [1989] 3 All E.R. 28. An employer is under a statutory duty to take out liability insurance in respect of employees employed in the U.K. under the Employers Liability (Compulsory Insurance) Act 1969. See *infra,* Chap. 19.

[84] *Van Oppen* v. *Bedford Charity Trustees* [1989] 1 All E.R. 273.

[85] *Wilkinson* v. *Coverdale* (1793) 1 Esp. 74.

[86] *Park* v. *Hammond* (1816) 6 Taunt. 495.

[87] *De Meza* v. *Apple* [1975] 1 Lloyd's Rep. 498.

with brokers who are members of Lloyd's. All brokers, including Lloyd's brokers, are the agents of the assured and not of the underwriters,[88] although the Court of Appeal has recently said that this rule bears no relation to the reality of the close relationship between Lloyd's brokers and underwriters and ought to be reconsidered.[89]

By a special custom of Lloyd's, which also operates in marine insurance, the broker and not the assured is liable to the underwriters for the premium,[90] and has a lien on the policy in respect of it. He may in such cases be regarded as an agent of the insurers for the purpose only of receiving the premium.[91] These rules have been given statutory force in the Marine Insurance Act 1906, ss.53–54.[92]

15–21 Duties of brokers

A broker's duties will depend upon his agreement with the assured, but will in general relate to obtaining insurance, completing the proposal, in general giving advice, and assisting with claims. In all cases the broker must act with the requisite care and skill in obeying his instructions.

The primary duty of a broker is to procure a contract of insurance in accordance with his instructions. The coverage of the policy must be sufficient[93] and it must be procured at the time required by the assured so far as this is possible.[94] However, if the assured does not give proper instructions, the broker will not be liable as long as all necessary care and skill is exercised by him in the circumstances.[95] The insurer chosen by the broker must not be financially unsound to the broker's knowledge,[96] and must be willing to insure the class of risk put forward by the assured.[97] The policy need not be the cheapest available on the market.[98]

Brokers often undertake the completion of the proposal form on the assured's behalf. In *O'Connor* v. *Kirby*[99] the Court of Appeal held that the assured had no remedy where he signed a proposal form containing an erroneous statement by the broker, as there was no evidence as to how the error came to be made and in any event the assured's failure to

---

[88] *Empress* v. *Bowring* (1905) 11 Com. Cas. 107, 112, *per* Kennedy J.; Scrutton L.J. in *Rozanes* v. *Bowen* (1928) 32 Ll.L.R. 98, 101. *Cf. Haylow* v. *Smith* (1950) 84 Ll.L.R. 504.

[89] *Roberts* v. *Plaisted* [1989] 2 Lloyd's Rep. 341.

[90] *Minett* v. *Forester* (1811) 4 Taunt. 541. This custom does not extend to non-Lloyd's brokers dealing with non-marine business: see *Wilson* v. *Avec Audio-Visual Ltd.* [1974] 1 Lloyd's Rep. 81, where a broker who paid on the assured's behalf was held to be unable to recover the premium money from the assured.

[91] *Equitable Life* v. *General Accident* (1904) 12 S.L.T. 348, 352.

[92] See *infra*, §§ 23–54–23–55.

[93] *Mallough* v. *Barber* (1815) 4 Cowp. 150; *Yuill* v. *Robson* [1908] 1 K.B. 270; *Zurich General* v. *Rowberry* [1954] 2 Lloyd's Rep. 55; *Ackbar* v. *Green* [1975] 2 Q.B. 582. It is no defence for the insurer to argue that the assured failed to examine the policy: *Dickson* v. *Devitt* (1916) 86 L.J.K.B. 291.

[94] *Turpin* v. *Bilton* (1843) 5 Man. & G. 455; *Hurrell* v. *Bullard* (1863) 3 F. & F. 445; *Cock, Russell* v. *Bray, Gibb* (1920) 3 Ll.L.R. 71.

[95] *Vale* v. *Van Oppen* (1921) 6 Ll.L.R. 167; *United Mills* v. *Bray* [1952] 1 All E.R. 225n.

[96] *Osman* v. *Moss* [1970] 1 Lloyd's Rep. 313. Here the plaintiff was able to recover damages equal to the fine and costs imposed upon him in criminal proceedings for driving uninsured: as the plaintiff believed that he had been insured, there was no objection on public policy grounds to such recovery. *Cf. Bell* v. *Lothiansure* (1990) *The Times*, February 2 (Ct. of Session).

[97] *McNealy* v. *Pennine Insurance* [1978] 2 Lloyd's Rep. 18, where the broker failed to warn the assured that various categories of motorist—including the class into which the assured himself fell as a part-time musician—would not be covered by the policy.

[98] *Moore* v. *Mourgue* (1776) 2 Cowp. 47.

[99] [1972] 1 Q.B. 90.

notice the error broke the chain of causation following the broker's allegedly negligent act. However, if the assured is not shown the completed proposal, for example where the broker completes the form by asking questions of the assured by telephone, the assured may recover from the broker if the insurer avoids for misrepresentation,[1] and a broker charged with the duty to renew a policy will be liable for failing to disclose material facts to the insurer on renewal.[2]

Incorrect advice given by the broker, whether as to the insurability of a risk[3] or as to the meaning of the policy[4] will render the broker liable in damages if he does not take adequate steps to verify the advice. Similarly, on renewal the broker is required to warn the assured of any material changes in the terms of the policy.[5]

Remedies for breach of duty   15–22

A broker who fails to procure or maintain valid insurance in accordance with his instructions, or who otherwise fails to exercise due care and skill, will be liable to the assured for the sum which the insurers would themselves have been liable for had the insurance been effective. If the insurers have an independent defence, the court must determine on the balance of probabilities how they would have treated the assured's claim in the light of that independent defence and award damages accordingly.[6] The broker's liability may sound in either contract or tort, and in either case appropriate deduction may be made for contributory negligence under the Law Reform (Contributory Negligence) Act 1945.[7] Under the Limitation Act 1980, as amended by the Latent Damage Act 1986, time will run against a broker as follows[8]:

(a) in an action in contract, six years from the date of the broker's breach of contract;

(b) in an action in tort, six years from the date of the broker's original negligence or three years from the date at which the assured ought to have discovered the broker's negligence, whichever is later.

Is insurer agent for assured?   15–23

The general answer to this question is obviously, no. There is no presumed agency relationship as between insurer and assured: whether

---

[1] *Warren* v. *Sutton* [1976] 2 Lloyd's Rep. 276. See also *Commonwealth Insurance* v. *Groupe Sprinks* [1983] 1 Lloyd's Rep. 67, where Lloyd J. was of the view that a broker would be liable for failing to add to the proposal material facts disclosed by the assured which had not been the subject of express questions.

[2] *Coolee* v. *Wing Heath* (1930) 47 T.L.R. 78; *Dunbar* v. *A. & B. Painters* [1986] 2 Lloyd's Rep. 38.

[3] *Sarginson* v. *Moulton* (1942) 73 Ll.L.R. 104.

[4] *King* v. *Chambers & Newman* [1963] 2 Lloyd's Rep. 130; *Melik* v. *Norwich Union* [1980] 1 Lloyd's Rep. 523.

[5] *Avondale Blouse* v. *Williamson* 91948) 81 Ll.L.R. 492; *Mint Securities* v. *Blair* [1982] 1 Lloyd's Rep. 188. Cf. *Cherry* v. *Allied* [1978] 1 Lloyd's Rep. 274, where the broker cancelled insurance but failed to replace it.

[6] *Fraser* v. *Furman* [1967] 1 W.L.R. 898; *Everett* v. *Hogg Robinson* [1973] 2 Lloyd's Rep. 217; *Dunbar* v. *A. & B. Painters* [1986] 2 Lloyd's Rep. 38.

[7] This was determined by Hobhouse J. in *Forsakringsiktieselskapet Vesta* v. *Butcher* [1986] 2 All E.R. 488, affirmed [1988] 2 All E.R. 43. The House of Lords did not deal with this point: [1989] 1 All E.R. 402.

[8] *Iron Trades Mututal* v. *Buckenham* [1989] 2 Lloyd's Rep. 85; *Islander Trucking Ltd.* v. *Hogg Robinson* [1990] 1 All E.R. 826.

agency exists is to be determined by the application of the ordinary rules of agency. Thus, where motor vehicle insurers arrange on their own behalf with repairers to repair a damaged car, and become insolvent, the repairers have no recourse against the assured.[9]

But in those cases the only argument put forward for the repairers was that the insurers contracted as agents for the assured, which was rejected. But where the assured initially takes the vehicle to a garage for repair, there is necessarily a contract between them on terms, *e.g.*, that the garage should properly and expeditiously do the work.[10] Thus in *Charnock* v. *Liverpool Corporation*[11] the insurers, under their separate contract with the repairers, had paid for the repairs, but the assured was clearly entitled to damages under his independent contract with the repairers, for delay in effecting the repairs. The more difficult question arose in *Brown & Davis* v. *Galbraith*.[12] There the insurer became insolvent and the relevant issue was whether the repairers were entitled to be paid by the assured, by an implied term in his contract with them. It was held hat the assured was not liable, as the implication of a term for payment by him was not necessary to give business efficacy to his contract with them.

15–24 Regulation of Lloyd's Brokers

Lloyd's is governed by a series of Acts of Parliament and bye-laws made under those Acts by Lloyd's itself. The most recent legislation, the Lloyd's Act 1982, creates a strict division between Lloyd's brokers and managing agents, the latter term being defined as meaning, in essence, any person involved with underwriting at Lloyd's. The Council of Lloyd's may not permit a person to act as a Lloyd's broker if he is a managing agent or associated with a managing agent, and the Council may not permit a person to act as a managing agent if he is a managing agent or associated with a managing agent.[13]

15–25 Regulation of other brokers

The Insurance Brokers (Registration) Act 1977, which implements European Council Directive 77/92, establishes a framework for the control of persons carrying on broking business under the title "insurance broker." The Act does not apply to persons carrying on broking business under some other title, such as consultant or adviser, although it is a criminal offence for any person not registered under the Act to use the title "insurance broker."[14] Compliance with the 1977 Act is, to that extent, voluntary, although any unregistered broker will in any event be subject to the ABI's Code of Conduct issued in 1989.[15]

The 1977 Act established the Insurance Brokers Registration Coun-

---

[9] *Godfrey Davis* v. *Culling* [1962] 2 Lloyd's Rep. 349; *Cooter and Green* v. *Tyrell* [1962] 2 Lloyd's Rep. 377. It is doubtful whether the assured would have an action against the repairers for delay, as the only loss would be enonomic loss. However, any physical depreciation caused by the repairers would clearly be actionable by the assured.

[10] Such terms would in any event be implied by the Supply of Goods and Services Act 1982.

[11] [1968] 2 Lloyd's Rep. 113.

[12] [1972] 2 Lloyd's Rep. 1.

[13] Lloyd's Act 1982, ss.10–12.

[14] s.22.

[15] *Supra.*, § 15–08.

cil. The Council maintains the register of brokers,[16] approves the educational qualifications necessary for registration,[17] and regulates the conduct of brokers by means of a Code of Conduct and the imposition of compulsory liability insurance.[18] Complex rules are laid down for the investigation of breaches of discipline[19] ultimately, the Council has the right to remove a broker from the register and thereby to prevent that person from describing himself as an "insurance broker."

---

[16] ss.1–5, 8–9.
[17] ss.6–7.
[18] ss.10–12. The Codes issued under the Act deal with ordinary business conduct and with the conduct of investment business.
[19] ss.13–20.

Part Three

SPECIAL TYPES OF INSURANCE

CHAPTER 16

LIFE INSURANCE

1. DEFINITIONS

Classes of Life Policy 16–01

Life policies may be of various types, but in general can be subdivided into three classes:

(a) endowment policies, whereby the primary liability of the insurers is to pay a fixed sum at the end of a fixed period or on the death of the life assured, whichever first occurs[1];

(b) whole life policies, where the sum insured is payable on death only, and not on the expiry of any fixed period;

(c) accident policies, which insure death by accident only.

It is to be noted that it is practically always a predetermined sum that **16–02** is payable on the happening of the contingency, and never an indemnity. Where an indemnity is payable on the death of a third party, for example under an employer's liability policy in respect of the death of an employee, it is not a case of life insurance at all.[2] Further, not all contracts under which liability is dependent on the happening of a contingency related to human life are contracts of life insurance. Thus a contract whereby two or more people purchase property as joint tenants with the object of the longest liver getting the benefit of survivorship would clearly not be a contract of insurance at all.[3]

Statutory Definitions 16–03

There are a number of statutes containing different definitions of life insurance for different purposes. Thus, the Policies of Life Assurance Act 1867, s.7[4] defines a "policy of life assurance" as "any instrument by which the payment of moneys by or out of the funds of an assurance company on the happening of any contingency depending on the duration of human life is assured or secured." The Life Assurance Companies (Payment into Court) Act 1896, s.2, defines "life policy" as including "any policy not foreign to the business of life assurance." The Life Assurance Act 1774[5] covers insurances on "lives or other events."[6]

Perhaps the most important definitions are those laid down for regula- **16–04** tory purposes. The Insurance Companies Act 1982 draws a distinction between long-term business (life and related contracts) and general

---

[1] See generally *Prudential* v. *C.I.R.* [1904] 2 K.B. 658; *Gould* v. *Curtis* [1913] 3 K.B. 84; *Joseph* v. *Law Integrity* [1912] 2 Ch. 581.

[2] See Bruce J. in *Lancashire Insurance* v. *Inland Revenue Commissioners* [1899] 1 Q.B. 353, 359.

[3] Channel J. in *Prudential* v. *C.I.R.* [1904] 2 K.B. 658, 664.

[4] Dealing with assignment of life policies: see *infra* 16–35 *et seq.*

[5] Which requires the assured to have insurable interest: see Chap. 3.

[6] After *Mark Rowlands* v. *Berni Inns* [1985] 3 All E.R. 473 it is clear that "other events" refers to other events concerned with life insurance and does not encompass any form of indemnity insurance.

business (all other forms of insurance). Seven types of long-term business are recognised in Schedule 1 of the 1982 Act: life and annuity ("effecting and carrying out contracts of insurance on human life or contracts to pay annuities on human life"); marriage and birth; linked long-term (*i.e.* life and annuity policies "where the benefits are wholly or partly to be determined by reference to the value of, or the income from, property of any description . . . "); permanent health; tontines; capital redemption; and pension fund management. All of these types of insurance are regulated as long-term business under the Insurance Companies Act 1982.[7]

Certain types of life insurance will also be regulated by the Financial Services Act 1986. That Act establishes a complex regulatory structure for all forms of "investment business" carried on in the United Kingdom. This term refers to contracts of insurance which constitute long-term business under the 1982 Act, but excluding: contracts under which benefits are payable only on death due to injury, sickness or infirmity; policies without surrender value or where only a single premium is required and the surrender value is less than that premium; and contracts under which no benefits are payable unless death occurs within ten years or before the life assured reaches a specified age not exceeding seventy years.[8]

16–05 Special cases

An arrangement whereby an insurance society distributes profits in the form of payments to the widow or widower of a member on the member's death is not life insurance business.[9] But where tea merchants offered annuities during widowhood to married women who bought their tea for a certain time before the death of their husbands, it was held that they granted annuities on human life within section 2 of the Life Assurance Companies Act 1870, and had to deposit £20,000 as required by section 3.[10]

2. THE RISK

16–06 The cover afforded by policies of life insurance, unlike that of other policies,[11] is not restricted to loss by accident: they cover also the death of the assured from disease or other natural causes. The exception of inherent vice, which might be compared with disease, and that of wear and tear, which might be compared with senile decay of the life insured, apply to insurance policies generally,[12] but do not apply in the case of life insurance.

16–07 Death caused by wilful misconduct of assured

But not even a life policy covers death caused by the wilful misconduct of the assured himself[13] unless the policy otherwise provides. Such

---

[7] See Chap. 13.
[8] Financial Services Act 1986, s.1 and Sched. 1, para. 10.
[9] *Hampton* v. *Toxteth Co-op* (1915) 1 Ch. 721.
[10] *Nelson* v. *Board of Trade* (1901) 84 L.T. 565; 17 T.L.R. 456; Act now repealed.
[11] Save for some livestock policies.
[12] See § 4–08 *supra.*
[13] Lord Atkin in *Beresford* v. *Royal* [1938] A.C. 586, 595.

misconduct is an implied exception to the risk, as in the case of insurance generally.[14]

The misconduct must be the proximate cause of the death and not merely the occasion of it, to exclude the death from the risk covered by the policy. Where the assured is executed at the hands of justice for committing a felony his personal representatives or his assignees in bankruptcy will be unable to recover under a policy taken out by him on his life.[15] In such a case the course of justice is only to be considered as the natural consequence of his own crime. But where the assured dies while engaged in an unlawful occupation, such as the slave trade, it has been held in an American case that the person for whose benefit the policy was taken out may recover.[16] A similar conclusion was reached in England where the assured was killed in a motor accident while driving while intoxicated and at excessive speeds.[17] Death resulting from a duel, on the other hand, would no doubt be excluded from the cover.[18]

Thus where the person whose life is insured is murdered by the person who took out the policy neither he nor anyone claiming through him will be entitled to recover, by reason of an implied term in the policy excepting loss caused by his wilful misconduct from the risk, quite irrespective of the questions of public policy arising.[19]

The exception does not apply where the misconduct is by a stranger to the original contract of insurance, even where such stranger is the beneficiary under the policy by reason of a trust in his favour.[20] An ordinary policy covers the risk of the assured being murdered by third parties just as it covers the risk of death by accident or disease, and there is no reason in such a case why the innocent assured, or his representatives, should not enforce the policy.[21] Thus where a policy was taken out on the joint lives of A and B, and was assigned to a building society, the building society was able to recover under the policy where A murdered B.[22] Had the assignment been merely of the right to recover under the policy, A would have remained the assured and no claim under the policy could have been presented by him.

Suicide   16–08

The misconduct must be wilful. Thus, while the sane suicide of the assured will, unless otherwise provided, be excluded from the risk covered by a life policy,[23] where the assured commits suicide while he is

---

[14] See §§ 4–03 *et seq.*, *supra*.

[15] *Amicable Insurance* v. *Bolland* (1830) 4 Bligh(N.S.) 194 (H.L.).

[16] *Lord* v. *Dall* (1815) 12 Mass. 118.

[17] *Marcel Beller* v. *Hayden* [1978] Q.B. 694.

[18] See Erskine J. in *Borradaile* v. *Hunter* (1843) 5 M. & G. 639, 658.

[19] See Lord Atkin in *Beresford* v. *Royal* [1938] A.C. 586, 595.

[20] *Cleaver* v. *Mutual Reserve* (1892) 1 Q.B. 147; but the person guilty of the misconduct will not be able to benefit and the proceeds will be held on resulting trust for the estate of the life assured.

[21] Lord Abinger in *Wainewright* v. *Bland* (1835) 1 Moo. & Rob. 481, 486.

[22] *Davitt* v. *Titcumb* [1989] 3 All E.R. 417. The building society used the funds to discharge the mortgage debt owing to it. When the mortgaged property was subsequently sold, it was held that the proceeds belonged entirely to B's estate. This result prevented A from deriving any benefit as the result of his wrongful act.

[23] Erskine J. in *Borradaile* v. *Hunter* (1843) 5 M. & G. 639, 658; Lord Atkin in *Beresford* v. *Royal* [1938] A.C. 586, 595. Where the assured, having insured his own life, wilfully takes it, that is "misconduct" for this purpose, although by the Suicide Act 1961, s.1, he commits no crime, as where he wilfully burns a chattel which he has insured against fire.

insane the insurers will be liable,[24] apart from any express exception in the policy on the matter.

16–09 Express term

There is nothing, however, to prevent the insurers from expressing the policy to cover even sane suicide by the assured, on the one hand, or from excepting all suicide, sane or insane, from the risk on the other,[25] provided they use apt words to do so. In the former case innocent assignees from the assured before his death will be entitled to recover,[26] and also assignees or others deriving title through him after his death; this follows from the Suicide Act 1961, s.1, which has abrogated the rule of law whereby it was a crime for a person to commit suicide. But no one can recover who assisted in the suicide, or otherwise committed the serious crime introduced by section 2 of the Act of 1961 (of assisting suicide by providing lethal drugs) that would be making a profit from his own crime.

Generally no suicide exception clause is inserted in life policies. If it does appear it is as a result of investigation revealing that the life assured's family has a history of suicide, or the life assured himself seems otherwise likely to take his own life. If an investigation is unfavourable to the assured on this point, he is usually given an option: he can either accept the policy with the exception clause, or pay a higher premium and have the clause excluded. When a suicide exception clause is inserted, there is a tendency for it to be limited so as to apply only for one or two years from the date of the policy. If the suicide clause does operate and the life assured take his own life whilst insane, the insurers might make an *ex gratia* return of premiums.

Although suicide is no longer a crime, the implied term that the assured is not entitled to recover where the loss is caused by his wilful misconduct is still applicable to life policies. Thus where an own-life policy is silent, sane suicide by the assured precludes recovery by his personal representatives. Insane suicide is not wilful, and the moneys are therefore payable.

16–10 Express exceptions

Exceptions of "*suicide*," or of death by the assured's "*own hands*," have been construed, in effect, to cover all cases of intentional self-destruction,[27] where the assured knew the nature of his act and the natural consequence of what he was doing.[28] Thus, like the implied exception of sane suicide, "suicide" so expressed does not cover cases in which the assured did not know what he was doing, for in such cases his act cannot be said to have been intentional, and his representatives will be entitled to recover. But, unlike the implied exception, such words will cover cir-

---

[24] *Horn* v. *Anglo-Australian Life* (1861) 30 L.J.Ch. 511.

[25] *Horn* v. *Anglo-Australian Life* (1861) 30 L.J.Ch. 511; see *White* v. *British Empire Mutual Life* (1868) L.R. 7 Eq. 394 and *Ellinger* v. *Mutual Life of New York* [1905] K.B. 31 for such exceptions.

[26] *Beresford* v. *Royal* [1938] A.C. 586, *per* Lord Atkin.

[27] *Borradaile* v. *Hunter* (1843) 5 Man. & G. 639; *Clift* v. *Schwabe* (1846) 3 C.B. 437; *Dufaur* v. *Professional Life* (1858) 25 Beav. 599; *Rowett, Leakey & Co.* v. *Scottish Provident* [1927] 1 Ch. 55.

[28] Maule J. in *Borradaile* v. *Hunter* (1843) 5 Man. & G. 639 at p. 654; Patteson J. in *Clift* v. *Schwabe* (1846) 3 C.B. 437 at p. 465; *Stormont* v. *Waterloo Life* (1858) 1 F. & F. 22.

cumstances such as those in *Borradaile* v. *Hunter*,[29] where the assured voluntarily threw himself into the Thames, knowing that he would destroy his life, but without being able at the time to judge between right and wrong. His act was held to amount to death by his own hands, within the meaning of the policy, although it did not amount to the (now abolished) crime of self-murder owing to his temporary moral insanity.

Burden of proof   16–11
The burden of proving that a loss falls within an excepted peril always falls upon the insurers,[30] and the exception of "suicide" in a life policy falls within this rule.[31] Thus where the only evidence before the Industrial Assurance Commissioner was a finding of an inquest of "suicide while temporarily of unsound mind" he held that the assured's death did not fall within the exception of death "by his or her own act."[32] Where sane suicide used to be alleged the presumption against crime laid a specially heavy burden of proof upon the insurers.[33] Since, however, the test has now veered from criminality to gravity, it is suggested that a similar approach would be used notwithstanding section 1 of the Act of 1961. Suicide remains a grave matter in the eye of the law, as is shown by section 2 of the Act.

Surrender of policy on suicide   16–12
Policies sometimes provide that in cases of suicide during insanity the policy shall not be paid in full, but treated as surrendered, and that its surrender value shall be paid to the deceased's representatives. By this means substantial justice is done, since the insurer avoids having his risk increased by the acceleration of death by suicide and the representatives of the assured are not deprived of the benefit of the policy so far as it has already been earned by the payment of premiums.

3. INSURABLE INTEREST

Life Assurance Act 1774   16–13
As is stated above,[34] in order that a life policy may be valid, the person taking out the policy must, by section 1 of this Act, have an insurable interest in the life insured, at the time of taking out the policy.[35] Moreover, by section 3 of this Act "no greater sum shall be recovered or received from the insurer or insurers, than the amount or value of the interest of the insured in such life." Thus if the assured has any interest at the time of taking out the policy it will be a valid one, but he will only be able to enforce it against the insurers to the extent of that interest. But if, his interest being already covered to its full extent by one policy, he takes out a second policy in respect of the same interest, the second

---

[29] See n. 27, *supra.*
[30] See § 4–43, *supra.*
[31] *Keeling* v. *Pearl Assurance* (1923) 129 L.T. 573.
[32] *Re Ives and Liverpool Victoria Friendly Society* [1929] 1 A.C. 14.
[33] *Harvey* v. *Ocean Accident* [1905] 2 Ir.R. 1; but see *supra*, § 4–44.
[34] See § 3–21, *supra.*
[35] *Dalby* v. *India & London Life* (1854) 15 C.B. 365.

policy will, apparently, be wholly void on the ground that he has no insurable interest left to support it.[36]

Provided the assured has an interest at the time of taking out the policy, section 3 does not prevent him from recovering if he should lose that interest before the policy matures, as where a creditor insures the life of his debtor and is paid before his death,[37] or where the debt becomes statute-barred before the life drops,[38] or where a company reinsures a life policy and before the life drops the original policy is surrendered.[39]

16–14 Insurable interest in own life

A person's insurable interest in his own life is considered to be sufficient to enable his personal representatives to recover whatever sum he may have insured it for, and this is so even if the insurance is for a portion only of his life.[40] There is nothing to prevent a person from insuring his own life for his own benefit as often as he pleases, even though he intends, when insuring, to assign the policy to another person.[41]

16–15 Fraudulent policies

But where the assured merely lends his name to another, that other paying the premium and taking the benefit of the policy, the insurance may be a fraudulent evasion of section 2 of the Life Assurance Act, and illegal.[42] The test is whether the insurance was effected by the party nominally insured at the instance of, and for the benefit of, another without interest who was to pay the premiums, in pursuance of an arrangement between them under which that other was immediately to secure the sole benefit of it, by assignment, bequest or otherwise.[43] Thus, where the assured sold for £5 a policy on his own life for £500, which he had not then taken out, the policy was held to be illegal under the Act.[44] But it has been held on the other hand that an insurance company lending money may validly agree with the borrower that he shall insure his life to a greater amount than the debt, and assign the policy to the company as security.[45]

16–16 Interest in life of another

A creditor has an insurable interest in the life of his debtor,[46] and can recover the full extent of the debt, and in general any sort of contractual or other relationship between two persons which gives one the legal right to pecuniary benefit from the other, gives him an insurable interest, *pro tanto*, in that other's life.

---

[36] *Simcock* v. *Scottish Imperial Insurance* (1902) 10 S.L.T. 286; see also *Hebdon* v. *West* (1863) 3 B. & S. 579.
[37] *Law* v. *London Indisputable Life* (1855) 1 K. & J. 223.
[38] *Garner* v. *Moore* (1855) 3 Drew. 277.
[39] *Dalby* v. *India & London Life* (1854) 15 C.B. 365.
[40] *Wainewright* v. *Bland* (1835) 1 Moo. & Rob. 481; (1836) 1 M. & W. 32.
[41] Pollock B. in *M'Farlane* v. *Royal London Friendly Society* (1886) 2 T.L.R. 755.
[42] See n. 40, *supra*.
[43] *Shilling* v. *Accidental Death* (1857) 27 L.J.Ex. 16; (1858) 1 F. & F. 116.
[44] *Macdonald* v. *National Mutual Life of Australasia* (1906) 14 S.L.T. 173, 249.
[45] *Downes* v. *Green* (1844) 12 M. & W. 481.
[46] See § 3–19, *supra*.

Master and servant   16–17

Thus a servant has an insurable interest in the life of his employer to the extent of any wages or salary to which he is entitled under a contract of service,[47] and an employer similarly has an interest in the life of his servant.[48] But the extent of such an interest is strictly limited by the contract of service; thus where the employment may be terminated by notice, though the expectation is that the relationship will last for a lifetime, the utmost extent of the employer's insurable interest is the value to him of the length of the notice period.[49]

Partners   16–18

Similarly partners have an insurable interest in each other's lives, and are in the practice of insuring against the loss likely to arise on the death of a co-partner by the withdrawal of his capital from the partnership.[50]

Husband and wife   16–19

A wife has an insurable interest in the life of her husband which is presumed in every case,[51] and a husband has similarly, as such, an insurable interest in the life of his wife.[52] The reciprocal rights and duties created by the marriage tie are alone sufficient to support both interests,[53] irrespective of their pecuniary relationship.[54] Thus evidence to show that either husband or wife stands to gain by the death of the other is inadmissible in rebuttal of this presumption, and the interest of one spouse in the life of the other is as unlimited as the interest of a man in his own life.[55] It is an interest which has been recognised by statute.[56]

Relatives   16–20

The general rule relating to relatives is that where one relative, who effects an insurance on the life of another, is so related to that other as to have against him a claim for support enforceable by law, the relationship gives an insurable interest. But natural love and affection arising out of kinship, however close, does not by itself do so; and unless there is some pecuniary interest enforceable by law, one relative cannot validly insure the life of another. Thus, a father has been held in England to have no insurable interest in the life of his son as such,[57] however much he may have expended on his education,[58] unless he has a pecuniary interest in it,[59] although it has been held otherwise in Scotland where a parent has, by Scottish law, the right to claim aliment from his children.[60] Similarly an adult son was held to have no insurable interest

---

[47] *Hebdon* v. *West* (1863) 3 B. & S. 579; *Turnbull* v. *Scottish Provident* (1876) 34 S.L.R. 146.
[48] *Simcock* v. *Scottish Imperial Insurance* (1902) 10 S.L.T. 286.
[49] *Ibid. per* Lord Pearson at p. 288.
[50] Vaughan Williams L.J. in *Griffiths* v. *Fleming* [1909] 1 K.B. 805, 815.
[51] Lord Kenyon in *Reed* v. *Royal Exchange* (1796) Peake Add.Cas. 70.
[52] *Griffiths* v. *Fleming* [1909] 1 K.B. 805, 819–821, *per* Kennedy L.J., and at pp. 814–817, *per* Vaughan Williams L.J.
[53] Manning J. in *Ronbach* v. *Piedmont Life* (1883) 48 Am.Rep. 239.
[54] Kennedy L.J. in *Griffiths* v. *Fleming* [1909] 1 K.B. 805, 820–823.
[55] See n. 49.
[56] *I.e.* the Married Women's Property Acts; see §§ 16–80 *et seq., infra.*
[57] *Halford* v. *Kymer* (1830) 10 B. & C. 724; *Att.-Gen.* v. *Murray* [1904] 1 K.B. 165.
[58] *Worthington* v. *Curtis* (1876) 1 Ch.D. 419, 423, *per* Mellish L.J.
[59] *Law* v. *London Indisputable Life* (1855) 1 K. & J. 223.
[60] *Carmichael's Case*, 1919 S.C. 636, 648, *per* Lord Salvesen.

in the life of his pauper father whom he supported,[61] and a son was held to have no interest in the life of his mother, whom he supported, even although she in fact performed the duties of housekeeper for him.[62] But an infant child entitled to be supported by his parents[63] would no doubt have an insurable interest in the life of both of them.

16–21   In *Barnes* v. *London, Edinburgh and Glasgow Life*[64] the plaintiff had taken out a life policy on a child. This child was her stepsister and she had promised its mother to maintain it. It was held that she had an insurable interest in the life of the child "so far as to secure the repayment of the expenses incurred by her."[65] In so far as this case implies that a mere moral obligation to repay one's benefactor can support an insurance it has been criticised,[66] and would not on principle appear correctly to represent the law.[67] The true rule appears to be that support given to a dependant does not give an insurable interest in his life unless it can be shown that he was liable to repay the money expended on him.[68]

16–22 Funeral expenses

It has been debated how far one has an insurable interest on the life of another on account of the expenses of burying him. Since every householder in whose house a dead body lies is bound by common law to inter the body decently according to Christian rites,[69] it would seem to follow that he has an insurable interest, *pro tanto*, in the lives of those living with him.[70] Industrial societies had for many years been in the practice of insuring parents against the funeral expenses of their children before the practice was, prior to its abolition, recognised by statute.[71]

16–23 Illegitimate child

The mother of an illegitimate child has the same interest in the life of her child,[72] and the illegitimate child has the same interest in the life of its mother,[73] as they would have had had the child been born in wedlock.

---

[61] *Shilling* v. *Accidental Death* (1858) 1 F. & F. 116; see also *Howard* v. *Refuge* (1886) 54 L.T. 644, 646; *Elson* v. *Crookes* (1911) 106 L.T. 462.
[62] *Harse* v. *Pearl Life* [1903] 2 K.B. 92. See also *Goldstein* v. *Salvation Army* [1917] 2 K.B. 291. But insurance might be made, up to £30, on the lives of parents by Sched. I. para. (2)(*d*), to Friendly Societies Act 1974, and s.72 thereof.
[63] See A. L. Smith J. in *Barnes* v. *London, Edinburgh & Glasgow Life* [1892] 1 Q.B. 864, 866.
[64] [1892] 1 Q.B. 864.
[65] *Ibid. per* Lord Coleridge C.J. at pp. 865, 866.
[66] See *per* Lord Alverstone C.J. in *Harse* v. *Pearl* [1903] 2 K.B. 92, 96; *per* Kennedy L.J. in *Griffiths* v. *Fleming* [1909] 1 K.B. 805, 819.
[67] See, for instance, Lord Eldon in *Lucena* v. *Craufurd*, (1806) 2 B. P. N.R. 269.
[68] See *Anctil* v. *Manufacturers' Life* [1899] A.C. 604 (P.C.); *Goldstein* v. *Salvation Army* [1917] 2 K.B 291, 295, *per* Rowlatt J.
[69] *R.* v. *Stewart* (1840) 12 Ad. & El. 773.
[70] Phillimore L.J. in *Tofts* v. *Pearl* [1915] 1 K.B. 189, 194.
[71] Shearman J. in *Hatley* v. *Liverpool Victoria Friendly Society* (1918) 88 L.J.K.B. 237, 239, 240. The payment of funeral expenses of the husband, wife or *child* of a member was recognised by s.1 of the Friendly Societies Act 1896 as one of the purposes of a friendly society, and s.3 of the Industrial Assurance Act 1923 authorised policies issued by collecting societies and industrial assurance companies to cover the funeral expenses of a parent, *child*, grandparent, grandchild, brother or sister. Insurance of funeral expenses under the above provisions was prohibited by s.1 of the Industrial Assurance and Friendly Societies Act 1948, and insurance under the Act of the life of a child under 10 was also prohibited: s.6(1).
[72] *Morris* v. *Britannic* [1931] 2 K.B. 125.
[73] *Re Swainbank and Co-operative Insurance* [1953] 1 A.C. 29.

Foster child   **16–24**
By section 9 of the Children Act 1958, a person undertaking for reward the nursing and maintenance of a child under the age of nine apart from its parents or having no parents is expressly "deemed to have no interest in the life of the child for the purposes of the Life Assurance Act 1774," and by the same section insurance by such a person on the life of such child is a criminal offence.

4. INQUIRIES MADE BY INSURERS

Health of insured   **16–25**
Life insurance is peculiar in that the assured is often ignorant as to the fact most material in assessing the premium—the state of his own health. Though he may have a general idea as to his own physical well-being, he may well be unaware of an incipient but deadly disease within his system that a doctor might have diagnosed. A man might not even know, it has been held, that he has gout.[74] And if an assured may be ignorant as to his own health, one who takes out a policy on the life of another is even less in a position to inform the insurers accurately as to the state of that other's health. The rule is, warranties apart, that the insurers may avoid the policy if the assured knowingly misrepresents his state of health, or that of the life insured.[75] Similarly he is bound to disclose no more than he actually knows,[76] though he is bound to disclose a serious disease of which he is aware.[77]

Insurance companies therefore put upon applicants for life insurance **16–26** the responsibility of disclosing the true state of their health or that of the life assured by asking them questions in the proposal on this matter, and by giving the assured's answers to them the force of warranties by means of a declaration in the proposal and a reference to it in the policy.[78] By the employment of such a scheme the assured is made responsible for the absolute truth of his answers,[79] irrespective of their materiality[80]; if they are not true, they will afford the insurers a ground for repudiating liability on the policy, even though he gave them innocently. Courts the world over, however, are slow to construe such answers as stating anything more than the belief of the assured,[81] but unless the questions are so framed as to require him to answer as to his own knowledge only, he

---

[74] *Fowkes* v. *Manchester and London Life* (1863) 3 B. & S. 917.
[75] See §§ 5–20 *et seq.*, *supra.*
[76] *Swete* v. *Fairlie* (1833) 6 C. & P. 1; Lord Campbell in *Wheelton* v. *Hardisty* (1857) 8 E. & B. 232, 269, 271–273; *Joel* v. *Law Union* [1908] 2 K.B. 863. See § 5–07, *supra.*
[77] *British Equitable Ins. Co.* v. *Musgrave* (1887) 3 T.L.R. 630. See also *Godfrey* v. *Britannic Ass. Co.* [1963] 2 Lloyd's Rep. 515.
[78] See § 6–18, *supra.*
[79] Blackburn J. in *Macdonald* v. *Law Union* (1874) L.R. 9 Q.B. 328, 332, 333; *Hutton* v. *Waterloo Life* (1859) 1 F. & F. 735.
[80] *Pawson* v. *Watson* (1778) 2 Cowp. 785.
[81] Burton J. in *Sceales* v. *Scanlan* (1843) 6 Ir.L.R. 367, 401; Cockburn C.J. in *Fowkes* v. *Manchester and London Life* (1863) 3 B. & S. 917, 925, 926; *Life Association of Scotland* v. *Forster* (1873) 11 M. (Ct. of Sess.) 351; *Thomson* v. *Weems* (1884) 9 App.Cas. 671; *Delahaye* v. *British Empire Mutual* (1897) 13 T.L.R. 245; *Fidelity Mutual Life* v. *Jeffords* (1901) 107 Fed.Rep. 402, 408, 409 (Georgia, U.S.A.). But see *National Mutual of Australasia* v. *Smallfield* [1922] N.Z.L.R. 1074; *Metropolitan Life* v. *Burno* (1941) 309 Mass. 7.

is advised to qualify his answers in this respect.[82] Where the assured warrants his answers to questions to be put to him in the future by the company's medical examiner to be true, this binds him to do no more than tell the truth to the best of his knowledge, and will be construed accordingly.[83] In fact it may be said in general that, unless the insurers put the matter beyond all doubt by using the clearest language in their policies, it is the accuracy—to the assured's knowledge—and not the truth of his answers that the assured warrants in life insurance.[84] And section 9 of the Industrial Assurance and Friendly Societies Act 1948 renders such warranties ineffective in the case of industrial assurance policies.

16–27 Past illnesses and medical attendance

Questions as to past illnesses and medical attendance are, however, in a different position from questions as to present state of health, since from their nature the insurers can expect the answers to be true in fact, and not mere matters of belief.[85] But even such questions have been construed to have a limited meaning.[86] Thus a question as to how long it was since the assured had been "attended" by a doctor has been construed not to include attendance for mere minor ailments[87]; and the question, "What medical men have you consulted?" has been construed not to extend to consultations during early childhood.[88] Similarly, questions as to the medical history of the assured's relatives will be given a reasonable and limited meaning.[89]

16–28   The principle upon which such decisions rest was clearly enunciated by the Privy Council in *Condogianis* v. *Guardian*[90]:

> "In a contract of insurance it is a weighty fact that the questions are framed by the insurer, and that if an answer is obtained to such a question which is upon a fair construction a true answer, it is not open to the insuring company to maintain that the question was put in a sense different from or more comprehensive than the proponents' answer covered. Where an ambiguity exists, the contract must stand if an answer has been made to the question on a fair and reasonable construction of that question. Otherwise the ambiguity would be a trap against which the insured would be protected by courts of law." Evasive answers, on the other hand, are as objectionable as ambiguous questions, and the assured will not be allowed to profit by them.[91]

16–29   English decisions on the construction of questions and answers in life insurance proposals are rare, owing to the arbitration clause contained in our policies although in recent years insurers have not sought to rely

---

[82] See *Wheelton* v. *Hardisty, supra*, at pp. 271–273, *per* Lord Campbell.
[83] *Delahaye* v. *British Empire Mutual Life* (1897) 13 T.L.R. 245.
[84] Fletcher Moulton L.J. in *Joel* v. *Law Union* [1908] 2 K.B. 863 at p. 884.
[85] *Huckman* v. *Fernie* (1838) 3 M. & W. 505; *Metropolitan Life* v. *Madden* (1941) 117 Fed.Rep. 446.
[86] Note, however, in *Kumar* v. *Life Ass. Co. of India* [1974] 1 Lloyd's Rep. 147. The deceased had had a Caesarian operation, consulted a doctor and was prescribed an oral contraceptive. She had taken out a life policy, declaring that she had not consulted a medical practitioner and had not had an operation. Kerr J. *held*, in an action on the policy, that it could be avoided. *Quaere*, whether a Caesarian is usually thought of as an operation, or getting "the pill" as "*consulting*" a "medical practitioner."
[87] *Connecticut Mutual* v. *Moore* (1881) 6 App.Cas. 644 (P.C.).
[88] *Joel* v. *Law Union* [1908] 2 K.B. 863.
[89] *Ibid*. See Fletcher Moulton L.J. at p. 891.
[90] [1921] 2 A.C. 125, 130.
[91] See §5–27, *supra*.

upon arbitration clauses in life and "consumer" policies. American and Commonwealth decisions are useful as a guide to the meaning of policies, but it must not be overlooked, as was stated in an Australian judgment,[92] that, generally speaking, American cases are more favourable to the assured than English cases, at all events, on matters of construction. Thus it has been held that questions as to past illnesses include diseases of the mind,[93] but not minor ailments.[94] "Afflections of the liver" do not include every disorder of that organ,[95] and "afflicted with fits" does not include a fit caused by an accident.[96] But the question "Have you ever had fits?" has a wider significance.[97] "Spitting of blood" means the disorder so called, but one act of spitting blood should be stated to the insurers.[98] A disorder is not one "tending to shorten life" simply from the circumstance that the assured dies from it.[99] Good health means reasonably good health.[1] A warranty of good health can "never mean that a man has not in him the seeds of some disorder. We are all born with the seeds of mortality in us."[2] But where a man suffering from tuberculosis, of which his mother, brother and sister had died, stated that he was in good health, the policy was held voidable.[3] "Paralysis" has been held to mean the shock of paralysis, and not local paralysis resulting in lameness caused by a fall.[4] Near-sightedness has been held not to be a bodily infirmity.[5]

The assured's "usual" medical attendant is not necessarily his last one,[6] but if he denies that he has a doctor, though one has attended him recently, he is precluded from recovering on his policy.[7]

Temperate habits   16–30

Questions are often asked as to the temperate habits of the assured.[8] No satisfactory judicial definition of "intemperance" has been given, but it has been held not to be limited to such intemperance as would impair the general health of the assured.[9] It is essentially a matter of degree as to what constitutes intemperance.[10] In an insurance policy it means habitual, immoderate indulgence in alcohol, or addiction to it,

---

[92] *Dalgety* v. *Australian Mutual* [1908] V.L.R. 481.
[93] *Connecticut Mutual* v. *Akens* 150 U.S. 468 (1893).
[94] *Connecticut Mutual* v. *Moore* (1881) 6 App.Cas. 644, 648.
[95] *Connecticut Mutual* v. *Union Trust Co.* 112 U.S. 250 (1884).
[96] *Chattock* v. *Shawe* (1835) 1 M. & R. 498; *Shilling* v. *Accidental Death* (1857) 27 L.J.Ex. 16; (1858) 1 F. & F. 116.
[97] *Aetna Life* v. *France* (1876) 94 U.S. 561.
[98] *Geach* v. *Ingall* (1845) 14 M. & W. 95.
[99] *Watson* v. *Mainwaring* (1813) 4 Taunt. 763.
[1] See *Yorke* v. *Yorkshire Insurance* [1918] 1 K.B. 662, 668–669 and *National Mutual* v. *Smallfield* [1922] N.Z.L.R. 1074.
[2] *Per* Lord Mansfield in *Willis* v. *Poole* (1780) 2 Park (8th ed.) 935.
[3] *Davian* v. *Canadian Order of Foresters* (1923) 61 Que.S.C. 492.
[4] *Cruikshank* v. *Northern Accident* (1895) 23 R.(Ct. of Sess.) 147.
[5] *Cotten* v. *Fidelity & Casualty Co.* (1890) 41 Fed.Rep. 506.
[6] *Huckman* v. *Fernie* (1838) 3 M. & W. 505; *Maynard* v. *Rhode* (1824) 1 C. & P. 360; *Scanlan* v. *Sceales* (1849) 13 Ir.L.R. 71; but see *Everett* v. *Desborough* (1829) 5 Bing. 503.
[7] *Palmer* v. *Hawes* (1841) Ellis, Ins. 131. See *Connecticut Mutual* v. *Moore* (1881) 6 App.Cas. 644; *British Equitable Ins. Co.* v. *Musgrave* (1887) 3 T.L.R. 630.
[8] *Hutton* v. *Waterloo Life* (1859) 1 F. & F. 735.
[9] Coleridge J. in *Southcombe* v. *Merriman* (1842) Car. & M. 286, 287.
[10] See *Scottish Widows' Fund* v. *Buist* (1876) 3 R. (Ct. of Sess.) 1078; *Scottish Equitable* v. *Buist* (1877) 4 R. (Ct. of Sess.) 1076, 1078, *per* Lord Young; *Thomson* v. *Weems* (1884) 9 App.Cas. 671— compare Lord Blackburn at p. 685 with Lord Watson at p. 696 and Lord Fitzgerald at pp. 697–698.

not immoderate consumption on an isolated occasion.[11] Intemperance implies intemperance in regard to alcohol, and not to the use of veronal or other soporific or narcotic drugs.[12] The exemption of death of or injury to the assured while "under the influences of liquor" sometimes to be found in accident policies raises a similar problem.[13] To fall within it "the balance of a man's mind or the intelligent exercise of his faculties"[14] must be disturbed.

16–31 Residence and occupation

In the absence of a warranty the failure by the assured to disclose his domicile[15] or occupation[16] is not normally fatal, though such omissions might be so were the occupation of the assured a particularly dangerous one, or had he been for a long period in an unhealthy climate. The term "residence" in a proposal for insurance means the place where the proposer is living or residing at the time of making the proposal, and not where he has been residing before or where he is going to reside afterwards. It is a matter of fact whether the assured's imprisonment is material and therefore to be disclosed.[17]

16–32 Age

The age of the assured is obviously material. If he misstates it a reasonable insurer will make a corresponding adjustment of the sum assured instead of avoiding the policy, but if he does neither and accepts further premiums after discovering the truth he is liable on the policy to the full extent.[18]

16–33 Threats against assured's life

It has been held in American cases that threats against the life of the assured need not generally be disclosed.[19] But it would appear, on an analogy with incendiarism cases,[20] that such threats would be material if he reasonably supposed they might be carried out, and that in that case he would be obliged to disclose them on taking out life insurance.

5. ASSIGNMENT OF LIFE POLICIES

16–34 Since practically all the decided cases on the assignment of insurance policies have been decisions on life policies and the matter is one of some difficulty, detailed consideration of it has been reserved for this

---

[11] *Ridley* v. *Bradford Ins.* [1971] R.T.R. 61. Thus, for the purpose of an exclusion clause in a private motor car insurance policy, in a case where there was 145 mg. of alcohol in 100 ml. of blood in a man of moderate drinking habits who died in a road accident, this could not be described as "intemperance."

[12] *Yorke* v. *Yorkshire Insurance* [1918] 1 K.B. 662, 666.

[13] See § 17–24, *infra.*

[14] *Mair* v. *Railway Passengers' Assurance* (1877) 37 L.T. 356; applied in *Louden* v. *British Merchants Ins.* [1961] 1 W.L.R. 798.

[15] *Grogan* v. *London and Manchester Industrial Assurance* (1855) 2 T.L.R. 75.

[16] *Lindenau* v. *Desborough* (1828) 8 B. & C. 586, 592. *Contra McNealy* v. *Pennine* [1978] 2 Lloyd's Rep. 18.

[17] *Huguenin* v. *Rayley* (1815) 6 Taunt. 186.

[18] *Hemmings* v. *Sceptre Life* [1905] 1 Ch. 365.

[19] *Connecticut Mutual* v. *McWhirter* 73 Fed.Rep. 444 (1896); *Penn Mutual Life* v. *Mechanics' Savings Bank* (1896) 72 Fed.Rep. 413.

[20] See § 18–20, *infra.*

chapter, but the fundamental principles of assignment are common to all policies.

A. Methods of assigning policies

(1) Legal assignments

(i) *Under the Policies of Assurance Act 1867.* This Act applies only to **16–35** life policies.[21] Assignments under this Act may be made either by indorsement on the policy, or by a separate instrument, in the form scheduled to the act, and this indorsement or instrument must be duly stamped.[22]

The assignee will have no right to sue the assurance company unless he gives them written notice of the assignment at their principal place of business,[23] which they are bound to specify in the policy.[24] The date on which such notice is received regulates the priority of claims under more than one assignment.[25] If the assignee fails to give such notice, a payment made by the company in good faith will be valid against him.[26]

(ii) *Under the Law of Property Act 1925, s.136.* This section applies **16–36** only to absolute assignments not purporting to be by way of charge only, and is in this respect narrower than the 1867 Act. An assignment subject to a trust in favour of the assignor is an absolute one.[27] Furthermore the section applies to all things in action capable of assignment, and would therefore include policies of assurance.

The essentials are:

(a) the assignment must be in writing under the hand of the assignor, *and*

(b) express notice in writing must be given to the debtor, *i.e.* to the insurers in the case of an insurance policy, but it does not matter if it is not given to them until after the death of the assured.[28]

Such an assignment, like one under the Act of 1867,[29] gives the assignee the legal right to sue the insurers in his own name without joining the assignee, and gives the insurers the power to discharge their liability by paying the assignee.

Form and stamp. A legal mortgage of a life policy, unless it is covered **16–37** by section 136 of the Law of Property Act 1925, must be in the form scheduled to the Policies of Assurance Act 1867. It should be by deed if the mortgagee wishes to have the advantage of the power of sale conferred by section 101 of the Law of Property Act 1925.

The assignee will have no right to sue on the assignment unless it is duly stamped,[30] and the insurer will be liable to penalties if he makes a

---

[21] As defined in s.7: see § 16–03, *supra.*
[22] s.5 of 1867 Act.
[23] *Ibid.* s.3.
[24] *Ibid.* s.4.
[25] *Ibid.* s.3.
[26] *Ibid.* n. 25.
[27] *Burlinson* v. *Hall* (1884) 12 Q.B.D. 347.
[28] *Walker* v. *Bradford Old Bank* (1884) 12 Q.B.D. 511.
[29] s.1.
[30] Stamp Act 1891, s.118(1).

payment on an assignment which is insufficiently stamped.[31] A bank lending money on the security of an assignment, and which, subsequent to the assignment, lends money in excess of the amount in respect of which the assignment was originally stamped, will be able to recover no more than that amount from the insurers, unless the assignment has been stamped with a further duty.[32]

16–38 (2) Equitable assignments

The statutes did nothing to take away the efficacy of equitable assignments.[33] They simply gave the assignee a more convenient remedy, and no alteration in the rights of the parties was contemplated.[34] Unless the assignor's interest in the policy is an equitable one only, no special form is required to constitute a valid equitable assignment. It may even be effected by word of mouth.[35] But an assignment of an equitable interest must be in writing signed by the assignor or his agent.[36] Such interests include that of an assignee under a previous equitable assignment and also that of a beneficiary for whom a policy is held on trust.

Equitable assignments may be made:

16–39 (i) *By delivery of the policy*.[37] This is provided an intention to assign may be inferred from the surrounding circumstances.[38]

The most common example of such an assignment is the deposit of a policy with a bank, or other creditor, by his debtor with the intention of giving him an equitable charge over it. The deposit of a policy by a borrower with his lender, without a word, written or spoken, on either side thus operates as an equitable mortgage of the policy.[39]

It will operate, moreover, not only as security for the repayment of any loan already advanced,[40] but also for any subsequent advances made on the same security,[41] and the court will presume that any subsequent advances were so made.[42] Such a deposit may, however, if such an intention is shown, give the lender no more than a lien on the policy.[43]

So also a valid equitable assignment by way of gift may be made by delivery of the policy to a donee,[44] provided the evidence shows that such an assignment was intended. But if the intention is merely to give the donee the authority, revocable during the donor's life, to receive the policy moneys after his death, such delivery will not even constitute an

---

[31] *Ibid.* subs. (2).
[32] *Re Waterhouse's Policy* [1937] Ch. 415.
[33] Lord Macnaghten in *Brandt's* v. *Dunlop* [1905] A.C. 454, 461.
[34] Lord Brammwell in *Pellas* v. *Neptune Marine* (1879) 5 C.P.C. 34.
[35] *Brandt's* v. *Dunlop* [1905] A.C. 454.
[36] Law of Property Act 1925, s.53(1)(c).
[37] *Dufaur* v. *Professional Life* (1858) 25 Beav. 599.
[38] *Chapman* v. *Chapman* (1851) 13 Beav. 308.
[39] *Per* Lord Eldon in *Ex p. Kensington* (1813) 2 V. & B. 79, 83; *Row* v. *Dawson* (1749) 1 Ves.Sen. 331; *Gurnell* v. *Gardner* (1863) 4 Giff. 626; *Green* v. *Ingham* (1867) L.R. 2 C.P. 525; *Shaw* v. *Foster* (1872) L.R. 5 H.L. 321.
[40] *Glaholme* v. *Rowntree* (1837) 6 A. & E. 710; *Ferris* v. *Mullins* (1854) 2 Sm. & Giff. 378; *Chowne* v. *Baylis* (1862) 31 Beav. 351; *Harrold* v. *Plenty* [1901] 2 Ch. 314.
[41] *Re Knight ex p. Langston* (1810) 17 Vest. 227.
[42] *Maugham* v. *Ridley* (1863) 8 L.T. 309, *per* Page-Wood V.-C.
[43] *Gibson* v. *Overbury* (1841) 7 M. & W. 555; *Chapman* v. *Chapman* (1851) 13 Beav. 308, 311.
[44] *Rummens* v. *Hare* (1876) 1 Ex.D. 169.

equitable assignment.[45] A court will not readily presume that an assignment is intended where the delivery is not for value. Thus the handing of a policy by a husband to his wife for her benefit on condition that she paid the premiums has been held to give her no interest in it.[46]

In general, bare physical possession of the policy itself, that is to say, the piece of paper upon which it is written, will not give the holder any rights under it unless there is some evidence of surrounding circumstances from which an assignment can be inferred.[47] Banks, for instance, frequently accept life policies for safe keeping, and such a deposit would not, by itself, operate as an assignment even if the owner subsequently borrowed money from the bank in question.

(ii) *By an agreement to assign.* A promise to assign a policy will not **16–40** operate as a statutory assignment,[48] but such a promise, made for a valuable consideration, will operate as a valid equitable assignment.[49] A decree of specific performance can be obtained in respect of such a promise,[50] although such a decree will only be necessary if the promise was to execute a legal assignment. In all cases the courts will regard the agreement as itself constituting a valid equitable assignment.[51]

A bare voluntary promise,[52] on the other hand, to make a gift of a policy, passes no interest, either in law or equity to the promisee,[53] for equity will never perfect an imperfect gift.[54]

Donatio mortis causa. There is one notable exception to this rule. If the owner of a policy, believing himself to be on the point of death, hands it to another, telling him at the same time that if he dies the policy is to be his, then, although the legal title will pass on the policy-holder's death to his personal representatives, it will be their duty to collect the money from the insurers and to hold it on trust for the person to whom the policy was delivered,[55] notwithstanding that it was always within the power of the giver to recall the gift and get back the policy during his lifetime.

Promise under seal. Furthermore, if a promise to assign is made under seal, the promisee will be entitled to damages if the policy is not duly assigned to him, even if the promise was a voluntary one.[56]

A bare intention to take out[57] or to assign a policy,[58] even although

---

[45] *Re Williams* [1919] W.C. & Ins.Rep. 122.
[46] *Howes* v. *Prudential* (1883) 49 L.T. 133.
[47] *Chapman* v. *Chapman* (1851) 13 Beav. 308; *Carter* v. *Wake* (1877) 4 Ch.D. 605. See also *Norris* v. *Wilkinson* (1806) 12 Ves. 192, and *Gibson* v. *Overbury* (1841) 7 M. & W. 555.
[48] *Spencer* v. *Clarke* (1878) 9 Ch.D. 137.
[49] *Thomas* v. *Harris* [1947] 1 All E.R. 444.
[50] *Ashley* v. *Ashley* (1829) 3 Sim. 149; *Godsal* v. *Webb* (1838) 2 Keen 99; *Jeston* v. *Key* (1871) L.R. 6 Ch. 610.
[51] *Spencer* v. *Clarke, supra*; *Re Moore* (1878) 8 Ch.D. 519.
[52] Romilly M.R. in *Pearson* v. *Amicable Assurance* (1859) 27 Beav. 229, 232.
[53] *Vavasseur* v. *Vavasseur* (1909) 25 T.L.R. 250.
[54] Turner L.J. in *Milroy* v. *Lord* (1862) 4 De G.F. & J. 264, 274.
[55] *Witt* v. *Amis* (1861) 1 B. & S. 109; *Amis* v. *Witt* (1863) 33 Beav. 619.
[56] *Ward* v. *Audland* (1846) 16 M. & W. 862; *Cox* v. *Barnard* (1850) 8 Hare 310.
[57] *Freme* v. *Brade* (1858) 2 De G. & J. 582.
[58] *Crossley* v. *City of Glasgow Life* (1876) 4 Ch.D. 421.

the proposed beneficiary is informed, can, of course, give him no rights whatever under it.[59]

16-41   (iii) *By a memorandum in writing.*[60] Like assignment by delivery, and unlike a mere agreement to assign, even an assignment by way of gift may be made in this way, and will be enforceable in equity even if it does not amount to a statutory assignment.

16-42   *Notice unnecessary.* There is no need for notice to be given to the insurers to give the assignee a good equitable title as against the assignor.[61] It follows that an assignment which fails under the Acts for lack of notice may nevertheless be good in equity.

16-43   *Assignments void for mistake.* While the right to sue the insurers in respect of a claim which has already arisen is freely assignable, where a policy is assigned in the belief that the life insured is still in being, and, unknown to both parties, the insured is already dead, the assignment is void on the ground of a common mistake of fact going to the basis of the contract.[62]

B. Priority between assignees: notice

16-44 Although notice is unnecessary to complete an equitable assignment it becomes important when the priority between successive assignees of the same policy comes to be considered.

The general rule is that, notice apart, the priority of assignments is governed by the order of date in which they were made.[63]

16-45 Rule in Dearle v. Hall[64]

But by giving notice to the insurers a bona fide assignee for value gains priority over earlier assignees who have not done so. In order to displace the general rule the later assignee must (i) have given value, and (ii) have acted in good faith, without notice, actual or constructive, of any earlier assignment.

(i) *Value.* Notice to the insurers by a mere volunteer can never give him priority over a previous assignee for value who has failed to give notice.[65]

(ii) *Good faith.* The rule does not operate if the later assignee knew, or ought to have known,[66] of the previous assignment at the date of his own assignment.[67] A man who fails to make a careful investigation as regards previous assignments is considered to have constructive knowledge of them.[68] Thus possession of the policy

---

[59] *Freme* v. *Brade* (1858) 2 De G. & J. 582.
[60] *Chowne* v. *Baylis* (1862) 31 Beav. 351.
[61] *Fortescue* v. *Barnett* (1834) 3 My. & K. 36; *Cook* v. *Black* (1842) 1 Hare 390; *Re King, Sewell* v. *King* (1879) 14 Ch.D. 179; *Holt* v. *Heatherfield Trust* [1942] 2 K.B. 1; *West of England Bank* v. *Batchelor* (1882) 51 L.J.Ch. 199.
[62] *Scott* v. *Coulson* [1903] 2 Ch.D. 249.
[63] *Spencer* v. *Clarke* (1878) 9 Ch.D. 137; *Re Weniger's Policy* [1910] 2 Ch. 291.
[64] (1828) 3 Russ. 1.
[65] *Le Feuvre* v. *Sullivan* (1855) 10 Moo.P.C. 1.
[66] *West of England* v. *Batchelor* (1882) 51 L.J.Ch. 199.
[67] See n. 63.
[68] See n. 66.

by a previous assignee amounts to constructive notice to the later assignee of his prior right,[69] and in such a case notice to the insurers will not assist the later assignee.

This rule is in fact the application of the equitable doctrine in *Dearle* v. *Hall*[70] to assignments of policies of insurance.

Legal assignments

16-46

As regards legal assignments, their priority, as between themselves, depends entirely on the date of notice to the insurers.[71] But this is only an application of the general rule that priority is governed by the order of date in which assignments are made, for a legal assignment is not complete until notice is given. Priority, on the other hand, between legal and equitable assignments depends on identically the same principles as those governing priority between equitable assignments alone, since the Acts do not affect the rights of the parties but only the procedure by which they are enforceable.[72] It follows therefore that a legal assignment completed by notice will not give the assignee priority over an earlier equitable assignment of which he had been aware at the date of the assignment to him.[73]

Assignment by operation of law

16-47

The rule giving assignees who give notice priority over earlier assignees who have not done so does not apply to such assignees as a trustee in bankruptcy, where the assignment is by operation of law. A trustee in bankruptcy takes subject to all existing equities[74] and he cannot, therefore, by giving notice to an insurance company, deprive a prior assignee who has not done so of his right in equity to the policy moneys.[75]

Precautions to be taken by assignee

16-48

It follows from the rule in *Dearle* v. *Hall*[76] that anyone proposing to lend money on the security of a life policy should first ask the insurance company whether it has had notice of any previous dealings with the policy.[77] He should also demand production of the original policy: the failure of the proposed assignor to produce it should operate as a warning to him that the policy may have been dealt with already and may constitute constructive notice to him of such previous dealings.[78] He should, if possible, retain possession of the policy after the assignment, as it will be necessary to him when he comes to collect the money from the insurers and his possession of it will operate as constructive notice of his interest should the assured seek to make a further assignment.[79]

---

[69] See n. 63.
[70] (1828) 3 Russ. 1.
[71] See § 16-35, *supra*.
[72] *Newman* v. *Newman* (1884) 28 Ch.D. 674; L.P.A. 1925, s.136(1).
[73] *Ibid*. n. 72.
[74] *Re Stories' Trust* (1859) 1 Giff. 94.
[75] *Re Wallis, ex p. Jenks* [1902] 1 K.B. 719.
[76] (1828) 3 Russ. 1.
[77] *Williams* v. *Thorp* (1828) 2 Sim. 257; *Re Weniger's Policy* [1910] 2 Ch. 291, 296, *per* Parker J.
[78] *Le Feuvre* v. *Sullivan* (1855) 10 Moo.P.C. 1; *Spencer* v. *Clarke* (1878) 9 Ch.D. 137; *West of England Bank* v. *Batchelor* (1882) 51 L.J.Ch. 199; *Re Weniger's Policy* [1910] 2 Ch. 291.
[79] *Rummens* v. *Hare* (1876) 1 Ex.D. 169; *Harrison* v. *Alliance Assurance* [1903] 1 K.B. 184.

16–49 Notice: how given

Notice must be given to the insurance company at its principal place of business or at one of its principal places of business to satisfy the Policies of Assurance Act 1867,[80] but for the purposes of the rule in *Dearle* v. *Hall* notice to a branch, or to an agent of the company who has authority to receive it, will be sufficient.[81]

16–50 Estoppel by acceptance of notice

Quite apart from questions of priority the acceptance of notice of an assignment by the insurers will estop them from subsequently repudiating the policy, if they were then aware of a breach of condition,[82] and will cast on them the duty of informing the assignee should they subsequently discover information entitling them to repudiate it.[83]

C. Effect of assignment

16–51 The general effect of an assignment of a policy of insurance is to pass the rights of the assignor, as against the insurers, to the assignee. Subject to the rule in *Dearle* v. *Hall* it will pass these rights only subject to existing equities of third parties: unless he is an assignee in good faith and for value and without notice actual or constructive the assignee stands in exactly the same position as the assignor in relation to equitable interests to which the policy is already subject.[84]

16–52 Assignments in fraud of creditors

Sections 423–425 of the Insolvency Act 1986[85] provide that the court may set aside any transaction, including an assignment, entered into by the assured at an undervalue[86] and with the intention of putting the subject matter beyond the reach of an actual or potential creditor.[87] If the subject matter has been the subject of a further assignment—by the assignee to a third party—the third party will obtain an unimpeachable title as long as he was a bona fide purchaser for value and without notice of the circumstances which resulted in the voidability of the original assignment.[88] An application under section 423 is to be made on behalf of the victims of the transaction, and may be made by the assignor's trustee in bankruptcy, the official receiver or any victim.[89] Sections 339, 341 and 342 of the Insolvency Act 1986[90] confer upon a bankrupt assignor's trustee in bankruptcy a similar power to apply to the court to set aside any transaction at an undervalue,[91] irrespective of the assignor's

---

[80] s.3; § 16–35 *supra*.

[81] *Gale* v. *Lewis* (1846) 9 Q.B. 730.

[82] *Mangles* v. *Dixon* (1852) 3 H.L.C. 702.

[83] *Scottish Equitable Life* v. *Buist* (1877) 4 R. (Ct. of Sess.) 176, 1081; (1878) 5 R. (Ct. of Sess.) (H.L.) 64.

[84] *Mangles* v. *Dixon* (1852) 3 H.L.C. 702.

[85] Replacing s.172 of the Law of Property Act 1925, which in turn replaced the Fraudulent Conveyances Acts 1571.

[86] Defined as a gift, a transaction in consideration of marriage, or a transaction which significantly undervalues the asset transferred: s.423(1).

[87] s.423(3).

[88] s.425(2), (3).

[89] s.424.

[90] Replacing s.42 of the Bankruptcy Act 1914.

[91] Defined in s.339(3) in a fashion identical to s.423(1), *supra* n. 86.

intentions when making the assignment, if the assignment was made within five years before the day on which the bankruptcy petition was presented.[92] A bona fide purchaser for value from the assignee will not be affected if he was not aware of the circumstances giving rise to the voidability of the original assignment.[93]

Assignee stands in assignor's shoes   16–53
Express provisions of the policy apart, an assignment of a policy can never give the assignee any larger rights against the insurers than those of the assignor. As against the insurers the assignee stands in his shoes. Thus in *British Equitable Ins. Co.* v. *G.W.R.*,[94] where a policy, voidable for non-disclosure, had been assigned to the defendant company, they could not, on suing the insurers be in any better position than that in which the assured would have been, and that his non-disclosure therefore precluded them from recovery of the policy moneys. So also where a policy is vitiated by the assured's fraud, and the insurers pay his assignee in ignorance of such fraud, they are, on discovering the fraud, entitled to recover the money so paid as money paid under a mistake of fact.[95] An insurance policy is not a negotiable instrument,[96] and can only be assigned "subject to equities," in the sense of that term as applied to bills of exchange.

Clause protecting suicide's assignee   16–54
This rule may result in injustice to assignees for value of policies which are expressed to be avoided by the suicide of the assured. In such cases, or where suicide is made an exception to the risk covered by the policy,[97] it is usual to add a clause in it protecting the interests of such assignees in the event of the suicide of the assured, and a compromise is thus effected whereby the assured is prevented from providing for his dependants by his suicide at the insurer's expense, while a great inducement to persons to insure, namely—the possibility of their disposing, if expedient, with their policies, is not removed.[98]

Such a clause has the effect that an assured with a defeasible title can transfer a perfectly complete title to somebody with whom he deals for value, and gives such policies one of the attributes of negotiability possessed by cheques and bills.[99] As we have seen,[1] there is nothing illegal about such a clause: that it may promote evil by leading to suicide is a very remote and improbable contingency, and it may frequently be very beneficial by rendering a life policy a safe security in the hands of an assignee.[2]

---

[92] s.341(1).
[93] s.342(2), (4).
[94] (1869) 38 L.J.Ch. 314.
[95] *Lefevre* v. *Boyle* (1832) 3 B. & Ad. 877.
[96] *Strachan* v. *M'Dougle* (1835) 13 S. (Ct. of Sess.) 954; *United Kingdom Life* v. *Dixon* (1838) 16 S. (Ct. of Sess.) 1277.
[97] See §§ 16–09 *et seq., supra.*
[98] Cockburn C.J. in *Jackson* v. *Forster* (1859) 29 L.J.Q.B. 8.
[99] See Sargant L.J. in *Rowett, Leakey* v. *Scottish Provident* [1927] 1 Ch. 55, 74.
[1] See §§ 3–58 and 16–09, *supra.*
[2] Lord Campbell C.J. in *Moore* v. *Woolsey* (1854) 4 E. & B. 243, 255.

16–55 Meaning of "value"

An assignment which is part of a marriage settlement is an assignment for valuable consideration within the meaning of such a clause.[3] But the mere fact that a debtor assigns a policy to his creditor as security does not make the transaction one for valuable consideration unless there is an agreement, express or implied, to give time or some further consideration or an actual forbearance to sue on the part of the creditor, which *ex post facto* may become the consideration to support it.[4]

16–56 Interests in policy covered by clause

A clause covering the interest of "another person who has acquired an interest in the policy" only refers to legal or equitable interests: it does not assist a creditor of the assured who has no charge or lien on the policy.[5] But where the protection extended to "a bona fide interest in the life assured to whom the policy has been assigned" it was held that an equitable charge was sufficient, a legal assignment being unnecessary.[6] Even the phrase "legally assigned" in a policy has similarly been held to cover an equitable assignment,[7] but this was before legal assignments *stricto sensu* of life policies were possible except to the Crown.

16–57 Whose interests are covered

Such a clause covering the interests of "third parties" has been held not to cover the interest of a person who becomes the assured's assignee by operation of law,[8] nor can the insurers themselves be such a third party where the assured assigns a policy to them by way of security for a loan.[9] But a well-drawn policy may even protect their interest, as where a policy expressed any "bona fide interest therein which at the time of the death should be vested in *any other person*" for a pecuniary consideration to be protected.[10] Such a clause may directly benefit the estate of the assured, as where it operates for the benefit of a mortgagee who has sufficient security apart from the policy in question.[11]

A clause protecting "onerous holders" protects assignees for valuable consideration only,[12] but it has been held to extend to the wife of the assured where he assigned his policy to her under an agreement condoning his infidelity.[13]

16–58 Effect of absolute assignment

The general rule is that the assignee under an absolute assignment takes all the rights of the assignor under the policy. Even if the assignor

---

[3] *Moore* v. *Woolsey* (1854) 4 E. & B. 243.
[4] *Wigan* v. *English & Scottish Law Life* [1909] 1 Ch. 291, 303, *per* Parker J.
[5] Lord Wright M.R. in *Beresford* v. *Royal* [1937] 2 K.B. 197, 208, 209.
[6] *Cook* v. *Black* (1842) 1 Hare 390.
[7] *Dufaur* v. *Professional Life* (1858) 25 Beav. 599.
[8] *Jackson* v. *Forster* (1859) 29 L.J.Q.B. 8; *Moore* v. *Woolsey* (1854) 4 E. & B. 243.
[9] *Royal London Mutual* v. *Barrett* [1928] Ch. 411.
[10] *White* v. *British Empire Mutual Life* (1868) L.R. 7 Eq. 394; see also *Cook* v. *Black* (1842) 1 Hare 390.
[11] *Solicitors Life* v. *Lamb* (1864) 1 H. & M. 716, 725.
[12] *Rowett, Leakey* v. *Scottish Provident* [1927] 1 Ch. 55.
[13] *Ballantyne's Trustees* v. *Scottish Amicable Life* [1921] W.C. & Ins.Rep. 262; 2 S.L.T. 75.

obtains an extension of the policy after the assignment he will be held to have done so as trustee for the assignee.[14]

Bonuses 16–59

Thus, whoever is obliged to pay the premiums, any bonus payable under the policy will belong to the assignee of the policy,[15] even where it can, under the terms of the policy, be applied in reduction of future premiums,[16] unless the intention of the parties was that bonuses should belong to the assignor.[17] This is commonly the case where a voluntary settlement is made of a life policy, the settlor continuing to pay the premiums. The fact that the policy is for a sum named in the settlement will not alone, however, entitle the settlor to retention of the bonuses.[18] But where a bequest was made of "£200 secured by a policy" it was held that no more than £200 were intended to pass, and the residuary legatee was therefore allowed to apply bonuses under it in reduction of the premiums.[19]

Liability of assignee as contributory 16–60

Whether an assignee from a contributing member of a mutual association is liable as a contributory depends on the rules of the association.[20]

Effect of assignment by way of mortgage 16–61

As regards assignment by way of mortgage or charge, a legal assignment passes the whole interest in the policy of the assignor to the assignee in law, but reserves to the assignor an equity of redemption. An equitable assignment, on the other hand, gives the assignee no more than an equitable charge on the policy to the extent of the sum secured, both the legal interest and the equity of redemption remaining in the assignee.

Even a legal assignment may give the assignee a right to sue the insurers for no more than a part of the policy moneys, where, for instance, it is insufficiently stamped, and in such a case the assignor will be entitled to sue them for the balance[21]; but otherwise a legal mortgagee is entitled, as against the insurers, to the whole of the insurance moneys.[22] An equitable mortgagee, on the other hand, since he cannot discharge the insurers without the concurrence of the assignor,[23] has in effect an interest in the policy strictly limited to the extent of his charge on it.

Limitation Act 1980 16–62

Since the right to sue the insurance company on a life policy does not arise until the death of the assured, an assignee's right will not become

---

[14] *Royal Exchange* v. *Hope* [1928] Ch. 179.

[15] *Courtney* v. *Ferrers* (1827) 1 Sim. 137; *Simpson* v. *Walker* (1832) 2 L.J.Ch. 55.

[16] *Macdonald* v. *Irvine* (1878) 8 Ch.D. 191, 118–120, *per* Bagallay L.J.; but see *Gilly* v. *Burley* (1856) 22 Beav. 619.

[17] *Lackersteen* v. *Lackersteen* (1861) 30 L.J.Ch. 5.

[18] *Courtney* v. *Ferrers, supra*; *Parkes* v. *Bott* (1838) 9 Sim. 388.

[19] *Re Edmed*; *Pettit* v. *Dunn* [1884] W.N. 152.

[20] *Re Albion Life* (1881) 18 Ch.D. 639; (1882) 20 Ch.D. 403.

[21] *Re Waterhouse's Policy* [1937] Ch. 415.

[22] *Holland* v. *Smith* (1806) 6 Esp. 11; *Re Waterhouse, supra*.

[23] See § 16–71, *infra*.

statute-barred simply because of the time that has elapsed between the assignment and the death. Thus time will only begin to run against the mortgagee of a life policy from the date of the assured's death.[24] This rule applies even where part of the mortgagee's security consists of land, and his rights against such land have become statute-barred.[25] But where real estate and a policy are included in one mortgage, and the mortgagee retains possession of the real estate for more than 12 years without acknowledging the mortgagor's interest so that his right to redeem is lost,[26] he loses also his right of redemption of the policy, because both are intended as one security for one debt.[27]

16–63 Special remedies of mortgagee

Apart from his right to sue the insurers when the policy matures, the mortgagee of a policy may have two other remedies should the mortgagor fail to repay the loan. These remedies are, (i) a power of sale and (ii) a foreclosure order.

(i) *Power of sale.* A mortgagee may have the right to sell any mortgaged property, including a policy of insurance, without resorting to the court, either from the express terms of the mortgage or by virtue of sections 101–106 of the Law of Property Act 1925. These sections only apply to mortgages made by deed. The right to sell under them arises so soon as the mortgage money becomes due,[28] but it may not be exercised unless the mortgagor is two months in arrears with interest, or three months in default after notice to pay the mortgage money, or unless he is in breach of some other covenant,[29] such as a breach of his covenant to keep up a policy. The power of sale under the Act may be varied or extended by the deed itself.[30]

The proceeds of such a sale, after meeting prior charges, are to be held in trust by the mortgagee, to be applied first in payment of his own claims, the residue being payable to the mortgagor.[31] Money received from the proceeds of securities comprised in a mortgage, such as life insurance policies, is to be applied in the same way.[32]

Either mortgagor or mortgagee may apply to the court for an order for sale under section 91 of the Law of Property Act 1925,[33] even where the mortgage is by deposit of the policy only.[34]

16–64

(ii) *Foreclosure.* By means of a decree of foreclosure the mortgagee may be able to get an absolute title to property mortgaged, free from the equity of redemption.

In the case of equitable mortgages, the proper remedy is to apply to the court for an order of sale,[35] foreclosure orders usually being granted

---

[24] *Re Haycock's Policy* (1876) 1 Ch.D. 611; *London & Midland Bank* v. *Mitchell* [1899] 2 Ch. 161.
[25] *Re Witham* [1922] 2 Ch. 413; *Re Jauncey* [1926] Ch. 471.
[26] Real Property Limitation Act 1874, s.7; Limitation Act 1980, s.16.
[27] *Charter* v. *Watson* [1899] 1 Ch. 175.
[28] s.101(1)(i).
[29] s.103.
[30] *Berry* v. *Halifax Commercial Banking Co.* [1901] 1 Ch. 188.
[31] See s.105.
[32] s.107(2).
[33] See *Dyson* v. *Morris* (1842) 1 Hare 413; *Union Bank* v. *Ingram* (1882) 20 Ch.D. 463.
[34] *Oldham* v. *Stringer* (1884) 51 L.T. 895.
[35] *Dyson* v. *Morris* (1842) 1 Hare 413, *per* Wigram V.-C.

only in the case of legal mortgages. However, in certain circumstances a decree of foreclosure will be given in the case of both types of mortgage of insurance policies.[36]

Covenant to pay premiums   16–65

The mere assignment of a policy, by itself, does not place the assignor under any obligation to pay the premiums[37] or otherwise to keep up the policy, and it is therefore desirable to include covenants in the instrument assigning the policy dealing with these matters. The mortgagee of a policy will generally require the mortgagor to covenant to pay all premiums, including any extra premiums that may be demanded for any reason, if, for instance, the assured leaves Europe,[38] under the policy.

The fact that the lender has kept the policy on foot for his own benefit by payment of the premiums will be no defence to a borrower who is in breach of his covenant to do so.[39] In such a case the lender will normally be entitled to the amount of the premiums paid by way of damages,[40] unless there is provision for adding such sums to the mortgage debt,[41] in which case he will only be entitled to nominal damages.[42] Where the mortgagee has obtained no such covenant, and pays the premiums voluntarily, the court may insist on his debtor repaying him as a condition of his enforcing his equity of redemption.[43] Such payments, though irrecoverable from the mortgagor personally, form a charge on the policy mortgaged.[44] Even where the mortgagor is bound to pay the premiums, the payment of them by the mortgagee on his refusal to do so will not deprive him of his ultimate equity of redemption in the policy.[45] But express provision should be made for adding premiums paid by the mortgagee to the debt secured, as he will not otherwise be able to recover them from the policy moneys to the detriment of later mortgagees.[46]

Bankruptcy of mortgagor   16–66

A mortgagee of a policy proving in the mortgagor's bankruptcy for the unsecured part of his debt is entitled to nothing in respect of the mortgagor's covenant to pay the premiums.[47] The ground of this is that his security having been assessed at its proper value, the courts will not allow a double proof in respect of one and the same liability. As Mellish L.J. put it in *Re Oriental Commercial Bank, ex p. European Bank*[48]: "The true principle is, that there is only to be one dividend in respect of what is in substance the same debt, although there may be two separate contracts."

---

[36] *Parker* v. *Anglesea* (1871) 25 L.T. 482; *Beaton* v. *Boulton* [1891] W.N. 30.
[37] *Pedder* v. *Moseley* (1862) 31 Beav. 159; *Prescott* v. *Prescott* [1906] 1 Ir.R. 155.
[38] *Vyse* v. *Wakefield* (1840) 6 M. & W. 442.
[39] *Winthrop* v. *Murray* (1850) 8 Hare 214.
[40] *Schlesinger* v. *Mostyn* [1932] 1 K.B. 349.
[41] See *Shaw* v. *Scottish Widows' Fund* (1917) 87 L.J.Ch. 76.
[42] *Brown* v. *Price* (1858) 4 Jur.(N.S.) 882; 6 W.R. 721.
[43] *Fitzwilliam* v. *Price* (1858) 31 L.T.(O.S.) 389; but see *Bellamy* v. *Brickenden* (1861) 2 J. & H. 137.
[44] See § 10–18, *supra*.
[45] *Drysdale* v. *Piggott* (1856) 8 De G.M. & G. 546.
[46] *Brooke* v. *Stone* (1865) 34 L.J.Ch. 251.
[47] *Derring* v. *Bank of Ireland* (1886) 12 App.Cas. 20.
[48] (1871) L.R. 7 Ch. 99, 103, 104.

In such a case the mortgagor is no longer bound to pay the premiums, but he may wish to pay them in order to preserve his equity of redemption. It has been held that such premiums are repayable, as against the mortgagee, out of the policy moneys, as salvage moneys,[49] but this decision has been questioned.[50] The court may, in any case, order the premiums so paid to be repaid by the trustees in bankruptcy when the policy matures as a matter of honesty and fair dealing irrespective of the strict position in equity.[51]

16–67 Settlor's covenant to keep up policy

Payment of premiums. Settlements of policies of insurance also usually contain a covenant by the settlor to continue to pay the premiums, although this obligation is not necessarily undertaken by him, especially where the settlement is a voluntary one.[52] If the settlor allows the policy to lapse by non-payment of premiums he, or his estate, will be liable, on the death of the life insured, for the policy moneys.[53] Where the settlor, in breach of his covenant, fails to pay the premiums, and the trustees of the settlement do so, they are entitled to damages from him in respect of the breach of covenant to the amount of the premiums paid by them.[54] They are entitled to prove in his bankruptcy for the same amount, even where the premiums were paid out of a special fund set aside against the event of his default.[55]

The trustees of the settlement are bound to do all they can to enforce payment under such a covenant,[56] unless they know or reasonably believe that the settlor is insolvent and unable to pay.[57] Where there is no such covenant, or the covenant is unenforceable, they are entitled to pay the premiums out of other funds which are settled on the same trusts under the same settlement,[58] and are liable to the beneficiaries if they do not do so.[59] But in the absence of such funds they are not bound to pay the premiums out of their own pocket.[60] They may do so, however, in which case they have a lien upon the policy for the premiums so paid.[61] Where the settlor is clearly unable to continue to perform his covenant to pay the premiums, as where he had been sentenced to transportation for life for forgery,[62] and there are no funds out of which they can be paid, the court will authorise the trustees to sell or surrender the policy.[63]

---

[49] *Shearman* v. *British Empire Mutual* (1872) L.R. 14 Eq. 4.
[50] *Saunders* v. *Dunman* (1878) 7 Ch.D. 825; *Falcke* v. *Scottish Imperial* (1886) 34 Ch.D. 234, *per* Fry L.J. at p. 254.
[51] See *Re Ryler* [1907] 1 K.B. 865.
[52] *Pedder* v. *Moseley* (1862) 31 Beav. 159; *Prescott* v. *Prescott* [1906] 1 Ir.R. 155.
[53] *Re Deane* (1889) 42 Ch.D. 9.
[54] *Schlesinger* v. *Mostyn* [1932] 1 K.B. 349.
[55] *Re Miller, ex p. Wardley* (1877) 6 Ch.D. 790.
[56] *Clack* v. *Holland* (1854) 19 Beav. 262.
[57] *Hobday* v. *Peters* (1860) 28 Beav. 603; *Kingdon* v. *Castleman* (1877) 46 L.J.Ch. 448.
[58] *Darcy* v. *Croft* (1858) 9 Ir.Ch. 19; *Clack* v. *Holland, supra, Re Winchilsea's Policy Trusts* (1888) 39 Ch.D. 168.
[59] *Marriott* v. *Kinnersley* (1839) Tam. 470.
[60] *Hobday* v. *Peters, supra.*
[61] *Clack* v. *Holland, supra; Johnson* v. *Swire* (1861) 3 Giff. 194; *Re Winchilsea, supra;* § 10–20, *supra.*
[62] *Beresford* v. *Beresford* (1857) 23 Beav. 292.
[63] *Hill* v. *Trenery* (1857) 23 Beav. 16.

Bankruptcy of settlor. On the bankruptcy of the settlor the trustees **16–68**
can prove for the actuarial value of his covenant to pay premiums under
section 322 of the Insolvency Act 1986[64] unless a special fund has been
set aside against the event of his failure, in which case they will only be
entitled to prove in respect of premiums which he has already failed to
pay.[65]

Other acts to keep up policy   **16–69**
    Where the policy is voidable on the assured doing or not doing certain
things, leaving Europe or committing suicide for instance, appropriate
covenants should be included in the assignment by which the assignor
undertakes to do, or refrain from doing, things which affect the liability
of the insurers under the policy. The covenants should be made sufficiently wide. A covenant to do all acts necessary to keep on foot the
policy does not, for instance, amount to a covenant not to do acts, such
as committing suicide, which will vitiate it.[66]
    Where the assignor allows the policy to drop in breach of his coven-
ant, the measure of damages will normally be:

(a) if the event on which the policy moneys were payable has already
    occurred—the amount of the policy moneys[67];
(b) if the event has not yet happened—the present value of the policy
    actuarially computed,[68] taking into account any sum which the
    insurers are bound to pay in respect of its surrender and the value
    of any covenant to pay future premiums.[69]

D. Whom insurers may pay

It is not always clear to the insurers whom they should pay on an insur- **16–70**
ance policy. Provided they have no notice of any assignment they can
safely pay the apparent owner who is able to produce the policy whether
or not they know him to be a trustee of the policy for someone else.[70] In
such a case an assignee's only remedy would be against the assignor[71]; if
he were insolvent the assignee would have no right to follow the insurance moneys, but would be in the position of an ordinary creditor. Nor
could he make any claim on the insurers. But where the insurers have
notice of an assignment, or the policy is lost, their position may be a difficult one.

Statutory assignee can give good discharge   **16–71**
    In the case of a legal assignment they may be safe in paying the
assignee. One of the principal advantages of a statutory assignment is
that in the event of a loss the assignee can give the insurers a good discharge for the insurance moneys without the concurrence of the assig-

---

[64] *Cf. Re Pannell, ex p. Bates* (1879) 11 Ch.D. 914 (covenant to pay annuity).
[65] *Re Miller, ex p. Wardley* (1877) 6 Ch.D. 790.
[66] *Dormay* v. *Borrodaile* (1847) 10 Beav. 335.
[67] *Garner* v. *Moore* (1855) 3 Drew. 277.
[68] *Hawkins* v. *Coulthurst* (1864) 5 B. & S. 343.
[69] *Ibid.* n. 68.
[70] *Fernie* v. *Maguire* (1844) 6 Ir.Eq.R. 137; *Ford* v. *Ryan* (1854) 4 Ir.Ch. 342.
[71] *Williams* v. *Sorrell* (1799) 4 Ves. 389; *Kingdon* v. *Castleman* (1877) 46 L.J.Ch. 448.

nor.[72] In the case of an equitable assignment such concurrence is essential.[73] The insurers are thus safe in paying a legal assignee, even where they suspect that the assignor is entitled to avoid the assignment, for fraud for instance, provided they have been given no notice of his intention to do so.[74] It is clear on the other hand that the company should refuse payment, even to a legal assignee, where they have notice of a prior equitable assignment, however long ago.[75]

16–72 "Executors, administrators or assigns"

Sometimes the insurers covenant to pay the executors, administrators or assigns of the assured. The use of this wording is simply, however, to avoid the awkwardness of making the policy moneys payable to a person already dead, and it does not apparently affect the contract. Thus a person otherwise entitled to recover by the foreign law applicable, though not technically an executor or administrator, would be entitled to recover despite such covenant; and the word "assigns" is apparently limited to legal assignees who can give the insurers a good discharge.[76]

16–73 Payment into court

Under the Life Assurance Companies (Payment into Court) Act 1896, life insurance companies,[77] not being friendly societies,[78] may pay into court "moneys payable by them under a life policy in respect of which, in the opinion of their board of directors, no sufficient discharge can otherwise be obtained."[79] By this means the rival claimants are left to apply for payment out, and the receipt of the proper officer of the court for the money paid in discharges the insurance company.[80] Apart from rival claims the company may pay the money into court under this provision where the policy has been lost.[81] Provided the opinion of the directors that no sufficient discharge can otherwise be obtained is an honest one, payment into court gives them an absolute discharge,[82] but where their opinion although honest is unreasonable, they may be made liable for the costs of payment out.[83] They will usually have to bear the costs of payment in.[84] If they are in doubt as to the law it is their duty to call in the aid of their legal advisers before paying in under the Act.[85]

Normally the insurance company will not be made a party to the application for payment out, but they may be where the claimant is claiming costs or interest from them,[86] or where the company does not

---

[72] Law of Property Act 1925, s.136(1)(c). Policies of Assurance Act 1867, ss.1 and 3.
[73] *Spencer* v. *Clarke* (1878) 9 Ch.D. 137; *Webster* v. *British Empire Mutual Life* (1880) 15 Ch.D. 169.
[74] *Walker* v. *Bradford Old Bank* (1884) 12 Q.B.D. 511.
[75] *Re Haycock's Policy* (1876) 1 Ch.D. 611.
[76] Scrutton J. in *Haas* v. *Atlas Assurance* [1913] 2 K.B. 209, 219.
[77] They could not pay into court under the Trustee Acts as they were not trustees: *Re Haycock's Policy* (1876) 1 Ch.D. 611; *Matthew* v. *Northern Assurance* (1878) 9 Ch.D. 80.
[78] s.2.
[79] s.3. ss.3 and 4 were amended by the Courts Act 1971, Sched. 11.
[80] s.4.
[81] *Harrison* v. *Alliance Assurance* [1903] 1 K.B. 184.
[82] See n. 74.
[83] See n. 76.
[84] R.S.C., Ord. 54c, r. 1(d).
[85] Lord Ardwell in *Allgemeine Deutsche Credit* v. *Scottish Amicable Life*, 1908 S.C. 33, 37.
[86] *Re Waterhouse's Policy* [1937] Ch. 415.

admit liability for the whole amount claimed.[87] Otherwise payment in of the full sum would amount to an admission that all of it is due to one or some of the claimants.[88]

The limitation on the Act of 1896 is that it applies only in the case of **16–74** life policies. The proviso to section 136 of the Law of Property Act 1925 now enables any insurer to pay money into court under provisions of the Trustee Act 1925 where (a) an assignment under the section is disputed by the assignor or any person claiming through him or (b) where the claim is by an assignee under the section and there is an opposing or conflicting claim to the policy.

Interpleader   **16–75**

If neither the Acts of 1896 nor 1925 are of assistance, the only remedy of insurers in the event of competing claims is by way of interpleader.[89] Where the company interpleads they may be wise to offer to pay interest,[90] which the court has a discretion to order them to pay up to the date of judgment.[91] They may be ordered to pay interest even where conflicting claims through no fault of theirs delay such payment.[92] However, the insurers are entitled to a full legal discharge, and interest will not be awarded against them for refusing to pay except in return for such discharge.[93]

E. Non-assignable life policies

As we have seen, the ordinary rights of assignment may be limited by **16–76** the terms of the policy,[94] and certain life assurances are not freely assignable. Such assurances are not in fact the full property of the assured at all, but comprise the type of insurance in which he has only a limited power of appointment of funds standing to his credit. Certain friendly society assurances are of this nature,[95] and certain policies against death by accident, newspaper policies in particular, fall in this class.[96]

6. OTHER DISPOSITIONS OF LIFE POLICIES

A. Dispositions by nomination

(1) Ineffective dispositions   **16–77**

It is common in the case of insurances on the assured's own life, for the assured to nominate a beneficiary at the time of taking out a policy.

---

[87] *Re City of Glasgow Life* (1914) 84 L.J.Ch. 684; *Re Loir's Policies* [1916] W.N. 87.
[88] *Re Jeffrey's Policy* (1872) 20 W.R. 857.
[89] *Prudential* v. *Thomas* (1867) L.R. 3 Ch. 74; *Randall* v. *Lithgow* (1884) 12 Q.B.D. 525.
[90] *Bignold* v. *Audland* (1840) 11 Sim. 23.
[91] Supreme Court Act 1981, s.35A.
[92] *French* v. *Royal Exchange* (1857) 6 Ir.Ch.R. 523; 7 Ir.Ch.R. 523.
[93] *Webster* v. *British Empire Mutual Life* (1880) 15 Ch.D. 169.
[94] See § 10–06, *supra*.
[95] See § 16–94, *infra*.
[96] *Law* v. *Newnes* (1894) 31 S.L.R. 888; *Hunter* v. *Hunter* (1904) 7 F. (Ct. of Sess.) 136.

Such a nomination does not, however, by itself, constitute the assured a trustee,[97] nor, since the person nominated is a stranger to the contract, has he any remedy at law. The property in such a policy will therefore pass, notwithstanding the nomination, to the personal representatives of the assured on his death[98] and the nominee has no rights whatsoever, unless—

(a) the nomination amounts to a declaration of trust,[99] or the person taking out the policy is merely the agent of the nominee,[1] or

(b) the nomination is made under section 11 of the Married Women's Property Act 1882,[2] or

(c) it is made under section 66 of the Friendly Societies Act 1974,[3] or

(d) the nomination creates a binding contract between insurer A and B to pay C on an event or contingency with (C not being a party to the contract). B can then use the equitable remedy of specific performance against A to obtain an order against him to pay what may be due to C, upon the event or contingency insured against. The law is now clear on this point,[4] as a matter of general law. What require consideration are the remedies which C might have against B to ensure that he pursues his right of action against A and what B might do with the money having obtained it for C.

16–78   This rule sometimes works considerable injustice, as where a person took out an endowment policy expressly for the benefit of his godson, but died before the policy matured, and it was held that the policy formed part of his general estate and that the godson had no title to it.[5] Since the policy holder, in such a case, does not generally wish to create a trust binding upon himself during his lifetime, it is important that he should provide by will that the policy should pass on his death to the nominee. He may, on the other hand, create a trust subject to his keeping up the policy.[6]

The same principles apply where a person takes out a policy on the life of another.[7] Such a policy may infringe the Life Assurance Act 1774, but this will not affect the property in the insurance moneys should the company pay them. Thus, where a father insured his son's life and paid the premiums, and after his death the son continued to pay the pre-

---

[97] *Re Engelbach's Estate* [1924] 2 Ch. 348 (wrongly decided: *Beswick* v. *Beswick* [1968] A.C. 58); *Re Burgess's Policy* (1915) 85 L.J.Ch. 273.

[98] The law of Scotland differs from the law of England in this respect; *Carmichael's Case*, 1920 S.C.(H.L.) 195; 57 S.L.R.(H.L.) 547.

[99] *Re Webb* [1941] Ch. 225. See § 16–79, *infra*.

[1] *Re Scottish Equitable Life Policy* [1902] 1 Ch. 282.

[2] See §§ 16–80 *et seq.*, *infra*. The dictum of Wallington J. in *Bown* v. *Bown* [1948] 2 All E.R. 778, 779, 780 that a husband can settle a policy on his wife without creating a trust, and apart from this section, appears to be wrong.

[3] See § 16–88, *infra*.

[4] *Beswick* v. *Beswick* [1968] A.C. 58; *Gurtner* v. *Circuit* [1968] 1 Lloyd's Rep. 171.

[5] *Re Sinclair's Policy* [1938] Ch. 799. This case decided that s.56(1) of the Law of Property Act 1925 did not affect the rule. See also *Re Clay's Policy* [1937] 2 All E.R. 548.

[6] *Pedder* v. *Moseley* (1862) 31 Beav. 159.

[7] *Worthington* v. *Curtis* [1876] 1 Ch.D. 419; *Hatley* v. *Liverpool Victoria* (1918) 88 L.J.K.B. 237.

miums, it was held that, upon the son's death, the policy passed to the personal representatives of the father.[8]

(2) Nominations creating trust or agency

16–79

It is a difficult question of construction to determine whether a nomination makes the nominator a trustee or agent of the nominee. In *Re Engelbach's Estate*[9] a testator had taken out an endowment policy under which a sum was expressed to be payable to his one-month-old daughter (described in the policy as "the nominee"), her executors, administrators or assigns if *she* should live 21 years. In the proposal form the testator inserted his own name as proposer "for his daughter . . . aged one month." It was held that he was not acting either as trustee or agent for his daughter, and that the policy did no more than to make the insurance company the mandatory of the father in making payment to her. In *Re Scottish Equitable Life Policy 6402*[10] a policy was taken out by A on his own life "for behalf of B," his wife's sister, and the policy provided that B, her executors, administrators and assigns, should be entitled to receive the policy moneys on A's death. A was held to have taken out the policy as B's agent. In *Re Gordon*[11] the question arose whether an officer's widow was entitled to retain a lump sum payable on his death from a fund of the Society for the Benefit of Widows of the Royal Regiment of Artillery, and it was held on the construction of the society's rules that they constituted a trust in her favour. Similarly in *Re Webb*[12] the terms of policies taken out by a father "on behalf and for the benefit" of his children clearly made him a trustee, although the words "on trust" or "as trustee" were not actually used. He was expressly given only limited powers of dealing with the policies, and limited rights in them which were to terminate on the children attaining 21.[13]

(3) Married Women's Property Act 1882, s.11

16–80

By section 11 of the Married Women's Property Act 1882, a policy effected by a married man or woman on his or her own life and expressed on its face to be for the benefit of his or her spouse or children is not to form a part of his or her estate, but is to enure for the benefit of such spouse or children.

Such policies may be expressed to be for the benefit of the assured's wife or husband, or children, or both.

The effect is that while the assured remains the legal owner of the policy, a trust is created in favour of the objects named in it, and the policy moneys when they become payable are not part of the assured's estate or subject to his debts "so long as any object of the trust remains unperformed."

---

[8] *Re Foster* [1938] 3 All E.R. 357.

[9] [1924] 2 Ch. 348, considered in *Re Schebsman* [1944] Ch. 83 by the C.A. See also *Green* v. *Russell* [1959] 2 Q.B. 226 (C.A.); *Bowskill* v. *Dawson* (*No. 2*) [1955] 1 Q.B. 13; *Dalton* v. *I.R.C.* [1958] T.R. 45. However, *Re Engelbach* was questioned in *Beswick* v. *Beswick* [1966] Ch. 538 (C.A.); [1968] A.C. 58 (H.L.), on the basis that the insurance moneys had been paid to the daughter: their Lordships held that actual payment to her precluded recovery by the testator's estate irrespective of the trust issue.

[10] [1902] 1 Ch. 282, criticised in *Re Slattery* [1917] 2 Ir.R. 278.

[11] [1940] Ch. 851.

[12] [1941] Ch. 225. See also *Re Foster's Policy* [1966] 1 W.L.R. 222, in which *Re Webb* was applied.

[13] See also *Re Foster's Policy* [1966] 1 W.L.R. 222; *Beswick* v. *Beswick*, [1968] A.C. 58.

16–81 *Effect of naming wife and children.* The nature of the interest of the beneficiaries under the policy depends on whether or not they are named. If named, they acquire an immediate vested interest in the policy, and, should they die before the assured, their interest will pass to their personal representatives,[14] unless the policy provides that they are only to be paid if living when the moneys fall in.

If not named, *e.g.* where the policy is simply expressed to be for the benefit of the assured's wife and children, only those of this class alive when the moneys become payable will be entitled to benefit, and the policy moneys will be divisible between them in equal shares,[15] whether in the case of children they were born before or after the policy was taken out.[16] Unnamed beneficiaries take only a contingent interest in the proceeds of the trust policy.[17] If the assured marries again after taking out the policy and his second wife survives him she will normally be entitled to a share of such moneys.[18] But a second wife may be expressly or impliedly[19] excluded by the terms of the policy.

16–82 *Exercise of options.* Where the assured has, by the terms of the policy, options in respect of its surrender or otherwise, such options must be exercised in the best manner for the benefit of all those who might be entitled.[20] In *Re Fleetwood*[21] when the husband exercised his option of surrender, the company paid the money into court, and it was held he could not take it out without the assent of his wife who was named as the person to benefit should she survive him.

16–83 *Creditors' rights in policy.* The creditors of the assured are unable to benefit from a policy to which the section applies "so long as any object of the trust remains unperformed,"[22] and all they can claim are premiums paid by the assured out of money which should have gone in payment of his debts to them, and this has been held to be so even where the assured took out a policy under the section in place of one under which his creditors might have benefited.[23]

16–84 *Policies covered.* The section, like the Policies of Assurance Act 1867, applies to policies against death by accident only.[24] It applies also to ordinary endowment policies, if the money is payable on the death of the *assured*.[25] It applies only however to policies taken out on the life of the assured himself: it does not therefore cover ordinary education policies.[26] "Children" includes illegitimate ones by the Family Law Reform Act 1969, s.19(1).

---

[14] *Cousins* v. *Sun Life* [1933] 1 Ch. 126, following *Prescott* v. *Prescott* [1906] 1 Ir.R. 155.
[15] *Re Seyton* (1887) 34 Ch.D. 511; *Re Davies' Policy* [1892] 1 Ch. 90.
[16] *Re Browne's Policy* [1903] 1 Ch. 188; *Re Parker's Policies* [1906] 1 Ch. 526.
[17] *Re Adams' Policy* (1883) 23 Ch.D. 525.
[18] See n. 16.
[19] *Re Griffith's Policy* [1903] 1 Ch. 739.
[20] *Re Equitable Life Policy* [1911] 27 T.L.R. 213.
[21] [1926] Ch. 48.
[22] See *Cousins* v. *Sun Life, supra* and *Cleaver* v. *Mutual Reserve Life* [1892] 1 Q.B. 147, 154.
[23] *Holt* v. *Everall* (1876) 2 Ch.D. 266.
[24] *Re Gladitz* (1937) 106 L.J.Ch. 254.
[25] *Re Ioakimidis' Policy* [1925] Ch. 403.
[26] On a policy dependent on a *child* attaining a specified age, see *Re Engelbach's Estate* [1924] 2 Ch. 348; *Beswick* v. *Beswick* [1968] A.C. 58.

Reservation of interest. The section applies even though the wife's **16–85** interest is only a contingent one, *e.g.* where the assured takes out an endowment policy which is to go to his wife should he die within 20 years,[27] or where the assured reserves the right to assign the policy.[27]

People covered. The section only covered policies for the benefit of **16–86** natural children, not adopted[28] nor godchildren,[29] but it was extended to cover children adopted under an adoption order by section 14(3) of the Adoption Act 1958; see now section 39 of the consolidating Adoption Act 1976. It was held under the corresponding Act applicable in Scotland[30] that a widower is a "married man" within the meaning of the section.[31]

Variation after divorce. A disposition under the section was a "settle- **16–87** ment" within what is now section 24(1)(*c*) of the Matrimonial Causes Act 1973, and may therefore be varied by the court after a divorce,[32] even though the interest of the wife was only a contingent one.[33] By section 24(1)(*c*) of the Act of 1973 a court, on granting a decree of divorce, nullity or judicial separation, may make

> "an order varying for the benefit of the parties to the marriage and of the children of the family or either or any of them any ante-nuptial settlement or post-nuptial settlement (including such a settlement made by will or codicil) made on the parties of the marriage; . . . "

These words appear equally adequate to cover a disposition under the Act of 1882.

(4) Friendly Societies Act 1974, s.66   16–88

A member of a friendly society who has reached the age of 16 has the right to nominate a person to receive any sum payable on his death up to, but not exceeding, £500.[34] The nomination must be in writing and delivered at, or sent to, the society.[35] It can be revoked or varied by the nominator, in the same way,[36] but not otherwise. Thus, a revocation by will would be inoperative.[37] The nomination is automatically revoked on the marriage of the nominator.[38] No more than £500 can be so nominated, and the general law of succession will apply to the excess.[39]

The right of nomination is not in substitution, but in addition to, the

---

[27] *Re Davies* [1892] 3 Ch. 63: Or the policy may be contingent on the wife surviving the husband, *Bown* v. *Bown* [1938] 2 All E.R. 778.

[28] *Re Clay's Policy* [1937] 2 All E.R. 548, a questionable decision, because the child was named, and it was perfectly obvious that a trust was intended. If it was right, it follows that only a child adopted under an order, and not one named and *de facto* adopted, can now benefit under the section.

[29] *Re Sinclair's Policy* [1938] 1 Ch. 799.

[30] Married Women's Policies of Assurance (Scotland) Act 1880.

[31] *Kennedy* v. *Sharpe* (1895) 30 S.L.T. 89.

[32] *Gunner* v. *Gunner* [1948] 2 All E.R. 771.

[33] *Lort-Williams* v. *Lort-Williams* [1951] P. 395.

[34] Friendly Societies Act 1974, s.66(2).

[35] *Ibid.* s.66(1).

[36] *Ibid.* s.66(6).

[37] *Bennett* v. *Slater* [1899] 1 Q.B. 45. See *Griffiths* v. *Eccles Provident* [1911] 2 K.B. 275; *Re Baxter* [1903] P. 12.

[38] s.66(7) of Friendly Societies Act 1896.

[39] See n. 34.

ordinary right of assignment. It does not prevent the member of a friendly society assigning his benefit, just as any other policy holder may,[40] or leaving it by will.[41]

But that principle only applies where the friendly society benefit is the property of the assured. Where, by the rules of the society, he can only deal with it in strictly limited ways, and in the event of his not doing so the society have a discretion to whom to pay it, quite different considerations apply. He can then only deal with the policy as the rules allow: if he fails to do so his personal representatives may be unable to claim upon it.[42] Thus where the society's rules entitled them to pay a number of persons including the deceased's sister in the absence of any specific bequest by him of the benefit, and they so paid her, it was held that she could hold such moneys as against his administrator.[43]

16–89 (5) Contract by A with B to pay C

B can sue A for specific performance whether A is an insurer or otherwise.[44] C has no right of action against A.[45] If B agrees to discharge the agreement with A, C has no remedy,[46] but if B pursues his remedy against A for specific performance or A pays C, C has a right to retain the proceeds.[47] But B, in the case of life assurance will usually not be B but B1 standing in B's shoes, the personal representative of B upon the death: B1 will then usually have a right, or be under a duty, as administrator or executor.[48]

B. Life policies to secure a debt

16–90 Where a creditor, neither he nor the debtor being under any obligation to do so, takes out a policy on the life of the debtor without consulting him and at his own expense, there can be no doubt that he has the full legal and equitable property in the policy.[49] It is as much his own property as anything else which he may have purchased,[50] even where an allowance for insurance is included in the consideration for the loan.[51]

16–91 Presumption in debtor's favour

But where the creditor, with the debtor's consent, takes out a policy on his life to secure the debt, the presumption is that, while he has the full legal title, he has in equity no more than a charge upon the policy for that purpose,[52] at any rate where the cost of the premiums is for the

---

[40] *Re Griffin* [1902] 1 Ch. 135.
[41] *Bennett* v. *Slater, supra.*
[42] *Ashby* v. *Costin* (1888) 21 Q.B.D. 401; *Re Davies* [1892] 3 Ch. 63.
[43] *Ashby* v. *Costin, supra.*
[44] *Beswick* v. *Beswick* [1968] A.C. 58.
[45] *Beswick* v. *Beswick, supra.*
[46] *Dunlop* v. *Selfridge* [1915] A.C. 847; *Midland Silicones* v. *Scruttons* [1962] A.C. 446. See *Beswick* v. *Beswick* [1968] A.C. 58, 96, *per* Lord Upjohn.
[47] See *ibid.* See also *per* Lord Reid at pp. 70 *et seq.*
[48] See *ibid. per* Lord Hodson, at pp. 81, 82.
[49] *Re Jacob, ex p. Lancaster* (1851) 4 De G. & Sm. 524, 525, *per* Shadwell V.-C.
[50] *Freme* v. *Brade* (1858) 2 De G. & J. 582.
[51] *Simpson* v. *Walker* (1832) 2 L.J.Ch. 55; *Drysdale* v. *Piggott* (1856) 8 De G.M. & G. 546; *Lea* v. *Hinton* (1854) 5 De G.M. & G. 823.
[52] *Ibid.* n. 51.

debtor's account.[53] In such a case the creditor will hold the policy in trust for the debtor.[54]

Whether insurance to secure a debt 16-92

This presumption only applies however in the case of insurances to secure a debt. Thus, where one partner in a firm of solicitors insured the life of another, the more usual presumption was applied that a policy effected on the life of another belongs to the person who effects it, whoever pays the premiums.[55]

The principle is illustrated by a number of cases in which A, in order to raise money, sold an annuity to B with a right of redemption, and B, by arrangement with A, insured A's life to secure the advance.

Special circumstances apart,[56] it was held that the sale of the annuity did not create a debtor-creditor relationship and that the vendor had therefore no equity in the policy taken out by the purchaser, unless provision was so made.[57] Thus, unlike the loan cases, provision for payment by the vendor of any additional premiums which might become payable, or for submission by him to a medical examination, did not, prima facie, give him an equity in the policy.[58] "As a general rule it is not disputed that where the grantee of an annuity insures the life of the grantor, the policy effected belongs to the grantee."[59]

Premiums 16-93

The presumption that a creditor has, in equity, no more than a charge on a policy taken out by him, by agreement with the debtor, to secure a debt can, however, be rebutted by the creditor if he is able to show:

(a) that he paid the premiums; and
(b) that he paid them on the understanding that the debtor should not be called upon to repay them.[60]

Thus, where the creditor insured the debtor's life with his knowledge and paid the premiums, but debited him with the sum paid, it was held the beneficial interest in the policy belonged to the debtor.[61] But where, in similar circumstances, the creditor agreed that he would pay the first and future premiums and not charge the debtor therewith, it was held both the legal and the beneficial interest in the policy belonged to him.[62] Where the creditor is liable for payment of the premiums in this way, it does not matter whether or not he promises to assign the policy to the

---

[53] *Bruce* v. *Garden* (1869) L.R. 5 Ch. 32, 35, *per* Hatherley L.C.; see also *Re Emmett, ex p. Andrews* (1816) 1 Madd. 573.

[54] *Ibid.* n. 53.

[55] *Triston* v. *Hardey* (1851) 14 Beav. 232.

[56] *Hawkins* v. *Woodgate* (1844) 7 Beav. 565; *Williams* v. *Atkyns* (1845) 2 Jones & Latouche (Ir.) 603; *Courtenay* v. *Wright* (1869) 2 Giff. 337. See Bacon V.-C. in *Preston* v. *Neele* (1879) 12 Ch.D. 760, 770.

[57] *Re Jacob, ex p. Lancaster* (1851) 4 De G. & Sm. 524; *Gottlieb* v. *Cranch* (1853) 4 De G.M. & G. 440; *Bashford* v. *Cann* (1863) 33 Beav. 109; *Knox* v. *Turner* (1870) L.R. 9 Eq. 155; *Preston* v. *Neele* (1879) 12 Ch.D. 760.

[58] *Gottlieb* v. *Cranch, supra.*

[59] *Ibid.* at p. 446, *per* Turner L.J.

[60] *Brown* v. *Freeman* (1851) 4 De G. & Sm. 444; Romilly M.R. in *Morland* v. *Isaac* (1855) 20 Beav. 389, 393. But see also *Bruce* v. *Garden* (1869) L.R. 5 Ch. 32.

[61] *Morland* v. *Isaac, supra*; see also *Pfleger* v. *Brown* (1860) 28 Beav. 391.

[62] *Brown* v. *Freeman, supra.*

debtor on repayment of the debt and the premiums. Until such assignment the whole property in the policy belongs to the creditor, and if the
debtor does not exercise his option within a reasonable time after repayment of the debt, he will lose all his rights under the policy.[63] But once
the debtor exercises his option the ultimate beneficial interest in the
policy passes to him and the creditor can no longer surrender it or otherwise deal with it as his own.[64]

16–94   In fact the ultimate test is, who is liable to bear the cost of the premiums? The position was summed up by Stuart V.-C. in *Courtenay* v.
Wright[65]:

> "Where the relation of debtor and creditor subsists and the true construc-
> tion of the instruments and the evidence of the real nature of the trans-
> action shows that the policy . . . was effected by the creditor as a security or
> indemnity, if the debtor directly or indirectly provides money to defray the
> expense of the security, he is, on a principle of natural equity, entitled to
> have the security delivered up to him when he pays his debt which it was
> directly or indirectly at his expense effected to secure."

16–95 Clog on equity of redemption

Where a mortgagor of property pays the premiums of a policy taken
out by his mortgagee as a collateral security, a provision that the proceeds of the policy shall belong unconditionally to the mortgagee is void
as a clog on the mortgagor's equity of redemption.[66]

16–96 Voidable transactions

The creditor on the other hand has an interest in such policies to
secure repayment of sums actually advanced even although the transaction is set aside on account of fraud, but in such a case premiums he
voluntarily pays to keep up the policy are not recoverable from the
debtor.[67]

16–97 Sureties

Where a creditor, whose debt is secured by sureties, insures the life of
the principal debtor, he is perfectly free to assign over such policy to a
person, whether debtor or surety, who pays the principal debt. But, as
between the sureties, no one of them can, by paying the debt, and
obtaining such assignment, appropriate the whole benefit of the policy
and claim contribution from his co-sureties as though such policy never
existed. To give him such a right, the other must abandon or disclaim all
benefit of the policy. But the surety who takes over the policy is entitled
in an action for contribution to deduct from the amount received on the
policy all sums spent by him in keeping it up, since as the benefit is joint,
the burden must be so also.[68]

---

[63] *Bashford* v. *Cann* (1863) 33 Beav. 109; *Lewis* v. *King* (1857) 44 L.J.Ch. 259. Bacon V.-C. in *Preston* v. *Neele* (1879) 12 Ch.D. 760, 771.
[64] *Hawkins* v. *Woodgate* (1844) 7 Beav. 565.
[65] (1869) 2 Giff. 337, 351.
[66] *Salt* v. *Marquis of Northampton* [1892] A.C. 1.
[67] *Pennell* v. *Millar* (1857) 23 Beav. 172; *Re Leslie, Leslie* v. *French* (1883) 23 Ch.D. 552. See p. 198,
1st ed. of this work.
[68] *Atkins* v. *Arcedeckne* (1883) 24 Ch.D. 709; *Re Denton's Estate* [1904] 2 Ch. 178.

C. Bankruptcy of assured

A policy of assurance belonging to a person who becomes bankrupt **16–98** passes with all other property in which he has a beneficial interest to his trustee or to the official receiver for the benefit of his creditors[69] even if its apparent value is insignificant[70] or if, owing to arrears of premium[71] the policy may be a liability rather than an asset; it is for his creditors and those acting for them to judge of the expediency, or otherwise, of taking possession of it.[72]

A policy taken out by a debtor after the date of his bankruptcy but before he has obtained his discharge may be claimed by the trustee.[73] The debtor will probably not be allowed to keep the proceeds of a policy existing at the date of his bankruptcy and disclaimed by his trustee but kept alive by premiums paid by the debtor before his discharge, unless they are paid by him out of moneys which belong to him and not to his creditors and which he was rightfully entitled to use for the purpose.[74]

If, however, the trustee or the official receiver, being aware of the existence of the policy, stands by and allows the debtor (after his discharge), or anyone else to pay the premiums,[75] or if an assignee for valuable consideration of the policy,[76] believing that he has a good title to it,[77] pays the premiums, or, if someone pays them under any other mistake, either of fact or of law,[78] the trustee or the official receiver, being an officer of the court[79] will not be allowed, afterwards, to act in a manner contrary to fair dealing[80]; therefore, the proceeds of the policy must be applied first to repayment of the premiums and the balance, only, will be available for distribution among the creditors of the bankrupt. This rule does not apply to cases where premiums are paid without the knowledge of the trustee or the official receiver.[81]

7. LIFE INSURANCE CONDITIONS

Territorial limitations and restrictions on occupation   16–99

We have already considered conditions in favour of assignees where the assured dies by suicide or some other excepted peril,[82] and conditions, not so confined to life policies however, making the undertaking

---

[69] Insolvency Act 1986, s.283.

[70] *Tapster* v. *Ward* (1909) 101 L.T. 503 (C.A.), where, at the date of the bankruptcy, there was a policy on which only one premium had been paid and which had no surrender value.

[71] *Schondler* v. *Wace* (1808) 1 Camp. 486. Onerous property may, however, be disclaimed subsequently under s. 315 of the Insolvency Act 1986.

[72] *Re Learmonth* (1866) 14 W.R. 628.

[73] Insolvency Act 1986, s.307.

[74] *Re Learmonth* (1866) 14 W.R. 628.

[75] *Re Tyler, ex p. Official Receiver* [1907] 1 K.B. 865.

[76] *Schondler* v. *Wace* (1808) 1 Camp. 486.

[77] *West* v. *Reid* (1843) 2 Hare 249.

[78] *Re Carnac, ex p. Simmonds* (1885) 16 Q.B.D. 308.

[79] *Ex p. James, re Condon* (1874) L.R. 9 Ch. 609, 614, James L.J.

[80] Cozens-Hardy M.R. in *Tapster* v. *Ward* (1909) 101 L.T. 503, 504; Atkin L.J. in *Re Thellusson* [1919] 2 K.B. 735, 765.

[81] *Re Hall, ex p. Official Receiver* [1907] 1 K.B. 875, *per* Farwell L.J. at p. 879; *Tapster* v. *Ward* (1909) 101 L.T. 503; *Re Phillips* [1914] 2 K.B. 689; *Re Stokes, ex p. Mellish* [1919] 2 K.B. 256; *Re Thellusson* [1919] 2 K.B. 735, 750.

[82] See §§ 16–54 *et seq.*, *supra*.

of the risk conditional on the truth of the answers made on the application to insure.[83] Another species of condition that once commonly appeared in life policies was a condition limiting the territory in which the assured might reside,[84] generally allowing him to go outside the specified geographical limits however on payment of an increased premium. Similarly restrictions may be made in the policy against the assured engaging in military service[85] or other such dangerous occupations unless he pays an increased premium. But there has long been a general tendency on the part of insurers to remove local restrictions and grant "whole-world" policies so as to avoid the obvious inconveniences of this old system. By questioning the assured as to his occupation and intentions they are able fairly to estimate the probable risk of his travelling to unhealthy localities, and can fix the premium accordingly. The answers to such questions amount to no more than an expression of intention and, if they are made in good faith, the policy will continue to be valid even if the assured changes his mind.[86] An insurer who wishes to restrict the assured's future conduct must obtain an express continuing warranty to this effect.[87]

As regards hazardous occupations, a motor racing driver insured his life under a policy excluding the recovery of full profits accruing under it if he were killed whilst engaging in "motor racing, motor speed hill climbs, motor trials or rallies." He died as the result of an accident in a sprint event. While "motor racing" covered sprint events as a matter of ordinary English, it was held, "motor racing" had a restricted meaning, known to the insurers, which did not cover sprint events, and they were liable in full on the policy.[88]

16–100 Indisputable life policies

Life insurance companies often advertise in their prospectus, and sometimes insert a statement in their policies, that they are "indisputable." If such a statement is included in a policy, or the assured can prove that he effected a policy on the faith of such a statement in a prospectus,[89] the company are precluded from relying on a breach of a warranty by him that his statements were true,[90] and the fact that he made a mistake in filling in the proposal offers them no defence. But it does not preclude the company from relying on their common law right to avoid the policy for fraudulent misrepresentation or concealment.[91] The words "except in the case of fraud" are sometimes added to the statement to make this position clear to the assured. Nor does such a statement preclude the company from alleging that the policy is void on the ground of no interest.[92]

---

[83] See Chap. 6, *supra*.
[84] *Wing* v. *Harvey* (1854) 5 De G.M. & G. 265.
[85] *Duckworth* v. *Scottish Widows' Fund* (1917) 33 T.L.R. 430.
[86] *Grant* v. *Aetna Assurance* (1862) 15 Moo.P.C.C. 516.
[87] See Chap. 6.
[88] Mocatta J. in *Scragg* v. *U.K. Temperance* [1976] 2 Lloyd's Rep. 227.
[89] *Wood* v. *Dwarris* (1856) 11 Ex. 493; *Wheelton* v. *Hardisty* (1858) 8 E. & B. 232.
[90] *Anstey* v. *British Natural Premium Life* (1908) 99 L.T. 765.
[91] *Re General Provincial, ex p. Daintree* (1870) 18 W.R. 396.
[92] *Anctil* v. *Manufacturers' Life* [1899] A.C. 604 (P.C.).

8. EFFECT OF WAR ON LIFE POLICY

A contract of life insurance with an enemy, unlike an insurance of prop- **16–101** erty, is not abrogated by the outbreak of war—at any rate, where the policy is expressed as an entire contract for life. This rule follows from the special character of a life policy as a piece of property; in this respect it is analogous to a lease.[93] Thus, in *Seligman* v. *Eagle Insurance*[94] a policy taken out by an enemy with the defendant company before the war had been mortgaged to the company, and it was held that the company were entitled to accept premiums from sureties. A contract of life insurance with an enemy made during a war is, by contrast, illegal and void as it amounts to trading with the enemy.

---

[93] As to which see *Halsey* v. *Lowenfeld* [1916] 2 K.B. 707.
[94] [1917] 1 Ch. 519.

CHAPTER 17

ACCIDENT INSURANCE

1. GENERAL

ACCIDENT insurance, as generally understood, is a branch of insurance **17–01** closely allied to life insurance, by which persons are enabled to provide against loss to themselves or their families in case they are injured or disabled for a time or permanently, or killed, by some cause operating on them from without.

Renewal

There is usually no obligation on the insurer to continue an accident policy, as there is in the case of a life policy.[1] And where a policy against accident is for one year, renewable from time to time by consent, each renewal is a new contract, and not a continuation of the original contract.[2]

Statutory definitions   **17–02**

A distinction is drawn, for regulatory purposes, between accident insurance and sickness insurance under the Insurance Companies Act 1982. Accident insurance provides benefits in the event of the person assured:

    (a) sustaining injury as the result of an accident or of an accident of a specified class; or

    (b) dying as the result of an accident or of an accident of a specified class; or

    (c) becoming incapacitated in consequence of disease or of disease of a specified class.[3]

Sickness insurance, by contrast, insures against "risks of loss to the persons insured attributable to sickness or infirmity."[4] Both classes constitute general business rather than long term business,[5] and are mutually exclusive.

Whether contract of indemnity   **17–03**

A policy of insurance against accidents, as usually drawn, is not a contract of indemnity. It is a contract to pay a certain fixed sum per week in case of injury, and a certain other fixed sum in case of death. But accident policies need not necessarily be drawn in this way. Thus in *Theobald* v. *Railway Passengers' Assurance*[6] there were two distinct contracts contained in the policy:

---

[1] *Simpson* v. *Accidental Death Ins. Co.* (1857) 26 L.J.C.P. 289.
[2] *Stokell* v. *Heywood* [1897] 1 Ch. 459.
[3] Insurance Companies Act 1982, Sched. 2, class 1.
[4] Insurance Companies Act 1982, Sched. 2, class 2.
[5] See Chap. 13.
[6] (1854) 10 Ex. 45.

(a) to pay £1,000 to the assured's executors if he was killed by accident, and

(b) to *compensate* him to any amount, not exceeding £1,000, for the expense and pain and loss caused to him by accident.

The second, though not the first, of these contracts was a contract of indemnity. So a policy insuring against personal accident to a third person was held to be a contract of indemnity in a case in which the employer of a lecturer insured her performances for £100 each against her absence owing to accident or illness.[7]

17–04 Interest

But whether a policy taken out against accidents to a third party is construed as a contract of indemnity or not, the person taking it out must have an interest at the time of taking it out in the health or life of the assured, as the Life Assurance Act 1774 applies to accident policies[8] except to those taken out by a local authority against accidents to members under section 140 of the Local Government Act 1972.[9]

17–05 Rights against tortfeasor

The fact that an injured person's loss is covered by an accident policy is no bar to his right to sue a tortfeasor who has injured him for damages,[10] nor can a tortfeasor, who has caused an accident, plead an insurance against accident in mitigation of damages.[11] This principle is common to all policies,[12] but applied to accident policies which are not policies of indemnity it may have the result that the assured makes a considerable profit out of an accident, as the doctrine of subrogation is not applicable.[13]

17–06 Fatal Accidents Acts

There used to be one exception to this principle in the case of accidents resulting in death, for the right of the deceased's dependents to sue the tortfeasor under section 2 of the Fatal Accidents Act 1846 was restricted to the actual pecuniary loss suffered by them, and this was held to mean that insurance moneys were to be deducted from the damages awardable under the Act.[14] It was subsequently enacted by section 1 of the Fatal Accidents (Damages) Act 1908, however, that in assessing such damages "there shall not be taken into account any sum paid or payable on the death of the deceased under any contract of assurance or insurance." The words "contract of . . . insurance" gave rise to difficulties in the case of sums paid under a pensions scheme. It was held that such payments were within the 1908 Act if paid under a contract[15] in the nature of life insurance, but sums falling outside the

---

[7] *Blascheck* v. *Bussell* (1916) 33 T.L.R. 74.
[8] *Shilling* v. *Accidental Death* (1857) 2 H. & N. 42.
[9] Replacing s.130 of the Local Government Act 1948.
[10] *Port Glasgow & Newark Sailcloth Co.* v. *Caledonian Ry.* (1892) 29 S.L.R. 577.
[11] *Bradburn* v. *G.W.R.* (1874) L.R. 10 Ex. 1.
[12] See § 8–09, *supra.*
[13] See Chap. 8, *supra.*
[14] *Hicks* v. *Newport, Abergaveny & Hereford Ry.* (1857) 4 B. & S. 403n.
[15] See Lord Hewart C.J. in *Carling* v. *Lebbon* [1927] 2 K.B. 108, 109; *Bowskill* v. *Dawson (No. 2)* [1955] 1 Q.B. 17.

Act included those paid under statutory pension funds,[16] and voluntary payments by the Crown[17] or from charitable funds.[18] However, it is now provided by section 4 of the Fatal Accidents Act 1976, replacing the earlier legislation, that in assessing damages "there shall not be taken into account any insurance money, benefit, pension or gratuity which has been or will or may be paid as a result of the death." These words clearly apply to moneys paid on the death of the husband under a policy taken out by his employer in which the deceased had no legal or equitable interest, if it was envisaged that they would be applied for his benefit.[19]

Time and voyage policies   17–07
Accident policies, like marine policies, may be divided into time and voyage policies. Railway and aviation insurance against accident are common instances of the latter type. Most accident policies are, however, for a fixed period.

Notice of other insurances   17–08
It is the practice to insert a condition in accident policies requiring notice of other insurances against the same risk.[20] Such notice is of special importance in the case of accident policies, since the principle of indemnity does not apply, and increased insurance encourages negligence or fraud by the assured without on the other hand giving the insurers the benefit of the principle of contribution.

2. THE RISK

Importance of "accident"   17–09
Accident policies define the insurer's liability in terms of an "accident" befalling the assured. Many questions arise concerning the true meaning of this word, and it is difficult to define the word so as to include the innumerable mishaps which occur in the daily course of human life. It is equally difficult to decide whether a mishap comes within the risk taken, or the exceptions made, by the terms of a particular policy; this is in essence a matter of causation.[21] In general terms, the courts have been generous to assureds and have held that the assured may claim when an accidental event gives rise to illness[22] or when illness gives rise to an accidental event,[23] as in both cases the loss is the result of

---

[16] *Baker* v. *Dalgleish SS Co.* [1922] 1 K.B. 361 (naval pension); *Carling* v. *Lebbon, supra* (widows' pension); *Lory* v. *G.W.R.* [1942] 1 All E.R. 230 (police pension); *Smith* v. *B.E.A.* [1951] 2 K.B. 893 (civil aviation pension); *O'Neill* v. *Smith* [1957] 1 W.L.R. 1204 (coal pension).
[17] *Baker* v. *Dalgleish, supra.*
[18] *Lory* v. *G.W.R., supra.*
[19] *Green* v. *Russell* [1959] 3 W.L.R. 17.
[20] See, *e.g. Marshall and Scottish Employers' Liability* (1901) 85 L.T. 757.
[21] See chap. 4.
[22] *Fitton* v. *Accidental Insurance* (1864) 17 C.B.N.S. 122; *Mardorf* v. *Accident Insurance* (1889) 22 Q.B.D. 504; *Mardorf* v. *Accident Insurance* [1903] 1 K.B. 584; *Re Etherington and Lancashire and Yorkshire Accident Insurance* [1909] 1 K.B. 591; *Smith* v. *Cornhill Insurance* [1938] 3 All E.R. 145. Contrast *Smith* v. *Accident Insurance* (1870) L.R. 5 Ex. 302.
[23] *Reynolds* v. *Accident Insurance* (1870) 22 L.T. 820; *Winspear* v. *Accident Insurance* (1880) 6 Q.B.D. 42; *Lawrence* v. *Accidental Insurance* (1882) 7 Q.B.D. 216. Contrast *Re Scarr and General Accident Assurance* [1905] 1 K.B. 387; *Fidelity and Casualty* v. *Mitchell* [1917] A.C. 592.

"accident" rather than sickness. Appropriate wording may, however, restrict the causation principle and may allow the assured to recover only where accident was the *sole* or *independent* cause of the loss.[24]

17–10 General definition of "accident"

Some guidance may be obtained from decisions under the Workmen's Compensation Acts, which were repealed in 1946. Lord Macnaghten said that this expression was used in the Workmen's Compensation Act 1897:

> "in the popular and ordinary sense of the word, as denoting an unlooked-for mishap or an untoward event which is not expected or designed,"

and Lord Shand, referring to the same Act, was of the opinion that it

> "denotes or includes any unexpected personal injury . . . from any unlooked-for mishap or occurrence."[25]

Thus in *Brintons* v. *Turvey*[26] a workman who was employed to sort wool became infected with anthrax, from which he died, by a *bacillus* passing from the wool to his eye. The House of Lords held this to be an "injury by accident" within the meaning of the 1897 Act. The term "accident," while not including sickness, will nevertheless encompass any form of unintended injury, including injury by exposure to contagious diseases.

17–11 Illustrations of "accidents"

If a man walks and stumbles, thus spraining his ankle, the injury is accidental for while he intends to walk he does not intend to stumble.[27] In *Hamlyn* v. *Crown Accidental Insurance*[28] the assured's injury was due to stooping forward to pick up a marble dropped by a child as it rolled from him. He stood with his legs together, separated his knees, leaned forward and made a grab at the marble, and in doing so wrenched his knee. The injury was held by the Court of Appeal to be accidental, on the ground that the assured did not intend to get into such a position that he might wrench his knee.

Further illustrations of an "accident" are provided by cases where the assured was drowned while bathing,[29] where he sprained the muscles of his back in lifting a heavy weight in the course of his employment[30] and where he took a poisonous mixture by mistake instead of medicine and died immediately.[31]

17–12 Accidental excludes disease

Although disease proximately caused by an accident will be covered by a personal accident policy,[32] it is well established that the word "acci-

---

[24] *Jason* v. *Batten* [1969] 1 Lloyd's Rep. 281.
[25] *Fenton* v. *Thorley* [1903] A.C. 433, 448, 451.
[26] [1905] A.C. 230.
[27] Bray J. in *Re Scarr, supra,* at p. 394.
[28] [1893] 1 Q.B. 750. See also *Voison* v. *Royal* 53 D.L.R. (4th) 299 (1989).
[29] *Trew* v. *Railway Passengers' Association* (1861) 6 H. & N. 839; *Reynolds* v. *Accidental Insurance* (1870) 22 L.T. 820.
[30] *Sinclair* v. *Maritime Passengers' Assurance* (1861) 3 E. & E. 478.
[31] *Cole* v. *Accident Insurance* (1889) 5 T.L.R. 736, although there the policy excluded death by poison.
[32] See n. 22.

dent" does not include disease and other natural causes, and implies that intervention of some cause which is brought into operation by chance and which can be described as fortuitous. Thus the word "accident" in an accident policy excludes sunstroke, which the court has classed with illness from malaria, exposure to the weather, etc.[33]

Latent diseases of which the assured is unaware do not constitute accidents. There was held to be nothing accidental in the assured pushing and pulling a drunken man from his premises, even though unknown to the assured, his heart was in a weak condition, and he died from the exertion.[34] Similarly, there is no accident where a person with a weak heart injures it by running to catch a bus.[35]

Accident includes negligence   17–13

It makes no difference that the accident was caused by the negligence of the assured (as opposed to his intentional act). Thus there is an accident where the assured crosses a railway line without exercising due care and is knocked down by an approaching train.[36] In fact, one of the commonest causes of accidents is negligence, and an accident policy applies, excepted perils apart, whether the injury is caused by the negligent act of the assured himself or of a third party.[37]

Accident excludes intentional act of assured   17–14

If the assured's deliberate act is intended to cause loss, he cannot recover. However, if the assured commits a deliberate act which results in unintended loss, such loss is accidental. Thus in *Marcel Beller* v. *Hayden*,[38] death was held to be accidental where the assured was killed while driving his car at high speeds while intoxicated, although recovery was ultimately denied on public policy grounds.[39]

"Violent"   17–15

In most of the above cases the policies insured against bodily injury caused "by violent, accidental, external and visible means only," but the decisions turned mainly on the question whether or not the particular injury was caused by accidental means. That was because such words as "violent," "external" and "visible" have been given wide meanings, practically co-extensive with "accidental."

Thus "violent" does not necessarily imply actual violence, as where the assured is bitten by a dog.[40] "Violent means" include any external, impersonal cause, such as drowning,[41] or the inhalation of gas,[42] or even

---

[33] *Sinclair* v. *Maritime Passengers' Assurance* (1861) 3 E. & E. 478.

[34] *Scarr* v. *General Accident* [1905] 1 K.B. 387.

[35] See *Appel* v. *Aetna Life* (1903) 86 App.Div.Rep. S.C.N.Y. 83, approved by Bray J. in *Scarr, supra*.

[36] *Cornish* v. *Accident Insurance* (1889) 23 Q.B.D. 453.

[37] Lord M'Laren in *Cildero* v. *Scottish Accident* (1892) 19 R. (Ct. of Sess.) 355, 363.

[38] [1978] Q.B. 694. *Contra* the South African decision in *C. Griessel* v. *S.A. Myn* 1952 (4) S.A. 473.

[39] But in *Gray* v. *Barr* [1971] 2 Q.B. 554 the Court of Appeal held, for the purposes of a liability policy, that a deliberate act with unintended consequences might be an accident in appropriate circumstances. It is suggested that this case is wrongly decided.

[40] See Wright J. in *Mardorf* v. *Accident Insurance* [1903] 1 K.B. 584, 588.

[41] *Trew* v. *Railway Passengers' Assurance* (1861) 6 H. & N. 839; *Reynolds* v. *Accidental Insurance* (1870) 22 L.T. 820.

[42] *Re United London & Scottish Insurance, Brown's Claim* [1915] 2 Ch. 167.

undue exertion on the part of the assured.[43] The word "violent" is merely used as an antithesis of "without any violence at all."[44]

17–16 "External" and "visible"

Similarly "external" is used to express anything which is not "internal,"[45] and any cause which is "external" in this sense is also "visible" within the meaning of an accident policy.[46] These words refer to the accident, not the injury, and are used to distinguish injuries covered by the policy from those due simply to such causes as disease or senility which arise in the body of the assured.

Thus the words "by violent, external and visible means" add little, if anything, to an accident policy and have been adversely criticised by the Court of Appeal.[47]

17–17 Limitations on cover

The cover afforded by an accident policy may be limited in two ways:

(a) by express words in the policy limiting the cover to particular kinds of accident, such as railway or transit accidents, or to particular kinds of injury such as total disablement;

(b) by means of inserting exceptions into the policy, such as poison and suicide.

17–18 "Railway accident"

Theobald v. *Railway Passengers' Assurance*,[48] in which the cover was limited to railway accidents, affords an illustration of the first type of limitation; it covers accidents arising out of an act immediately connected with the assured being a passenger.

17–19 Injuries in discharge of duty

Sometimes the cover is limited to injuries sustained by the assured in the discharge of his duty. This will not be limited to his ordinary everyday duties. Thus a signalman, so insured, was held to be covered when he was injured trying to stop a train, one of the carriages of which was broken.[49]

17–20 Total disablement

Where an insurance is limited to accidents wholly disabling the assured from following his *usual* business or occupation, the necessary condition for compensation under it is proof that an accident has so far disabled the assured that he can no longer follow his occupation, business and pursuits in the manner in which he usually carried it or them on before.[50] It is not necessary to prove that the assured cannot do any part of his business.

---

[43] *Hamlyn* v. *Crown Accidental Insurance* [1893] 1 Q.B. 750.
[44] *Ibid. per* Lord Esher M.R. at p. 753.
[45] *Ibid.* n. 44.
[46] *Hamlyn* v. *Crown Accidental Insurance* [1893] 1 Q.B. 750, *per* Lopes L.J. at p. 754.
[47] See n. 42, *supra*.
[48] (1854) 10 Exch. 45, 57, 58.
[49] *Pugh* v. *L.B. & S.C. Ry.* [1896] 2 Q.B. 248; *Wilkinson* v. *Downton* [1897] 2 Q.B. 57.
[50] *Hooper* v. *Accidental Death* (1860) 5 H. & N. 546, 557.

Loss of sight 17–21

Complete loss of sight is another particular peril sometimes specifically insured against. This may occur where a one-eyed man loses his remaining eye in an accident.[51] In a Canadian case it was held that the assured had "irrevocably lost" the "entire sight of one eye" so as to recover for it under a policy when he has lost all useful sight of the eye, although still able to distinguish light from darkness and to "see a shadow" if an object was placed close to his injured eye.[52]

Exceptions cover negligent acts 17–22

An injury to the assured otherwise falling within an exception to the policy will do so even though it is caused by his negligence or mistake, unless the express words of the exception clearly read otherwise. Thus where the policy excepted "poison or intentional self-injury," and the assured drank some poison by mistake and died, it was held that his representatives could not recover under the policy.[53] So where in the policy there was a clause excepting liability where the injury was caused by "anything . . . inhaled," and the assured accidentally inhaled coal gas, it was held that the injury was within the exception, which could not be read as being limited to "anything *voluntarily* inhaled."[54]

"Voluntary exposure to obvious risk" 17–23

The most interesting type of exception has arisen where the insurers have attempted to exclude injuries due to the assured's own fault. "Voluntary exposure to obvious risk" is an example.[55] Such an exception will exempt the insurers from liability where the risk would have been obvious to the assured had he been paying reasonable attention to what he was doing. Thus, in *Cornish* v. *Accident Insurance*,[56] the assured had crossed a main line and waited for one train to pass, and was re-crossing when a second train killed him. There was no crossing at the place and nothing to obstruct his view. The assured's death was held to fall within an exception of "exposure of the insured to obvious risk of injury." In the absence of negligence however such an exception has no application.[57] It does not apply merely because one travels[58] in a vehicle along the road,[59] or crosses the street,[60] or where a skilled swimmer goes out for a swim, even on a chilly night.[61]

The exception applies, on the other hand, where one takes a short cut along a railway line,[62] or goes too near the edge of a cliff whilst gathering flowers and falls over.[63]

---

[51] *Bawden* v. *London, Edinburgh & Glasgow Insurance* [1892] 2 Q.B. 534.

[52] *Shaw* v. *Globe Indemnity* [1921] 1 W.W.R. 332 (British Columbia, C.A.).

[53] *Cole* v. *Accident Insurance* (1889) 5 T.L.R. 736.

[54] *Re United London & Scottish Insurance* [1915] 2 Ch. 167.

[55] *Shilling* v. *Accidental Death* [1857] 2 H. & N. 42.

[56] (1889) 23 Q.B.D. 453.

[57] *Ibid. per* Lindley L.J. at p. 456.

[58] But it would appear to be negligent to travel as a passenger in a car knowing that the driver is unfit to drive owing to the consumption of intoxicating liquor: *Owens* v. *Brimmel* [1976] 3 All E.R. 765, Cardiff Assizes, Tasker Watkins J.

[59] See n. 54, *supra*.

[60] See n. 56, *supra*.

[61] *Sangster's Trustees* v. *General Accident* (1896) 24 R. (Ct. of Sess.) 56.

[62] *Lovell* v. *Accident Insurance* (1875) 39 J.P.J. 293.

[63] *Walker* v. *Railway Passengers' Assurance* (1910) 129 L.T. 64.

17–24 Influence of liquor

Another common exception excludes injuries while the assured is under the influence of liquor. It does not matter whether or not the assured's drunkenness caused the accident: it is enough for the insurers, relying on this exception, to show that the assured was under the influence of liquor when he received the injury.[64] The expression "under the influence of liquor" in accident policies has been held to refer to circumstances where "a man's conduct is banefully influenced by the liquor he has drunk"[65] or where he is "under such influence of intoxicating liquor as disturbs the balance of a man's mind or the intelligent exercise of his faculties."[66]

17–25 Return of total disablement payment

In *Alder* v. *Moore*[67] a group personal accident policy for professional football players provided that no claim for permanent total disablement should be paid unless the claimant signed a declaration that he would not play professionally in the future "and that in the event of infringement of this condition he will be subject to a penalty of the amount paid him. . . . " The Court of Appeal (Devlin L.J. dissenting) held that such repayment was to be regarded as a payment by way of damages and not a penalty, and was therefore enforceable.

[64] *Mair* v. *Railway Passengers' Assurance* (1877) 37 L.T. 356; *Louden* v. *British Merchants Ins.* [1961] 1 W.L.R. 798. See § 16–34, *supra*.
[65] *MacRobbie* v. *Accident Assurance* (1886) 23 S.L.R. 391.
[66] See n. 64, *supra*.
[67] [1960] 2 Lloyd's Rep. 325.

CHAPTER 18

FIRE AND PROPERTY INSURANCE

1. DEFINITIONS

Insurance Companies Act 1982   18–01
The insurance of "fire and natural forces" is classified in Schedule 2 to
the Act of 1982 as a business of which the nature is effecting and carrying out contracts of insurance against loss of or damage to property
(other than property to which classes 3 to 7 below relate) due to fire,
explosion, storm, natural forces other than storm, nuclear energy or
land subsidence. Classes 3 to 7 relate to land vehicles, railway rolling
stock, aircraft and ships respectively.

Same rules apply to fire and other property insurance   18–02
Apart from special statutory definitions fire insurance has not, unlike
marine insurance, for instance,[1] been closely defined, and the rules
applicable to it are applicable to property insurance generally. Thus, the
rule that fire insurance is not subject to average unless expressed to be
so, and the definitions of the various excepted perils such as war and
civil commotion, are common also to burglary, plate-glass insurance and
the like.

2. FIRE INSURANCE—THE RISK

Meaning of "fire"   18–03
An insurance policy is a mercantile contract, and the words used in it
must be given their plain meaning[2] unless the surrounding circumstances or the nature of the contract make a special construction necessary. Thus, the word "fire," in contracts of fire insurance, is taken in its
ordinary signification. It is not confined to any technical and restricted
meaning, which might be applied to it on a scientific analysis of its
nature and properties, nor should it receive that general and extended
meaning which, by a kind of figure of speech, is sometimes applied to
the term, but it should be construed in its ordinary, popular sense.

Actual ignition necessary. So unless there be actual ignition, and the 18–04
loss be proximately caused by such ignition, the insurers are not liable;
for example, where sugar was spoilt by great heat, through a register in
the chimney being closed, but where there was no actual ignition, it was
held that the assured could not recover.[3] Thus, the heat of the sun often
contracts timber, but that would not be considered a loss by fire, unless

---

[1] See ss.1–3 of M.I.A. 1906, *supra*, Chap. 23.
[2] See Atkinson J. in *Harris* v. *Poland* [1941] 1 K.B. 462 at p.468.
[3] *Austin* v. *Drewe* (1816) 4 Camp. 360. *cf. Tempus Shipping* v. *Dreyfus* [1930] 1 K.B. 699; *Fleming* v.
Hislop (1886) 11 App.Cas. 686.

there was ignition, and the loss arose from actual fire.[4] But so long as something, not intended to be so, is consumed[5] it does not matter that the fire does not break its bounds, as where a manuscript accidentally falls into a domestic fire, or where the assured hid jewellery in her fire-place and subsequently, forgetting she had done so, set light to the fire.[6] The ignition must be ignition in its popular, not its scientific, sense. An explosion may not be a fire within the meaning of a policy,[7] although an explosion may be, scientifically speaking, only a rapid form of ignition.

18–05   *Origin of fire immaterial.* The origin of the fire is immaterial, unless that origin is a peril excepted by the policy. If the loss happens by fire, it matters not, apart from special conditions in the policy, how the flame is kindled, whether it be the result of accident or design.

If the assured has deliberately set fire to his own property, his loss is nonethless one by fire, although public policy will prevent him, or any person claiming through him from recovering under the policy.[8] How-ever, public policy will not always operate this way in the case of delib-erate incendiarism by the assured. Thus, setting fire to a vessel to evade capture,[9] or because of an apprehension that she has plague on board[10] would fall within the risk of fire and would constitute a recoverable loss.

18–06   *Spontaneous combustion.* It would appear that a loss by spontaneous combustion of a substance, at any rate if the substance has a peculiar vice or infirmity, is not a loss under a fire policy covering that sub-stance,[11] but if any other substance catch fire there is a loss under the policy as regards that other substance.[12] This principle would apply in the case of spontaneous combustion of a hayrick.

18–07   *All losses proximately caused by fire covered.* As we have seen[13] once there is a fire in the sense above, all losses proximately caused by it will fall within the cover afforded by the policy.

Thus all damage due to efforts to arrest the spread of a fire is covered by the fire risk, provided the danger is imminent and the efforts are made in good faith. Such efforts may include the spoiling of goods by water,[14] the throwing of furniture out of a window, or even the blowing up of part of the premises.[15] Even unnecessary damage can be included under this head where the insurers enter into possession for the purpose of minimising damage.[16] In such a case they cannot be heard to say that damage while they were in possession was not the natural and direct consequence of the fire, as was held by the Privy Council in a case in

---

[4] *Babcock* v. *Montgomery Fire* (1849) 6 Barb.(N.Y.) 637.

[5] Atkinson J. in *Harris* v. *Poland, supra,* at p. 475.

[6] *Harris* v. *Poland, supra.* Contrast U.S. decisions (1946) 46 *Columbia Law Review,* pp. 362, 363.

[7] *Everett* v. *London Assurance* (1865) 19 C.B.(N.S.) 126. But see *Taunton* v. *Royal* (1864) 2 Hem. & M. 135, where it was held that a company could as a matter of business pay for such loss if it seemed in their interest. See also § 18–08, *infra.*

[8] *The Alexion Hope* [1988] 1 F.T.L.R. 270.

[9] *Gordon* v. *Rimmington* (1807) 1 Camp. 123.

[10] Emerigon, tom. 1, p. 434.

[11] See § 4–09, *supra,* by the implied exception of inherent vice.

[12] *Angell on Insurance,* p. 155.

[13] § 4–41, *supra.*

[14] *Johnston* v. *West of Scotland Insurance* (1828) 7 S. (Ct. of Sess.) 52, 55n.

[15] Kelly C.B. in *Stanley* v. *Western Insurance* (1868) L.R. 3 Ex. 71, 74.

[16] See § 18–33, *infra.*

which the insurers in possession allowed machinery damaged by water to deteriorate.[17]

The principle applies even where there is no actual ignition of the subject-matter insured[18] provided other property is burnt.[19] Thus, the blowing up of a house to stop a fire which has not yet reached it will be covered by a policy covering it against fire.[20] If a tenement catches fire, damage by water, both to that tenement and to the tenement below it, will be covered by fire policies on the respective tenements.[21]

Explosion. Apart from any special provision in the fire policy the **18–08** insurers will be liable, under the proximity rule, for loss due:

(a) to explosion caused by fire,[22] as where a burning match is dropped into a keg of gunpowder,[23] provided the damage is not too remote[24]; and

(b) to fire following an explosion.[25]

They will not, however, be liable for loss due to an explosion, even though, scientifically, it must have been preceded by ignition, if it was not caused by fire in the popular sense. Even where the explosion is caused by fire, only damage so caused that is proximate to the fire will be included. Thus, where in the course of the fire of a building an explosion occurs, damage so caused in the building will be included in the risk of fire, but damage to other buildings will not.[26] When fire follows on an explosion the insurers will be liable for the damage caused by it, notwithstanding that the explosion makes the fire burn more strongly.[27]

Where, however, explosion is an excepted peril, the position is differ- **18–09** ent, for in this case explosion causing a fire will be the proximate cause of any loss due to that fire,[28] and explosion caused by a fire will be the proximate cause of all damage due to the explosion. Thus where an explosion occurs while a house is on fire, damage caused by it to the house would not be covered by a policy excepting explosion from the risk.[29]

Where, conversely, explosion is covered and fire is excepted, the policy will not cover a fire following on an explosion, even though caused by it.[30] For there the fire is the proximate cause of the loss. But where a policy covered loss on the property of the assured damaged by accident to a turpentine-bleaching tank, but excepted loss from fire, and the tank door blew off and the gas, uniting with the air, became ignited

---

[17] *Ahmedbhoy* v. *Bombay Fire* (1912) 29 T.L.R. 96.

[18] *Symington* v. *Union Insurance of Canton* (1928) 97 L.J.K.B. 646.

[19] See § 18–04, *supra.*

[20] Kelly C.B. in *Stanley* v. *Western, supra,* at p. 74.

[21] *Geisek* v. *Crescent Mutual* (1867) 19 Louis Ann. 297.

[22] Scrutton L.J. in *Re Hooley Hill Rubber Co.* [1920] 1 K.B. 257, 271, 272; Lord Dunedin in *Curtis's & Harvey* v. *North British* [1921] 1 A.C. 303, 309, 310 (P.C.).

[23] *Hobbs* v. *Guardian* (1886) 12 Can.S.C. 631.

[24] *Everett* v. *London Assurance* (1865) 19 C.B.(N.S.) 126; see § 4–41, *supra.*

[25] *Stanley* v. *Western* (1868) L.R. 3 Ex. 71. An explosion is a physical or chemical reaction, as opposed to some mechanical defect: see *Commonwealth Smelting* v. *G.R.E.* [1984] 2 Lloyd's Rep. 608.

[26] See n. 24.

[27] Masters B. in *Stanley* v. *Western, supra.*

[28] *Stanley* v. *Western, supra.*

[29] *Stanley* v. *Western; Re Hooley Hill; Curtis's & Harvey* v. *North British; supra.*

[30] *Abasand Oils* v. *Boiler Inspection Co.* (1949) 65 T.L.R. 713 (P.C.).

and exploded, the Privy Council held that the explosion was caused by the accident to the tank, *and* that the insurers could not rely on the exception of fire.[31] The fire was merely an incident in the explosion.

18–10   *Lightning and electricity*. The same rules apply to damage by lightning or electricity: unless the subject-matter is actually burnt by a fire, in which case it does not matter that lightning[32] or electricity caused it, the assured is not covered under an insurance against fire only. Neither by itself amounts to a "fire" in the popular sense. A clause exempting the insurer from damage by lightning unless it fires the subject-matter no more than sets out his common law liability.[33]

18–11 Excepted risks

Not only such risks as spontaneous combustion, explosion, lightning and earthquakes,[34] and other natural causes, but also such human risks as incendiarism, riot, civil commotion and war risks are often excepted in fire and other property insurances.

18–12   *"Incendiarism."* Where a policy contains the condition that it shall not cover loss occasioned by incendiarism,[35] and premises are set on fire by an incendiary whereby insured goods on adjoining premises are accidentally destroyed, the insurers will not be liable.[36]

18–13   *"Riot."* Prior to 1986 it had become established that the word "riot" in a policy was to be understood in its strict common law sense[37] and not in its popular signification. Thus where four armed men obtained admittance by trick into the assured's place of business, and terrorised the persons employed there with revolvers, and carried off a large sum in cash, without any outward noise or disturbance, the House of Lords held that the loss was caused by riot and was not covered by a burglary policy excepting that risk.[38] The meaning of "riot" was, however, altered by the Public Order Act 1986, section 1, so that violent conduct on the part of *twelve* persons acting in a common purpose is now required. The new meaning takes effect in marine policies, by an amendment to the schedule to the Marine Insurance Act 1906, r. 10, effected by the 1986 Act. It is unclear whether the word riot in non-marine policies bears the old or new meaning, but it is thought likely that the new meanng would prevail.

Where a riot exception does prevent recovery under the policy, the assured's remedy is against the relevant compensation authority under

---

[31] *Boiler Inspection Co.* v. *Sherwin-Williams* [1951] A.C. 319.

[32] Ellenborough L.C.J. in *Gordon* v. *Rimmington* (1807) 1 Camp. 123, 124.

[33] See *Everett* v. *London Assurance, supra; Babcock* v. *Montgomery Fire Co.* (1849) 6 Barb.N.Y. 637.

[34] See *Tootal* v. *London & Lancashire Insurance, The Times,* May 21, 1908; Welford, *Fire,* (3rd ed.), pp.498–500; *Scottish Union* v. *Pawsey, The Times,* October 17, 1908.

[35] See *Gorman* v. *Hand-in-Hand* (1877) Ir.Rep. 11 C.L. 224; *Walker* v. *London & Provincial* (1888) 22 L.R.Ir. 572.

[36] *Walker* v. *London & Provincial, supra.*

[37] See *Field* v. *Receiver for the Metropolitan Police District* [1907] 2 K.B. 853 for the common law definition: this was, in essence, violence or threats of violence by three or more persons.

[38] *London & Lancashire Fire* v. *Bolands* [1924] A.C. 836; see also *Gliksten* v. *State* (1922) 10 Ll.L.R. 604; *Cooper* v. *General Accident* (1922) 39 T.L.R. 113; *Motor Union* v. *Boggan* (1923) 130 L.T. 588; *Lycoming Fire* v. *Schwenk* (1880) 40 Am.Rep. 629.

the Riot (Damages) Act 1886 (as amended by the Police Act 1964 and the Local Government Act 1972).[39] If, on the other hand, riot is not excepted and the insurers pay, they will be entitled by way of subrogation to recover under that Act.[40]

"Civil commotion." "Civil commotion," a term without any such **18–14** strict legal meaning, was first introduced as an exception in London Assurance fire policies in 1720.[41] It is defined by Lord Mansfield as "an insurrection of the people for general purposes, though it may not amount to a rebellion."[42] It does not cover an organised conspiracy to commit criminal acts, without any actual commotion or disturbance, as was decided in a case dealing with certain suffragette activities.[43] Civil strife amounting to warfare, as the Sackville Street (Dublin) affair of 1916 is, on the other hand, something more than mere civil commotion.[44] Although a civil commotion may, technically speaking, also constitute a riot,[45] the phrase is used to indicate a stage between a riot and a civil war.[46] While the element of turbulence or tumult is essential, it is not necessary to show the existence of any outside organisation at whose instigation the acts were done although some form of common objective is required.[47]

Once civil commotion is proved, all losses proximately caused thereby will be excepted. Thus where the assured's motor car was taken in Ireland, with a show of force, at a time when there was a civil commotion in the neighbourhood, although not at the actual place, and there was evidence that motor cars were much used by those engaged in the commotion, it was held by the House of Lords that the court was justified in finding that the loss fell within the exception of civil commotion.[48]

Military or usurped power. The exception of military or usurped **18–15** power does not include a mere civil commotion,[49] but refers to such occasions as invasion from abroad, or an internal rebellion where armies are employed to support it.[50] An example of damage caused by military power is that suffered in an enemy air-raid,[51] but it also includes acts done by our own forces in repelling the enemy or suppressing a rebellion.[52] A common mob can be distinguished from a rebellious mob in that the former commits riot, the latter treason.[53] There must be a rebel-

---

[39] See as to ships, the Merchant Shipping Act 1894, s.515.
[40] s.2; this remedy was analogous to their common law right of recovery from the hundred; see *Mason* v. *Sainsbury* (1782) 3 Doug. 61; *Langdale* v. *Mason* (1780) 2 Marshall, 2nd ed., 791, 794.
[41] *Langdale* v. *Mason, supra;* see also *Drinkwater* v. *London Assurance* (1767) 2 Wils. 363; *Mason* v. *Sainsbury, supra.*
[42] *Ibid.* n. 41.
[43] *London & Manchester Plate Glass* v. *Heath* [1913] 3 K.B. 411; see *Cooper* v. *General Accident, supra, per* Cave L.C.at p. 116; see also *Craig* v. *Eagle Star* (1922) 56 Ir.L.T. 145.
[44] *Curtis* v. *Mathews* [1919] 1 K.B. 425.
[45] *Per* Lord Birkenhead in *Motor Union* v. *Boggan, supra,* at p. 591.
[46] Farwell L.J. in *Bolivia Republic* v. *Indemnity Mutual* [1909] 1 K.B. 785, 800. See also *Spinney's* v. *Royal Insurance Co.* [1980] 1 Lloyd's Rep. 406.
[47] *Levy* v. *Assicurazioni Generali* [1940] A.C. 791; *Spinney's supra.*
[48] *Cooper* v. *General Accident, supra,* see also *Motor Union* v. *Boggan, supra.*
[49] *Curtis* v. *Mathews, supra.*
[50] *Drinkwater* v. *London Assurance* (1767) 2 Wils. 363, 365, *per* Wilmot C.J. See also *Spinney's* v. *Royal Insurance Co.* [1980] 1 Lloyd's Rep. 404.
[51] *Rogers* v. *Whittaker* [1917] 1 K.B. 942.
[52] See n. 49, *supra.*
[53] See n. 50, *supra.*

lion, conducted by authority, to constitute "usurped power."[54] "Usurped power" does not include the act of a civil magistrate who exceeds his lawful powers[55] or an act of a government *de facto* recognised by the British Government.[56]

18–16   "*War*." Where war risks are excepted "war" is not used in any technical meaning; thus, on the commencement of the China incident it was held that there was a "war," for the purposes of a charterparty, between China and Japan, irrespective of whether H.M. Government recognised a state of war or whether diplomatic relationships had been broken.[57] So the Irish rebellion was held to amount to "war" within the meaning of insurance policies,[58] and the revolutionaries were held to be "king's enemies."[59] "The word 'war' in a policy of insurance includes civil war unless the context makes it clear that a different meaning should be given to the word."[60]

18–17   "*Destruction by government*." "Destruction by government" means deliberate and intentional destruction, in the sense of confiscation, and not incidental damage caused in the course of military operations against rebels or a foreign enemy.[61]

18–18 Termination of fire risk by notice
     Where a fire policy is subject to a condition that "if by any reason of a change in the risk, or from any other cause whatever," the insurers desire to terminate the assurance, it should be lawful for them to do so on refunding a rateable proportion of the premium, the policy is determinable at the will of the insurers.[62]

3. NON-DISCLOSURE AND MISREPRESENTATION

18–19 The rule making policies voidable for non-disclosure or misrepresentation of a material fact[63] applies in the case of fire insurance policies[64] as to insurance generally.

18–20 Facts increasing risk
     The risk of fire may be increased either by the peculiar structure of the building or by the nature of the goods insured or by the nature or state of surrounding structures. Such facts will then be material and must be disclosed. Such are the facts that a building near to a house insured has recently been on fire,[65] or the structure and situation of the garage of an insured car,[66] or that a wooden building behind a ware-

---

[54] Lord Mansfield in *Langdale* v. *Mason, supra*, at p. 792.
[55] *City Fire* v. *Corlies* (1836) 21 Wend.N.Y. 367.
[56] *White, Child and Beney* v. *Eagle Star* (1922) 127 L.T. 571, 583, *per* Bankes L.J.
[57] *Kawasaki, etc.* v. *Bantham SS. Co.* [1939] 2 K.B. 544.
[58] *Curtis* v. *Mathews* [1919] 1 K.B. 425.
[59] *Secretary of State for War* v. *Midland Great Western Railway of Ireland* [1923] 2 Ir.R. 102.
[60] *Pesquerias* v. *Beer* (1949) 82 Ll.L.R. 501, 514, *per* Lord Morton.
[61] *Curtis* v. *Mathews, supra*.
[62] *Sun Fire* v. *Hart* (1889) 14 App.Cas. 98.
[63] See Chap. 5, *supra*.
[64] See *Bufe* v. *Turner* (1815) 6 Taunt. 338.
[65] *Bufe* v. *Turner, supra*.
[66] *Dawsons* v. *Bonnin* [1922] 2 A.C. 413, 429, *per* Viscount Finlay.

house insured against fire is used as a kitchen.[67] On the other hand where buildings were described as built of brick and slated, but it turned out that one of the buildings was in fact roofed with tarred felt, it was held that this mis-description was immaterial as no higher premium would have been charged had the truth been disclosed.[68] Threats to set fire to a property may be material.[69]

Description of property insured   **18–21**
The description of one room occupied by a lodger as a "dwelling-house" has been held not to be inaccurate.[70] A coffee-house has been held not to come under the description of "inn,"[71] and a "garage" has been held not to include an unroofed yard,[72] though furniture in lifts in a yard covered by tarpaulins has been held to be "in store."[73]

4. ALTERATIONS IN RISK OF FIRE

While the assured is bound to disclose all material facts relating to the **18–22** structure or the contents of buildings insured, and any material alterations therein, up to the time of the completion of the contract, the policy, in the absence of any express condition on the matter, is not in any way invalidated by any subsequent increase in the risk. Thus, in *Pim* v. *Reid*[74] Pim carried on the business of a papermaker, and effected an insurance on the premises in which the business was carried on. Subsequently, a large quantity of cotton waste was cleaned and dyed there. A fire occurred when some of it was in the mill and, though it appeared that insurance offices generally declined to insure premises where cotton waste was kept or used, the company was held liable. The principle applies even where the assured warrants his description of the premises, or of the use he puts them to, to be true,[75] provided always that such warranty does not relate to the future.[76] So a statement by the assured as to the use to which he is going to put the subject-matter of the insurance, even if warranted to be true, will not bind him subsequently if he honestly changes his mind, unless his statement amounts to a warranty that the subject-matter is only to be so used.[77]

---

[67] *Barsalou* v. *Royal*, 15 Lr.Can.Rep. 1.
[68] *Re Universal Non-Tariff Fire* (1875) L.R. 19 Eq. 485.
[69] *Watt* v. *Union Ins. Co.* (1884) 5 N.S.W.L.R. 48; *North American Fire Ins. Co.* v. *Throop* (1871) 7 Am.Rep. 638. *Cf. Bufe* v. *Turner* (1815) 6 Taunt. 338. See also *Greet* v. *Citizens' Ins. Co.* (1880) 5 U.C.Er. & App. 596, 601; *Herbert* v. *Mercantile Fire Ins. Co.* (1873) 43 U.C.Q.B. 384; *Campbell* v. *Victoria Mutual Fire Ins. Co.* (1880) 45 U.C.Q.B 412.
[70] *Friedlander* v. *London Assurance* (1832) 1 Moo. & R. 171.
[71] *Doe* d. *Pitt* v. *Laming* (1814) 4 Camp. 73.
[72] *Barnett* v. *National Parcels Insurance* [1942] 1 All E.R. 221.
[73] *Wulfson* v. *Switzerland General* (1940) 163 L.T. 136. And see §§ 4–17 *et seq., supra.*
[74] (1843) 6 M. & G. 1. Thus in *Exchange Theatre* v. *Iron Trades Mutual Ins.* [1983] 1 Lloyd's Rep. 674 a bingo hall was insured against fire in March 1977. In January 1978 the hall was destroyed by fire. The insurers denied liability on the ground, *inter alia*, that the assured without first obtaining the agreement of the insurers, had installed a petrol generator which increased the risk. Lawson J. held that that was not an unauthorised alteration to the building entitling the insurers to avoid the policy, and the assured were entitled to judgment.
[75] *Shaw* v. *Robberds* (1837) 6 Ad. & El. 75, 82, *per* Denman L.C.J.
[76] *Sillem* v. *Thornton* (1854) 3 E. & B. 868. This seems to have been the effect of such a warranty in *Whitehead* v. *Price* (1835) 2 Cr.M. & R. 447, and possibly also in *Dobson* v. *Sotherby* (1827) 1 M. & M. 90, 92, 93.
[77] *Provincial* v. *Morgan* [1933] A.C. 240; *Grant* v. *Aetna Insurance* (1862) 15 Moo.P.C.C. 516.

18–23 Conditions as to alteration of risk

Temporary alterations to risk. It is usual, therefore, for a condition to be included in fire insurance policies that subsequent alterations in the fire risk should be notified to the insurers,[78] and sometimes that their consent should be obtained to such alterations. Such a condition usually refers only to permanent and habitual alterations.[79] Thus in *Shaw* v. *Robberds*[80] the assured took out a policy containing such a condition on a granary containing a kiln for drying corn. Without notifying the insurers he gratuitously allowed the owner of some bark to dry it in this kiln to oblige him, with the result that the mill was burnt down. The jury found that bark drying was more dangerous than corn drying, but, since the use of the kiln for drying bark was only temporary and not in the way of business, it was held that the assured was entitled to recover. Similarly, in *Dobson* v. *Sotheby*,[81] where the condition was against the use of the premises insured for storing hazardous goods, tar was brought into the building for the purpose of tarring it, and the building was consequently set on fire, but it was held that the condition did not apply to the temporary introduction of hazardous materials, and that the insurers again were liable. Again, in *Thompson* v. *Equity Fire*[82] the Privy Council held that a clause excepting loss or damage occurring while gasoline was stored or kept in the building insured did not apply where a stove burning gasoline was used in a drug store, and the fire was caused by gasoline used in it.

The principle is that, as in the construction of other conditions,[83] if the insurers wish to make it a condition precedent to the validity of the policy that there shall be no alteration in the risk, they must do so in distinct terms.[84]

18–24   *Promissory and descriptive conditions*. Unless the condition otherwise expressly provides, is is to be construed as referring to the assured's present intentions and will not constitute a promise that its terms will be adhered to throughout the currency of the policy. In *Farnham* v. *Royal Insurance*[84A] the condition was in usual form against "any alteration after the commencement of this insurance . . . whereby the (fire) risk of destruction or damage is increased." Farm buildings were insured against the fire risk of carriers and transit warehousing. The assured allowed a third party to arrange for repairs on the premises to cargo containers stored there, and a fire occurred. Ackner J. held that the insurers were entitled to avoid the policy for breach of condition. To the knowledge of the assured, repair work involving the use of welding equipment

---

[78] *Shaw* v. *Robberds* (1837) 6 Ad. & El. 75.

[79] Denman L.C.J. in *Shaw* v. *Robberds, supra*, at p. 83. This case was disapproved by Parke B. in *Glen* v. *Lewis* (1853) 8 Ex. 607, 619, but was cited with apparent approval by Lord Wright in *Provincial* v. *Morgan* [1933] A.C. 240, 255. The cases are distinguishable on the ground stated in the text and also on the test whether the use was in the ordinary course of business.

[80] See n. 77, *supra*.

[81] (1827) 1 M. & M. 90.

[82] [1910] A.C. 592.

[83] See §§ 2–11 *et seq., supra*.

[84] Martin B. in *Baxendale* v. *Harvey* (1859) 4 H. & N. 445, 450, citing *Stokes* v. *Cox* (1856) 1 H. & N. 533.

[84A] [1976] 2 Lloyd's Rep. 437.

took place within the barn, and that, the judge found, increased the risk.

By contrast, in *Hair* v. *Prudential Ass.*[85] the assured completed in September 1977 a "Hearth and Home" proposal form stating (1) that the buildings were kept in a good state of repair, (2) that the premises were inhabited by the proposer's son, and (3) that they were regularly left unattended. The value was given at £8,000. In November 1978 a serious fire gutted the property: the Prudential denied liability on the grounds that the premises were not in a good state of repair, were not occupied, were uninhabitable, and that the assured had paid £230 for the property because there was a closing order in existence. Woolf J., giving judgment in her favour for £8,000 on the assured's suit, held that (1) when the form was signed the evidence on a balance of probability showed that the property *was* in a good state of repair (and did not materially change thereafter); (2) although the property did become uninhabited for long periods, the questions in the proposal form were directed towards the state of affairs when the form was signed, there was no warranty by the proposer that the position would not change thereafter; and (3) his Lordship would not be adverse to her in failing to disclose the closing order.

A condition requiring notification of any increase in the risk does not **18–25** apply to increases which might be taken to be within the contemplation of the parties at the time of taking out the insurance.[86] Thus where the insurers had allowed the assured to use a store room insured to boil varnish, the introduction of boilers for this purpose was held not to fall within the condition,[87] and the same was held where the insurers allowed the erection of a steam engine, even where it was used for a purpose they had not actually anticipated and which was specially dangerous.[88]

Where the assured states the trade for which premises are to be used, the insurers may be taken to know all facts relating to the general course of such trade.[89]

In the case of all such conditions the burden is on the insurers to prove the prohibited alteration of the risk[90] and the absence of notice[91] to or consent by them.

Conditions prohibiting introduction of specified thing   **18–26**

The result of these decisions has been the introduction of clauses into fire policies forbidding not only alterations in the risk, construed to mean permanent alterations without the consent of the insurers, but also the introduction of stipulated dangerous things such as steam

---

[85] [1983] 2 Lloyd's Rep. 661.
[86] *Law Guarantee Trust* v. *Munich Reinsurance* [1912] 1 Ch. 138, 154.
[87] *Barrett* v. *Jermy* (1849) 3 Ex. 535.
[88] *Baxendale* v. *Harvey* (1859) 4 H. & N. 445; see also *Whitehead* v. *Price* (1835) 2 Cr.M. & R. 447; *Mayall* v. *Mitford* (1837) 6 A. & E. 670.
[89] Shee J. in *Bates* v. *Hewitt* (1867) L.R. 2 Q.B. 595, 610.
[90] *Whitehead* v. *Price* (1835) 2 Cr.M. & R. 447, 456, *per* Parke B.
[91] *Barrett* v. *Jermy* (1849) 3 Ex. 535, 542, *per* Parke B.

engines, stoves, etc.[92] Such a condition applies even to a temporary
introduction of the prohibited thing, and the fact that it does not cause
the loss is immaterial.[93] Such a clause prevents decisions such as *Stokes*
v. *Cox*,[94] in which the jury found that the introduction of a steam engine
did not constitute a breach of a condition prohibiting an increase in the
risk.

Such conditions, unlike conditions against variation of the risk,[95] are
strictly construed. Thus, in *McEwan* v. *Guthridge*,[96] the Privy Council
held that the assured could not recover where he kept more than 56 lb of
gunpowder on the insured premises contrary to a condition in the
policy.

Sometimes such risks are provided against by way of exception, *e.g.*
to risk of fire by installation of dangerous plant.

18–27 Leaving premises unoccupied

It is a question of fact in each case whether leaving a building unoccupied amounts to an increase in the risk of fire.[97] "A house may be so
situated that to leave it vacant for any length of time would expose it to
be fired by some malicious or wantonly wicked person. On the other
hand, it may be so situated that its want of occupancy may be to reduce
the danger."[98] In any case the burden of proving that leaving a house
unoccupied increases the risk lies on the insurer.[99]

It might be thought that leaving a house unoccupied in a civilised
country where neighbours did not often burn each other's houses out of
spite generally reduced the risk of fire, and express provisions excepting
fires while the insured building is unoccupied are, in fact, rare in policies
issued in Great Britain, though continuous occupancy is frequently
made a condition in burglary policies.[1] In North America and the Dominions,[2] on the other hand, fire policies often contain such provisions,
and the insurers are not always content to rely on a general condition as
to alteration of the risk.

A condition that premises shall remain "occupied" is not broken
where the assured seeks refuge in a shelter during an air-raid,[3] or in case
of temporary absence on business or for family convenience,[4] and
absence for as much as three days was held not to constitute a breach of
such condition in a Canadian case.[5] But "occupation" means actual use
as a dwelling-house, mere use for storage is not enough,[6] nor is employment of a night watchman to observe an empty building from outside it.[7]

---

[92] Parke B. in *Glen* v. *Lewis* (1853) 8 Ex. 607, 619.
[93] *Glen* v. *Lewis* (1853) 8 Ex. 607.
[94] (1856) 1 H. & N. 533.
[95] See § 2–11, *supra.*
[96] (1860) 13 Moo.P.C.C. 304; see also *Beacon Life & Fire* v. *Gibb* (1862) 1 Moo.P.C.C.(N.S.) 73.
[97] *Cooper* v. *Toronto Casualty Insurance* [1928] 2 D.L.R. 1007.
[98] Harrison C.J. in *Abrahams* v. *Agricultural Mutual* (1876) 40 U.C.Q.B. 175, 182.
[99] *Foy* v. *Aetna Insurance* (1854) 8 N.B.R. (3 All.) 29.
[1] *Winicofsky* v. *Army & Navy General Assurance* (1919) 88 L.J.K.B. 1111.
[2] See *London & Lancashire* v. *Honey* (1876) 2 Vict.L.R. 7.
[3] *Winicofsky* v.*Army & Navy General Assurance* (1919) 88 L.J.K.B. 1111.
[4] *Shackleton* v. *Sun Fire* (1884) 54 Am.Rep. 379.
[5] *Canada Landed Credit Co.* v. *Canada Agricultural Insurance* (1870) 17 Grant (U.C.) 418.
[6] *Ashworth* v. *Builders' Mutual* (1873) 17 Am.Rep. 117.
[7] *Marzouca* v. *Atlantic and British Commercial Ins.* [1971] 1 Lloyd's Rep. 449. "The occupation to be
effectual must be actual not constructive," p. 453 (P.C., appeal from Jamaica).

5. AVERAGE CONDITIONS

Partial loss   **18–28**

Under an ordinary fire or other non-marine policy the assured is entitled to recover, within the limits of the sum insured, the whole amount of any loss or damage.[8] Thus, although the assured obtains the insurance at a small premium by under-insuring, the insurers may, nevertheless, be bound to pay him the whole amount of a loss of part only of the subject-matter insured. In this respect fire and other non-marine insurance differs from marine insurance,[9] and by section 81 of the Marine Insurance Act 1906,[10] where the assured is insured for an amount less than the insurable value, he is deemed to be his own insurer in respect of the uninsured balance. Thus, if goods worth £300 are insured for £200, and half only of them are lost, the assured would be entitled to recover £150 under a fire policy but only £100 under a marine-policy. In the latter case he would be deemed to his own insurer as to £100, the uninsured balance, and he would have, therefore, to bear £50 of the partial loss. But under a non-marine policy the assured bears no part of the loss until the sum assured is exhausted.[11]

In order to prevent under-insurance a condition may therefore be inserted in a fire policy making it "subject to average." Such a condition is not uncommon in fire policies on goods,[12] for in such a case the probability of a partial loss only is high. The use of the term "subject to average" in fire policies should be distinguished from special uses of the word "average" in marine insurance law. "Subject to average" in a fire policy implies that the policy is subject to a condition similar to section 81 of the Marine Insurance Act. The condition is an old one[13] and is specially necessary in floating policies.[14] Thus policies on goods in lighters generally include such a clause applying the marine rule.[15]

Lloyd's first average condition   **18–29**

Thus in 1904, the words "subject to average" in a Lloyd's fire policy imported the following standard clause into the policy:[16]

> "Whenever a sum insured is declared to be subject to average, if the property shall, at the breaking out of any fire, be collectively of greater value than such sum insured, then the insured shall be considered as being his own insurer for the difference, and shall bear a rateable share of the loss accordingly."

This was the first or *pro rata* condition of average used by Lloyd's

---

[8] *Fifth Building Society* v. *Travellers Insurance* (1893) 9 T.L.R. 221; *Newman* v. *Maxwell* (1899) 80 L.T. 681.

[9] *Joyce* v. *Kennard* (1871) L.R. 7 Q.B. 78.

[10] Set out § 23–82, *infra*.

[11] Campbell L.C.J. in *Sillem* v. *Thornton* (1854) 3 E. & B. 868, 888; Walton J. in *Anglo-Californian Bank* v. *London Marine & General* (1904) 10 Com.Cas. 1, 9.

[12] Bailhache J. in *Carreras* v. *Cunard SS. Co.* [1918] 1 K.B. 118, 122. The practice is today less common than was once the case.

[13] See 9 Geo. 4, c. 13 (Stamps on fire insurances) ss.1–3, repealed by 32 & 33 Vict. c. 14 (Revenue), making such a condition necessary in order that the value for stamp duty could be ascertained; *Hare* v. *Barstow* (1844) 8 Jur. 928.

[14] See § 14–40, *supra*.

[15] *Crowley* v. *Cohen* (1832) 3 B. & Ad. 478; contrast *Joyce* v. *Kennard*.

[16] *Acme Wood Flooring* v. *Marten* (1904) 20 T.L.R. 229.

underwriters; a modified or special condition was also in force making the assured his own insurer only where the proportion of the sum insured to the value of the property insured fell below a stated percentage.

18–30 Average clauses and double insurance

The fact that the assured has insured the same property with other insurers will not enable him to recover any more under such a policy. Thus, where timber worth £36,000 was insured under policy A for £12,000, subject to average, and under other policies for a further £30,000, and the assured suffered a loss of timber amounting to £12,000 in value, it was held that he was entitled to recover no more than £4,000 under policy A.[17] In such a case the assured is bound therefore to sue each insurer separately, he cannot claim to recover the whole loss from one insurer, leaving him to obtain contribution from the others. In fact the effect of the average clause in that case was similar to that of a clause limiting the liability of the insurers to their rateable share of the loss.[18]

In cases of double insurance an insurer without benefit of an average clause may be prejudiced by an average clause in other policies, hence, it is common to insert an average clause to take effect only where there is other insurance which is subject to average,[19] or where the other insurance is subject to any other provision whereby it may be excluded from contributing rateably to the whole loss.

18–31 Clauses having similar effect

A condition throwing a specified proportion[20] or a specified amount[21] of the loss on the assured is sometimes inserted in a policy in place of an ordinary average clause, especially in the case of reinsurance policies.[22]

6. RIGHTS AFTER LOSS

18–32 Duty of assured to minimise loss[23]

If the assured's house takes fire he must use reasonable efforts to extinguish the flames and to save his goods. He is not entitled to look on and let them burn because he is insured. His loss would in such a case be to a great extent the direct consequence of his own act, for which he would not be entitled to recover under the policy.[24] Such conduct might even amount to fraud, in which case he would not be entitled to recover anything under the policy, even in respect of other losses.

---

[17] *Acme Wood Flooring* v. *Marten, supra.*
[18] See § 8–36, *supra.*
[19] See *North British* v. *London, Liverpool & Globe* (1877) 5 Ch.D. 569.
[20] *Williamson* v. *Gore District Mutual Fire* (1866) 26 U.C.Q.B. 145; *McCulloch* v. *Gore* (1872) 32 U.C.Q.B. 610.
[21] Especially in motor-vehicle policies where the driver is inexperienced, *Zurich* v. *Morrison* [1942] 2 K.B. 53.
[22] *Traill* v. *Baring* (1864) 4 De G.J. & Sm 318. As to insurance of rent see *Buchanan* v. *Liverpool, London & Globe* (1884) 21 S.L.R. 696.
[23] See also § 4–38, *supra.*
[24] Scrutton L.J. in *City Tailors* v. *Evans* (1921) 38 T.L.R. 230, 233, 234.

Insurer's right of entry 18–33

As soon as a fire breaks out the insurers have an obvious interest in fighting it and saving what they can from the flames. However, their common law right of entry on to the premises for this purpose is vague, although they probably have some such right.[25] Besides, their right to retain insured property as salvage will only arise after they have paid the assured under the policy. A provision is therefore usually included in the policy allowing them to enter and take possession of the premises or its contents in the event of a fire.

But by doing so they may lay themselves open to claims in respect of loss of, or damage to, the property of the assured while they are in possession.[26]

Another disadvantage of entry under such a provision is that it may,[27] though it will not necessarily,[28] amount to an affirmation of the validity of the assured's claim by which they will be estopped from contesting it.

Sue and labour clause 18–34

The sue and labour clause[29] in marine policies is occasionally introduced into fire policies.[30] The aim of the clause is to induce the assured to do all he can to save the insured property by promising to recoup him for expenses reasonably incurred for the preservation of the thing insured from loss,[31] but it is not a contract to indemnify him against any claims made by other people against him.[32]

The condition in *Thompson* v. *Montreal Insurance Co.*[33] was that in case of removal to escape conflagration the insurer would contribute rateably with the assured and other insurers to the loss and expenses "attending the act of salvage." Robinson C.J. said: "That clause was surely not intended to deprive the assured of any portion of his claim under the general terms of his policy, but is a condition wholly for his advantage, and intended to afford him a remedy for something in addition to the compensation for his goods destroyed, injured, or lost in consequence of the fire." The law laid down in this case with regard to a fire insurance seems quite in accordance with the view of Lord Blackburn in *Aitchison* v. *Lohre*[34] on the effect of the sue and labour clause in a marine policy.

---

[25] See notes to *Oldfield* v. *Price* (1860) 2 F. & F. 80.
[26] See, *e.g. Oldfield* v. *Price, supra*; *Norton* v. *Royal Fire* (1885) 1 T.L.R. 460; *Ahmedbhoy* v. *Bombay Fire* (1912) 29 T.L.R. 96 (P.C.).
[27] *Yorkshire Insurance* v. *Craine* [1922] 2 A.C. 541 (P.C.).
[28] *Locker & Woolf* v. *Western Australian Insurance* [1936] 1 K.B. 408.
[29] *Kidston* v. *Empire Marine Ins. Co.* (1866) L.R. 1 C.P. 535; affirmed (1867) L.R. 2 C.P. 357. See generaly s.78 of the M.I.A. 1906, *infra*, § 23–79.
[30] *Thompson* v. *Montreal Ins. Co.* (1850) 6 U.C.Q.B. 319; M.I.A. 1906, s.78.
[31] *Aitchison* v. *Lohre* (1879) 4 App.Cas. 755; *Thompson* v. *Montreal Ins. Co.*, *supra*.
[32] *Johnston* v. *Salvage Association* (1887) 19 Q.B.D. 458, 460.
[33] (1850) 6 U.C.Q.B. 319.
[34] (1879) 4 App.Cas. 755, 764.

CHAPTER 19

LIABILITY INSURANCE

1. GENERAL

A person may insure himself not only against the risk of death and per- **19–01**
sonal injury, or damage to his property, but also against the risk of
incurring liability to third parties. Though such insurance may be an
insurance on property for some purposes,[1] the risk of liability in connection with the use of goods or other property is one which must be specifically insured against and is not covered by a simple insurance on goods.
Where a policy is capable of being construed either on goods or on liability—as in the case of a policy taken out by a carrier or other bailee—
there is a presumption that the amount recoverable is the value of the
goods and not the lesser amount of the assured's liability to the owner in
respect of the goods.[2]

Contract of indemnity   **19–02**
An insurance against liability is a contract of indemnity.[3] Insurance
against liability for accidents arising in connection with the use of motor
vehicles, or against liability to the public by the owners of business and
employers' liability insurance furnish examples of such insurance. Professional men, such as solicitors and doctors, may also insure against
liabilities which may be incurred in the course of their practices. Liability insurance is required by various pieces of legislation—most importantly in relation to motor vehicles (Road Traffic Act 1988),[4] employers'
liability (Employers Liability (Compulsory Insurance) Act 1969),[5] solicitors (Solicitors Act 1974) and nuclear installations (Nuclear Installations Act 1965)—and may be imposed by the governing bodies of
certain professions (*e.g.* in relation to insurance brokers and other insurance intermediaries).[6]

Forms of liability policy   **19–03**
Liability policies generally fall within one of two classes. First, the
policy may protect the assured against all losses occurring during the
currency of the policy; in such a case the insurer accepts liability for
causes of action against the assured which may have arisen prior to the
inception of the policy, but which give rise to an award of damages
against him during the currency of the policy. The insurer will, therefore, prior to the making of the contract require disclosure of any events

---

[1] *Williams* v. *Baltic* [1924] 2 K.B. 282; *Prudential Staff Union* v. *Hall* [1947] K.B. 685.
[2] *Tomlinson* v. *Hepburn* [1966] A.C. 451.
[3] Fletcher Moulton L.J. in *British Cash & Parcel Conveyors* v. *Lamson Store Service* [1908] 1 K.B.
1006, 1014. See also *Goddard and Smith* v. *Frew* [1939] 4 All E.R. 358.
[4] *Infra*, Chap. 20.
[5] *Infra*, § 19–14 *et seq.*
[6] *Supra*, Chap. 15.

known to the assured and likely to give rise to a claim during the currency of the policy.[7] Moreover, the insurer may also refuse to accept liability for any loss flowing from an event which has been notified to another insurer under an earlier policy.[8]

The second class of liability policy imposes liability on the insurer for any event occurring or notified to the insurer during the currency of the policy; the fact that damages are not awarded against the assured until after the policy has run off is immaterial in such a case. It was held by the Court of Appeal in *Thorman* v. *New Hampshire Insurance*[9] that the issue of a writ against the assured, rather than its subsequent service, is the notifiable "occurrence," and that it is immaterial that the claims under the writ as issued are not particularised until some later date.

It will be appreciated that the former class of policy deals to some extent with retroactive liability, whereas the latter deals with prospective liability.

19–04 Forms of liability covered

Liability policies are frequently expressed as providing indemnity against "liability at law." This phrase is undoubtedly aimed primarily at negligence liability, but is not so confined. In *M/S Aswan Engineering* v. *Iron Trades Mutual*[10] it was held by the Court of Appeal that the term covered liability in contract, under the Sale of Goods Act 1979, as well as liability in tort.[11] Again, in *Wimpey Construction* v. *Poole*[12] Webster J. held that insurers were liable to indemnify a building contractor who had incurred liability to a third party for the faulty design of a structure even though the fault did not amount to negligence.

Moreover, the liability covered may not be the kind for which the remedy is an action for damages against the assured. It may affect his property, as where the assured insures against a restrictive covenant being enforced so as to make intended development impractical. Where such a policy insured against any persons claiming to be entitled to enforce the covenant, and adjoining landlords sought an injunction against building, it was held that the policy applied.[13]

Liability policies normally cover only legal liability and will not, for example, provide cover for *ex gratia* payments by the assured. However, it has been held that a liability which becomes effective only through a waiver of diplomatic immunity is nevertheless within a liability policy.[14]

19–05 Misconduct by the assured

As the main purpose of a liability policy is to permit the assured to recover for negligence, the policy presumes that there will have been

---

[7] *Tilley* v. *Dominion Insurance* [1987] 2 E.G.L.R. 34.
[8] *National Employers Mutual* v. *Heydon* [1980] 2 Lloyd's Rep. 149.
[9] [1988] 1 Lloyd's Rep. 7.
[10] [1989] 1 Lloyd's Rep. 289.
[11] *Contra* the position taken in Canada in *Canadian Indemnity* v. *Andrews and George* [1952] 4 D.L.R. 690 and *Dominion Bridge* v. *Toronto General Insurance* [1964] 1 Lloyd's Rep. 194.
[12] [1984] 2 Lloyd's Rep. 499. See also *Mills* v. *Smith* [1964] 1 Q.B. 30, where Paull J. held that the word "accident" in a householders' comprehensive policy covered nuisance liability which had occurred without any fault on the assured's part.
[13] It was further held that the assured could recover even though a threat of action had been made prior to the inception of the policy: "claiming" involved more than an assertion of a right.
[14] *Dickinson* v. *Del Solar* [1930] 1 K.B. 376.

some misconduct on the assured's part. Consequently, in the absence of any express provision restricting the insurer's liability, the assured will be able to recover unless his liability is attributable to an *intentional* criminal act on his part.[15] The mere fact of criminality is not sufficient to prevent recovery: the courts have recognised that the true beneficiary of a liability policy is the third party victim, and have, with notable exceptions,[16] allowed the assured to recover despite the criminal nature of his conduct.[17]

While it is contrary to public policy for the assured to insure against liability for his own criminal conduct, a policy may be effective to cover the criminal acts of the assured's employee. However, a policy merely providing cover in respect of a clerk's "neglect, omission or error" will not extend to loss occasioned by his fraud or criminal acts.[18]

Express clauses may limit the insurer's obligations in the event of the assured's misconduct. It is common for the consequences of criminality to be excluded, although the courts have generally confined such an exclusion to deliberate criminal misconduct.[19] Similarly, where a policy requires the assured to take "reasonable precautions" against the incurring of liability, it has been held consistently that nothing short of recklessness will bring the exception into play, as any other interpretation would defeat the entire purpose of the policy from the assured's point of view.[20]

Loss 19–06

The assured's right to recover under a third party policy comes into being as soon as he has furnished proof of his liability in accordance with the terms of his policy; he has no need to prove that he has discharged such liability by payment to the third party.[21] Clear wording will be needed to oust this principle,[22] although the rules of P & I Clubs universally contain "pay to be paid" provisions which have been held by the courts to be enforceable as against the member-assureds.[23]

"Events," "Occurrences" and "Accidents" 19–07

The liability of a liability insurer is normally qualified by the imposition on the assured of an excess in respect of each "event," "occurrence" or "accident" resulting in loss. It is important to know, therefore, whether the relevant term refers to the cause of the loss, or

---

[15] *Haseldine* v. *Hosken* [1933] 1 K.B. 822.

[16] *Gray* v. *Barr* [1971] 2 Q.B. 554.

[17] See in particular the motor manslaughter cases, *Tinline* v. *White Cross Insurance* [1921] 3 K.B. 327 and *James* v. *British General Insurance* [1927] 2 K.B. 311.

[18] *Davies* v. *Hosken* (1937) 53 T.L.R. 798. See also *Goddard and Smith* v. *Frew* [1939] 4 All E.R. 358; *West Wake Price* v. *Ching* [1957] 1 W.L.R. 45; *Warrender* v. *Swain* [1960] 2 Lloyd's Rep. 111.

[19] *Marcel Beller* v. *Hayden* [1978] Q.B. 694; *Linden Alimak* v. *British Engine Insurance* [1984] 1 Lloyd's Rep. 416.

[20] *Fraser* v. *Furman* [1967] 3 All E.R. 57; *Woolfall & Rimmer* v. *Moyle* [1942] 1 K.B. 66; *Linden Alimak* v. *British Engine Insurance* [1984] 1 Lloyd's Rep. 416; *M/S Aswan Engineering* v. *Iron Trades Mutual Insurance* [1989] 1 Lloyd's Rep. 289.

[21] *Johnston* v. *Salvage Association* (1887) 19 Q.B.D. 458. See also *Lancashire Insurance* v. *I.R.C.* [1899] 1 Q.B. 353, 359, *per* Bruce J.

[22] *Cf.* the refusal of the courts to treat the reinsurance wording "pay as may be paid thereon" as obliging the reinsured to pay before claiming indemnity: *Re Eddystone Marine* [1892] 2 Ch. 423.

[23] But not against third party claimants under the Third Parties (Rights against Insurers) Act 1930. See *infra*, § 19–19 *et seq.*

the individual losses resulting from it, as this will determine how many excesses the assured must bear. The word "occurrence" has been held to mean the negligent act of the assured rather than the individual injuries that each negligent act causes. Thus where a vehicle was negligently driven into a crowd of bystanders, there was held to be only one "occurrence" despite the fact that some forty people had been injured,[24] and where a solicitor gave two separate pieces of negligent advice, resulting in his client being unable to bring an action for damages against a third party, it was held that each piece of advice constituted an "occurrence."[25] Similarly, an "event" is the cause of a loss and not the loss itself.[26] By contrast, an "accident" is the individual loss suffered by the third party and not the wrongful act. Thus where a cart ran down two men in a single accident, it was ruled that there had been two "accidents."[27] The term "accident" may also appear in another context, namely, in defining the quality of the event for which the insurer is liable. It has been held that for these purposes an "accident" is an unexpected misfortune, for example, the natural growth of tree roots which cause damage to neighbouring land.[28]

Where a firm of accountants was insured against "claims," it was held that the claim against it was the totality of the sums sought by the third party and not each individual cause of action making up the total loss.[29]

19–08 Householders' comprehensive insurance

Householders' comprehensive policies cover liabilities incurred as "occupier" or as "owner." In *Sturge* v. *Hackett*[30] the policy covered the assured "as occupier" of a flat. Fire, owing to his negligence, damaged other property. McNair J. held that the words "as occupier" connoted that occupation was an essential ingredient of the liability insured against; that the fire started by the assured (to a birds' nest) did not originate in the flat itself; and that, since the assured was personally negligent, and not because he was occupier in breach of duty as occupier, he could not obtain an indemnity. This conclusion was reversed by the Court of Appeal, but only on the basis that the fire did in fact begin on the assured's premises so that the liability attached to him as occupier.

This decision was followed in *Rigby* v. *Sun Alliance*.[31] Here the relevant policy covered the assured's liability "solely as owner (not occupier)." An action was brought against the assured in nuisance, and Mustill J. held that the assured could not recover: nuisance liability attached to occupiers as well as owners, so that it could not be said that the assured had incurred liability "solely as occupier." The assured was, however, able to recover under a second policy which governed liability as occupier.

[24] *South Staffordshire Tramways* v. *Sickness and Accident Assurance* [1891] 1 Q.B. 402. See also *Allen* v. *London Guarantee* (1912) 28 T.L.R. 254.
[25] *Forney* v. *Dominion Insurance* [1969] 1 W.L.R. 928.
[26] *Kelly* v. *Norwich Union* [1989] 2 All E.R. 888.
[27] *Allen* v. *London Guarantee* (1912) 28 T.L.R. 254.
[28] *Mills* v. *Smith* [1964] 1 Q.B. 30.
[29] *West Wake Price* v. *Ching* [1957] 1 W.L.R. 45.
[30] [1962] 1 W.L.R. 1257. These cases were distinguished in *Turner* v. *Manx Line* [1990] 1 Lloyd's Rep. 137.
[31] [1980] 1 Lloyd's Rep. 359.

In *Oei* v. *Foster*[32] the policy covered injury or damage arising directly or indirectly from "occupation." A house belonging to the assured's neighbour was damaged by fire, due to the negligence of the assured's wife who was at the relevant time staying in the house while the neighbour was away. It was held that the assured's wife was in occupation of the neighbour's house, so that the policy covered the loss.

2. DEFENCE BY INSURER FOR ASSURED

Provision in policy   19–09

Since the insurers cannot make use of their ordinary rights of subrogation to contest the assured's liability as against a third party unless they first pay the assured the full amount of his estimated loss,[33] the policy usually specifically reserves their right to conduct litigation in connection with the assured's liability on his behalf. If the insurers deny liability under the policy, the assured will be free to accept their repudiation and defend or settle a third-party claim in breach of such a condition, reserving his right to proceed against the insurers.[34]

In *Barrett Bros.* v. *Davies*[35] the policy insured a motor-cyclist against liability for damage to another vehicle. He damaged a taxi. It was a condition of the policy that he should give full particulars in writing to the insurers. He did not, but the insurers knew all about it from the police. It was held by the Court of Appeal that the insurers had waived the condition by not asking for the relevant documents during which Lord Denning M.R. said that: "The law never compels a person to do that which is useless and unnecessary."

Costs   19–10

The insurers usually agree, in the policy, to indemnify the assured in respect of costs incurred by or awarded against him in his defence.[36] A later agreement by the assured to pay part of his costs will then be unenforceable for want of consideration.[37] Insurers who insist on defending the assured, without consulting him,[38] are liable to him for costs in any event. The assured is entitled to any costs reasonably incurred by him in resisting a claim, by way of damages, where the insurers wrongfully repudiate liability on the policy.[39]

Conduct of proceedings   19–11

Where the insurers do in fact take control of the litigation on the defendant's behalf they must do so in his name and not in their own.[40] The policy often gives the insurers a wide discretion as to the conduct of the assured's defence and the settlement of claims against him. They are

---

[32] [1982] 2 Lloyd's Rep. 170.
[33] See § 8–19, *supra*.
[34] *General Omnibus Co.* v. *London General Ins.* (1932) 66 Ir.L.T. 96.
[35] [1966] 1 W.L.R. 1334.
[36] See Lord Birkenhead in *British General* v. *Mountain* (1919) 36 T.L.R. 171 (H.L.).
[37] *Knight* v. *Hosken* (1942) 75 Ll.L.R. 74.
[38] *Allen* v. *London Guarantee* (1912) 28 T.L.R. 254.
[39] *Pictorial Machinery* v. *Nicolls* (1940) 67 Ll.L.R. 524.
[40] *Murfin* v. *Ashbridge* [1941] 1 All E.R. 231.

bound, however, to take into account the interests of the assured in its exercise.[41] Thus, if they make a settlement in good faith instead of contesting a claim the assured cannot complain,[42] but it is otherwise if they unreasonably accept liability.[43]

The exercise by the insurers of their right to conduct litigation on the assured's behalf cannot give the third party any rights against them except in respect of costs,[44] nor will they be liable to him for the tort of maintenance.[45] Nor does the insurers' undertaking to indemnify the assured against costs preclude him from recovering the costs of his defence against an unsuccessful third party.[46]

19–12 Disadvantages of interference by insurers

Where the insurers wish to dispute liability on a policy they should be cautious in the exercise of such a power, as where they continue the conduct of such proceedings after knowledge of facts which show that they are not liable they may be estopped from denying liability.[47] Moreover, even though the insurers subsequently successfully deny liability on the policy, they may be liable to the assured in damages if they have failed to exercise due care in defending the assured against the third party's action.[48] On the other hand, where insurer Y allowed the assured to send a writ, in breach of a condition of the policy to send it to Y, to insurer X, who defended a third party claim, Y was held not estopped from subsequently relying on the condition.[49]

19–13 Queen's Counsel clause

Sometimes, by "a Queen's Counsel clause," the insurer agrees to pay any claim without requiring the assured to dispute it unless leading counsel advises that it can be successfully contested. Where the policy covered liability for negligence only, this clause was held not to cover a mixed claim of fraud and negligence.[50]

3. THE RIGHTS OF THIRD PARTIES

Third Parties (Rights Against Insurers) Act 1930

19–14   At common law third party liability insurance gave no security to the third party that he would be able to recover in full if the assured became bankrupt or went into liquidation, as the case may be. Even if, in those circumstances, the assured recovered the insurance money in full, the

---

[41] *Groom* v. *Croker* [1939] 1 K.B. 194.

[42] *Beacon Insurance* v. *Langdale* [1939] 4 All E.R. 204; 65 Ll.L.R. 57 (C.A.).

[43] See n. 41, *supra*.

[44] *Nairn* v. *South-East Lancashire Insurance*, 1930 S.C. 606; *Vandepitte* v. *Preferred Accident Assurance* [1933] A.C. 70 (P.C.).

[45] Moulton L.J. in *British Cash & Parcel Conveyors* v. *Lamson Store Service* [1908] 1 K.B. 1006, 1015.

[46] *Cornish* v. *Lynch* (1910) 3 B.W.C.C. 343 (C.A.).

[47] *Hansen* v. *Marco Engineering* [1948] V.L.R. 198; *Etchells* v. *Eagle Star* (1928) 72 S.J. 242; *Evans* v. *Employers Mutual* [1936] 1 K.B. 505; contrast *McCormick* v. *National Motor Ins.* (1934) 50 T.L.R. 528. In *Soole* v. *Royal* [1971] 2 Lloyd's Rep. 332 Shaw J. was of the view that an insurer who does intervene will not be estopped from denying liability on grounds wholly unconnected with the claim.

[48] See *Groom* v. *Crocker* [1939] 1 K.B. 194; *Patteson* v. *Northern Accident* [1901] 2 Ir.R. 262.

[49] *Canadian Bank of Commerce* v. *London & Lancs.* (1958) 14 D.L.R. (2d) 623.

[50] *West Wake Price* v. *Ching* [1957] 1 W.L.R. 45.

injured third party had no right to that money, but could only prove as a creditor against the general assets of the assured.[51]

To remedy that state of affairs, the Third Parties (Rights Against Insurers) Act 1930 was passed, in the first instance to give support to the fledgling compulsory motor insurance scheme introduced by the Road Traffic Act 1930.[52] The broad effect of the 1930 Act is, on the happening of specified events indicating the assured's insolvency, to transfer to the third party the assured's rights against the insurer: this is in essence a form of statutory subrogation.

"Contract of insurance"   19–15

The 1930 Act applies to "any contract of insurance" (section 1(1)), whether in the form of a liability policy proper or in the form of the rules of a mutual association.[53] If the insurer is not under any legal obligation to make payment under the contract, but is merely required to consider claims in good faith, the contract is not one of insurance at all and the 1930 Act will not apply to it.[54]

It is unclear whether the proper law of the insurance must be English law, or whether it is sufficient that the policy moneys are payable in England or that the assured has been put into bankruptcy or liquidation in England.[55]

The 1930 Act, by section 1(5), is stated not to apply to reinsurance.

The assured's bankruptcy or liquidation   19–16

The rights of the assured are transferred to the third party under section 1(1) where the assured is made bankrupt or reaches a composition with his creditors or, in the case of a company, where the assured is wound up voluntarily or by the court, becomes subject to an administration order or where debenture holders appoint a receiver or manager or authorise the taking of the assured's property. The 1930 Act will also be brought into play by the approval of a voluntary arrangement under Part I of the Insolvency Act 1986 in respect of a corporate assured.

If a corporate assured, with no assets in England other than a liability policy, has failed to meet its liability to a third party, the English court has jurisdiction to make a winding up order in the third party's favour simply to allow the third party to proceed against the assured's liability insurer. This is so even though the company has previously been wound up in another jurisdiction, as the English courts accept jurisdiction to wind up any company with assets in England.[56]

Establishing the assured's liability   19–17

It is a condition precedent to the insurer's liability under the 1930 Act that the third party has established the assured's liability to it. Thus in

---

[51] *Re Harrington Motor Co.* [1928] Ch. 105; *Hood's Trustees* v. *Southern Union General Insurance* [1928] Ch. 793; *Ward* v. *British Oak* [1932] 1 K.B. 392.
[52] See Chap. 20.
[53] *Wooding* v. *Monmouth Mutual Indemnity Society* [1939] 4 All E.R. 570.
[54] *C.V.G. Siderugicia* v. *London Steamship Owners Mutual* [1979] 1 Lloyd's Rep. 557.
[55] *Irish Shipping* v. *Commercial Union, The Irish Rowan* [1989] 2 Lloyd's Rep. 144.
[56] *Re Compania Merabello* [1973] Ch. 75; *Re Allobrogia Steamship Corporation* [1978] 3 All E.R. 423; *The Irish Rowan* [1989] 2 Lloyd's Rep. 144.

Post Office v. *Norwich Union Fire*[57] the Court of Appeal dismissed an action by the third party against the insurer, as the assured's liability had not at that point been established by legal process.

The *Norwich Union* principle can give rise to particular difficulty where the assured is a company and has been dissolved before the third party has been able to establish its liability. This occurred in *Bradley* v. *Eagle Star*,[58] where the third party employee failed in her action against her ex-employer's liability insurers, on the ground that once the assured employer had been dissolved it became impossible for it to be sued and its liability towards her established. This problem may be less acute in future years as a result of changes made to section 651 of the Companies Act 1985 by the Companies Act 1989. Under the unamended provision the dissolution of a company could be reversed by the court on application by any interested person. The relevant two year period had elapsed in *Bradley*, so that this provision was of little use. However, under the amended section 651 the court may on application reverse the dissolution of a company at any time following dissolution in the case of an action for damages for death or personal injury. In future cases the proper procedure will be to apply to the court under section 651 for an order revoking dissolution: an action may then be brought against the company and, ultimately, against its liability insurer.

19–18 Effect of the statutory transfer

A third party who can claim the benefit of the 1930 Act receives precisely the same rights against the insurer as were possessed by the assured himself. The third party is thus bound to go to arbitration if the policy so provides,[59] and any defence which the insurer could have raised against the assured may also be pleaded against the third party.[60] This is of particular importance in relation to conditions which have to be fulfilled by the assured following loss, for example, the submission of a timeous claim.[61] If the premium has not been paid by the assured, the third party is obliged to pay it only if such payment is a condition precedent to the insurer's liability.[62]

Where the sums payable under the policy exceed the third party's loss, the surplus accrues to the assured's trustee in bankruptcy or liquidator. Conversely, if the policy moneys are inadequate to meet the third party's claim, the third party has the right, following payment by the insurer, to prove in the assured's bankruptcy or liquidation for the uninsured loss (section 1(4)).

If the insurer includes in its contract a provision whereby the assured is not entitled to be paid until it has first made payment to the assured,

---

[57] [1967] 1 All E.R. 577.

[58] [1989] 2 W.L.R. 568.

[59] *Freshwater* v. *Western Australian Assurance* [1933] 1 K.B. 515; *Dennehy* v. *Bellamy* [1938] 2 All E.R. 262; *Smith* v. *Pearl Assurance* [1939] 1 All E.R. 95; *The Padre Island (No. 1)* [1984] 2 Lloyd's Rep. 408.

[60] *Cunningham* v. *Anglian Insurance* 1934 S.L.T. 273; *McCormick* v. *National Motor* (1934) 40 Com. Cas. 76; *Cleland* v. *London General* (1935) 51 Ll.L.R.156.

[61] *Hassett* v. *Legal and General* (1939) 63 Ll.L.R. 278; *Farrell* v. *Federated Employers* [1970] 1 W.L.R. 1400; *Monksfield* v. *Vehicle and General* [1971] 1 Lloyd's Rep. 139; *Pioneer Concrete* v. *National Employers Mutual* [1985] 2 All E.R. 395.

[62] *Murray* v. *Legal and General* [1970] 2 Q.B. 495.

and the assured has gone into liquidation before payment, the third party can nevertheless rely upon the 1930 Act. The Court of Appeal has held that the third party has transferred to him the contingent right of the assured to be paid subject to payment, and that as the third party cannot be expected to pay itself, the contingency is to be disregarded and the insurer is liable.[63]

Alteration of rights on insolvency   19–19
In so far as a contract of insurance purports to avoid the contract or to alter the rights of the parties on the bankruptcy or liquidation of the assured, the contract is of no effect (section 1(3)). It is thus not possible for the insurer to contract out of the 1930 Act. The rules of a P & I Club may not, therefore, provide that a member's membership is to terminate on his insolvency, although a "pay to be paid" clause does not offend section 1(3) as the assured's rights are always the same whether or not it is insolvent.[63]

Contracts between assured and insurer   19–20
Section 3 of the 1930 Act provides that once the assured has become bankrupt, gone into liquidation or another relevant event has occurred, and liability to the third party has been incurred, the assured shall not enter into any agreement with the insurer the effect of which is to limit the rights of the third party against the insurer. Any such agreement is avoided by section 3. The provision does not, however, apply to any agreement made between insurer and assured prior to the assured's bankruptcy, winding up, etc., which restricts the insurer's liability to the assured, even if the plain effect of the agreement is to limit the rights of a third party in respect of a claim which was pending when the agreement was made.[64]

Supplemental   19–21
Where a third party has rights under the 1930 Act, he must be informed of those rights by the person administering the assured's affairs (section 2).

4. EMPLOYERS' LIABILITY INSURANCE

Sources of liability to employees   19–22
An employer may face liability to his employees, in respect of personal injury or death, from a number of sources. First, the common law obliges employers to take reasonable care to safeguard their employees. Secondly, the Health and Safety at Work Act 1974, as amended by the Consumer Protection Act 1987, imposes both general and industry-specific standards of care upon employers. Thirdly, the Employers' Liability (Defective Equipment) Act 1969 provides that where an employee suffers personal injury in consequence of a defect in equip-

---

[63] *The Fanti and the Padre Island* [1989] 1 Lloyd's Rep. 239. "Pay to be paid" clauses are universally found in P & I Club rules.
[64] *Normid Housing Association* v. *Ralphs* (1988) *The Times*, July 18.

ment provided by his employer, and the defect is attributable wholly or partly to the fault of a third party, the injury is deemed to have been caused by the negligence of the employer[65]; contracting out of this Act is expressly forbidden.[66]

In order to ensure that the employer is able to meet any judgment against him, the Employers' Liability (Compulsory Insurance) Act 1969 requires employers to procure insurance against liability for the death of, or personal injury to, their employees.

19–23 Compulsory insurance

By section 1(1) of the Act of 1969:

> " . . . every employer carrying on any business in Great Britain shall insure, and maintain insurance, under one or more approved policies with an authorised insurer or insurers, against liability for bodily injury or disease sustained by his employees, and arising out of and in the course of their employment in Great Britain in that business, but, except in so far as regulations otherwise provide, not including injury or disease suffered or contracted outside Great Britain."

Scope of the 1969 Act

19–24 *Employers within the legislation.* All employers, other than those not having a place of business in Great Britain,[67] local authorities,[68] nationalised industries[69] and those expressly exempted by regulations under the Act,[70] must take out the required insurance.

19–25 *Employees within the legislation.* The 1969 Act requires insurance only in respect of employees. This term is defined in section 2(1) as meaning:

> "an individual who has entered into or works under a contract of service or apprenticeship with an employer whether by way of manual labour, clerical work or otherwise, whether such contract is expressed or implied, oral or in writing."

The Act thus requires the usual distinction between a "contract of service" and a "contract for services" to be made. There is no single test for determining whether a worker is employed, although the degree of control exercised by the employer over the manner in which the work is performed has always been regarded as a crucial factor and the courts are prepared to allow the parties to reach genuine agreement on the matter. The real test is whether the worker is in business on his own account or for the employer.[71]

---

[65] s.1(1).
[66] s.1(2).
[67] s.1(3)(d).
[68] s.3(1)(a), (2).
[69] s.3(1)(b).
[70] s.3(1)(c). The relevant regulations, the Employers Liability (Compulsory Insurance) Exemption Regulations S.I. 1971 No. 1933, as amended by S.I. 1974 No. 208, exclude various governmental bodies and shipowners' mutual insurers.
[71] *Ready Mixed Concrete* v. *Minister of Pensions* [1968] 2 Q.B. 497; *Global Plant* v. *Secretary of State for Social Security* [1972] 1 Q.B. 139; *Ferguson* v. *Dawson Ltd.* [1976] 2 Lloyd's Rep. 669; *Massey* v. *Crown Life* [1978] 1 W.L.R. 676; *B.S.M.* v. *Secretary of State for Social Services* [1978] A.C. 894; *W.H.P.T. Housing Association* v. *Secretary of State for Social Services* [1981] I.C.R. 737.

The Act does not require an employer to insure close relatives[72] or employees not ordinarily resident in England.[73] In the latter case, however, regulations provide that an employee must be insured if he has been present in Great Britain in the course of employment for a continuous period of fourteen days.[74]

Carrying on business in Great Britain. The employer must carry on **19–26** business[75] in Great Britain in that he must have a place of business in Great Britain.[76] By way of exception, however, an employer is within the legislation as regards his offshore installations such as oil rigs and similar structures used for underwater exploration and exploitation of mineral resources.[77]

Liability arising out of and in the course of employment. There is a **19–27** good deal of authority on the meaning of this wording, as it appears in social security legislation as well as being the accepted formula for determining the employer's liability to employees and his vicarious liability to third parties for the actions of employees.

Many of the difficulties arise in the course of the employee's transit to and from work. This matter has recently been given detailed consideration by the House of Lords in *Smith* v. *Stages*,[78] where the following principles were laid down:

(a) An employee travelling to and from work is not generally to be regarded as doing so in the course of his employment unless he was required by contract to use transport provided by his employer.[79]

(b) Any travelling during working hours between different premises owned by the employer is in the course of the employee's employment, although any deviation would take the employee outside the course of his employment.

(c) If an employee is paid ordinary wages or salary (as opposed to a transport allowance) while travelling, such travelling will be in the course of employment even though the employee is given discretion as to the mode of transport to be used.

(d) Travel in the employer's time and on the employer's instructions from the employee's residence to a place other than the employee's normal place of work will be in the course of his employment.

Once an employee has arrived at the place of work it does not follow

---

[72] Defined as the employer's hunsband, wife, father, mother, grandfather, grandmother, step-father, step-mother, son, daughter, grandson, granddaughter, stepson, stepdaughter, brother, sister, half-brother or half-sister: s.2(2)(*a*).

[73] s.2(2)(*b*).

[74] Employers Liability (Compulsory Insurance) General Regulations 1971, S.I. 1971 No. 1117 (as amended by S.I. 1974 No. 208 and S.I. 1975 No. 191), reg. 4.

[75] This word is defined in its usual sense of trade or profession: s.1(3)(*b*).

[76] s.1(3)(*d*).

[77] Employers Liability (Compulsory Insurance) Offshore Installations Regulations 1975, S.I. 1975 No. 1289.

[78] [1989] 1 All E.R. 833.

[79] *St. Helen's Colliery Co.* v. *Hewitson* [1924] A.C. 59; *Black* v. *Aitkenhead* 1938 S.C. 291; *Weaver* v. *Tredegar Co.* [1940] A.C. 955; *Paterson* v. *Costain & Press (Overseas) Ltd.* [1979] 2 Lloyd's Rep. 204; *Vandyke* v. *Fender* [1970] 2 Q.B. 292.

that any accident befalling him while there is suffered in the course of employment. In *R.* v. *National Insurance Commissioner, ex p. East*[80] the employee arrived at her place of employment, donned overalls supplied and required by her employers to be worn at work, and went to the canteen for her midday meal prior to "clocking on" for her noon shift. While there she slipped on some custard and was injured. The Divisional Court ruled that the employee's course of employment had commenced upon her donning her overalls, and that there had been no sufficient interruption by her visit to the canteen to take her out of such a course of employment.

Activities related to work carried on outside the hours of employment will be within the course of employment only if reasonably incidental to the work. This was so held by the Court of Appeal in *R* v. *National Insurance Commissioner, ex p. Michael*,[81] where an injury suffered by a police constable playing football for his force's team was held to have arisen out of his employment but not in the course of it.

19–28   *Approved policy issued by authorised insurer.* A policy will comply with the 1969 Act only if it is approved and if it has been issued by an authorised insurer. An approved policy is one which does not contain terms outlawed by regulations under the 1969 Act; these are discussed *infra* para. 19–32.[82] An authorised insurer is one authorised to carry on insurance business under the Insurance Companies Act 1982.[83]

19–29   *Coverage and amount.* The policy need cover only "bodily injury or disease" and not any liability which the employer may incur in respect of property belonging to employees, although a property extension is commonly found in such policies. The minimum amount of insurance is £2 million in respect of all claims arising out of any one occurrence.[84]

19–30 The employer's obligations

Penalty for failure to insure. Section 5 provides that an employer who is not insured on any day when required in accordance with the Act to be so, shall be liable on summary conviction to a fine not exceeding £500. If such an offence is committed by a corporation, any director or other officer of it who consented to it, connived at it, or by neglect or default facilitated it, will also to be liable.

19–31   *Certificate of insurance.* Section 4(1) of the 1969 Act provides for the making of regulations securing that prescribed certificates are issued by insurers entering into insurance contracts under the Act, and for the surrender of such certificates.

Regulation 5 of the General Regulations 1971 made under this section[85] provides that every employer entering into a contract of insurance in accordance with the requirements of the Act shall be issued by the insurer with whom he contracts a certificate of insurance in the form

---

[80] [1976] I.C.R. 206.
[81] [1977] 1 W.L.R. 109.
[82] s.1(3)(*a*).
[83] s.1(3)(*b*).
[84] *Ibid.* 1971 Regulations, reg. 3.
[85] 1971 Regulations, (S.I. 1971 No. 1117).

specified in the Schedule to the General Regulations. No such certificate shall be issued later than 30 days after the date on which the insurance commences or is renewed. The regulations, under the authority of section 4(2) of the 1969 Act, go on to require the employer to display copies of the certificate for the information of employees,[86] to produce the certificate or copies of it on demand to any inspector of the Health and Safety Executive[87] and to permit inspection of the certificate or a copy of it by any inspector appointed by the Secretary of State.[88] By section 4(3) of the 1969 Act, the maximum fine for failure to comply with these requirements is £200.

Prohibition of certain policy conditions. A policy of employers liab- **19–32** ility insurance must, to comply with the Act of 1969,[89] not contain any provisions which exclude the insurer's liability:

(a) in the event of some specified thing being done or omitted to be done after the happening of the event giving rise to a claim under the policy[90];

(b) unless the policy holder takes reasonable care to protect his employees against the risk of bodily injury or disease in the course of their employment[91];

(c) unless the policy holder complies with the requirements of any enactment for the protection of employees against the risk of bodily injury or disease in the course of their employment; and

(d) unless the policy holder keeps specified records or provides the insurer with or makes available to him information therefrom.[92]

---

[86] *Ibid.*, reg. 6.
[87] *Ibid.*, reg. 7.
[88] *Ibid.*, reg. 8.
[89] *Ibid.*, reg. 2.
[90] Notice provisions in respect of claims are thus prohibited if they permit the insurer to avoid liability following a late claim.
[91] Such clauses were in any event prior to the 1969 Act held to be effective only where the employer was reckless: *Woolfall and Rimmer* v. *Moyle* [1942] 1 K.B. 66; *Fraser* v. *Furman* [1967] 1 W.L.R. 898.
[92] Where the premium is adjusted according to wages paid by the employer, there will be an obligation imposed on him by the insurer to keep a wages book. The insurer cannot now avoid liability where the assured fails to maintain the required records, although it has been held that such a provision is not in any event to be construed as a condition precedent to the insurer's liability in the absence of clear words: *Re Bradley and Essex Accident* [1912] 1 K.B. 415.

CHAPTER 20

MOTOR VEHICLE INSURANCE

1. ROAD TRAFFIC ACT 1988

Background 20–01

The insurance of motor vehicles against the risk of liability for injury to, or the death of, third parties caused by the driver's negligence has been compulsory since 1930. In the intervening period the scope of compulsory insurance has gradually expanded, either as the result of deficiencies in the legislation demonstrated by judicial decisions or as the result of the United Kingdom's obligations under the Treaty of Rome. Thus, the insurance of passengers was brought within the scheme in 1971, the extension of compulsory insurance to other Member States was achieved in 1973[1] and, most importantly, the introduction of compulsory insurance for property damage occurred in 1988.[2] These changes were incorporated into Part VI of the Road Traffic Act 1972, but on the passing of new road traffic legislation in 1988 the opportunity was taken to consolidate the pre-existing law.[3] The relevant provisions are, therefore, now to be found in Part VI of the Road Traffic Act 1988, sections 143 to 161. The draftsman has, so far as is possible, followed the section numbering contained in the 1972 Act.

The 1988 Act is concerned only with compulsory insurance as regards the lives and property of third parties. Policies on motor vehicles are, however, generally wider in their scope than the Act requires and may cover also damage to the motor vehicle itself[4] and the death of, or injury to, the assured himself.

Motor vehicle 20–02

"Motor vehicle" is defined by section 185(1) of the Road Traffic Act 1972 as "a mechanically propelled vehicle intended or adapted for use on roads."

"Intended or adapted for use on roads." The expression has been held not to cover a diesel dumper used for constructing roads[5] but to cover an

---

[1] By the Motor Vehicles (Compulsory Insurance) Regulations 1973 (S.I. 1973 No. 1820), as subsequently replaced by the Motor Vehicles (Compulsory Insurance) (No. 2) Regulations 1973 (S.I. 1973 No. 2143); the latter were in turn subsequently amended. The Regulations implemented Council Directive 72/166, as amended by Council Directive 72/430.

[2] By the Motor Vehicles (Compulsory Insurance) Regulations 1987 (S.I. 1987 No. 2171), implementing Council Directive 84/5.

[3] It should be said, however, that the European Communities have proposed further changes in the law, so that future amendments may have to be introduced.

[4] The insurer may include in the policy an option to repair damage to the motor vehicle. It is an implied term of such an option that the insurer causes the vehicle to be repaired in a reasonable time: *Davidson* v. *Guardian Royal Exchange* [1979] 1 Lloyd's Rep. 406; *Llynf Motor Services* v. *Western National Omnibus Co.* [1983] 6 C.L., § 100.

[5] *MacDonald* v. *Carmichael*, 1941 S.C.(J.) 27.

agricultural tractor.[6] That a vehicle, obviously not adapted for use on roads, should be capable of use on roads, does not bring it within the definition of "motor vehicle." If a vehicle is unfit for use on roads, and has not been adapted—which means "altered" or "fit and apt" for such use—it is not a "motor vehicle" because it is used on a road.[7]

Thus two dumpers, used in the ordinary way for the construction of works, were held, although mechanically propelled vehicles, not to be "motor vehicles" only because they happened to be propelled on a road.[8]

20–03 *"Mechanically propelled vehicle."* A motor car remains a "mechanically propelled vehicle" even where the engine has been temporarily removed[9] (by theft or otherwise), or is for any reason undrivable under its own power,[10] unless there is no reasonable prospect of it ever being made mobile again.[11]

An auto-pedal cycle with vital parts of its auxiliary motor removed was held not to be a "motor vehicle" within the Act[12]; but such a motor assisted pedal cycle has been held to be "mechanically propelled" even though the engine had been turned off at the material time.[13]

20–04 The key provision: section 143

Section 143 of the Act of 1988 is the key operative provision of Part VI of the Act, and provides:

(1) Subject to the provisions of this Act—
  (a) a person must not use a motor vehicle on a road unless there is in force in relation to the use of the vehicle by that person such a policy of insurance or such a security in respect of third party risks as complies with the requirements of this Part of this Act, and
  (b) a person must not cause or permit any other person to use a motor vehicle on a road unless there is in force in relation to the use of the vehicle by that other person such a policy of insurance or such a security in respect of third party risks as complies with the requirements of this Act.

(2) If a person acts in contravention of subsection (1) he is guilty of an offence.

Subsection (3) provides a defence to a person innocently "using the vehicle in the course of his employment" or who proves that the vehicle did not belong to him and was not in his possession under a contract of hiring or of loan, or who can show that he neither knew nor had any reason to believe that there was not in force in relation to the vehicle such a policy of insurance or security as is mentioned in subsection (1) above. By subsection (4), this Part of the Act does not apply to invalid carriages. In addition, the compulsory insurance requirement does not extend to vehicles owned by various public authorities, including certain

---

[6] *Woodward* v. *Young* 1958 S.L.T. 289, but not a trailer: *Rogerson* v. *Stephens* [1950] 2 All E.R. 144. "Trailer" means a vehicle drawn by a motor vehicle; s.185(1) of Act of 1988.
[7] *Burns* v. *Currell* [1963] 2 Q.B. 435 (the Go-Kart case).
[8] *Daley* v. *Hargreaves* [1961] 1 W.L.R. 487.
[9] *Newberry* v. *Simmonds* [1961] 2 Q.B. 345.
[10] *Law* v. *Thomas* (1964) 62 L.G.R. 195.
[11] *Smart* v. *Allan* [1963] 1 Q.B. 291.
[12] *Lawrence* v. *Howlett* [1952] 2 All E.R. 74.
[13] *Floyd* v. *Bush* [1953] 1 W.L.R. 242.

local authorities, the Metropolitan Police, armed forces vehicles, national health service vehicles and vehicles being driven on a journey to effect marine salvage.[14]

General effect of Act   20–05

Required scope of insurance. Part VI of the Act obliges every person who runs[15] a motor vehicle not to use or to cause or permit its use unless the following forms of liability, listed in section 143(2), are insured against under a policy issued by an authorised insurer[16]:

(a) such person, persons or classes of persons as may be specified in the policy in respect of any liability which may be incurred by him or them in respect of the death of or bodily injury to any person[17] or damage to property caused by, or arising out of, the use of the vehicle on a road[18] in Great Britain, and

(b) must insure him or them in respect of any liability which may be incurred by him or them in respect of the use of the vehicle and of any trailer, whether or not coupled, in the territory other than Great Britain and Gibraltar of each of the member States of the Communities according to the law on compulsory insurance against civil liability in respect of the use of vehicles of the State where the liability may be incurred, and

(c) must also insure him or them in respect of any liability which may be incurred by him or them under the provisions of this Part of the Act[19] relating to payment for emergency treatment.

Limitations. A compulsory policy need not cover any of the following **20–06** forms of loss or liability[20]:

(a) liability in respect of the death of, or bodily injury to, an employed person arising out of the course of his employment;

(b) insurance in excess of £250,000 in respect of damage to the property of a third party;

(c) liability in respect of damage to the insured vehicle;

(d) liability in respect of damage to goods carried for hire or reward in or on the vehicle or on any trailer drawn by the insured vehicle;

---

[14] s.144(2).

[15] Greer L.J. in *Monk* v. *Warbey* [1935] 1 K.B. 75, 80.

[16] s.145(2). "Authorised insurer" is defined by s.145(5) as meaning an insurer authorised to carry on motor insurance business under the Insurance Companies Act 1982 and who is a member of the Motor Insurers' Bureau: see *infra*, § 20–33 *et seq.* If an insurer ceases to be a member of the M.I.B., policies previously issued by it remain within the 1988 Act: s.145(6).

[17] In *Digby* v. *General Accident* [1943] 2 A.C. 121 the House of Lords was divided on the question whether "any person" included the policy holder. A person driving with the owner's consent is not "any person": *Cooper* v. *Motor Insurers' Bureau* [1985] 1 All E.R. 449.

[18] A "road" is any highway and any other road to which the public has access, and includes bridges over which a road passes—s.192(1). An accident occurring in a private road after a vehicle has left the road is not one "*arising out of*" its user on the road: *Lister* v. *Romford Ice* [1957] A.C. 555. What is a "road" is a question of fact. In *Griffin* v. *Squires* [1958] 1 W.L.R. 180 it was held to be open to magistrates to find that a car-park to which the public had access and habitually used was *not* a road, and in *Thomas* v. *Dando* [1951] 2 K.B. 620 the forecourt of a corner shop used, but not habitually, by the public was held *not* to be a road. By contrast, in *Bugge* v. *Taylor* [1941] 1 K.B. 198 the forecourt of a hotel was held to be a road as the proprietors allowed it to be used as part of a road, and in *Chapman* v. *Parlby* (1964) 62 L.G.R. 150 it was held that a highway to a depot used by the War Department was a road, as it was available for the public to use as a turning point for motor vehicles.

In *Randall* v. *Motor Insurers' Bureau* [1968] 2 Lloyd's Rep. 553 Megaw J. held that a lorry driven from private property with its front wheels on a public highway was on a road, even though the victim was on the private property at the time of the accident.

[19] ss. 157–159, *infra* § 20–19.

[20] s.145(4).

    (e) the liability of any person in respect of damage to property in his custody or under his control.
    (f) contractual liability.

20–07 *Breach of duty to insure.* The breach of the duty to insure imposed by the 1988 Act lays the owner open to criminal penalties. In addition, the courts have held that failure to insure will render the owner liable for breach of statutory duty to an injured person who is deprived of any other effective remedy through his failure to comply with the Act.[21] The injured person must prove, however, that it was on account of the negligent driver's impecuniosity that he had no effective remedy and not, for example, because he had allowed his action to become time-barred.[22]

20–08 *"Causes or permits."* An insurance company which issues a policy on a motor car which it is entitled to rescind for breach of condition is not a person who "causes or permits" the use of the car.[23] Nor is a person who has sold the car to another a person who permits that other to use it.[24]

    The meaning of "permit" was considered by the House of Lords in *Kelly* v. *Cornhill Insurance Co.*[25] The owner of a motor car authorised his son to use the car but died during the currency of the policy. The son continued to use the car and was involved in an accident. The House held, by a majority, that he was then still driving with the permission of his father. The word "permission," it was held, did not imply that the permission must be one which there was power to revoke, or could endure only so long as the grantor was in a position to revoke it.[26] The construction of the word is a question "of the ordinary use of the English Language."[27] It is only if the personal representatives of the deceased sell or otherwise transfer the property in the car (during the currency of the policy) that the permission ceases: the son would then have required the permission of the new owner.[28]

    In *Sheldon Deliveries* v. *Willis*[29] the insured company who delivered motor cars for reward, were insured against third party risks in respect of vehicles bearing trade plates. They instructed an employee to take a car bearing trade plates home, suitably park it, and deliver it early on Monday morning. Unknown to the company he went in the car on a frolic of his own, without trade plates, on Sunday. The company was convicted by justices of "permitting" the offence. Allowing the company's appeal, the Divisional Court held that permitting the use of an uninsured car essentially connoted either knowledge, or deliberate blindness or recklessness.

    But it is not only the owner who can give such permission; any person

---

[21] *Monk* v. *Warbey* [1935] 1 K.B. 75, impliedly approved by the House of Lords in *McLeod* v. *Buchanan* [1940] 2 All E.R. 179. Such actions are now largely unnecessary, as the Motor Insurers' Bureau accepts liability where the owner is uninsured, but they have nevertheless survived the advent of the Bureau: *Corfield* v. *Groves* [1950] 1 All E.R. 488.

[22] *Daniels* v. *Vaux* [1938] 2 K.B. 203.

[23] *Richards* v. *Port of Manchester Ins.* (1934) 152 L.T. 413.

[24] *Peters* v. *General Accident* [1938] 2 All E.R. 267; see also *Watkins* v. *O'Shaughnessy* [1939] 1 All E.R. 385; *Smith* v. *Ralph* [1963] 2 Lloyd's Rep. 439.

[25] [1964] 1 W.L.R. 158.

[26] *Per* Lord Dilhorne L.C. [1964] 1 W.L.R. 158 at p. 161. See also *per* Lord Reid at p. 165.

[27] *Ibid.* p. 167, *per* Lord Reid.

[28] See *ibid.* pp. 168, 174.

[29] [1972] R.T.R. 217.

who is responsible for the care, management or control of a vehicle will, for instance, commit an offence under the Act if he permits another person to use it uninsured against third party risks.[30]

The person in whose name the car is registered is not necessarily the owner.[31] The owner will be in breach of his duty if, the vehicle being insured for a limited purpose only, he gives another permission to use it which is not so limited.[32] But it does not matter if the personal liability of the driver of the vehicle is not covered if the vicarious liability of the owner is.[33] Where a man who had no licence to drive his car was instructing a woman (and both were held to be drivers), there was held to be no breach of the statute, though the man's policy did not cover the woman, on the ground that the man could have been sued (and would have been covered) if an accident had occurred.[34]

An owner's honest but mistaken belief that a driver is covered by his (the owner's) insurance, *e.g.* on the ground that he holds a driving licence which he in fact does not, is not a defence to a charge of permitting him to drive uninsured[35]; the imposition of a condition that he will not drive unless covered by insurance is.[36]

"*Use.*" It is the user of the vehicle, not the driver, that must be **20–09** covered.[37] "Use" on a road by a person for the purpose of the Act requires an element of controlling, managing or operating the vehicle at the relevant time[38]; to "use" means to "have the use of a motor vehicle on a road."[39] Thus, in *Elliot* v. *Grey*,[40] the owner of a car which had broken down immobilised it and left it in the road outside his house until it could be repaired. *Held*, that as the car could be moved, albeit not driven, the owner had the "use" of it on the road within the meaning of the Act.

In most circumstances a passenger in or on a motor vehicle will not be **20–10** a "user" of it. Thus in *Brown* v. *Roberts*[41] a passenger opened a van door, injuring a pedestrian on the pavement. It was held that the passenger did not use the van, for the control, management or operation of

---

[30] *Lloyd* v. *Singleton* [1953] 1 Q.B. 357, disapproving a dictum of Mackinnon L.J. in *Goodbarne* v. *Buck* [1940] 1 K.B. 771, 774; see also *D.* v. *Parsons* [1960] 1 W.L.R. 797, pillion rider held not aiding and abetting offence under section, and *Thompson* v. *Lodwick* [1983] R.T.R. 76.

[31] *James* v. *British General* [1927] 2 K.B. 311; *Goodbarne* v. *Buck*, *supra*.

[32] *McLeod* v. *Buchanan* [1940] 2 All E.R. 179.

[33] *Ellis* v. *Hinds* [1947] K.B. 475; *Marsh* v. *Moores* (1949) 65 T.L.R. 318.

[34] *Langman* v. *Valentine* [1952] 2 T.L.R. 713 (Lord Goddard C.J. and Finnemore J., McNair J. dissenting). See also *Rendlesham* v. *Dunne* [1964] 1 Lloyd's Rep. 192 (learner driver driving alone with provisional licence held by county court "licence to drive" within meaning of policy).

[35] *Baugh* v. *Crago* [1975] R.T.R. 453, [1976] 1 Lloyd's Rep. 563 (D.C.). See also *Ferrymaster* v. *Adams* [1980] R.T.R. 139.

[36] *Newbury* v. *Davis* [1974] R.T.R. 367 (D.C.).

[37] s.143(1) of Act of 1988. *Ellis* v. *Hinds*, *supra*; *Lees* v. *Motor Insurers' Bureau* [1952] 2 T.L.R. 356, where it was held that an employee driver need not be separately covered though liability to a fellow employee is excluded from the cover of the employer's policy. See also *Lister* v. *Romford* [1957] A.C. 555, 582, 593.

[38] *Per* Megaw J. in *Brown* v. *Roberts* [1965] 1 Q.B. 1, 15.

[39] *Per* Lord Parker C.J. in *Elliot* v. *Grey* [1960] 1 Q.B. 367, 372. So in *Williams* v. *Jones* [1975] R.T.R. 433 (D.C.) a van which had been driven with trade plates abandoned in a lay by was held to be "used" on a road.

[40] [1960] 1 Q.B. 367.

[41] [1965] 1 Q.B. 1.

a door by a passenger did not amount to the necessary control, management or operation of the vehicle itself. However, an owner "uses" his car when being carried as a passenger in it,[42] and a passenger "uses" a car which he has helped to steal.[43] A passenger is not, however, guilty of an offence if he learns on the journey that the driver is without insurance cover.[44]

20–11   *Policy required by 1988 Act.* In order to satisfy section 143, there must be a policy issued by an authorised insurer covering the risks specified in section 145(3). It is sufficient that a policy exists: the fact that it is voidable is immaterial,[45] at least until it has been avoided,[46] although a policy void *ab initio* clearly does not satisfy the Act. A "cover note" is a policy for the purposes of the Act,[47] as long as it contains an enforceable contract of insurance. Thus in *Taylor* v. *Allon*[48] a temporary cover note to extend existing insurance was sent to the assured, but he did not rely upon it and sought alternative insurance. It was held that he had not intended to accept the insurer's offer in the cover note, so that no contract of insurance existed.

The required policy, in the case of visitors from abroad, may consist of a "Green Card"[49] or a document issued under the Motor Vehicles (Third Party Risks) Regulations.[50]

20–12   *Security required by Act.* By section 146(3) a security, in lieu of a policy (subject to conditions therein), may be given to make good "any failure by the owner of the vehicle or such other person or classes of persons as may be specified in the security duly to discharge any liability which may be incurred by him or them being a liability required under section 145 of this Act to be covered by a policy of insurance." By section 146(2) the security must be given by an authorised insurer or some body of persons which carries on in the United Kingdom the business of giving securities of like kind and keeps deposited with the Accountant General of the Supreme Court £15,000 in respect of that business. By subsection (4) the undertaking must be "(*a*) in the case of . . . public service vehicles . . . of not less than £25,000, (*b*) in any other case, of not less than £5,000."

20–13   *Certificate of insurance.* A policy is of no effect for the purpose of the Act of 1972 unless and until there is delivered by the insurer to the person by whom the policy is effected[51] a "certificate of insurance," such as is prescribed.[52] Without such certificate or a "certificate of security,"[53]

---

[42] *Cobb* v. *Williams* [1973] R.T.R. 113.
[43] *Leathley* v. *Tatton* [1980] R.T.R. 358.
[44] *B.* v. *Knight* [1981] R.T.R. 136.
[45] *Goodbarne* v. *Buck* [1940] 1 K.B. 771, affirming Hilbery J. at [1939] 4 All E.R. 107.
[46] *Adams* v. *Dunne* [1978] R.T.R. 281; *Evans* v. *Lewis* [1964] 1 Lloyd's Rep. 258.
[47] s.161(1).
[48] [1966] 1 Q.B. 304.
[49] Under the Motor Vehicles (International Motor Insurance Card) Regulations 1971 (S.I. 1971 No. 792), as amended by the Motor Vehicles (International Motor Insurance Card) (Amendment) Regulations 1977 (S.I. 1977 No. 895).
[50] S.I. 1972 No. 1217, as amended.
[51] Or his agent, see *Starkey* v. *Hall* [1936] 2 All E.R. 18.
[52] s.147(1).
[53] s.147(2).

the owner is unable to obtain a vehicle licence for his car,[54] and by section 165 a police constable may require production of the certificate.

Alternatively, the owner may deposit £15,000 with the Accountant General of the Supreme Court, in which case the Act will not apply when the vehicle is being driven under his control.[55] Or he may obtain a "certificate of security,"[56] consisting of an undertaking in the terms of section 146(3) of the Act or make good the failure of the owner to discharge his liability to third parties, from an authorised insurer or other person specified in section 146(2) of the Act, in which case his obligation under section 143(1) of the Act is satisfied.

The issue of a certificate under the Act does not estop the insurers from subsequently pleading, either against the insurer or third parties, that the policy was obtained by fraud.[57]

Section 165(1)(a) empowers a constable to require a person (inter alia) driving on a road a motor vehicle to give his name and address and the name and address of the owner of the vehicle and produce for examination the relevant certificate of insurance or security (or other prescribed evidence that the vehicle was not being driven in contravention of section 143). A person not complying commits an offence. By subsection (4) it is a defence to produce[58] the certificate at such police station as he specified when asked to produce it.

By section 174 it is an offence, for the purpose of obtaining the issue of a certificate of insurance or security, to make a false statement or withhold any material information; and by section 175 it is an offence to issue such a certificate which is false in any material particular to the knowledge of the person issuing it. An ante-dated certificate has been held not to fall within the latter provisions.[59]

A certificate of insurance, unlike a cover note, is not a "policy of insurance" for the purpose of the Act. Thus where in *Biddle* v. *Johnston*[60] the terms of the certificate did not agree with those of the policy it was held that the contract of insurance was constituted by and contained in the policy alone.

Evidence of insurance: onus of proof. On a charge of driving or permitting to drive without a valid policy of insurance covering third party risks in contravention of section 143 the onus is on the defendant to satisfy the court that he was covered at the material time. Thus, where in *Leathley* v. *Drummond*[61] the justices found that the certificate produced to the police did not relate to the vehicles concerned at all, the defendants submitted that the prosecution had failed to show that there was no valid insurance policy in force, and those submissions were upheld by the justices. On appeal by the prosecutor, it was held that that onus **20–14**

---

[54] s.156 referring to regulations under s.37 of the Vehicles (Excise) Act 1971.

[55] s.144(1).

[56] s.147(2).

[57] *McCormick* v. *National Motor Insurance* (1934) 40 Com.Cas. 76.

[58] The policeman must be given reasonable time to inspect it and take details: *Tremelling* v. *Martin* [1971] R.T.R. 196 (D.C.).

[59] *Ocean Accident* v. *Cole* [1932] 2 K.B. 100.

[60] [1965] 2 Lloyd's Rep. 121.

[61] [1972] R.T.R. 293 (D.C.).

was on the defendants. That decision was applied in *Davey* v. *Towle*,[62] where a driver failed to produce a vehicle's insurance certificate to the police. The driver argued that he could not, since the vehicle belonged to someone else; and that the onus of proving that he failed to produce a certificate and that he had no insurance was on the prosecutor. The Divisional Court held that the driver must be convicted.

20–15 Statutory contract between insurer and driver

The simplest method of giving the cover required by the Act where the owner himself is not driving is by an extension in his policy covering not only his liability but that of the actual driver also. It was held in *Williams* v. *Baltic*[63] that the driver's name need not be inserted in the policy under section 2 of the Life Assurance Act 1774,[64] since motor vehicle policies are not within that Act, and by section 148(7) of the Act of 1988 which to some extent preserves that decision[65]:

> Notwithstanding anything in any enactment, a person issuing a policy under section 145 of this Act shall be liable to indemnify the persons or classes of persons specified in the policy in respect of any liability which the policy purports to cover in the case of those persons or classes of persons.

The insurer may by virtue of this provision be made liable to indemnify any specified class of driver, but is not thereby liable to the injured third party himself.[66] As to actions against the insurers by a driver of the class specified in the policy, it has now been decided that his right to sue the insurers is not, on account of this provision, dependent on the owner insuring as his trustee or as his agent.[67] Thus, where the policy was expressed to cover "any person who is driving on the assured's order or with his permission" it was held that any such person might sue the insurers direct on the policy.[68]

Such person is bound by the conditions of the policy; he must take it as he finds it,[69] and cannot excuse his breach of a condition by his ignorance of its terms. The effect of section 148(7) in fact, is to create a contract[70] between the insurers and any driver of the vehicle who is of a class covered by the policy.

20–16   *Extensions to policy.* A satisfactory form of policy will, therefore, afford a main cover to the policy holder in respect of liability incurred by him while driving his own car, and will extend also to indemnify in like manner:

    (a) the policy holder while driving other cars; and
    (b) other persons while driving the policy holder's car.

---

[62] [1973] R.T.R. 328 (D.C.).
[63] [1924] 2 K.B. 282.
[64] Motor policies were treated as goods rather than liability policies, and thus fell within the exception in s.4 of the 1774 Act. It is now clear from *Mark Rowlands* v. *Berni Inns* [1985] 3 All E.R. 473 that all indemnity policies are outside the 1774 Act.
[65] Goddard J. in *Tattersall* v. *Drysdale* [1935] 2 K.B. 174, 180.
[66] *McCormick* v. *National Motor Insurance* (1934) 40 Com. Cas. 76.
[67] *Tattersall* v. *Drysdale* [1935] 2 K.B. 174; approved by Greene M.R. in *Austin* v. *Zurich* [1945] 1 K.B. 250, 255.
[68] See n. 91.
[69] *Guardian* v. *Sutherland* (1939) 55 T.L.R. 576; *Austin* v. *Zurich, supra, per* Greene M.R. at p. 257.
[70] Atkinson J. in *Sutch* v. *Burns* (1943) 60 T.L.R. 1, 2.

In *Digby* v. *General Accident*[71] Miss Merle Oberon took out just such a policy. She was injured when driven negligently in her own car, and obtained judgment against her chauffeur, and the question arose whether he was entitled to recover under the policy. The main cover was expressed to extend to "claims by any person" against the policy holder. It was held[72] that "any person" included the policy holder, and that the chauffeur could therefore recover under the second extension in respect of his liability to the policy holder. In Lord Porter's words: "Miss Merle Oberon was a third party in reference to her authorised driver."

The main cover may exclude the liability of the policy holder to persons in his employment, in which case, it has been held,[73] the second extension excludes liability by other drivers of the car to their employees at the time of the accident.

A common form of policy wording effecting an extension is to afford cover to any person driving the vehicle "with the consent of the assured." In *Singh* v. *Rathour*[74] R borrowed a vehicle ostensibly for business purposes but in fact used it for social purposes. An accident for which R incurred liability occurred while the vehicle was being used for this unauthorised purpose, and the question was whether R's liability was covered by the insurer. The Court of Appeal held that, while R had obtained consent to drive the vehicle, the consent was conditional only; on that basis the consent ceased to operate and R was not covered by the policy.

Sale of car ends policy. The main cover will usually be by reference to **20–17** a specified car, owned by the policy holder. The whole policy will then only remain effective while he retains an interest in that car.[75] Even if it contains an extension in respect of the use by the policy holder of any car being used at the time of the accident "instead of the insured car" this extension will cease to be effective once he has parted with the car insured.[76]

While complete change of ownership of a vehicle will put an end to the policy, this is not so when the additional partner joins a partnership in whose name a vehicle is insured.[77]

Double insurance of driver. The second extension is usually limited in **20–18** its scope to persons who are not protected against liability by any other insurance. Where the driver is covered by two policies in each of which is a clause excluding liability if cover is afforded by another policy, both the insurers will be liable to contribute rateably towards the loss notwithstanding such clauses.[78] If either of such insurers pays the whole of the loss, he will be entitled to bring an action for contribution, which should be in his own name,[79] against the other.

---

[71] [1943] A.C. 121.
[72] By a three to two majority in the House of Lords reversing the Court of Appeal and restoring Atkinson J.'s decision.
[73] *Richards* v. *Cox* [1943] 1 K.B. 139 *Cf. Lees* v. *Motor Insurers' Bureau* [1952] 2 T.L.R. 356.
[74] [1988] 1 W.L.R. 422.
[75] *Rogerson* v. *Scottish Automobile* (1931) 146 L.T. 26.
[76] *Tattersall* v. *Drysdale* [1935] 2 K.B. 174; *Boss* v. *Kingston* [1963] 1 W.L.R. 99.
[77] Goddard J. in *Jenkins* v. *Deane* (1933) 103 L.J.K.B. 250, 255.
[78] *Weddell* v. *Road Transport and General* [1932] 2 K.B. 563.
[79] *Austin* v. *Zurich* [1945] K.B. 250, 258.

20–19   *Rights of hospital and doctors.* The hospital treating a person injured in a motor accident is given certain rights for expenses reasonably incurred in treating him, as against the insurer, or owner where security has been given, by section 157(1) of the Act of 1988.

Further provision for the payment of a doctor for emergency treatment on the scene of the accident by the driver is made by sections 158 and 159 of the Act, and by section 145(3)(*c*) such liability must be covered by the policy.

2. RIGHTS OF THIRD PARTIES

20–20 The assured's insolvency

The statutory rights, as against the insurers, of an injured third party are governed by the Third Parties (Rights against Insurers) Act 1930.[80] This Act does not diminish the third party's rights under the Road Traffic Act 1988 where the assured becomes insolvent, so that the third party can sue the insolvent assured's insurer under the 1988 Act in the manner described in the following paragraphs irrespective of the assured's insolvency.[81]

20–21 Right of action against the insurer

The general principle. By section 151 of the 1988 Act the third party is given a direct right of action against the insurer on obtaining judgment against the assured or a person driving the assured's vehicle. Unlike the position under the Third Parties (Rights against Insurers) Act 1930, the right under section 151 is in no way dependent upon the assured's insolvency. Under the original terms of the 1972 Act, the direct action against the insurer was limited to cases in which the third party had obtained judgment against the assured or a person covered by the assured's policy, so that if the vehicle was being driven by an unauthorised driver or other person not covered by the assured's policy the third party had no cause of action against the insurer. However, the 1988 Act, consolidating amendments introduced in 1987, now makes the insurer responsible for certain liabilities incurred by persons driving the assured's car but not within the terms of the assured's policy. The insurer is thus obliged to meet both insured and certain uninsured liabilities.

20–22   *Insured liabilities.* The insurer is directly liable to the third party for insured liabilities if the following conditions are satisfied:

(a) a certificate of insurance or security must have been delivered to the policy holder under section 147 (section 151(1)).

(b) judgment must have been obtained[82] against any insured under

---

[80] § 19–14 *et seq., supra.*
[81] Road Traffic Act 1988, s.153.
[82] *Carpenter* v. *Ebblewhite* [1939] 1 K.B. 347 holds that judgment must actually have been obtained and not satisfied by the assured.

the policy or person whose liability is covered by the security (section 151(2)(*a*)).

(c) the liability is covered by the terms of the policy (s.151(2)). This, however, is subject to section 148, which prevents the insurer from relying upon breach of specific conditions or warranties listed in that section.[83]

Uninsured liabilities. The insurer is directly liable to the third party if **20–23** the following conditions are satisfied:

(a) A certificate of insurance or security must have been delivered to the policy holder under section 147 (section 151(1)).

(b) Judgment must have been obtained against a person who would have been covered by the policy had the policy covered all persons (section 151(2)(*b*)). Consequently, the insurer is liable in respect of any person driving the vehicle, whether or not that person was covered by the policy, and in particular the insurer is liable for a person driving without a driving licence (section 151(3)). This does not extend to an "excluded liability," *i.e.* liability to a person (for death, personal injury or property damage) who at the time of the use giving rise to the liability was allowing himself to be carried in the vehicle knowing or having reason to believe that it had been stolen or unlawfully taken (section 151(4)).[84]

(c) The liability is, subject to section 148, covered by the terms of the policy (section 151(2)).

Extent of the insurer's liability. Where the insurer faces liability under **20–24** section 151, the third party is entitled to claim the following sums[85]:

(a) as regards death or bodily injury, any sum payable under the judgment plus interest;

(b) as regards property damage, any sum payable under the judgment up to a maximum of £250,000 plus interest.

Avoidance of liability. The insurer faces liability under section 151 **20–25** even though it would otherwise have been entitled to avoid or cancel the policy (section 151(5)); this contrasts with the position under the Third Parties (Rights against Insurers) Act 1930, where the third party gets no better rights than those possessed by the assured himself. In such a case, the insurer is nevertheless entitled to recover the sums paid to the third party from the person in respect of whom the insurer incurred liability (section 151(7)–(8)). However, the wide rights conferred by section 151 on the third party are curtailed by section 152.

By section 152(1), no sum shall be payable by an insurer under section 151 where:

(a) he had not been given notice within seven days after the com-

---

[83] See *infra*, § 20–28 *et seq.*

[84] If the third party did not become aware, or had no reason to believe, that the vehicle had been stolen or unlawfully taken until after the journey had commenced, he can recover as long as he had no reasonable opportunity to alight from it before the event giving rise to his loss.

[85] s.151(5)–(6).

mencement of the proceedings[86] in which judgment was given,[87] of the beginning of the proceedings; or

(b) execution of the judgment is stayed pending an appeal; or
(c) before the assured's liability to the third party arose, the policy was cancelled by mutual consent or by virtue of any provision in it and the certificate was surrendered.

In addition, under section 152(2), where, apart from any provision contained in the policy, the insurer is entitled to avoid, or has avoided the policy, on the ground that it was obtained by the non-disclosure of a material fact or by a representation of fact that was false in some material particular,[88] the insurer can prevent the operation of section 151 by:

(a) obtaining a declaration to the above effect[89] in an action commenced before, or within three months after,[90] the third party's action against the assured, and
(b) giving notice of the action for the declaration within seven days of its commencement to the third party, who shall be entitled, if he thinks fit, to be made a party thereto.

20–26 The notice under section 152(2) should specify every instance of non-disclosure or misrepresentation on which the insurer proposes to rely, as he will not be able to rely upon further instances not so specified as against the third party,[91] but only against the assured.

The admissions of the assured are not evidence as against the third party in an action by the insurer for such a declaration.[92]

Since the right to avoid for non-disclosure or misrepresentation of a material fact does not arise out of the policy itself, the better view appears to be that a clause to the effect that nothing in the policy is to affect third party rights under the Road Traffic Act does not affect the insurer's right to a declaration under section 152.[93]

A further limitation on the third party's wide rights under section 151 is the insurer's ability to apply for an order setting aside a judgment obtained by the third party against the assured where it was obtained in default of appearance.[94]

---

[86] Mere notification of a claim is not sufficient: *McGoona* v. *Motor Insurers' Bureau* [1969] 2 Lloyd's Rep. 34, and *cf. Herbert* v. *Railway Passengers Association* [1938] 1 All E.R. 650. Further, it is not enough for the third party's solicitors to inform the insurer that the third party has been advised by them to institute proceedings: *Harrington* v. *Link Motor Policies* [1989] 2 Lloyd's Rep. 310. There is no need, however, for every detail of the claim to be specified as long as the notice is unconditional: *Ceylon Motor* v. *Thambugala* [1953] A.C. 584.

[87] Within seven days of delivery of counterclaim if the judgment was on a counterclaim: *Cross* v. *British Oak* [1938] 2 K.B. 167.

[88] "Material" bears its ordinary meaning, namely, "of such a nature as to influence the judgment of a prudent insurer in determining whether he will take the risk and, if so, at what premium": s.151(9). However, the policy must have been "obtained" by non-disclosure or misrepresentation of a material fact, which indicates that the *actual* insurer's judgment must have been influenced. See *Zurich* v. *Morrison* [1942] 1 All E.R. 529.

[89] *National Farmers' Mutual* v. *Tully* 1935 S.L.T. 547; *Guardian* v. *Sutherland* (1939) 55 T.L.R. 576.

[90] *Croxford* v. *Universal Insurance* [1936] 2 K.B. 253.

[91] *Zurich* v. *Morrison* [1942] 1 All E.R. 529.

[92] *Merchants' Marine* v. *Hunt* [1941] 1 K.B. 295.

[93] Atkinson J. in *Zurich* v. *Morrison* [1942] 1 All E.R. 529, 535; *Merchants' Assurance* v. *Hunt* [1941] 1 K.B. 295.

[94] *Windsor* v. *Chalcraft* [1939] 1 K.B. 279.

Reliance on policy provisions 20–27

By section 148 the assured may recover from the insurer notwith-standing any clause in the policy limiting the cover provided by it in one or more specified respects. If the insurer is obliged to make payment despite the presence of a clause limiting recovery, the amount of its payment may be recovered from the assured (section 148(4)).

Conditions to be disregarded. The conditions upon which the insurer 20–28 may not rely, listed in section 148(2), comprise:

(a) the age or physical or mental condition of persons driving the vehicle,

(b) the condition of the vehicle,

(c) the number of persons that the vehicle carries,

(d) the weight or physical characteristics of the goods that the vehicle carries,

(e) the time at which or the areas within which the vehicle is used,

(f) the horsepower or cylinder capacity or value of the vehicle,

(g) the carrying on the vehicle of any particular apparatus, or

(h) the carrying on the vehicle of any particular means of identification required to be carried by or under the Vehicles (Excise) Act 1971.

Car-sharing arrangements. Where a policy on a vehicle not adapted to 20–29 carry more than eight passengers restricts cover to social, domestic or pleasure purposes, it is deemed to be used for such purposes on any journey in respect of which fares charged did not include any element of profit and were fixed before the commencement of the journey (section 150). The effect of this clause is to make it clear that car-sharing arrangements between fellow-workers travelling to and from work do not remove the protection of the policy.

Post-loss misconduct. If the assured fails to comply with a policy con- 20–30 dition after the loss has taken place—for example, if the required notices are not provided or the claim is made out of time[95]—the insurer is unable to rely upon the condition. However, the insurer may, if the policy so provides, reclaim from the assured sums paid by it under this form of statutory liability (section 148(5)–(6)).

Liability towards passengers 20–31

Under earlier versions of the Road Traffic Acts passengers were entitled to the benefit of compulsory insurance only if not being carried "for hire or reward," an exclusion which was omitted in 1972. However, the position of even these passengers was weak, as the common law permitted the driver to exclude liability by contract or by a tortious disclaimer.[96] The 1988 Act retains the change made in 1972 deleting the "hire or reward" exception, and section 149 goes further and avoids certain agreements or arrangements under which the assured's liability towards passengers is limited. The effect of section 149 is:

---

[95] *Revell* v. *London General* (1935) 152 L.T. 258; *Bright* v. *Ashfold* [1932] 2 K.B. 153; Slesser L.J. in *Croxford* v. *Universal* [1936] 2 K.B. 253, 268 *et seq.*
[96] *Nettleship* v. *Weston* [1971] 2 Q.B. 691; *Owens* v. *Brimmell* [1977] Q.B. 859.

(a) to render ineffective any agreement or understanding between driver and passenger, whether or not intended to be legally binding, which negatives or restricts the former's liability to the latter;

(b) to treat a passenger who has willingly accepted the risk of negligence as not having waived any right to sue the driver.[69a]

20–32 Duty of assured to inform third party

Section 154 of the Act of 1988 places persons against whom claims are made under a duty of giving the third party the necessary information as to their insurance.

3. RECOVERY FROM THE MOTOR INSURERS' BUREAU

20–33 History of the Motor Insurers' Bureau agreements

The law stated above on the "Rights of Third Parties" is supplemented by three agreements between the Secretary of State for Transport and the Motor Insurers' Bureau. The Bureau consists of and is funded by all authorised motor insurers, and provides payments to a third party where for some reason recovery from the wrongdoer's insurers is not possible. Two situations are covered: recovery where the loss is caused by an uninsured driver; and recovery where the loss is caused by an untraced driver. The primary agreement, now of December 21, 1987, but originally of June 17, 1946, (replaced on November 22, 1972) deals with uninsured drivers, and its broad effect is to permit the third party to recover from the Bureau if a judgment in his favour is not met within seven days. The second agreement, of November 22, 1972, (originally April 21, 1969) deals with untraced drivers, and similarly allows recovery from the Bureau, but only in respect of death or personal injury and not property damage. The supplementary agreement, of December 7, 1977, provides an accelerated procedure for settlements where the claim does not exceed £20,000.

20–34 The 1987 Agreement: Compensation of Victims of Uninsured Drivers

The full text of this Agreement is set out in the following paragraphs.

20–35 Definitions

1. In this Agreement—

"contract of insurance" means a policy of insurance or a security;

"insurer" includes the giver of a security;

"relevant liability" means a liability in respect of which a policy of insurance must insure a person in order to comply with Part VI of the Road Traffic Act 1988

20–36 Satisfaction of claims by M.I.B.

2.—(1) If judgment in respect of any relevant liability[97] is obtained against any person or persons in any Court in Great Britain whether or not such a person or persons be in fact covered by a contract of insur-

---

[96a] But see *Pitts* v. *Hunt* (1990) *The Times*, April 13.

[97] As defined in Clause 1. Where the assured has deliberately caused injury to the third party the rule of public policy prevent the assured from seeking an indemnity from his insurers. However, the third party has an action against the assured, and this constitutes a "relevant liability" for the purposes of an action against the Bureau: *Hardy* v. *Motor Insurers' Bureau* [1964] 2 Q.B. 745; *Gardner* v. *Moore* [1984] A.C. 548.

ance and any such judgment is not satisfied in full within seven days from the date upon which the person or persons in whose favour the judgment was given became entitled to enforce it then M.I.B. will, subject to the provisions of paragraphs (2), (3) and (4) below and to Clauses 4, 5 and 6 hereof, pay or satisfy or cause to be paid or satisfied to or to the satisfaction of the person or persons in whose favour the judgment was given any sum payable or remaining payable thereunder in respect of the relevant liability including any sum awarded by the Court in respect of interest on that sum and any taxed costs or any costs awarded by the Court without taxation (or such proportion thereof as is attributable to the relevant liability) whatever may be the cause of the failure of the judgment debtor to satisfy the judgment.[98]

(2) Subject to paragraphs (3) and (4) below and to Clauses 4, 5 and 6 hereof, M.I.B. shall incur liability under paragraph (1) above in respect of any sum awarded under such a judgment in respect of property damage not exceeding £250,000 or in respect of the first £250,000 of any sum so awarded exceeding that amount.

(3) Where a person in whose favour a judgment in respect of a relevant liability which includes liability in respect of damage to property has been given, has received or is entitled to receive in consequence of a claim he has made, compensation from any source in respect of that damage, M.I.B. may deduct from the sum payable or remaining payable under paragraph (1) above an amount equal to the amount of that compensation in addition to the deduction of £175 by virtue of paragraph (4) below. The reference to compensation includes compensation under insurance arrangements.

(4) M.I.B. shall not incur liability under paragraph (1) above in respect of any amount payable or remaining payable under the judgment in respect of property damage liability where the total of amounts so payable or remaining payable is £175 or less, or, where the total of such amounts is more than £175, in respect of the first £175 of such total.

Period of agreement   20–37
3. This Agreement shall be determinable by the Secretary of State at any time or by M.I.B. on twelve months' notice without prejudice to the continued operation of the Agreement in respect of accidents occurring before the date of termination.

Recoveries   20–38
4. Nothing in this Agreement shall prevent insurers from providing by conditions in their contracts of insurance that all sums paid by them or by M.I.B. by virtue of the Principal Agreement or this Agreement in or towards the discharge of the liability of their insured shall be recoverable by them or by M.I.B. from the insured or from any other person.

Conditions precedent to M.I.B.'s liability   20–39
5.—(1) M.I.B. shall not incur any liability under Clause 2 of this Agreement unless—

(a) notice in writing of the bringing of the proceedings is given within seven days after the commencement of the proceedings—
   (i) to M.I.B. in the case of proceedings in respect of a relevant liability which is either not covered by a contract of insurance or covered by a contract of insurance with an insurer whose identity cannot be ascertained, or
   (ii) to the insurer in the case of proceedings in respect of a relevant liability which is covered by a contract of insurance with an insurer whose identity can be ascertained;
   Such notice shall be accompanied by a copy of the writ, summons or other document initiating the proceedings;

---

[98] This clause is exhaustive of the Bureau's obligations. In particular the Bureau is not liable to make interim payments under R.S.C. Ord. 29: *Powney* v. *Coxage* (1988) *The Times*, March 8.

(*b*) the person bringing the proceedings furnishes to M.I.B.—

    (i) such information (in such form as M.I.B. may specify) in relation thereto as M.I.B. may reasonably require; and

    (ii) such information (in such form as M.I.B. may specify) as to any insurance covering any damage to property to which the claim or proceedings relate and any claim made in respect of that damage under the insurance or otherwise and any report which may have been made or notification which may have been given to any person in respect of that damage or the use of the vehicle giving rise thereto, as M.I.B. may reasonably require;

(*c*) the person bringing the proceedings has demanded the information and, where appropriate, the particulars specified in section 154 of the Road Traffic Act 1988 in accordance with that section or, if so required by M.I.B., has authorised M.I.B. to do so on his behalf;

(*d*) if so required by M.I.B. and subject to full indemnity from M.I.B. as to costs[99] the person bringing the proceedings has taken all reasonable steps to obtain judgment against all the persons liable in respect of the injury or death or damage to property and, in the event of any such person being a servant or agent, against his principal; and

(*e*) the judgment referred to in Clause 2 of this Agreement and any judgment referred to in paragraph (*d*) of this Clause which has been obtained (whether or not either judgment includes an amount in respect of a liability other than a relevant liability) and any order for costs are assigned to M.I.B. or their nominee.

(2) In the event of any dispute as to the reasonableness of a requirement by M.I.B. for the supply of information or that any particular step should be taken to obtain judgment against other persons it may be referred to the Secretary of State whose decision shall be final.

(3) Where a judgment which includes an amount in respect of a liability other than a relevant liability has been assigned to M.I.B. or their nominee in pursuance of paragraph (1)(*e*) of this Clause M.I.B. shall apportion any monies received in pursuance of the judgment according to the proportion which the damages in respect of the relevant liability bear to the damages in respect of the other liabilities and shall account to the person in whose favour the judgment was given in respect of such monies received properly apportionable to the other liabilities. Where an order for costs in respect of such a judgment has been so assigned monies received pursuant to the order shall be dealt with in the same manner.

20–40 Exceptions

6.—(1) M.I.B. shall not incur any liability under Clause 2 of this Agreement in a case where—

(*a*) the claim arises out of the use of a vehicle owned by or in the possession of the Crown, except where any other person has undertaken responsibility for the existence of a contract of insurance under Part VI of the Road Traffic Act 1988 (whether or not the person or persons liable be in fact covered by a contract of insurance) or where the liability is in fact covered by a contract of insurance;

(*b*) the claim arises out of the use of a vehicle the use of which is not required to be covered by a contract of insurance by virtue of section 144 of the Road Traffic Act 1988, unless the use is in fact covered by such a contract;

(*c*) the claim is in respect of a judgment or any part thereof which has been obtained by virtue of the exercise of a right of subrogation by any person;

---

[99] The court has a discretion in such cases to make a full order for costs against the defendant notwithstanding that he is legally aided: *Godfrey* v. *Smith* [1955] 1 W.L.R. 692.

(d) the claim is in respect of damage to property which consists of damage to a motor vehicle or losses arising therefrom if at the time of the use giving rise to the damage to the motor vehicle there was not in force in relation to the use of that vehicle when the damage to it was sustained such a policy of insurance as is required by Part VI of the Road Traffic Act 1988 and the person or persons claiming in respect of the loss or damage either knew or ought to have known that that was the case;

(e) at the time of the use which gave rise to the liability the person suffering death or bodily injury or damage to property was allowing himself to be carried in or upon the vehicle and either before the commencement of his journey in the vehicle or after such commencement if he could reasonably be expected to have alighted from the vehicle he—

    (i) knew or ought to have known that the vehicle had been stolen or unlawfully taken,[1] or

    (ii) knew or ought to have known that the vehicle was being used without there being in force in relation to its use such a contract of insurance as would comply with Part VI of the Road Traffic Act 1988.

(2) The exception specified in sub-paragraph (1)(e) of this Clause shall apply only in a case where the judgment in respect of which the claim against M.I.B. is made was obtained in respect of a relevant liability incurred by the owner or a person using the vehicle in which the person who suffered death or bodily injury or sustained damage to property was being carried.

(3) For the purposes of these exceptions—

(a) a vehicle which has been unlawfully removed from the possession of the Crown shall be taken to continue in that possession whilst it is kept so removed;

(b) references to a person being carried in a vehicle include references to his being carried in or upon or entering or getting on to or alighting from the vehicle; and

(c) "owner" in relation to a vehicle which is the subject of a hiring agreement of a hire-purchase agreement, means the person in possession of the vehicle under that agreement.

Agents   20–41

7.—Nothing in this Agreement shall prevent M.I.B. performing their obligations under this Agreement by Agents.

Operation   20–42

8.—This Agreement shall come into operation on December 31, 1988, in relation to accidents occurring on or after that date. The Agreement made on November 22, 1972, between the Secretary of State and M.I.B. shall cease and determine except in relation to claims arising out of accidents occurring before December 31, 1988.

Notes   20–43

The following notes are for the guidance of those who may have a claim on the Motor Insurers' Bureau under the Agreement, and of their legal advisers, but they must not be taken as rendering unnecessary a careful study of the Agreement itself. Communications on any matter connected with the Agreement should be addressed to the Motor Insurers' Bureau whose address is New Garden House, 78 Hatton Garden, London EC1N 8JQ.

1. The Agreement, which operates from December 31, 1988 supersedes earlier Agreements made on 17 June 1946 (which was operative from 1 July 1946), on

---

[1] This wording alters the 1972 wording "had reason to believe," which proved to be unduly hard on the third party: *Porter* v. *Motor Insurers' Bureau* [1978] 2 Lloyd's Rep. 463

February 1 1971 (which was operative from March 1, 1971) and on November 22, 1972 (which was operative from 1 December 1972) in relation to claims arising out of accidents occurring on or after 31 December 1988.

2. If damages are awarded by a Court in respect of death or personal injury or damage to property arising out of the use of a motor vehicle on a road in circumstances where the liability is one which was, at the time the accident occurred, required to be covered by insurance and such damages, or any part of them, remain unpaid seven days after the judgment becomes enforceable, the Bureau will, subject to the limit specified in Clause 2(2), which corresponds with the limited insurance requirement in section 145(4)(*b*) of the Road Traffic Act 1988, and the exceptions in paragraphs (3) and (4) of Clause 2 and Clause 6 of the Agreement, pay the unrecovered amount (including any interest awarded by the Court and costs) to the person in whose favour the judgment has been given against an assignment of the judgment debt. This applies whether the judgment debtor is a British resident or a foreign visitor.

3. Clause 1 defines "relevant liability" as a liability in respect of which a policy of insurance must insure a person in order to comply with Part VI of the Road Traffic Act 1988, which includes liability in respect of property damage caused by, or arising out of, the use of a motor vehicle on a road in Great Britain. This provision gives effect to Article 1.1 of Council Directive (84/5/EEC) of 30 December 1983 on the approximation of the laws of Member States relating to insurance against civil liability in respect of the use of motor vehicles (OJ No. L8, 11.1.84, p. 17). In the context of the Directive "damage to property" means damage to material property. Accordingly in this Agreement the reference to damage to property is understood in that sense. With regard to liability in respect of such damage which is covered by the Agreement, M.I.B. would expect to meet the consequential loss elements of a claim flowing from damage to the claimant's material property which a Court would allow. It must be emphasised that M.I.B.'s obligation does not extend to those liabilities not required to be covered by the policy under section 145(4) of the Road Traffic Act 1988.

4. Nothing in the Agreement affects the position at law of the parties to an action for damages arising out of the driving of a motor vehicle. The Bureau's liability under the Agreement can only arise when the plaintiff has successfully established his case against the person or persons liable in the usual manner and judgment has been given in his favour. There is, of course, nothing to exclude the acceptance of compensation by the plaintiff under a settlement of his claim negotiated between the plaintiff and the alleged person liable or the Bureau.

5. The purpose of Clause 2(3) is to oblige any claimant in respect of property damage to give credit for compensation which he may have received or be entitled to receive under a claim he has made on another source or sources relative to that damage. The most common instances will involve compensation recovered under comprehensive motor or household policies. Policyholders with these covers cannot be forced to claim under them but will normally wish to do so for their convenience. Furthermore legal liability for the accident will not affect that claim and the M.I.B. excess of £175 (Clause 2(4)) will not apply. Where such a claim has been made successfully M.I.B. will only be concerned with the claimant's uninsured losses *e.g.* any excess he may have under his own policy, or loss of use of his vehicle subject to legal liability and the M.I.B. excess of £175.

6. WHERE THERE IS A POLICY. In cases where it is ascertained that there is in existence a policy issued in compliance with the Road Traffic Act 1988, the insurer will act as the agent of the Bureau even if entitled to repudiate liability under the policy and, subject to notice being given as provided for in Clause 5(1)(*a*)(ii), will handle claims within the terms of the Agreement.

In many cases, particularly where the vehicle was being used without the policyholder's authority, the provisions of the Road Traffic Act preclude repudiation by the insurer of a victim's claim. Victims and those acting on their behalf are expressly reminded of the requirements as to the giving of notice to the insurer if the protection afforded to third parties by section 151 of the Road Traffic Act 1988 is sought.

It must be stressed that the above arrangements are without prejudice to any rights insurers may have against their policyholders and, to avoid any possible misunderstanding, it is emphasised that there is nothing in this Agreement affecting any obligations imposed on a policyholder by his policy. Policyholders are not released from their contractual obligations to their insurers, although the Road Traffic Act and M.I.B. protect THIRD PARTY VICTIMS from the consequences of failure to observe them. For example, if a policyholder fails to notify claims to his insurers as required by his policy or permits an unauthorised person to drive, he may be liable to his insurers.

WHERE THERE IS NO POLICY OR THE IDENTITY OF THE INSURER CANNOT BE ASCERTAINED. In cases where there is no policy, or for any reason the existence of a policy is in doubt or where there is a policy but the identity of the insurer cannot be ascertained, the victim or those acting on his behalf must notify the Bureau, and in practice it is desirable to inform the Bureau in all cases where the name of the insurer is not speedily forthcoming. It is a condition of the Bureau's liability that they should be given notification in writing (with relevant documents) within seven days after the commencement of proceedings against the alleged person liable. It should always be remembered that the requirement for notice of issue of proceedings under Clause 5(1)(a)(i) and (ii) must be complied with strictly. Notice should be given immediately on issue of the proceedings, and such notice must be accompanied by copies of the writ or summons.

7. Claims arising out of the use of uninsured vehicles owned by or in the possession of the Crown will in the majority of cases be outside the scope of the Bureau's liability (see Clause 6 of the Agreement—Exceptions). In such cases the approach should be made to the responsible authority in the usual way. The same benefits in respect of compensation will normally be afforded by the Crown to the victims in such cases as they would receive were the accident caused by a private vehicle, except where the victim is a serviceman or servicewoman whose death or injury gives rise to an entitlement to a pension or other compensation from public funds.

8. The purpose of Clause 6(1)(c) is to relieve M.I.B. of liability to meet judgments in respect of damage to property obtained by persons who have compensated the victim such as the victim's own insurers. Such insurers have the right to attempt to recoup their outlay by requiring an insured to lend his name to proceedings against the person responsible, but M.I.B. will not meet such claims as the victim has already been compensated.

9. Claims for damage to a vehicle or for losses arising therefrom for which a policy of insurance issued in compliance with Part VI of the Road Traffic Act 1988 is required, are excluded from the Agreement if the vehicle was not insured and the claimant knew or ought to have known that it was not. See Clause 6(1)(d). The claim may also be excluded under Clause 6(1)(e).

10. It should be noted that the monetary limit applicable to property damage claims by virtue of Clause 2(2) corresponding with the insurance limit in section 145(4)(b) of the Road Traffic Act 1988, and the excess prescribed by Clauses 2(3) and (4) of this Agreement will be subject to review from time to time.

11. The Bureau have no liability UNDER THIS AGREEMENT to pay compensation in respect of any person who may suffer bodily injury or death or may sustain damage to property resulting from the use on a road of a vehicle, the owner or driver of which cannot be traced. A separate Agreement between the Secretary of State for Transport and the Bureau for the Compensation of Victims of Untraced Drivers in respect of bodily injury and death applies, but this Agreement does not embrace damage to property.

The 1972 Agreement: Compensation of Victims of Untraced Drivers   20–44

The original Motor Insurers' Bureau agreement of 1946 was limited to uninsured drivers, and specifically excluded untraced "hit-and-run" drivers. This exclusion was highlighted by Sachs J. in *Adams* v. *Andrews*,[2]

---

[2] [1964] 2 Lloyd's Rep. 347.

who described it as "lamentable" and demanding of action.[3] This decision resulted in an agreement in 1969, replaced, in its current form, in 1972. The Untraced Drivers Agreement is applicable only where the wrongdoer cannot be identified: if the wrongdoer is identified but cannot be contacted, the victim must proceed under the Uninsured Drivers Agreement.[4]

The 1972 Agreement is procedurally complex and only its most important provisions are set out in the following paragraphs:

20-45   1.—(1) Subject to paragraph (2) of this Clause, this agreement applies to any case in which an application is made to M.I.B. for payment in respect of the death of or bodily injury to any person caused by or arising out of the use of a motor vehicle on a road in Great Britain and the case is one in which the following conditions are fulfilled,[5] that is to say,—

(a) the event giving rise to the death or injury occurred on or after December 1, 1972;

(b) the applicant for the payment either—
  (i) is unable to trace any person responsible for the death or injury, or
  (ii) in a case to which Clause 5 hereof applies where more than one person was so responsible, is unable to trace one of those persons.[6]
  (Any person so untraced is hereinafter referred to as "*the untraced person*");

(c) the death or injury was caused in such circumstances that on the balance of probabilities[6] the untraced person would be liable to pay damages to the applicant in respect of the death or injury;

(d) the liability of the untraced person to pay damages to the applicant is one which is required to be covered by insurance or security under Part VI of the Road Traffic Act 1988, it being assumed for this purpose, in the absence of evidence to the contrary, that he vehicle was being used in circumstances in which the user was required by the said Part VI to be insured or secured against third party risks;

(e) the death or injury was not caused by the use of the vehicle by the untraced person as a weapon, that is to say, in a deliberate attempt to run the deceased or injured person down[7];

(f) the application is made in writing *within three years*[8] from the date of the event giving rise to the death or injury.

(2) This Agreement does not apply to a case in which—

(a) the death or bodily injury in respect of which any such application is made was caused by or arose out of the use of a motor vehicle which at the time of the event giving rise to the death or bodily injury was owned by or in the possession of the Crown, unless the case is one in which some other person has undertaken responsibility for the existence of a contract of insurance under Part VI of the Road Traffic Act 1972;

(b) at the time of the accident the person suffering death or bodily injury in respect of which the application is made was allowing himself to be carried in a vehicle and—

---

[3] *Ibid.* at pp. 351 *et seq.*

[4] *Gurtner* v. *Circuit* [1968] 2 Q.B. 587; *Clarke* v. *Vedel* [1979] R.T.R. 26.

[5] It is for the M.I.B. to decide whether these conditions are fulfilled. If they refuse to make an award (*e.g.* under cl. 1(1) (c) on the ground that the untraced person could not be liable), the applicant's only remedy is to arbitrate under cl. 11. He has no right of action against the Board; *Persson* v. *London Country Buses* [1974] 1 W.L.R. 569 (C.A.).

[6] For an illustration, see *Elizabeth* v. *Motor Insurers' Bureau* [1981] R.T.R. 405.

[7] This is really an exception such as those in cl. 1(1). No corresponding exception is made in the uninsured drivers' agreement. It is oddly worded, and appears difficult to justify. Note 3, states, more simply that the Board will not deal with deliberate "running down" cases. Such conduct may be commendable—*e.g.* to avoid a major catastrophic pile-up, or prevent the escape of a convict—but it does not follow that it is not criminal. Even if it is, why should the victim be prejudiced?

[8] The three years contrasts with the seven days maximum notice to be given M.I.B. by cl. 5(1)(a) of the uninsured drivers' agreement.

(i) knew or has reason to belief that the vehicle had been taken without the consent of the owner or other lawful authority, except in a case where—
(A) he believed or had reason to believe that he had lawful authority to be carried or that he would have had the owner's consent if the owner had known of his being carried and the circumstances of his carriage; or
(B) he had learned of the circumstances of the taking of the vehicle since the commencement of the journey and it would be unreasonable to expect him to have alighted from the vehicle; or
(ii) being the owner of or being a person using the vehicle he was using or causing or permitting the vehicle to be used without there being in force in relation to such use a policy of insurance or such security as would comply with Part VI of the Road Traffic Act 1972, knowing or having reason to believe that no such policy or security was in force.

(3) The exception from the application of this Agreement specified in subparagraph (2)(*b*) of this Clause shall apply only in a case where the application is made to M.I.B. in respect of a liability arising out of the use of the vehicle in which the person who suffered death or bodily injury was being carried.

(4) For the purpose of paragraph (2) of this Clause—
(*a*) a vehicle which has been unlawfully removed from the possession of the Crown shall be taken to continue in that possession whilst it is kept so removed;
(*b*) references to a person being *carried* in a vehicle include references to his being carried in or upon, or entering or getting on to or alighting from the vehicle;
(*c*) "owner" in relation to a vehicle which is the subject of a hiring agreement or a hire purchase agreement means the person in possession of the vehicle under the agreement.

2.—(1) An application to M.I.B. for a payment in respect of the death of or **20–46** bodily injury to any person may be made either by the person for whose benefit that payment is to be made (hereinafter called "the applicant") or by any solicitor acting for the applicant or by any other person whom M.I.B. may be prepared to accept as acting for the applicant.

(2) Any decision, award or payment given or made or other thing done in accordance with this Agreement to or by a person acting as aforesaid on behalf of the applicant, or in relation to an application made by such a person, shall, whatever may be the age, or the circumstances affecting the capacity, of the applicant, be treated as having the same effect as if it had been done to or by, or in relation to an application made by, an applicant of full age and capacity.

Clauses 3 et seq. of the Agreement. These clauses are mainly procedural, **20–47** *and are accordingly mentioned only briefly below.*

Clauses 3 and 4 provide for the *assessment of damages* by M.I.B. on an application made to them in respect of the relevant death or injury.[9] They shall simply by clause 3 award the applicant a payment, as assessed by a court of law (in England and Wales, or Scotland, where the victim suffered the relevant injury or death), save that by clause 4(*a*) loss of expectation of life or pain or suffering may be ignored as may, in Scotland, a relative's grief[10] and, by paragraph (*b*), payments of earnings for work he was unable to do shall be deducted from loss of earnings even though he undertook to reimburse his employer if he re-recovered damages.

---

[9] Cl. 5(1) defines "the relevant loss or injury" as referring in cl. 5 only, to any case where the death or bodily injury in respect of which an application has been made to M.I.B. under this Agreement." It can conveniently be used more generally.
[10] Solatium.

20–48   Clause 5 provides for the situation where the relevant death or injury was caused partly by "the untraced person" and partly (A) by some other identified person or persons, *or* (B) some other untraced person or persons whose master or principal can be identified, *and* in circumstances making (A) the identified person(s), *or* (B) such master or principal, liable for the relevant death or injury.

That being by Clause 5(1) the situation, by paragraph (2) the amount to be awarded to "the applicant" by M.I.B., if condition (3)(*a*) *or* (*b*) is satisfied, is determined by paragraph (4).

The paragraph (3) conditions are:

(*a*) that the applicant has *obtained judgment*, against at least one identified person *or* master or principal of any other person, *which has not been satisfied in full within three months, or*

(*b*) that the applicant (i) has not obtained and has not been required by M.I.B. to obtain judgment against any such person or master or principal of such person as (*a*) applies to, *and* (ii) has not received payment by compensation from any such person(s).

By paragraph (4) the amount to be awarded shall be:

(*a*) if the para. (3)(*a*) condition is satisfied, and the judgment wholly unsatisfied, an amount of equal to '*the untraced person's contribution*'[11] to a '*full award*.'[12]

(*b*) but if the judgment is satisfied in part only, the amount is to be adjusted as specified;

(*c*) if the para. (3)(*b*) condition is satisfied, an amount equal to the untraced person's contribution to a full award.

Paragraph (5) provides for the situation where an appeal is begun against a paragraph 3(*a*) judgment, and also in the event of a further appeal following it.

By clause 5(6), in this clause:

(*a*) '*full award*' means the amount which would have fallen to be awarded under clause 3 if the untraced person had been wholly responsible for the relevant death or injury; and

(*b*) '*untraced person's contribution*' means the proportion of such 'full award' which on the balance of probabilities would have been apportioned by a court as being the untraced person's share had suit been brought against all the persons having a share in the responsibility for the relevant death or injury.

Clause 5(7) finally provides that M.I.B. shall not be liable for the relevant death or injury under the Agreement if the applicant is entitled to compensation therefore under the Agreement for Compensation of Victims of Uninsured Drivers.

20–49   Clause 6 sets out conditions precedent to any liability falling on the M.I.B. upon an application under the untraced drivers Agreement in respect of any death or injury.

Applicant's duties. Clause 6(1) imposes duties on the applicant. He must:

(*a*) assist the M.I.B. as reasonably required to enable any investigation under

---

[11] Defined by cl. 5(6)(*b*), *infra.*
[12] Defined by cl. 5(6)(*a*), *infra.*

the Agreement to be carried on—including furnishing statements and information.

(b) If so required by the M.I.B. the applicant must take all reasonable steps required to obtain judgment against any identified person(s) or the master or principal of any person in respect of liability for the relevant death or injury, at any time before the M.I.B. have communicated their decision to the applicant; and

(c) assign any judgment obtained by him whether or not under subpara. (b), to the M.I.B. or their nominee in respect of the relevant death or injury on terms securing that the M.I.B. (or its nominee) will be accountable to the applicant for any amount by which the net total[13] recovered under the judgment exceeds the amount payable by the M.I.B. to the applicant under the Agreement.

Clause 6(2)(a) imposes the *correlative duty on the M.I.B.* to indemnify the applicant against all costs reasonably incurred in complying with the clause 6(1)(b) requirement:

unless the result of those proceedings materially contributes to establish that the untraced person did not cause or contribute to the relevant death or injury.

Subparagraph (b) provides that the applicant shall, if required by the M.I.B. and at their expense, furnish the M.I.B. with a transcript of any official shorthand note taken in such proceedings of evidence or judgment.

Disputes. Clause 6(3) provides that any dispute between the applicant and the M.I.B. as to the reasonableness of any requirement by the M.I.B. under paragraph (1)(b) or whether costs were reasonably incurred under subparagraph (c), shall be referred to the Secretary of State whose decision shall be final; and that such a dispute as to whether the M.I.B. are required to indemnify the applicant under paragraph (2)(a) shall be referred to the arbitrator.

By clause 7 the M.I.B. shall cause any application made to them for **20–50** payment under the untraced drivers Agreement to be investigated, and (unless they decide on preliminary investigation to reject the application since it is not a case to which the Agreement applies) they shall cause a report to be made on the application:

and on the basis of that report the M.I.B. shall decide whether to make an award and, if so, the amount of the award which shall be calculated in accordance with the foregoing provisions of this Agreement.

Clause 8 provides that before coming to such a decision, the M.I.B. **20–51** may request the applicant to furnish them with a statutory declaration of the facts and circumstances[14] on which his claim is based or such of them as may be specified by the M.I.B.

By clause 9(2) the M.I.B. shall give notice of a decision, with reasons, **20–52** that they will not indemnify the applicant against costs on the ground of the exception to clause 6(2)(a) and furnish him, if they consider it relevant, with any transcript as is mentioned in clause 6(2)(b).

---

[13] The aggregate of all sums recovered by M.I.B. or its nominee under the said judgment (after deducting all reasonable expenses incurred in effecting such recovery).

[14] "Setting out to the best of his knowledge, information and belief the facts and circumstances."

Clause 9 provides:

(1) The M.I.B. shall notify their decision to the applicant and when so doing shall—

(*a*) if the application is rejected because a preliminary investigation has disclosed that it is not one made in a case to which this Agreement applies, give their reasons for the rejection; or

(*b*) if the application has been fully investigated furnish him with a statement setting out—

    (i) the circumstances in which the death or injury occurred and the evidence bearing thereon,

    (ii) the circumstances relevant to the assessment of the amount to be awarded to the applicant under the Agreement and the evidence bearing thereon, and

    (iii) if they refuse to make an award, their reasons for that refusal; and

(*c*) in a case to which Clause 5[15] of this Agreement applies specify the way in which the amount of that award has been computed and its relation to those provisions of Clause 5 which are relevant to its computation.[16]

20–53   Clause 10 provides as follows:

Subject to the provisions of this Agreement, M.I.B. shall,—

(*a*) on being notified by the applicant that M.I.B.'s award is accepted; or

(*b*) if at the expiration of the period during which the applicant may give notice of an appeal under Clause 11 hereof there has not been given to M.I.B. either any such notification as aforesaid of the acceptance of M.I.B.'s award or a notice of an appeal under the said Clause 11,

pay the applicant the amount of that award, and such payment shall discharge M.I.B. from all liability under this Agreement in respect of the death or injury in respect of which that award has been made.

20–54   By clause 11:

The applicant shall have a right of appeal to an arbitrator against any decision notified to him under Clause 9 hereof on any of the following grounds, that is to say,—

(*a*) that the case is one to which this Agreement applies and that his application should be fully investigated by M.I.B. with a view to their deciding whether to make an award to the applicant and, if so, the amount of that award; or

(*b*) where the application has been fully investigated—

    (i) that M.I.B. were wrong in refusing to make an award, or

    (ii) that the amount they have awarded to the applicant is insufficient; or

(*c*) in a case where a decision not to indemnify the applicant against the costs of any proceedings has been notified under Clause 9(2) hereof, that that decision was wrong,

if, within six weeks from the date when notice of the decision against which he wishes to appeal was given to him, the applicant, not having previously notified M.I.B. that he wishes to appeal against their decision.

20–55   Clauses 12 to 22 are mainly concerned with the procedure on appeal, and the costs of it.

Clause 18 provides:

"The arbitrator by whom any such appeal as aforesaid shall be decided shall be an arbitrator to be selected by the Secretary of State from two panels of Queen's Counsel appointed respectively by the Lord Chancellor and the Lord Advocate for the purpose of determining appeals under this Agreement, the arbitrator to be selected from the panel appointed by the Lord

---

[15] *Supra*, § 20–48.

[16] cl. 5(4) to (6), *supra*, § 20–48.

Chancellor in cases where the event giving rise to the death or injury occurred in England or Wales and from the panel appointed by the Lord Advocate where that event occurred in Scotland.''

If in any case it appears to the M.I.B. that by reason of the applicant **20–56** being under the age of majority or of any other circumstances affecting his capacity to manage his affairs it would be in the interest of the applicant that all or some part of the amount which would otherwise be payable to him under an award made under this Agreement should be administered for him by the Family Welfare Association or by some other body or person under a trustee, the M.I.B. may establish for that purpose a trust of the whole part of the said amount to take effect for such period and subject to such provisions as may appear to the M.I.B. appropriate in the circumstances of the case.

The Agreement may be determined at any time by the Secretary of **20–57** State or by the M.I.B. by either of them giving to the other not less than 12 months' previous notice in writing.

Right to recover from Bureau   **20–58**
This arises *ex facie* the (uninsured drivers) agreement if (1) the third party obtains judgment against the tortfeasor in respect of liability required by Part VI of the Road Traffic Act 1988, to be covered by insurance, and (2) the judgment is not satisfied in full within seven days.

The third party has no right in law to sue the Bureau in his own name, since he was not a party to the agreements of 1946, 1969, 1972 and 1987 between the government and the Bureau.[17]

This consideration is, however, partly academic. The courts in a series of cases have allowed the third party to sue the Bureau direct: in case after case the Bureau has either submitted to arbitration or not contested the jurisdiction of the court in an action against it on the agreement by the third party.

In *Coward* v. *M.I.B.*[18] Upjohn L.J. said, in a case of a third party suing the Bureau in his own name: "No point is taken by the defendants that the plaintiff was not privy to 'the agreement' or that the Minister of Transport should have been a party. As we understand other actions have been maintained in circumstances similar to this in the High Court, this court has not thought it necessary to raise any such objection independently. . . . ''

"I trust," said Lord Denning M.R. in *Hardy* v. *Motor Insurers' Bureau*[19] "no such point will ever be taken. This agreement [of 1946] is as important as any statute.''[20]

It may be, however, that by joining the Secretary of State, the third **20–59** party can sue on it as a person interested in an insurance on goods[21] effected by the Secretary of State for his benefit.[22] The question, upon

---

[17] *Midland Silicones* v. *Scruttons* [1962] A.C. 446; *Gurtner* v. *Circuit* [1968] 1 Lloyd's Rep. 171.
[18] [1963] 1 Q.B. 259, 265.
[19] [1964] 2 Q.B. 745.
[20] *Ibid*. 757. But see *Persson* v. *London Country Buses* [1974] 1 W.L.R. 569 (C.A.).
[21] *Williams* v. *Baltic* [1924] 2 K.B. 282.
[22] *Prudential Staff Union* v. *Hall* [1947] K.B. 685.

the authorities as they stand, appears to be whether the Secretary of State according to the construction of the agreement, intended to insure the interests of third parties. Since the agreement states[23] that the Bureau was set up "to secure compensation to third party victims in cases where, notwithstanding the provisions of the Road Traffic Acts relating to compulsory insurance, the victim is deprived . . . of effective insurance," it would appear that that was the intention. No question of consideration arises because the agreement was under seal. Prima facie, accordingly, it appears to be enforceable in the courts, in any event, in the name of the Secretary of State.

20–60   Thus in *Gurtner* v. *Circuit*[24] the Court of Appeal gave leave to the Bureau to be joined as a defendant in a case where the injured third party was suing a motor cycle driver who had left the country, and could not be served personally with the writ. Neither the first defendant nor his insurers (Lloyd's underwriters) could be traced; the police failed to take down the name of the syndicate which had issued the certificate. But while the Bureau was allowed to be joined it was made clear by all the court that the only person entitled to enforce the agreement was the Minister; it conferred no right of action against the Bureau upon any unsatisfied judgment creditor.[25] The Minister could sue for specific performance of it and compel the Bureau to honour its agreement by paying the third person.[26]

20–61   It is no defence to an action by an injured third party against the owner of a vehicle for breach of statutory duty to insure (on the *Monk* v. *Warber*[27] principle) that the third party may be able to recover from the Bureau, where he was injured by the negligence of someone permitted to drive an uninsured vehicle.[28]

4. CLAUSES RESTRICTING COVER

20–62 Clauses restricting cover to specified circumstances, such as where a lorry is used to carry coal, should be distinguished from conditions precedent to liability, such as that a lorry should be used for no other purpose. If the vehicle is used in circumstances which the policy does not cover, the policy remains effective under circumstances covered by it, but breach of a condition entitles the insurers to terminate the policy for breach.[29]

A few examples of how the more common of such restrictions have been construed by the courts are instructive. Since, unless they fall

---

[23] Recitals to (uninsured drivers) Agreement of 1987.
[24] [1968] 1 Lloyd's Rep. 171, overruling *Fire Auto and Marine Ins. Co.* v. *Greene* [1964] 2 Q.B. 687.
[25] *Per* Diplock L.J. at p. 177.
[26] *Per* Lord Denning M.R. at p. 176. Salmon L.J. agreed with both judgments. Lord Denning also said, at p. 176: "If the Minister of Transport should hesitate to sue, I think it may be open to the plaintiff to make him a defendant: and thus compel performance." This appears to support the text above.
[27] [1935] 1 K.B. 75.
[28] *Corfield* v. *Groves* [1950] 1 All E.R. 488.
[29] *Provincial Insurance* v. *Morgan* [1933] A.C. 240; contrast *Dawsons* v. *Bonnin* [1922] 2 A.C. 413. See also *Farr* v. *Motor Mutual* [1920] 3 K.B. 669; *Roberts* v. *Anglo-Saxon* (1927) 137 L.T. 243. See generally the discussion in § 6–07 *et seq.*

within the compulsory insurance requirements of section 148(1) of the
Road Traffic Act 1988, they are binding, such restrictions are a popular
way of limiting liability in modern motor policies.

Roadworthiness   20–63

In *Barrett* v. *London General*,[30] Goddard J. held that a provision
restricting the cover to accidents while the car is in a safe and roadworthy condition means roadworthy at the commencement of its journey, not at the time of the accident, on the analogy of the implied
warranty of seaworthiness in marine policies.[31] His reasoning, however,
was disapproved by the Privy Council in *Trickett* v. *Queensland Insurance*[32] on the ground that such an analogy is unsound. The principle that
may be deduced from these two cases is that where the unroadworthiness, *e.g.* the failure of a footbrake,[32] occurs only at the moment of the
accident, the policy is effective, but that it is not so where the unroadworthiness *e.g.* failure of lights, occurs some time before the accident.
Knowledge by the assured of the unroadworthiness is irrelevant. In
some factual situations, however, the law of seaworthiness is of assistance in determining whether or not a vehicle is roadworthy. Thus in
Clarke v. *National Insurance*,[33] the Court of Appeal held that a car over-
loaded with passengers was "unroadworthy" by analogy to the rule that
overloading or bad stowage can render a ship unseaworthy.

"In efficient condition"   20–64

A condition that the assured should maintain the vehicle in "an
efficient condition,"[34] or other such words, is to be contrasted with
cover which is restricted to a roadworthy vehicle. Thus in *Conn* v. *Westminster Motor Insurance Association*[35] it was held, in the context of the
policy, that the insurers were not liable for an accident which had
nothing to do with the condition of the tyres of the vehicle (visibly inef-
ficient). "In efficient condition," it was held, meant "in roadworthy condition." On the other hand, the fact that the brakes were defective was
held not to be a breach of condition, since their state could only be dis-
cerned by dismantling them.

In *Liverpool Corporation* v. *Roberts*[36] the policy provided that the
assured "shall take due and reasonable precautions to safeguard the
property insured, and to keep it *in a good state of repair*." *Held*, that his
words imposed only a personal obligation on the assured to take due
and reasonable precautions; if only a casual negligence or failure on the
part of an employee to carry out his duty had been proved against the
assured, there would have been no breach of this provision.

In *New India Ass.* v. *Yeo Beng Chow*[37] a comprehensive policy contained a condition that the assured should "take all reasonable steps to

---

[30] [1935] 1 K.B. 238.
[31] See M.I.A. 1906, s.39, *infra*, § 23–40.
[32] [1936] A.C. 159.
[33] [1964] 1 Q.B. 199.
[34] See *Brown* v. *Zurich* [1954] 2 Lloyd's Rep. 243.
[35] [1966] 1 Lloyd's Rep. 407, C.A. See also *Brown* v. *Zurich* [1954] 2 Lloyd's Rep. 243; *McInnes* v.
National Motor and Accident Ins. Union [1963] 2 Lloyd's Rep. 415.
[36] [1965] 2 Lloyd's Rep. 219, 224, *per* Cumming-Bruce J.
[37] [1972] 1 W.L.R. 786 (P.C.).

safeguard the motor vehicle from loss or damage and to maintain it" in
"efficient condition." Section I of the policy form provided cover
against loss or damage, and Section II against "Liability to Third Parties." Section I was deleted, and the question was whether the condition
to maintain remained as affecting Section II. The Judicial Committee of
the Privy Council held that although these parts of the condition which
related to loss or damage might have been inserted in the policy bearing
in mind that it was drafted to provide comprehensive cover, it did not
follow that it was to be implied from the deletion of Section I that the
condition was altered; the condition could and did survive the deletion,
in their Lordships' opinion.

Such provisions as to roadworthiness fall within head (b) of section
148(1) of the Act of 1988, but most of the following restrictions escape
the operation of this section.

20–65 Private purposes, etc.

A clause restricting the use of a vehicle to private purposes only
includes use for pleasure such as carrying tools or timber for use in a garden.[38] It is generally expressed also to include "business or professional" use by the assured, but such cover does not extend to business
use by others,[39] even though the vehicle is used at the same time in the
assured's business.[40] Use for the purposes of a particular trade may be
excluded.[41] Where the cover extends to private and limited business
purposes it has been held not to extend to other business purposes,[42] but
to extend to use for the limited *and* other business purposes contempor-
aneously.[43] *Quare*, whether use for agricultural purposes includes taking
a show pony to a show.[44]

A policy applicable only to a motor car or private personal use contained (*inter alia*) conditions that the car was not covered (1) if and when
it was being used in connection with any trade or business, or otherwise
than for the private personal purposes of the assured; and (2) while the
car was (*inter alia*) let out for hire or was used for any other than the private personal purposes of the assured. The insured car was used for private hiring and was destroyed by fire while standing idle in a garage. It
was held that the use of the car for private hiring did not avoid the contract, but rendered the car not covered by the policy on the occasion of
the fire, as owing to its use for private hiring, it could not be described as
a car for private personal use.[45]

In *English* v. *Weston*[46] it was held by a majority of the Court of

---

[38] *Piddington* v. *Co-operative Ins.* [1934] 2 K.B. 236.

[39] *Pailor* v. *Co-op Ins.* (1930) 38 Ll.L.R. 237.

[40] *Passmore* v. *Vulcan Boiler* (1935) 52 T.L.R. 193.

[41] *Gray* v. *Blackmore* [1934] 1 K.B. 95. *Cf. Samuelson* v. *National Insurance* [1986] 3 All E.R. 417,
where use "in connection with the motor trade" was excluded.

[42] *Jones* v. *Welsh Ins.* (1937) 54 T.L.R. 22.

[43] *Kellerher* v. *Chistopherson* (1956) 91 Ir.L.T. 191. But see *Browning* v. *Phoenix* [1960] 2 Lloyd's
Rep. 360, where Pilcher J. suggested that where a car is used simultaneously for two purposes, one
excluded, it is not covered.

[44] *Henderson* v. *Robson* (1949) 113 J.P. 313.

[45] *Murray* v. *Scottish Automobile and General Ins. Co.*, 1929 S.C. 49. *Cf. Provincial Ins. Co.* v. *Morgan* [1933] A.C. 240.

[46] [1940] 1 K.B. 145. In *Calverley* v. *Gore* (1959) 18 D.L.R. (2d) 598 an absconding servant was held
not to be a person in the *household* of the assured.

Appeal that the assured's *household* in a policy excluding liability for death of or injury to members of it means not a household which the assured is in, but the household of which the assured is the head. It did not therefore include a brother's liability for injury to his sister.

In *Wood* v. *General Accident*[47] the cover only extended to the user of a motor car for social, domestic and pleasure purposes. It was held that a Daimler car was not being so used when the policy holder was being driven in it with the object of making a business contract at the end of his journey, although it was a pleasurable way of making the journey.

Hire or reward[48]   20–66

The meaning of these words as words excluding liability in a policy where a vehicle is used for hire or reward now presents some difficulty. Most recent cases depend not on the meaning of the simple and meaningful phrase but on the construction of the words in the Road Traffic Act 1960, s.203, replacing similar words in the Act of 1934, requiring compulsory insurance of passengers only "in the case of a vehicle in which passengers are carried for hire or reward." The statute did not say "when passengers are carried for hire or reward." By using the phrase "in the case of a vehicle in which passengers are carried," the legislature denoted a vehicle whose habitual or normal use was for the carriage of passengers for hire or reward.[49]

The words "hire or reward" in that context caused great judicial difficulty culminating in the decision of the House of Lords in *Albert* v. *Motor Insurers' Bureau*[50] that "hire or reward" connoted a reward payable under a legally binding contract.

In 1972 the legislature neatly severed this Gordian knot by cutting out *in toto* both the exception of passengers and the "hire or reward" proviso.

In *Coward* v. *Motor Insurers' Bureau*[51] the Court of Appeal set out a   **20–67** principle that carriage for hire or reward refers to carriage in consideration of a monetary payment to be made to the carrier "and legally enforceable by him." An arrangement to carry a fellow-workman on the pillion of a motor-cycle for a weekly sum, it was held, was contemplated by neither party (both dead by reason of an accident ensuing) as a legally binding contract.

This decision appears supportable in construing the meaning, not of "in the case of a vehicle in which passengers are carried for hire or

---

[47] (1948) 65 T.L.R. 53. *Cf. Seddon* v. *Binions* [1978] 1 Lloyd's Rep. 381 (C.A.). In *Lee* v. *Poole* [1954] Crim. L.R. 942 the carriage of furniture without payment was held to be within such cover. The mere fact that the driver is fulfilling a duty to his employers by driving a car does not prevent it being used for a "*social purpose*," *e.g.* conveyance by clerk to a council of foreign visitors in England to discuss town-twinning arrangement, *Moody* v. *Iron Trades Mutual* [1971] R.T.R. 120, [1971] 1 Lloyd's Rep. 386; Wrangham J. *Cf. Willesden Corporation* v. *Municipal Mutual* (1945) 172 L.T. 245. See now s.150 of the 1988 Act, *supra* § 20–29, which deems car-sharing arrangements to be social arrangements.

[48] For the meaning of the words "hire or reward" in connection with the carriage of goods see *Hammond* v. *Hall and Ham River* [1965] A.C. 1049.

[49] *Connell* v. *M.I.B.* [1969] 2 Lloyd's Rep. 1, 3 (C.A.).

[50] [1972] A.C. 301–378. See also *M.I.B.* v. *Meanen* [1971] 2 Lloyd's Rep. 251 (H.L.). Earlier decisions on the effect of these words are referred to in previous editions of this work.

[51] [1963] 1 Q.B. 259.

reward" in section 203 of the Act of 1960, but of the meaning *per se* of the words "hire or reward"; in construing the latter words only the existance or not of a binding contract is relevant.[52]

Thus, apart from the Road Traffic Acts, a policy excluding liability while the car is used for hire or reward has been held to afford cover where passengers contribute to the cost of petrol and other out-of-pocket expenses,[53] but not where they regularly pay an amount equivalent to the train fare in respect of a journey, even if they only pay voluntarily,[54] or where a passenger is carried for payment on an isolated occasion.[55] Thus "private hire" has been held to include driving one's fellow workmen to and from work for a weekly payment.[56]

20–68 Driver

Persons may not be entitled to drive a vehicle because the owner has excluded them in taking out third-party insurance cover to satisfy section 143 of the Act of 1988. The driver may be named in the certificate of insurance and in effect in the policy by the incorporation of such specification in the certificate therein. A clause in the policy may then seek to except the insurers from liability while the vehicle is driven by any other person.[57] Such an exclusion is now only partly effective as section 151 of the Road Traffic Act 1988, discussed in paragraph 20–30 earlier, makes the insurer liable to a third party whether or not the driver is authorised under the policy. Moreover, section 148(2)(a) prevents reliance on a condition relating to the age or condition of the driver: see paragraph 20–28 above.

A condition that the assured should exercise care in the employment of steady and competent drivers has been held not to apply where he himself drives in a drunken condition.[58]

"Paid driver." A policy covering the assured "or his paid driver" has been held to include a driver, in the pay of a third party, borrowed by the assured.[59] A clause excluding from cover a driver "disqualified from holding a licence" was held not to apply to a person who was unable to renew his licence owing to a mental disability.[60] But such a clause does apply to an infant prohibited by reason of his age from driving.[61] The words "being driven by the insured" in a policy taken out by a limited company mean "being driven by or on behalf of the insured."[62]

Driver not specified in certificate of insurance. An exception in a policy exempting the insurers from liability while a car was being driven by a person not specified in the certificate issued by them under the Acts was

---

[52] See, *e.g. ibid. per* Upjohn L.J. at p. 274.

[53] *McCarthy* v. *British Oak* [1938] 3 All E.R. 1.

[54] *Bonham* v. *Zurich* [1945] 1 K.B. 292.

[55] *Wyatt* v. *Guildhall Insurance* [1937] 1 K.B. 635.

[56] *Lyons* v. *Denscombe* [1941] 1 All E.R. 977.

[57] *G.F.P. Units* v. *Monksfield* [1972] 2 Lloyd's Rep. 79, Roskill L.J.

[58] *Robertson* v. *London Guarantee*, 1915 1 S.L.T. 195. But contrast *National Farmers' Union Mutual* v. *Dawson* [1941] 2 K.B. 424.

[59] *Bryan* v. *Forrow* [1950] 1 All E.R. 294.

[60] *Edwards* v. *Griffiths* [1953] 1 W.L.R. 1199.

[61] *Mumford* v. *Hardy* [1956] 1 W.L.R. 163.

[62] *Lester Bros. Ltd.* v. *Avon Insurance* (1942) 72 Ll.L.R. 109. "Person" includes limited company: *Briggs* v. *Gibson's Bakery* [1948] N.I. 165.

held to apply when another person took the car on an unauthorised joy-ride without consent and damaged it. The exception could not be construed as though it contained the words "with consent."[63]

20–69 Load

A clause excluding liability "whilst the car is conveying any load in excess of that for which it was constructed" has been held not to apply where more passengers were carried than a motor car was designed to carry; it covered only cases where there was a specific weight which must not be exceeded, as in the case of lorries or vans.[64]

20–70 Precautions against theft

It is common, particularly in the case of cars regularly visiting the metropolis, for insurers to require an alarm system or special locks to be fitted to the relevant vehicle. In the case of a jeweller's all risk insurance against loss of jewellery it was held (i) that "fitted with locks and alarm systems approved by underwriters and in operation" meant "approved," not by the insurers, but by underwriters generally; (ii) that "locks" meant, in the context, locks of a greater security value than those supplied by car manufacturers; and (iii) that the alarm system was "in operation" notwithstanding that two switches were faulty.[65]

20–71 Vehicle used

The policy often covers the assured when driving a vehicle other than that specified in the policy. Thus in *Boss* v. *Kingston*[66] it was stipulated that the "company will also indemnify the insured when driving any motor-cycle not belonging to him." But it was held, on the construction of the policy, that it lapsed when he sold the specified motor-cycle.

"Cars owned by assured" has been held to include a car hired by him under a hire-purchase agreement, but to exclude cars hired by him without option to purchase.[67]

[63] *Greenleaf* v. *Monksfield* [1972] R.T.R. 451, Roskill L.J.
[64] *Houghton* v. *Trafalgar Ins.* [1954] 1 Q.B. 247.
[65] *De Maurier (Jewels)* v. *Bastion Ins. Co.* [1967] 2 Lloyd's Rep. 550.
[66] [1963] 1 W.L.R. 99.
[67] *De Maurier (Jewels)* v. *Bastion Ins. Co.* [1967] 2 Lloyd's Rep. 550.

CHAPTER 21

GUARANTEE INSURANCE

1. CONTRACTS OF GUARANTEE AND INSURANCE DISTINGUISHED

INSURANCE companies and Lloyd's underwriters engage in a consider- **21–01** able amount of guarantee business. It includes guarantees of servants' honesty, by means of fidelity bonds and policies, guarantees for the due completion of contracts,[1] and guarantees for the payment of debts. There are two distinct legal arrangements by which such guarantees may be effected: either,

  (a) the company or underwriter may stand surety for the servant's fidelity, for the completion of the contract, or for the payment of the debt, or

  (b) they may insure their client against loss arising from specified dishonesty, non-completion of a contract, or non-payment of a debt.

It is only the second arrangement with which the present work is concerned.[2]

It might be noted, however, that credit insurance, miscellaneous financial loss insurance and suretyship are all forms of general insurance business for the purposes of the Insurance Companies Act 1982. The distinction between insurance and guarantee is thus important for contractual and not regulatory purposes.

Guarantee insurance should be distinguished from guarantee by a **21–02** surety. A surety promises a creditor that he will be paid; an insurer promises to indemnify him if he is not. In neither case does the surety or insurer come under any obligation to pay unless or until the debtor is in default. But while payment by a surety discharges the principal debt, payment by an insurer does not affect it. In the former case the surety has a direct right in equity against the debtor, in the latter case the insurer is only subrogated to the rights of the assured against him. The rules of guarantee insurance are a part of the law of contract and were developed in the courts of common law. Suretyship does not necessarily depend upon a contract,[3] and its rules were developed in courts of equity. While these two branches of the law have developed on similar lines, and it is often immaterial to which of the two classes a contract

---

[1] See *Trade Indemnity Co.* v. *Workington Harbour Board* [1937] A.C. 1.
[2] See *Chitty on Contracts* (26th ed.) Vol. II, §§ 5010–5074, for contracts of suretyship.
[3] See *Rowlatt on Principal and Surety* (3rd ed.) p. 4.

belongs,[4] their principles sometimes differ in their effect. Thus the doctrine of subrogation has been carried further in suretyship cases.[5]

21–03 Non-disclosure

It is still uncertain how far a surety is entitled to full disclosure from the creditor, since where the relation of principal and surety arises out of a contract it is not clear how far that contract is one of the utmost good faith.[6]

Whatever the position as between surety and creditor the rule requiring full disclosure of material facts applies to guarantee insurance as to contracts of insurance generally.[7] As regards what is material, where the subject-matter of the insurance was the repayment of a loan it was held that the rate of interest was not material, even though it was exceptionally high.[8] The financial position of the debtor, on the other hand, is always material, though the assured need not disclose it where the insurer is already acquainted with it.[9]

21–04 Section 4 of the Statute of Frauds

Another difference between the two classes of contract is that by section 4[10] of the Statute of Frauds 1677, contracts of guarantee, to be enforceable, must be in writing,[11] while contracts of insurance (other than marine insurances) may be oral.[12]

21–05 Whether contract one of insurance or guarantee

It is often a difficult question whether a given contract is one of guarantee or of insurance and the matter came before the House of Lords in *Trade Indemnity Co.* v. *Workington Harbour Board*.[13] There an insurance company for a financial consideration subscribed to a money bond conditioned for the performance of a contract, and it was held that the contract was a guarantee and not an insurance policy.[14] This case, however, provides little guidance in principle, and Romer L.J.'s judgment in *Seaton* v. *Heath*[15] provides a more detailed statement of principle.

The difference between the two classes of contract, he states, does not

---

[4] Kay J. in *Dane* v. *Mortgage Insurance* [1894] 1 Q.B. 54, 62; Kennedy J. in *Re Law Guarantee Trust* [1914] 2 Ch. 617, 636; Lord Robertson in *Seaton* v. *Burnand* [1900] A.C. 135, 148; Warrington J. in *Shaw* v. *Royce Ltd.* [1911] 1 Ch. 138, 147.

[5] See *Rowlatt on Principal and Surety* (3rd ed.), Chap. IX.

[6] See *Seaton* v. *Heath* [1899] 1 Q.B. 782, 792, *per* Romer L.J., unaffected by *Seaton* v. *Burnand*, *supra*, on one hand, and *Railton* v. *Mathew* (1844) 10 Cl. & F. 934 and *L.G.O.C.* v. *Holloway* [1912] 2 K.B. 72, on the other. The question remained unresolved in *Trade Indemnity* v. *Workington Harbour Board* [1937] A.C. 1.

[7] *Allis Chalmers Co.* v. *Fidelity Deposit* (1916) 32 T.L.R. 263 (H.L.).

[8] *Seaton* v. *Burnand* [1900] A.C. 135.

[9] *Anglo-Californian Bank* v. *London & Provincial Marine* (1904) 20 T.L.R. 665.

[10] 29 Car. 2, c. 3, s.4, is still in force in relation to such contracts, *viz.*: "any special promise to answer for the debt, default or miscarriage of another person." This part of s.4 was left unrepealed by the Law Reform (Enforcement of Contracts) Act 1954 and the Law of Property (Miscellaneous Provisions) Act 1989.

[11] *Eastwood* v. *Kenyon* (1840) 11 Ad. & E. 438; *Hargreaves* v. *Parsons* (1844) 13 M. & W. 561, 570.

[12] See § 1–22, *supra*.

[13] [1937] A.C. 1.

[14] See Lord Atkin *ibid.* at pp. 16, 17.

[15] [1899] 1 Q.B. 782, 792, 793. Reversed [1900] A.C. 135 on other grounds. Romer L.J.'s judgment was approved in the Court of Appeal in *Re Denton's Estate* [1904] 2 Ch. 178, 188, *per* Vaughan Williams L.J.

depend on the mere use of the words "insurance" or "guarantee,"[16] but they can generally be distinguished by the way in which they are effected.

> "Contracts of insurance are generally matters of speculation, where the person desiring to be insured has means of knowledge as to the risk, and the insurer has not the means or not the same means. The insured generally puts the risk before the insurer as a business transaction, and the insurer on the risk stated fixes a proper price to remunerate him for the risk to be undertaken; and the insurer engages to pay the loss incurred by the insured in the event of certain specified contingencies occurring. On the other hand . . . [in contracts of guarantee] the creditor does not himself go to the surety, or represent, or explain the surety, the risk to be run. The surety often takes the position from motives of friendship, and generally not as the result of any direct bargaining between him and the creditor, or in consideration of any remuneration passing to him from the creditor."

The lack of premium rating by the "insurer," and of consideration **21–06** passing from the "assured" to the "insurer" are clearly important factors, and were recognised as such by Sheen J. in *The Zuhal K and the Selin*.[17] In that case a further factor found to be relevant was the existence of a term whereby the issuer of a bond was entitled to a counter-indemnity from the beneficiary of the bond; in the view of Sheen J. the presence of a counter-indemnity is wholly inconsistent with the notion of insurance.

The question must, therefore, ultimately depend upon the expressed intention of the parties in each case.[18] Where the intention is that the surety should on the default of the debtor pay the original debt, the contract is one of guarantee; where the intention is that a new debt should arise on default, the contract is one of insurance.[19]

2. FIDELITY POLICIES

Fidelity policies are the most common type of guarantee insurance. **21–07** They are usually intended to protect a master against breaches of confidence on the part of his servant, and have displaced the arrangement by which relatives of employees stood surety for their honesty.

Fidelity and liability policies distinguished   21–08

Fidelity policies should be distinguished from policies against liability incurred through a servant's negligence. Thus a policy against "all losses . . . by reason of any act, neglect . . . or error" of the assured's employees has been held to be a liability policy only, and not to extend to a loss due to embezzlement by an employee.[20] Liability policies are normally restricted to liability incurred through negligence.[21] Fidelity

---

[16] See *Re Denton's Estate*, [1904] 2 Ch. 178, where a contract expressed to be of insurance in fact operated as a contract of guarantee. *Contra, Dane* v. *Mortgage Insurance* [1894] 1 Q.B. 54, and *Finlay* v. *Mexican Investment* [1897] 1 Q.B. 517.

[17] [1987] 1 Lloyd's Rep. 151. See also *Travel and General Insurance* v. *Barron* (1988) *The Times*, November 25.

[18] Lord Esher in *Dane* v. *Mortgage Insurance* [1894] 1 Q.B. 54 at p. 60.

[19] See also *Re Law Guarantee* [1914] 2 Ch. 617.

[20] *Goddard & Smith* v. *Frew* [1939] 4 All E.R. 358.

[21] See *Davies* v. *Hosken* (1937) 53 T.L.R. 798; § 19–05, *supra*.

policies are essentially aimed at losses due to criminal disappropriation of money or securities[22] by an employee.[23] The same policy may, however, cover both these types of loss.[24] And banks frequently insure against loss by reason of securities turning out to be invalid, where the fraud, if any, is that of a stranger.[25]

21–09 Risk covered

The acts of the employee covered vary considerably from policy to policy. Some are restricted to "theft," which must be construed within the strict meaning of the criminal law,[26] unless the policy itself provides an interpretation.

A policy covering a bank against losses by reason of currency being taken out of their possession by fraudulent means does not include the case where the bank is induced by fraud to give credit and afterwards pay out the money[27]; and a policy covering "making away with" securities does not include fraud by an employee where no security is physically made away with.[28] Some policies cover any form of dishonesty.[29] By a Lloyd's policy of insurance, the plaintiff was insured against "loss or deprivation of bonds, debentures, stocks, scrip, shares, transfers, certificates, coupons, warrants or other securities, cash, cheques, bank notes, bills of exchange, promissory notes, or any documents of value," by robbery, theft, fire, explosion, embezzlement, burglary or abstraction, whether with or without violence, or any other loss whatsoever through theft or any other dishonesty. The plaintiff was induced by false representations to discount bills of exchange which were afterwards dishonoured. It was held that the plaintiff's loss was caused by dishonesty within the meaning of the policy and that he was entitled to recover.[30]

21–10 Generally limited to particular employment

Since the risk of loss under a fidelity policy depends on the opportunity to be dishonest afforded by a servant's employment, the risk covered is generally restricted to losses occurring while he is employed in a specified capacity in which case the policy will not extend to misappropriation by him after the scope of his duties has been enlarged,[31] or where he is employed in a different capacity.[32]

---

[22] Jessel M.R. in *Re Norwich Provident* (1878) 8 Ch.D. 334, 341.

[23] See *Walker* v. *British Guarantee Association* (1852) 21 L.J.Q.B. 257. They appear to be a form of *property insurance*; see definition of property insurance business in s.83(8) of the Insurance Companies Act 1974, *supra*, Chap. 13.

[24] *Wasserman* v. *Blackburn* (1926) 43 T.L.R. 95; *Lazard Bros.* v. *Brooks* (1932) 38 Com.Cas. 46 (H.L.).

[25] *Equitable Trust Co. of N.Y.* v. *Henderson* (1930) 47 L.T.R. 90; *Philadelphia National Bank* v. *Price* (1938) 43 Com.Cas. 238; *Lazard Bros.* v. *Brooks, supra*.

[26] *Grundy (Teddington)* v. *Fulton* [1983] 1 Lloyd's Rep. 16; *Dobson* v. *General Accident* [1989] 3 All E.R. 927.

[27] *Century Bank* v. *Young* (1914) 84 L.J.K.B. 385.

[28] *Liberty National Bank* v. *Bolton* (1925) 21 Ll.L.R. 3.

[29] *Ravenscroft* v. *Provident Clerks' Ass.* (1885) 5 T.L.R. 3; *American Surety Co.* v. *Wrightson* (1910) 103 L.T. 663.

[30] *Wasserman* v. *Blackburn* (1926) 43 T.L.R. 95. For a policy of insurance against loss incurred through acting on any document which might prove "to have been forged" see *Equitable Trust Co. of New York* v. *Henderson* (1930) 47 T.L.R. 90.

[31] *Wembley U.D.C.* v. *Poor Law Mutual* (1901) 17 T.L.R. 516.

[32] See *Cosford Union* v. *Poor Law Mutual* (1910) 103 L.T. 463.

Term of policy **21–11**

Fidelity policies are usually made for a term of one or more years. It is sometimes stipulated that unless notice to terminate be given, the policy shall be treated as a renewal contract of like nature and conditions.[33] The effect of this is merely to continue the contract for a second term. At the end of that term, if no notice to continue is given, or other arrangement made, the policy drops.

Where one of the conditions indorsed was that all guarantees, whatever might be the original term, should from the expiration of such original term be treated as a renewal contract of the like nature and conditions, unless either the member interested therein or the board of directors should give two calendar months' notice of an intention not to renew the same, it was held that the renewed contract was not itself to be deemed to contain this particular condition as to renewal, and that therefore, even in the absence of notice, the contract did not extend beyond one renewal. "A" renewal is one renewed contract.[33]

The fact that the rules of the company, on the faith of which the assured took the guarantee,[34] are altered, will not have the effect of determining such a renewed contract if no notice to terminate has been given by either party,[35] and the insurers will be entitled to the renewal premium.

The liability of the guarantors will generally be for a default of the employee within the period for which the guarantee is given, whether found out within the period or after its expiration, unless limited by apt words to a default committed and discovered within the period.[36]

Conditions **21–12**

It is usual in fidelity insurance, as in insurance generally to give the assured's answers in the proposal form the force of warranties,[37] but a mere declaration of the course intended by the assured to be pursued in checking the accounts of an employee only relates to his present intention, and a warranty based on it will not therefore be broken simply because this course is not subsequently pursued.[38]

Prosecution of an employee who has been guilty of a criminal offence such as embezzlement is not a condition precedent to recovery under a fidelity policy unless such policy expresses it to be so.[39]

Notice of loss may be made a condition precedent to liability under the policy,[40] but the employer is not usually under any duty to notify the insurer of mere suspicion that a servant has been dishonest until he has satisfied himself that his suspicions are justified.[41]

No condition can be a condition precedent to payment which only

---

[33] *Solvency Mutual Guarantee Co.* v. *Froane* (1861) 7 H. & N. 5.

[34] *Solvency Mutual Guarantee Co.* v. *Freeman* (1861) 7 H. & N. 17.

[35] *Solvency Mutual Guarantee Co.* v. *York* (1858) 3 H. & N. 588.

[36] *Fanning* v. *London Guarantee and Accident Co.* (1884) 10 Vict. L.R. 8.

[37] *Towle* v. *National Guardian* (1861) 30 L.J.Ch. 900; *Haworth* v. *Sickness & Accident Ass.* (1891) 28 S.L.R. 394.

[38] *Bedham* v. *United Guarantee Co.* (1852) 7 Ex. 744; *Hearts of Oak Building Society* v. *Law Union* [1936] 2 All E.R. 619; contrast *Haworth* v. *Sickness & Accident Ass.* (1891) 28 S.L.R. 394.

[39] *London Guarantee Co.* v. *Fearnley* (1880) 5 App.Cas. 911.

[40] See *Clydebank Water Trustees* v. *Fidelity Co. of Maryland*, 1915 S.C. 362, insurance against non-completion of contract.

[41] See *Ward* v. *Law Property* (1856) 4 W.R. 605.

relates to matters to be done after payment, such as a condition that the employer shall give assistance to enable the company to obtain reimbursement from the employed.[42]

21–13 Calculation of indemnity

Fidelity policies generally contain an excess clause whereby the insurer's liability in respect of every "loss" or "occurrence" arises only where the loss exceeds a stated sum. In the case of fraud by an employee, it will be necessary to determine whether the fraud consists of a number of single "occurrences," so that the insurer can apply the excess to each claim, or whether the fraud is part of a single course of conduct, so that the assured bears only one excess. In *Philadelphia National Bank* v. *Poole*[43] it was held that each individual fraud constituted a "loss or occurrence" for the purposes of the policy; in the result the assured was unable to recover any of its loss of $300,000, as each individual "loss or occurrence" was within the excess limit of $25,000. This decision followed that of Greer J. in *Equitable Trust of New York* v. *Whittaker*,[44] where it was held that the excess of £2,500 carried in respect of "each and every loss" applied to each of the seven individual occurrences of fraud taking place under one master agreement.

21–14 Subrogation

The insurer is entitled to the benefit of the assured's rights against the wrongdoer. Thus, under an employers' fidelity policy, the insurer is usually entitled to deduct any money which would have been payable to the employee but for the misappropriation. However, where the loss exceeds the sum insured, he is only entitled to so much of such money, if any, as exceeds the difference, after payment of the sum insured.[45]

Under a fidelity guarantee the surety is entitled on payment to any stolen property recovered after deducting the costs of recovery.[46] It would seem on principle[47] that an insurer would be similarly subrogated to the assured's rights against his employee.[48]

3. INSURANCE OF DEBTS

21–15 Wherever a debt exists, or is contemplated,[49] the creditor may insure its due payment.

Subrogation

Policies insuring against the non-payment of a debt are contracts of indemnity, and if the debt is not paid on the date when it falls due the

---

[42] *London Guarantee* v. *Fearnley* (1880) 5 App.Cas. 911. See also Humphreys J. in *Pictoria Machinery* v. *Nichols* (1940) 45 Com.Cas. 334.

[43] [1938] 2 All E.R. 199.

[44] (1923) 17 Ll.L.R. 153, following *Pennsylvania Co.* v. *Mumford* [1920] 2 K.B. 537.

[45] *Liverpool Starr-Bowkett Building Society* v. *Travellers' Accident Insurance* (1893) 9 T.L.R. 221.

[46] *Hatch, Mansfield & Co.* v. *Weingott* (1906) 22 T.L.R. 366.

[47] The employer's right to proceed against the employee was established in *Lister* v. *Romford Ice* [1957] A.C. 555.

[48] See, however, Scott L.J.'s language in *Goddard & Smith* v. *Frew* [1939] 4 All E.R. 358, contrasting fidelity policies with contracts of indemnity.

[49] *Seaton* v. *Burnand* [1900] A.C. 135, 141; *Anglo-Californian Bank* v. *London & Provincial Marine* (1904) 10 Com.Cas. 1.

insurers will, on payment, be subrogated to the assured's rights against the debtor.[50]

The premium

The term of such policies usually extends to the date on which payment becomes due, annual premiums being regarded rather as instalments of the total premium than renewal premiums. Hence, where the premium is payable by the debtor his failure to pay it does not necessarily put an end to the policy.[51] Where, however, such payment is made a condition precedent to liability, it will not avail the assured that the risk of non-payment insured against has already become a certainty.[52]

The loss

Such policies sometimes cover non-payment from specified causes only,[53] but where the insurance is simply against non-payment of a debt on a specified date it is immaterial to consider the cause of the default.[54] The policy moneys become payable immediately on such default; the assured is not bound to sue the debtor or enforce his securities first,[55] unless it is the deficiency only after he has done so that is insured.[56]

Schemes of arrangement 21–16

Nor will the fact that the creditor has assented to a scheme of arrangement with the debtor avail the insurers.[57] Such arrangement is a form of non-payment, not an alteration of the risk vitiating the policy.[58] In such a case they will be subrogated on payment to the creditor's rights under the scheme.[59] The same principle applies where the holder of a debenture insures payment thereunder, and by a special resolution of debenture-holders such payment is postponed,[60] or where a bank whose debts a creditor has insured becomes insolvent and forms a realisation company.[61]

Shaw v. *Royce*[62] must be contrasted with these decisions. In that case the assured, a debenture-holder, was held to be bound, as against the insurers of the debentures, by a scheme of arrangement to which the insurers were a party substituting new uninsured debentures for those whose payment they had insured. This case may be distinguished from

---

[50] *Meacock* v. *Bryant and Co.* (1942) 59 T.L.R. 51; *Parr's Bank* v. *Albert Mines* (1900) 5 Com.Cas. 116. Prior to payment by the insurer, however, the assured cannot—in the absence of some express policy term—be prevented from taking such action to recover the debt as he thinks reasonable: see *AB Exportkredit* v. *New Hampshire Insurance* March 1989, unreported, C.A. The Court of Appeal further held that a "reasonable care" clause does not alter this general principle.
[51] Warrington J. in *Shaw* v. *Royce Ltd.* [1911] 1 Ch. 138, 148.
[52] *Employers' Insurance* v. *Benton* (1897) 24 R. (Ct. of Sess.) 908; see *Simpson* v. *Mortgage Ins.* 1893 38 S.C. 99.
[53] *Hambro* v. *Burnand* [1904] 2 K.B. 10, 19, *per* Collins M.R.; *Waterkeys* v. *Eagle Star* (1920) 5 Ll.L.R. 42.
[54] Hawkins J. in *Mortgage Ins.* v. *I.R.C.* (1887) 57 L.J.Q.B. 174, 181; Lord Maclaren in *Laird* v. *Securities Insurance* (1895) 22 R. (Ct. of Sess.) 452.
[55] Lord Esher in *Dane* v. *Mortgage Insurance* [1894] 1 Q.B. 54, 61.
[56] *Murdock* v. *Heath* (1899) 80 L.T. 50; *Re Law Guarantee Trust* [1914] 2 Ch. 617.
[57] *Dane* v. *Mortgage Insurance* [1894] 1 Q.B. 54; *Laird* v. *Securities Insurance* (1895) 22 R. 452.
[58] See *Law Guarantee* v. *Munich Reinsurance* [1912] 1 Ch. 138.
[59] See n. 57.
[60] *Finlay* v. *Mexican Investment Co.* [1897] 1 Q.B. 517.
[61] *Murdock* v. *Heath* (1899) 80 L.T. 50.
[62] [1911] 1 Ch. 138.

those above on the ground that the original contract of insurance was a tripartite one between the insurers, the company and the debenture-holders providing for such a scheme.

21–17 Insurance of completion of contract

Due completion of a contract may similarly be insured.[63] Where A employed B to do a job and A insured with C against loss arising out of failure duly to complete, and by a condition of the policy A was required to notify C in writing of any non-performance or non-observance on the part of B of the terms of the contract between A and B which might involve a loss for which C would be responsible under the contract of insurance, and where it was a term of the contract between A and B that the work should be done at a definite rate, and it was not, but the failure so to do on the part of B was not notified by A to C, and then B went bankrupt and A had to complete at a loss, it was held that C was not liable.[64]

The modern practice in relation to specific forms of contracts, notably large-scale building works (frequently to be carried out in other countries), is for the contractor rather than the employer to procure "insurance" against the contractor's default, by the means of a performance bond. Such bonds are issued by insurers, banks and surety companies. Where the construction contract calls for a bond, it will be the contractor's obligation to procure a bond from an issuer, payable to the employer. The bond will normally be payable on demand, and will not require the employer to prove that the contractor is in breach of contract: consequently, it is possible for the contractor to find that the issuer has been called upon by the employer to honour the bond even though there was no objective justification for the employer's demand, and the contractor is unable in English law to prevent the issuer from making payment.[65] Contractors are, therefore, reluctant to agree to an obligation to procure a bond, although it may be that such an obligation is the price of obtaining a potentially lucrative contract: to overcome the possibility of fraud or abuse by the employer, some insurers have developed for the benefit of contractors "unfair calling" insurance policies.

4. MORTGAGEES' INTEREST INSURANCE

21–18 Nature

Mortgagees' interest insurance is a specific form of guarantee insurance, presently operating almost exclusively in the marine market. Where a vessel is mortgaged to a bank or other lender as security for a loan for facilitating the purchase of the vessel, the bank will normally either take an assignment of the proceeds of the policy or be joined as a co-assured under the policy. Consequently, if the vessel is lost, the bank's loan is satisfied out of the policy proceeds. However, if the insurer has a defence against the assured, on the basis of, for example,

---

[63] See *Trade Indemnity* v. *Workington Harbour Board* [1937] A.C. 1.

[64] *Clydebank Water Trustees* v. *Fidelity & Deposit Co. of Maryland*, [1915] S.C. 362.

[65] See, as illustrative of the many cases on the point, *Edward Owen Engineering Ltd.* v. *Barclays Bank* [1978] 1 All E.R. 976.

non-disclosure, misrepresentation, breach of warranty, fraud or wilful destruction, such defence will also prevail against the bank,[66] so that the value of the policy as additional security is in essence dependent upon the honesty of the assured. The bank may to some extent protect its position by requesting the insurer to issue to it a letter of undertaking, specifying *inter alia* that the bank will be informed if the insurance ceases, but it was held by the Court of Appeal in *The Good Luck* that such wording does not obliged the insurer to inform the bank of the availability of a defence under the policy until that defence has actually been exercised.[67]

The purpose of mortgagees' interest insurance is, therefore, to allow the bank to recover from its own secondary insurer in the event that the assured's insurer has a defence against the bank, based on the assured's misconduct, under the primary policy.

Typical terms 21–19

Prior to 1986 there were no standard London market terms for this form of guarantee insurance. Two early cases demonstrated the need for such terms. In *Continental Illinois Bank* v. *Bathurst, The Captain Panagos*.[68] Mustill J. construed such a policy as an unvalued marine, rather than financial guarantee, policy, with the effect that the mortgagee bank was restricted to recovering the value of the vessel at the time of its loss[69] rather than the higher amount of its outstanding loan. In *The Alexion Hope*[70] the question to be determined was the point at which the primary insurer had refused to meet the bank's claim, thereby putting on risk the mortgagees' interest insurer: Staughton J. held that on the wording of the policy the latter insurer became liable as soon as an average adjustment had been made and accepted.

The post-1986 position is generally governed by the Institute Mortgagees' Interest Clauses, which are applicable only to hulls. These treat the policy as a marine policy, but fix the bank's recovery as both the amount irrecoverable under the primary policy *and* the remaining outstanding indebtedness of the assured. The time at which the mortgagees' interest insurer becomes liable is either when a final judgment is delivered against the assured under the primary policy, or at such earlier time as the bank can demonstrate that there is no reasonable prospect of recovery under the primary policy (in the event of dispute, the matter will be referred to arbitration).

---

[66] See: *Samuel* v. *Dumas* [1924] A.C. 431 (wilful casting away by the assured—no "peril of the sea"); *Black King Shipping* v. *Massie, The Litsion Pride* [1985] 1 Lloyd's Rep. 437 (fraudulent claim); *The Alexion Hope* [1988] 1 Lloyd's Rep. 311 (wilful casting away); *Bank of Nova Scotia* v. *Hellenic Mutual War Risks Association, The Good Luck* [1989] 3 All E.R. 628.

[67] In *The Good Luck* the Court of Appeal rejected a variety of alternative arguments by the bank, based on (a) an implied term in the letter of undertaking, imposing upon the insurer a "duty to speak," (b) the suggestion that the letter of undertaking was itself a contract of utmost good faith, and (c) a tortious "duty to speak" running parallel with the insurer's contractual obligation in the letter of undertaking.

[68] [1985] 1 Lloyd's Rep. 625.

[69] The ordinary rule that the assured can recover the value of the vessel at the date of the inception of the risk—M.I.A. 1906, s.16—was held by Mustill J. to have been ousted by contrary intention.

[70] [1986] 2 F.T.L.R. 655 (this point was not dealt with on appeal, [1988] 1 Lloyd's Rep. 311).

Chapter 22

GUARANTEES FOR POLICYHOLDERS

Policyholders Protection Act 1975   **22–01**

The main effect of the Act of 1975 is to guarantee to the policyholders of an insurance company in liquidation that the obligations of the company will be met either fully or substantially by the insurance industry as a whole. The Act is administered by the Policyholders Protection Board, which has the duty to ensure payment and to raise the funds from which payment is to be made.

1. POLICYHOLDERS PROTECTION BOARD

Constitution   **22–02**

The Policyholders Protection Act 1975, section 1(1) and (5) and Schedule 1 establish the constitution of the Board, as consisting of five persons appointed by the Secretary of State. At least three must be directors, chief executives or managers of authorised insurance companies, and one qualified to represent policyholders' interests. Alternative members—with similar qualifications—may be appointed in respect of each member to act in his absence.

Functions   **22–03**

By section 1(2)(*a*) of the Act the Board must arrange for policyholders to be indemnified in whole or in part should they be prejudiced by the inability of an *authorised* insurance company carrying on business in the United Kingdom to meet its liabilities (sections 6 to 16). In addition, it may give financial assistance to insurance companies in difficulty (sections 16 and 17). The remainder of the section provides for finance to do that, in accordance with sections 17 to 21: the Board must impose levies on companies and others engaged in the insurance industry in the United Kingdom (subsection (2)(*b*)) and may (by subsection (3)) borrow, but not in excess of £10 million.

The Secretary of State may, by section 2, give guidance to the Board in writing, after consultation with them, as to the performance of any such function: such guidance must first have been approved by a resolution of each House of Parliament (by section 2(2)).

2. PREREQUISITES OF THE RIGHTS OF POLICYHOLDERS

Authorised insurance companies   **22–04**

By section 3(1) the functions of the Board "shall be exercisable in relation to policyholders and others who have been or may be prejudiced in consequence of the inability" of "authorised insurance companies" to meet their liabilities under policies issued or securities given by them. Subsection (2) defines an authorised insurance company as any company authorised, in accordance with the Insurance Companies Act 1982, to carry on insurance business of any class in the United Kingdom. The policyholders of unauthorised insurers thus do not derive protection from the Act.

22–05 United Kingdom policy

By section 4(1) a policyholder is eligible for the assistance or protection of the Board only in respect of a "United Kingdom policy." Subsection (2) provides that a policy of insurance is a United Kingdom policy:

> when the performance by the insurer of any of his obligations under the contract evidenced by the policy would constitute the carrying on by the insurer of insurance business of any class in the United Kingdom.

3. COMPANIES IN LIQUIDATION

22–06 Meaning of liquidation

By section 5(1) the functions of the Board under sections 6 to 11 are exercisable in the case of any authorised insurance company in liquidation, provided that the beginning of the liquidation, *i.e.* the passing of the resolution for voluntary winding up, or the making of a compulsory winding up order by the court,) was after October 29, 1974 (subsections (2) to (3)).

The jurisdiction of the Board over a company attaches as soon as the company has passed a resolution for voluntary winding up, or, in the absence of such a resolution, on the making of a winding up order by the court (subsections (4) and (5)). This marks the "beginning of the liquidation," a term which occurs at regular points in the 1975 Act.

22–07 Compulsory insurance

Compulsory insurance enactments. By section 6(1) the section applies to any policy which satisfies the requirements of the Riding Establishments Act 1964, the Nuclear Installations Act 1965, the Employers' Liability (Compulsory Insurance) Act 1969 and the Road Traffic Act 1988. By section 6(2), the section also applies to a security in lieu of policy under the Road Traffic Act 1988.

22–08 *Duties under compulsory policies.* Section 6(4) states the general principle of the section:

> it shall be the duty of the Board to secure that a sum equal to the full amount of any liability of a company in liquidation towards any policyholder or security holder under the terms of any policy or security to which this section applies is paid to the policyholder or security holder as soon as reasonably practicable after the beginning of the liquidation.

This duty applies only to those liabilities within the policy which are subject to compulsory insurance, so that other liabilities covered by the policy fall outside this particular provision (subsections (3) and (5)). These excluded risks are dealt with by a more limited provision, contained in section 6(5): the policyholder is entitled to recover 90 per cent. of the insurer's liability from the Board. However, this right is extended only to a "private policyholder," a term defined in subsection (7) as meaning an individual or a partnership of which all the partners are individuals. Corporate assureds cannot, therefore, claim for non-compulsory risks insured under a policy also covering compulsory risks.

Extension to third parties. Section 7 provides that the benefit of section 6(4) applies to a sum payable to a person entitled to the benefit of a judgment under the Road Traffic Act 1988.[1] Third parties are not entitled to the protection of the Board in respect of any other form of compulsory insurance or in respect of non-compulsory policies, even though the third party may have had an action against the insurer under the Third Parties (Rights against Insurers) Act 1930 following the insolvency of the assured himself.[2] **22–09**

Limitations. The Board is, by section 9, relieved from the liability to make payments under sections 6 and 7 where the liability of the insurance company in liquidation is duplicated by the coverage of another United Kingdom policy. The Board's duties are also modified by sections 13 and 14, discussed later. **22–10**

General insurance **22–11**

Section 8 applies to general (as opposed to long term) policies other than those covering compulsory risks falling within section 6, reinsurance contracts, and marine, aviation and transport policies. Under section 8(2):

> it shall be the duty of the Board to secure that a sum equal to ninety per cent. of the amount of any liability of a company in liquidation towards a private policyholder under the terms of the policy to which this section applies was a United Kingdom policy at the beginning of the liquidation is paid to the policyholder as soon as is reasonably practicable after the beginning of the liquidation.

The liability of the Board under non-compulsory general policies is thus limited to private policyholders, as defined in section 6(7), and covers only 90 per cent. of the insurer's liability. In addition, the provisions of section 9 apply here, so that the Board is discharged from liability where the assured's loss is covered by another policy.

Modifications under sections 13 and 14 are discussed later.

Long-term liabilities **22–12**

Duties of the Board. Section 10(2), which applies to any long term policy not being a contract of reinsurance (section 10(1)), imposes upon the Board the duty:

> to secure that a sum equal to ninety per cent. of the amount of any liability of a company in liquidation towards any policyholder under the terms of a long term policy which was a United Kingdom policy at the beginning of the liquidation is paid to the policyholder as soon as reasonably practicable after the beginning of the liquidation.

This duty is not limited to private policyholders. Thus a company may insure the life of an irreplaceable company officer for its own benefit or,

---

[1] See Chap. 20.
[2] See Chap. 19.

more importantly, may insure adequate amenities for its employees and still rely on 90 per cent. security from the Board in the event that the employer's own insurer should fail.

22–13 *Continuity of insurance.* Section 11 makes special provision for future benefits under long term policies. By subsection (1), "future benefit" in this context

> means any benefit provided for under the policy which has not fallen due to be paid by the company before the beginning of the liquidation

save that, by subsection (2), any bonus provided for under a policy shall not be treated as a future payment unless it was declared before the beginning of the liquidation.

Subsection (3) is the operative provision here:

> it shall be the duty of the Board, as soon as is reasonably practicable after the beginning of the liquidation, to make arrangements . . . for securing continuity of insurance for every policyholder of a company in liquidation who is a policyholder in respect of a long term policy which was a United Kingdom policy at the beginning of the liquidation.

The assured must, however, be willing to comply with his contractual obligations to pay premiums (subsection (11)).

22–14 The arrangements to be made by the Board in furtherance of its duty to secure continuance are those which appear to it to be appropriate:

> (a) for securing or facilitating the transfer of the long term business of the company, or of any part of that business, to another authorised insurance company; or
>
> (b) for securing the issue by another authorised insurance company to the policyholders in question of policies in substitution for their existing policies.

The continuance of the policy benefits by either of these means is subject to the usual 90 per cent. qualification, in that the Board must ensure that the policyholder will receive 90 per cent. of future benefits (section 11(4)). If the policy contains terms relating to matters other than future benefits, the Board's duty, by virtue of subsection (6), extends only to securing that a transfer of business or substituted policy contains terms which correspond so far as appears to the Board "reasonable in the circumstances" to the earlier terms.

By subsection (7) it is the Board's duty to secure a 90 per cent. payment to the policyholder, as soon as is reasonably practicable, of any benefit which would have fallen due to be paid while the Board is seeking to secure continuity of insurance for him: payment relieves the Board of any duty to secure continuity in that respect (subsection (8)). The Board's duty to secure payment is, however, subject to compliance by the assured with contractual obligation to pay premiums (subsection (11)).

22–15 Subsection (9) provides for the case in which the Board is in difficulty as regards obtaining continuity of insurance. If it appears to the Board that securing continuity is not reasonably practicable, it is the Board's duty:

to pay the policyholder a sum equal to ninety per cent. of the value attributed to his policy for the purposes of any claim in respect of his policy in the winding up of the company, as soon as reasonably practicable after any such claim is admitted.

Subsection (10), however, empowers the Secretary of State by statutory instrument to make alternative arrangements to meet this particular problem.

Actuarial considerations. The Board is directed, by section 12, to refer **22–16** the terms of the policy to an independent actuary if it appears to the Board that the benefits may be excessive, having regard to the premiums paid and the other terms of the policy. The company may, for example, have made excessive allocations to policyholders under section 30 of the Insurance Companies Act 1982. Section 12 goes on to regulate: details of the matters for actuarial considerations; the form of the actuary's report; the Board's powers following the report; and the Board's power to treat as reduced any claim under the policy for "future benefit" under section 11.

General provisions as to the Board's liability   22–17

Payment by the Board. The Board must make payment to the assured (section 13(1)), although payment will normally be arranged through a nominated authorised insurer (section 13(2)). In the event that the Board's funds are insufficient to meet its liabilities, payment may be postponed (section 13(3)). It will generally be a condition of payment by the Board that the assured assigns to the Board his interests under the policy issued by the insolvent insurer: this permits the Board to seek to recover what it can in the insurer's liquidation (section 13(4) to (7)).

Interim payments. Section 15(3) empowers the Board: (a) to make **22–18** payments to or on behalf of policyholders (under a general or long term policy) of a company in liquidation in respect of policies which were United Kingdom policies at the beginning of liquidation, on such terms (including full or partial repayment) and on such conditions as the Board thinks fit; or (b) to secure such payments to be made by the liquidator by giving him an indemnity covering any such payments. Similar relief may also be extended where the company is merely in *provisional liquidation.*[3]

Payments by other persons. Section 14 modifies the duties of the **22–19** Board where payments are made to the policyholder by any person other than the Board in relation to the policy or to assist the policyholder. The Board may then take such payments into account in determining the extent of its liability under the 1975 Act.

4. COMPANIES IN FINANCIAL DIFFICULTIES

Companies in difficulties   22–20
Sections 16 and 17 empower the Board to assist or protect policyholders of companies not yet in liquidation which have been in effect

---

[3] See § 22–20, *infra.*

recognised by the court as being in financial difficulty. The sections only apply to an authorised insurance company, not being a company in liquidation. The Board's powers come into operation in three cases: first, where the company is in "provisional liquidation" (a company is in "provisional liquidation" for present purposes if a provisional liquidator has been appointed under section 135 of the Insolvency Act 1986); secondly, if the company has been shown in winding up proceedings to be unable to pay its debts; or, thirdly, if an application has been made to the court for the sanctioning of a compromise or arrangement under section 425 of the Companies Act 1985.

22–21 Consequent rights of policyholders

Section 16(2) empowers the Board generally to take any measures for the purposes of safeguarding policyholders eligible for assistance or protection "against loss arising from the financial difficulties of the company," in the following ways. The powers are, in the case of long term business, subject to section 17. This has two consequences: section 16 powers cannot be exercised in respect of long term business if it would be cheaper to require the insurer to reduce benefits under the relevant long term policies to 90 per cent.; and excessive benefits under long term policies may be reduced following actuarial analysis.[4]

Under section 16(3) the Board may secure or facilitate the transfer of the company's business in whole or part to another authorised insurance company on terms (including reduction of liabilities or benefits under a policy).

Under subsection (4) it may give assistance to the company to enable it to continue to carry on insurance business; such assistance may, under subsection (5), be conditional on reduction of liabilities or benefits.

The powers exercisable under subsections (3) and (4) may not be exercised where it appears that persons who were members of the company at the "relevant time," *i.e.* the commencement of the statutory "financial difficulties," and persons who had responsibility for or who may have profited from the company's financial difficulties, would benefit from the exercise of those powers in any capacity other than that of policyholders (subsections (6) and (7)). In addition, the Board shall not, under subsection (8), take measures in pursuance of subsections (3) and (4) where it appears to the Board that measures under sections 6 to 11 in the event of the company's liquidation would cost less.

22–22 Long term business

The powers contained in section 16(3) and (4) are exercisable in respect of long term policies, but only where such exercise would be cheaper than reducing the benefits under the relevant long term policies to 90 per cent. (section 17(1) and (2)). Consequently, a policy cannot be continued by transfer or otherwise if it would be cheaper to reduce its benefits (and the premiums payable thereunder) to 90 per cent.

In addition, section 17 provides a procedure for reducing liability under a long term policy are in the opinion of the Board excessive. The

---

[4] See § 22–22, *infra.*

Board may, under subsection (4), refer the matter to an independent actuary. Following the actuary's report, the Board may determine that the benefit should be treated as reduced or disregarded for the purposes of section 16(3) and (4).

5. LEVIES

Finance functions of Board 22–23

By section 1(2)(*b*) the functions of the Board, for the purpose of financing their functions under sections 6 to 16 of the Act, include:

> to impose levies, in accordance with sections 19, 20 and 21 below and Schedules 2 and 3 to this Act, on insurance companies and other persons engaged in the insurance industry in the United Kingdom

and otherwise in carrying out the provisions of the Act.

Section 18 classifies expenditure of the Board in the performance of their functions into "general" and "long term" business expenditure as follows:

18.—(1) In this Act "general business expenditure" means—
  (*a*) any expenditure of the Board under section 6, 7 or 8 above; and
  (*b*) any expenditure attributed by the Board under subsection (3) below to general business expenditure.
(2) In this Act "long term business expenditure" means—
  (*a*) any expenditure of the Board under section 10 or 11 above; and
  (*b*) any expenditure attributed by the Board under subsection (3) below to long term business expenditure.
(3) The Board may, in the case of—
  (*a*) any expenditure under section 15 or 16 above;
  (*b*) any expenditure in repaying or servicing any loans; and
  (*c*) any expenditure on their administrative expenses in performing their functions under this Act;
attribute that expenditure to general business expenditure or to long term business expenditure, or partly to the one and partly to the other, in such manner as may appear to them to be reasonable in the circumstances of the case.

Finance by levy 22–24

The Board is empowered by the Act to finance their expenditure by the imposition of levies on "accountable intermediaries" (section 19) and authorised insurers in business in the United Kingdom (section 21). The Board *shall* (section 19(1)) impose a levy on intermediaries, where empowered to do so, and *may* from time to time impose levies on authorised insurance companies (section 21(1) and (2)).

Levies on intermediaries 22–25

By section 19(1) "it shall be the duty of the Board to impose a levy" in accordance with this section and Schedule 2 to the Act where:

  (*a*) the Board have incurred or propose to incur any long term business expenditure in relation to a company in liquidation or a company which is a company in financial difficulties within the meaning of section 16 above; and (*b*) it appears to the Board that the company in question has accountable intermediaries:

"An accountable intermediary" so leviable is defined in section 19(2), and is one if—

(*a*) he has acted as an intermediary for the company in relation to any relevant long term contract of the company; and

(*b*) his income from the company in respect of his services (whether as an intermediary or otherwise) in relation to any such contracts (hereafter in this section and in section 20 below referred to as "relevant services") for either or each of the two years comprised in the period of two years ending immediately before the time mentioned below in this subsection exceeded his exempt income level for the year in question.

Subsection (3) excludes from the species of accountable intermediaries an individual if the services in question under subsection (2)(*b*) were performed in pursuance of a contract of exclusive agency with the company.

Subsection (8) provides:

> For the purposes of this section a person acts as an intermediary for a company in relation to a long term contract if, otherwise than as an employee of the company—
>
> (*a*) he invites any other person to take any step with a view to entering into a long term contract with the company;
>
> (*b*) he introduces any other person to the company with a view to his entering into such a contract with the company; or
>
> (*c*) he takes any other action with a view to securing that any other person will enter into such a contract with the company.

22–26 Accountability of intermediary

An intermediary is accountable only where his income from the company in respect of relevant services exceeded his exempt income level[5] for the year in question.

By section 19(4), for the purposes of section 20:

> Subject to section 20 and subsection (5) below, the income of an accountable intermediary of a company which is liable to levy under this section shall be—
>
> (*a*) one-half of any amount by which his income from the company in respect of relevant services for the later of the two years mentioned in subsection (2) above exceeded his exempt income level for that year; and
>
> (*b*) one quarter of any amount by which his income from the company in respect of relevant services for the earlier of those two years exceeded his exempt income level for that year;
>
> and in relation to any intermediary, his income liable to levy for either of those years or, where he had income liable to levy for each of those years, the aggregate of his income liable to levy for both of those years, is hereafter in this Act referred to as income of the intermediary which is income liable to levy."

and by subsection (5)

> a person's income from a company in respect of relevant services for any year is the total amount of the sums paid or allowed to that person by the company in respect of relevant services which were recorded as debits in the company's accounts during that year; but no account shall be taken for

---

[5] *Infra*, § 22–27.

those purposes of any sums recorded in a company's accounts at any time before 1st January 1976.

Exempt income level 22–27

Section 20 defines "exempt income level of an intermediary for any year" for the purposes of section 19. Such income level, by section 20(1) is:

(*a*) where no other person is linked with the intermediary, £5,000; and
(*b*) in any other case, that proportion of £5,000 which is equal to the proportion which the intermediary's income from the company in respect of relevant services for the year in question bears to the total amount of the group's income from the company in respect of such services for that year.

"Person linked with an intermediary" is defined by subsections (3) to (5) of section 20 as follows:

(3) The following are persons linked with an intermediary for the purposes of this section, whether the intermediary is a company or a person other than a company—
(*a*) any partner of the intermediary and any partnership of which the intermediary is a member;
(*b*) any company of which the intermediary is a director; and
(*c*) any director of any company which is linked with the intermediary.
(4) Where the intermediary in question is a company the following are also persons linked with the intermediary for the purposes of this section—
(*a*) any person other than a company who has a controlling interest in the intermediary and any company other than the intermediary in which any such person also has a controlling interest;
(*c*) any subsidiary of the intermediary; and
(*d*) any director of the intermediary.
(5) Where the intermediary in question is a person other than a company the following are also persons linked with the intermediary for the purposes of this section—
(*a*) any company in which the intermediary has a controlling interest;
(*b*) any company of which a company linked with the intermediary by virtue of subsection (3)(*b*) or paragraph (*a*) above is a subsidiary and any other subsidiary of any such company;
(*c*) any subsidiary of any company linked with the intermediary by virtue of subsection (3)(*b*) or paragraph (*a*) above; and
(*d*) where the intermediary is a partnership, each of its members.

By section 20(6) of the Act of 1975:

A person other than a company shall be treated as having a controlling interest in a company for the purposes of subsections (4)(*a*) and (5)(*a*) above if, but only if, that company would be a subsidiary of the person in question if that person were a company.

By subsections (7) and (8) of section 20:

(7) In determining for the purposes of subsection (6) above whether a company would be a subsidiary of any person other than a company, any shares held or power exercisable by either of two spouses or by both spouses jointly shall be treated as held or exercisable by each spouse.
(8) In subsections (3) to (7) above "company" has the same meaning as in section 154 of the Companies Act 1948 (meaning of "holding company" and "subsidiary").[6]

---

[6] Now replaced by ss. 736, 736A and 736B of the Companies Act 1985, as inserted by s. 144 of the Companies Act 1989.

22–28   *Imposition and enforcement of levy.* Section 19(10) provides that "Schedule 2 to the Act shall have effect with respect to the imposition and enforcement of levies under this section."

By Schedule 2, paragraph 1, no levy shall be imposed under section 19 in respect of any company *after* the end of the period of two years beginning with (*a*) the beginning of the liquidation (defined in section 5(5), see paragraph 22–06) if the company is one "in liquidation" (defined in section 5(4); see paragraph 22–06 or (*b*) the "relevant time" as defined by section 16(6) (see paragraph 22–21).

22–29   *Rate of levy.* By paragraph 2(1) where the long term business expenditure (defined in section 18(2) see paragraph 22–23) incurred (or estimated under sub-paragraph (2)) by the Board in relation to that company is less than "the total amount of the income liable to levy" (defined in sub-paragraph (3) to mean the total of the income of all persons appearing to be accountable intermediaries liable to it), is to be (*a*) a percentage equal to the percentage of that amount which the Board's expenditure represents; and (*b*) in any other case, 100 per cent.

22–30   *Statements.* Paragraph 3(1) and (2) empower the Board to require any person who "appears . . . to be an intermediary" of any company mentioned in paragraph 10 to submit a statement giving them information appearing to them necessary to determine a linkage matter. Paragraph 4 makes false information therein an offence.

22–31   *Enforcement of levy.* Paragraph 5 *inter alia* requires the Board to send notice of the levy to every person appearing to them to be an accountable intermediary, and specifying the rate. By paragraph 7 a notice under paragraphs 3 or 5 may be sent by post and a "letter containing such a notice shall be deemed to be properly addressed if it is addressed to the person to whom it is sent at his last known place of business in the United Kingdom."

22–32 Levies on insurance companies

Section 21 (*Levies on authorised insurance companies*) by subsection (1) provides:

> Subject to the following provisions of this section and to Schedule 3 to this Act, the Board may from time to time, for the purposes of financing general business expenditure, impose a levy on authorised insurance companies carrying on general business in the United Kingdom (hereafter in this Act referred to as a "general business levy").

Subsection (2) likewise provides for a "long term business levy" for the purpose of financing long term expenditure imposed on such insurance companies "carrying on long term business."

By subsection (3):

> The amount each insurance company may be required to pay under general business levies imposed in any financial year shall be calculated by reference to the net premium income of the company for the year ending last before the beginning of that financial year in respect of general policies which were United Kingdom policies at the relevant time; and any such income is hereafter in this Act referred to, in relation to any company, as income of the company for the year in question which is income liable to the general business levy.

Subsection (4) provides how income liable to the long term business levy should likewise be calculated.

"Net premium income" in subsections (3) and (4) means by subsection (5):

> the gross amounts recorded in the company's accounts during that year as paid or due to the company by way of premiums under policies of that description which were United Kingdom policies at the time when the amounts in question were so recorded, less any amounts deductible for that year in respect of policies of that description in accordance with subsection (6) or (7).

Subsection (6) provides:

> In calculating a company's net premium income for any year in respect of policies of any description any rebates or refunds recorded in the company's accounts during that year as allowed or given in respect of any amounts so recorded during that or any previous year as paid or due to the company by way of premiums under policies of that description which were United Kingdom policies at the time when the rebates or refunds were so recorded shall be deductible.

By subsection (7) in such calculation in respect of general policies within section 8:

> any sums recorded in the company's accounts during that year as paid by or due from the company by way of premiums for reinsuring its liabilities towards policyholders under general policies which were United Kingdom policies at the time when the sums in question were so recorded shall be deductible.

By subsection (8):

> The proceeds of general business levies may be applied by the Board only on general business expenditure and those of long term business levies only on long term business expenditure.

By subsection (9):

> Schedule 3 to the Act shall have effect with respect to the imposition and enforcement of general business levies and long term business levies and the other matters there mentioned.

By Schedule 3, paragraph 1 (restrictions on imposition) no levy may be imposed before the beginning of the financial year ending with March 31, 1977. By paragraph 2(1) general business levies and (2) long term business levies imposed in any financial year shall not exceed "one per cent. of any income of the company for the year ending last before the beginning of that financial year" which is income liable to the respective levy. Paragraph 3 restricts finance of *future* expenditure:

> The Board may not impose a levy for the purpose of financing expenditure of any description unless—
> (*a*) [it] has already been incurred by the Board; or
> (*b*) it appears to the Board that [it] will be incurred within twelve months of the imposition of the levy.

Paragraphs 4 and 5 cover statements of premium income. By paragraph 4 every authorised insurance company shall send to the Secretary of State for Trade before March 1 annually a statement of any income of the company for the previous year liable to (1) the general business levy;

(2) the long term business levy (in separate statements where the company is thus required to send statements of income of both descriptions: sub-paragraph (3)). This information must accompany the accounting information to be sent to the Secretary of State under the Insurance Companies Act 1982 (see Chapter 13).

Sub-paragraphs 5(1) and (2) create criminal offences.

By sub-paragraph (3) failure of an insurance company to comply with paragraph 4 confers a power on the Secretary of State to intervene and petition for its winding up in accordance with the terms of the Insurance Companies Act 1982. Other enforcement powers are contained in paragraphs 6 and 7.

CHAPTER 23

MARINE INSURANCE

The Marine Insurance Act 1906 {23-01}

The M.I.A. 1906, which was the work of Sir Mackenzie Chalmers, sought to codify the pre-existing common law of marine insurance. The Act remains the governing provision, and has significance far beyond England as much of the world's marine insurance business is transacted in London and is governed expressly or impliedly by English law. This chapter consists of the text, and a brief synopsis, of the M.I.A. 1906. When reading the text of the M.I.A. 1906 it should be borne in mind that a number of subsequent decisions have had need to construe Chalmers' language and have on occasion put surprising glosses on it, that some aspects of marine insurance practice referred to by implication in the M.I.A. 1906 have long been modified or abandoned, and that the standard marine clauses used by the institute of London Underwriters—as varied from time to time—at various points contract out of the Act's provisions. The M.I.A. 1906 is not, therefore, by any means the entire story. The reader is referred, for greater detail, to Arnould's *Law of Marine Insurance and Average*, 16th edition, 1981. Many of the principles contained in the M.I.A. 1906 are equally applicable to other forms of insurance. The principal differences were listed in Chapter 1 of this work.

1. GENERAL DEFINITIONS

Marine insurance defined {23-02}

1. A contract of marine insurance is a contract whereby the insurer undertakes to indemnify the assured in the manner and to the extent thereby agreed, against marine losses, that is to say, the losses incident to marine adventure.

Mixed sea and land risks {23-03}

2.—(1) A contract of marine insurance may, by its express terms, or by usage or trade, be extended so as to protect the assured against losses on inland waters or on any land risk which may be incidental to any sea voyage.

(2) Where a ship in course of building, or the launch of a ship, or any adventure analagous to a marine adventure, is covered by a policy in the form of a marine policy, the provisions of this Act, in so far as applicable, shall apply thereto; but, except as by this section provided, nothing in this Act shall alter or affect any rule of law applicable to any contract of insurance other than a contract of marine insurance as by this Act defined.

Commentary. Section 2 provides that a marine policy need not cover marine risks, exclusively and that ancillary risks may be covered. Subsection (1) recognises the practice, still current, of insuring cargo on a "warehouse to warehouse" basis.

23–04 Marine adventure and maritime perils defined

3.—(1) Subject to the provisions of this Act, every lawful marine adventure may be the subject of a contract of marine insurance.

(2) In particular there is a marine adventure where—

(*a*) any ship goods or other movables are exposed to maritime perils. Such property is in this Act referred to as "insurable property";

(*b*) the earning or acquisition of any freight, passage money, commission, profit, or other pecuniary benefit, or the security for any advances, loan, or disbursements, is endangered by the exposure of insurable property to maritime perils;

(*c*) any liability to a third party may be incurred by the owner of, or other person interested in or responsible for, insurance property, by reason of maritime perils.

"Maritime perils" means the perils consequent on, or incidental to, the navigation of the sea, that is to say, perils of the seas, fire, war perils, pirates, rovers, thieves, captures, seizures, restraints, and detainments of princes and peoples, jettisons, barratry, and any, other perils, either of the like kind or which may be designated by the policy.

Commentary. The various terms used in section 3 are defined in Schedule 1, set out below. The words "incidental to the navigation of the seas" have the effect of deeming a peril which occurs at sea to be a marine peril, although the concluding words "other perils of the like kind which may be designated by the policy" do not allow anything other than incidental land risks to be insured under a marine policy.[1]

2. INSURABLE INTEREST

23–05 Avoidance of gaming or wagering contracts

4.—(1) Every contract of marine insurance by way of gaming or wagering is void.

(2) A contract of marine insurance is deemed to be a gaming or wagering contract—

(*a*) where the assured has not an insurable interest as defined by this Act, and the contract is entered into with no expectation of acquiring such an interest; or

(*b*) where the policy is made "interest or no interest," or "without further proof of interest than the policy itself," or "without benefit of salvage to the insurer," or subject to any other like term:

Provided that, where there is no possibility of salvage, a policy may be effected without benefit of salvage to the insurer.

Commentary. A policy is void if the assured neither has an insurable interest at its inception, nor has a reasonable expectation of obtaining one: mere overvaluation of a valid or anticipated interest does not render the policy one by way of gaming or wagering.[2] A policy in p.p.i. and similar form is void, even if made on valid or anticipated interest.[3] Void policies may give rise to criminal offences under the Marine Insurance (Gambling Policies) Act 1909.

---

[1] *Continental Illinois Bank* v. *Bathurst, The Captain Panagos* [1985] 1 Lloyd's Rep. 625.
[2] *Glapki Shipping* v. *Pinios Shipping* [1984] 1 Lloyd's Rep. 660.
[3] *Cheshire* v. *Vaughan* [1920] 3 K.B. 240.

Insurable interest defined

20–06

5.—(1) Subject to the provisions of this Act, every person has an insurable interest who is interested in a marine adventure.

(2) In particular a person is interested in a marine adventure where he stands in any legal or equitable relation to the adventure or to any insurable property at risk therein, in consequence of which he may benefit by the safety or due arrival of insurable property, or may be prejudiced by its loss, or by damage thereto, or by the detention thereof, or may incur liability in respect thereof.[4]

When interest must attach

23–07

6.—(1) The assured must be interested in the subject-matter insured at the time of the loss though he need not be interested when the insurance is effected:

Provided that where the subject-matter is insured "lost or not lost," the assured may recover although he may not have acquired his interest until after the loss, unless at the time of effecting the contract of insurance the assured was aware of the loss, and the insurer was not.

(2) Where the assured has no interest at the time of the loss, he cannot acquire interest by any act or election after he is aware of the loss.

Commentary. Subsection (1) emphasises the indemnity nature of a marine policy by providing that the assured must prove his interest at the time of loss if he is to recover: the absence of insurable interest at the inception of the policy is immaterial, although if the assured has no expectation of acquiring an interest the policy will be void under section 4. The assured cannot exercise any option in respect of the insured subject matter once he becomes aware of a loss (subsection (2)). The proviso to subsection (1) makes a saving for "lost or not lost" policies.

Defeasible or contingent interest

23–08

7.—(1) A defeasible interest is insurable, as also is a contingent interest.

(2) In particular, where the buyer of goods has insured them, he has an insurable interest, notwithstanding that he might, at his election, have rejected the goods, or have treated them as at the seller's risk, by reason of the latter's delay in making delivery or otherwise.

Partial interest

23–09

8. A partial interest of any nature is insurable.

Reinsurance

23–10

9.—(1) The insurer under a contract of marine insurance has an insurable interest in his risk, and may re-insure in respect of it.

(2) Unless the policy otherwise provides, the original assured has no right or interest in respect of such re-insurance.[5]

Bottomry

23–11

10. The lender of money or bottomry or respondentia has an insurable interest in respect of the loan.

---

[4] This definition follows the broad view expressed in *Lucena* v. *Craufurd* (1808) 1 Taunt. 325, discussed in Chap. 3.
[5] See the discussion in Chap. 12.

23–12 Master's and seamen's wages

11. The master or any member of the crew of a ship has an insurable interest in respect of his wages.

23–13 Advanced freight

12. In the case of advance freight, the person advancing the freight has an insurable interest, in so far as such freight is not repayable in case of loss.

23–14 Charges of insurance

13. The assured has an insurable interest in the charges of any insurance which he may effect.

23–15 Quantum of interest

14.—(1) Where the subject-matter insured is mortgaged, the mortgagor has an insurable interest in the full value thereof, and the mortgagee has an insurable interest in respect of any sum due or to become due under the mortgage.

(2) A mortgagee, consignee, or other person having an interest in the subject-matter may insure on behalf and for the benefit of other persons interested as well as for his own benefit.

(3) The owner of insurable property has an insurable interest in respect of the full value thereof, notwithstanding that some third person may have agreed, or be liable, to indemnify him in case of loss.

Commentary. These rules are identical to those operating in respect of non-marine policies concerning insurance of limited interests.[6] Subsection (3) preserves the common law right of the assured to recover from the insurer despite being entitled to a contractual indemnity: the point is of particular significance in cargo claims, as the owner of cargo will have a contractual right to sue the carrier for loss in addition to a claim under the policy, although the former right will accrue to the insurer by way of subrogation. Where various interests are insured under a single policy, the claimant may recover the entire policy moneys but must hold those in excess of his own interest on trust for the owners of the other interests.[7]

23–16 Assignment of interest

15. Where the assured assigns or otherwise parts with his interest in the subject-matter insured, he does not thereby transfer to the assignee his rights under the contract of insurance unless there be an express or implied agreement with the assignee to that effect.

But the provisions of this section do not affect a transmission of interest by operation of law.

Commentary. A marine policy, unlike a non-marine property policy is assignable *unless* assignment is restricted by contract (M.I.A., section 50): other policies can be assigned only with the insurer's consent.[8] However, section 15—which is a rule applicable in marine and non-marine insurance alike—prevents a mere sale of the insured subject matter from transferring the policy unless there is agreement to that effect between seller and buyer.

---

[6] See Chap. 14.
[7] *Hepburn* v. *Tomlinson* [1966] A.C. 410.
[8] See Chap. 10.

2. INSURABLE VALUE

Measure of insurable value   **23–17**

16. Subject to any express provision or valuation in the policy, the insurable value of the subject-matter insured must be ascertained as follows:

(1) in insurance on ship, the insurable value is the value, at the commencement of the risk, of the ship, including her outfit, provisons and stores for the officers and crew, money advanced for seamen's wages, and other disbursements (if any) incurred to make the ship fit for the voyage or adventure contemplated by the policy, plus the charges of insurance upon the whole.

The insurable value, in the case of a steamship, includes also the machinery, boilers, and coals and engine stores if owned by the assured, and, in the case of a ship engaged in a special trade, the ordinary fittings requisite for that trade:

(2) in insurance on freight, whether paid in advance or otherwise, the insurable value is the gross amount of the freight at the risk of the assured, plus the charges of insurance:

(3) in insurance on goods or merchandise, the insurable value is the prime cost of the property insured, plus the expenses of and incidental to shipping and the charges of insurance upon the whole:

(4) in insurance on any other subject-matter, the insurable value is the amount at the risk of the assured when the policy attaches, plus the charges of insurance.

Commentary. This definition is important, as it fixes the amount recoverable by the assured under an undervalued policy (see section 67(1), which defines the insurable value as the assured's measure of indemnity). In non-marine insurance the value of insured subject matter is taken to be that immediately prior to the loss. In marine insurance, however, the value is taken to be that an earlier stage. In the case of the vessel, freight and any subject matter other than cargo, the relevant value is that at the inception of the risk (subsections (1), (2) and (4)). The rule is, however, contrary to express provision.[9] In the case of cargo the relevant measure is "prime cost." This is generally taken to be the invoice price paid by the assured,[10] although the assured is free to demonstrate that the prime cost is not the true value of the cargo.[11]

3. DISCLOSURE AND REPRESENTATIONS[12]

Insurance is uberrimae fidei   **23–18**

17. A contract of marine insurance is a contract based upon the utmost good faith, and, if the utmost good faith be not observed by either party, the contract may be avoided by the other party.

Disclosure by assured   **23–19**

18.—(1) Subject to the provisions of this section, the assured must disclose to the insurer, before the contract is concluded, every material circumstance which is known to the assured, and the assured is deemed to know every cir-

---

[9] *Continental Illinois Bank* v. *Bathurst, supra.* n. 1, is an illustration of the basic rule being held inconsistent with the policy, there a mortgagee's interest policy.

[10] *Williams* v. *Atlantic* [1933] 1 K.B. 81.

[11] *Berger* v. *Pollock* [1973] 2 Lloyd's Rep. 442.

[12] See generally Chap. 5.

cumstance which, in the ordinary course of business, ought to be known by him. If the assured fails to make such disclosure, the insurer may avoid the contract.

(2) Every circumstance is material which would influence the judgment of a prudent insurer fixing the premium, or determining whether he will take the risk.

(3) In the absence of inquiry the following circumstances need not be disclosed, namely:

(*a*) Any circumstance which diminishes the risk;

(*b*) Any circumstance which is known or presumed to be known to the insurer. The insurer is presumed to know matters of common notoriety or knowledge, and matters which an insurer in the ordinary course of his business, as such, ought to know;

(*c*) Any circumstances as to which information is waived by the insurer;

(*d*) Any circumstance which it is superfluous to disclose by reason of any express or implied warranty.

(4) Whether any particular circumstance, which is not disclosed, be material or not is in each case, a question of fact.

(5) The term "circumstance" includes any communication made to, or information received by, the assured.

23–20 Disclosure by agent effecting insurance

19. Subject to the provisions of the preceding section as to circumstances which need not be disclosed, where an insurance is effected for the assured by an agent, the agent must disclose to the insurer—

(*a*) Every material circumstance which is known to himself, and an agent to insure is deemed to know every circumstance which in the ordinary course of business ought to be known by, or to have been communicated to, him; and

(*b*) Every material circumstance which the assured is bound to disclose, unless it come to his knowledge too late to communicate it to the agent.

23–21 Representations pending negotiation of contract

20.—(1) Every material representation made by the assured or his agent to the insurer during the negotiations for the contract, and before the contract is concluded, must be true. If it be untrue the insurer may avoid the contract.

(2) A representation is material which would influence the judgment of a prudent insurer in fixing the premium, or determining whether he will take the risk.

(3) A representation may be either a representation as to a matter of fact, or as to a matter of expectation or belief.

(4) A representation as to a matter of fact is true, if it be substantially correct, that is to say, if the difference between what is represented and what is actually correct would not be considered material by a prudent insurer.

(5) A representation as to a matter of expectation or belief is true if it be made in good faith.

(6) A representation may be withdrawn or corrected before the contract is concluded.

(7) Whether a particular representation be material or not is, in each case, a question of fact.

23–22 When contract is deemed to be concluded

21. A contract of marine insurance is deemed to be concluded when the proposal of the assured is accepted by the insurer whether the policy be then issued or not; and, for the purpose of showing when the proposal was accepted, reference may be made to the slip or covering note or other customary memorandum of the contract . . .

Commentary. The date at which the policy is concluded is crucial, as it marks the point at which the duty of utmost good faith in respect of the risk comes to an end. A contract of marine insurance initiated by a Lloyd's broker's slip comes into effect when the slip is initialled by the underwriter, and not at the later date at which the policy is issued: *General Reinsurance* v. *Fenna Patria*.[13]

4. THE POLICY

Contract must be embodied in policy   23–23

22. Subject to the provisions of any statute, a contract of marine insurance is inadmissible in evidence unless it is embodied in a marine policy in accordance with this Act. The policy may be executed and issued either at the time when the contract is concluded, or afterwards.

Commentary. A slip is probably not sufficient to constitute a *policy* of insurance, even though it is a *contract* of insurance.

What policy must specify   23–24

23. A marine policy must specify—
(1) The name of the assured, or of some person who effects the insurance on his behalf . . .

Signature of insurer   23–25

24.—(1) A marine policy must be signed by or on behalf of the insurer, provided that in the case of a corporation the corporate seal may be sufficient, but nothing in this section shall be construed as requiring the subscription of a corporation to be under seal.
(2) Where a policy is subscribed by or on behalf of two or more insurers, each subscription, unless the contrary be expressed, constitutes a distinct contract with the assured.

Voyage and time policies   23–26

25. Where the contract is to insure the subject-matter "at and from," or from one place to another or others, the policy is called a "voyage policy," and whether the contract is to insure the subject-matter for a definite period of time the policy is called a "time policy." A contract for both voyage and time may be included in the same policy.

Commentary. The distinction between time and voyage policies is important for a number of reasons: the risk under the two types of policy commences and terminates at different times; the assured under a voyage policy is obliged to commence and maintain the voyage without delay, deviation or change of voyage,[14] and there is no implied warranty of seaworthiness in a time policy.[15] The distinction between time and voyage policies is normally obvious, particularly as standard forms are used,[16] although a policy is a time policy notwithstanding the fact that it

---

[13] [1983] 2 Lloyd's Rep. 287. See *supra*, §§1–29—1–30.
[14] ss.42–49, *infra*.
[15] s.39, *infra*.
[16] But see *Dudgeon* v. *Pembroke* (1877) 2 App.Cas. 284, where the House of Lords held that a policy in voyage policy standard form was in fact a time policy, in accordance with the actual intentions of the parties.

may be extended,[17] and a policy may be a "mixed" time and voyage policy.

23–27 Designation of subject matter

26.—(1) The subject-matter insured must be designated in a marine policy with reasonable certainty.

(2) The nature and extent of the interest of the assured in the subject-matter insured need not be specified in the policy.

(3) Where the policy designates the subject-matter insured in general terms, it shall be construed to apply to the interest intended by the assured to be covered.

(4) In the application of this section regard shall be had to any usage regulating the designation of the subject-matter insured.

Commentary. Section 26(2) relieves an assured with insurable interest from the need to state precisely what his interest is. Thus, where a marine policy insures specific subject-matter, the assured need not disclose that it is his liability in respect of that subject-matter, rather than the subject-matter itself, which is intended to be covered.[18] Subsection (3) appears to allow the assured to recover only for those interests intended by him to be insured, but the Court of Appeal has nevertheless held that the assured can recover for any interests insured under the policy even if it was not his intention at the outset to insure all of those interests.[19]

23–28 Valued policy

27.—(1) A policy may be either valued or unvalued.

(2) A valued policy is a policy which specifies the agreed value of the subject-matter insured.

(3) Subject to the provisions of this Act, and in the absence of fraud, the value fixed by the policy is, as between the insurer and assured, conclusive of the insurable value of the subject intended to be insured, whether the loss be total or partial.

(4) Unless the policy otherwise provides, the value fixed by the policy is not conclusive for the purpose of determining whether there has been a constructive total loss.

Commentary. The distinction between valued and unvalued policies was discussed in Chapter 1. The conclusiveness of the valuation, set out in section 27(3), is subject to express exceptions for fraudulent overvaluation and for calculating the value of the subject-matter to determine if there has been a constructive total loss under section 60 (section 27(4)). In addition, section 27(3) is overridden by section 18, so that gross overvaluation not amounting to fraud must be disclosed by the assured.[20]

23–29 Unvalued policy

28. An unvalued policy which does not specify the value of the subject-matter insured, but, subject to the limit of the sum insured, leaves the insurable value to be subsequently ascertained, in the manner hereinbefore specified.

---

[17] *The Eurysthenes* [1977] Q.B. 49.
[18] *Crowley* v. *Cohen* (1832) 3 B. & Ald. 478; *Mackenzie* v. *Whitworth* (1875) L.R. 1 Ex. P. 36.
[19] *Reliance Marine* v. *Duder* [1913] 1 K.B. 265.
[20] *Inversiones Manria* v. *Sphere Drake* [1989] 1 Lloyd's Rep. 69.

Floating policy by ship or ships   23–30

29.—(1) A floating policy is a policy which describes the insurance in general terms, and leaves the name of the ship or ships and other particulars to be defined by subsequent declaration.

(2) The subsequent declaration or declarations may be made by endorsement on the policy, or in other customary manner.

(3) Unless the policy otherwise provides, the declarations must be made in the order of dispatch or shipment. They must, in the case of goods, comprise all consignments within the terms of the policy, and the value of the goods or other property must be honestly stated, but an omission or erroneous declaration may be rectified even after loss or arrival, provided the omission or declaration was made in good faith.

(4) Unless the policy otherwise provides, where a declaration of value is not made until after notice of loss or arrival, the policy must be treated as an unvalued policy as regards the subject-matter of that declaration.

Commentary. A floating policy allows the assured to insure an unascertained cargo on an unspecified vessel, although when the details of the cargo and the vessel become clear they must be declared to the insurer. As declarations are made after the policy has been made, the duty of utmost good faith has no part to play, and is sufficient if declarations are made honestly.[21]

Construction of terms in policy   23–31

30.—(1) A policy may be in the form of the First Schedule to this Act.

(2) Subject to the provisions of this Act, and unless the context of the policy otherwise requires, the terms of expressions mentioned in the First Schedule to this Act shall be construed as having the scope and meaning in that schedule assigned to them.

Commentary. The policy form set out in the First Schedule was superseded in the London market, by a far simpler form, as from 1984. The terms defined in the First Schedule are nevertheless still of importance, as they are used in the modern form of policy as well as in various parts of the M.I.A. 1906.

Premium to be arranged   23–32

31.—(1) Where an insurance is effected at a premium to be arranged, and no arrangement is made, a reasonable premium is payable.

(2) Where an insurance is effected on the terms that an additional premium is to be arranged in a given event, and that event happens but no arrangement is made, then a reasonable additional premium is payable.

Commentary. Subsection (2) is of particular importance under the "held covered" provisions of the standard marine clauses established by the Institute of London Underwriters. The courts will fix a reasonable premium by reference to the market rate for the degree of risk in question,[22] although if there is no market rate and the risk is uninsurable, the held covered protection cannot apply.[23]

---

[21] *Ionides* v. *Pacific Fire* (1871) L.R. 6 Q.B. 674.
[22] *Hewitt* v. *London General* (1925) 23 Ll. & L.R. 243.
[23] *Liberian Insurance Agency* v. *Mosse* [1977] 2 Lloyd's Rep. 560.

5. DOUBLE INSURANCE

23–33 Double insurance

32.—(1) Where two or more policies are effected by or on behalf of the assured on the same adventure and interest or any part thereof, and the sums insured exceed the indemnity allowed by this Act, the assured is said to be over-insured by double insurance.

(2) Where the assured is over-insured by double insurance—

    (*a*) The assured, unless the policy otherwise provides, may claim payment from the insurers in such order as he may think fit, provided that he is not entitled to receive any sum in excess of the indemnity allowed by this Act;

    (*b*) Where the policy under which the assured claims is a valued policy, the assured must give credit as against the valuation for any sum received by him under any other policy without regard to the actual value of the subject-matter insured;

    (*c*) Where the policy under which the assured claims is an unvalued policy he must give credit, as against the full insurable value, for any sum received by him under any other policy;

    (*d*) Where the assured receives any sum in excess of the indemnity allowed by this Act, he is deemed to hold such sum in trust for the insurers, according to their right of contribution among themselves.[24]

6. WARRANTIES, ETC.

23–34 Nature of warranty

33.—(1) A warranty, in the following sections relating to warranties, means a promissory warranty, that is to say, a warranty by which the assured undertakes that some particular thing shall or shall not be done, or that some condition shall be fulfilled, or whereby he affirms or negatives the existence of a particular state of facts.

(2) A warranty may be express or implied.

(3) A warranty, as above defined, is a condition which must be exactly complied with, whether it be material to the risk or not. If it be not so complied with, then, subject to any express provision in the policy, the insurer is discharged from liability as from the date of the breach of warranty, but without prejudice to any liability incurred by him before that date.[25]

23–35 When breach of warranty excused

34.—(1) Non-compliance with a warranty is excused when, by reason of a change of circumstances, the warranty ceases to be applicable to the circumstances of the contract, or when compliance with the warranty is rendered unlawful by any subsequent law.

(2) Where a warranty is broken, the assured cannot avail himself of the defence that the breach has been remedied, and the warranty complied with, before loss.

(3) A breach of warranty may be waived by the insurer.

23–36 Express warranties

35.—(1) An express warranty may be in any form of words from which the intention to warrant is to be inferred.

---

[24] This section restates the common law applicable to all forms of insurance: see Chap. 8.
[25] This and the following two sections restate the common law applicable to all forms of insurance: see Chap. 6. Sections 36 to 41 are unique to marine insurance.

(2) An express warranty must be included in, or written upon, the policy, or must be contained in some document incorporated by reference into the policy.

(3) An express warranty does not exclude an implied warranty, unless it be inconsistent therewith.

Warranty of neutrality 23–37

36.—(1) Where insurable property, whether ship or goods, is expressly warranted neutral, there is an implied condition that the property shall have a neutral character at the commencement of the risk, and that, so far the assured can control the matter, its neutral character shall be preserved during the risk.

(2) Where a ship is expressly warranted "neutral" there is also an implied condition that, so far as the assured can control the matter, she shall be properly documented, that is to say, that she shall carry the necessary papers to establish here neutrality, and that she shall not falsify or supress her papers, or use simulated papers. If any loss occurs through breach of this condition, the insurer may avoid the contract.

No implied warranty of nationality 23–38

37. There is no implied warranty as to the nationality of a ship, or that her nationality shall not be changed during the risk.

Warranty of good safety 23–39

38. Where the subject-matter insured is warranted "well" or "in good safety" on a particular day, it is sufficient if it be safe at any time during that day.

Warranty of seaworthiness of ship 23–40

39.—(1) In a voyage policy there is an implied warranty that at the commencement of the voyage the ship shall be seaworthy for the purpose of the particular adventure insured.

(2) Where the policy attaches while the ship is in port, there is also an implied warranty that she shall, at the commencement of the risk, be reasonably fit to encounter the ordinary perils of the port.

(3) Where the policy relates to a voyage which is performed in different stages, during which the ship requires different kinds of or further preparation or equipment, there is an implied warranty that at the commencement of each stage the ship is seaworthy in respect of such preparation or equipment for the purposes of that stage.

(4) A ship is deemed to be seaworthy when she is reasonably fit in all respects to encounter the ordinary perils of the seas of the adventure insured.

(5) In a time policy there is no implied warranty that the ship shall be seaworthy at any stage of the adventure, but where, with the privity of the assured, the ship is sent to sea in an unseaworthy state, the insurer is not liable for any loss attributable to unseaworthiness.

Commentary. Section 39 draws a distinction between time and voyage policies. There is no implied warranty of seaworthiness under a time policy, although under subsection (5) the assured is precluded from recovering if the vessel was sent to sea in an unseaworthy condition and the proximate cause of the loss was unseaworthiness of which the assured had been aware.[26] If the vessel is unseaworthy to the knowledge

---

[26] In *Compania Maritima San Basilio* v. *Oceanus Mutual, The Eurysthenes* [1976] 2 Lloyd's Rep. 171 the Court of Appeal held that "privity" in section 39(5) meant either actual knowledge or "turning a blind eye": *per* Lord Denning M.R. at p. 179.

of the assured, but it is lost as the result of a different form of unseaworthiness of which he was not aware, he can nevertheless recover.[27]

In the case of a voyage policy there is a warranty of seaworthiness at the commencement of voyage. If the voyage is in stages, the warranty applies to the commencement of each stage. The warranty is not broken by a vessel becoming unseaworthy in the course of a voyage.[28] There is no fixed standard of seaworthiness, as all depends upon the purposes of the adventure and the reasonable fitness of the vessel to meet its perils. A vessel may be rendered unfit on a number of grounds, including the insufficiency of navigational equipment, the incompetence of the master or crew, and the overloading of the vessel.

23–41 No implied warranty that goods are seaworthy

40.—(1) In a policy on goods or other movables there is no implied warranty that the goods or movables are seaworthy.

(2) In a voyage policy on goods or other movables there is an implied warranty that at the commencement of the voyage the ship is not only seaworthy as a ship, but also that she is reasonably fit to carry the goods or other movables to the destination contemplated by the policy.

23–42 Warranty of legality

41. There is an implied warranty that the adventure insured is a lawful one, and that, so far as the assured can control the matter, the adventure shall be carried out in a lawful manner.

Commentary. There is no authority on the scope of this warranty, and it is probably the case that the principle is subsumed by the general rules relating to illegality and public policy, discussed in Chapter 3. Insofar as section 42 does have independent effect, it is confined to marine insurance.[29]

7. THE VOYAGE[30]

23–43 Implied condition as to commencement of risk

42.—(1) Where the subject-matter is insured by a voyage policy "at and from" or "from" a particular place, it is not necessary that the ship should be at that place when the contract is concluded, but there is an implied condition that the adventure shall be commenced within a reasonable time, and that if the adventure be not so commenced the insurer may avoid the contract.

(2) The implied condition may be negatived by showing that the delay was caused by circumstances known to the insurer before the contract was concluded, or by showing that he waived the condition.

Commentary. Section 42(1) is in essence negative in operation, as it merely provides that the insurer is discharged if the adventure under a voyage policy does not commence within a reasonable time. The precise time at which the risk attaches depends upon the provisions of Schedule 1, paragraphs 2 and 3. Paragraph 2 deals with adventures "from" a

---

[27] *Thomas* v. *Tyne and Wear Steamship* (1917) 117 L.T. 55.
[28] *Bermon* v. *Woodbridge* (1781) 2 Doug. 781.
[29] *Euro-Diam* v. *Bathurst* [1988] 2 All E.R. 23.
[30] The following sections necessarily apply only to voyage policies.

named part, and provides that the risk attaches when the voyage commences. Paragraph 3 deals with "at and from" policies, and provides that the risk attaches as and when the vessel is in port "in good safety."[31] The latter form of policy thus with port risks as well as voyage risks.

Alteration of port of departure

23–44

43. Where the place of departure is specified by the policy, and the ship instead of sailing from that place sails from any other place, the risk does not attach.

Sailing for different destination

23–45

44. Where the destination is specified in the policy, and the ship, instead of sailing for that destination, sails for any other destination, the risk does not attach.

Change of voyage

23–46

45.—(1) Where, after the commencement of the risk, the destination of the ship is voluntarily changed from the destination contemplated by the policy, there is said to be a change of voyage.

(2) Unless the policy otherwise provides, where there is a change of voyage, the insurer is discharged from liability as from the time of change, that is to say, as from the time when the determination to change it is manifested; and it is immaterial that the ship may not in fact have left the course of voyage contemplated by the policy when the loss occurs.

Commentary. Change of voyage, governed by section 45, should be distinguished from deviation (section 46), whereby the assured retains the same ultimate destination but adopts a non-contractual route.

A change of voyage discharges the insurer only where it was voluntary,[32] and section 45(2) reaffirms the common law rule that a manifest intention to change voyage is sufficient.[33]

The standard marine clauses offer "held covered" protection following change of voyage, subject to the assured giving prompt or immediate notice and agreeing to any new policy conditions (including an additional premium).

Deviation

23–47

46.—(1) Where a ship, without lawful excuse, deviates from the voyage contemplated by the policy, the insurer is discharged from liability as from the time of deviation, and it is immaterial that the ship may have regained her route before any loss occurs.

(2) There is a deviation from the voyage contemplated by the policy—
- (*a*) Where the course of the voyage is specifically designated by the policy, and that course is departed from; or
- (*b*) Where the course of the voyage is not specifically designated by the policy, but the usual and customary course is departed from.

---

[31] A vessel may be "in good safety" despite being damaged or liable to seizure: *Lidgett* v. *Secretan* (1870) L.R. 5 C.P. 190; *Lockyer* v. *Offley* (1786) 1 T.R. 252.

[32] See *Rickards* v. *Forrestal Land* [1942] A.C. 50, where the change was forced by government orders.

[33] *Tasker* v. *Cunningham* (1819) 1 Bligh. 87.

(3) The intention to deviate is immaterial; there must be a deviation in fact to discharge the insurer from his liability under the contract.

Commentary. Deviation is in essence the taking of a non-contractual route by the vessel. Unlike change of voyage, there must be an actual deviation and not merely an intention to deviate (subsection (3)). The possibility of deviation depends upon the terms of the policy: section 46(2) deals with agreed and customary routes, while section 47 is concerned with deviation where ports of call, or an area consisting of different ports, have been specified.

It is unclear whether deviation is an automatically discharging event, but it is certain that if deviation is operative the insurer can escape liability even though no loss has occurred and the vessel has regained its route.

The reference to "lawful excuse" refers to section 49, which lists the grounds on which deviation is justified. In addition, the standard marine insurance clauses provide "held covered" protection in the event of deviation.

23–48 Several ports of discharge

47.—(1) Where several ports of discharge are specified by the policy, the ship may proceed to all or any of them, but, in the absence of any usage or sufficient cause to the contrary, she must proceed to them, or such of them as she goes to, in the order designated by the policy. If she does not there is a deviation.

(2) Where the policy is to "ports of discharge," within a given area, which are not named, the ship must, in the absence of any usage of sufficient cause to the contrary, proceed to them, or such of them as she goes to, in their geographical order. If she does not there is a deviation.

23–49 Delay

48. In the case of a voyage policy, the adventure insured must be prosecuted throughout its course with reasonable despatch, and, if without lawful excuse it is not so prosecuted, the insurer is discharged from liability as from the time when the delay became unreasonable.

Commentary. At common law delay was a form of deviation; the Act indeed affords the same defences in section 49. Section 48 is confined to the voyage policies, and is to be read in conjunction with section 42, which prevents the risk from attaching in the event of pre-voyage delay. It should also be noted that loss proximately caused by delay is irrecoverable in all forms of marine policy: section 55(2)(*b*).

23–50 Excuses for deviation or delay

49.—(1) Deviation or delay in prosecuting the voyage contemplated by the policy is excused—
    (*a*) Where authorised by any special term in the policy; or
    (*b*) Where caused by circumstances beyond the control of the master and his employer; or
    (*c*) Where reasonably necessary in order to comply with an express or implied warranty; or
    (*d*) Where reasonably necessary for the safety of the ship or subject-matter insured; or

(e) For the purpose of saving human life, or aiding a ship in distress where human life may be in danger; or

(f) Where reasonably necessary for the purpose of obtaining medical or surgical aid for any person on board the ship; or

(g) Where caused by the barratrous conduct of the master or crew, if barratry be one of the perils insured against.

(2) When the cause excusing the deviation or delay ceases to operate, the ship must resume her course, and prosecute her voyage, with reasonable despatch.

Commentary. Ground (a) is in practice the most important, as various waivers and "held covered" provisions are contained in the standard Institute Clauses used on the London Marine Market. Circumstances beyond the control of the master under ground (b) include government orders[34] and weather conditions.[35] Ground (c) is apparently intended to enable the assured to secure compliance with the implied warranty of seaworthiness for a journey in stages, by delay for refitting if necessary.[36] The purpose of ground (g) is to make it clear that if the delay or deviation is the result of fraud or misconduct by the crew (barratry), and barratry is an insured peril, the assured can nevertheless recover.

8. ASSIGNMENT OF POLICY[37]

When and how policy is assignable   23–51

50.—(1) A marine policy is assignable unless it contains terms expressly prohibiting assignment. It may be assigned either before or after the loss.

(2) Where a marine policy has been assigned so as to pass the beneficial interest in such policy, the assignee of the policy is entitled to sue thereon in his own name; and the defendant is entitled to make any defence arising out of the contract which he would have been entitled to make if the action had been brought in the name of the person by or on behalf of whom the policy was effected.

(3) A marine policy may be assigned by indorsement thereon or in other customary manner.

Commentary. Marine policies, unlike other policies of indemnity, are assignable unless there are express terms to the contrary. Subsection (2) states a general rule applicable to all valid assignments.

51. Where the assured has parted with or lost his interest in the subject-   **23–52**
matter insured, and has not, before or at the time of so doing, expressly or impliedly agreed to assign the policy, any subsequent assignment of the policy is inoperative:

Provided that nothing in this section affects the assignment of a policy after loss.

Commentary. This rule is an obvious corollary of insurable interest: if the assignor loses insurable interest, the policy lapses and there is thus nothing to assign. In the converse case, where the assured assigns the

---

[34] *Rickards* v. *Forrestal, supra,* n. 32.
[35] *Delany* v. *Stoddart* (1785) 1 T.R. 22.
[36] *Bouillon* v. *Lupton* (1863) 33 L.J. C.P. 37.
[37] See generally, Chap. 10.

policy without assigning the subject-matter, the assignee has no insurable interest and is thus unable to sue on the policy.[38]

9. THE PREMIUM[39]

23–53 When premium is payable

52. Unless otherwise agreed, the duty of the assured or his agent to pay the premium, and the duty of the insurer to issue the policy to the assured or his agent, are concurrent conditions, and the insurer is not bound to issue the policy until payment or tender of the premium.

Commentary. Section 52 does not say that there is no contract or cover, until the premium is paid, but merely that the policy need not be issued. The effect of non-issue is, in addition to any express terms suspending cover, to prevent the assured from mounting an action on the contract: see section 22, above.

23–54 Policy effected through broker

53.—(1) Unless otherwise agreed, where a marine policy is effected on behalf of the assured by a broker, the broker is directly responsible to the insurer for the premium, and the insurer is directly responsible to the assured for the amount which may be payable in respect of losses, or in respect of returnable premium.

(2) Unless otherwise agreed, the broker has, as against the assured, a lien upon the policy for the amount of the premium and his charges in respect of effecting the policy; and, where he has dealt with the person who employs him as a principal, he has also a lien on the policy in respect of any balance on any insurance account which may be due to him from such person, unless when the debt was incurred he had reason to believe that such person was only an agent.

Commentary. Subsection (1) is a rule unique to marine insurance and to other policies issued by Lloyd's. It is based on the fiction that the broker has passed the premium paid by the assured to the underwriter, and the underwriter has loaned it back to the broker. As a result, the underwriter is the broker's creditor.[40]

23–55 Effect of receipt on policy

54. Where a marine policy effected on behalf of the assured by a broker acknowledges the receipt of the premium, such acknowledgment is, in the absence of fraud, conclusive as between the insurer and the assured, but not as between the insurer and broker.

Commentary. The usual course of dealing at Lloyd's provides for quarterly settlements between brokers and underwriters. In practice, therefore, brokers will not forward premiums to underwriters, but policies will nevertheless be issued acknowledging receipt. Section 54 in effect provides that the broker's failure to settle obliges the underwriter to look to the broker or its liquidator, and not to the assured (who will have previously paid the broker).

---

[38] *Lloyd* v. *Fleming* (1872) L.R. 7 Q.B. 299.

[39] See generally, Chap. 7. For return of premium, see sections 82 to 84, *infra*.

[40] *Power* v. *Butcher* (1829) 10 B. & C. 329, *per* Parke J. at p. 347; *Universo of Milan* v. *Merchants Marine Insurance* [1897] 2 Q.B. 93.

10. LOSS AND ABANDONMENT

Included and excluded losses 23–56

55.—(1) Subject to the provisions of this Act, and unless the policy otherwise provides, the insurer is liable for any loss proximately caused by a peril insured against, but subject as aforesaid, he is not liable for any loss which is not proximately caused by a peril insured against.

(2) In particular,—

(*a*) The insurer is not liable for any loss attributable to the wilful misconduct of the assured, but, unless the policy otherwise provides, he is liable for any loss proximately caused by a peril insured against, even though the loss would not have happened but for the misconduct or negligence of the master or crew;

(*b*) Unless the policy otherwise provides the insurer on ship or goods is not liable for any loss proximately caused by delay, although the delay be caused by a peril insured against;

(*c*) Unless the policy otherwise provides, the insurer is not liable for ordinary wear and tear, ordinary leakage and breakage, inherent vice or nature of the subject-matter insured, or for any loss proximately caused by rats or vermin, or for any injury to machinery not proximately caused by maritime perils.

Commentary. Subsection (1) reproduces the ordinary principle of proximate cause.[41] Subsection (2)(*a*) sets out the general rules of illegality: the assured may not recover for a loss caused by his own wilful misconduct, but that of his agents is no defence to the insurers.[42] Subsection (2)(*b*) maintains the common law distinction between hulls and cargo, in respect of which delay is not an insured peril, and freight, in respect of which delay is an insured peril. However, the Institute Freight Clauses now contain what has become known as the "time charter" clause: this excludes "any claim consequent on loss of time" and has the effect of preventing recovery of freight lost by delay in the absence of an event which frustrates the charterer's obligation to pay freight to the assured.[43] Subsection (2)(*c*) provides that inherent vice and related perils are not covered unless the policy expressly or impliedly confers cover. The House of Lords has decided that a policy against "the risks of heat, sweat and spontaneous combustion" insured, on its proper construction, those forms of loss even if arising from inherent vice.[44]

Partial and total loss 23–57

56.—(1) A loss may be either total or partial. Any loss other than a total loss, as hereinafter defined, is a partial loss.

(2) A total loss may be either an actual total loss or a constructive total loss.

(3) Unless a different intention appears from the terms of the policy, an insurance against total loss includes a constructive, as well as an actual, total loss.

(4) Where the assured brings an action for a total loss and the evidence proves only a partial loss, he may, unless the policy otherwise provides, recover for a partial loss.

---

[41] See Chap. 4.
[42] See Chap. 3.
[43] *Naviera de Canarias* v. *National Hispanica* [1978] A.C. 853.
[44] *Soya* v. *White* [1983] 1 Lloyd's Rep. 122. External causes of loss cannot constitute inherent vice: *Noten* v. *Harding* [1989] 2 Lloyd's Rep. 527.

(5) Where goods reach their destination in specie, but by reason of oblite-
ration of marks, or otherwise, they are incapable of identification, the loss, if
any, is partial, and not total.

Commentary. Non-marine insurance recognises total and partial
losses. Marine insurance recognises an intermediate form of loss, constructive total loss, This concept, defined in section 60, is in essence an
"economic" total loss, in that the subject matter, while not destroyed, is
for all practical purposes not repairable or recoverable. The assured
may treat a constructive total loss as an actual loss—by serving a notice
of abandonment under section 62—or as a partial loss, at his option.

23–58 Actual total loss

57.—(1) Where the subject-matter insured is destroyed, or so damaged as
to cease to be a thing of the kind insured, or where the assured is irretrievably
deprived thereof, there is an actual total loss.
(2) In the case of an actual total loss no notice of abandonment need be
given.

Commentary. Section 57(2) confirms that a notice of abandonment is
necessary only for the purpose of converting a constructive total loss
into an actual total loss. It is the practice, however, to serve a notice of
abandonment in all cases for the avoidance of doubt.

23–59 Missing ship

58. Where the ship concerned in the adventure is missing and after the lapse
of a reasonable time no news of her has been received, an actual total loss may
be presumed.

23–60 Effect of transhipment

59. Where, by a peril insured against, the voyage is interrupted at an intermediate port or place, under such circumstances as, apart from any special stipulation in the contract of affreightment, to justify the master in landing and re-
shipping the goods or other moveables, or in transhipping them, and sending
them on to their destination, the liability of the insurer continues, notwithstanding the landing or transhipment.

23–61 Constructive total loss defined

60.—(1)Subject to any express provision in the policy, there is a constructive total loss where the subject-matter insured is reasonably abandoned on
account of its actual total loss appearing to be unavoidable, or because it
could not be preserved from actual total loss without an expenditure which
would exceed its value when the expenditure had been incurred.
(2) In particular, there is a constructive total loss—
   (i) Where the assured is deprived of the possession of his ship or goods
       by a peril insured against, and (*a*) it is unlikely that he can recover the
       ship or goods, as the case may be, or (*b*) the cost of recovering the
       ship or goods, as the case may be, would exceed their value when
       recovered; or
   (ii) In the case of damage to a ship, where she is so damaged by a peril
        insured against that the cost of repairing the damage would exceed
        the value of the ship when repaired.
        In estimating the cost of repairs, no deduction is to be made in

respect of general average contributions to those repairs payable by other interests, but account is to be taken of the expense of future salvage operations and of any future general average contributions to which the ship would be liable if repaired; or

(iii) In the case of damage to goods, where the cost of repairing the damage and forwarding the goods to their destination would exceed their value on arrival.

Commentary. Subsection (1) countenances two forms of constructive total loss: reasonable abandonment, which is to be assessed on objective grounds,[45] and the occurrence of damage which renders the vessel beyond economic repair. In the case of a valued policy, the value of the vessel is its actual market value and not its agreed value: See section 27(4).

Subsection (2)(i)(*a*) has been taken to mean that recovery must be unlikely *within a reasonable time.* This will commonly be taken to be one year, although the period may be less if the policy covers loss of profits.

The time at which the classification of a loss as an actual or constructive total loss is to be made, is when the notice of abandonment has been accepted or rejected by the insurer.[46]

Effect of constructive total loss 23–62

61. Where there is a constructive total loss the assured may either treat the loss as a partial loss, or abandon the subject-matter insured to the insurer and treat the loss as if it were an actual total loss.

Abandonment 23–63

62.—(1) Subject to the provisions of this section, where the assured elects to abandon the subject-matter insured to the insurer, he must give notice of abandonment. If he fails to do so the loss can only be treated as a partial loss.

(2) Notice of abandonment may be given in writing, or by word of mouth or partly in writing and partly by word of mouth and may be given in any terms which indicate the intention of the assured to abandon his insured interest in the subject-matter insured unconditionally to the insurer.

(3) Notice of abandonment must be given with reasonable diligence after the receipt of reliable information of the loss, but where the information is of a doubtful character the assured is entitled to a reasonable time to make inquiry.

(4) Where notice of abandonment is properly given, the rights of the assured are not prejudiced by the fact that the insurer refuses to accept the abandonment.

(5) The acceptance may be either express or implied from the conduct of the insurer. The mere silence of the insurer after notice is not an acceptance.

(6) Where notice of abandonment is accepted the abandonment is irrevocable. The acceptance of the notice conclusively admits liability for the loss and the sufficiency of the notice.

(7) Notice of abandonment is unnecessary where, at the time when the assured receives information of the loss, there would be no possibility of benefit to the insurer if notice were given to him.

(8) Notice of abandonment may be waived by the insurer.

(9) Where an insurer has reinsured his risk, no notice of abandonment need be given by him.

---

[45] *Marstrand Fishing* v. *Beer* [1937] 1 All E.R. 158.
[46] *The Bamburi* [1982] 1 Lloyd's Rep. 312.

Commentary. Subsection (6) is subject to the general rules of common mistake. Thus if the insurer accepts a notice of abandonment in the genuine belief that the loss had occurred as the result of an insured peril, but the loss was in fact caused by an uninsured peril, the notice is ineffective and its acceptance a nullity.[47]

23–64 Effect of abandonment

63.—(1) Where there is a valid abandonment the insurer is entitled to take over the interest of the assured in whatever may remain of the subject-matter insured, and all proprietary rights incidental thereto.

(2) Upon the abandonment of a ship, the insurer thereof is entitled to any freight in course of being earned, and which is earned by her subsequent to the casualty causing the loss, less the expenses of earning it incurred after the casualty; and, whether the ship is carrying the owner's goods, the insurer is entitled to a reasonable remuneration for the carriage of them subsequent to the casualty causing the loss.

Commentary. The right of an insurer to take, by way of abandonment, whatever may remain of the subject-matter, applies to both actual and constructive total losses, although section 63(1) implies that abandonment is relevant only to the latter. In practice abandonment will be more significant in cases of constructive total loss, as actual total loss by its very definition will leave very little of the subject-matter available for salvage.

The power of an insurer to exercise the legal rights of the assured against third parties is conferred by section 74 (subrogation).

11. PARTIAL LOSSES

23–65 Particular average loss

64.—(1) A particular average loss is a partial loss of the subject-matter insured, caused by a peril insured against, and which is not a general average loss.

(2) Expenses incurred by or on behalf of the assured for the safety or preservation of the subject-matter insured, other than general average and salvage charges, are called particular charges. Particular charges are not included in particular average.

Commentary. The Marine Insurance Act 1906 distinguishes between two forms of partial loss: particular average and general average. A general average act is defined in section 66 as any sacrifice or expenditure on the assured's behalf reasonably made for the purpose of preserving other imperilled property. Loss resulting from such an act falls within the terms of an ordinary marine policy, although the assured (and thus the insurer, by way of subrogation) is entitled to claim a rateable proportion of this loss by way of contribution from the persons whose property was preserved as a result of the general average act. By the same token, if the assured is the beneficiary of the general average act of another, he is obliged to make a general average contribution under section 66, but may recover it from the insurer as a marine partial loss: section 73.

---

[47] *Norwich Union* v. *Price* [1934] A.C. 555.

Particular average is, under section 64(1), any form of partial loss other than a general average loss. Recovery excludes "particular charges," as defined in section 64(2). Particular charges are expenses incurred in the preservation of the assured subject-matter, and are recoverable not under the contract of marine insurance as such but under the supplementary contract in the "suing and labouring" clause (see section 78). "Salvage charges" are not "particular charges" (section 64(2)) and are thus recoverable under the policy as part of particular average (section 65(1)). "Salvage charges" are defined in section 65(2) as maritime—as opposed to contractual—salvage charge. Consequently, non-contractual salvage charges are recoverable under the policy itself, while contractual charges are recoverable under the "suing and labouring" clause. Most salvage operations are today conducted under the "Lloyd's Open Form," which is generally accepted to be contractual salvage and thus outside sections 64 and 65 but within section 78.

Salvage charges 23–66

65.—(1) Subject to any express provision in the policy, salvage charges incurred in preventing a loss by perils insured against may be recovered as a loss by those perils.

(2) "Salvage charges" means the charges recoverable under maritime law by a salvor independently of contract. They do not include the expenses of services in the nature of salvage rendered by the assured or his agents, or any person employed for hire by them for the purposes of averting a peril insured against. Such expenses, where properly incurred, may be recovered as particular charges or as a general average loss, according to the circumstances under which they were incurred.[48]

General average loss 23–67

66.—(1) A general average loss is a loss caused by or directly consequential on a general average act. It includes a general average expenditure as well as a general average sacrifice.

(2) There is a general average act where any extraordinary sacrifice or expenditure is voluntarily and reasonably made or incurred in time of peril for the purposes of preserving the property imperilled in the common adventure.

(3) Where there is a general average loss, the party on whom it falls is entitled, subject to the conditions imposed by maritime law, to a rateable contribution from the other parties interested, and such contribution is called a general average contribution.

(4) Subject to any express provision in the policy, where the assured has incurred a general average expenditure, he may recover from the insurer in respect of the proportion of the loss which falls upon him; and, in the case of general average sacrifice, he may recover from the insurer in respect of the whole loss without having enforced his right of contribution from the other parties liable to contribute.

(5) Subject to any express provision in the policy, where the assured has paid, or is liable to pay, a general average contribution in respect of the subject insured, he may recover therefor from the insurer.

(6) In the absence of express stipulation, the insurer is not liable for any general average loss or contribution where the loss was not incurred for the purpose of avoiding, or in connection with the avoidance of, a peril insured against.

---

[48] See the note to s.64.

(7) Where ship, freight, and cargo, or any two of those interests, are owned by the same assured, the liability of the insurer in respect of general average losses or contributions is to be determined as if those subjects were owned by different persons.[49]

12. MEASURE OF INDEMNITY

23–68 Extent of liability of insurer for loss

67.—(1) The sum which the assured can recover in respect of a loss on a policy by which he is insured, in the case of an unvalued policy to the full extent of the insurable value, or, in the case of a valued policy to the full extent of the value fixed by the policy, is called the measure of indemnity.

(2) Where there is a loss recoverable under the policy, the insurer, or each insurer if there be more than one, is liable for such proportion of the measure of indemnity as the amount of his subscription bears to the value fixed by the policy in the case of a valued policy, or to the insurable value in the case of an unvalued policy.

Commentary. Section 67 simply provides that the assured can recover only the measure of indemnity. This is defined in sections 68 to 77.

23–69 Total loss

68. Subject to the provisions of this Act and to any express provision in the policy, where there is a total loss of the subject-matter insured,—

(1) If the policy be a valued policy, the measure of indemnity is the sum fixed by the policy:

(2) If the policy can be an unvalued policy, the measure of indemnity is the insurable value of the subject-matter insured.

Commentary. Most policies are valued, and losses fall to be assessed in accordance with the valuation, which is in most cases conclusive: see the note to section 27. In other cases the measure of indemnity is based on the "insurable" value of the subject-matter, as defined by section 16.

23–70 Partial loss of ship

69. Where a ship is damaged, but is not totally lost, the measure of indemnity, subject to any express provision in the policy, is as follows;

(1) Where the ship has been repaired, the assured is entitled to the reasonable cost of the repairs, less the customary deductions, but not exceeding the sum insured in respect of any one casualty:

(2) Where the ship has been only partially repaired, the assured is entitled to the reasonable cost of such repairs, computed as above, and also to be indemnified for the reasonable depreciation, if any, arising from the unrepaired damage, provided that the aggregate amount shall not exceed the cost of repairing the whole damage, computed as above:

(3) Where the ship has not been repaired, and has not been sold in her damaged state during the risk, the assured is entitled to be indemnified for the reasonable depreciation arising from the unrepaired damage, but not exceeding the reasonable cost of repairing such damage, computed as above.

Commentary. Section 69 does not deal with the case in which an unrepaired vessel has been sold. However, it had been established prior to the 1906 Act[50] that the measure is *either* the reasonable cost of repairs

---

[49] See the note to s.64.
[50] In *Pitman* v. *Universal Marine* (1882) 9 Q.B.D. 192.

(less customary deduction) *or* the difference between unrepaired market value and actual sale price, whichever is less.

"Customary deduction" was fixed by the common law as one-third. However, the Institute Hulls Clauses presently provide for payment "without deduction new for old."

Partial loss of freight 23–71

70. Subject to any express provision the policy, where there is a partial loss of freight, the measure of indemnity is such proportion of the sum fixed by the policy in the case of a valued policy or of the insurable value in the case of an unvalued policy, as the proportion of freight lost by the assured bears to the whole freight at the risk of the assured under the policy.

Partial loss of goods, merchandise, etc. 23–72

71.—Where there is a partial loss of goods, merchandise, or other moveables, the measure of indemnity, subject to any express provision in the policy, is as follows:

(1) Where part of the goods, merchandise or other moveables insured by a valued policy is totally lost, the measure of indemnity is such proportion of the sum fixed by the policy as the insurable value of the whole, ascertained as in the case of an unvalued policy:

(2) Where part of the goods, merchandise, or other moveables insured by an unvalued policy is totally lost, the measure of indemnity is the insurable value of the part lost, ascertained as in case of total loss:

(3) Where the whole or any part of the goods or merchandise insured has been delivered damaged at its destination, the measure of indemnity is such proportion of the sum fixed by the policy in the case of a valued policy, or of the insurable value in the case of an unvalued policy, as the difference between the gross sound and damaged values at the place of arrival bears to the gross sound value:

(4) "Gross value" means the wholesale price or, if there be no such price, the estimated value, with, in either case, freight, landing charges, and duty paid beforehand; provided that, in the case of goods or merchandise customarily sold in bond, the bonded price is deemed to be the gross value. "Gross proceeds" means the actual price obtained at a sale where all charges on sale are paid by the sellers.

Apportionment of valuation 23–73

72.—(1) Where different species of property are insured under a single valuation, the valuation must be apportioned over the different species in proportion to their respective insurable values, as in the case of an unvalued policy. The insured value of any part of a species is such proportion of the total of the total insured value of the same as the insurable value of the part bears to the insurable value of the whole, ascertained in both cases as provided by this Act.

(2) Where a valuation has to be apportioned, and particulars of the prime cost of each separate species, quality or description of goods cannot be ascertained, the division of the valuation may be made over the net arrived sound values of the different species, qualities, or descriptions of goods.

General average contributions and salvage charges 23–74

73.—(1) Subject to any express provision in the policy, where the assured has paid, or is liable for, any general average contribution, the measure of indemnity is the full amount of such contribution, if the subject-matter liable to contribution is insured for its full contributory value; but, if such subject-matter be not insured for its full contributory value, or if only part of it be insured, the indemnity payable by the insurer must be reduced in proportion to the under insurance, and where there has been a particular average loss which constitutes a deduction from the contributory value, and for which the insurer is liable, that amount must be deducted from the insured value in order to ascertain what the insurer is liable to contribute.

(2) Where the insurer is liable for salvage charges the extent of his liability must be determined on the like principle.

Commentary. See the note to section 64. Section 73(1) incorporates the general principle that the assured is deemed to be his own insurer to the extent to which he is underinsured: section 81.

23–75 Liabilities to third parties

74. Where the assured has effected an insurance in express terms against any liability to a third party, the measure of indemnity, subject to any express provision in the policy, is the amount paid or payable by him to such third party in respect of such liability.

23–76 General provisions as to measure of indemnity

75.—(1) Where there has been a loss in respect of any subject-matter not expressly provided for in the foregoing provisions of this Act, the measure of indemnity shall be ascertained, as nearly as may be, in accordance with those provisions, in so far as applicable to the particular case.

(2) Nothing in the provisions of this Act relating to the measure of indemnity shall affect the rules relating to double insurance, or prohibit the insurer from disproving interest wholly or in part, or from showing that at the time of the loss the whole or any part of the subject-matter insured was not at risk under the policy.

23–77 Particular average warranties

76.—(1) Where the subject-matter insured is warranted free from particular average, the assured cannot recover for a loss of part, other than a loss incurred by a general average sacrifice, unless the contract contained in the policy be apportionable; but, if the contract be apportionable, the assured may recover for a total loss of any apportionable part.

(2) Where the subject-matter insured is warranted free from particular average, either wholly or under a certain percentage, the insurer is nevertheless liable for salvage charges, and for particular charges and other expenses properly incurred pursuant to the provisions of the suing and labouring clause in order to avert a loss insured against.

(3) Unless the policy otherwise provides, where the subject-matter insured is warranted free from particular average under a specified percentage, a general average loss cannot be added to a particular average loss to make up the specified percentage.

(4) For the purpose of ascertaining whether the specified percentage has been reached, regard shall be had only to the actual loss suffered by the subject-matter insured. Particular charges and the expenses of and incidental to ascertaining and proving the loss must be excluded.

Commentary. An "f.p.a." warranty confines the assured to recovering for total losses only, subject to the ordinary rules concerning the recovery of general average losses and salvage charges. Such warranties have fallen into disuse in England.

23–78 Successive losses

77.—(1) Unless the policy otherwise provides, and subject to the provisions of this Act, the insurer is liable for successive losses, even though the total amount of such losses may exceed the sum insured.

(2) Where, under the same policy, a partial loss, which has not been

repaired or otherwise made good, is followed by a total loss, the assured can only recover in respect of the total loss:

Provided that nothing in this section shall affect the liability of the insurer under the suing and labouring clause.

Commentary. It follows from subsection (2) that if an insured partial loss is followed by an uninsured total loss, the assured cannot recover the policy moneys but is able to recover suing and labouring costs in respect of the partial loss.[51]

Suing and labouring clause   23–79

78.—(1) Where the policy contains a suing and labouring clause, the engagement thereby entered into is deemed to be supplementary to the contract of insurance, and the assured may recover from the insurer any expenses properly incurred pursuant to the clause, notwithstanding that the insurer may have paid for a total loss, or that the subject-matter may have been warranted free from particular average, either wholly or under a certain percentage.

(2) General average losses and contributions and salvage charges, as defined by this Act, are not recoverable under the suing and labouring clause.

(3) Expenses incurred for the purpose of averting or diminishing any loss not covered by the policy are not recoverable under the suing and labouring clause.

(4) It is the duty of the assured and his agents, in all cases, to take such measures as may be reasonable for the purpose of averting or minimising a loss.

Commentary. Subsections (1)–(3) are operative only where the policy itself contains a suing and labouring clause. They provide that a suing and labouring clause is a contract supplementary to the policy itself, so that the sums payable under the clause are additional to the policy indemnity. Irrecoverable under the suing and labouring clause are: general average losses and contributions (which are recoverable under the policy itself—see the notes to sections 64 and 73); non-contractual salvage charges (see the note to section 64); and expenses incurred in averting an uninsured loss. In the last-mentioned case, however, the assured can recover the costs of his attempts to mitigate as long as he reasonably anticipated the occurrence of an insured peril, even if his anticipation is subsequently proved to have been mistaken.[52]

The standard clause presently operating in England, under the Institute Clauses, obliges the insurer to contribute to charges "properly and reasonably incurred" in mitigating or preventing a loss. However, if the assured is underinsured, so that the assured is deemed to be his own insurer for the uninsured balance, the same proportionate deduction is applied to the suing and labouring expenses.

Subsection (4), which is stated to apply in all cases (including, presumably those rare cases in which there is no suing and labouring clause), imposes a duty on the assured and his agents to take reasonable steps to avert or minimise a loss. This sits uneasily alongside section 55(2)(a), which allows the assured to recover irrespective of negligence: this conflict was resolved by Mocatta J. in *Astrovlanis* v. *Linard*,[53] where

---

[51] *Livie* v. *Janson* (1810) 2 East 648.
[52] *Integrated Container Service* v. *British Traders Insurance* [1984] 1 Lloyd's Rep. 154.
[53] [1972] 2 Lloyd's Rep. 187.

it was held that section 78(4) did not impose a duty of care on the master and crew, but only on the assured himself and his immediate agents. Where the duty does apply, the assured owes the standard of care reasonably to be expected of a person in charge of a vessel of the type in question[54] and must take such steps as would a reasonable man seeking to preserve his own property.[55]

13. RIGHTS OF INSURER ON PAYMENT

23–80 Right of subrogation

   79.—(1) Where the insurer pays for a total loss, either of the whole, or in the case of goods of any apportionable part, of the subject-matter insured, he thereupon becomes entitled to take over the interest of the assured in whatever may remain of the subject-matter so paid for, and he is thereby subrogated to all the rights and remedies of the assured in and in respect of that subject-matter as from the time of the casualty causing the loss.

   (2) Subject to the foregoing provisions, where the insurer pays for a partial loss, he acquires no title to the subject-matter insured, or such part of it as may remain, but he is thereupon subrogated to all rights and remedies of the assured in and in respect of the subject-matter insured as from the time of the casualty causing the loss, in so far as the assured has been indemnified, according to this Act, by such payment for the loss.[56]

23–81 Right of contribution

   80.—(1) Where the assured is over-insured by double insurance, each insurer is bound, as between himself and the other insurers, to contribute rateably to the loss in proportion to the amount for which he is liable under his contract.

   (2) If any insurer pays more than his proportion of the loss, he is entitled to maintain an action for contribution against the other insurers, and is entitled to the like remedies as a surety who has paid more than his proportion of the debt.[57]

23–82 Effect of under insurance

   81. Where the assured is insured for an amount less than the insurable value or, in the case of a valued policy, for an amount less than the policy valuation, he is deemed to be his own insurer in respect of the uninsured balance.

   Commentary. This section entrenches the principle of average in marine insurance. It is operative where the assured is underinsured under an unvalued policy and suffers a partial loss: he may in this situation recover only that proportion of his loss which the sum insured bears to the insurable value of the subject-matter.

14. RETURN OF PREMIUM

23–83 Enforcement of return

   82. Where the premium or a proportionate part thereof is, by this Act, declared to be returnable,—

---

[54] *Stephen* v. *Scottish Boatowners Mutual* [1989] 1 Lloyd's Rep. 535.
[55] *I.C.S.* v. *British Traders Insurance, supra,* n. 52.
[56] See generally Chap. 8.
[57] See generally Chap. 8.

(*a*) If already paid, it may be recovered by the assured from the insurer; and

(*b*) If unpaid, it may be retained by the assured or his agent.

Return by agreement

23–84

83. Where the policy contains a stipulation for the return of the premium, or a proportionate part thereof, on the happening of a certain event, and that event happens, the premium, or, as the case may be, the proportionate part thereof, is thereupon returnable to the assured.

Return for failure of consideration

23–85

84.—(1) Where the consideration for the payment of the premium totally fails, and there has been no fraud or illegality on the part of the assured or his agents, the premium is thereupon returnable to the assured.

(2) Where the consideration for the payment of the premium is apportionable and there is a total failure of any apportionable part of the consideration, a proportionate part of the premium is, under the like conditions, thereupon returnable to the assured.

(3) In particular—

(*a*) Where the policy is void, or is avoided by the insurer as from the commencement of the risk, the premium is returnable, provided that there has been no fraud or illegality on the part of the assured; but if the risk is not apportionable, and has once attached, the premium is not returnable:

(*b*) Where the subject-matter insured, or part thereof, has never been imperilled, the premium, or, as the case may be, a proportionate part thereof, is returnable:

Provided that where the subject-matter has been insured "lost or not lost" and has arrived in safety at the time when the contract is concluded, the premium is not returnable unless, at such time, the insurer knew of the safe arrival.

(*c*) Where the assured has no insurable interest throughout the currency of the risk, the premium is returnable, provided that this rule does not apply to a policy effected by way of gaming or wagering;

(*d*) Where the assured has a defeasible interest which is terminated during the currency of the risk, the premium is not returnable;

(*e*) Where the assured has over-insured under an unvalued policy, a proportionate part of the premium is returnable;

(*f*) Subject to the foregoing provisions, where the assured has over-insured by double insurance, a proportionate part of the several premiums is returnable:

Provided that, if the policies are effected at different times, and any earlier policy has at any time borne the entire risk, of a claim has been paid on the policy in respect of the full sum insured thereby, no premium is returnable in respect of that policy, and when the double insurance is effected knowingly by the assured no premium is returnable.[58]

15. MUTUAL INSURANCE

Modification of Act in case of mutual insurance

23–86

85.—(1) Where two or more persons mutually agree to insure each other against marine losses there is said to be a mutual insurance.

(2) The provisions of this Act relating to the premium do not apply to mutual insurance, but a guarantee, or such other arrangement as may be agreed upon, may be substituted for the premium.

---

[58] See generally Chap. 7.

(3) The provisions of this Act, in so far as they may be modified by the agreement of the parties, may in the case of mutual insurance be modified by the terms of the policies issued by the association, or by the rules and regulations of the association.

(4) Subject to the exceptions mentioned in this section, the provisions of this Act apply to a mutual insurance.

Commentary. The insurance ponds of mutual insurers are constituted not by premiums as such, but by "calls" upon members in the event that the initial periodic subscription proves to be inadequate. In other respects the rules of mutual insurance association operate in much the same way as policy terms.

16. SUPPLEMENTARY

23–87 Ratification by assured

86. Where a contract of marine insurance is in good faith effected by one person on behalf of another, the person on whose behalf it is effected may ratify the contract even after he is aware of a loss.[59]

23–88 Implied obligations varied by agreement or usage

87.—(1) Where any right, duty, or liability, would arise under a contract of marine insurance by implication of law, it may be negatived or varied by express agreement, or by usage, if the usage be such as to bind both parties to the contract.

(2) The provisions of this section extend to any right, duty, or liability declared by this Act which may be lawfully modified by agreement.

23–89 Reasonable time, etc. a question of fact

88. Where by this Act any reference is made to reasonable time, reasonable premium, or reasonable diligence, the question what is reasonable is a question of fact.

23–90 Slip as evidence

89. Where there is a duly stamped policy, reference may be made, as heretofore, to the slip or covering note, in any legal proceeding.

23–91 Interpretation of terms

90. In this Act, unless the context or subject-matter otherwise requires—
"Action" includes counter-claim and set off:
"Freight" includes the profit derivable by a shipowner from the employment
   of his ship to carry his own goods or moveables, as well as freight payable
   by a third party, but does not include passage money:
"Moveables" means any moveable tangible property, other than the ship, and
   includes money, valuable securities, and other documents:
"Policy" means a marine policy.

23–92 Schedule 1—Rules for Construction of Policy

The following are the rules referred to by this Act for the construction of a policy in the above or other like form, where the context does not otherwise require:

---

[59] Ths rule is confined to marine insurance: *Grover* v. *Matthews* [1910] 2 K.B. 401.

Lost or not lost

1. Where the subject-matter is insured "lost or not lost," and the loss has occurred before the contract is concluded, the risk attaches unless, at such time the assured was aware of the loss, and the insurer was not.

From

2. Where the subject-matter is insured "from" a particular place, the risk does not attach until the ship starts on the voyage insured.

At and from

3.—(*a*) Where a ship is insured "at and from" a particular place, and she is at that place in good safety when the contract is concluded, the risk attaches immediately.

(*b*) If she be not at that place when the contract is concluded the risk attaches as soon as she arrives there in good safety, and, unless the policy otherwise provides, it is immaterial that she is covered by another policy for a specified time after arrival.

(*c*) Where chartered freight is insured "at and from" a particular place, and the ship is at that place in good safety when the contract is concluded, the risk attaches immediately. If she be not there when the contract is concluded, the risk attaches as soon as she arrives there in good safety.

(*d*) Where freight, other than chartered freight, is payable without special conditions and is insured "at and from" a particular place, the risk attaches pro rata as the goods or merchandise are shipped; provided that if there be cargo in readiness which belongs to the shipowner, or which some other person has contradicted with him to ship, the risk attaches as soon as the ship is ready to receive such cargo.

From the loading thereof

4. Where goods or other moveables are insured "from the loading thereof," the risk does not attach until such goods or moveables are actually on board, and the insurer is not liable for them while in transit from the shore to the ship.

Safely landed

5. Where the risk on goods or other moveables continues until they are "safely landed," they must be landed in the customary manner and within a reasonable time after arrival at the port of discharge, and if they are not so landed the risk ceases.

Touch and stay

6. In the absence of any further licence or usages, the liberty to touch and stay "at any port of place whatsoever" does not authorise the ship to depart from the course of her voyage from the port of departure to the port of destination.

Perils of the seas

7. The term "perils of the seas" refers only to fortuitous accidents or casualties of the seas. It does not include the ordinary action of the winds and waves.

Pirates

8. The term "pirates" includes passengers who mutiny and rioters who attack the ship from the shore.

Thieves

9. The term "thieves" does not cover clandestine theft or a theft committed by any one of the ship's company, whether crew or passengers.

Restraint of princes

10. The term "arrests. &c., of kings, princes, and people" refers to political or executive acts, and does not include a loss caused by a riot or by ordinary judicial process.

Barratry

11. The term "barratry" includes every wrongful act wilfully committed by the master or crew to the prejudice of the owner, or, as the case may be, the charterer.

All other perils

12. The term "all other perils" includes only perils similar in kind to the perils specifically mentioned in the policy.

Average unless general

13. The term "average unless general" means a partial loss of the subject-matter insured other than a general average loss, and does not include "particular charges."

Stranded

14. Where the ship has stranded, the insurer is liable for the excepted losses, although the loss is not attributable to the stranding, provided that when the stranding takes place the risk has attached, and, if the policy be on goods, that the damaged goods are on board.

Ship

15. The term "ship" includes the hull, materials and outfit, stores and provisions for the officers and crew, and, in the case of vessels engaged in a special trade, the ordinary fittings requisite for the trade, and also, in the case of a steamship, the machinery, boilers, and coals and engine stores, if owned by the assured.

Freight

16. The term "freight" includes the profit derivable by the shipowner from the employment of his ship to carry his own goods or moveables, as well as freight payable by a third party, but does not include passage money.

Goods

17. The term "goods" means good in the nature of merchandise and does not include personal effects or provisions and stores for use on board.

In the absence of any usage to the contrary, deck cargo and living animals must be insured specifically, and not under the general denomination of goods.

17. MARINE INSURANCE (GAMBLING POLICIES) ACT 1909

23–93 Prohibition of gambling on loss by maritime perils

Section 1(1) of this Act defines a contract "deemed to be a contract by way of gambling on loss by maritime perils," see paragraph 3–30, and continues: and the person effecting it shall be guilty of an offence and shall be liable, on summary conviction, to imprisonment, with or without hard labour, for a term not exceeding six months or to a fine not exceeding one hundred pounds, and in either case to forfeit to the Crown any money he may receive under the contract.

(2) Any broker or other person through whom, and any insurer with whom, any such contract is effected shall be guilty of an offence and liable on summary conviction to the like penalties if he acted knowing that the contract was by way of gambling on loss by maritime perils within the meaning of this Act.

(3) Proceedings under this Act shall not be instituted without the consent in England of the Attorney-General, in Scotland of the Lord Advocate, and in Ireland of the Attorney-General for Ireland.

(4) Proceedings under this Act shall not be instituted under this Act against a person (other than a person in the employment of the owner of the ship in relation to which the contract was made) alleged to have effected a contract by way of gambling on loss by maritime perils until an opportunity has been afforded him of showing that the contract was not such a contract as aforesaid, and any information given by that person for that purpose shall not be admissible in evidence against him in any prosecution under this Act.

(5) If proceedings under this Act are taken against any person (other than a person in the employment of the owner of the ship in relation to which the contract was made) for effecting such a contract, and the contract was made "interest or no interest" or "without further proof of interest than the policy itself," or "without benefit of salvage to the insurer," or subject to any other like term, the contract shall be deemed to be a contract by way of gambling on loss by maritime perils unless the contrary is proved.

(6) For the purpose of giving jurisdiction under this Act, every offence shall be deemed to have been committed either in the place in which the same actually was committed or in any place in which the offender may be.

(7) Any person aggrieved by an order or decision of a court of summary jurisdiction under this Act, may appeal to quarter sessions.

(8) For the purposes of this Act the expression "owner" includes charterer.

(9) Subsection (7) of this section shall not apply to Scotland.

Short title   23–94

2. This Act may be cited as the Maritime Insurance (Gambling Policies) Act 1909, and the Marine Insurance Act 1906, and this Act may be cited together as the Marine Insurance Acts 1906 and 1909.

APPENDIX

LIFE ASSURANCE ACT 1774[1]

(14 Geo. 3, c. 48)

An Act for regulating Insurances upon Lives, and for prohibiting all such Insur- **A–01** ances except in cases where the Persons insuring shall have an Interest in the Life or Death of the Persons insured.

Whereas it hath been found by experience that the making insurances on lives or other events wherein the assured shall have no interest hath introduced a mischievous kind of gaming:

No insurance to be made on lives, etc., by persons having no interest, etc.

From and after the passing of this Act no insurance shall be made by any person or persons, or on any other event or events whatsoever, wherein the person or persons for whose use, benefit, or on whose account such policy or policies shall be made, shall have no interest, or by way of gaming or wagering; and that every assurance made contrary to the true intent and meaning hereof shall be null and void to all intents and purposes whatsoever.

No policies on lives without inserting the names of persons interested, etc.

2. And . . . it shall not be lawful to make any policy or policies on the life or lives of any person or persons, or other event or events, without inserting in such policy or policies the person or persons name or names interested therein, or for whose use, benefit, or on whose account such policy is so made or underwrote.

How much may be recovered where the insured hath interest in lives

3. And . . . in all cases where the insured hath interest in such life or lives, event or events, no greater sum shall be recovered or received from the insurer or insurers than the amount of value of the interest of the insured in such life or lives, or other event or events.

Not to extend to insurances on ships, goods, etc.

4. Provided, always, that nothing herein contained shall extend or be construed to extend to insurances bona fide made by any person or persons on ships, goods, or merchandises, but every such insurance shall be as valid and effectual in the law as if this Act has not been made.

Amendment of 1973   A–02

By section 50 of the Insurance Companies Amendment Act 1973:

(1) Section 2 of the Life Assurance Act 1774 (policy on life or lives or other event or events not valid unless name or names of assured etc. inserted when policy is made) shall not invalidate a policy for the benefit of unnamed persons from time to time falling within a specified class or description if the class or description is stated in the policy with sufficient particularity to make it possible to establish the identity of all persons who at any given time are entitled to benefit under the policy.

(2) This section applies to policies effected before the passing of this Act as well as to policies effected thereafter.

---

[1] The Act applies to Scotland. It was extended to Ireland by the Life Insurance (Ireland) Act 1866.

FIRE PREVENTION (METROPOLIS) ACT 1774

(14 Geo. 3, c. 78)

A–03 Money insured on houses burnt how to be applied

83. And in order to deter and hinder ill-minded persons from wilfully setting their house or houses or other buildings on fire with a view of gaining to themselves the insurance money, whereby the lives and fortunes of many families may be lost or endangered: Be it further enacted . . . that it shall and may be lawful to and for the respective governors or directors of the several insurance officers for insuring houses or other buildings against loss by fire, and they are hereby authorised and required, upon the request of any person or persons interested in or intitled unto any house or houses or other buildings which may hereafter be burnt down, demolished or damaged by fire, or upon any grounds of suspicion that the owner or owners, occupier or occupiers, or other person or persons who shall have insured such house or houses or other buildings have been guilty of fraud, or of wilfully setting their house or houses or other buildings on fire, to cause the insurance money to be laid out and expended as far as the same will go, towards rebuilding, reinstating or repairing such house or houses or other buildings so burnt down, demolished or damaged by fire, unless the party or parties claiming such insurance money shall, within sixty days next after his, her or their claim is adjusted, give a sufficient security to the governors or directors of the insurance office where such house or houses or other buildings are insured, that the same insurance money shall be laid out and expended as aforesaid, or unless the said insurance money shall be in that time settled and disposed of to and amongst all the contending parties, to the satisfaction and approbation of such governors or directors of such insurance office respectively.

A–04 No action to lie against a person where the fire accidentally begins[2]

86. And . . . no action, suit or process whatever shall be had, maintained, or prosecuted against any person in whose house, chamber, stable barn or other building or on whose estate any fire shall . . . accidentally[3] begin, nor shall any recompence be made by such person for any damage suffered thereby, any law, usage or custom to the contrary notwithstanding: And in such case, if any action be brought, the defendant may plead the general issue, and give this Act and the special matter in evidence at any trial thereupon to be had; . . . provided that no contract or agreement made between landlord and tenant shall be hereby defeated or made void.[4]

---

[2] At common law, *semble*, a householder was absolutely responsible to others for a fire originating on his premises, act of God, or a stranger only excepted: see *Beaulieu* v. *Fingham* (1401) Y.B. 2 Hen. 4, fo. 18, pl. 6; *Turberville* v. *Stamp* (1698) 1 Ld. Raym. 264; Lord Goddard C.J. in *Balfour* v. *Bart-King* [1957] 1 Q.B. 496. This provision of 1794 replaces the Apprehension of Housebreakers Act 1706 (6 Anne, c 31) and like s.83 is of general application in England and Wales at least: *Richards* v. *Easto* (1846) 3 Dow. & L. 515; *Filliter* v. *Phippard* (1847) 11 Q.B. 347. (As to Ireland, see Accidental Fires Act (Northern Ireland) 1944 (c. 5) (N.I.), s.1.)

[3] The provision protects the householder only if the fire "accidentally" began; he remains liable at common law for damage done by fire to the property of his neighbours or his landlord caused by (1) his negligence or (2) that of his servants: *Filliter's case (supra)*; *Musgrove* v. *Pandelis* [1919] 2 K.B. 43 or (3) that of an independent contractor whom he invites onto his premises to carry out work there; *Balfour* v. *Barty-King* [1957] 1 Q.B. 496, which shows how advisable it is for a householder specially to insure against this liability.

See also *Sturge* v. *Hackett* [1962] 1 W.L.R. 1257, applying those cases; *Mason* v. *Levy Auto Parts of England* [1967] 2 Q.B. 530 (fire caused by non-natural use of land not "accidental"); *Goldman* v. *Hargrave* [1967] 1 A.C. 645 (negligence in dealing with fire of tree which originally was accidental: occupier held liable).

[4] *Semble*, a householder's liability for fire cannot otherwise be increased by contract; thus an innkeeper is not liable to a guest for the destruction of his goods in an accidental fire: *Williams* v. *Owen* [1955] 1 W.L.R. 1293.

GAMING ACT 1845

(8 & 9 Vict. c. 109)

18. And be it enacted, that all contracts or agreements, whether by parole **A–05** or in writing, by way of gaming or wagering, shall be null and void; and that no suit shall be brought or maintained in any court of law or equity for recovering any sum of money or valuable thing alleged to be won upon any wager, or which shall have been deposited in the hands of any person to abide the event on which any wager shall have been made: provided always, that this enactment shall not be deemed to apply to any subscription or contribution, or agreement to subscribe or contribute, for or toward any plate, prize, or sum of money to be awarded to the winner or winners of any lawful game, sport, pastime, or exercise.

POLICIES OF ASSURANCE ACT 1867[5]

(30 & 31 Vict. c. 144)

An Act to enable Assignees of Policies of Life Assurance to sue thereon in their **A–06** own names.   [20th August 1867]

Assignees of life policies, empowered to sue

1. Any person or corporation now being or hereafter becoming entitled, by assignment or other derivative title, to a policy of life assurance, and possessing at the time of action brought the right in equity to receive and the right to give an effectual discharge to the assurance company liable under such policy for monies thereby assured or secured, shall be at liberty to sue at law in the name of such person or corporation to recover such monies.

Defence or reply on equitable grounds

2. In any action on a policy of life assurance, a defence on equitable grounds, or a reply to such defence on similar grounds, may be respectively pleaded and relied upon in the same manner and to the same extent as in any other personal action.

Notice of assignment

3. No assignment after the passing of this Act of a policy of life assurance shall confer on the assignee therein named, his executors, administrators, or assigns, any right to sue for the amount of such policy, or the monies assured or secured thereby, until a written notice of the date and purport of such assignment shall have been given to the assurance company liable under such policy at their principal place of business for the time being, or in case they have two or more principal places of business, than at some one of such principal places of business, either in England or Scotland or Ireland; and the date on which such notice shall be received shall regulate the priority of all claims under any assignment[6]; and a payment bona fide made in respect of any policy by any assurance company before the date on which such notice shall have been received shall be as valid against the assignee giving such notice as if this Act had not been passed.

Principal place of business to be specified on polices

4. Every assurance company shall, on every policy issued by them after the thirtieth day of September one thousand eight hundred and sixty-seven, specify

---

[5] This Act applies to Northern Ireland.

[6] This does not affect rights of claimants *inter se* on equitable grounds: *Newman* v. *Newman* (1885) 28 Ch.D. 674; § 16–50, *supra*.

their principal place or principal places of business at which notices of assignment may be given in pursuance of this Act.

Mode of assignment

5. Any such assignment may be made either by endorsement on the policy or by a separate instrument in the words or to the effect set forth in the schedule hereto, such endorsement or separate instrument being duly stamped.[7]

A–07 Receipt of notice of assignment

6. Every assurance company to whom notice shall have been duly given of the assignment of any policy under which they are liable shall, upon the request in writing of any person by whom any such notice was given or signed, or of his executors or administrators, and upon payment in each case of a fee not exceeding five shillings, deliver an acknowledgement in writing under the hand of the manager, secretary, treasurer, or other principal officer of the assurance company, of their receipt of such notice; and every such written acknowledgment, if signed by a person being de jure or de facto the manager, secretary, treasurer, or other principal officer of the assurance company whose acknowledgement the same purports to be, shall be conclusive evidence as against such assurance company of their having duly received the notice to which such acknowledgement relates.

Interpretation

7. In the construction and for the purposes of this Act the expression "policy of life assurance" or "policy" shall mean any instrument by which the payment of monies by or out of the funds of an assurance company, on the happening of any contingency depending on the duration of human life, is assured or secured[8]; and the expression "assurance company" shall mean and include every corporation, association, society, or company[9] now or hereafter carrying on the business of assuring lives, or survivorships, either alone or in conjunction with any other object or objects.

Saving of contracts under 16 & 17 Vict. c. 45, or 27 & 28 Vict. c. 43. and of engagements by friendly societies

8. Provided always, that this Act shall not apply to any policy of assurance granted or to be granted or to any contract for a payment on death entered into or to be entered into in pursuance of the provisions of the Government Annuities Act 1853, and the Government Annuities Act 1864,[10] or either of those Acts, or to any engagement for payment on death by any friendly society.

Short title

9. For all purposes this Act may be cited as "The Policies of Assurance Act 1867."

SCHEDULE

I, *A.B.*, of, &c., in consideration of, &c., do hereby assign unto *C.D.*, of &c., his executors, administrators, and assigns, [the within] policy of assurance granted, &c [*here describe the policy*]. In witness, &c.

---

[7] See Stamp Act 1891, s.118.
[8] Including policies against death by accident only, *Re Turcan* (1888) 40 Ch.D. 5.
[9] The Act would not apply to a policy issued by Lloyd's underwriters: see, *e.g. Re Gladitz* (1937) 106 L.J. Ch. 254.
[10] Now Government Annuities Act 1929, as amended.

MARRIED WOMEN'S PROPERTY ACT 1882[11]

(45 & 46 Vict. c. 75)

**Moneys payable under policy of assurance not to form part of estate of   A–08
assured**

11. A married woman may affect a policy upon her own life or the life of her
husband for her own benefit; and the same and all benefit thereof shall ensure
accordingly.

A policy of assurance effected by any man on his own life, and expressed to be
for the benefit of his wife, or of his children, or of his wife and children or any of
them, or by any woman on her own life, and expressed to be for the benefit of
her husband, or of her children, or of her husband and children, or any of them,
shall create a trust in favour of the objects therein named, and the money payable under any such policy shall not, so long as any object of the trust remains
unperformed, form part of the estate of the insured, or be subject to his or her
debts: Provided that if it shall be proved that the policy was effected and the premiums paid with intent to defraud the creditors of the insured, they shall be
entitled to receive, out of the moneys payable under the policy, a sum equal to
the premiums so paid. The insured may by the policy, or by any memorandum
under his or her hand, appoint a trustee or trustees of the moneys, payable
under the policy, and from time to time appoint a new trustee or new trustees
thereof, and may make provision for the appointment of a new trustee or new
trustees thereof, and for the investment of the moneys payable under such
policy. In default of any such appointment of a trustee, such policy, immediately
on its being effected, shall vest in the insured and his or her legal personal representatives, in trust for the purposes aforesaid. If, at the time of the death of
the insured, or at any time afterwards, there shall be no trustee, or it shall be
expedient to appoint a new trustee or new trustees, a trustee or trustees or a new
trustee or new trustees may be appointed by any court having jurisdiction under
the provisions of the Trustee Act 1850, or the Acts amending and extending the
same.[12] The receipt of a trustee or trustees duly appointed, or in default of any
such appointment, or in default of notice to the insurance office, the receipt of
the legal personal representative of the insured shall be a discharge to the office
for the sum secured by the policy, or for the value thereof, in whole or in part.

THIRD PARTIES (RIGHTS AGAINST INSURERS) ACT 1930

(20 & 21 Geo. 5, c. 25)

An Act to confer on third parties rights against insurers of third–party risks in   **A–09**
the event of the insured becoming insolvent, and in certain other events.

[10th July 1930.]

**Rights of third parties against insurers on bankruptcy, etc. of the
insured**

1.—(1) Where under any contract of insurance a person (hereinafter
referred to as the insured) is insured against liabilities to third parties which
he may incur, then—

(a) in the event of the insured becoming bankrupt or making a composition or arrangement with his creditors; or

(b) in the case of the insured being a company, in the event of a winding-
up order [or an administration order] being made, or a resolution for
a voluntary winding-up being passed, with respect to the company, or

---

[11] As amended by the Law Reform (Married Women and Tortfeasors) Act 1935.
[12] See now Trustee Act 1925, s.41.

of a receiver or manager of the company's business or undertaking being duly appointed, or of profession being taken, by or on behalf of the holders of any debentures secured by a floating charge, of any property comprised in or subject to the charge [or of a voluntary arrangement proposed for the purposes of Part I of the Insolvency Act 1986 being approved under that part];

if, either before or after the event, any such liability as aforesaid is incurred by the insured, his rights against the insurer under the contract in respect of the liability shall, notwithstanding anything in any Act or rule of law to the contary, be transferred to and vest in the third party to whom the liability was so incurred.

(2) Where [the estate of any person falls to be administered in accordance with an order under section 421 of the Insolvency Act 1986], then, if any debt provable in bankruptcy [(in Scotland, any claim accepted in the sequestration)] is owing by the deceased in respect of a liability against which he was insured under a contract of insurance as being a liability to a third party, the deceased debtor's rights against the insurer under the contract in respect of that liability shall, notwithstanding anything in [any such order], be transferred to and vest in the person to whom the debt is owing.

(3) In so far as any contract of insurance made after the commencement of this Act in respect of any liability of the insured to third parties purports, whether directly or indirectly, to avoid the contract or to alter the rights of the parties thereunder upon the happening to the insured of any of the events specified in paragraph (a) or paragraph (b) of subsection (1) of this section or upon the [estate of any person falling to be administered in accordance with an order under section 421 of the Insolvency Act 1986], the contract shall be of no effect.

(4) Upon a transfer under subsection (1) or subsection (2) of this section, the insurer shall, subject to the provisions of section three of this Act, be under the same liability to the third party as he would have been under to the insured, but—

(a) if the liability of the insurer to the insured exceeds the liability of the insured to the third party, nothing in this Act shall affect the rights of the insured against the insurer in respect of the excess; and
(b) if the liability of the insurer to the insured is less than the liability of the insured to the third party, nothing in this Act shall affect the rights of the third party against the insured in respect of the balance.

(5) For the purposes of this Act, the expression "liabilities to third parties," in relation to a person insured under any contract of insurance, shall not include any liability of that person in the capacity of insurer under some other contract of insurance.

(6) This Act shall not apply—

(a) where a company is wound up voluntarily merely for the purposes of reconstruction or of amalgamation with another company; or
(b) to any case to which subsections (1) and (2) of section seven of the Workmen's Compensation Act 1925 applies.

Duty to give necessary information to third parties

2.—(1) In the event of any person becoming bankrupt or making a composition or arrangement with his creditors, or in the event of [the estate of any person falling to be administered in accordance with an order under section 421 of the Insolvency Act 1986] or in the event of a winding-up order [or an administration order] being made, or a resolution for a voluntary winding-up being passed, with respect to any company or of a receiver or manager of the company's business or undertaking being duly appointed or of possession being taken by or on behalf of the holders of any debentures secured by a floating charge of any property, comprised in or subject to the charge it shall be the duty of the bankrupt, debtor, personal representative of the deceased debtor or company, and, as the case may be, of the trustee in bankruptcy, trustee, liquidator, [administrator], receiver, or manager, or person in possession of the property to give at the request of any person claiming that the bankrupt, debtor, deceased debtor, or company is under a liability to him such information as may reasonably be required by him for the purpose of ascertaining whether any rights have been transferred to and vested in him by this Act and for the purpose of enforcing such rights, if any, and any contract of insurance, in so far as it purports, whether directly or indirectly, to avoid the contract or to alter the rights of the parties thereunder upon the giving of any such information in the events aforesaid or otherwise to prohibit or prevent the giving thereof in the said events shall be of no effect.

[(1A) The reference in subsection (1) of this section to a trustee includes a reference to the supervisor of a voluntary arrangement proposed for the purposes of, and approved under, Part I or Part VIII of the Insolvency Act 1986.]

(2) If the information given to any person in pursuance of subsection (1) of this section discloses reasonable ground for supposing that there have or may have been transferred to him under this Act rights against any particular insurer, that insurer shall be subject to the same duty as is imposed by the said subsection on the persons therein mentioned.

(3) The duty to give information imposed by this section shall include a duty to allow all contracts of insurance, receipts for premiums, and other relevant documents in the possession or power of the person on whom the duty is so imposed to be inspected and copies thereof to be taken.

Settlement between insurers and insured persons

3. Where the insured has become bankrupt or where in the case of the insured being a company, a winding-up order [or an administration order] has been made or a resolution for a voluntary winding-up has been passed, with respect to the company, no agreement made between the insurer and the insured after liability has been incurred to a third party and after the commencement of the bankruptcy or winding-up [or the day of the making of the administration order], as the case may be, nor any waiver, assignment, or other disposition made by, or payment made to the insured after the commencement [or day] aforesaid shall be effective to defeat or affect the rights transferred to the third party under this Act, but those rights shall be the same as if no such agreement, waiver, assignment, disposition or payment had been made.

Application to Scotland

4. In the application of this Act to Scotland—

(a) [. . .]
(b) any reference to [an estate falling to be administered in accordance with an order under section 421 of the Insolvency Act 1986] shall be deemed to include a reference to an award of sequestration of the estate of a deceased debtor, and a reference to an appointment of a judicial factor, under section [11A of the Judicial Factors (Scotland) Act 1889], on the insolvent estate of a deceased person.

Short title

5. This Act may be cited as the Third Parties (Rights Against Insurers) Act 1930.

INDEX